Andy Warner's

Oddball Histories

SPICES and SPUDS

HOW PLANTS MADE OUR WORLD

About This Book

This book was edited by Andrea Colvin. The production was supervised by Bernadette Flinn, and the production editor was Lindsay Walter-Greaney. The text was set in fonts created by Andy Warner from his handwriting.

Colorist: Eleri Harris and Luke Healy

Little, Brown and Company
Hachette Book Group
1290 Avenue of the Americas, New York, NY 10104
Visit us at LBYR.com

First Edition: November 2024

Little, Brown Ink is an imprint of Little, Brown and Company. The Little, Brown Ink name and logo are registered trademarks of Hachette Book Group, Inc.

The publisher is not responsible for websites (or their content) that are not owned by the publisher.

Little, Brown and Company books may be purchased in bulk for business, educational, or promotional use. For information, please contact your local bookseller or the Hachette Book Group Special Markets Department at special.markets@hbgusa.com.

ISBNs: 978-0-316-49826-5 (hardcover), 978-0-316-49827-2 (paperback), 978-0-316-49825-8 (ebook), 978-0-316-15193-1 (ebook), 978-0-316-15208-2 (ebook)

PRINTED IN JOHOR, MALAYSIA

PCF

Hardcover: 10 9 8 7 6 5 4 3 2 1
Paperback: 10 9 8 7 6 5 4 3 2 1

For Kathy, Steve, Lisa, Aron, Valentine, Shern, Ben, and everyone else I ever tried to make a home and plant a garden with.

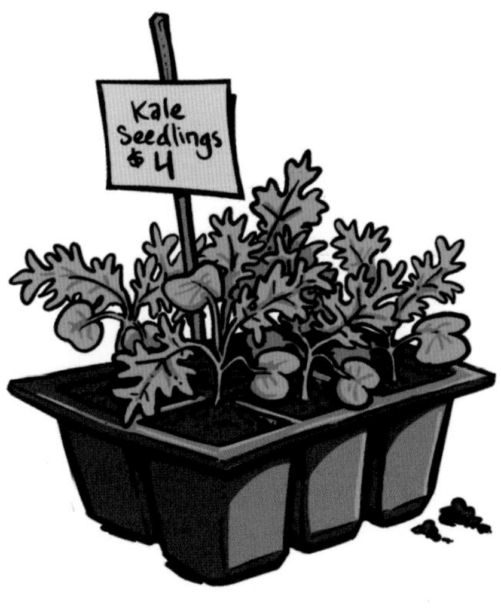
Kale
Seedlings
$4

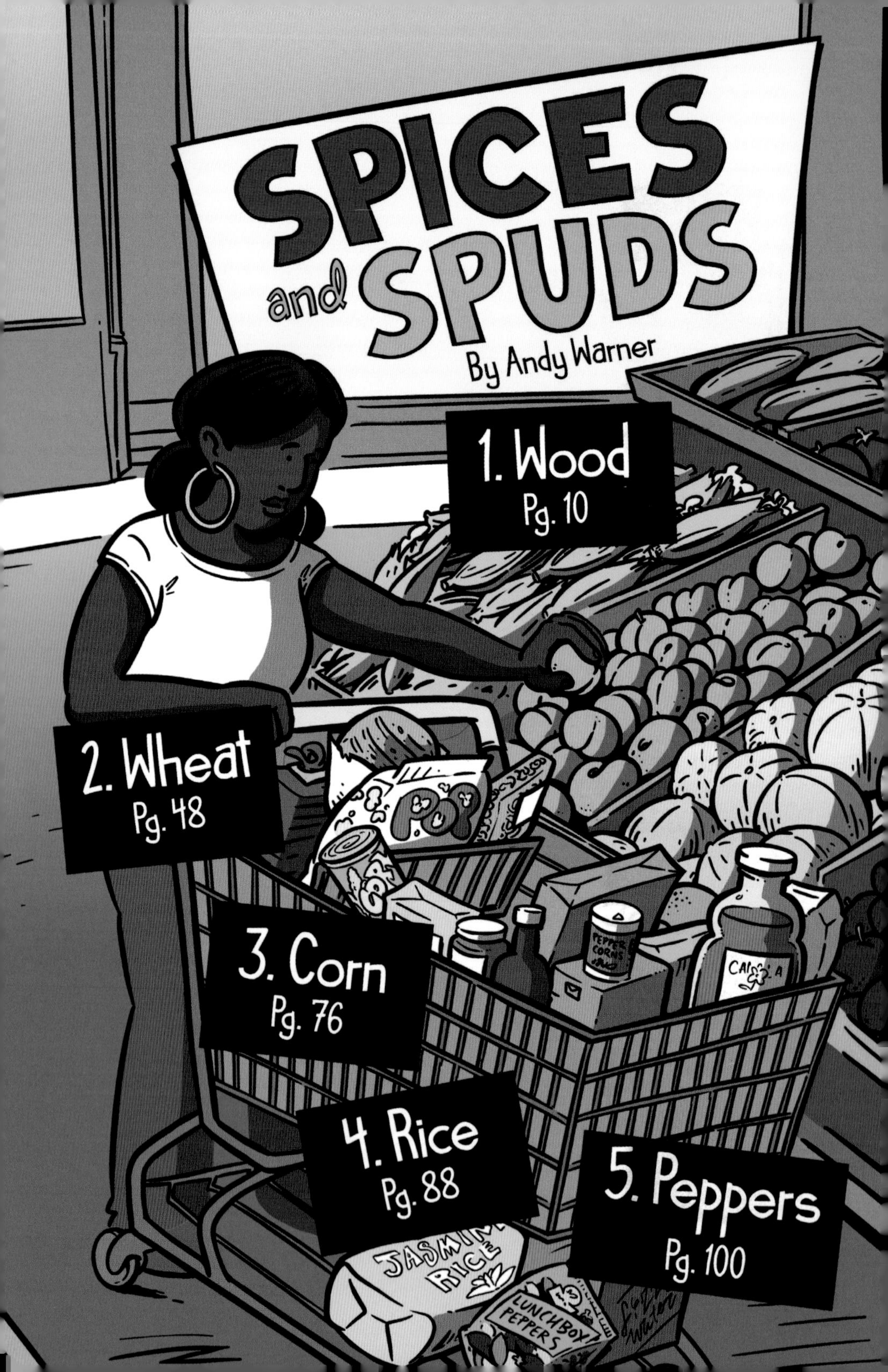
SPICES and SPUDS
By Andy Warner
1. Wood
Pg. 10
2. Wheat
Pg. 48
3. Corn
Pg. 76
4. Rice
Pg. 88
5. Peppers
Pg. 100
POP
PEPPER CORNS
JASMIN
RICE
LUNCHBOX PEPPERS

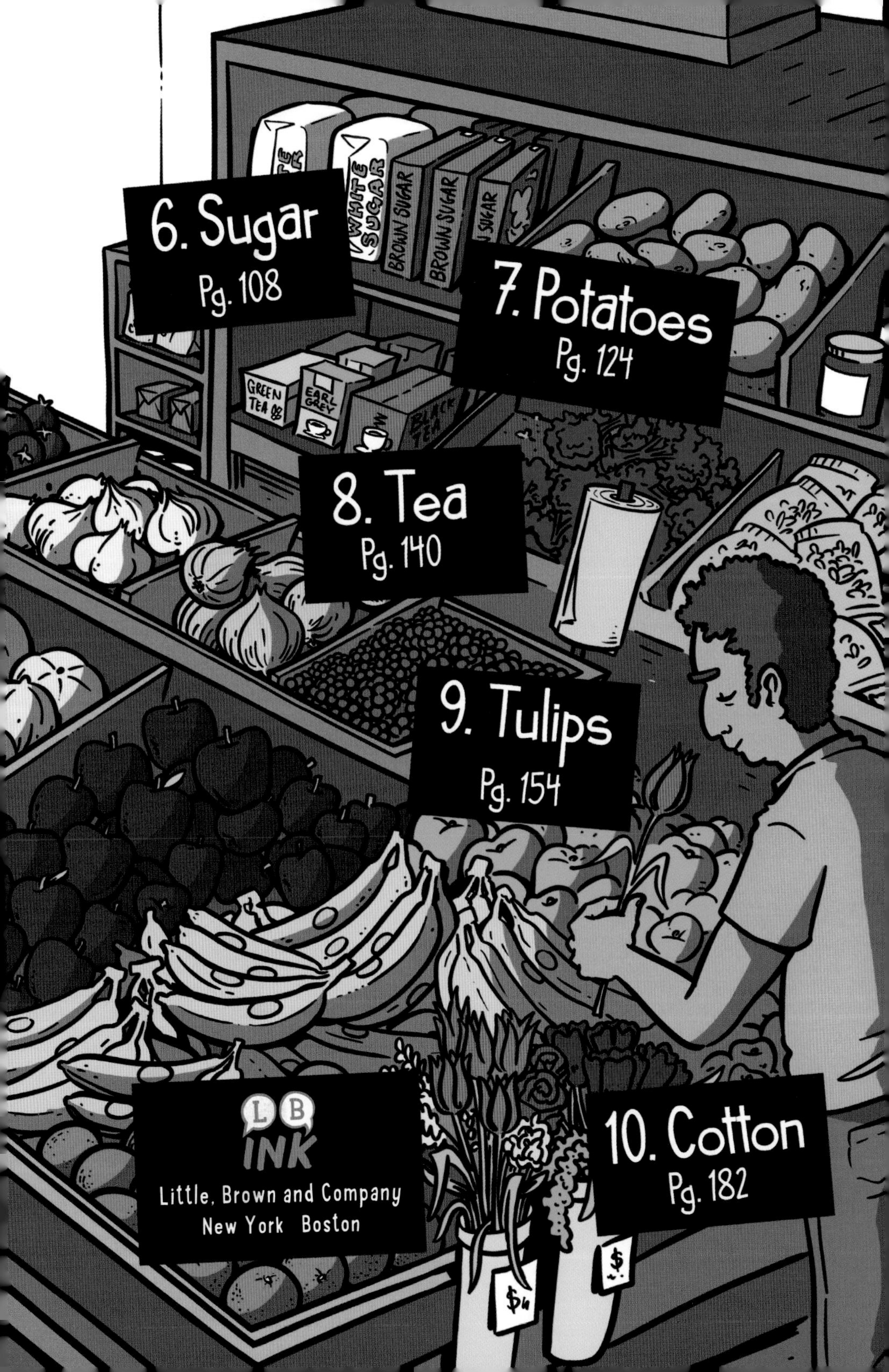
6. Sugar
Pg. 108
WHITE SUGAR
BROWN SUGAR
BROWN SUGAR
7. Potatoes
Pg. 124
GREEN TEA
EARL GREY
BLACK TEA
8. Tea
Pg. 140
9. Tulips
Pg. 154
LB INK
Little, Brown and Company
New York Boston
10. Cotton
Pg. 182
$4
$

INTRODUCTION

In every memory I have of it, the garden of my parents' house in Southern California was bursting with life—plant, bird, insect, and (to my parents' annoyance) animal.

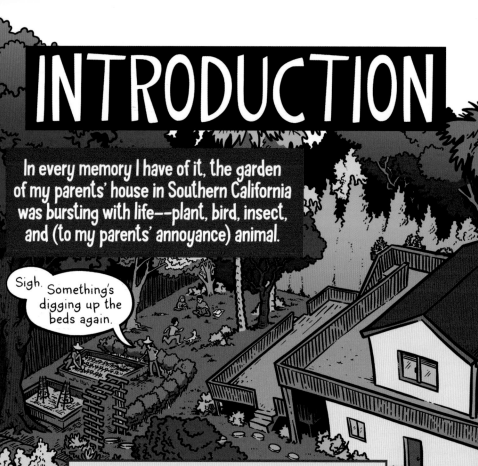

Sigh. Something's digging up the beds again.

Each season brought baskets overflowing with fruits and vegetables, jam making and carrot pulling.

I got my hands dirty until the age when fantasy novels and comics got more interesting than digging.

Get this: The dragons can cast magic.

Whoa....

I'll get the traps.

I'm playing a wizard.

But even then, I loved to be in, and around, their plants.

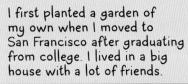

I first planted a garden of my own when I moved to San Francisco after graduating from college. I lived in a big house with a lot of friends.

I found a deep fryer on the street! Let's throw a party and call it Deep-Fry Day Friday!

Cool.

Ew.

There had just been a big financial crisis, and many of us were either out of work or not working enough.

I just lost another client.

Well, the kale needs to be weeded....

So we gardened.

Planting things, caring for them, and watching them change the landscape give you the time and the space to think about things separate from the bustle of the day-to-day.

It also connects your hands directly to one of the strangest and most magical aspects of our life here on Earth: that all of us depend on the ability of plants to capture sunlight and use it to grow.

I'm gonna try to deep-fry the kale!

This ability, called **PHOTOSYNTHESIS**, originates in an event from a really long time ago when things got a little weird.

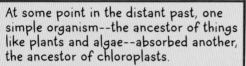

At some point in the distant past, one simple organism--the ancestor of things like plants and algae--absorbed another, the ancestor of chloroplasts.

What are chloroplasts? They're the place that photosynthesis happens.

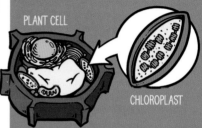

PLANT CELL

CHLOROPLAST

Once inside the bigger cell, the chloroplasts stayed. That move-in turned out to be essential to all of us.

Chloroplasts capture the sun's energy and use it to forge carbon dioxide and water into sugars, which plants use for energy, often releasing oxygen as a by-product.

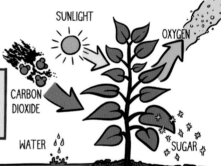

SUNLIGHT

OXYGEN

CARBON DIOXIDE

WATER

SUGAR

SUNLIGHT + CARBON DIOXIDE + WATER = OXYGEN SUGAR

The simple organism with the chloroplast stuck inside evolved into all the different complicated kinds of plants on Earth. The chloroplasts came along with them.

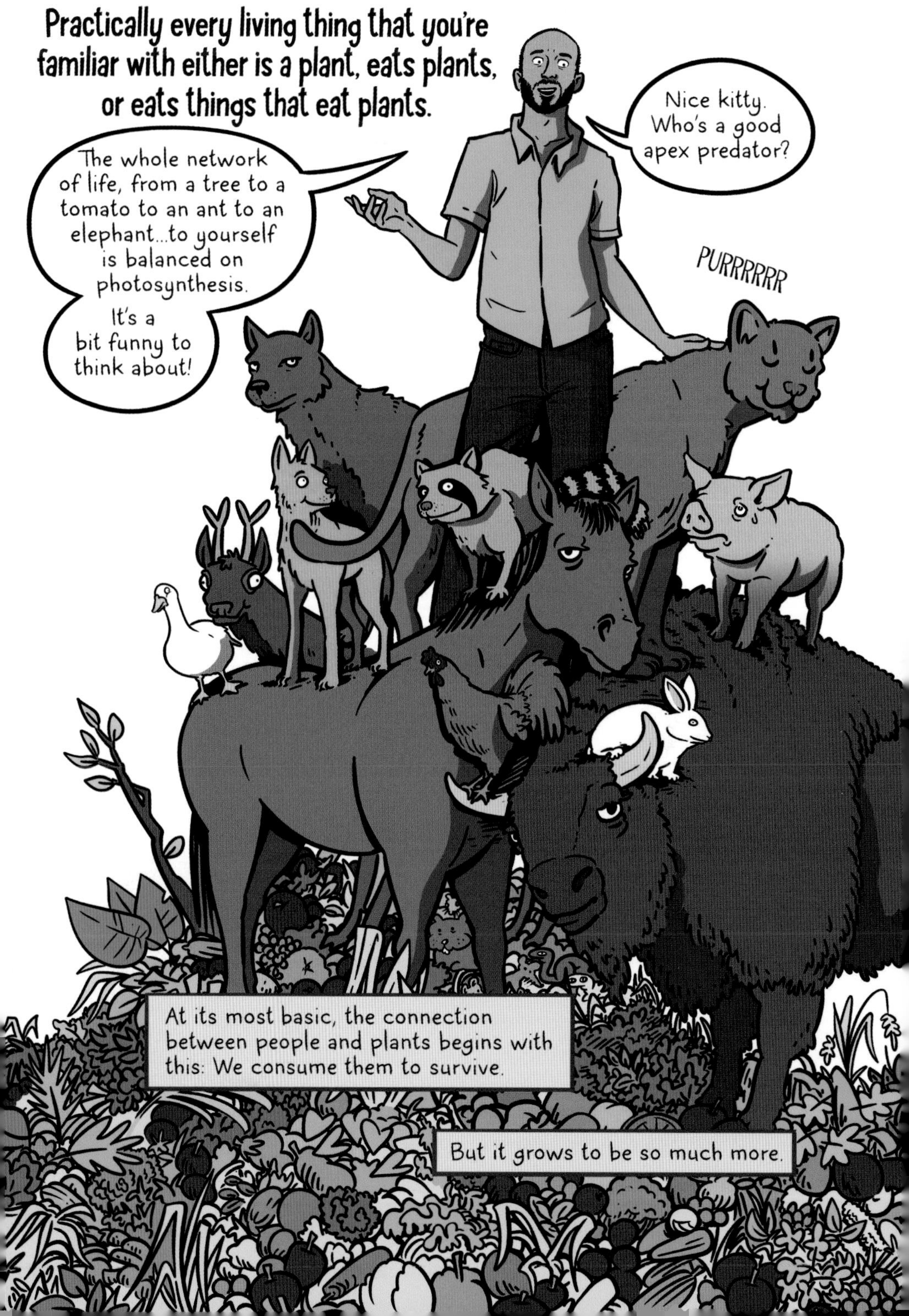
Practically every living thing that you're familiar with either is a plant, eats plants, or eats things that eat plants.
The whole network of life, from a tree to a tomato to an ant to an elephant...to yourself is balanced on photosynthesis.
It's a bit funny to think about!
Nice kitty. Who's a good apex predator?
PURRRRRR
At its most basic, the connection between people and plants begins with this: We consume them to survive.
But it grows to be so much more.

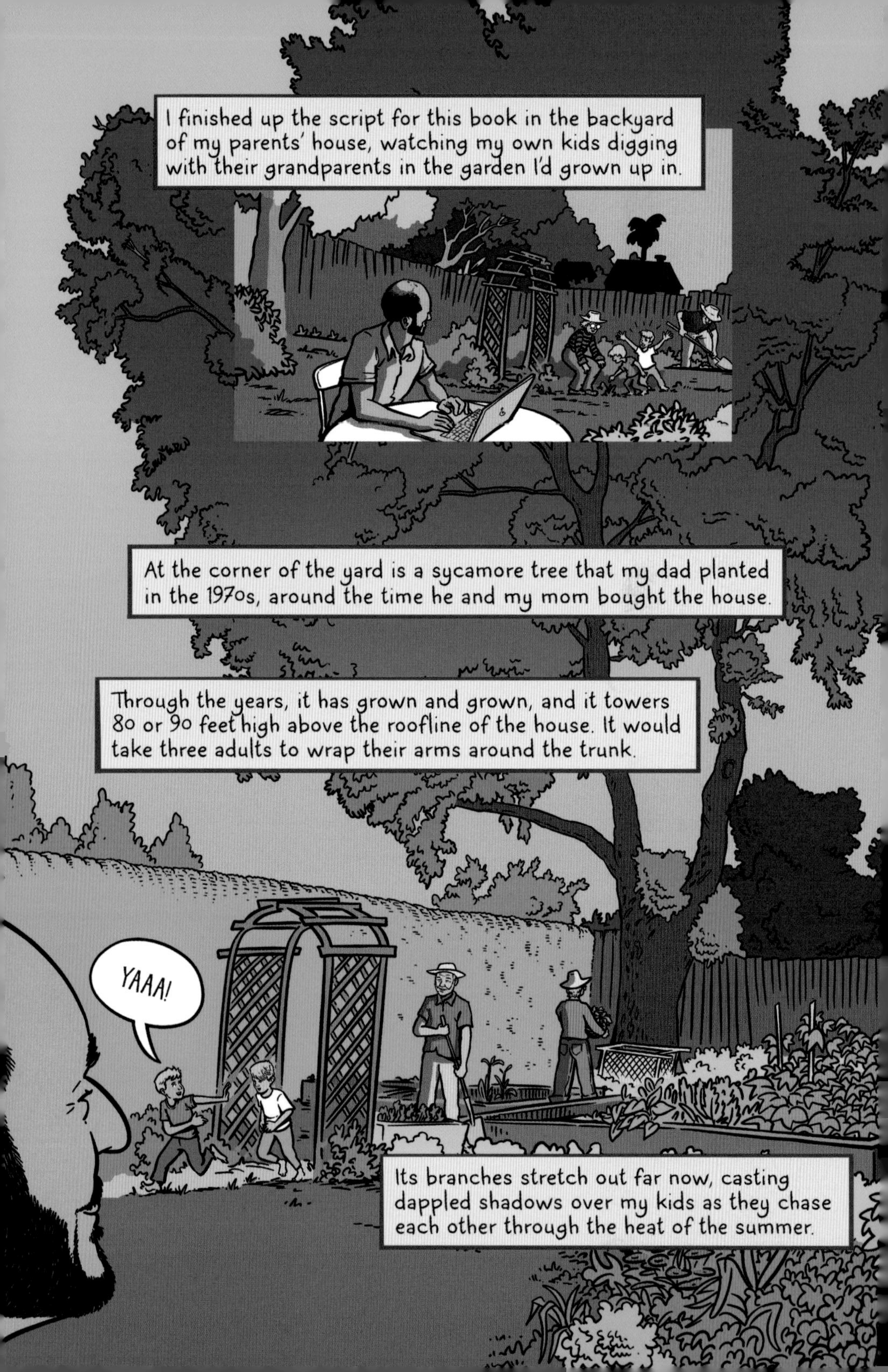
I finished up the script for this book in the backyard of my parents' house, watching my own kids digging with their grandparents in the garden I'd grown up in.
At the corner of the yard is a sycamore tree that my dad planted in the 1970s, around the time he and my mom bought the house.
Through the years, it has grown and grown, and it towers 80 or 90 feet high above the roofline of the house. It would take three adults to wrap their arms around the trunk.
YAAA!
Its branches stretch out far now, casting dappled shadows over my kids as they chase each other through the heat of the summer.

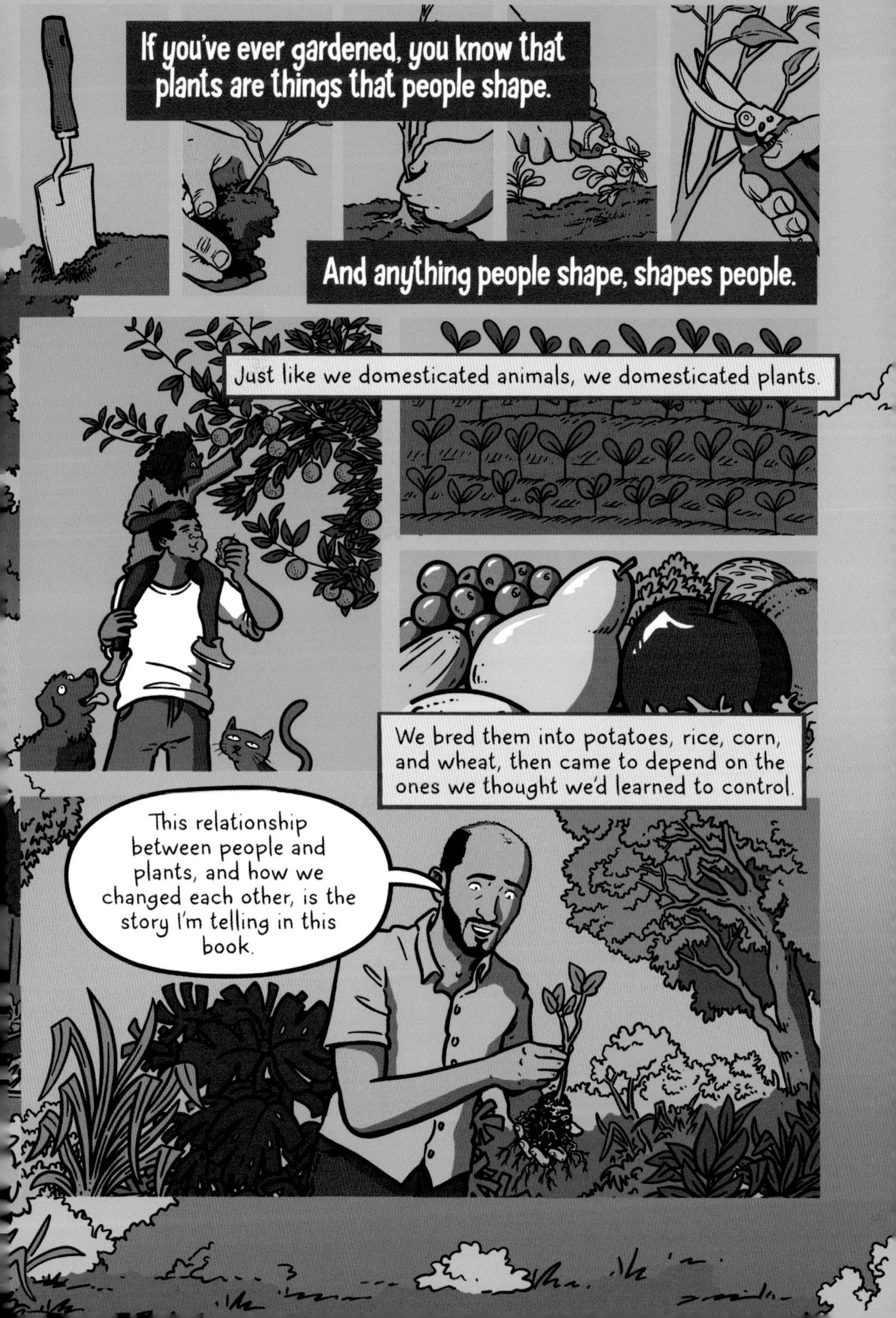
If you've ever gardened, you know that plants are things that people shape.
And anything people shape, shapes people.
Just like we domesticated animals, we domesticated plants.
We bred them into potatoes, rice, corn, and wheat, then came to depend on the ones we thought we'd learned to control.
This relationship between people and plants, and how we changed each other, is the story I'm telling in this book.

The plants we build with, the plants we eat, the plants we wear, and the plants we just like to look at move our history in ways that's sometimes not visible in textbooks or television shows.

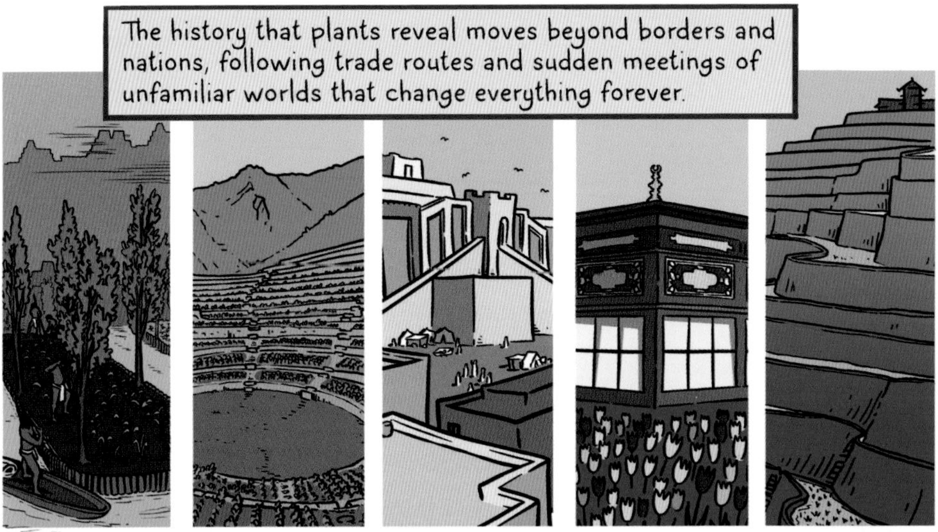
The history that plants reveal moves beyond borders and nations, following trade routes and sudden meetings of unfamiliar worlds that change everything forever.

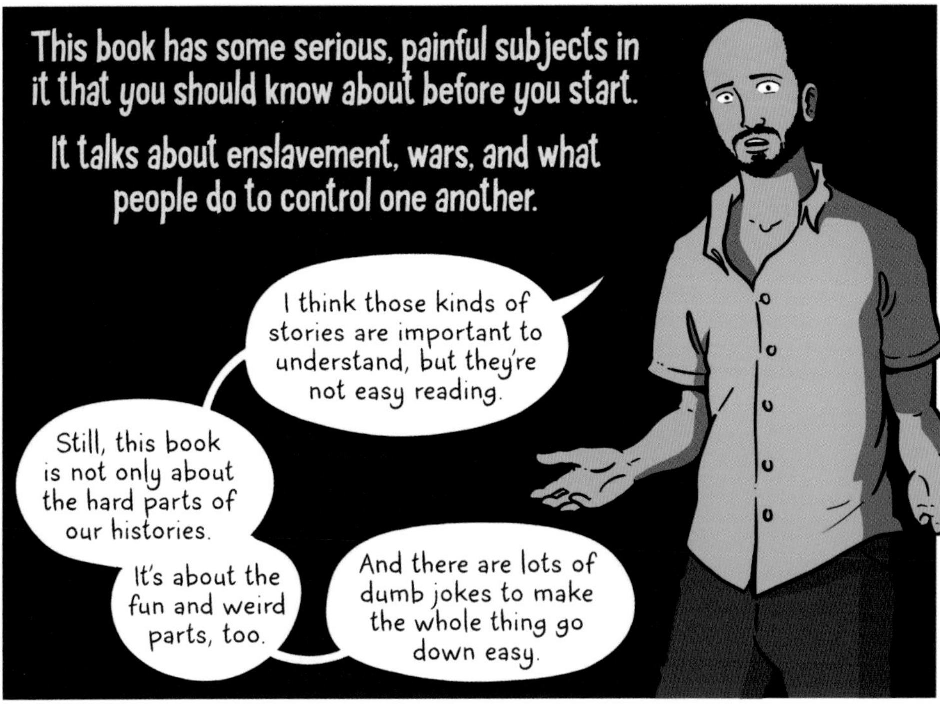
This book has some serious, painful subjects in it that you should know about before you start.
It talks about enslavement, wars, and what people do to control one another.
I think those kinds of stories are important to understand, but they're not easy reading.
Still, this book is not only about the hard parts of our histories.
It's about the fun and weird parts, too.
And there are lots of dumb jokes to make the whole thing go down easy.

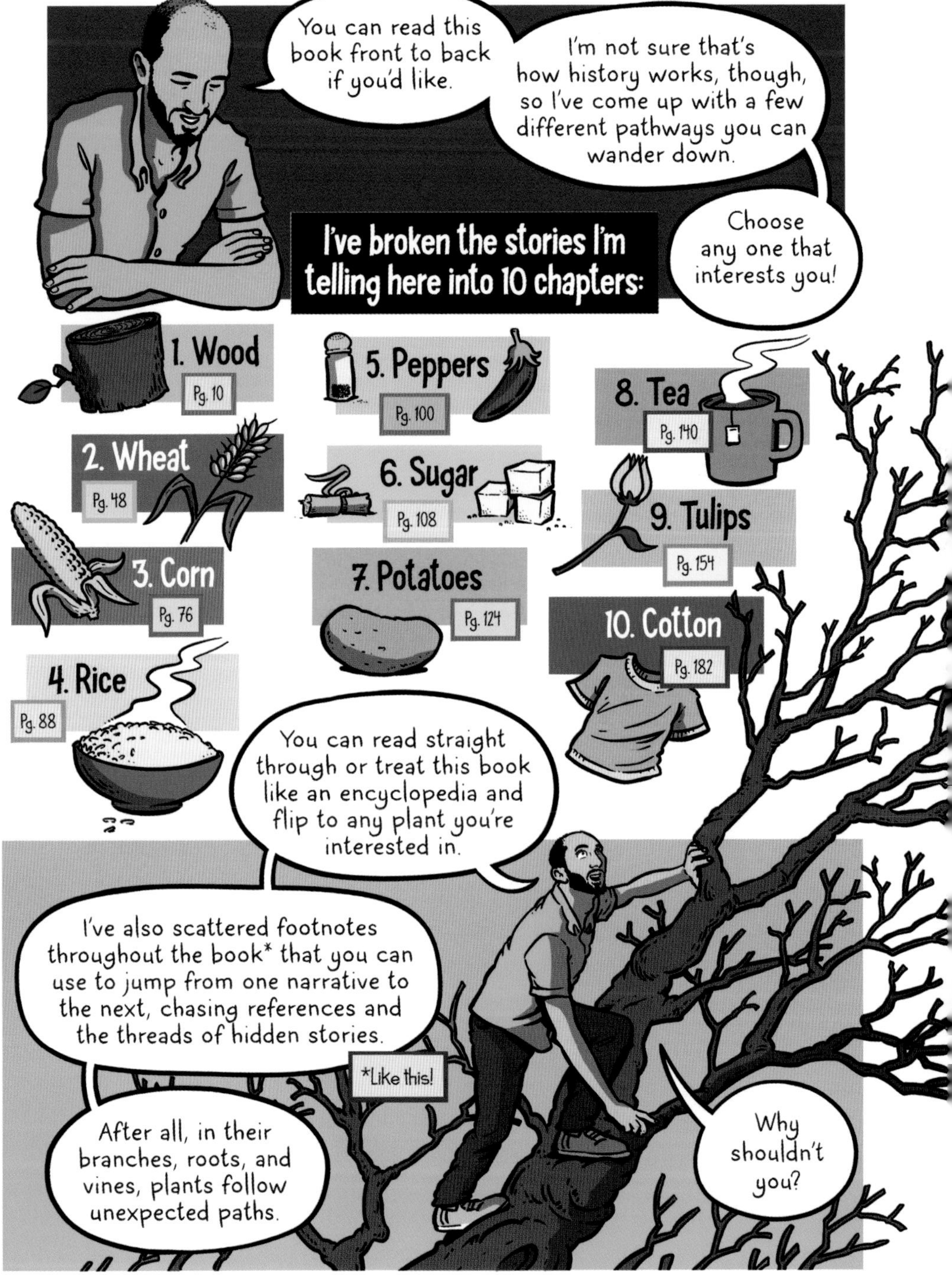
You can read this book front to back if you'd like.
I'm not sure that's how history works, though, so I've come up with a few different pathways you can wander down.
Choose any one that interests you!
I've broken the stories I'm telling here into 10 chapters:
1. Wood Pg. 10
2. Wheat Pg. 48
3. Corn Pg. 76
4. Rice Pg. 88
5. Peppers Pg. 100
6. Sugar Pg. 108
7. Potatoes Pg. 124
8. Tea Pg. 140
9. Tulips Pg. 154
10. Cotton Pg. 182
You can read straight through or treat this book like an encyclopedia and flip to any plant you're interested in.
I've also scattered footnotes throughout the book* that you can use to jump from one narrative to the next, chasing references and the threads of hidden stories.
*Like this!
After all, in their branches, roots, and vines, plants follow unexpected paths.
Why shouldn't you?

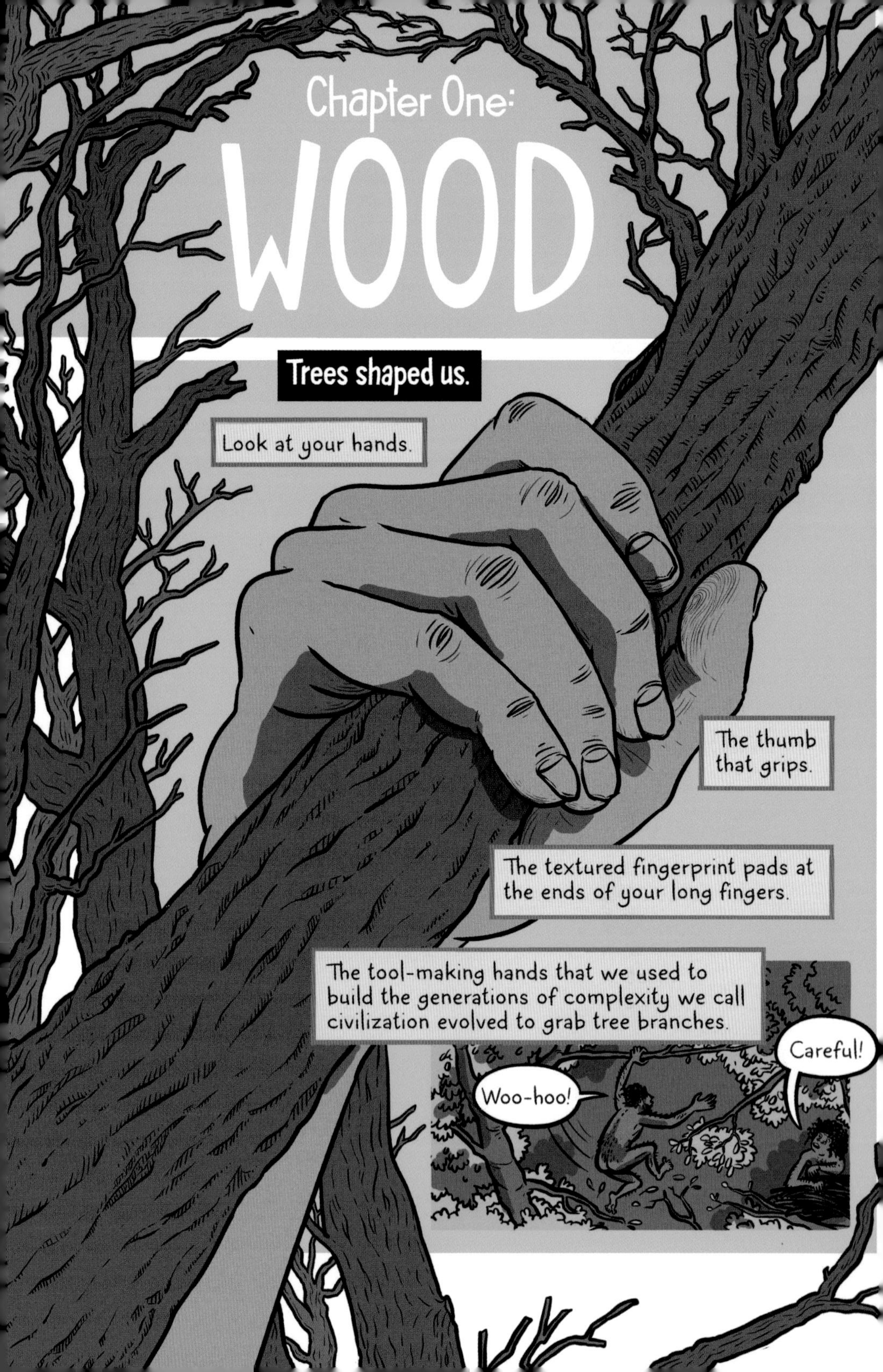
Chapter One:
WOOD
Trees shaped us.
Look at your hands.
The thumb that grips.
The textured fingerprint pads at the ends of your long fingers.
The tool-making hands that we used to build the generations of complexity we call civilization evolved to grab tree branches.
Woo-hoo!
Careful!

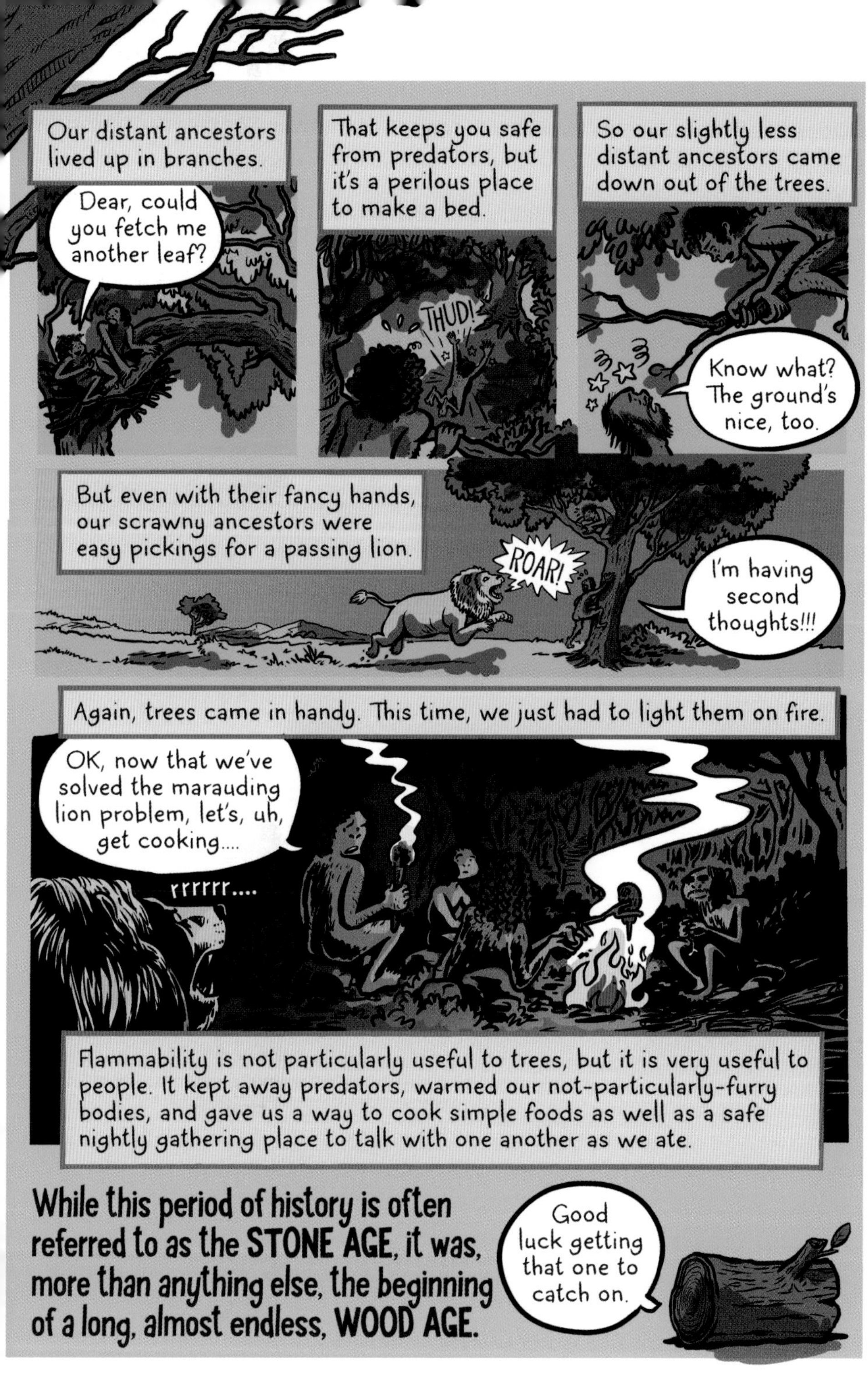
Our distant ancestors lived up in branches.
Dear, could you fetch me another leaf?
That keeps you safe from predators, but it's a perilous place to make a bed.
THUD!
So our slightly less distant ancestors came down out of the trees.
Know what? The ground's nice, too.
But even with their fancy hands, our scrawny ancestors were easy pickings for a passing lion.
ROAR!
I'm having second thoughts!!!
Again, trees came in handy. This time, we just had to light them on fire.
OK, now that we've solved the marauding lion problem, let's, uh, get cooking....
rrrrrr....
Flammability is not particularly useful to trees, but it is very useful to people. It kept away predators, warmed our not-particularly-furry bodies, and gave us a way to cook simple foods as well as a safe nightly gathering place to talk with one another as we ate.
While this period of history is often referred to as the STONE AGE, it was, more than anything else, the beginning of a long, almost endless, WOOD AGE.
Good luck getting that one to catch on.

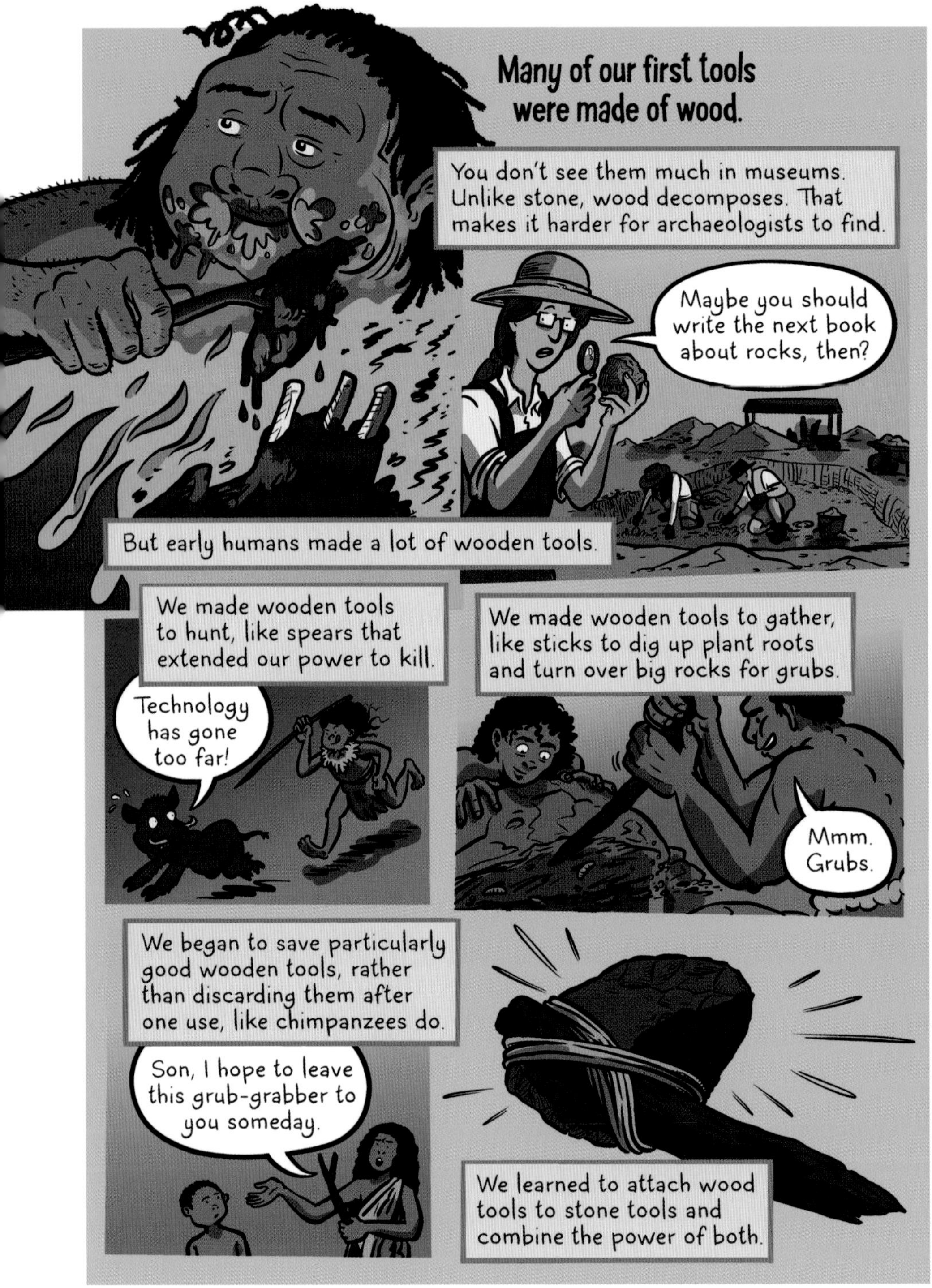
Many of our first tools were made of wood.
You don't see them much in museums. Unlike stone, wood decomposes. That makes it harder for archaeologists to find.
Maybe you should write the next book about rocks, then?
But early humans made a lot of wooden tools.
We made wooden tools to hunt, like spears that extended our power to kill.
Technology has gone too far!
We made wooden tools to gather, like sticks to dig up plant roots and turn over big rocks for grubs.
Mmm. Grubs.
We began to save particularly good wooden tools, rather than discarding them after one use, like chimpanzees do.
Son, I hope to leave this grub-grabber to you someday.
We learned to attach wood tools to stone tools and combine the power of both.

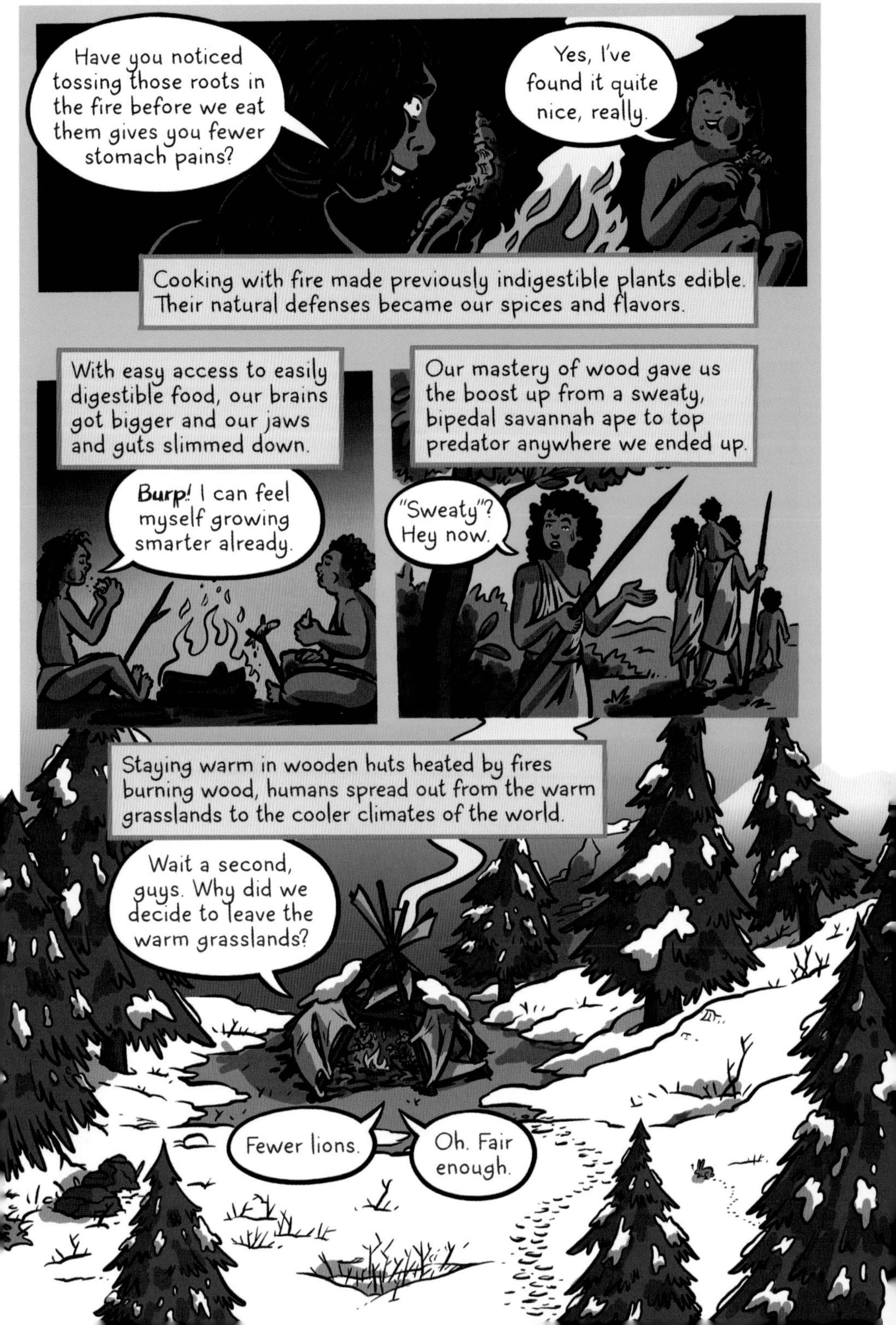
Have you noticed tossing those roots in the fire before we eat them gives you fewer stomach pains?
Yes, I've found it quite nice, really.
Cooking with fire made previously indigestible plants edible. Their natural defenses became our spices and flavors.
With easy access to easily digestible food, our brains got bigger and our jaws and guts slimmed down.
Burp! I can feel myself growing smarter already.
Our mastery of wood gave us the boost up from a sweaty, bipedal savannah ape to top predator anywhere we ended up.
"Sweaty"? Hey now.
Staying warm in wooden huts heated by fires burning wood, humans spread out from the warm grasslands to the cooler climates of the world.
Wait a second, guys. Why did we decide to leave the warm grasslands?
Fewer lions.
Oh. Fair enough.

And as ancient humans spread around the world, they encountered trees in such numbers and sizes that it boggles the mind.

Faced with such grandeur, many humans began to worship these ancient giants.

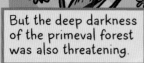

But the deep darkness of the primeval forest was also threatening.

THUD!

Ow, my head!

Humans worked the soil with wooden tools when they developed agriculture,* which happened again and again in many different places.

Agriculture requires fields to grow crops. To get those fields, humans had to get good at cutting down trees.

OK, now I'll grant you the sweaty bit.

*See Pg. 50

Grrr....

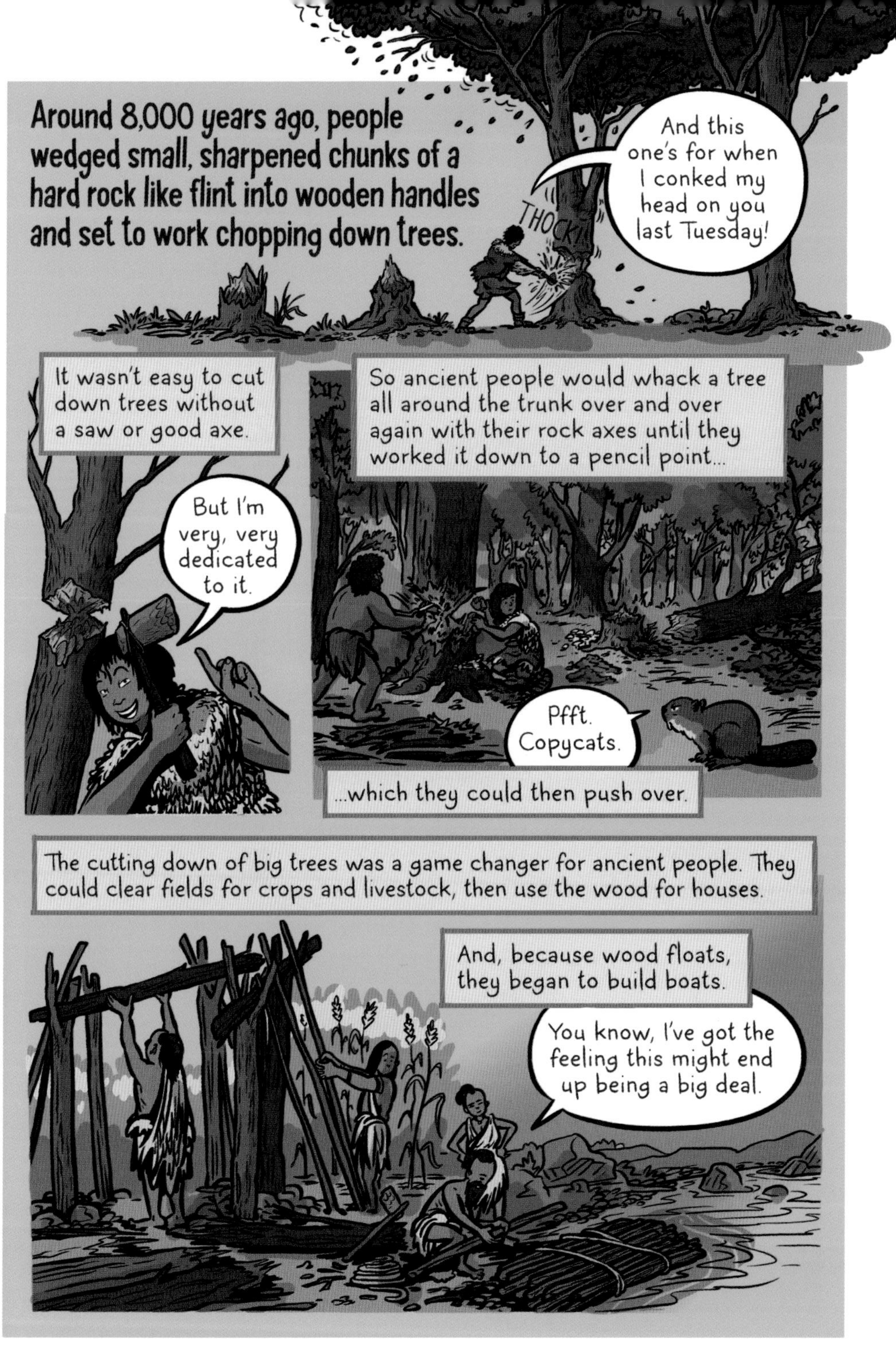

Around 8,000 years ago, people wedged small, sharpened chunks of a hard rock like flint into wooden handles and set to work chopping down trees.
THOCK!
And this one's for when I conked my head on you last Tuesday!
It wasn't easy to cut down trees without a saw or good axe.
But I'm very, very dedicated to it.
So ancient people would whack a tree all around the trunk over and over again with their rock axes until they worked it down to a pencil point...
Pfft. Copycats.
...which they could then push over.
The cutting down of big trees was a game changer for ancient people. They could clear fields for crops and livestock, then use the wood for houses.
And, because wood floats, they began to build boats.
You know, I've got the feeling this might end up being a big deal.

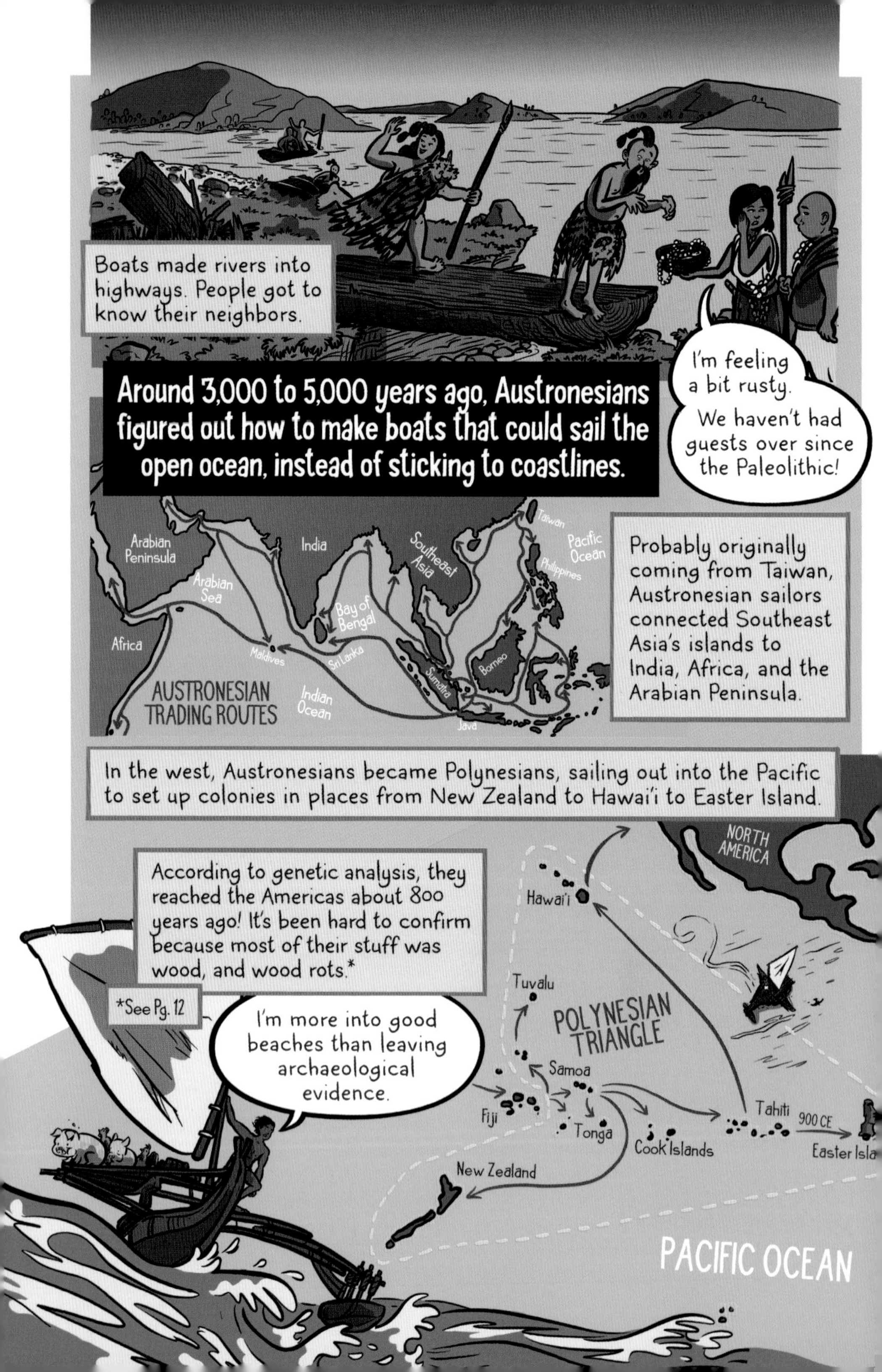

Boats made rivers into highways. People got to know their neighbors.
I'm feeling a bit rusty.
We haven't had guests over since the Paleolithic!
Around 3,000 to 5,000 years ago, Austronesians figured out how to make boats that could sail the open ocean, instead of sticking to coastlines.
Probably originally coming from Taiwan, Austronesian sailors connected Southeast Asia's islands to India, Africa, and the Arabian Peninsula.
AUSTRONESIAN TRADING ROUTES
Arabian Peninsula
Arabian Sea
Africa
India
Maldives
Sri Lanka
Bay of Bengal
Indian Ocean
Southeast Asia
Sumatra
Java
Borneo
Taiwan
Philippines
Pacific Ocean
In the west, Austronesians became Polynesians, sailing out into the Pacific to set up colonies in places from New Zealand to Hawai'i to Easter Island.
According to genetic analysis, they reached the Americas about 800 years ago! It's been hard to confirm because most of their stuff was wood, and wood rots.*
*See Pg. 12
I'm more into good beaches than leaving archaeological evidence.
NORTH AMERICA
Hawai'i
Tuvalu
POLYNESIAN TRIANGLE
Samoa
Fiji
Tonga
Cook Islands
Tahiti
900 CE
Easter Isla
New Zealand
PACIFIC OCEAN

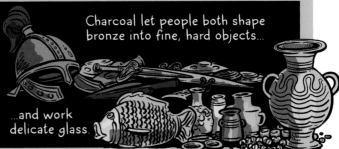

Back in Eurasia, folks figured out that limiting air to burning wood gets charcoal. And charcoal means power.

WOOM!

Whoa! Too much power!

I like the sound of power!

Charcoal is portable, light, and can heat things to temperatures hotter than plain burning wood.

Charcoal let people both shape bronze into fine, hard objects...

...and work delicate glass.

With bronze axes, people cut down more and bigger trees.

And they used these trees to build bigger, more complicated things.

This seems like something we can just sustain forever, right?

Absolutely.

CHOP!

Like bigger boats.

Wooooo!

Blarg!

Bronze technology let people saw planks and build ships big enough to haul lots of stuff across bodies of water.

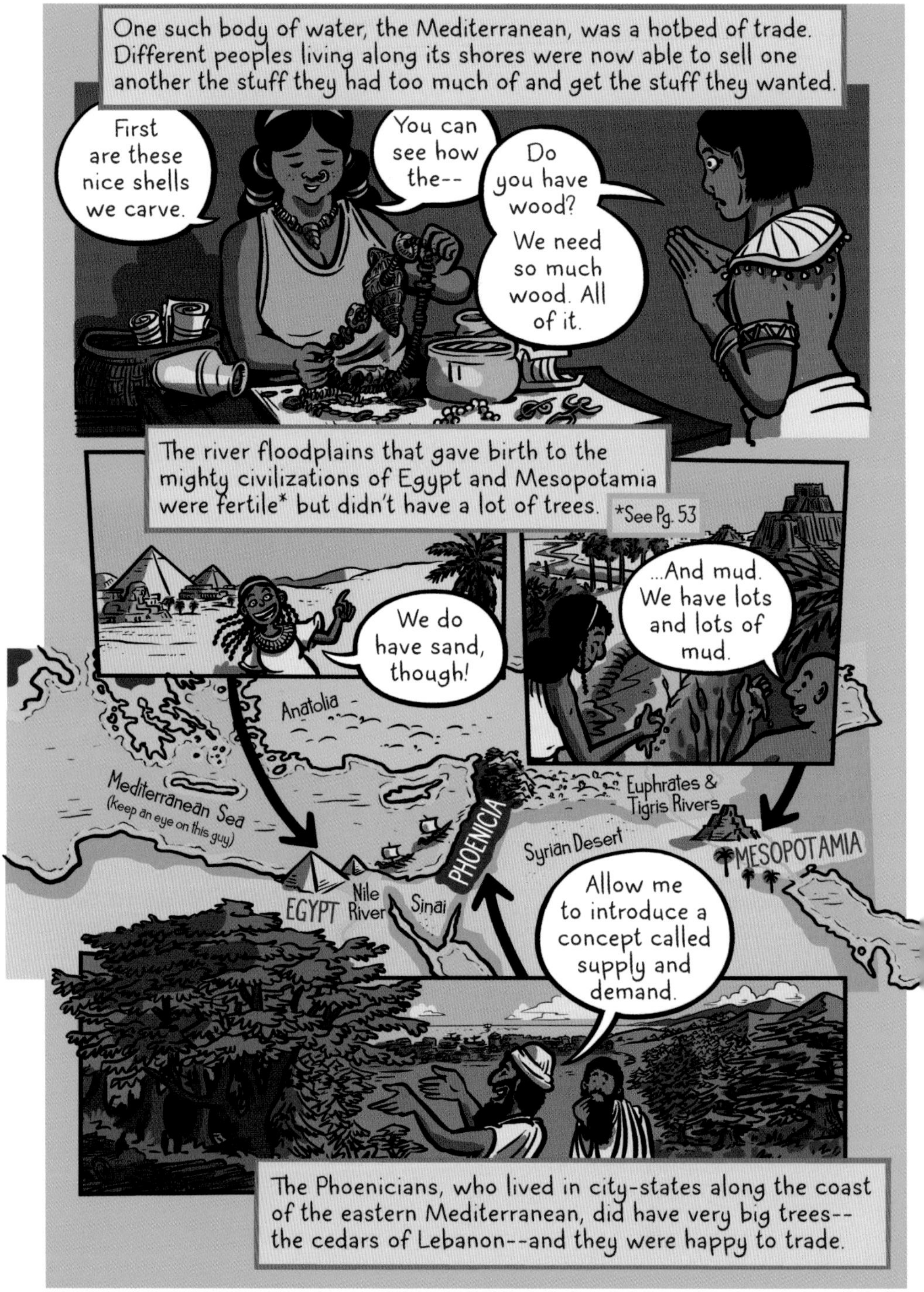
One such body of water, the Mediterranean, was a hotbed of trade. Different peoples living along its shores were now able to sell one another the stuff they had too much of and get the stuff they wanted.
First are these nice shells we carve.
You can see how the--
Do you have wood?
We need so much wood. All of it.
The river floodplains that gave birth to the mighty civilizations of Egypt and Mesopotamia were fertile* but didn't have a lot of trees.
*See Pg. 53
We do have sand, though!
...And mud. We have lots and lots of mud.
Anatolia
Mediterranean Sea
(Keep an eye on this guy)
Euphrates & Tigris Rivers
PHOENICIA
Syrian Desert
MESOPOTAMIA
EGYPT
Nile River
Sinai
Allow me to introduce a concept called supply and demand.
The Phoenicians, who lived in city-states along the coast of the eastern Mediterranean, did have very big trees--the cedars of Lebanon--and they were happy to trade.

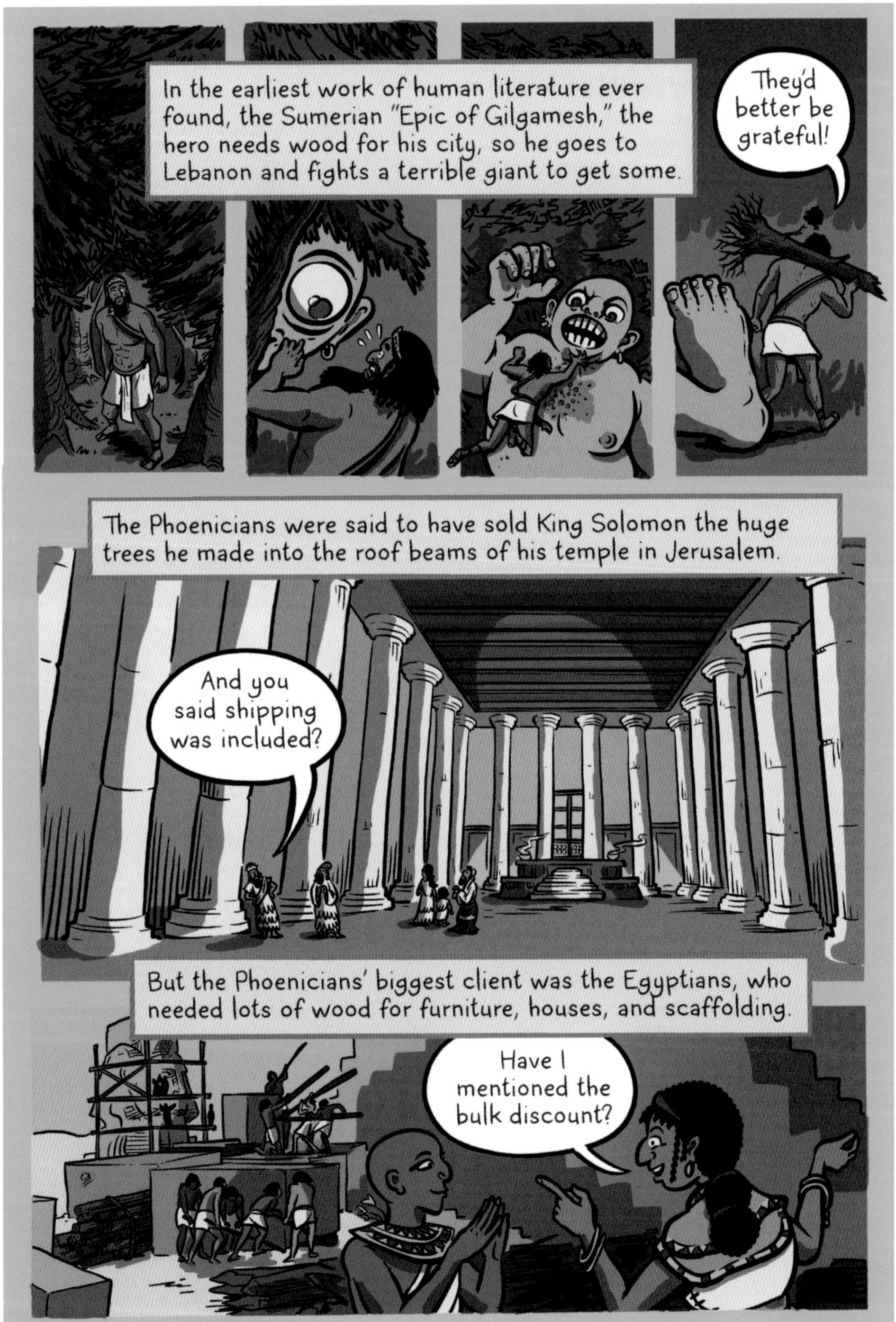
In the earliest work of human literature ever found, the Sumerian "Epic of Gilgamesh," the hero needs wood for his city, so he goes to Lebanon and fights a terrible giant to get some.
They'd better be grateful!
The Phoenicians were said to have sold King Solomon the huge trees he made into the roof beams of his temple in Jerusalem.
And you said shipping was included?
But the Phoenicians' biggest client was the Egyptians, who needed lots of wood for furniture, houses, and scaffolding.
Have I mentioned the bulk discount?

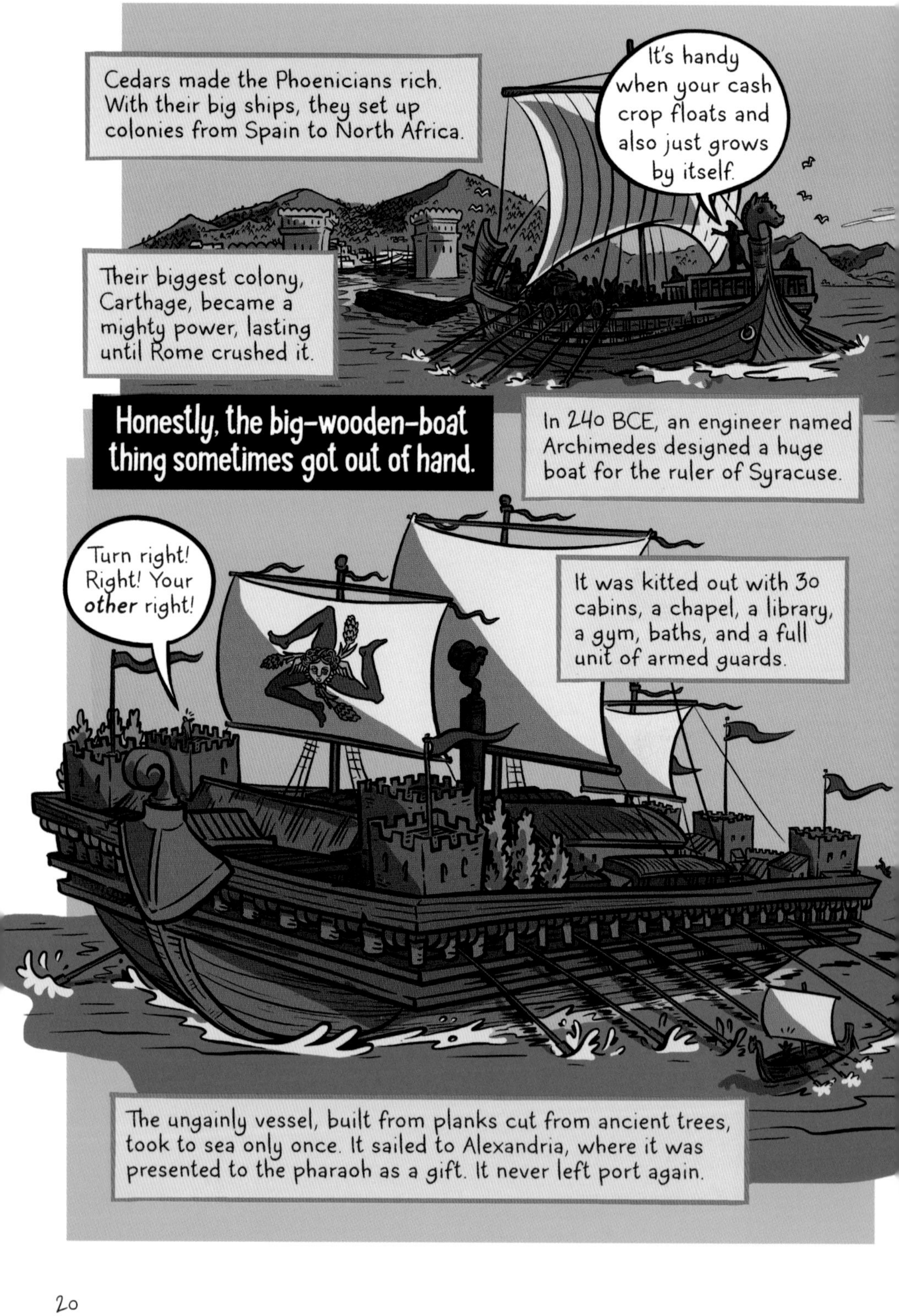

Cedars made the Phoenicians rich. With their big ships, they set up colonies from Spain to North Africa.
It's handy when your cash crop floats and also just grows by itself.
Their biggest colony, Carthage, became a mighty power, lasting until Rome crushed it.
Honestly, the big-wooden-boat thing sometimes got out of hand.
In 240 BCE, an engineer named Archimedes designed a huge boat for the ruler of Syracuse.
Turn right! Right! Your *other* right!
It was kitted out with 30 cabins, a chapel, a library, a gym, baths, and a full unit of armed guards.
The ungainly vessel, built from planks cut from ancient trees, took to sea only once. It sailed to Alexandria, where it was presented to the pharaoh as a gift. It never left port again.

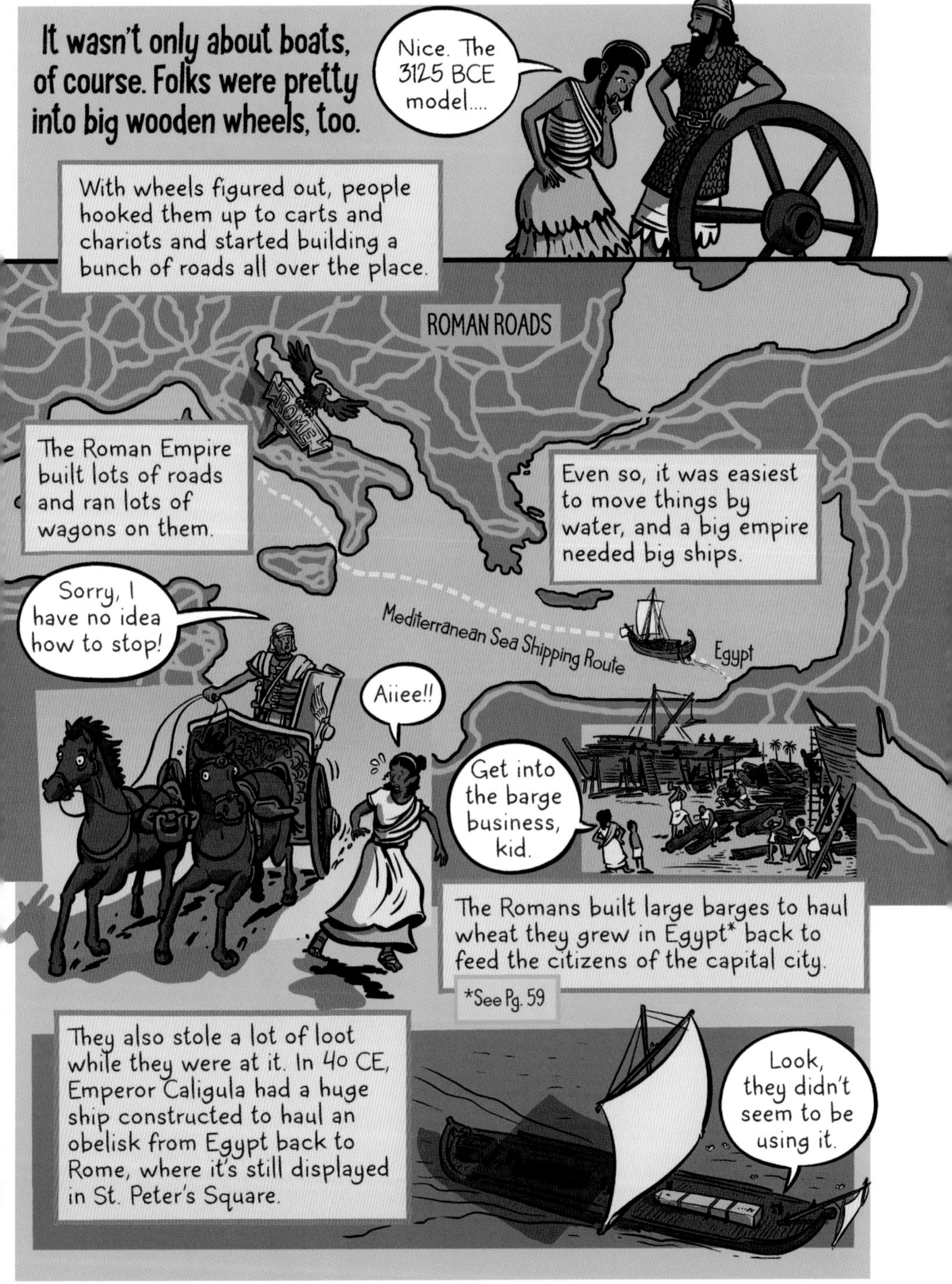
It wasn't only about boats, of course. Folks were pretty into big wooden wheels, too.
Nice. The 3125 BCE model....
With wheels figured out, people hooked them up to carts and chariots and started building a bunch of roads all over the place.
ROMAN ROADS
ROME
The Roman Empire built lots of roads and ran lots of wagons on them.
Even so, it was easiest to move things by water, and a big empire needed big ships.
Sorry, I have no idea how to stop!
Mediterranean Sea Shipping Route
Egypt
Aiiee!!
Get into the barge business, kid.
The Romans built large barges to haul wheat they grew in Egypt* back to feed the citizens of the capital city.
*See Pg. 59
They also stole a lot of loot while they were at it. In 40 CE, Emperor Caligula had a huge ship constructed to haul an obelisk from Egypt back to Rome, where it's still displayed in St. Peter's Square.
Look, they didn't seem to be using it.

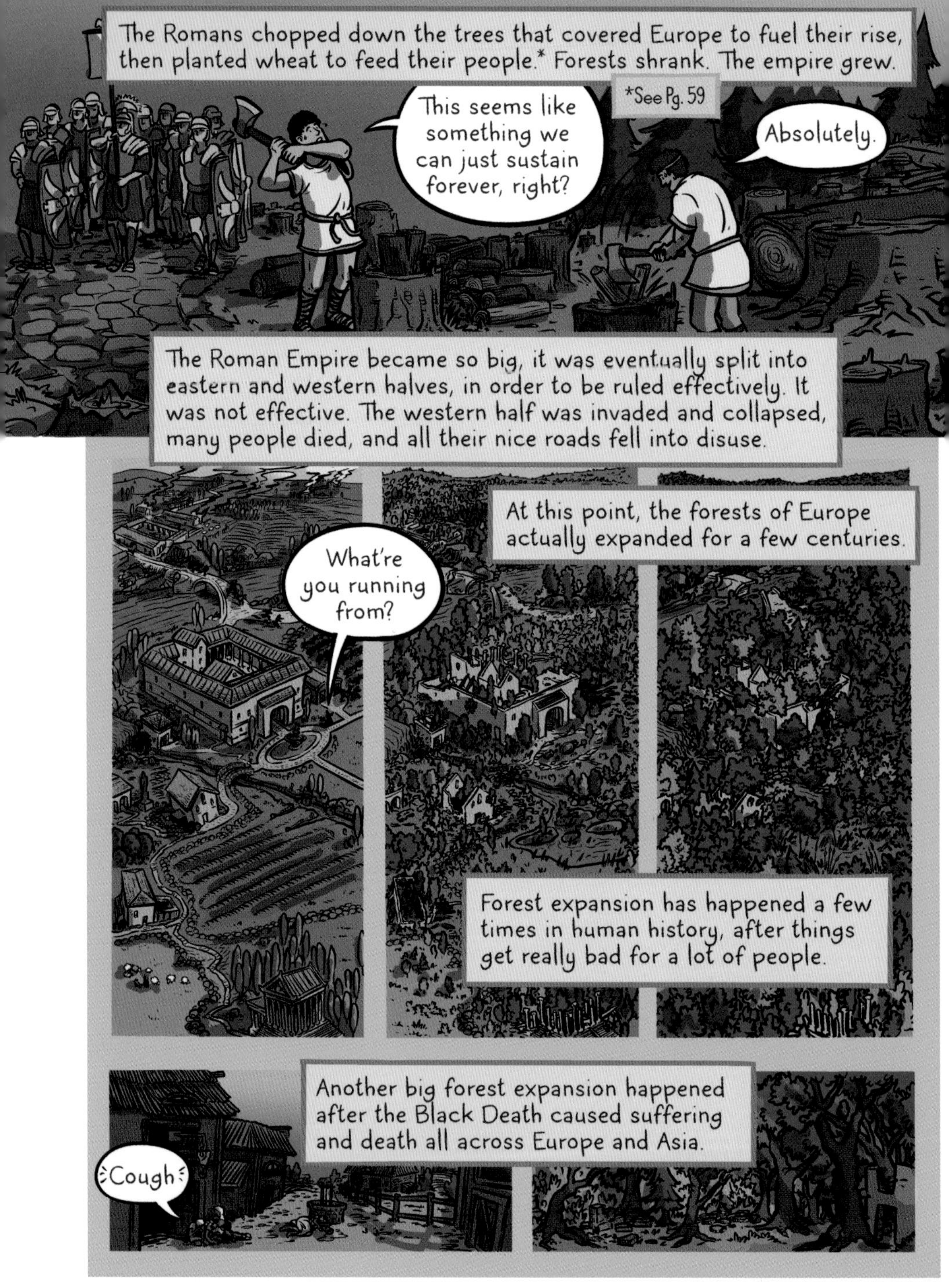
The Romans chopped down the trees that covered Europe to fuel their rise, then planted wheat to feed their people.* Forests shrank. The empire grew.
This seems like something we can just sustain forever, right?
*See Pg. 59
Absolutely.
The Roman Empire became so big, it was eventually split into eastern and western halves, in order to be ruled effectively. It was not effective. The western half was invaded and collapsed, many people died, and all their nice roads fell into disuse.
What're you running from?
At this point, the forests of Europe actually expanded for a few centuries.
Forest expansion has happened a few times in human history, after things get really bad for a lot of people.
Another big forest expansion happened after the Black Death caused suffering and death all across Europe and Asia.
Cough

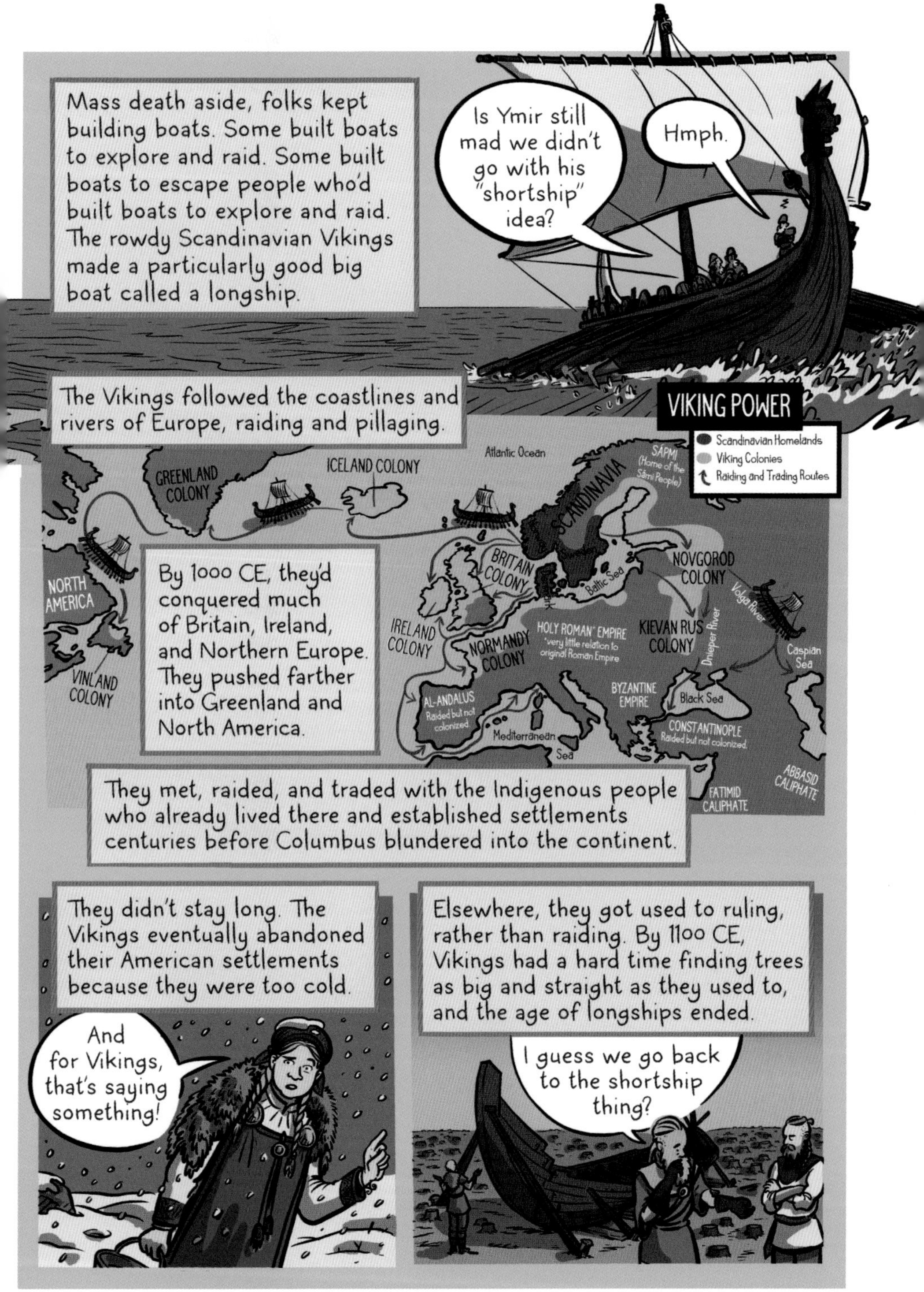
Mass death aside, folks kept building boats. Some built boats to explore and raid. Some built boats to escape people who'd built boats to explore and raid. The rowdy Scandinavian Vikings made a particularly good big boat called a longship.
Is Ymir still mad we didn't go with his "shortship" idea?
Hmph.
The Vikings followed the coastlines and rivers of Europe, raiding and pillaging.
VIKING POWER
Scandinavian Homelands
Viking Colonies
Raiding and Trading Routes
Atlantic Ocean
GREENLAND COLONY
ICELAND COLONY
SÁPMI (Home of the Sámi People)
SCANDINAVIA
NORTH AMERICA
VINLAND COLONY
BRITAIN COLONY
Baltic Sea
NOVGOROD COLONY
Volga River
IRELAND COLONY
NORMANDY COLONY
HOLY ROMAN* EMPIRE
*very little relation to original Roman Empire
KIEVAN RUS COLONY
Dnieper River
Caspian Sea
BYZANTINE EMPIRE
Black Sea
AL-ANDALUS
Raided but not colonized
Mediterranean Sea
CONSTANTINOPLE
Raided but not colonized.
FATIMID CALIPHATE
ABBASID CALIPHATE
By 1000 CE, they'd conquered much of Britain, Ireland, and Northern Europe. They pushed farther into Greenland and North America.
They met, raided, and traded with the Indigenous people who already lived there and established settlements centuries before Columbus blundered into the continent.
They didn't stay long. The Vikings eventually abandoned their American settlements because they were too cold.
And for Vikings, that's saying something!
Elsewhere, they got used to ruling, rather than raiding. By 1100 CE, Vikings had a hard time finding trees as big and straight as they used to, and the age of longships ended.
I guess we go back to the shortship thing?

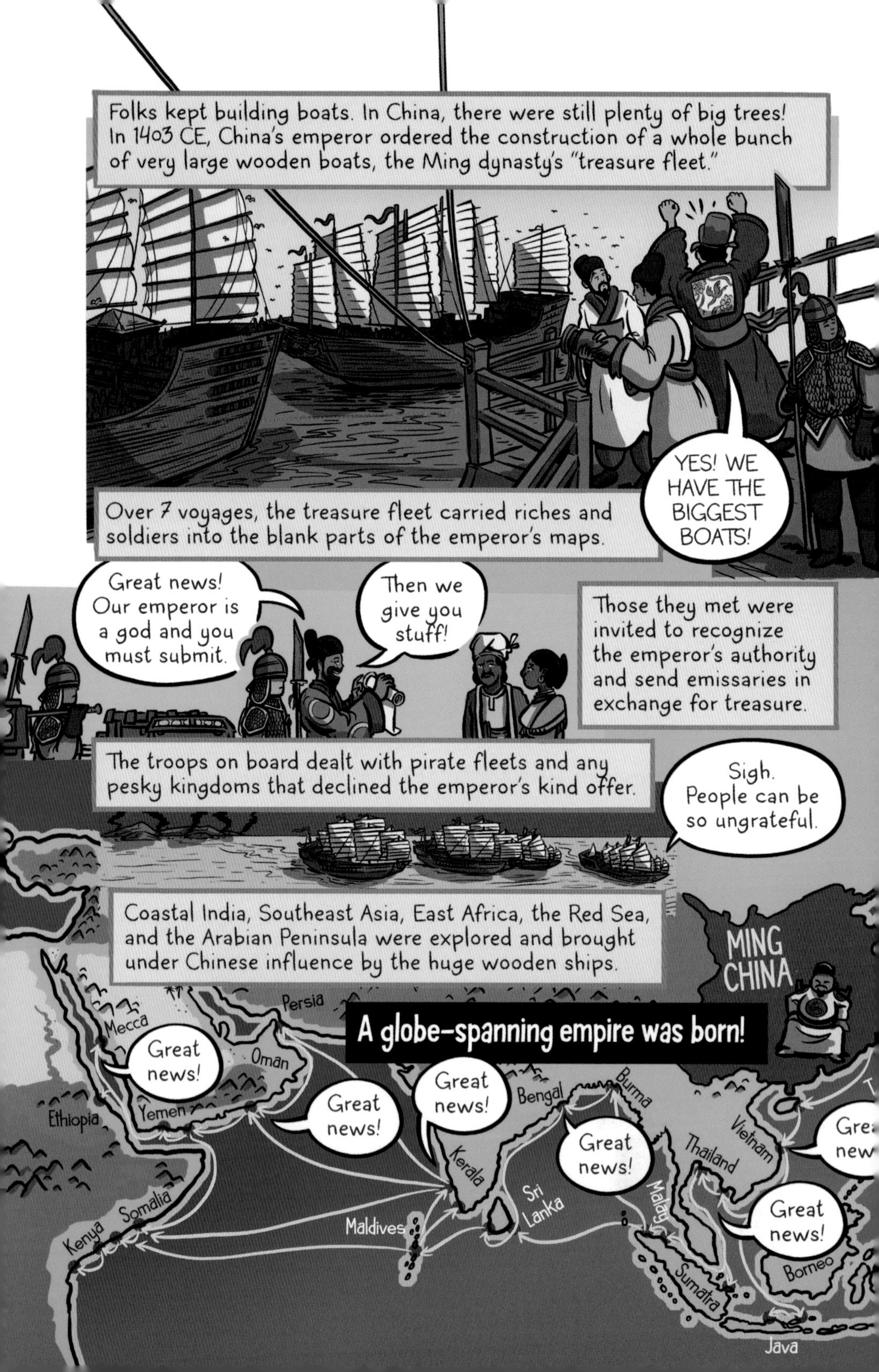
Folks kept building boats. In China, there were still plenty of big trees! In 1403 CE, China's emperor ordered the construction of a whole bunch of very large wooden boats, the Ming dynasty's "treasure fleet."
YES! WE HAVE THE BIGGEST BOATS!
Over 7 voyages, the treasure fleet carried riches and soldiers into the blank parts of the emperor's maps.
Great news! Our emperor is a god and you must submit.
Then we give you stuff!
Those they met were invited to recognize the emperor's authority and send emissaries in exchange for treasure.
The troops on board dealt with pirate fleets and any pesky kingdoms that declined the emperor's kind offer.
Sigh. People can be so ungrateful.
Coastal India, Southeast Asia, East Africa, the Red Sea, and the Arabian Peninsula were explored and brought under Chinese influence by the huge wooden ships.
MING CHINA
A globe-spanning empire was born!
Persia
Mecca
Great news!
Oman
Ethiopia
Yemen
Great news!
Great news!
Bengal
Burma
Great news!
Vietnam
Thailand
Kerala
Sri Lanka
Malay
Somalia
Kenya
Maldives
Great news!
Borneo
Sumatra
Java

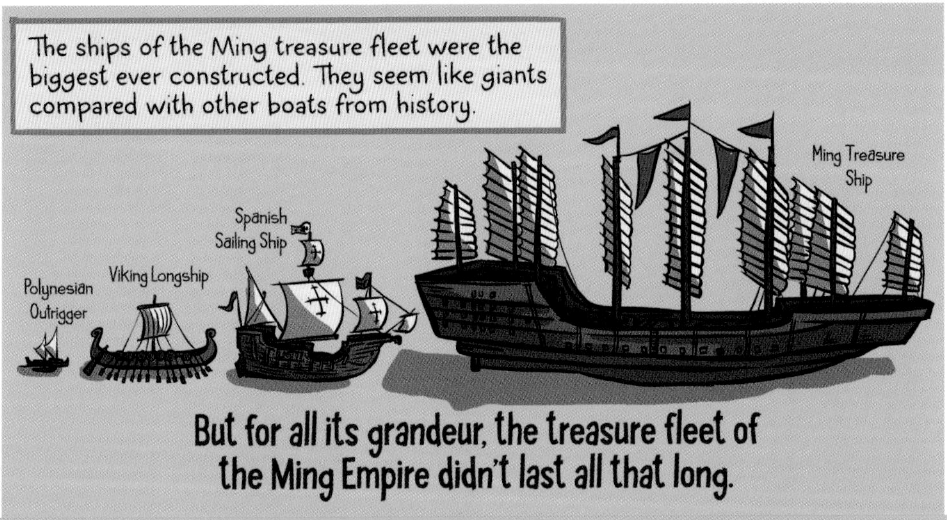
The ships of the Ming treasure fleet were the biggest ever constructed. They seem like giants compared with other boats from history.
Ming Treasure Ship
Spanish Sailing Ship
Viking Longship
Polynesian Outrigger
But for all its grandeur, the treasure fleet of the Ming Empire didn't last all that long.

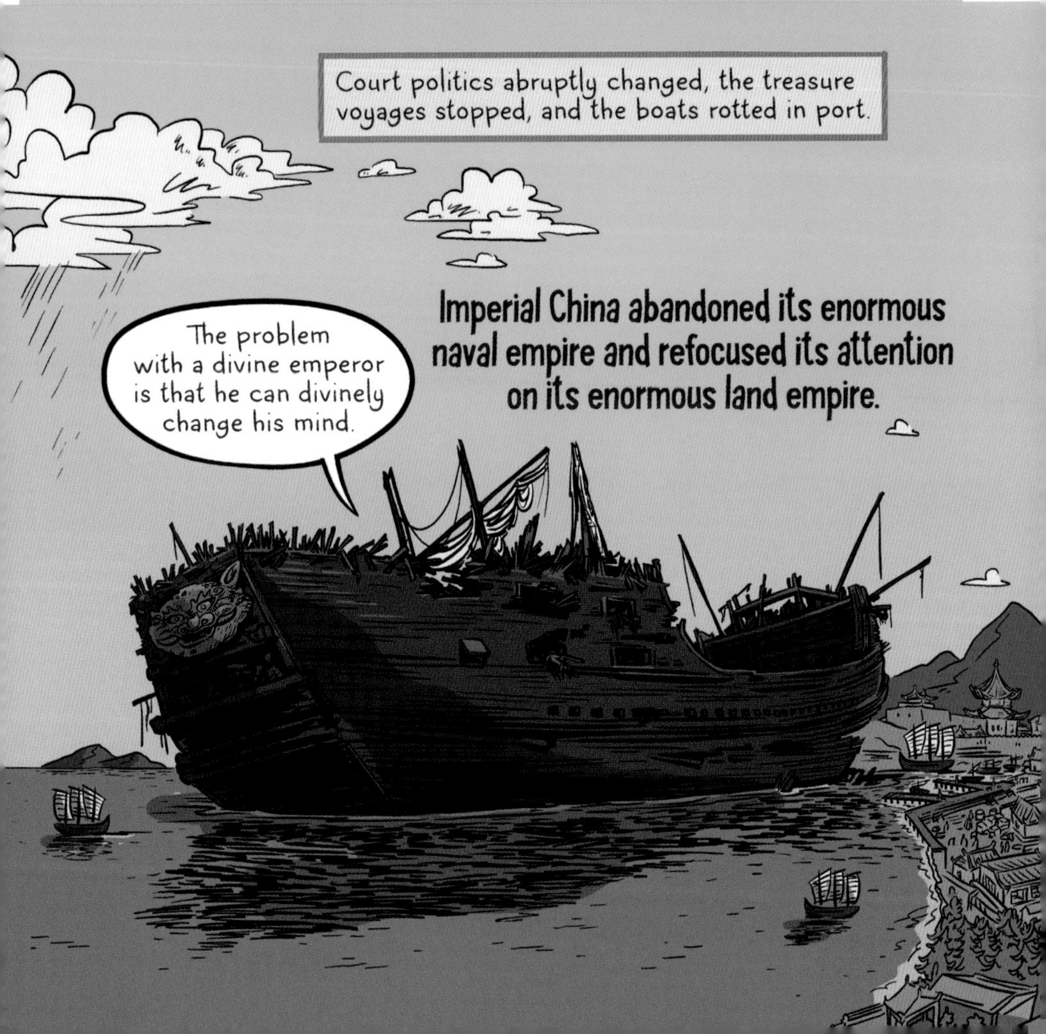
Court politics abruptly changed, the treasure voyages stopped, and the boats rotted in port.
Imperial China abandoned its enormous naval empire and refocused its attention on its enormous land empire.
The problem with a divine emperor is that he can divinely change his mind.

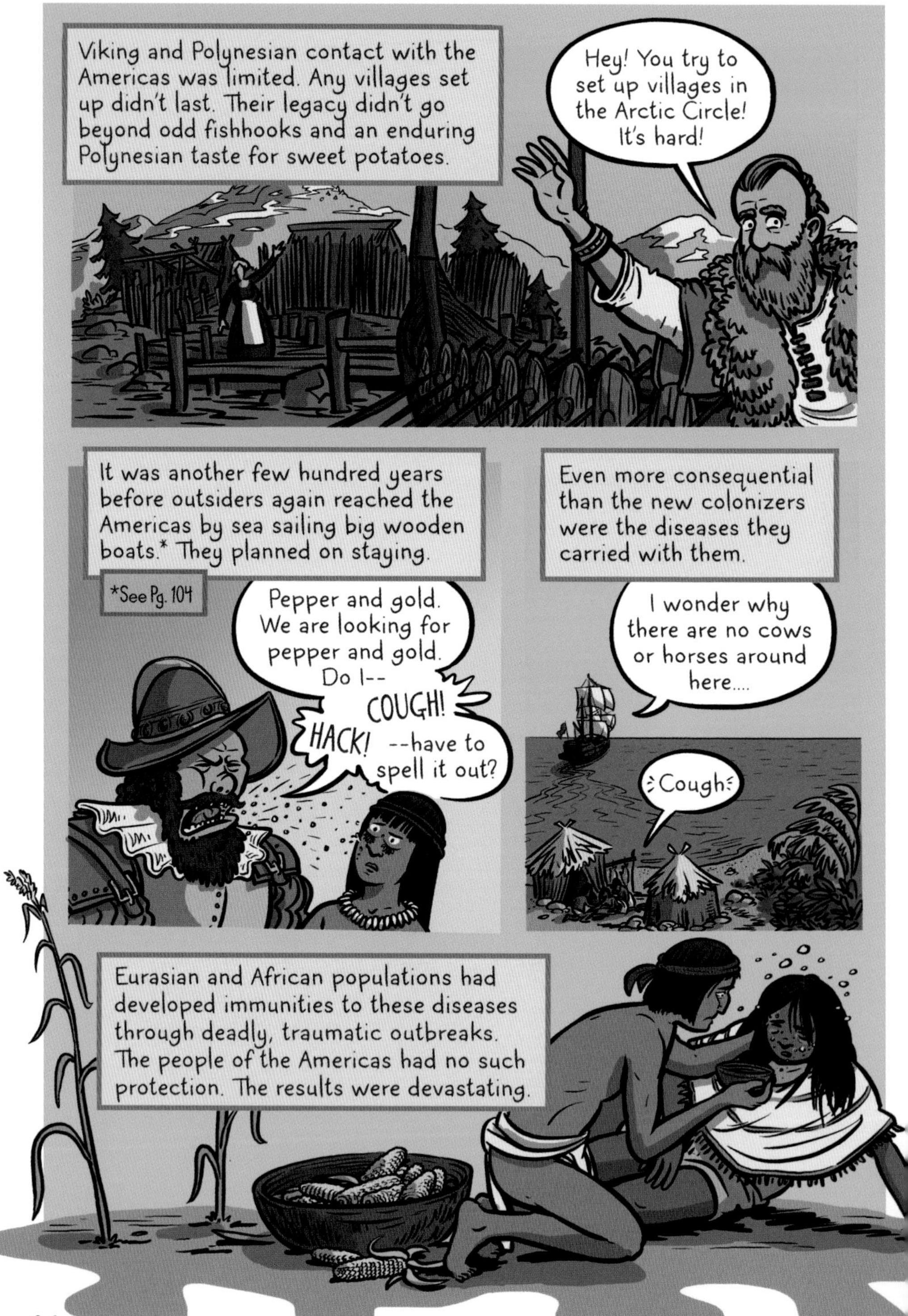

Viking and Polynesian contact with the Americas was limited. Any villages set up didn't last. Their legacy didn't go beyond odd fishhooks and an enduring Polynesian taste for sweet potatoes.
Hey! You try to set up villages in the Arctic Circle! It's hard!
It was another few hundred years before outsiders again reached the Americas by sea sailing big wooden boats.* They planned on staying.
*See Pg. 104
Pepper and gold. We are looking for pepper and gold. Do I--
COUGH!
HACK!
--have to spell it out?
Even more consequential than the new colonizers were the diseases they carried with them.
I wonder why there are no cows or horses around here....
Cough
Eurasian and African populations had developed immunities to these diseases through deadly, traumatic outbreaks. The people of the Americas had no such protection. The results were devastating.

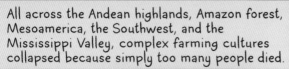 

The Indigenous population of the Americas fell from an estimated high of 60 million at first contact to 6 million in a little over a hundred years.

All across the Andean highlands, Amazon forest, Mesoamerica, the Southwest, and the Mississippi Valley, complex farming cultures collapsed because simply too many people died.

;Cough;

;Cough;

;Cough;

;Cough;

And, just like after Rome and the Black Death, the forests came back.

The thing is, forests suck in carbon dioxide. And so many forests came back during the Great Dying in the Americas, over such a broad swath of land, that global carbon levels dropped.

This in turn probably* contributed to a cooling of the earth known as the Little Ice Age.

Only called "little" because it didn't last as long. Not because it was any less cold and unpleasant!

Crop failures and famines led to unrest, wars, and religious violence across Europe in the 17th century. Religious minorities fled persecution and chaos to the colonies in the New World.

*Also maybe volcanoes? Causes of global temperature changes are hard enough to figure out even in modern times!

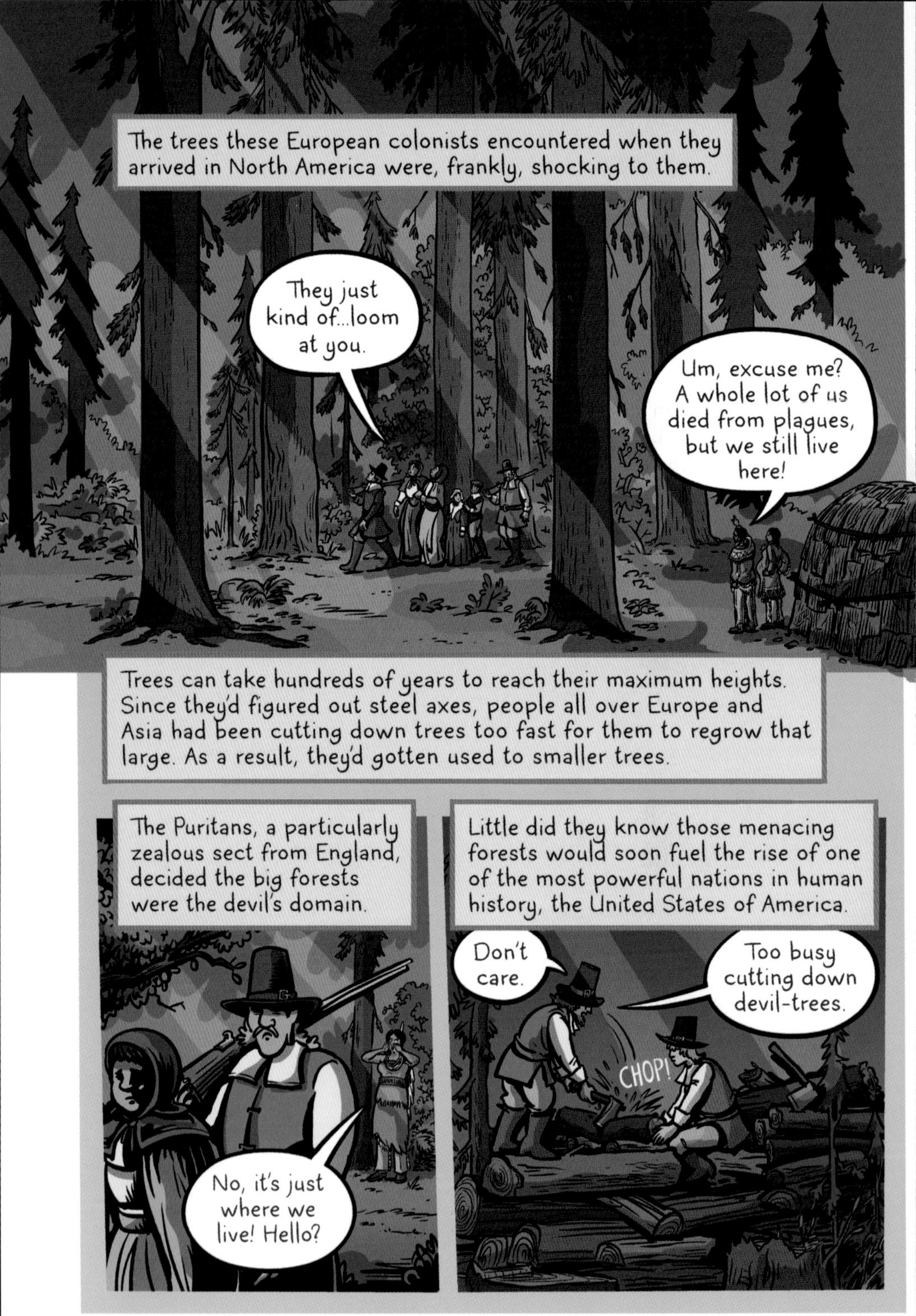
The trees these European colonists encountered when they arrived in North America were, frankly, shocking to them.
They just kind of...loom at you.
Um, excuse me? A whole lot of us died from plagues, but we still live here!
Trees can take hundreds of years to reach their maximum heights. Since they'd figured out steel axes, people all over Europe and Asia had been cutting down trees too fast for them to regrow that large. As a result, they'd gotten used to smaller trees.
The Puritans, a particularly zealous sect from England, decided the big forests were the devil's domain.
No, it's just where we live! Hello?
Little did they know those menacing forests would soon fuel the rise of one of the most powerful nations in human history, the United States of America.
Don't care.
Too busy cutting down devil-trees.
CHOP!

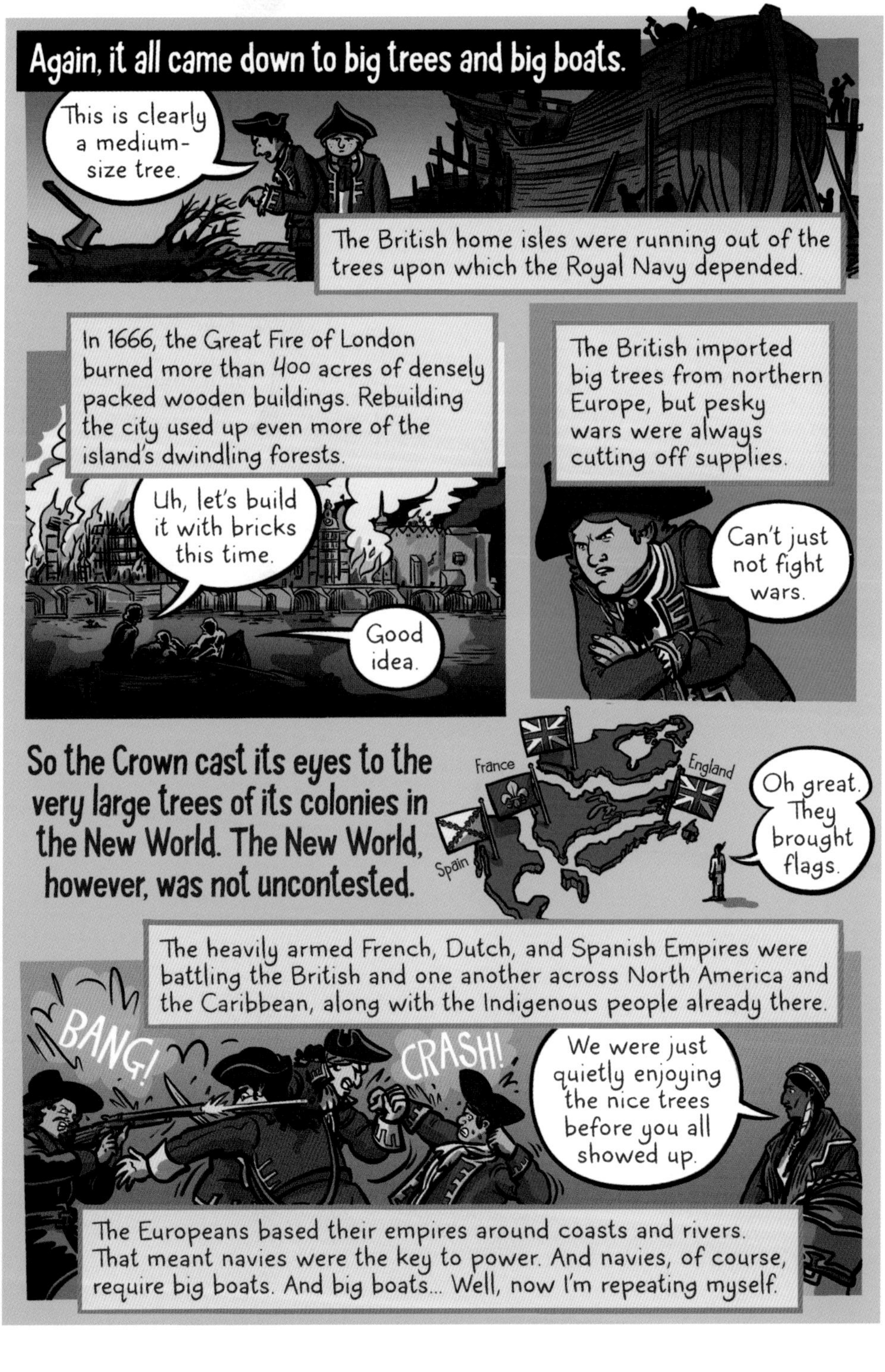
Again, it all came down to big trees and big boats.
This is clearly a medium-size tree.
The British home isles were running out of the trees upon which the Royal Navy depended.
In 1666, the Great Fire of London burned more than 400 acres of densely packed wooden buildings. Rebuilding the city used up even more of the island's dwindling forests.
Uh, let's build it with bricks this time.
Good idea.
The British imported big trees from northern Europe, but pesky wars were always cutting off supplies.
Can't just not fight wars.
So the Crown cast its eyes to the very large trees of its colonies in the New World. The New World, however, was not uncontested.
France
England
Spain
Oh great. They brought flags.
The heavily armed French, Dutch, and Spanish Empires were battling the British and one another across North America and the Caribbean, along with the Indigenous people already there.
BANG!
CRASH!
We were just quietly enjoying the nice trees before you all showed up.
The Europeans based their empires around coasts and rivers. That meant navies were the key to power. And navies, of course, require big boats. And big boats... Well, now I'm repeating myself.

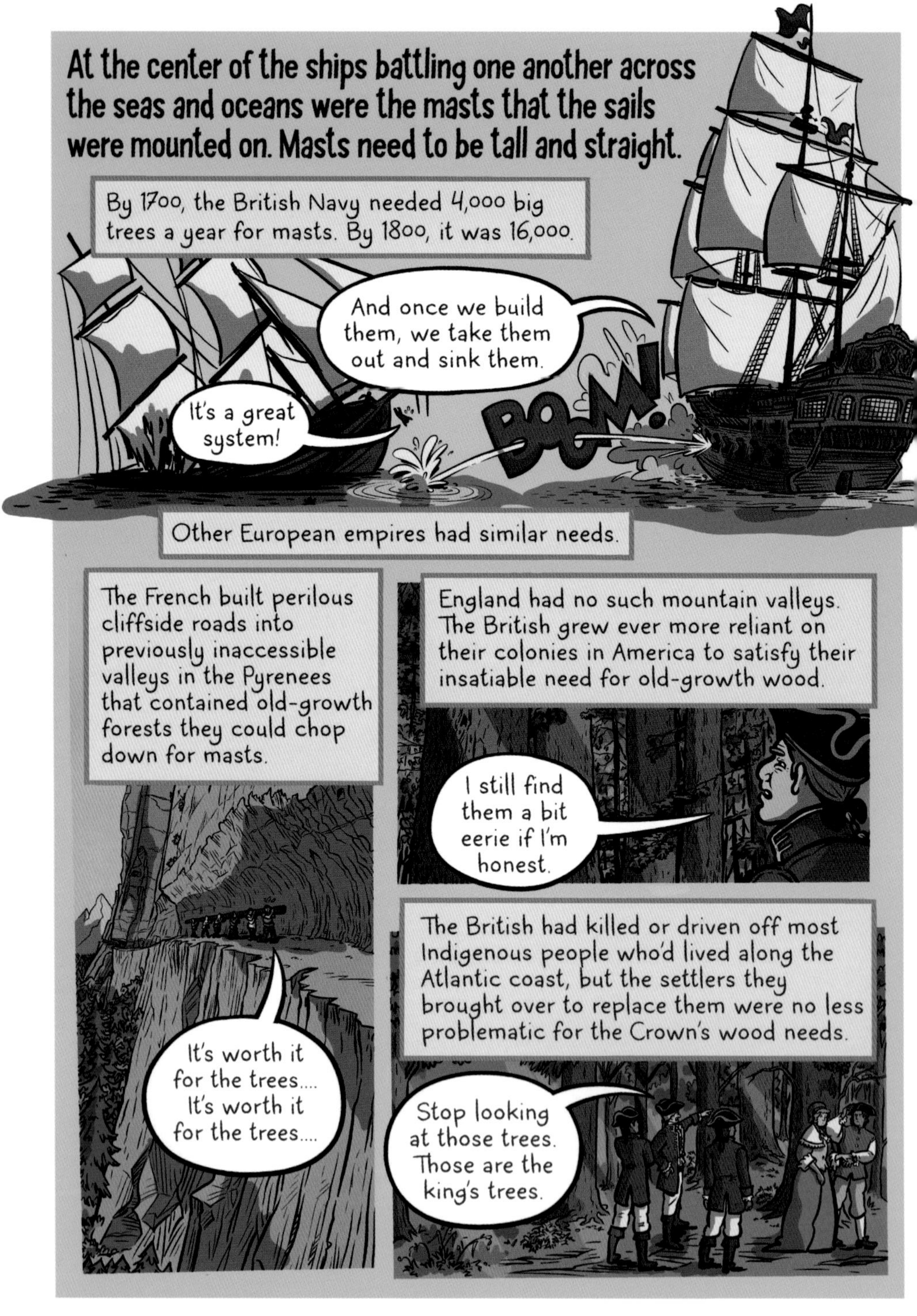
At the center of the ships battling one another across the seas and oceans were the masts that the sails were mounted on. Masts need to be tall and straight.
By 1700, the British Navy needed 4,000 big trees a year for masts. By 1800, it was 16,000.
And once we build them, we take them out and sink them.
It's a great system!
BOOM!
Other European empires had similar needs.
The French built perilous cliffside roads into previously inaccessible valleys in the Pyrenees that contained old-growth forests they could chop down for masts.
It's worth it for the trees.... It's worth it for the trees....
England had no such mountain valleys. The British grew ever more reliant on their colonies in America to satisfy their insatiable need for old-growth wood.
I still find them a bit eerie if I'm honest.
The British had killed or driven off most Indigenous people who'd lived along the Atlantic coast, but the settlers they brought over to replace them were no less problematic for the Crown's wood needs.
Stop looking at those trees. Those are the king's trees.

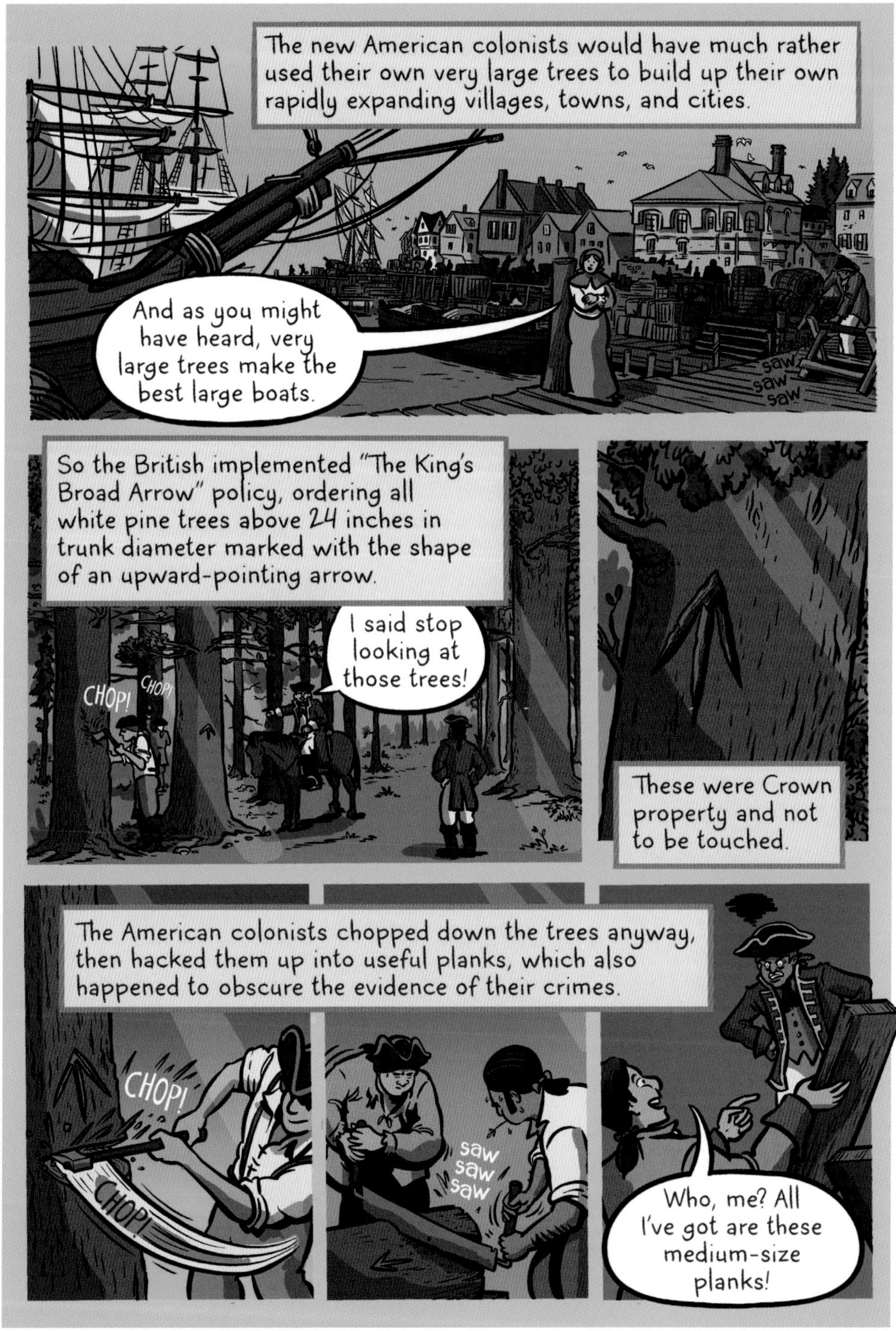
The new American colonists would have much rather used their own very large trees to build up their own rapidly expanding villages, towns, and cities.
And as you might have heard, very large trees make the best large boats.
saw saw saw
So the British implemented "The King's Broad Arrow" policy, ordering all white pine trees above 24 inches in trunk diameter marked with the shape of an upward-pointing arrow.
CHOP! CHOP!
I said stop looking at those trees!
These were Crown property and not to be touched.
The American colonists chopped down the trees anyway, then hacked them up into useful planks, which also happened to obscure the evidence of their crimes.
CHOP!
CHOP!
saw saw saw
Who, me? All I've got are these medium-size planks!

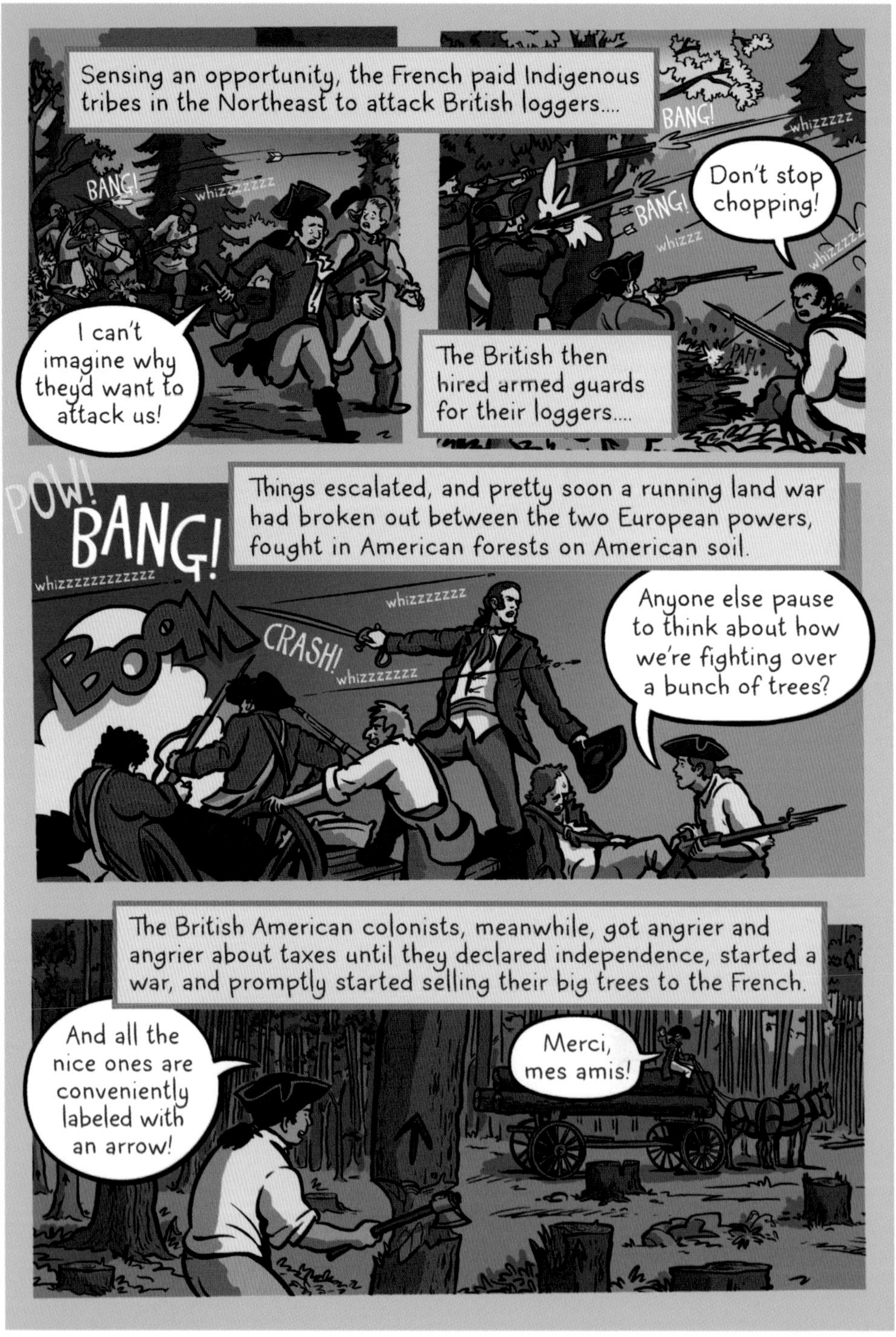

Sensing an opportunity, the French paid Indigenous tribes in the Northeast to attack British loggers....
BANG!
whizzzzzzz
I can't imagine why they'd want to attack us!
BANG!
whizzzzz
BANG!
whizzz
Don't stop chopping!
PAF!
The British then hired armed guards for their loggers....
POW!
BANG!
whizzzzzzzzzzzz
Things escalated, and pretty soon a running land war had broken out between the two European powers, fought in American forests on American soil.
whizzzzzzz
BOOM
CRASH!
whizzzzzzz
Anyone else pause to think about how we're fighting over a bunch of trees?
The British American colonists, meanwhile, got angrier and angrier about taxes until they declared independence, started a war, and promptly started selling their big trees to the French.
And all the nice ones are conveniently labeled with an arrow!
Merci, mes amis!

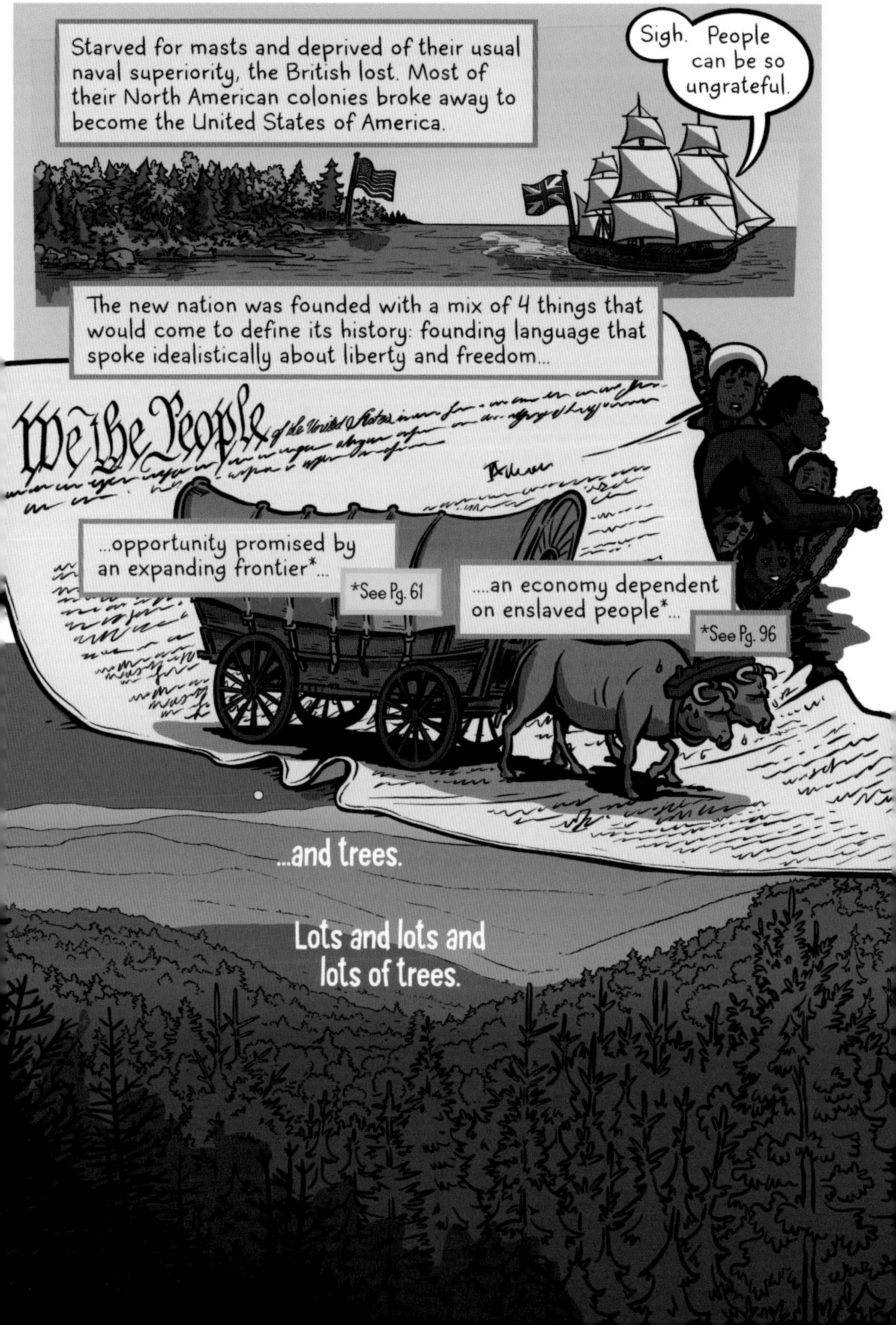

Starved for masts and deprived of their usual naval superiority, the British lost. Most of their North American colonies broke away to become the United States of America.
Sigh. People can be so ungrateful.
The new nation was founded with a mix of 4 things that would come to define its history: founding language that spoke idealistically about liberty and freedom...
We the People
...opportunity promised by an expanding frontier*...
*See Pg. 61
....an economy dependent on enslaved people*...
*See Pg. 96
...and trees.
Lots and lots and lots of trees.

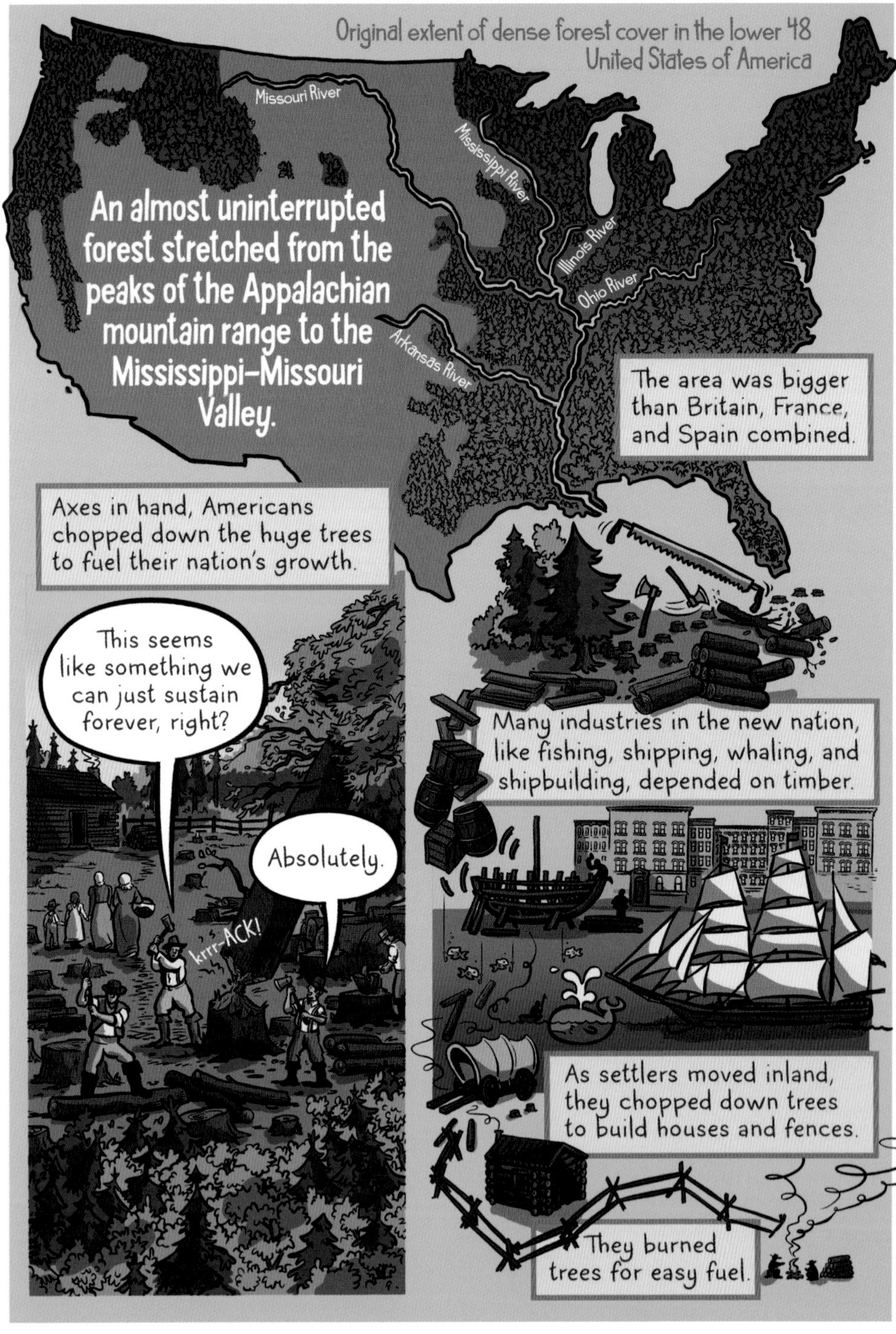
Original extent of dense forest cover in the lower 48 United States of America
Missouri River
Mississippi River
Illinois River
Ohio River
Arkansas River
An almost uninterrupted forest stretched from the peaks of the Appalachian mountain range to the Mississippi-Missouri Valley.
The area was bigger than Britain, France, and Spain combined.
Axes in hand, Americans chopped down the huge trees to fuel their nation's growth.
This seems like something we can just sustain forever, right?
Absolutely.
krrr-ACK!
Many industries in the new nation, like fishing, shipping, whaling, and shipbuilding, depended on timber.
As settlers moved inland, they chopped down trees to build houses and fences.
They burned trees for easy fuel.

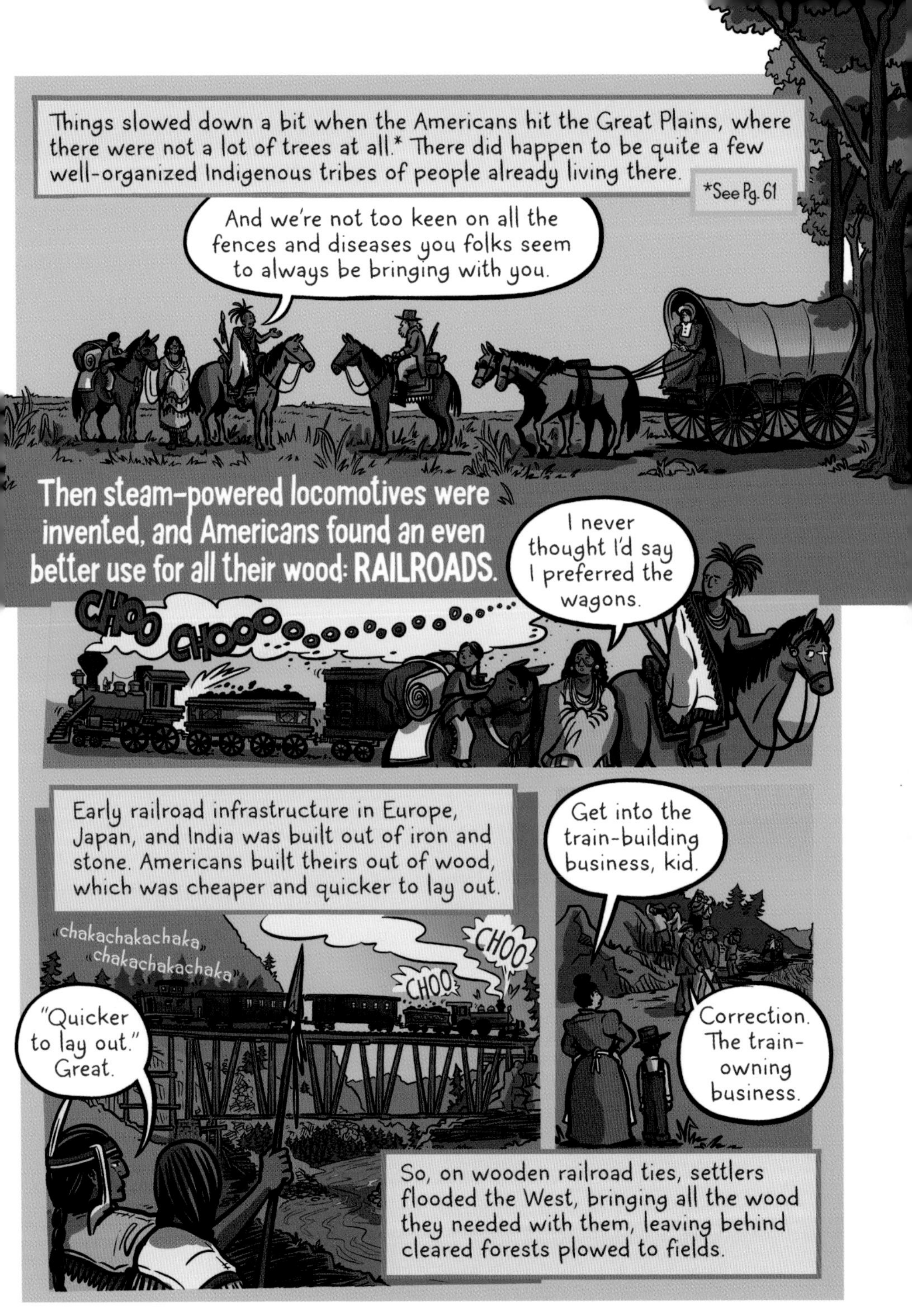

Things slowed down a bit when the Americans hit the Great Plains, where there were not a lot of trees at all.* There did happen to be quite a few well-organized Indigenous tribes of people already living there.
*See Pg. 61
And we're not too keen on all the fences and diseases you folks seem to always be bringing with you.
Then steam-powered locomotives were invented, and Americans found an even better use for all their wood: RAILROADS.
I never thought I'd say I preferred the wagons.
CHOO CHOOOOO...
Early railroad infrastructure in Europe, Japan, and India was built out of iron and stone. Americans built theirs out of wood, which was cheaper and quicker to lay out.
«chakachakachaka»
«chakachakachaka»
CHOO
CHOO
"Quicker to lay out." Great.
Get into the train-building business, kid.
Correction. The train-owning business.
So, on wooden railroad ties, settlers flooded the West, bringing all the wood they needed with them, leaving behind cleared forests plowed to fields.

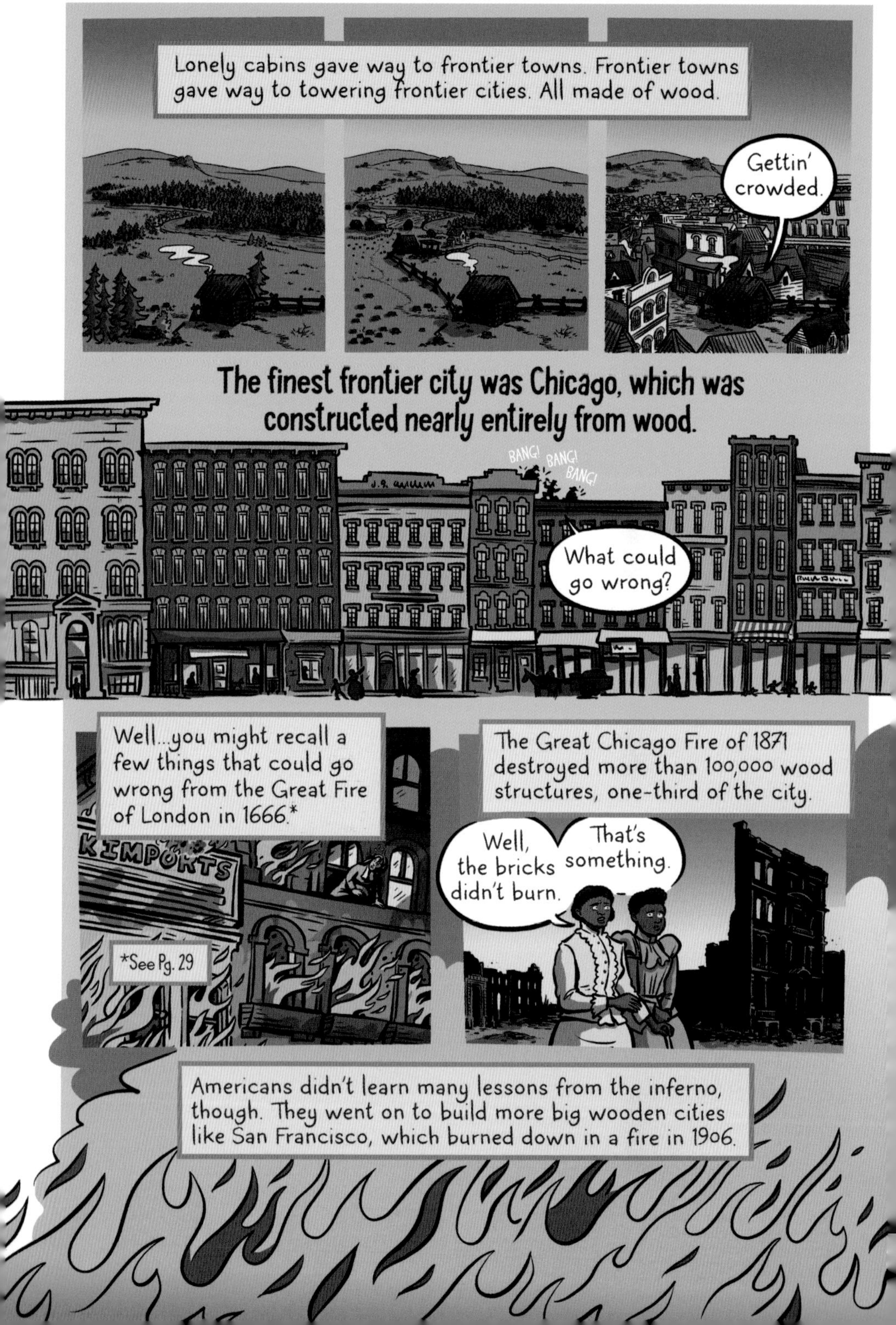
Lonely cabins gave way to frontier towns. Frontier towns gave way to towering frontier cities. All made of wood.
Gettin' crowded.
The finest frontier city was Chicago, which was constructed nearly entirely from wood.
BANG! BANG! BANG!
What could go wrong?
Well...you might recall a few things that could go wrong from the Great Fire of London in 1666.*
KIMPORTS
*See Pg. 29
The Great Chicago Fire of 1871 destroyed more than 100,000 wood structures, one-third of the city.
Well, the bricks didn't burn.
That's something.
Americans didn't learn many lessons from the inferno, though. They went on to build more big wooden cities like San Francisco, which burned down in a fire in 1906.

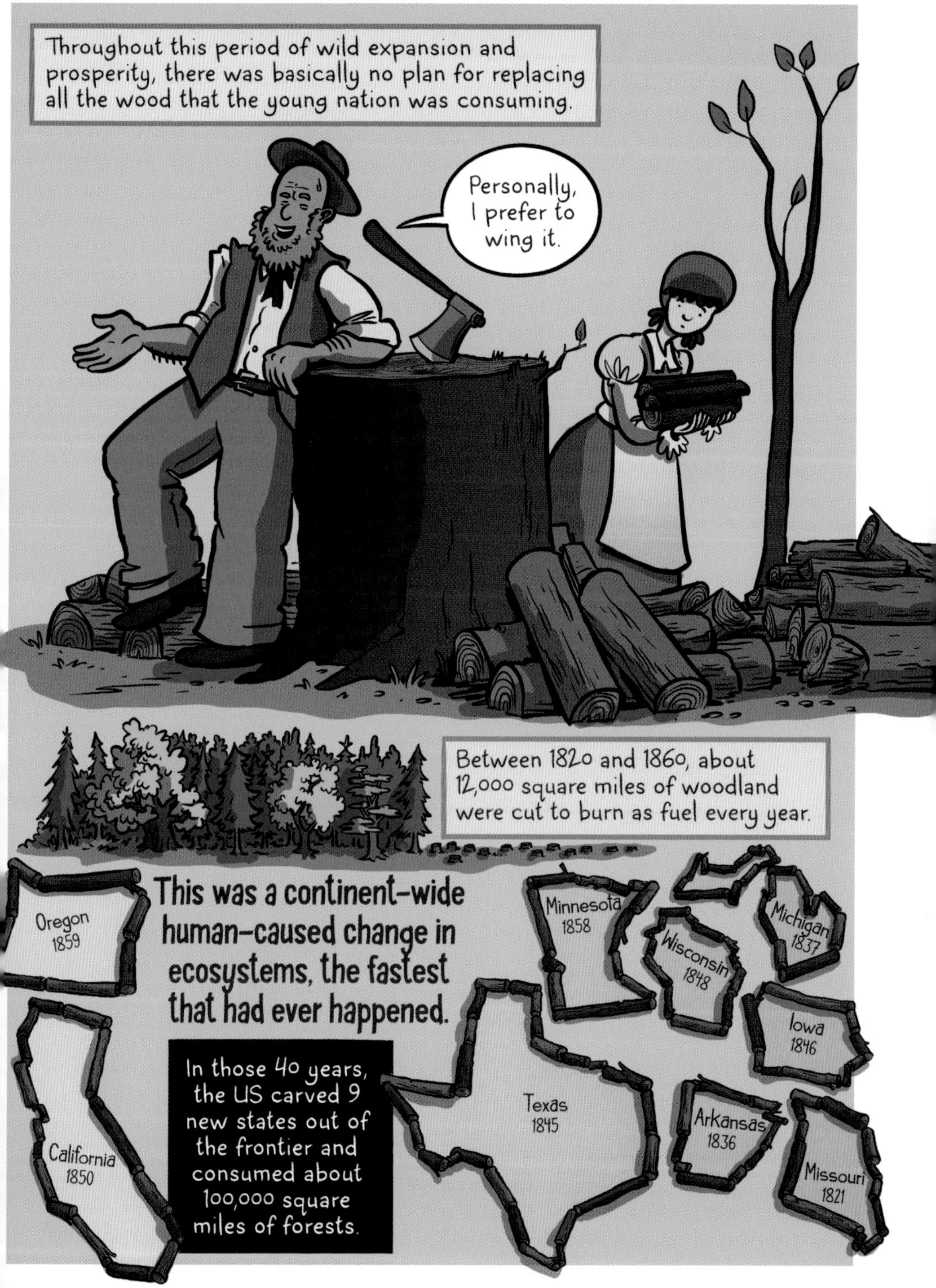
Throughout this period of wild expansion and prosperity, there was basically no plan for replacing all the wood that the young nation was consuming.
Personally, I prefer to wing it.
Between 1820 and 1860, about 12,000 square miles of woodland were cut to burn as fuel every year.
This was a continent-wide human-caused change in ecosystems, the fastest that had ever happened.
In those 40 years, the US carved 9 new states out of the frontier and consumed about 100,000 square miles of forests.
Oregon 1859
California 1850
Minnesota 1858
Wisconsin 1848
Michigan 1837
Iowa 1846
Texas 1845
Arkansas 1836
Missouri 1821

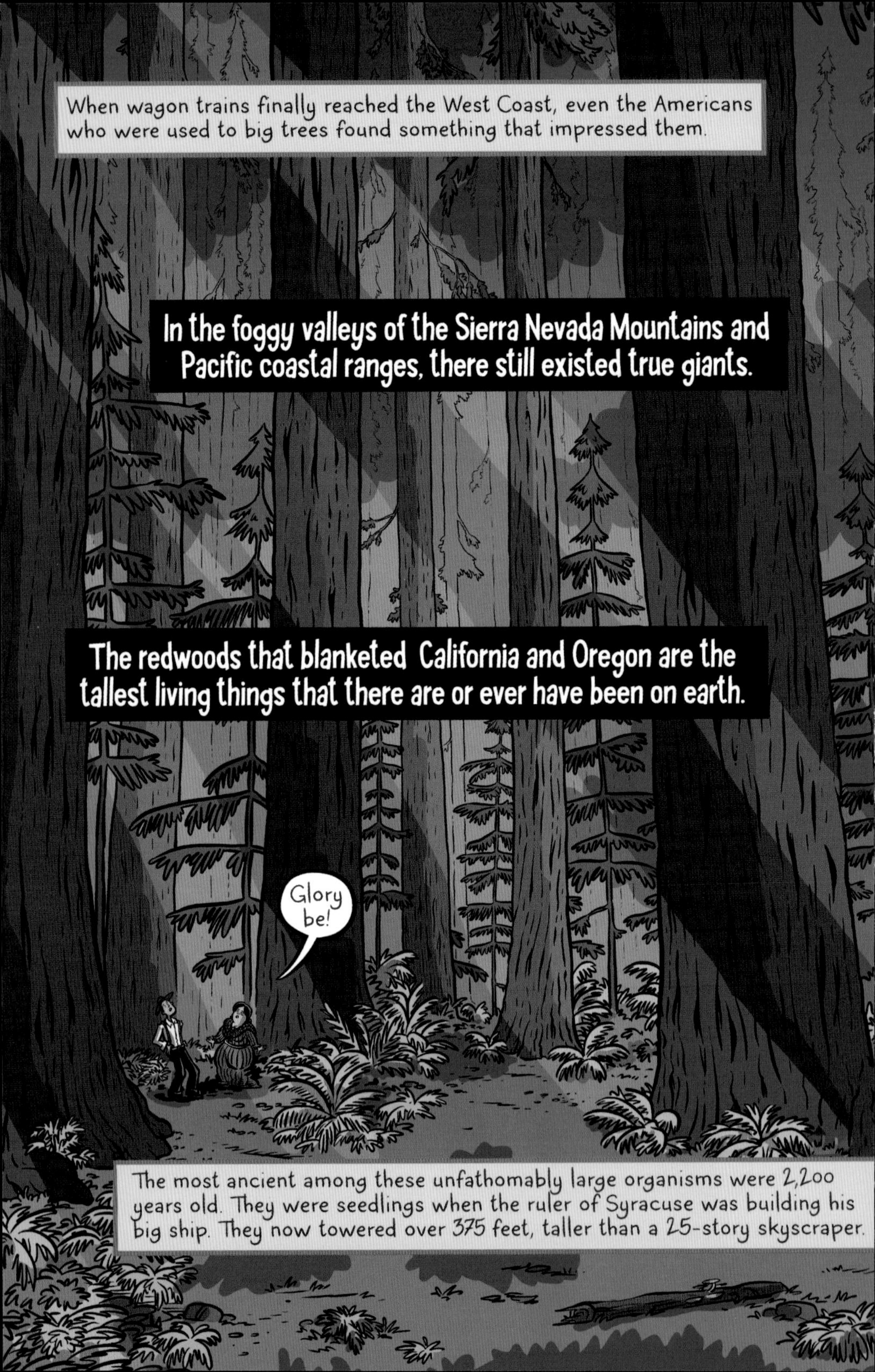

When wagon trains finally reached the West Coast, even the Americans who were used to big trees found something that impressed them.
In the foggy valleys of the Sierra Nevada Mountains and Pacific coastal ranges, there still existed true giants.
The redwoods that blanketed California and Oregon are the tallest living things that there are or ever have been on earth.
Glory be!
The most ancient among these unfathomably large organisms were 2,200 years old. They were seedlings when the ruler of Syracuse was building his big ship. They now towered over 375 feet, taller than a 25-story skyscraper.

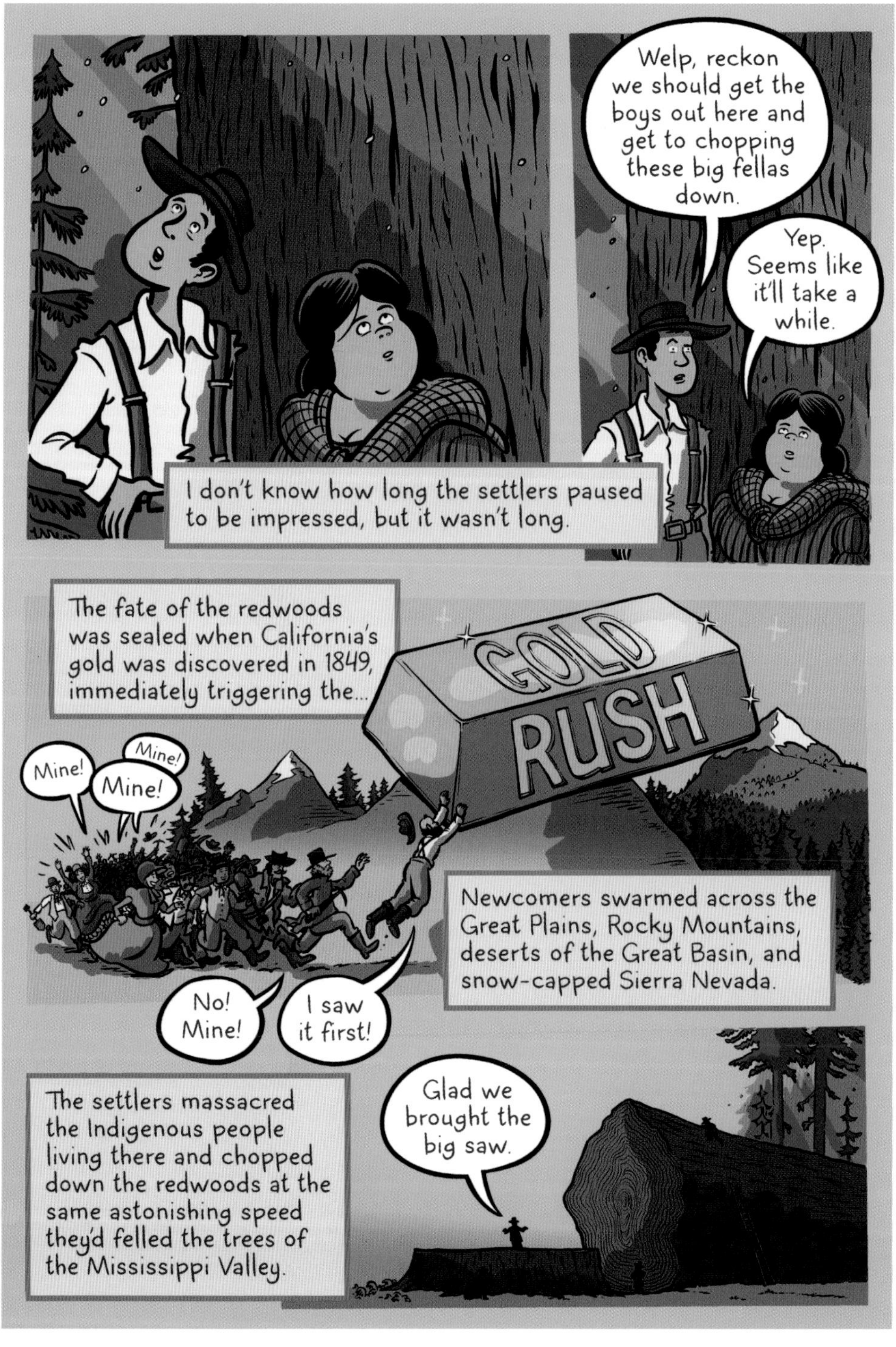
I don't know how long the settlers paused to be impressed, but it wasn't long.
Welp, reckon we should get the boys out here and get to chopping these big fellas down.
Yep. Seems like it'll take a while.
The fate of the redwoods was sealed when California's gold was discovered in 1849, immediately triggering the...
GOLD RUSH
Mine!
Mine!
Mine!
No! Mine!
I saw it first!
Newcomers swarmed across the Great Plains, Rocky Mountains, deserts of the Great Basin, and snow-capped Sierra Nevada.
The settlers massacred the Indigenous people living there and chopped down the redwoods at the same astonishing speed they'd felled the trees of the Mississippi Valley.
Glad we brought the big saw.

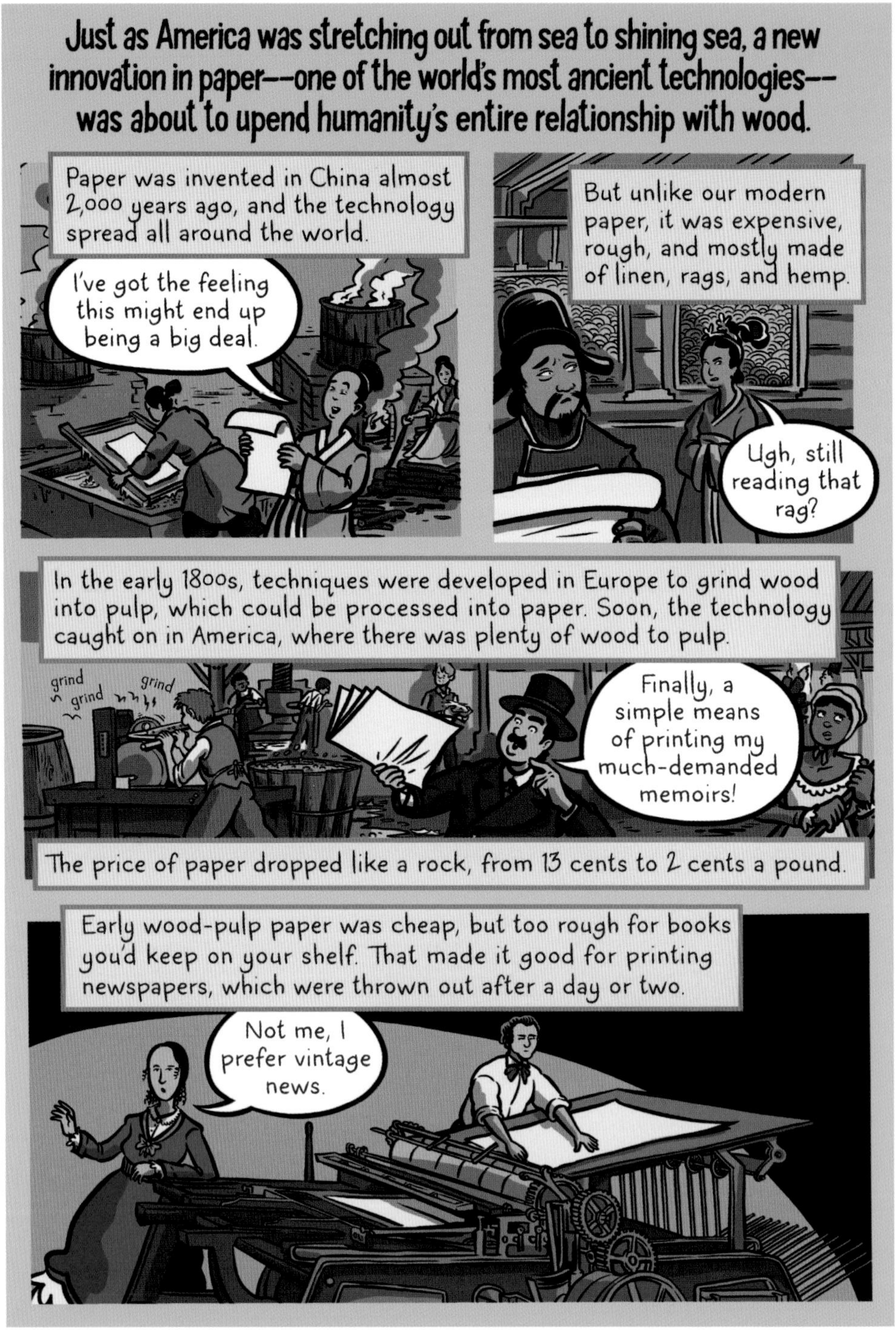
Just as America was stretching out from sea to shining sea, a new innovation in paper--one of the world's most ancient technologies--was about to upend humanity's entire relationship with wood.
Paper was invented in China almost 2,000 years ago, and the technology spread all around the world.
I've got the feeling this might end up being a big deal.
But unlike our modern paper, it was expensive, rough, and mostly made of linen, rags, and hemp.
Ugh, still reading that rag?
In the early 1800s, techniques were developed in Europe to grind wood into pulp, which could be processed into paper. Soon, the technology caught on in America, where there was plenty of wood to pulp.
grind grind grind
Finally, a simple means of printing my much-demanded memoirs!
The price of paper dropped like a rock, from 13 cents to 2 cents a pound.
Early wood-pulp paper was cheap, but too rough for books you'd keep on your shelf. That made it good for printing newspapers, which were thrown out after a day or two.
Not me, I prefer vintage news.

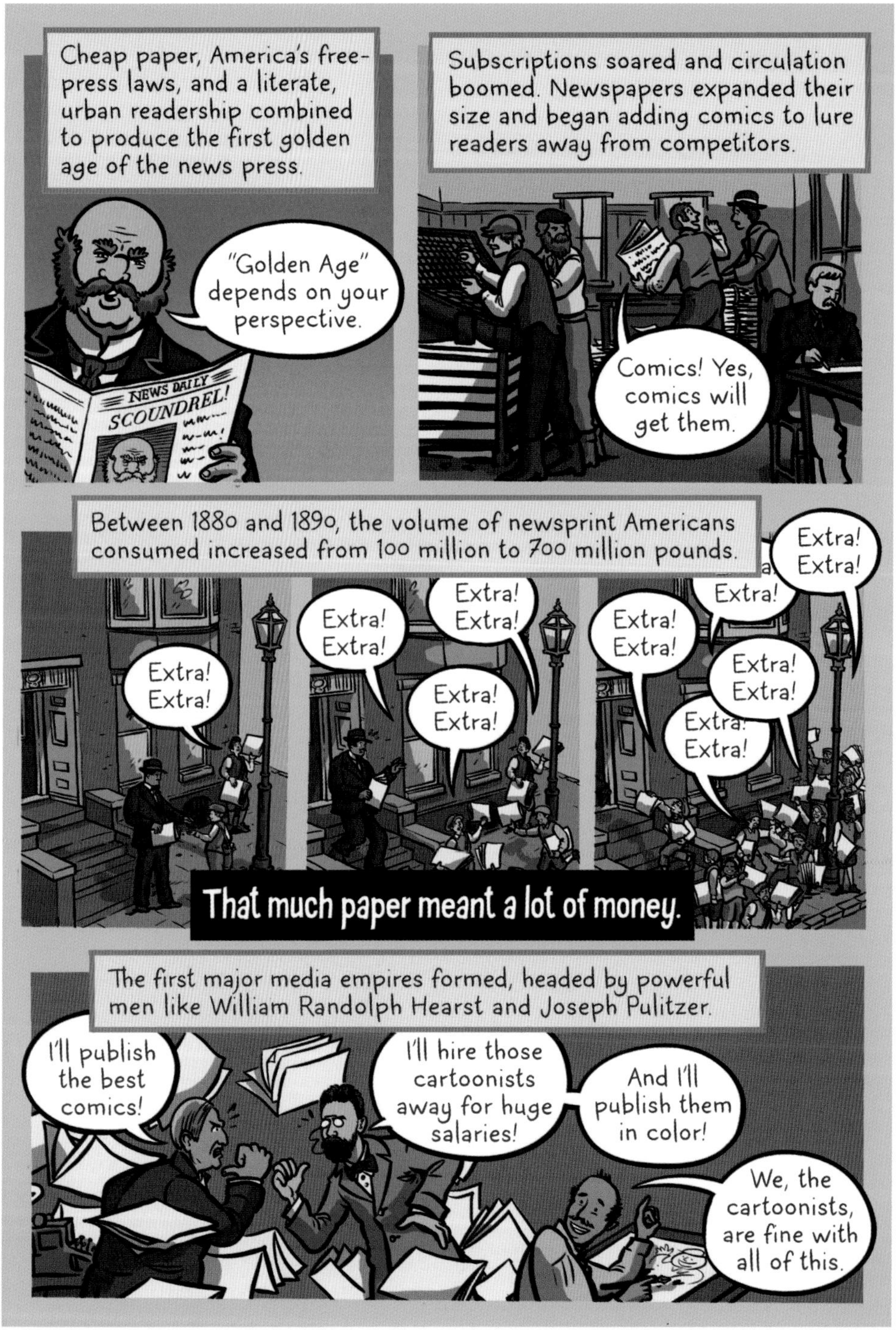

Cheap paper, America's free-press laws, and a literate, urban readership combined to produce the first golden age of the news press.
"Golden Age" depends on your perspective.
NEWS DAILY
SCOUNDREL!
Subscriptions soared and circulation boomed. Newspapers expanded their size and began adding comics to lure readers away from competitors.
Comics! Yes, comics will get them.
Between 1880 and 1890, the volume of newsprint Americans consumed increased from 100 million to 700 million pounds.
Extra! Extra!
Extra! Extra!
Extra! Extra!
Extra! Extra!
Extra! Extra!
Extra!
Extra! Extra!
Extra! Extra!
Extra! Extra!
That much paper meant a lot of money.
The first major media empires formed, headed by powerful men like William Randolph Hearst and Joseph Pulitzer.
I'll publish the best comics!
I'll hire those cartoonists away for huge salaries!
And I'll publish them in color!
We, the cartoonists, are fine with all of this.

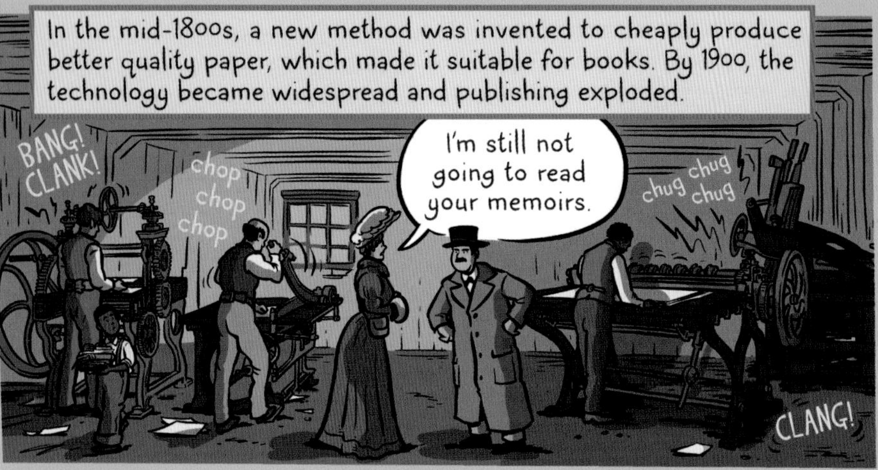
In the mid-1800s, a new method was invented to cheaply produce better quality paper, which made it suitable for books. By 1900, the technology became widespread and publishing exploded.
BANG! CLANK!
chop chop chop
I'm still not going to read your memoirs.
chug chug chug
CLANG!

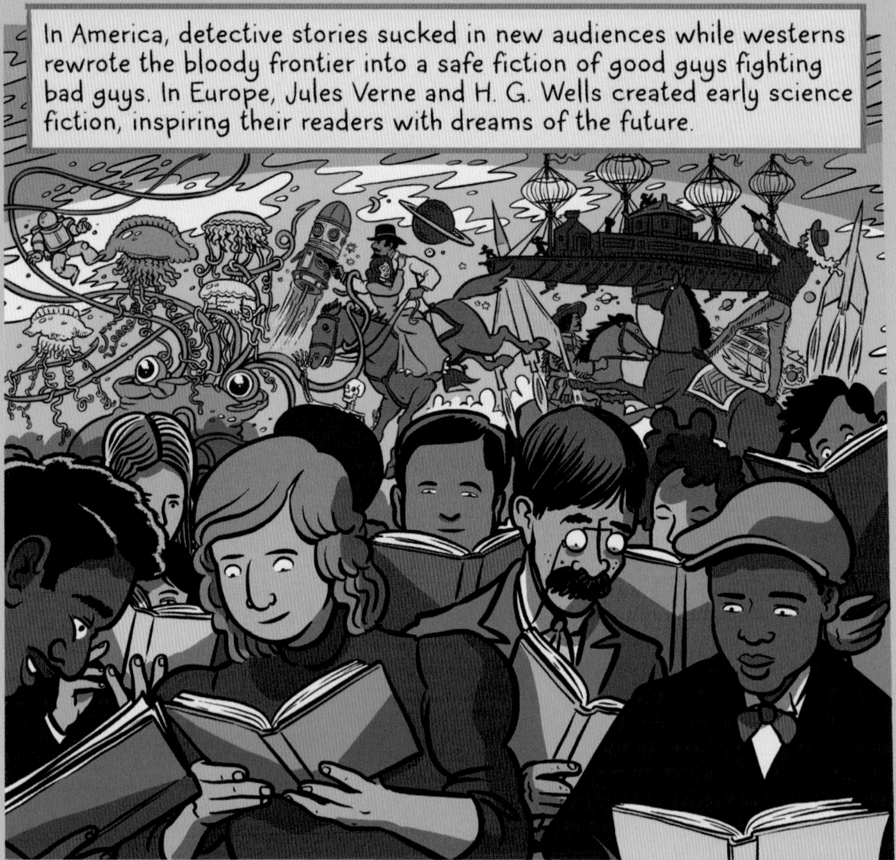
In America, detective stories sucked in new audiences while westerns rewrote the bloody frontier into a safe fiction of good guys fighting bad guys. In Europe, Jules Verne and H. G. Wells created early science fiction, inspiring their readers with dreams of the future.

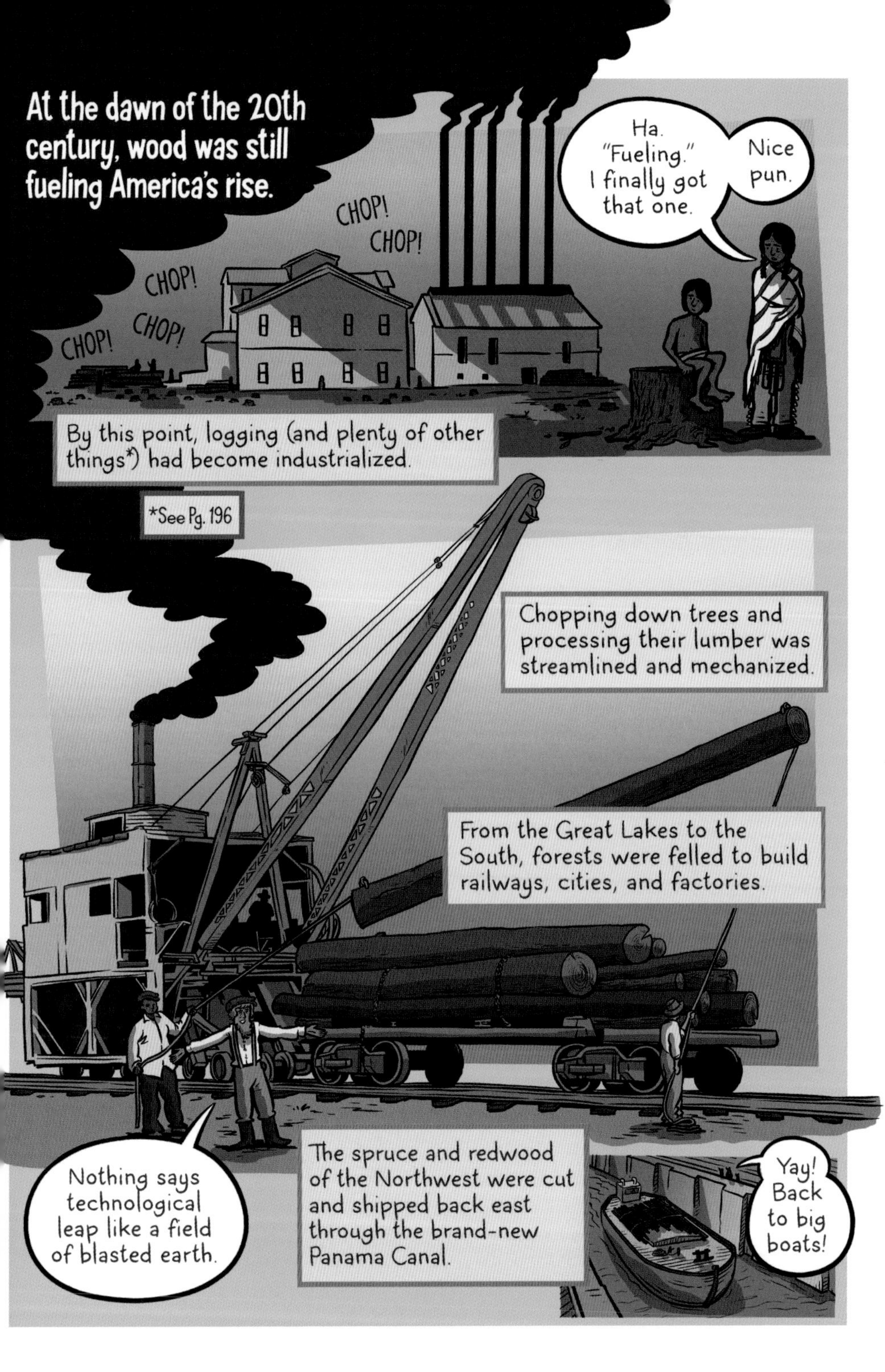
At the dawn of the 20th century, wood was still fueling America's rise.
CHOP! CHOP!
CHOP! CHOP! CHOP!
Ha. "Fueling." I finally got that one.
Nice pun.
By this point, logging (and plenty of other things*) had become industrialized.
*See Pg. 196
Chopping down trees and processing their lumber was streamlined and mechanized.
From the Great Lakes to the South, forests were felled to build railways, cities, and factories.
Nothing says technological leap like a field of blasted earth.
The spruce and redwood of the Northwest were cut and shipped back east through the brand-new Panama Canal.
Yay! Back to big boats!

In the 1940s, industrialized logging spread across the world. Chain saws and bulldozers cut roads into the dense old growth of the tropics, clearing green hills and valleys at ever faster speeds.

This seems like something we can just sus--

Look.

We get it.

VRRRRRRRRRR

rrumble

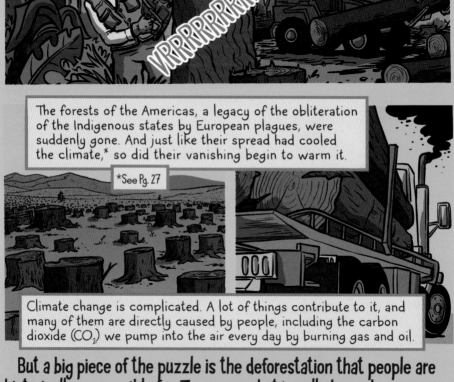

The forests of the Americas, a legacy of the obliteration of the Indigenous states by European plagues, were suddenly gone. And just like their spread had cooled the climate,* so did their vanishing begin to warm it.

*See Pg. 27

Climate change is complicated. A lot of things contribute to it, and many of them are directly caused by people, including the carbon dioxide (CO_2) we pump into the air every day by burning gas and oil.

But a big piece of the puzzle is the deforestation that people are historically responsible for. Trees are what is called a carbon reserve. When they're gone, the carbon in them goes into the atmosphere.

By the 1950s, scientists had started to figure this out.

Most other people didn't pay too much attention.

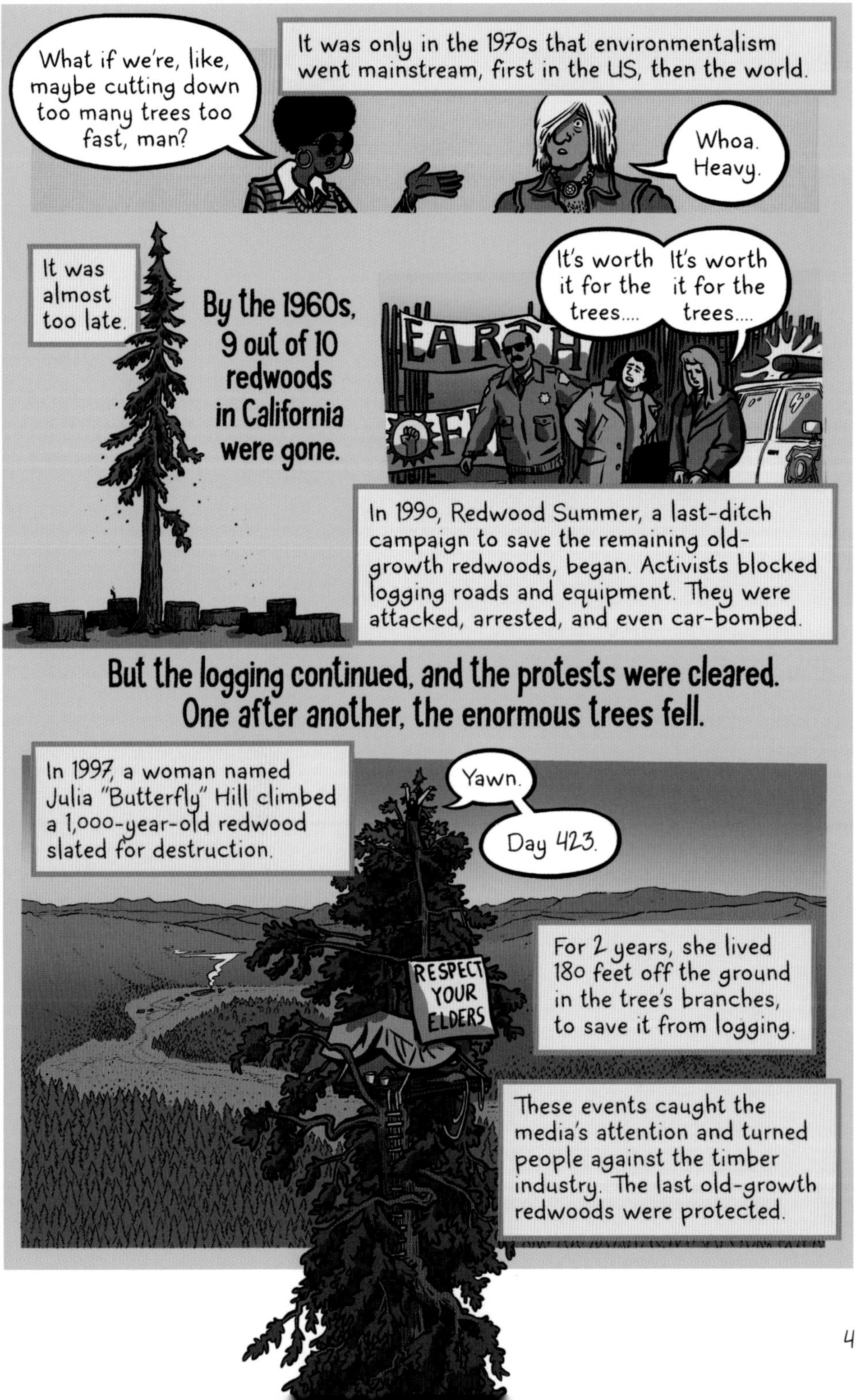
It was only in the 1970s that environmentalism went mainstream, first in the US, then the world.
What if we're, like, maybe cutting down too many trees too fast, man?
Whoa. Heavy.
It was almost too late.
By the 1960s, 9 out of 10 redwoods in California were gone.
EARTH
It's worth it for the trees....
It's worth it for the trees....
In 1990, Redwood Summer, a last-ditch campaign to save the remaining old-growth redwoods, began. Activists blocked logging roads and equipment. They were attacked, arrested, and even car-bombed.
But the logging continued, and the protests were cleared. One after another, the enormous trees fell.
In 1997, a woman named Julia "Butterfly" Hill climbed a 1,000-year-old redwood slated for destruction.
Yawn.
Day 423.
RESPECT YOUR ELDERS
For 2 years, she lived 180 feet off the ground in the tree's branches, to save it from logging.
These events caught the media's attention and turned people against the timber industry. The last old-growth redwoods were protected.

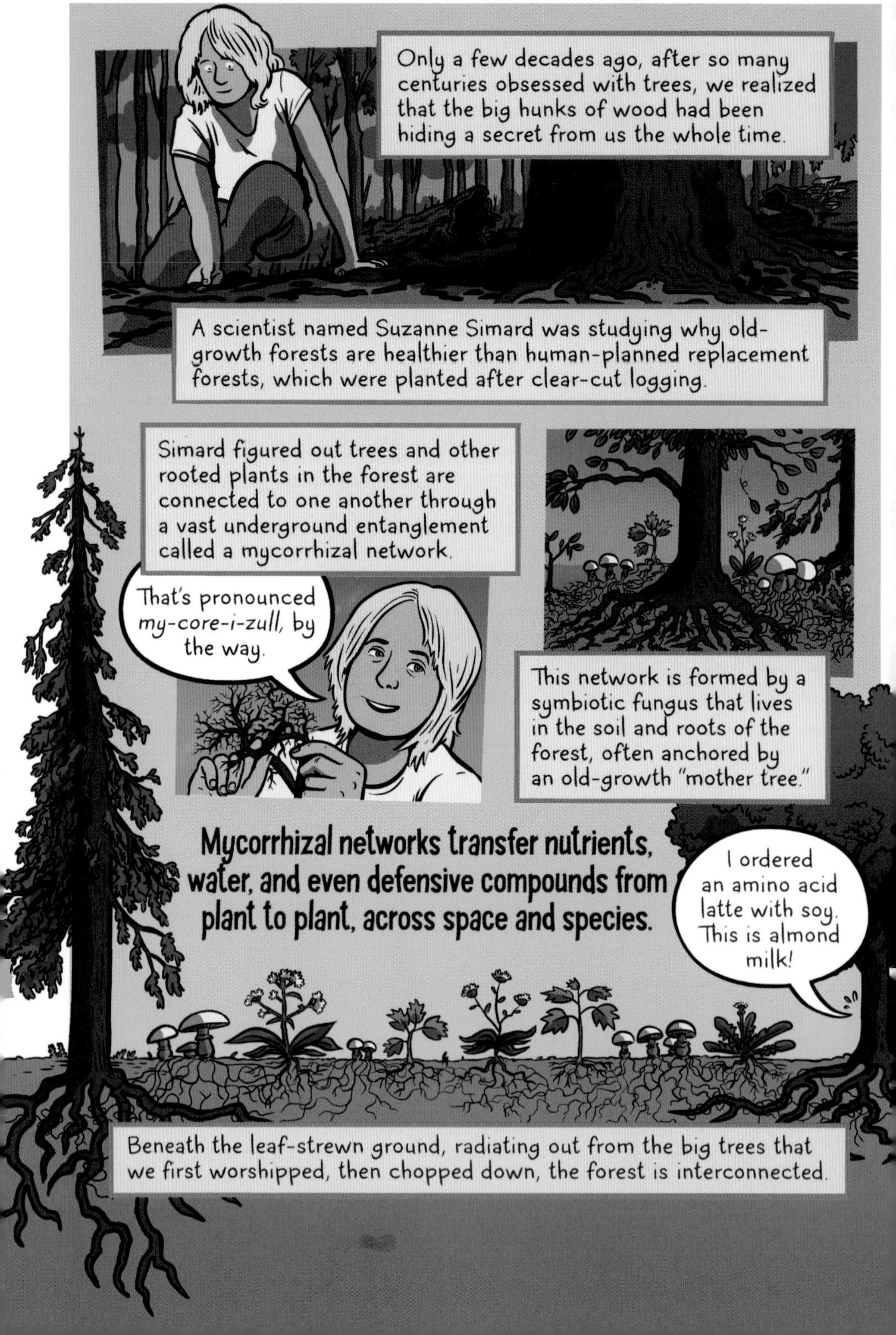
Only a few decades ago, after so many centuries obsessed with trees, we realized that the big hunks of wood had been hiding a secret from us the whole time.
A scientist named Suzanne Simard was studying why old-growth forests are healthier than human-planned replacement forests, which were planted after clear-cut logging.
Simard figured out trees and other rooted plants in the forest are connected to one another through a vast underground entanglement called a mycorrhizal network.
That's pronounced my-core-i-zull, by the way.
This network is formed by a symbiotic fungus that lives in the soil and roots of the forest, often anchored by an old-growth "mother tree."
Mycorrhizal networks transfer nutrients, water, and even defensive compounds from plant to plant, across space and species.
I ordered an amino acid latte with soy. This is almond milk!
Beneath the leaf-strewn ground, radiating out from the big trees that we first worshipped, then chopped down, the forest is interconnected.

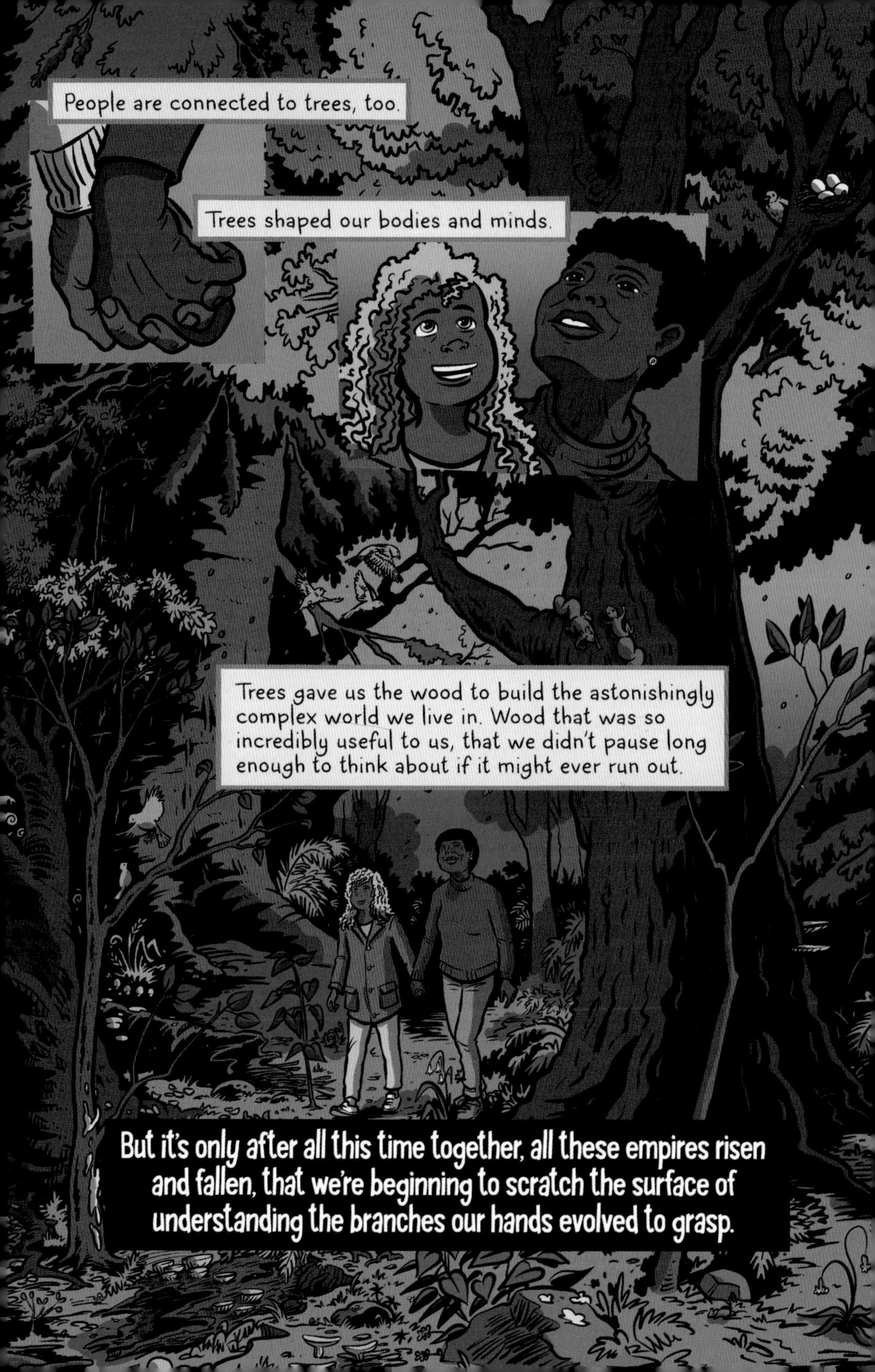
People are connected to trees, too.
Trees shaped our bodies and minds.
Trees gave us the wood to build the astonishingly complex world we live in. Wood that was so incredibly useful to us, that we didn't pause long enough to think about if it might ever run out.
But it's only after all this time together, all these empires risen and fallen, that we're beginning to scratch the surface of understanding the branches our hands evolved to grasp.

Chapter Two: WHEAT

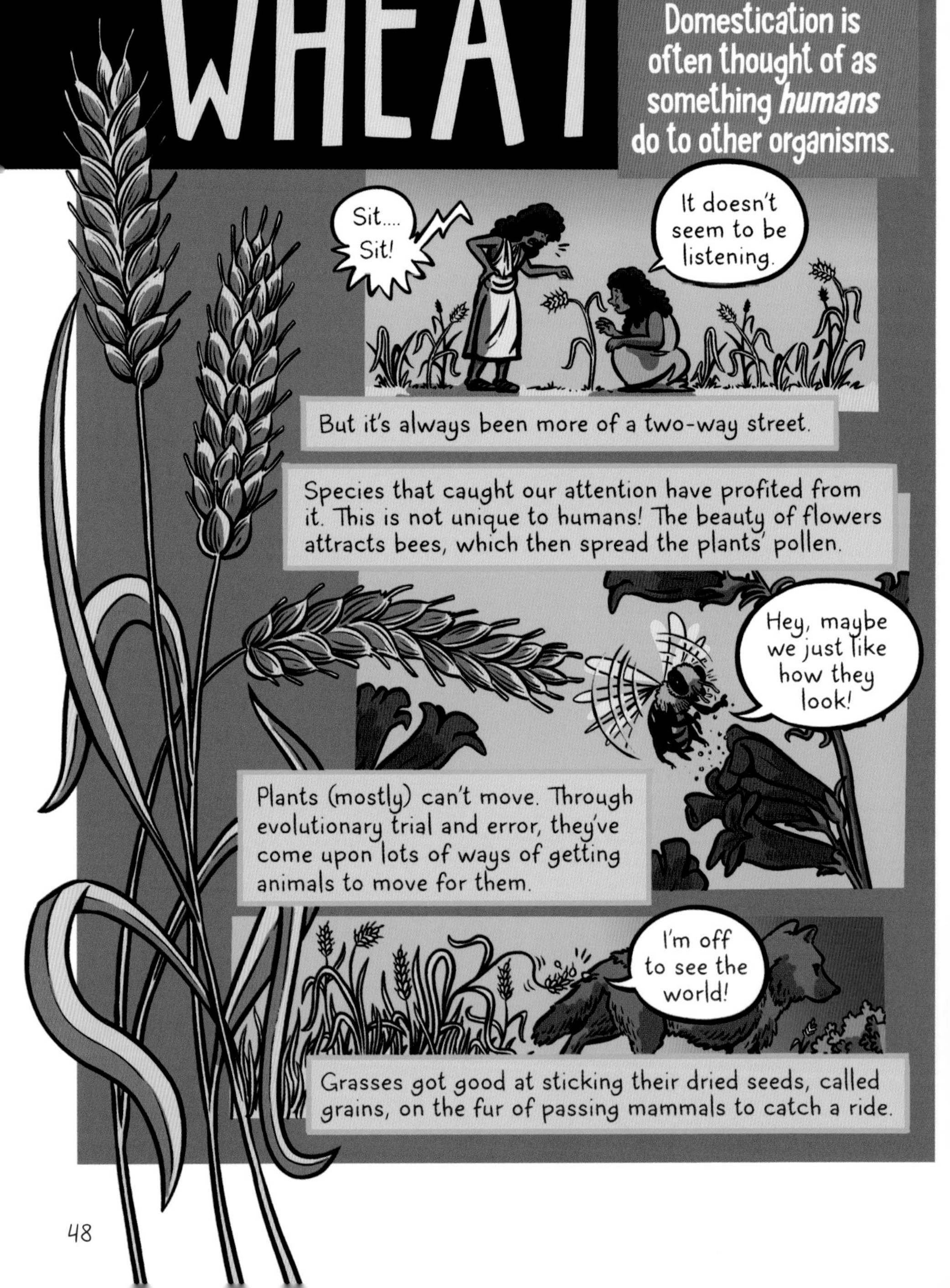

Domestication is often thought of as something ***humans*** do to other organisms.
Sit.... Sit!
It doesn't seem to be listening.
But it's always been more of a two-way street.
Species that caught our attention have profited from it. This is not unique to humans! The beauty of flowers attracts bees, which then spread the plants' pollen.
Hey, maybe we just like how they look!
Plants (mostly) can't move. Through evolutionary trial and error, they've come upon lots of ways of getting animals to move for them.
I'm off to see the world!
Grasses got good at sticking their dried seeds, called grains, on the fur of passing mammals to catch a ride.

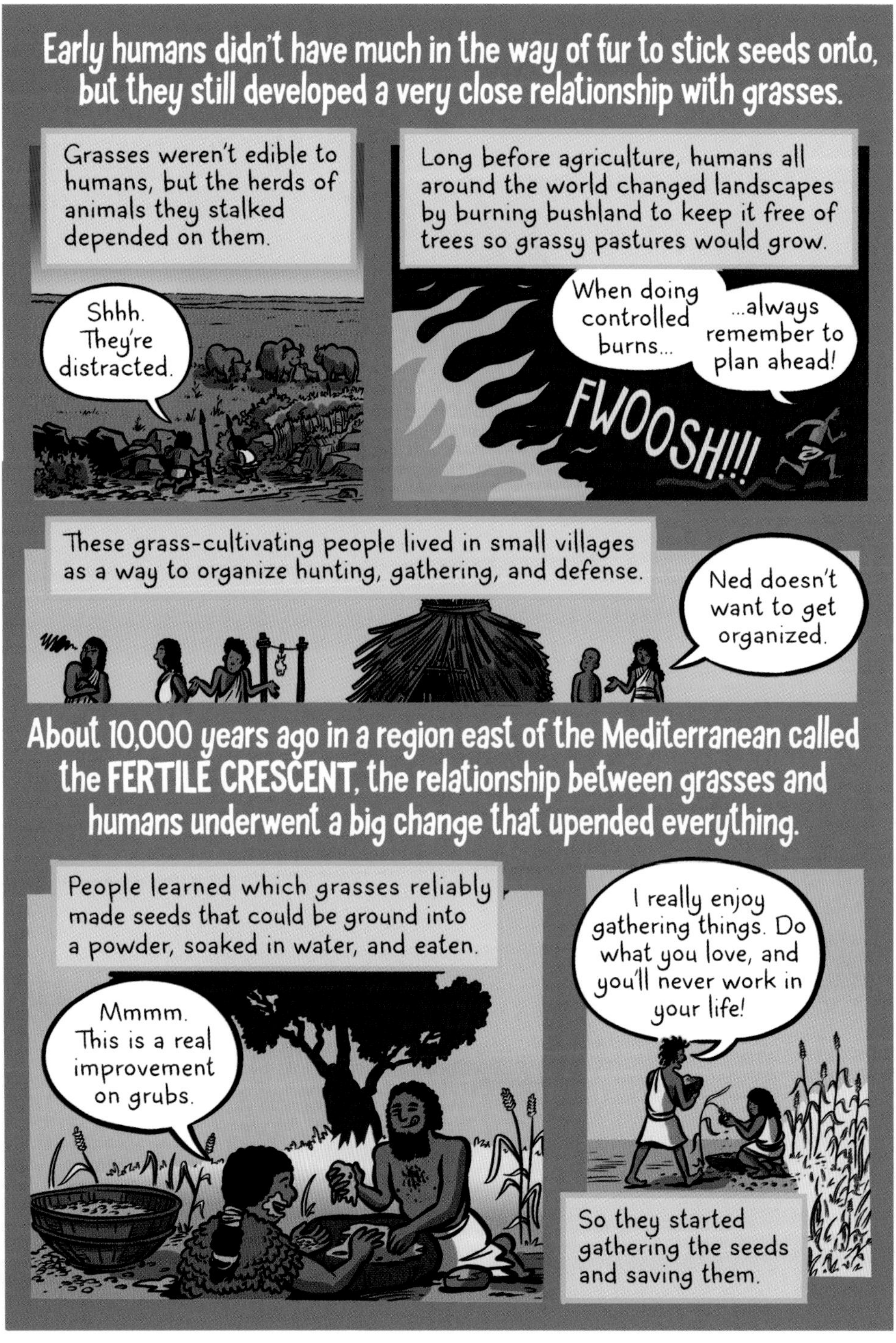
Early humans didn't have much in the way of fur to stick seeds onto, but they still developed a very close relationship with grasses.
Grasses weren't edible to humans, but the herds of animals they stalked depended on them.
Shhh. They're distracted.
Long before agriculture, humans all around the world changed landscapes by burning bushland to keep it free of trees so grassy pastures would grow.
When doing controlled burns...
...always remember to plan ahead!
FWOOSH!!!
These grass-cultivating people lived in small villages as a way to organize hunting, gathering, and defense.
Ned doesn't want to get organized.
About 10,000 years ago in a region east of the Mediterranean called the FERTILE CRESCENT, the relationship between grasses and humans underwent a big change that upended everything.
People learned which grasses reliably made seeds that could be ground into a powder, soaked in water, and eaten.
Mmmm. This is a real improvement on grubs.
I really enjoy gathering things. Do what you love, and you'll never work in your life!
So they started gathering the seeds and saving them.

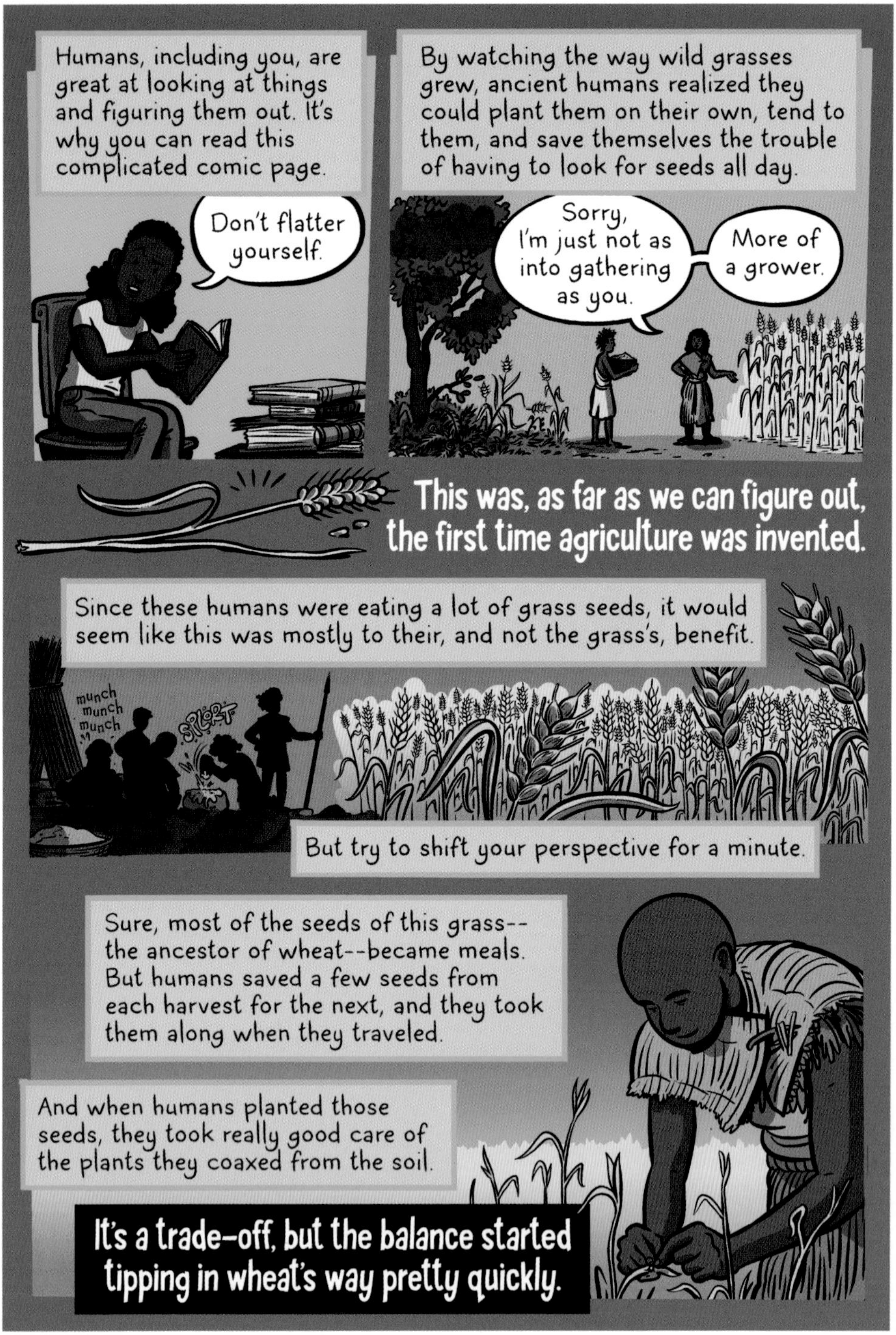
Humans, including you, are great at looking at things and figuring them out. It's why you can read this complicated comic page.
Don't flatter yourself.
By watching the way wild grasses grew, ancient humans realized they could plant them on their own, tend to them, and save themselves the trouble of having to look for seeds all day.
Sorry, I'm just not as into gathering as you.
More of a grower.
This was, as far as we can figure out, the first time agriculture was invented.
Since these humans were eating a lot of grass seeds, it would seem like this was mostly to their, and not the grass's, benefit.
munch munch munch
SPLORT
But try to shift your perspective for a minute.
Sure, most of the seeds of this grass--the ancestor of wheat--became meals. But humans saved a few seeds from each harvest for the next, and they took them along when they traveled.
And when humans planted those seeds, they took really good care of the plants they coaxed from the soil.
It's a trade-off, but the balance started tipping in wheat's way pretty quickly.

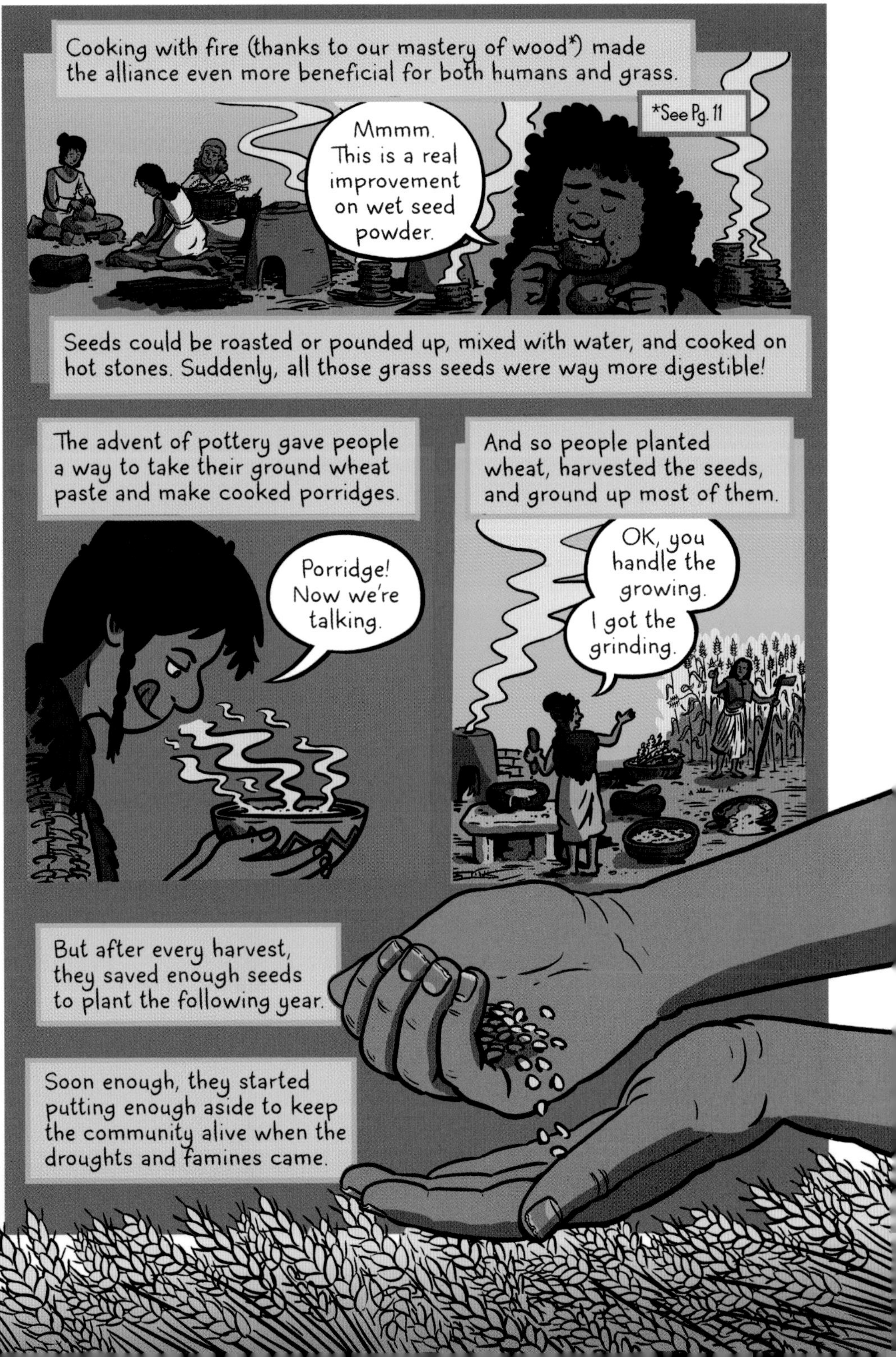
Cooking with fire (thanks to our mastery of wood*) made the alliance even more beneficial for both humans and grass.
*See Pg. 11
Mmmm. This is a real improvement on wet seed powder.
Seeds could be roasted or pounded up, mixed with water, and cooked on hot stones. Suddenly, all those grass seeds were way more digestible!
The advent of pottery gave people a way to take their ground wheat paste and make cooked porridges.
Porridge! Now we're talking.
And so people planted wheat, harvested the seeds, and ground up most of them.
OK, you handle the growing.
I got the grinding.
But after every harvest, they saved enough seeds to plant the following year.
Soon enough, they started putting enough aside to keep the community alive when the droughts and famines came.

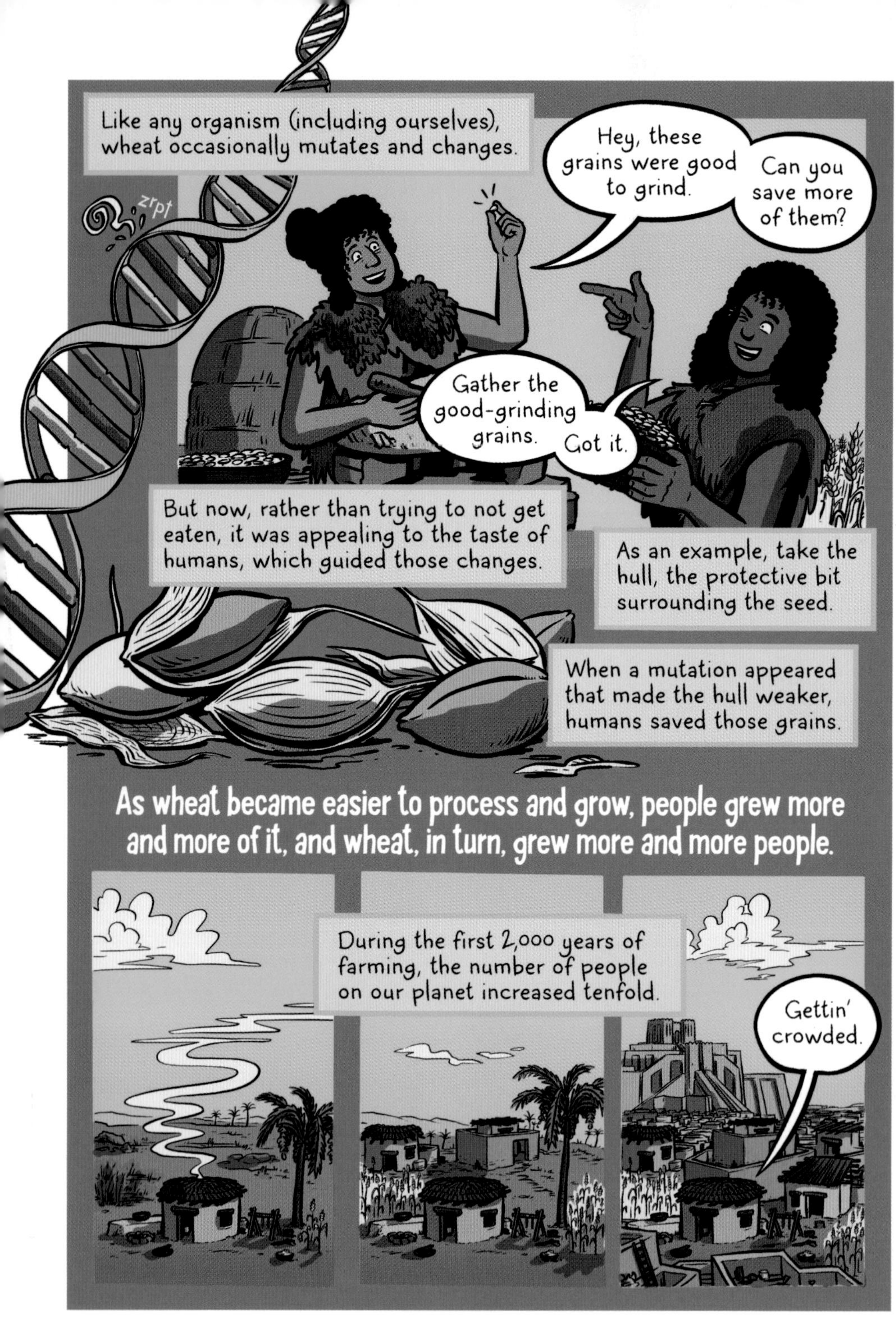
Like any organism (including ourselves), wheat occasionally mutates and changes.
zrpt
Hey, these grains were good to grind.
Can you save more of them?
Gather the good-grinding grains.
Got it.
But now, rather than trying to not get eaten, it was appealing to the taste of humans, which guided those changes.
As an example, take the hull, the protective bit surrounding the seed.
When a mutation appeared that made the hull weaker, humans saved those grains.
As wheat became easier to process and grow, people grew more and more of it, and wheat, in turn, grew more and more people.
During the first 2,000 years of farming, the number of people on our planet increased tenfold.
Gettin' crowded.

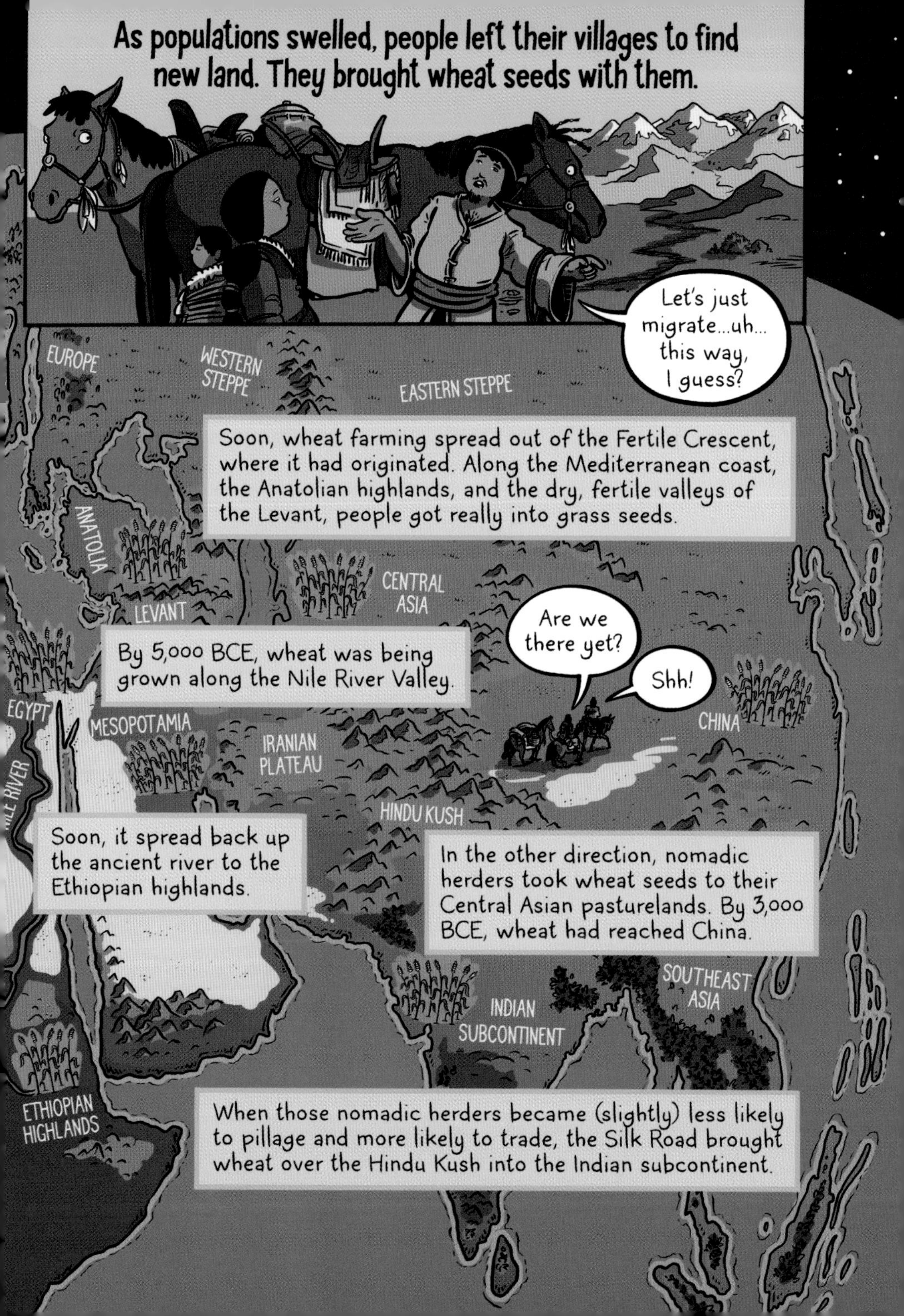
As populations swelled, people left their villages to find new land. They brought wheat seeds with them.
Let's just migrate...uh... this way, I guess?
EUROPE
WESTERN STEPPE
EASTERN STEPPE
Soon, wheat farming spread out of the Fertile Crescent, where it had originated. Along the Mediterranean coast, the Anatolian highlands, and the dry, fertile valleys of the Levant, people got really into grass seeds.
ANATOLIA
CENTRAL ASIA
LEVANT
By 5,000 BCE, wheat was being grown along the Nile River Valley.
Are we there yet?
Shh!
EGYPT
MESOPOTAMIA
IRANIAN PLATEAU
CHINA
HINDU KUSH
Soon, it spread back up the ancient river to the Ethiopian highlands.
In the other direction, nomadic herders took wheat seeds to their Central Asian pasturelands. By 3,000 BCE, wheat had reached China.
SOUTHEAST ASIA
INDIAN SUBCONTINENT
ETHIOPIAN HIGHLANDS
When those nomadic herders became (slightly) less likely to pillage and more likely to trade, the Silk Road brought wheat over the Hindu Kush into the Indian subcontinent.

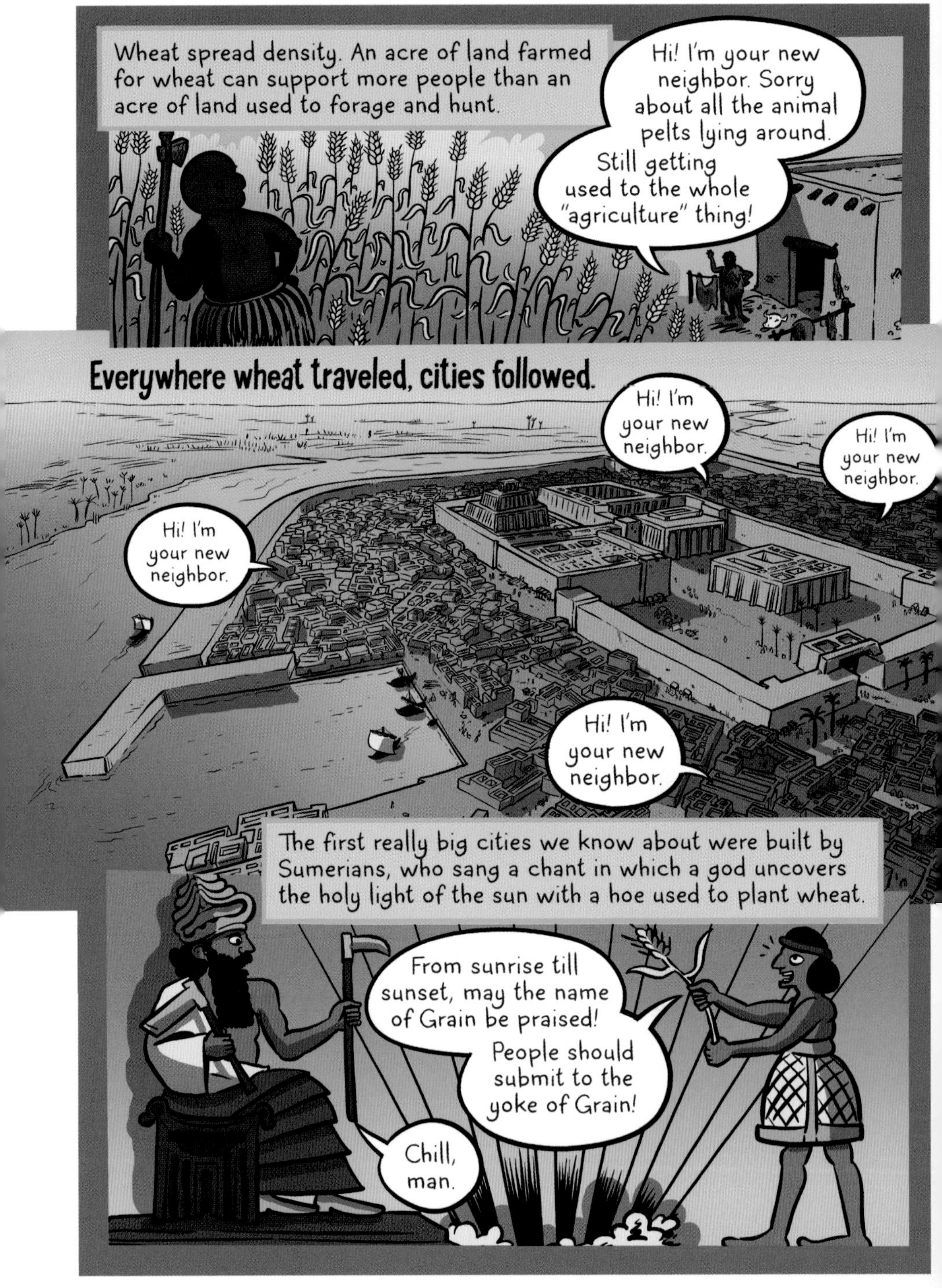

Wheat spread density. An acre of land farmed for wheat can support more people than an acre of land used to forage and hunt.
Hi! I'm your new neighbor. Sorry about all the animal pelts lying around.
Still getting used to the whole "agriculture" thing!
Everywhere wheat traveled, cities followed.
Hi! I'm your new neighbor.
Hi! I'm your new neighbor.
Hi! I'm your new neighbor.
Hi! I'm your new neighbor.
The first really big cities we know about were built by Sumerians, who sang a chant in which a god uncovers the holy light of the sun with a hoe used to plant wheat.
From sunrise till sunset, may the name of Grain be praised!
People should submit to the yoke of Grain!
Chill, man.

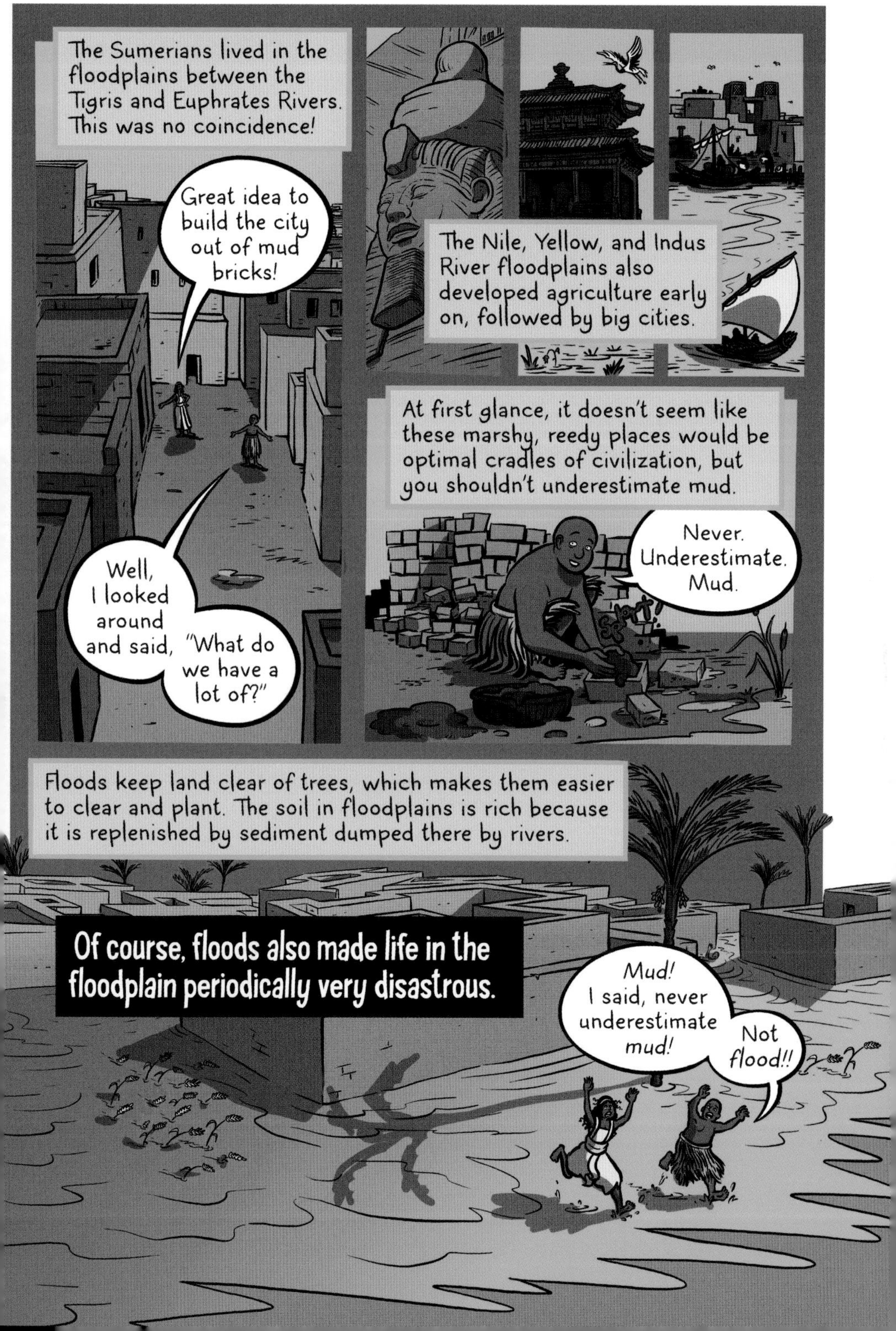
The Sumerians lived in the floodplains between the Tigris and Euphrates Rivers. This was no coincidence!
Great idea to build the city out of mud bricks!
Well, I looked around and said, "What do we have a lot of?"
The Nile, Yellow, and Indus River floodplains also developed agriculture early on, followed by big cities.
At first glance, it doesn't seem like these marshy, reedy places would be optimal cradles of civilization, but you shouldn't underestimate mud.
Never. Underestimate. Mud.
Floods keep land clear of trees, which makes them easier to clear and plant. The soil in floodplains is rich because it is replenished by sediment dumped there by rivers.
Of course, floods also made life in the floodplain periodically very disastrous.
Mud! I said, never underestimate mud!
Not flood!!

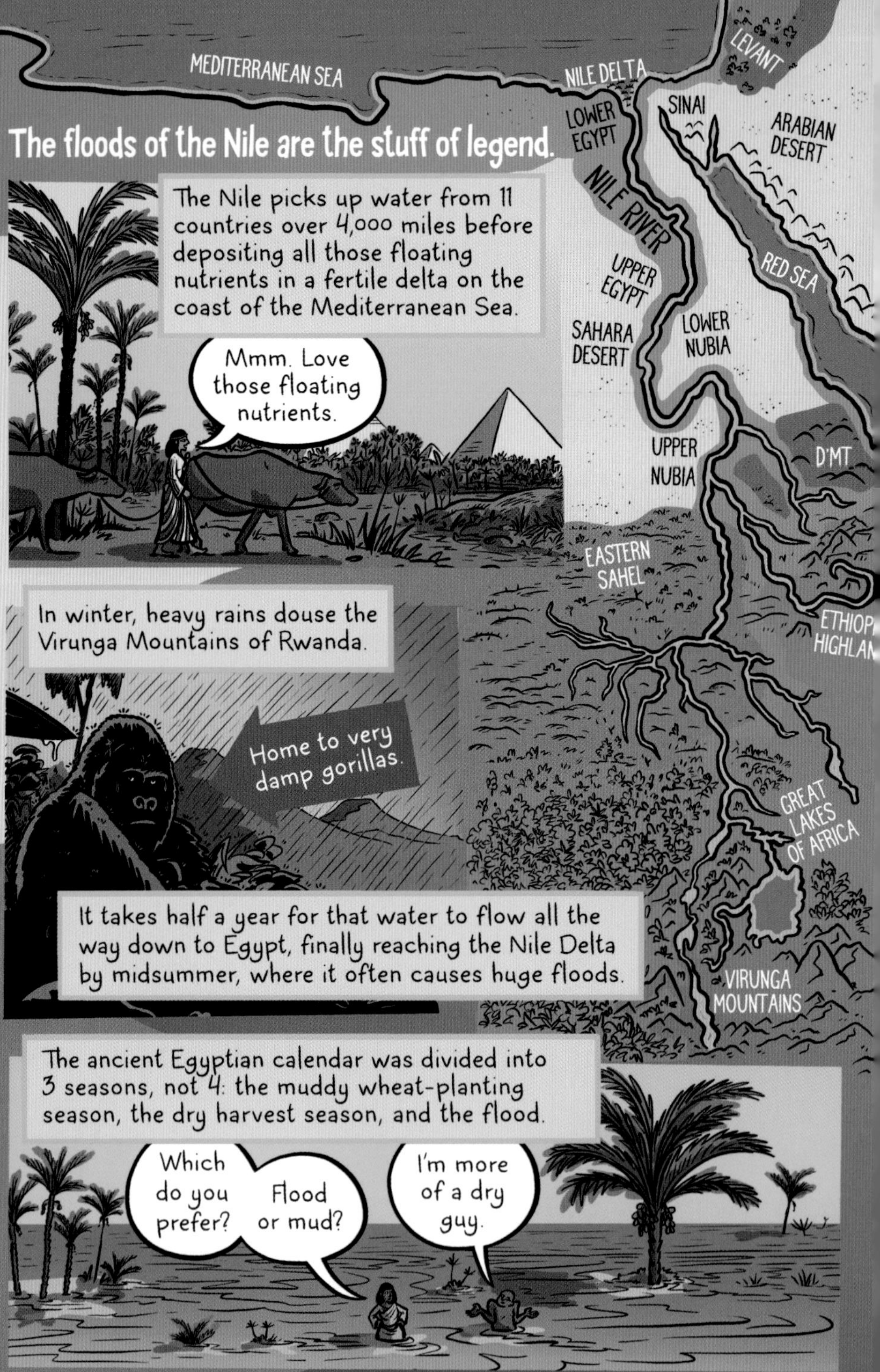
MEDITERRANEAN SEA
NILE DELTA
LEVANT
LOWER EGYPT
SINAI
ARABIAN DESERT
NILE RIVER
UPPER EGYPT
RED SEA
SAHARA DESERT
LOWER NUBIA
UPPER NUBIA
D'MT
EASTERN SAHEL
GREAT LAKES OF AFRICA
VIRUNGA MOUNTAINS
The floods of the Nile are the stuff of legend.
The Nile picks up water from 11 countries over 4,000 miles before depositing all those floating nutrients in a fertile delta on the coast of the Mediterranean Sea.
Mmm. Love those floating nutrients.
In winter, heavy rains douse the Virunga Mountains of Rwanda.
Home to very damp gorillas.
It takes half a year for that water to flow all the way down to Egypt, finally reaching the Nile Delta by midsummer, where it often causes huge floods.
The ancient Egyptian calendar was divided into 3 seasons, not 4: the muddy wheat-planting season, the dry harvest season, and the flood.
Which do you prefer?
Flood or mud?
I'm more of a dry guy.

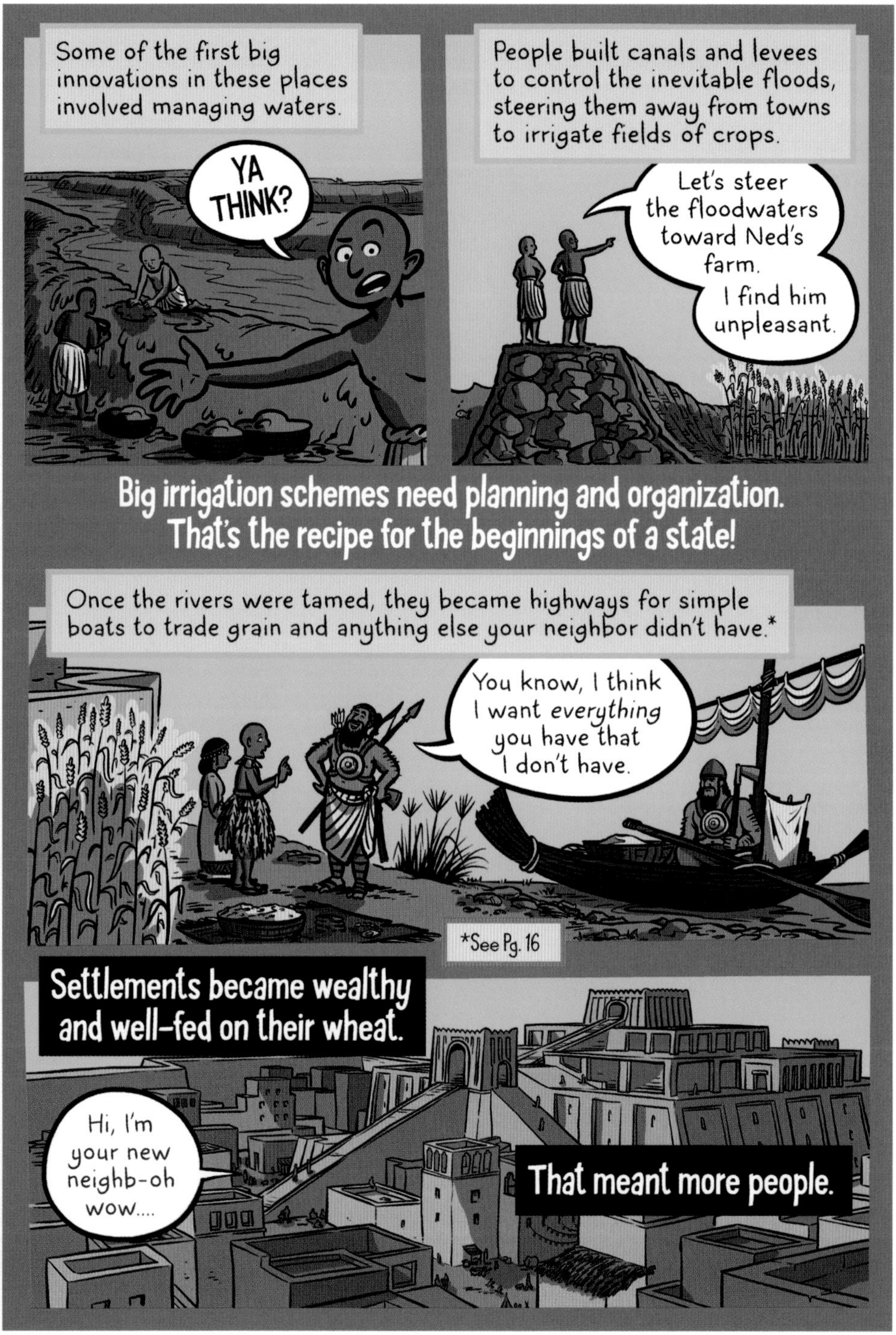
Some of the first big innovations in these places involved managing waters.
YA THINK?
People built canals and levees to control the inevitable floods, steering them away from towns to irrigate fields of crops.
Let's steer the floodwaters toward Ned's farm.
I find him unpleasant.
Big irrigation schemes need planning and organization. That's the recipe for the beginnings of a state!
Once the rivers were tamed, they became highways for simple boats to trade grain and anything else your neighbor didn't have.*
You know, I think I want *everything* you have that I don't have.
*See Pg. 16
Settlements became wealthy and well-fed on their wheat.
Hi, I'm your new neighb-oh wow....
That meant more people.

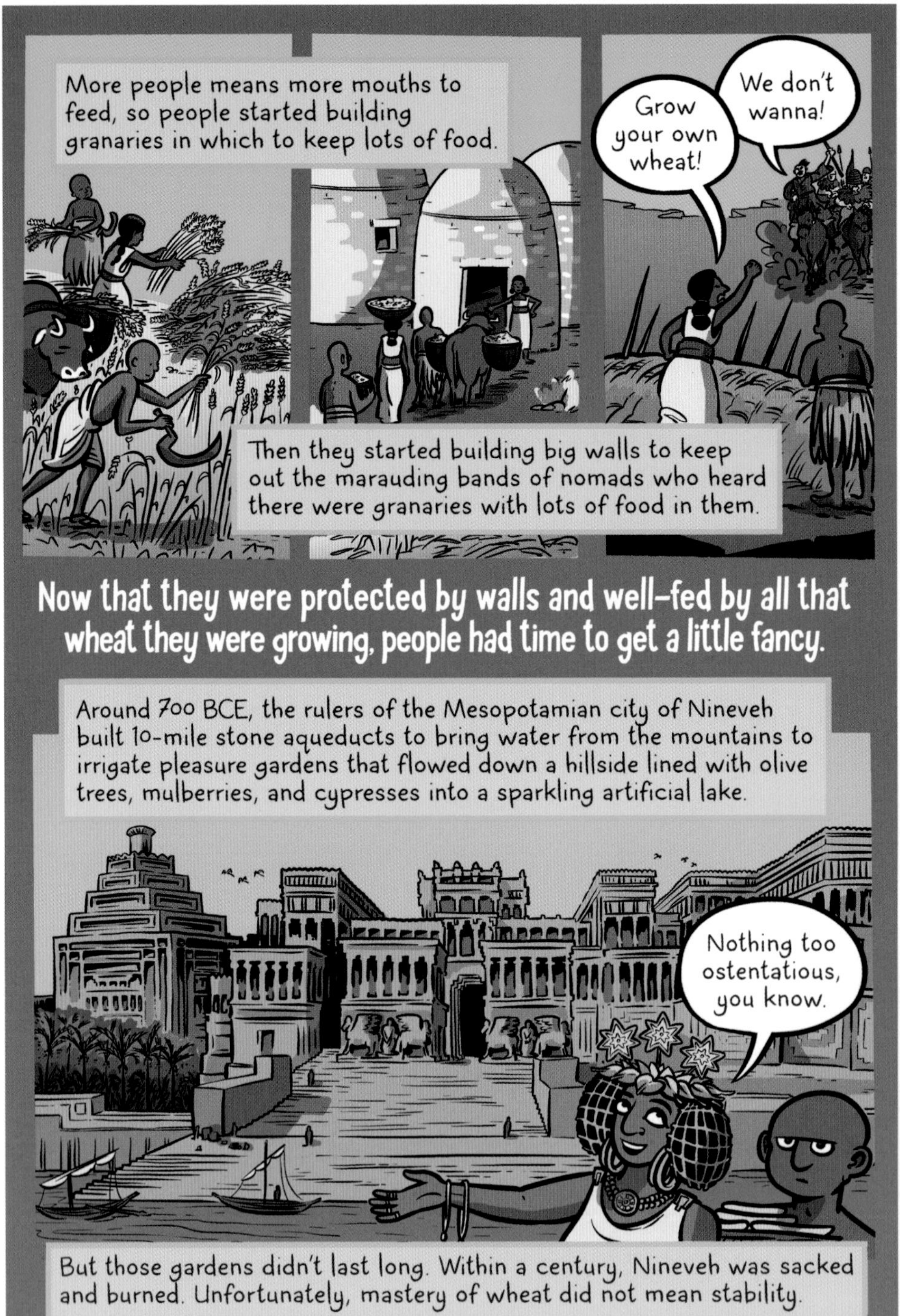
More people means more mouths to feed, so people started building granaries in which to keep lots of food.
Grow your own wheat!
We don't wanna!
Then they started building big walls to keep out the marauding bands of nomads who heard there were granaries with lots of food in them.
Now that they were protected by walls and well-fed by all that wheat they were growing, people had time to get a little fancy.
Around 700 BCE, the rulers of the Mesopotamian city of Nineveh built 10-mile stone aqueducts to bring water from the mountains to irrigate pleasure gardens that flowed down a hillside lined with olive trees, mulberries, and cypresses into a sparkling artificial lake.
Nothing too ostentatious, you know.
But those gardens didn't last long. Within a century, Nineveh was sacked and burned. Unfortunately, mastery of wheat did not mean stability.

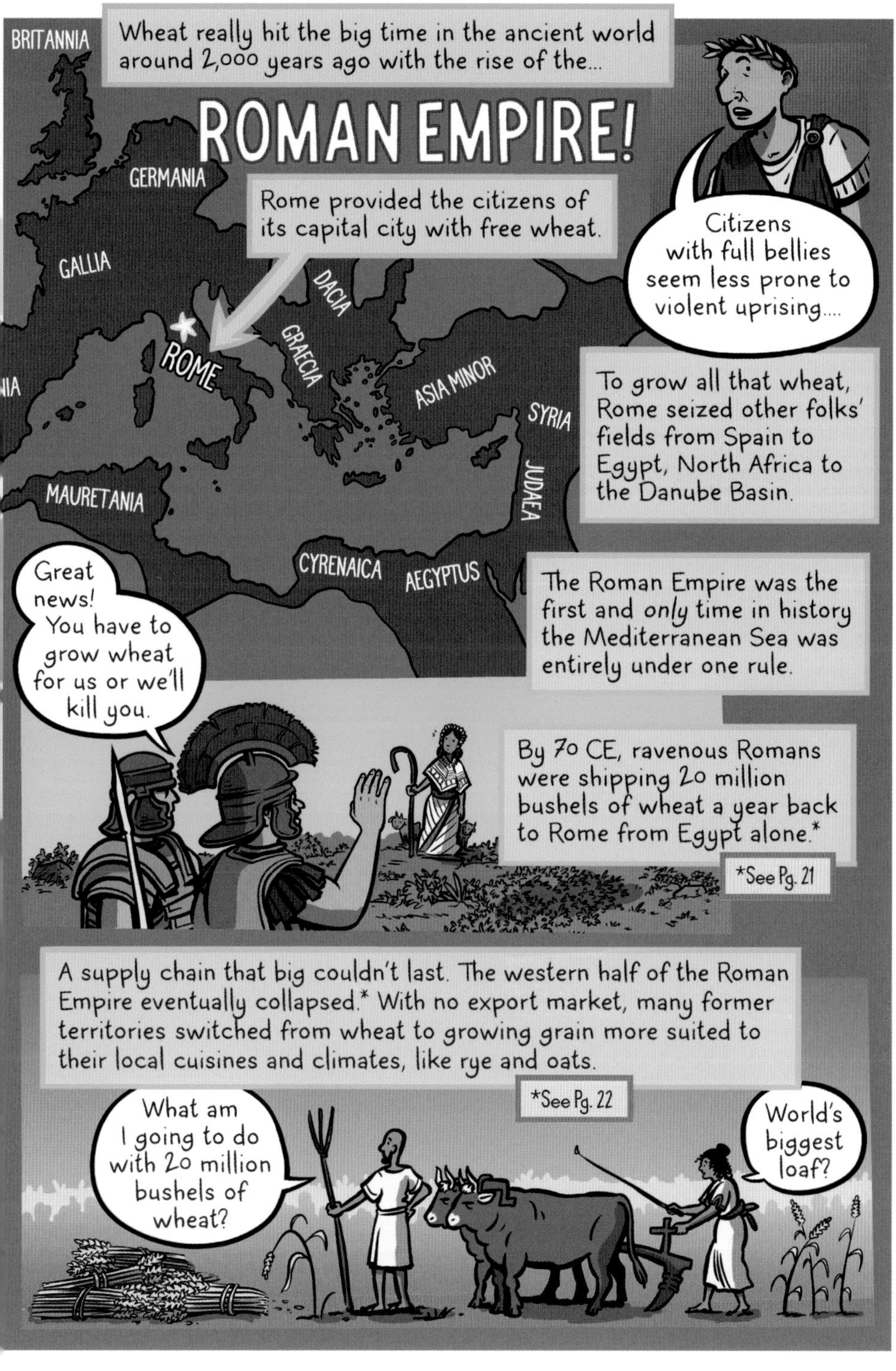
Wheat really hit the big time in the ancient world around 2,000 years ago with the rise of the...
ROMAN EMPIRE!
BRITANNIA
GERMANIA
GALLIA
Rome provided the citizens of its capital city with free wheat.
Citizens with full bellies seem less prone to violent uprising....
DACIA
GRAECIA
ROME
ASIA MINOR
SYRIA
JUDAEA
MAURETANIA
To grow all that wheat, Rome seized other folks' fields from Spain to Egypt, North Africa to the Danube Basin.
CYRENAICA
AEGYPTUS
The Roman Empire was the first and *only* time in history the Mediterranean Sea was entirely under one rule.
Great news! You have to grow wheat for us or we'll kill you.
By 70 CE, ravenous Romans were shipping 20 million bushels of wheat a year back to Rome from Egypt alone.*
*See Pg. 21
A supply chain that big couldn't last. The western half of the Roman Empire eventually collapsed.* With no export market, many former territories switched from wheat to growing grain more suited to their local cuisines and climates, like rye and oats.
*See Pg. 22
What am I going to do with 20 million bushels of wheat?
World's biggest loaf?

But it's hard to shake a taste for wheat once you've got it.

And as the technology to plough rocky soils developed, Europeans began to grow more wheat again, although not as much as they had under Roman rule for quite a while.

Not a fair comparison!

They had barges.

Wheat reached the Americas when a bunch of pepper-crazed Spaniards blundered into them in the 1400s.* But the Spanish were more focused on plunder than finding good wheat fields.

*See Pg. 105

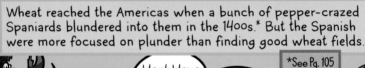

Hey! Have you seen any gold?

Why does nobody here speak Spanish?!

The Puritan colonists in the 1660s tried to grow wheat but didn't account for the weather in New England being completely different weather than back in Old England.

Personally, I blame the menacing trees.

Their wheat, adapted for damp England, proved no match for America's early, brutal winters followed by sweaty summers.

Fine. We'll eat your corn.

I still blame the trees, though.

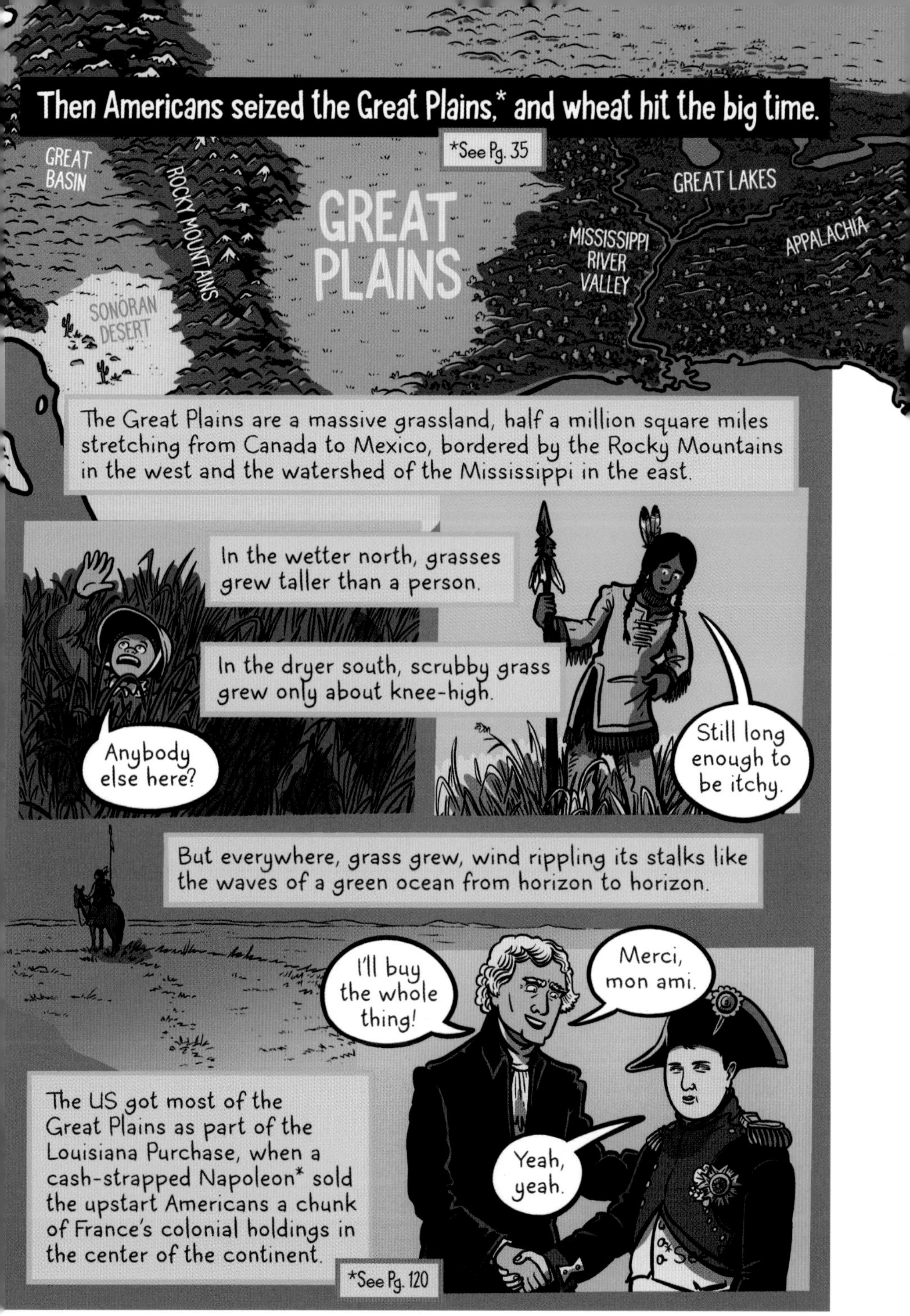
Then Americans seized the Great Plains,* and wheat hit the big time.
*See Pg. 35
GREAT BASIN
ROCKY MOUNTAINS
GREAT PLAINS
SONORAN DESERT
MISSISSIPPI RIVER VALLEY
GREAT LAKES
APPALACHIA
The Great Plains are a massive grassland, half a million square miles stretching from Canada to Mexico, bordered by the Rocky Mountains in the west and the watershed of the Mississippi in the east.
In the wetter north, grasses grew taller than a person.
In the dryer south, scrubby grass grew only about knee-high.
Anybody else here?
Still long enough to be itchy.
But everywhere, grass grew, wind rippling its stalks like the waves of a green ocean from horizon to horizon.
I'll buy the whole thing!
Merci, mon ami.
Yeah, yeah.
The US got most of the Great Plains as part of the Louisiana Purchase, when a cash-strapped Napoleon* sold the upstart Americans a chunk of France's colonial holdings in the center of the continent.
*See Pg. 120

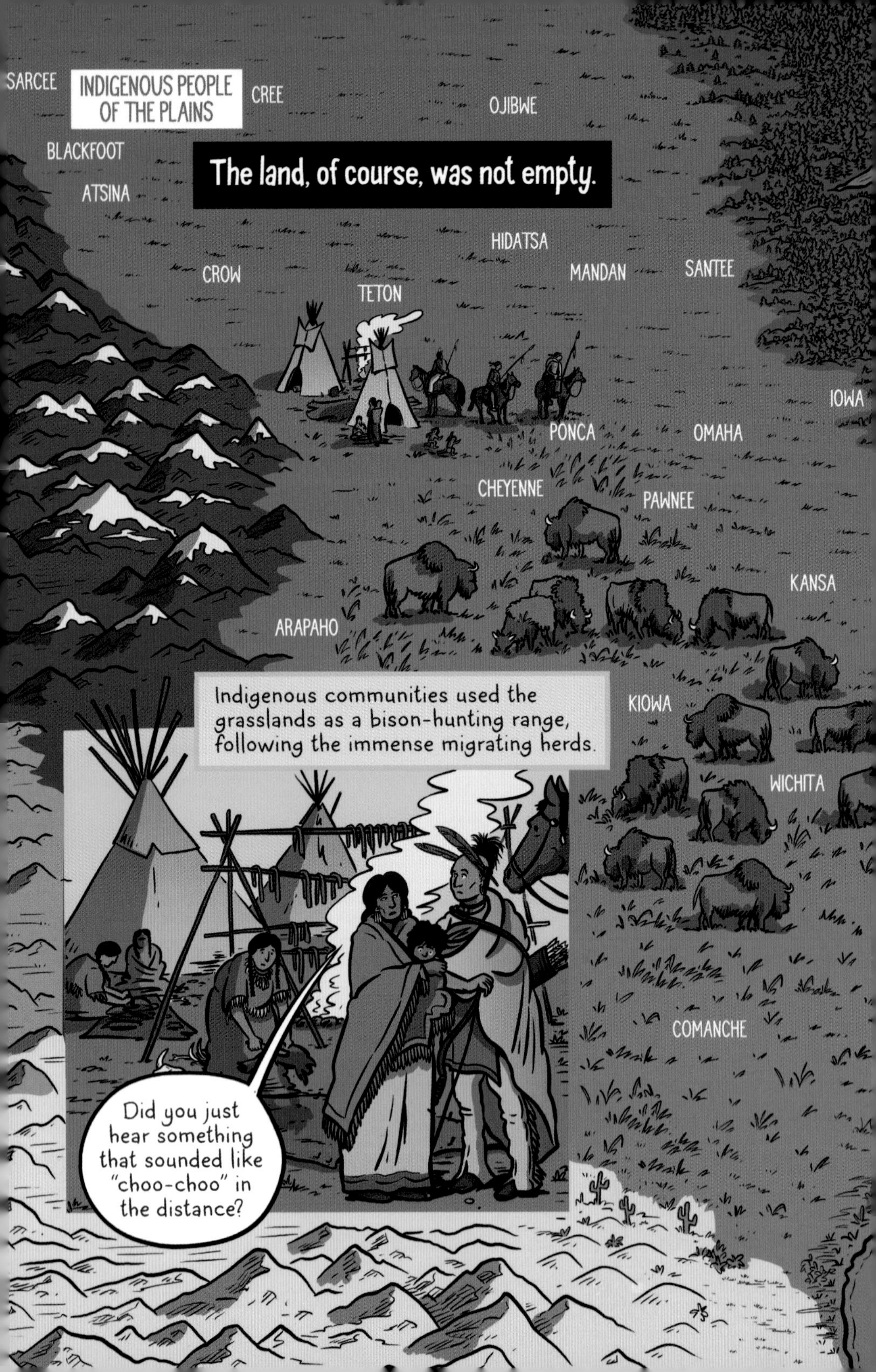
INDIGENOUS PEOPLE OF THE PLAINS
SARCEE
CREE
OJIBWE
BLACKFOOT
ATSINA
The land, of course, was not empty.
HIDATSA
CROW
MANDAN
SANTEE
TETON
IOWA
PONCA
OMAHA
CHEYENNE
PAWNEE
KANSA
ARAPAHO
Indigenous communities used the grasslands as a bison-hunting range, following the immense migrating herds.
KIOWA
WICHITA
COMANCHE
Did you just hear something that sounded like "choo-choo" in the distance?

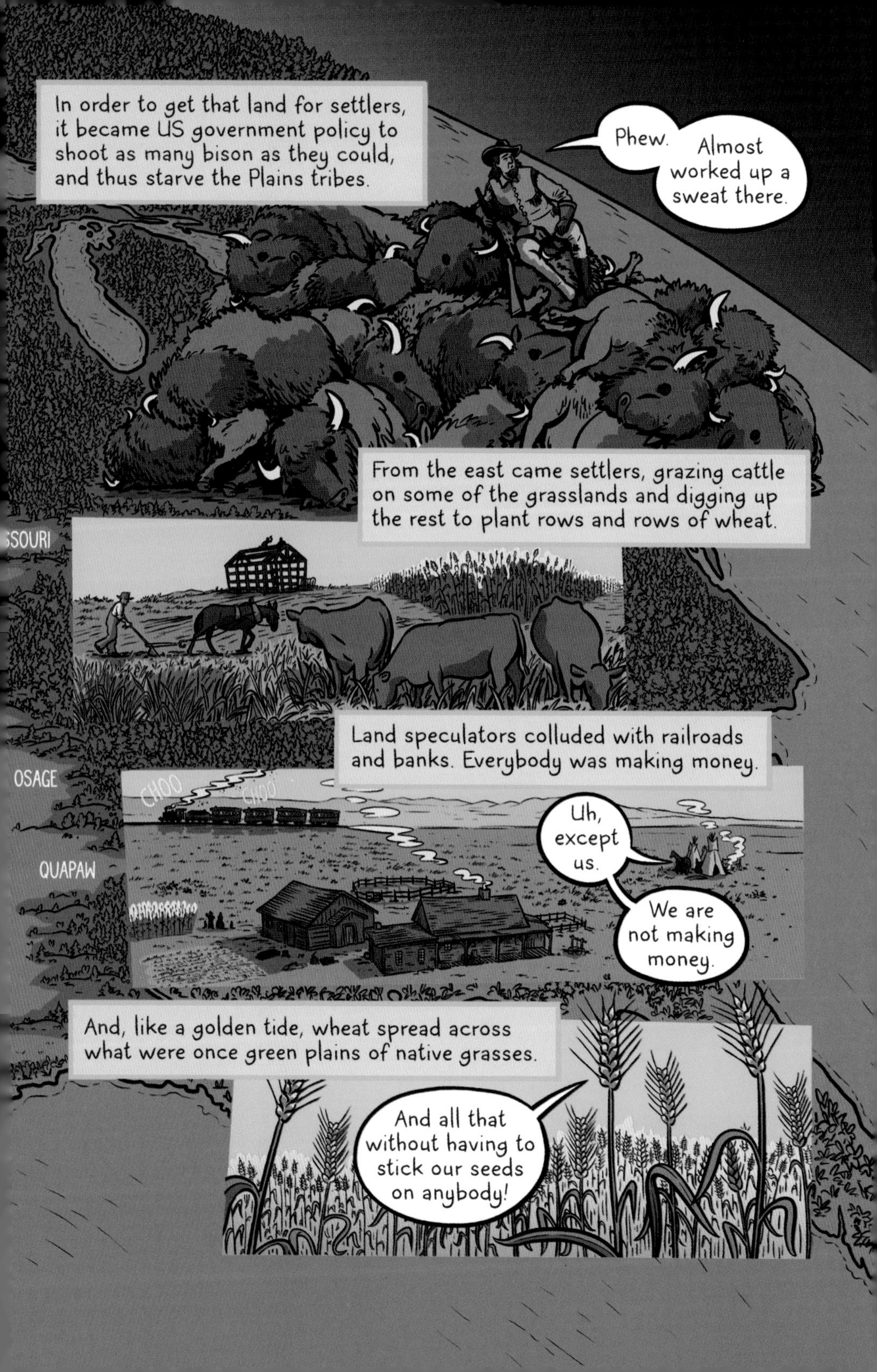
In order to get that land for settlers, it became US government policy to shoot as many bison as they could, and thus starve the Plains tribes.
Phew.
Almost worked up a sweat there.
From the east came settlers, grazing cattle on some of the grasslands and digging up the rest to plant rows and rows of wheat.
SSOURI
Land speculators colluded with railroads and banks. Everybody was making money.
OSAGE
CHOO
CHOO
Uh, except us.
QUAPAW
We are not making money.
And, like a golden tide, wheat spread across what were once green plains of native grasses.
And all that without having to stick our seeds on anybody!

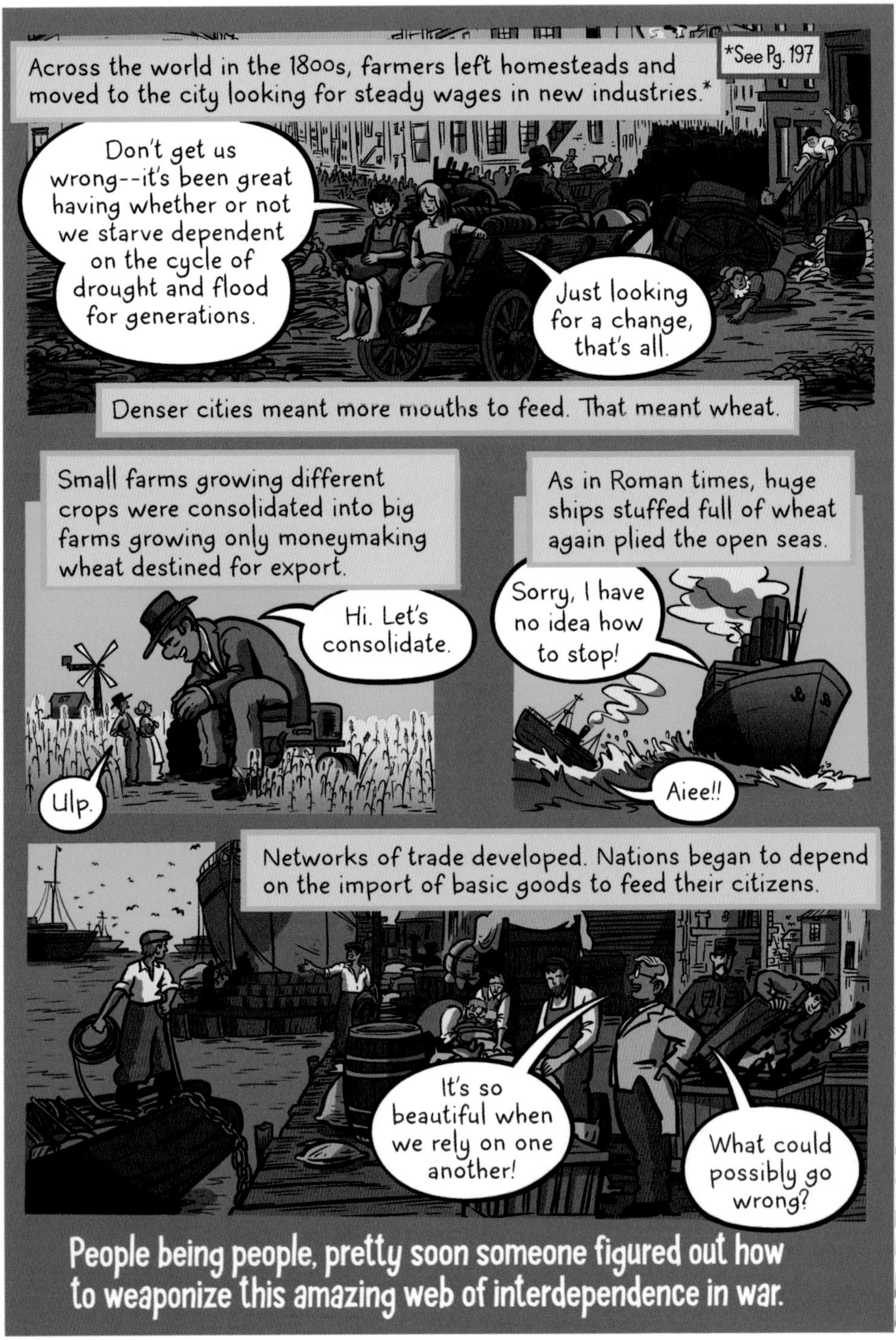
Across the world in the 1800s, farmers left homesteads and moved to the city looking for steady wages in new industries.*
*See Pg. 197
Don't get us wrong--it's been great having whether or not we starve dependent on the cycle of drought and flood for generations.
Just looking for a change, that's all.
Denser cities meant more mouths to feed. That meant wheat.
Small farms growing different crops were consolidated into big farms growing only moneymaking wheat destined for export.
Hi. Let's consolidate.
Ulp.
As in Roman times, huge ships stuffed full of wheat again plied the open seas.
Sorry, I have no idea how to stop!
Aiee!!
Networks of trade developed. Nations began to depend on the import of basic goods to feed their citizens.
It's so beautiful when we rely on one another!
What could possibly go wrong?
People being people, pretty soon someone figured out how to weaponize this amazing web of interdependence in war.

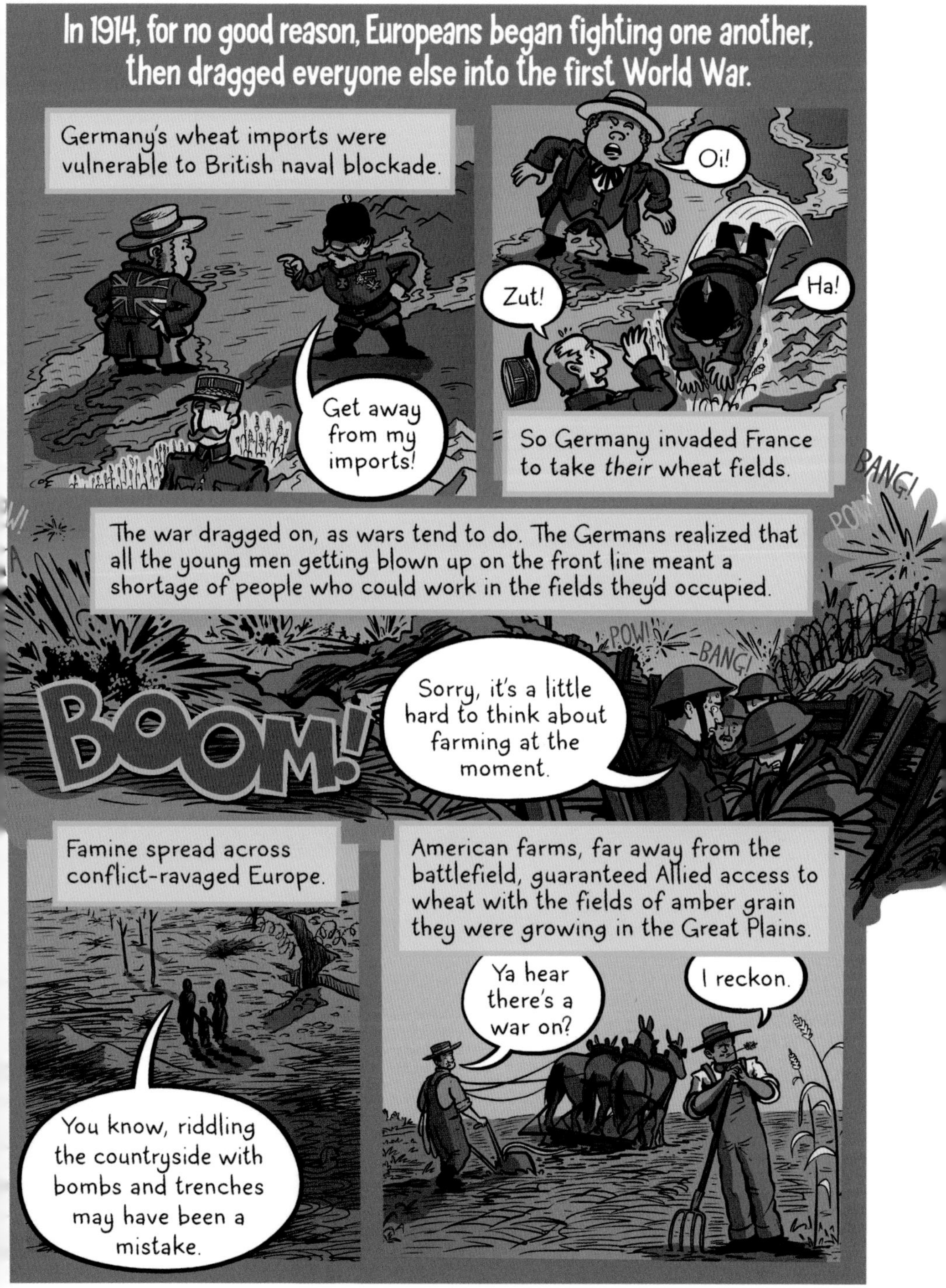
In 1914, for no good reason, Europeans began fighting one another, then dragged everyone else into the first World War.
Germany's wheat imports were vulnerable to British naval blockade.
Get away from my imports!
Oi!
Zut!
Ha!
So Germany invaded France to take *their* wheat fields.
The war dragged on, as wars tend to do. The Germans realized that all the young men getting blown up on the front line meant a shortage of people who could work in the fields they'd occupied.
BANG!
POW!
BOOM!
POW!
BANG!
Sorry, it's a little hard to think about farming at the moment.
Famine spread across conflict-ravaged Europe.
You know, riddling the countryside with bombs and trenches may have been a mistake.
American farms, far away from the battlefield, guaranteed Allied access to wheat with the fields of amber grain they were growing in the Great Plains.
Ya hear there's a war on?
I reckon.

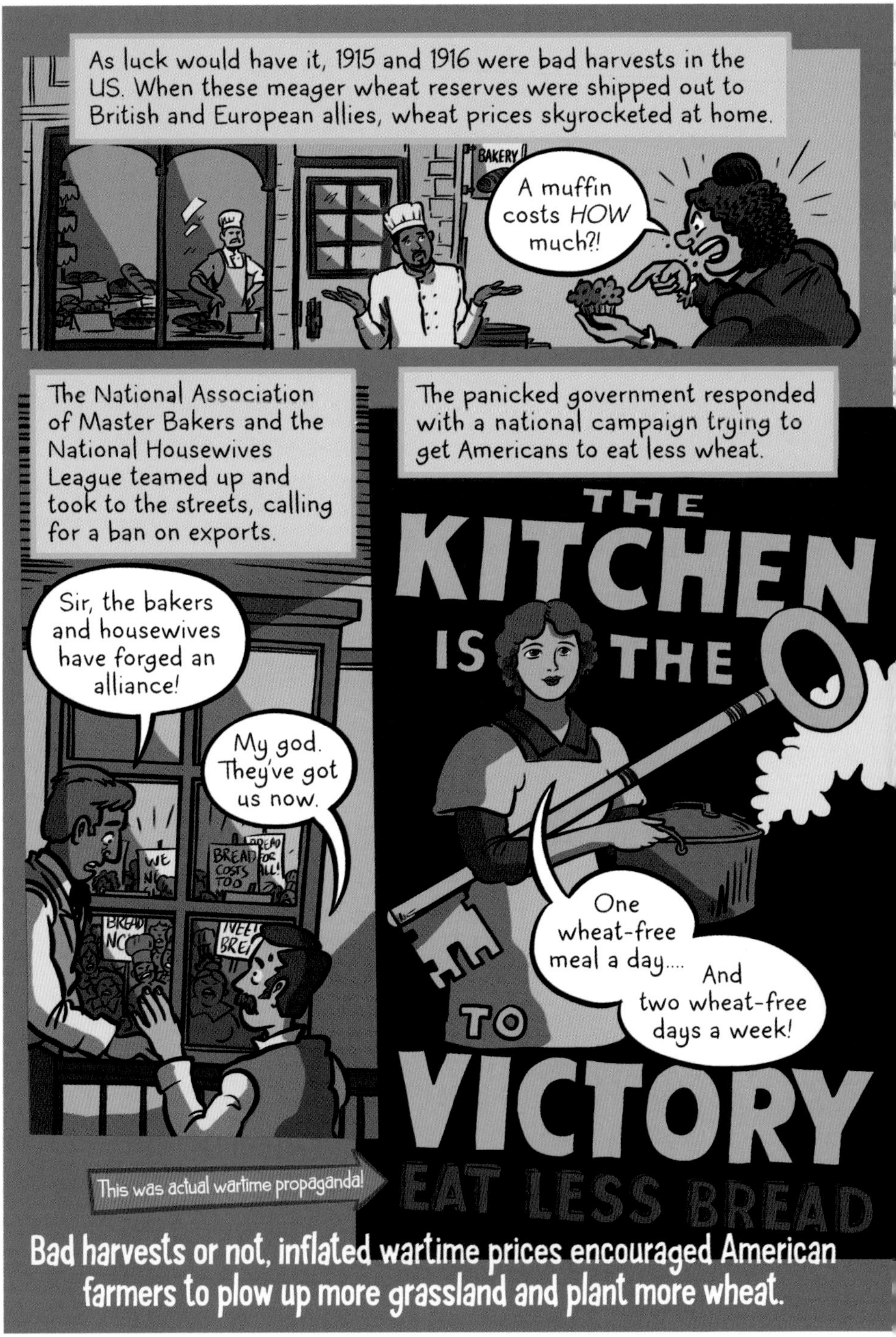

As luck would have it, 1915 and 1916 were bad harvests in the US. When these meager wheat reserves were shipped out to British and European allies, wheat prices skyrocketed at home.
BAKERY
A muffin costs *HOW* much?!
The National Association of Master Bakers and the National Housewives League teamed up and took to the streets, calling for a ban on exports.
Sir, the bakers and housewives have forged an alliance!
My god. They've got us now.
BREAD COSTS TOO
BREAD FOR ALL!
The panicked government responded with a national campaign trying to get Americans to eat less wheat.
THE KITCHEN IS THE KEY TO VICTORY
EAT LESS BREAD
One wheat-free meal a day....
And two wheat-free days a week!
This was actual wartime propaganda!
Bad harvests or not, inflated wartime prices encouraged American farmers to plow up more grassland and plant more wheat.

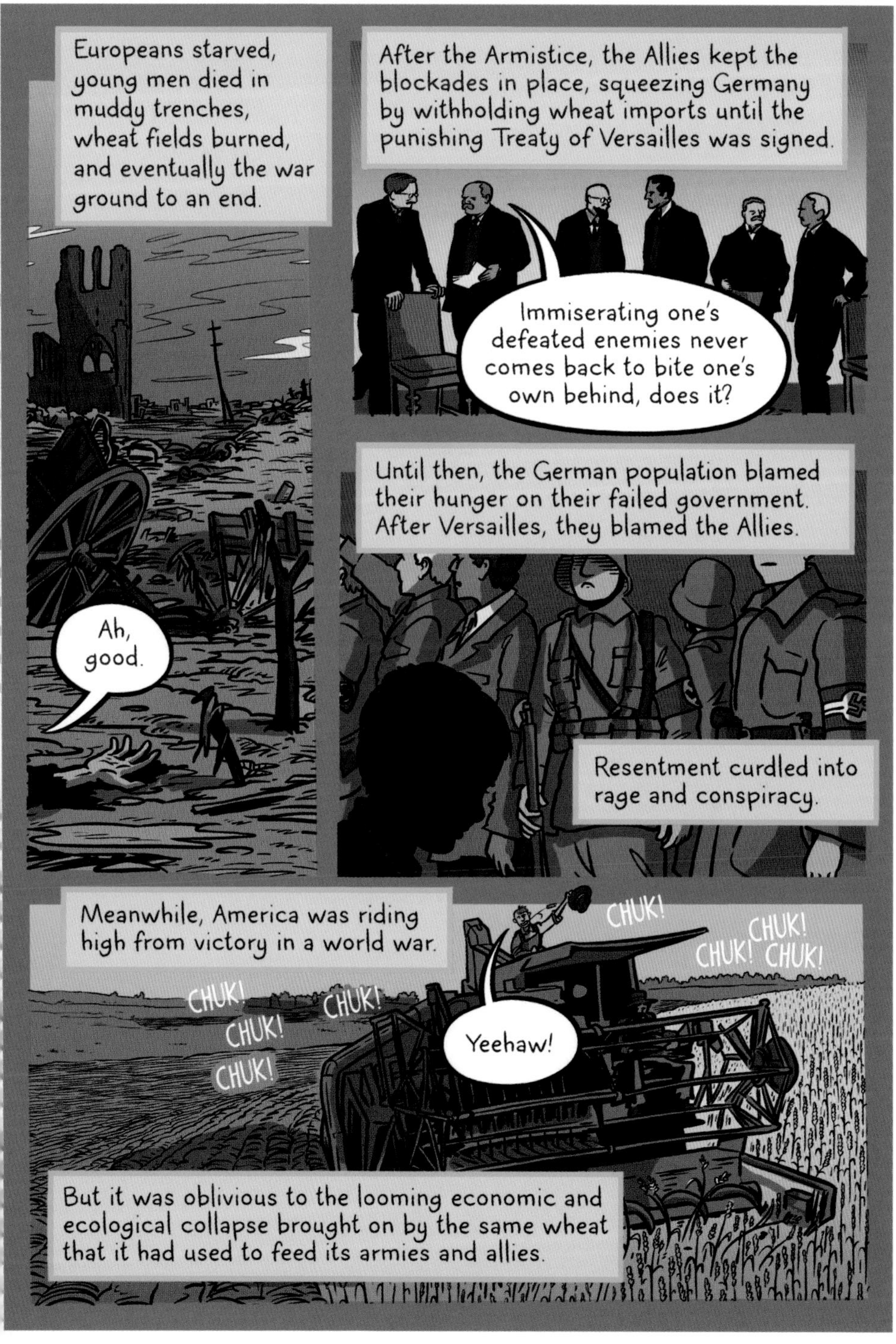

Europeans starved, young men died in muddy trenches, wheat fields burned, and eventually the war ground to an end.
Ah, good.
After the Armistice, the Allies kept the blockades in place, squeezing Germany by withholding wheat imports until the punishing Treaty of Versailles was signed.
Immiserating one's defeated enemies never comes back to bite one's own behind, does it?
Until then, the German population blamed their hunger on their failed government. After Versailles, they blamed the Allies.
Resentment curdled into rage and conspiracy.
Meanwhile, America was riding high from victory in a world war.
CHUK!
CHUK!
CHUK!
CHUK!
CHUK!
CHUK!
CHUK!
Yeehaw!
But it was oblivious to the looming economic and ecological collapse brought on by the same wheat that it had used to feed its armies and allies.

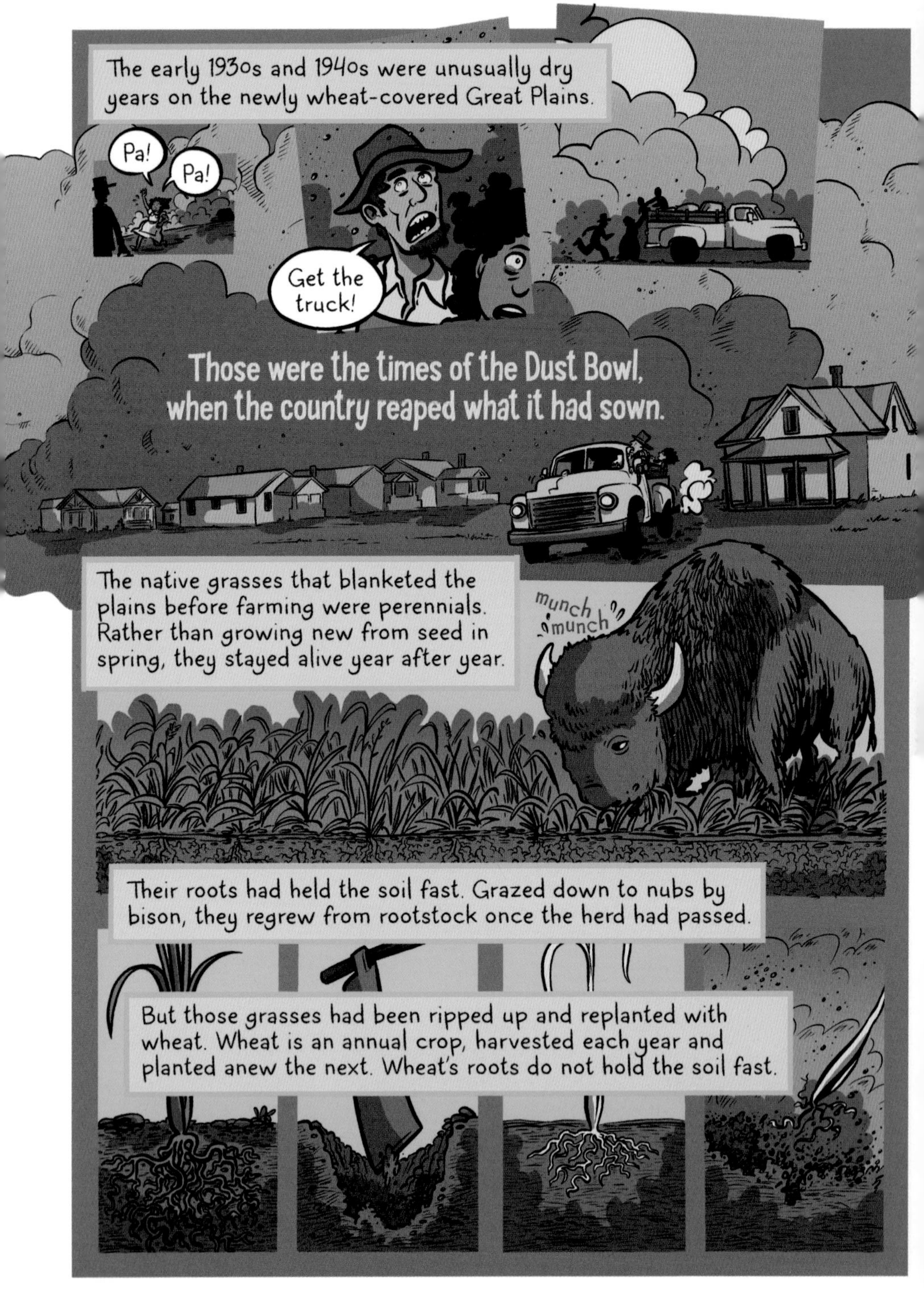

The early 1930s and 1940s were unusually dry years on the newly wheat-covered Great Plains.
Pa!
Pa!
Get the truck!
Those were the times of the Dust Bowl, when the country reaped what it had sown.
The native grasses that blanketed the plains before farming were perennials. Rather than growing new from seed in spring, they stayed alive year after year.
munch munch
Their roots had held the soil fast. Grazed down to nubs by bison, they regrew from rootstock once the herd had passed.
But those grasses had been ripped up and replanted with wheat. Wheat is an annual crop, harvested each year and planted anew the next. Wheat's roots do not hold the soil fast.

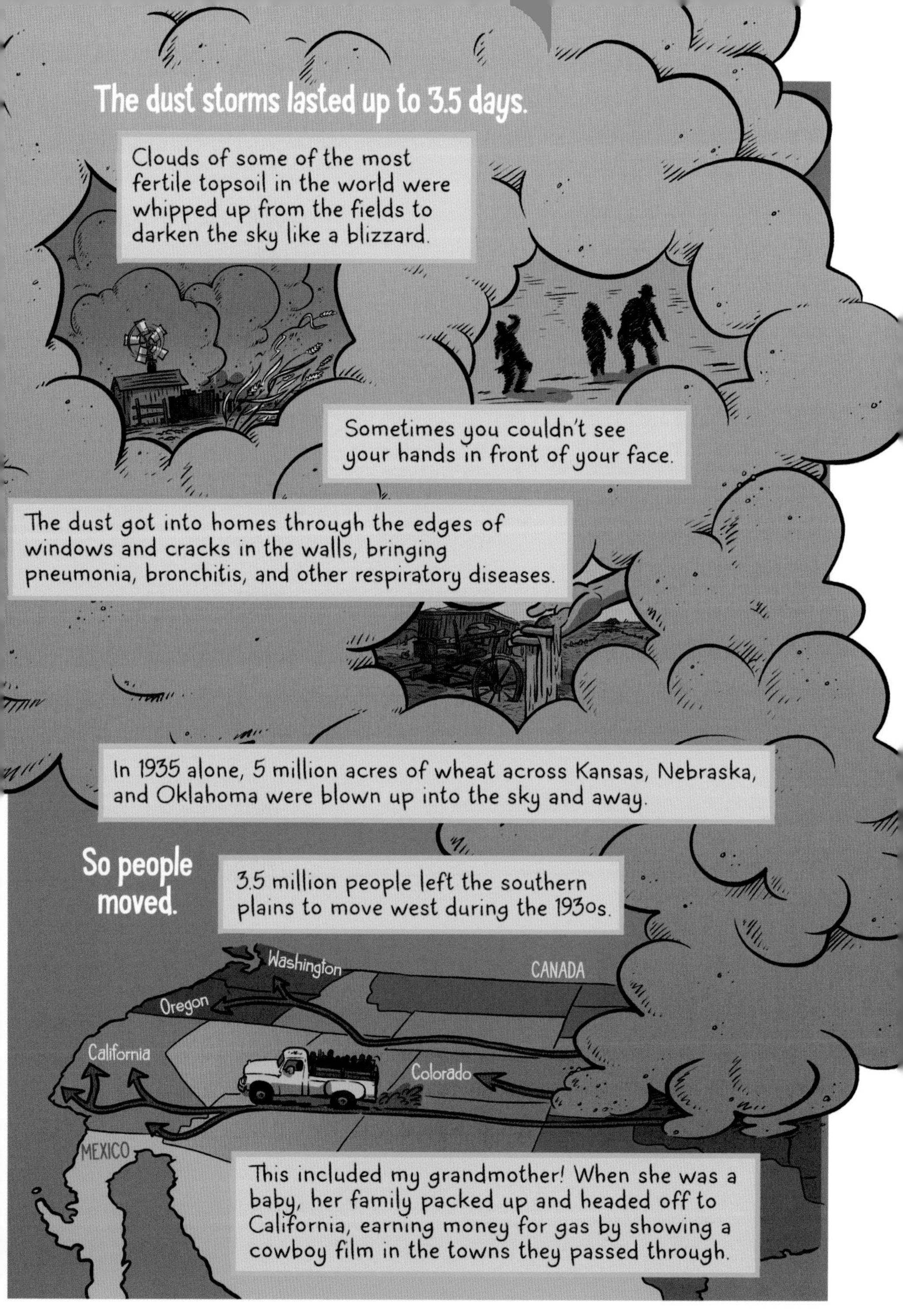
The dust storms lasted up to 3.5 days.
Clouds of some of the most fertile topsoil in the world were whipped up from the fields to darken the sky like a blizzard.
Sometimes you couldn't see your hands in front of your face.
The dust got into homes through the edges of windows and cracks in the walls, bringing pneumonia, bronchitis, and other respiratory diseases.
In 1935 alone, 5 million acres of wheat across Kansas, Nebraska, and Oklahoma were blown up into the sky and away.
So people moved.
3.5 million people left the southern plains to move west during the 1930s.
Washington
CANADA
Oregon
California
Colorado
MEXICO
This included my grandmother! When she was a baby, her family packed up and headed off to California, earning money for gas by showing a cowboy film in the towns they passed through.

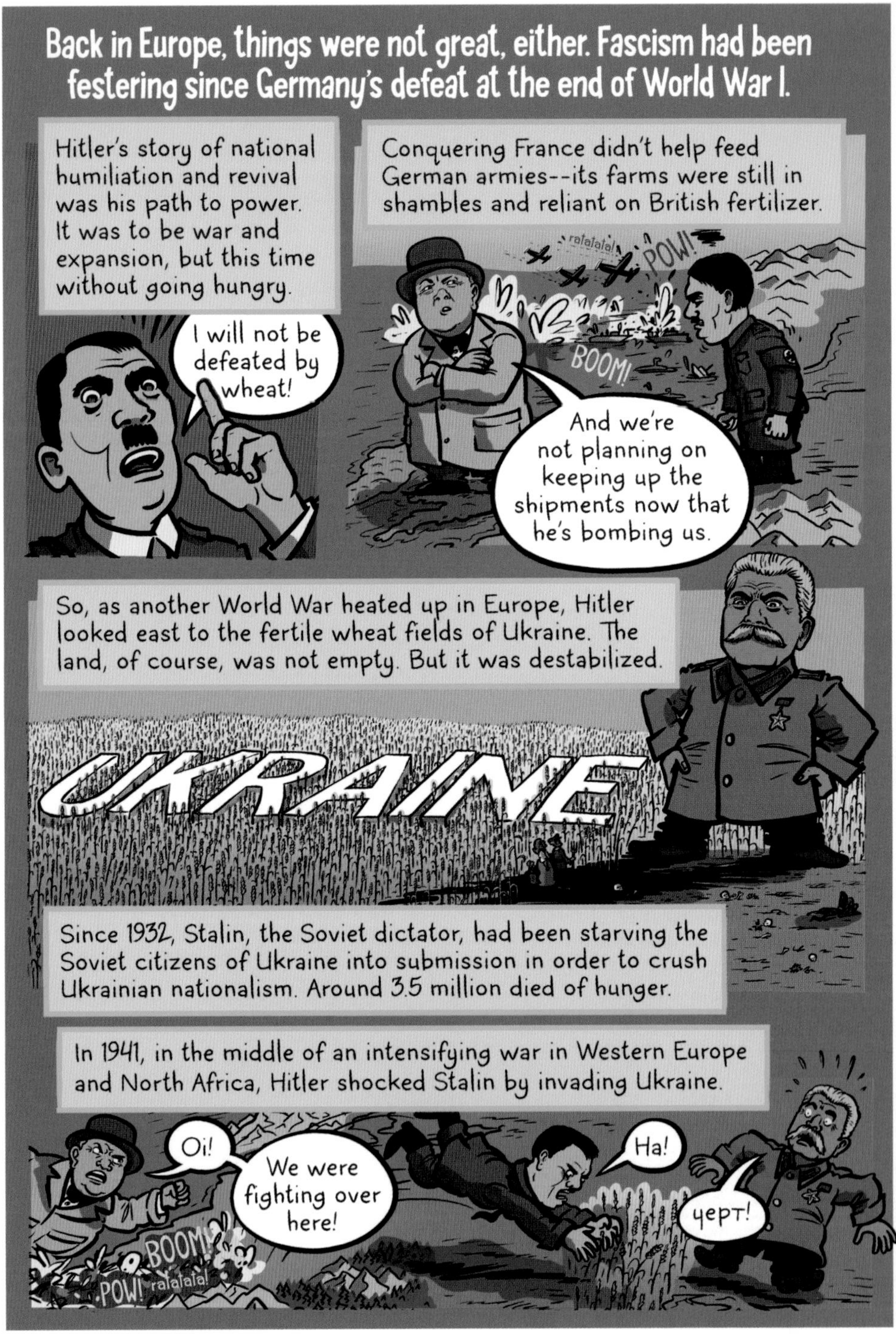
Back in Europe, things were not great, either. Fascism had been festering since Germany's defeat at the end of World War I.
Hitler's story of national humiliation and revival was his path to power. It was to be war and expansion, but this time without going hungry.
I will not be defeated by wheat!
Conquering France didn't help feed German armies--its farms were still in shambles and reliant on British fertilizer.
ratatata!
POW!
BOOM!
And we're not planning on keeping up the shipments now that he's bombing us.
So, as another World War heated up in Europe, Hitler looked east to the fertile wheat fields of Ukraine. The land, of course, was not empty. But it was destabilized.
UKRAINE
Since 1932, Stalin, the Soviet dictator, had been starving the Soviet citizens of Ukraine into submission in order to crush Ukrainian nationalism. Around 3.5 million died of hunger.
In 1941, in the middle of an intensifying war in Western Europe and North Africa, Hitler shocked Stalin by invading Ukraine.
Oi!
We were fighting over here!
BOOM!
POW!
ratatata!
Ha!
черт!

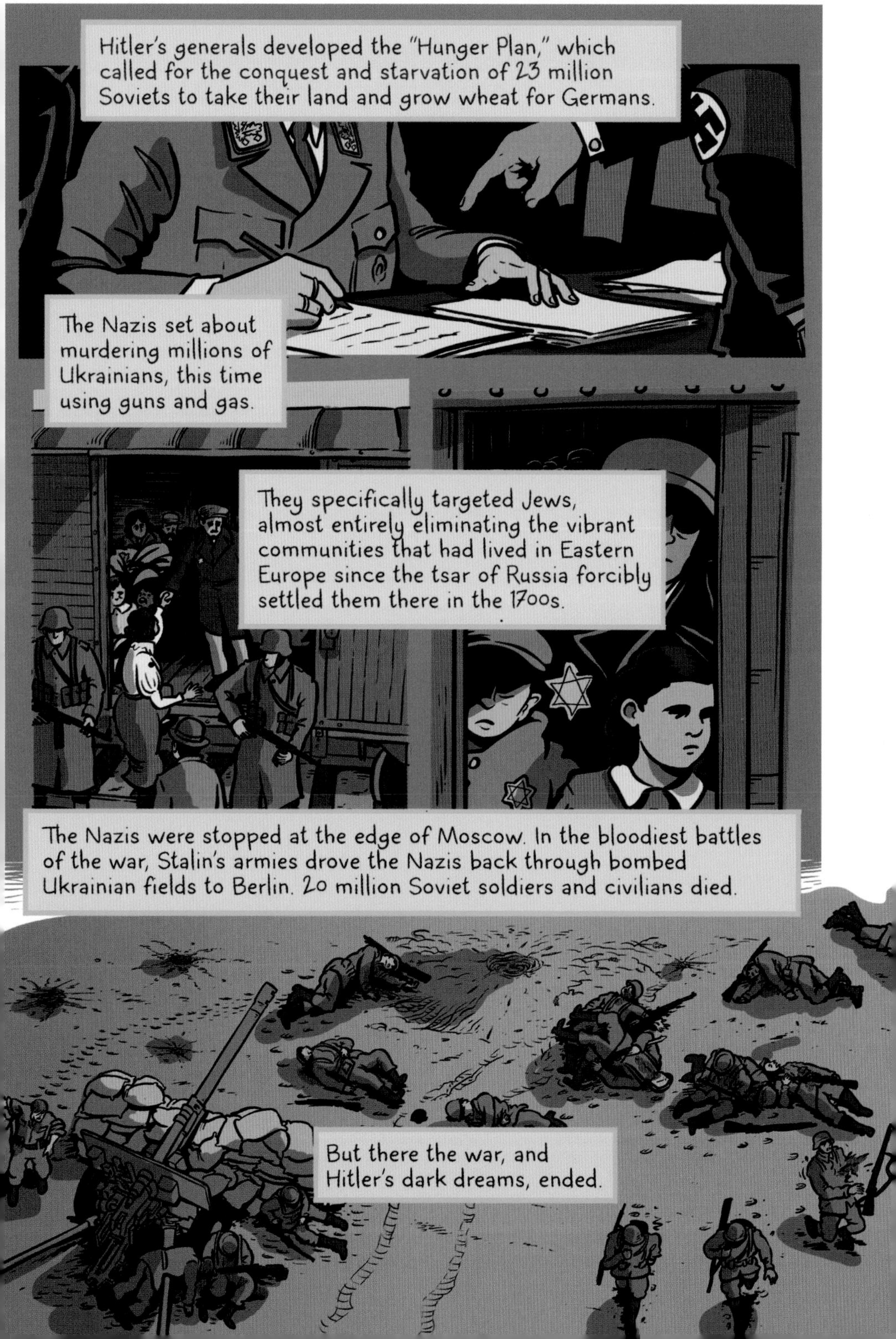

Hitler's generals developed the "Hunger Plan," which called for the conquest and starvation of 23 million Soviets to take their land and grow wheat for Germans.
The Nazis set about murdering millions of Ukrainians, this time using guns and gas.
They specifically targeted Jews, almost entirely eliminating the vibrant communities that had lived in Eastern Europe since the tsar of Russia forcibly settled them there in the 1700s.
The Nazis were stopped at the edge of Moscow. In the bloodiest battles of the war, Stalin's armies drove the Nazis back through bombed Ukrainian fields to Berlin. 20 million Soviet soldiers and civilians died.
But there the war, and Hitler's dark dreams, ended.

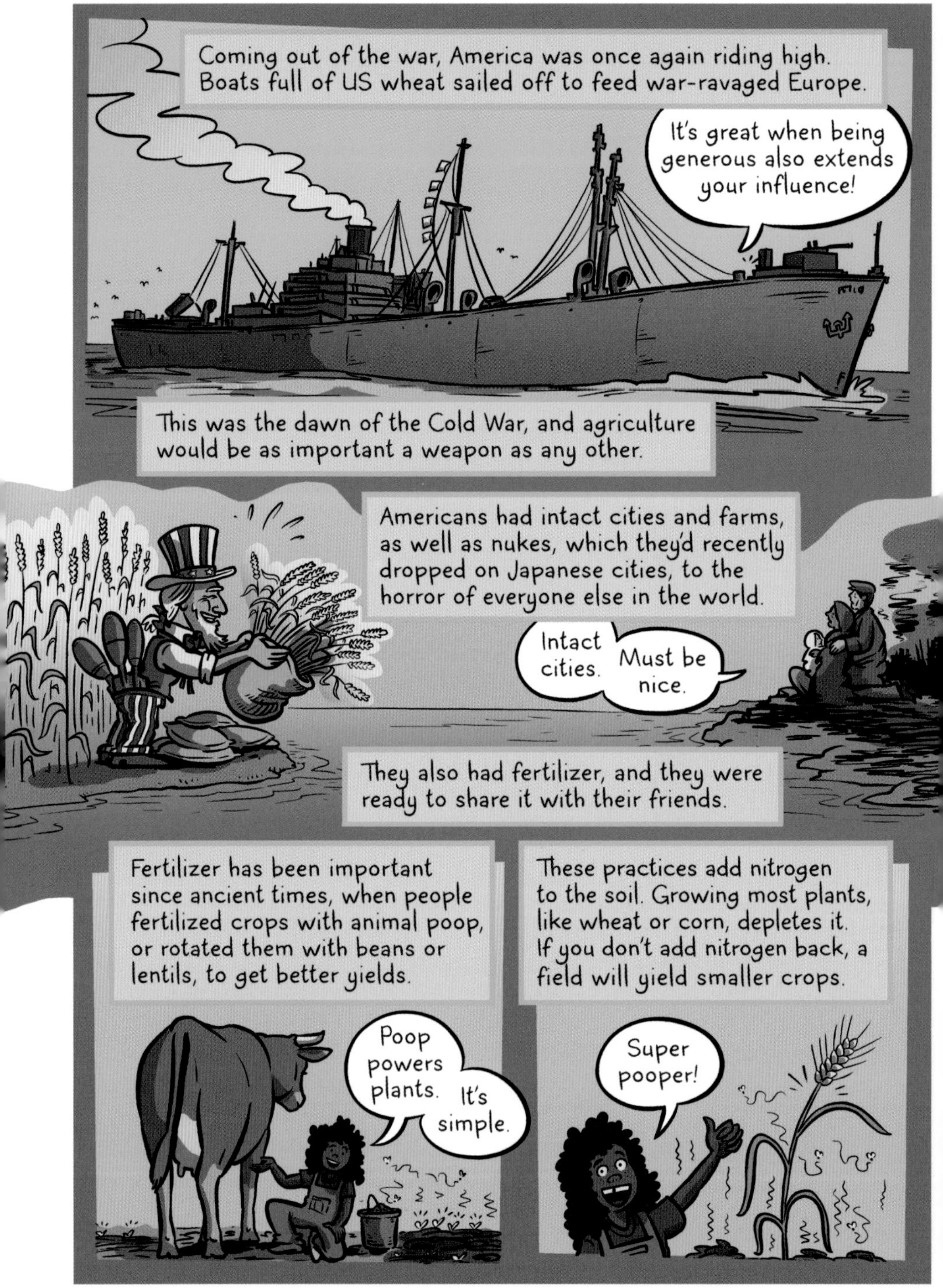
Coming out of the war, America was once again riding high. Boats full of US wheat sailed off to feed war-ravaged Europe.
It's great when being generous also extends your influence!
This was the dawn of the Cold War, and agriculture would be as important a weapon as any other.
Americans had intact cities and farms, as well as nukes, which they'd recently dropped on Japanese cities, to the horror of everyone else in the world.
Intact cities.
Must be nice.
They also had fertilizer, and they were ready to share it with their friends.
Fertilizer has been important since ancient times, when people fertilized crops with animal poop, or rotated them with beans or lentils, to get better yields.
Poop powers plants.
It's simple.
These practices add nitrogen to the soil. Growing most plants, like wheat or corn, depletes it. If you don't add nitrogen back, a field will yield smaller crops.
Super pooper!

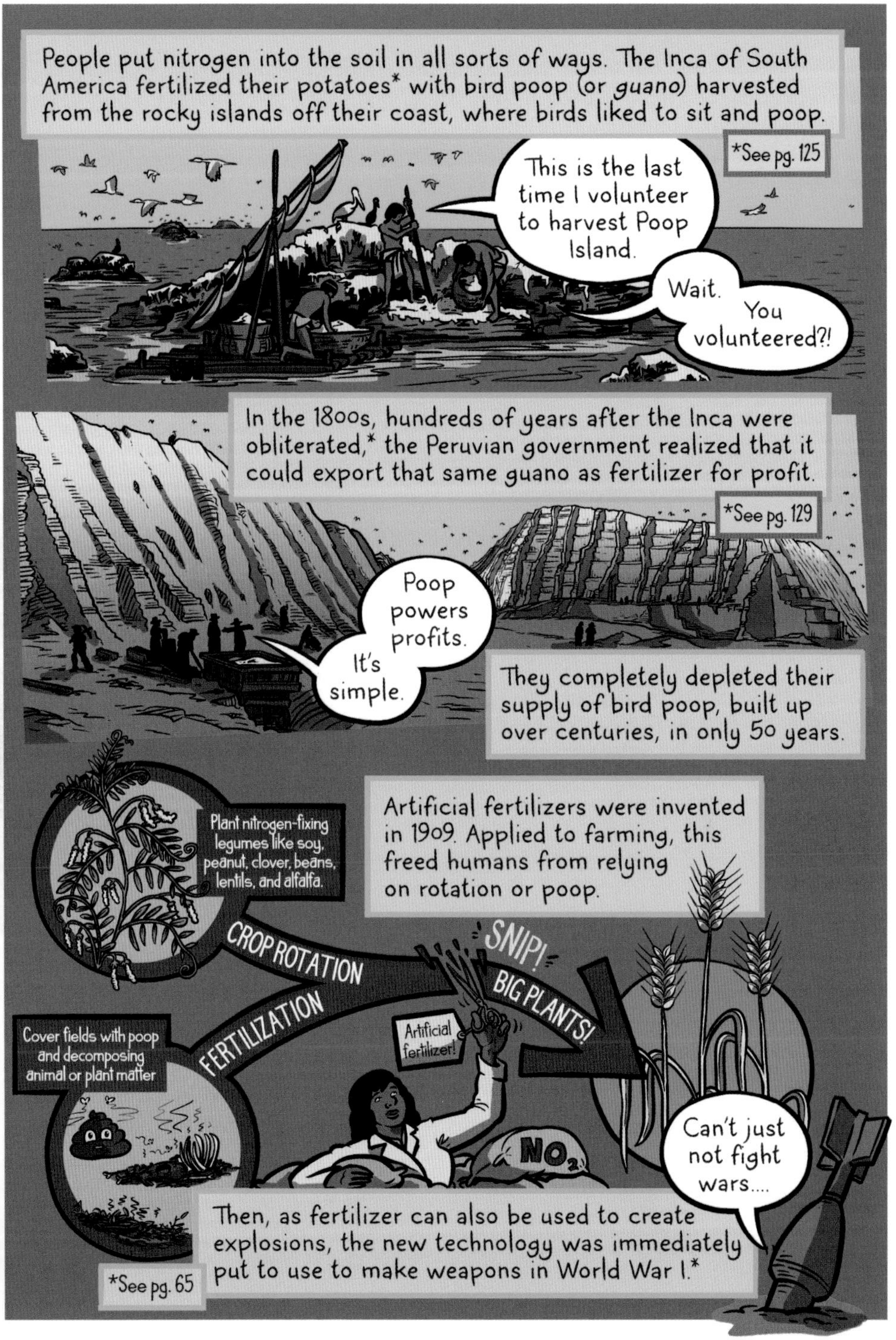
People put nitrogen into the soil in all sorts of ways. The Inca of South America fertilized their potatoes* with bird poop (or *guano*) harvested from the rocky islands off their coast, where birds liked to sit and poop.
*See pg. 125
This is the last time I volunteer to harvest Poop Island.
Wait. You volunteered?!
In the 1800s, hundreds of years after the Inca were obliterated,* the Peruvian government realized that it could export that same guano as fertilizer for profit.
*See pg. 129
Poop powers profits.
It's simple.
They completely depleted their supply of bird poop, built up over centuries, in only 50 years.
Plant nitrogen-fixing legumes like soy, peanut, clover, beans, lentils, and alfalfa.
Artificial fertilizers were invented in 1909. Applied to farming, this freed humans from relying on rotation or poop.
CROP ROTATION
SNIP!
BIG PLANTS!
FERTILIZATION
Artificial fertilizer!
Cover fields with poop and decomposing animal or plant matter
NO2
Can't just not fight wars....
Then, as fertilizer can also be used to create explosions, the new technology was immediately put to use to make weapons in World War I.*
*See pg. 65

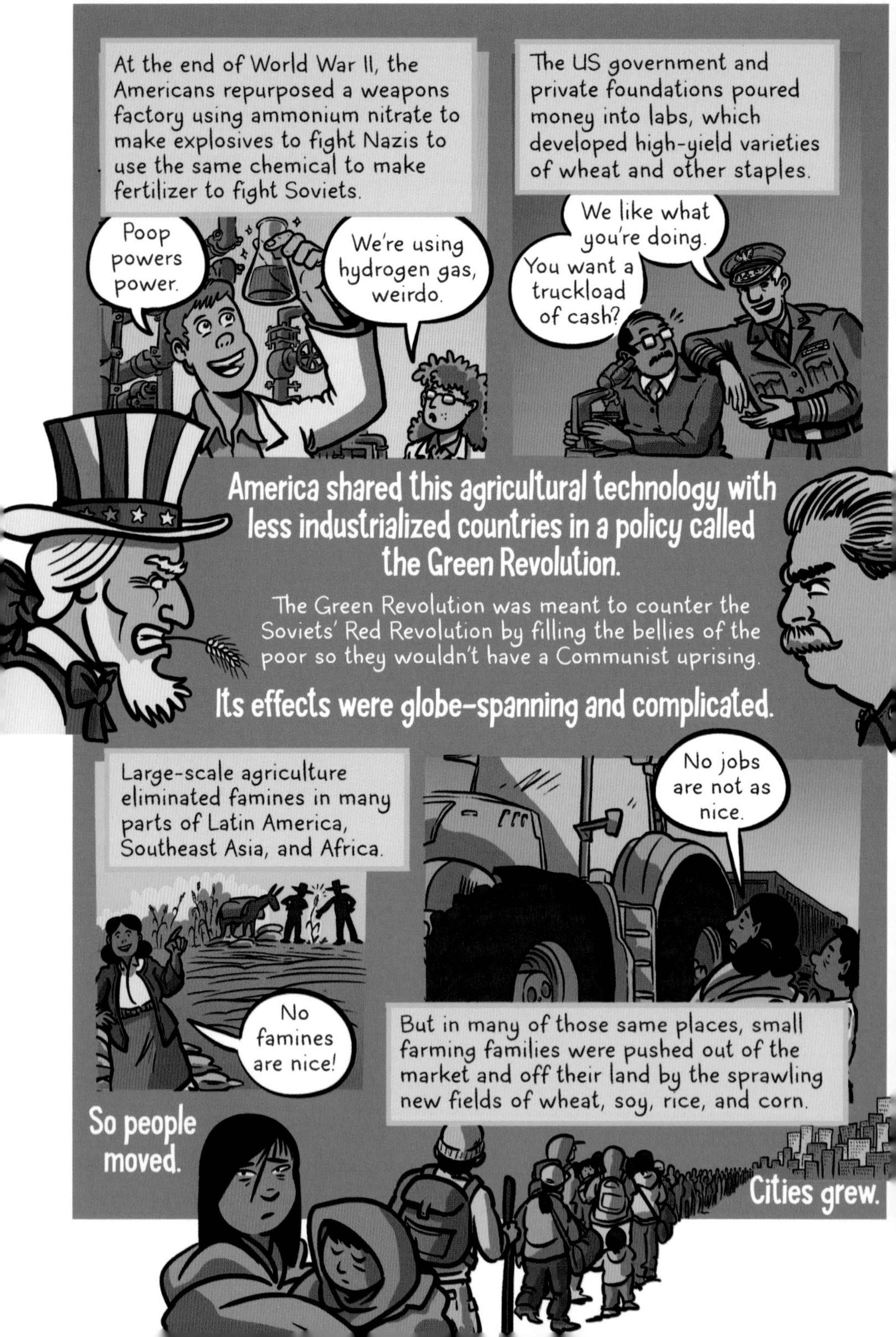
At the end of World War II, the Americans repurposed a weapons factory using ammonium nitrate to make explosives to fight Nazis to use the same chemical to make fertilizer to fight Soviets.
Poop powers power.
We're using hydrogen gas, weirdo.
The US government and private foundations poured money into labs, which developed high-yield varieties of wheat and other staples.
We like what you're doing.
You want a truckload of cash?
America shared this agricultural technology with less industrialized countries in a policy called the Green Revolution.
The Green Revolution was meant to counter the Soviets' Red Revolution by filling the bellies of the poor so they wouldn't have a Communist uprising.
Its effects were globe-spanning and complicated.
Large-scale agriculture eliminated famines in many parts of Latin America, Southeast Asia, and Africa.
No famines are nice!
No jobs are not as nice.
But in many of those same places, small farming families were pushed out of the market and off their land by the sprawling new fields of wheat, soy, rice, and corn.
So people moved.
Cities grew.

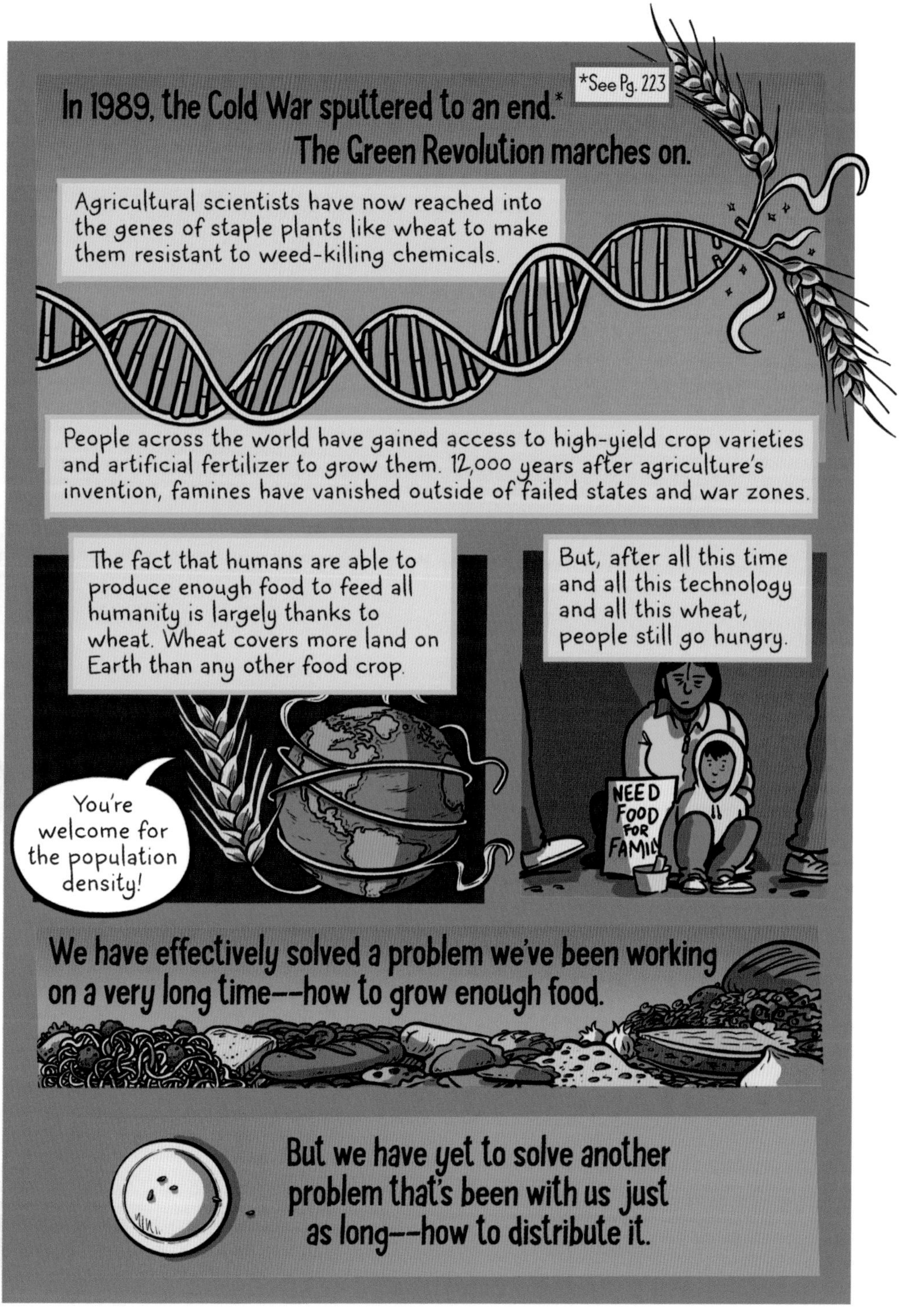
In 1989, the Cold War sputtered to an end.*
*See Pg. 223
The Green Revolution marches on.
Agricultural scientists have now reached into the genes of staple plants like wheat to make them resistant to weed-killing chemicals.
People across the world have gained access to high-yield crop varieties and artificial fertilizer to grow them. 12,000 years after agriculture's invention, famines have vanished outside of failed states and war zones.
The fact that humans are able to produce enough food to feed all humanity is largely thanks to wheat. Wheat covers more land on Earth than any other food crop.
You're welcome for the population density!
But, after all this time and all this technology and all this wheat, people still go hungry.
NEED FOOD FOR FAMIL
We have effectively solved a problem we've been working on a very long time--how to grow enough food.
But we have yet to solve another problem that's been with us just as long--how to distribute it.

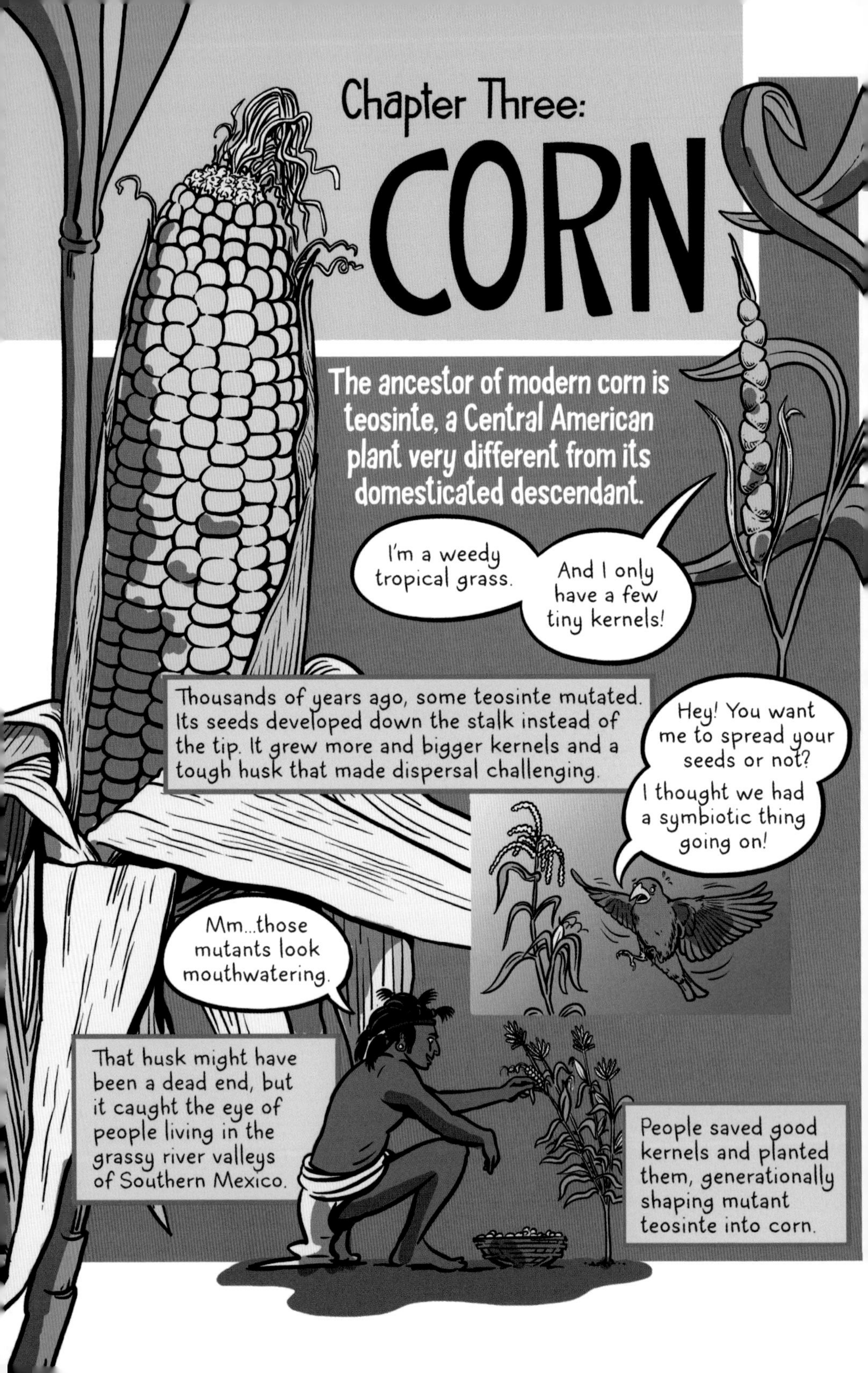
Chapter Three:
CORN
The ancestor of modern corn is teosinte, a Central American plant very different from its domesticated descendant.
I'm a weedy tropical grass.
And I only have a few tiny kernels!
Thousands of years ago, some teosinte mutated. Its seeds developed down the stalk instead of the tip. It grew more and bigger kernels and a tough husk that made dispersal challenging.
Hey! You want me to spread your seeds or not?
I thought we had a symbiotic thing going on!
Mm...those mutants look mouthwatering.
That husk might have been a dead end, but it caught the eye of people living in the grassy river valleys of Southern Mexico.
People saved good kernels and planted them, generationally shaping mutant teosinte into corn.

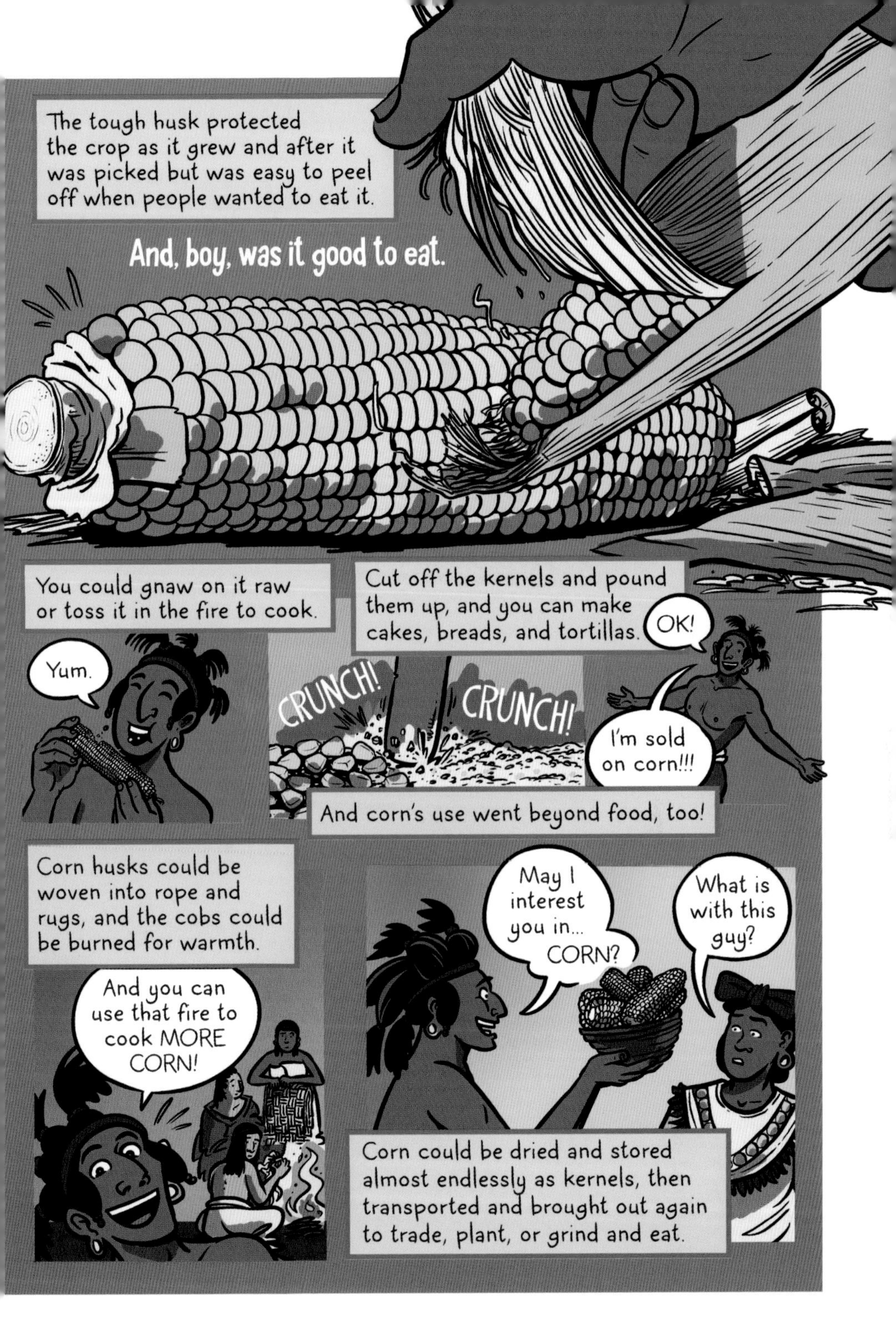

The tough husk protected the crop as it grew and after it was picked but was easy to peel off when people wanted to eat it.
And, boy, was it good to eat.
You could gnaw on it raw or toss it in the fire to cook.
Yum.
Cut off the kernels and pound them up, and you can make cakes, breads, and tortillas.
CRUNCH!
CRUNCH!
OK!
I'm sold on corn!!!
And corn's use went beyond food, too!
Corn husks could be woven into rope and rugs, and the cobs could be burned for warmth.
And you can use that fire to cook MORE CORN!
May I interest you in... CORN?
What is with this guy?
Corn could be dried and stored almost endlessly as kernels, then transported and brought out again to trade, plant, or grind and eat.

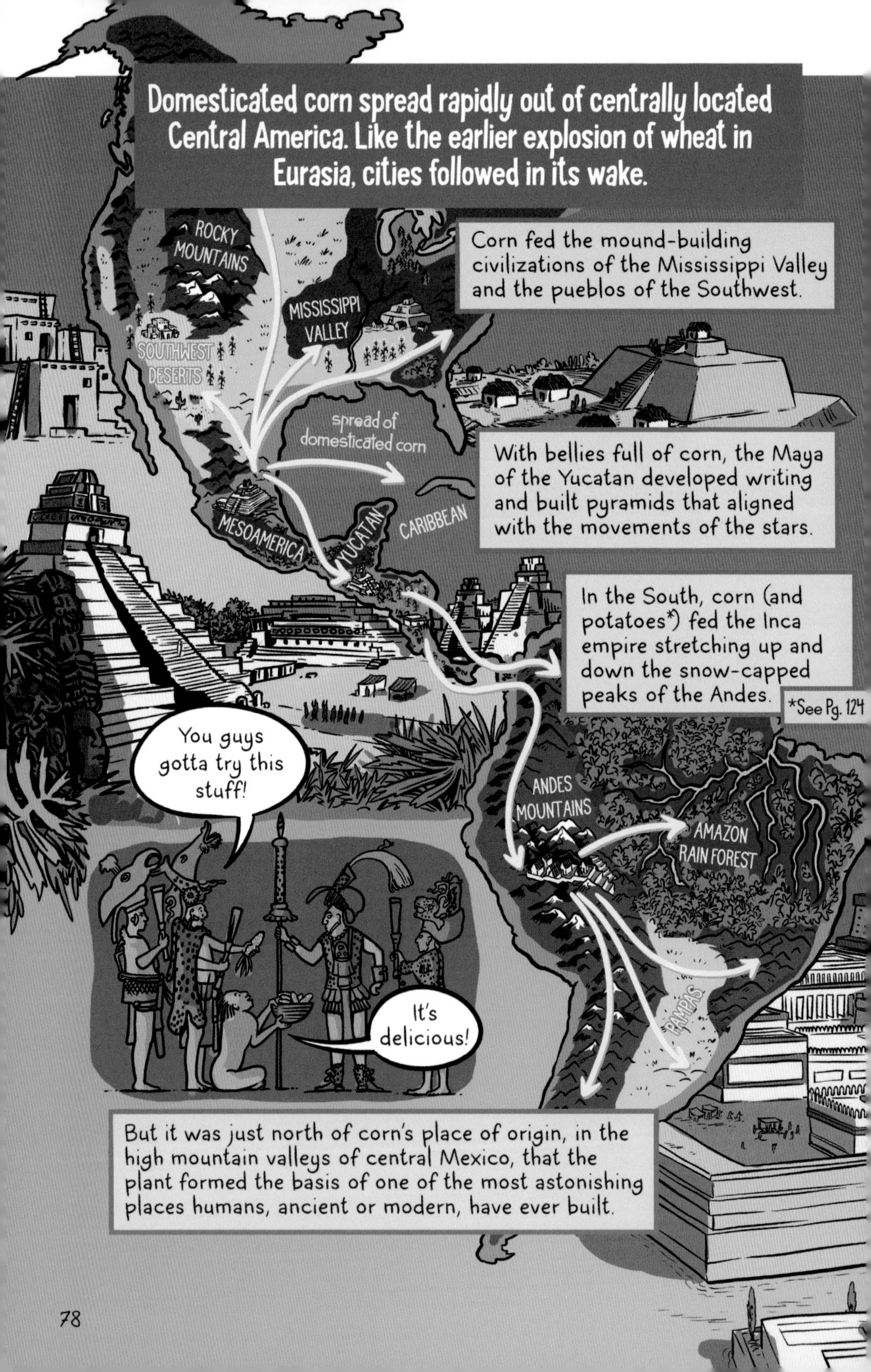
Domesticated corn spread rapidly out of centrally located Central America. Like the earlier explosion of wheat in Eurasia, cities followed in its wake.
ROCKY MOUNTAINS
SOUTHWEST DESERTS
MISSISSIPPI VALLEY
Corn fed the mound-building civilizations of the Mississippi Valley and the pueblos of the Southwest.
spread of domesticated corn
With bellies full of corn, the Maya of the Yucatan developed writing and built pyramids that aligned with the movements of the stars.
MESOAMERICA
YUCATAN
CARIBBEAN
In the South, corn (and potatoes*) fed the Inca empire stretching up and down the snow-capped peaks of the Andes.
*See Pg. 124
You guys gotta try this stuff!
ANDES MOUNTAINS
AMAZON RAIN FOREST
It's delicious!
PAMPAS
But it was just north of corn's place of origin, in the high mountain valleys of central Mexico, that the plant formed the basis of one of the most astonishing places humans, ancient or modern, have ever built.

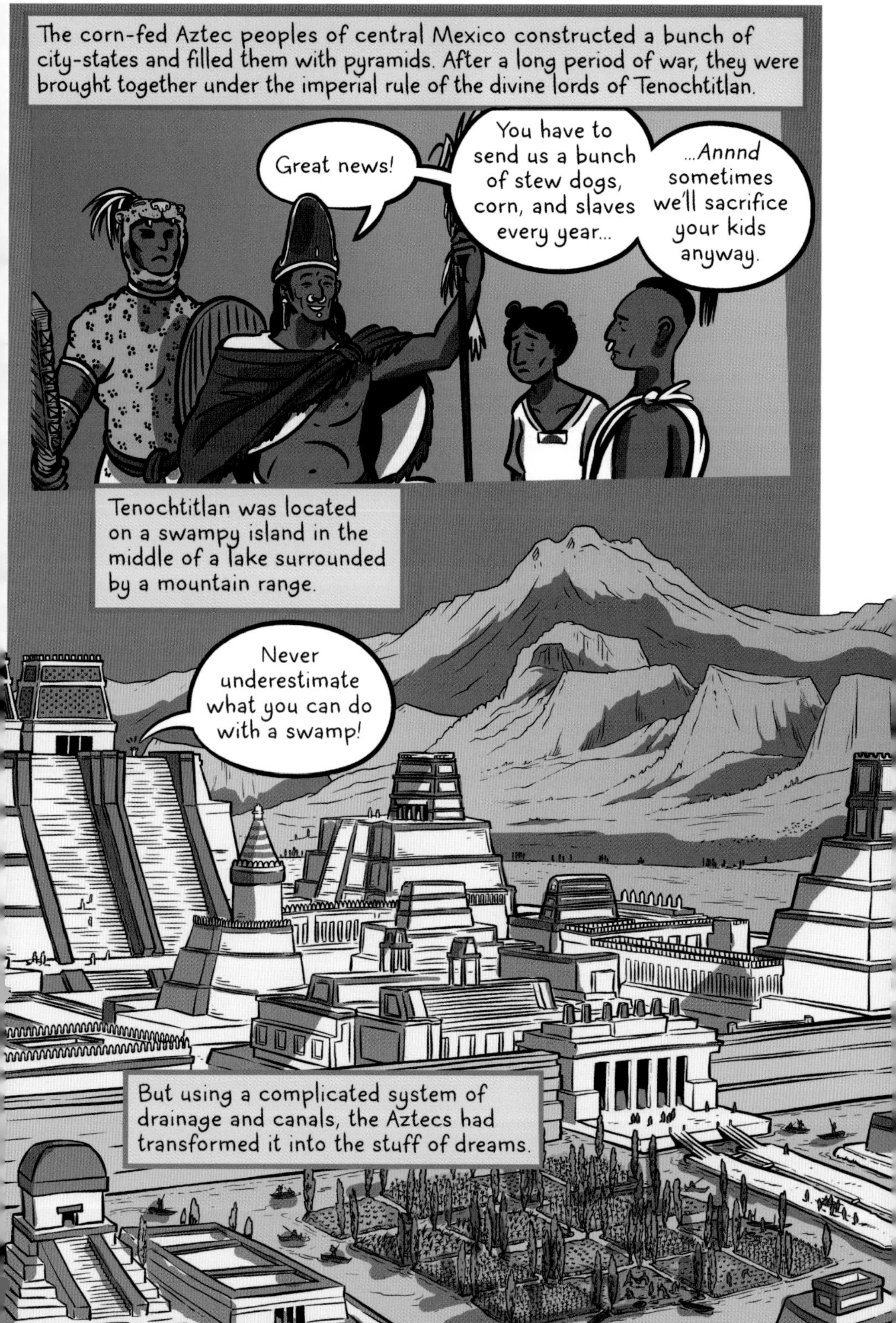
The corn-fed Aztec peoples of central Mexico constructed a bunch of city-states and filled them with pyramids. After a long period of war, they were brought together under the imperial rule of the divine lords of Tenochtitlan.
Great news!
You have to send us a bunch of stew dogs, corn, and slaves every year...
...Annnd sometimes we'll sacrifice your kids anyway.
Tenochtitlan was located on a swampy island in the middle of a lake surrounded by a mountain range.
Never underestimate what you can do with a swamp!
But using a complicated system of drainage and canals, the Aztecs had transformed it into the stuff of dreams.

To a visitor, Tenochtitlan appeared to be a floating city, rising from the shimmering lake surface as if it were a mirage.

Long, human-made causeways connected the city to the mainland. A towering temple complex stood at the very center where the lines converged.

It's good to be at the very center!

Floating fields, called *chinampas*, ringed the city in a gridded pattern.

Yes, very convenient.

These were created by floating big rectangular baskets made of juniper trees in shallow water. They were then filled with mud, manure, and compost, which sunk them to the lake bed.

Remind me why we moved to the middle of a lake?

Then trees were planted, anchoring the chinampas.

I dunno. Few jaguars?

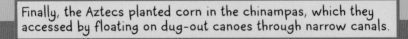

Finally, the Aztecs planted corn in the chinampas, which they accessed by floating on dug-out canoes through narrow canals.

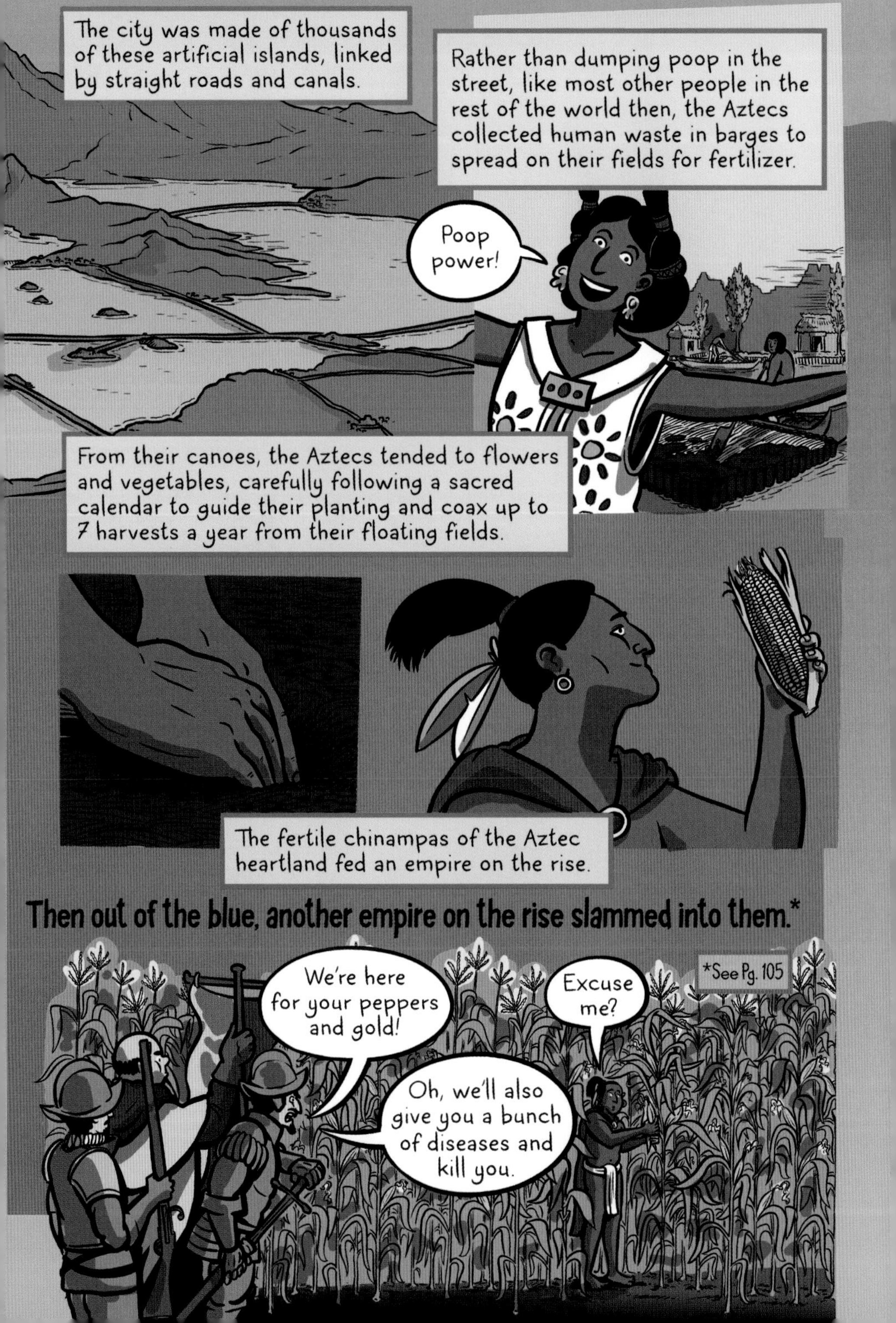
The city was made of thousands of these artificial islands, linked by straight roads and canals.
Rather than dumping poop in the street, like most other people in the rest of the world then, the Aztecs collected human waste in barges to spread on their fields for fertilizer.
Poop power!
From their canoes, the Aztecs tended to flowers and vegetables, carefully following a sacred calendar to guide their planting and coax up to 7 harvests a year from their floating fields.
The fertile chinampas of the Aztec heartland fed an empire on the rise.
Then out of the blue, another empire on the rise slammed into them.*
*See Pg. 105
We're here for your peppers and gold!
Excuse me?
Oh, we'll also give you a bunch of diseases and kill you.

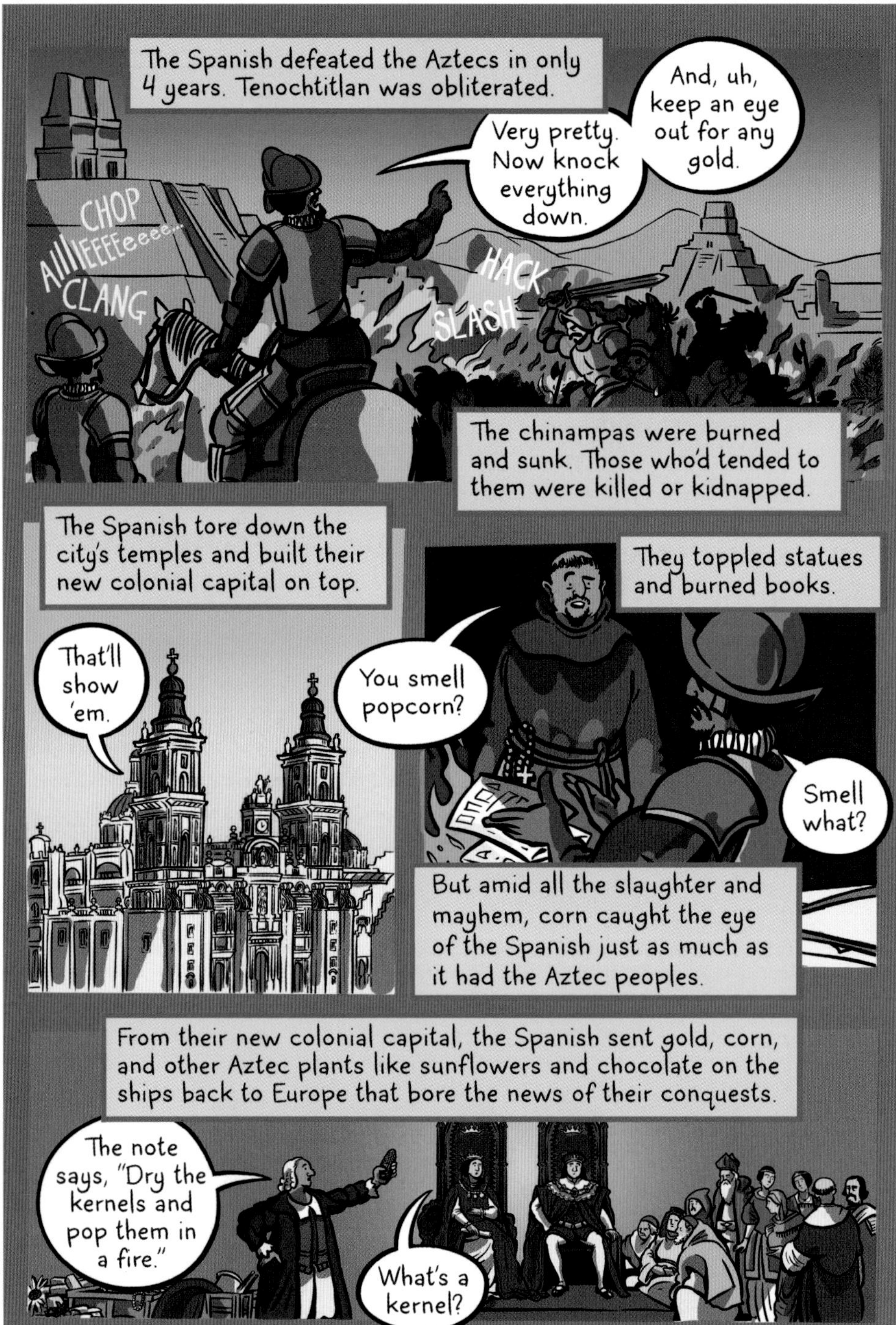

The Spanish defeated the Aztecs in only 4 years. Tenochtitlan was obliterated.
Very pretty. Now knock everything down.
And, uh, keep an eye out for any gold.
CHOP
AIIIIEEEEeeee...
CLANG
HACK
SLASH
The chinampas were burned and sunk. Those who'd tended to them were killed or kidnapped.
The Spanish tore down the city's temples and built their new colonial capital on top.
That'll show 'em.
They toppled statues and burned books.
You smell popcorn?
Smell what?
But amid all the slaughter and mayhem, corn caught the eye of the Spanish just as much as it had the Aztec peoples.
From their new colonial capital, the Spanish sent gold, corn, and other Aztec plants like sunflowers and chocolate on the ships back to Europe that bore the news of their conquests.
The note says, "Dry the kernels and pop them in a fire."
What's a kernel?

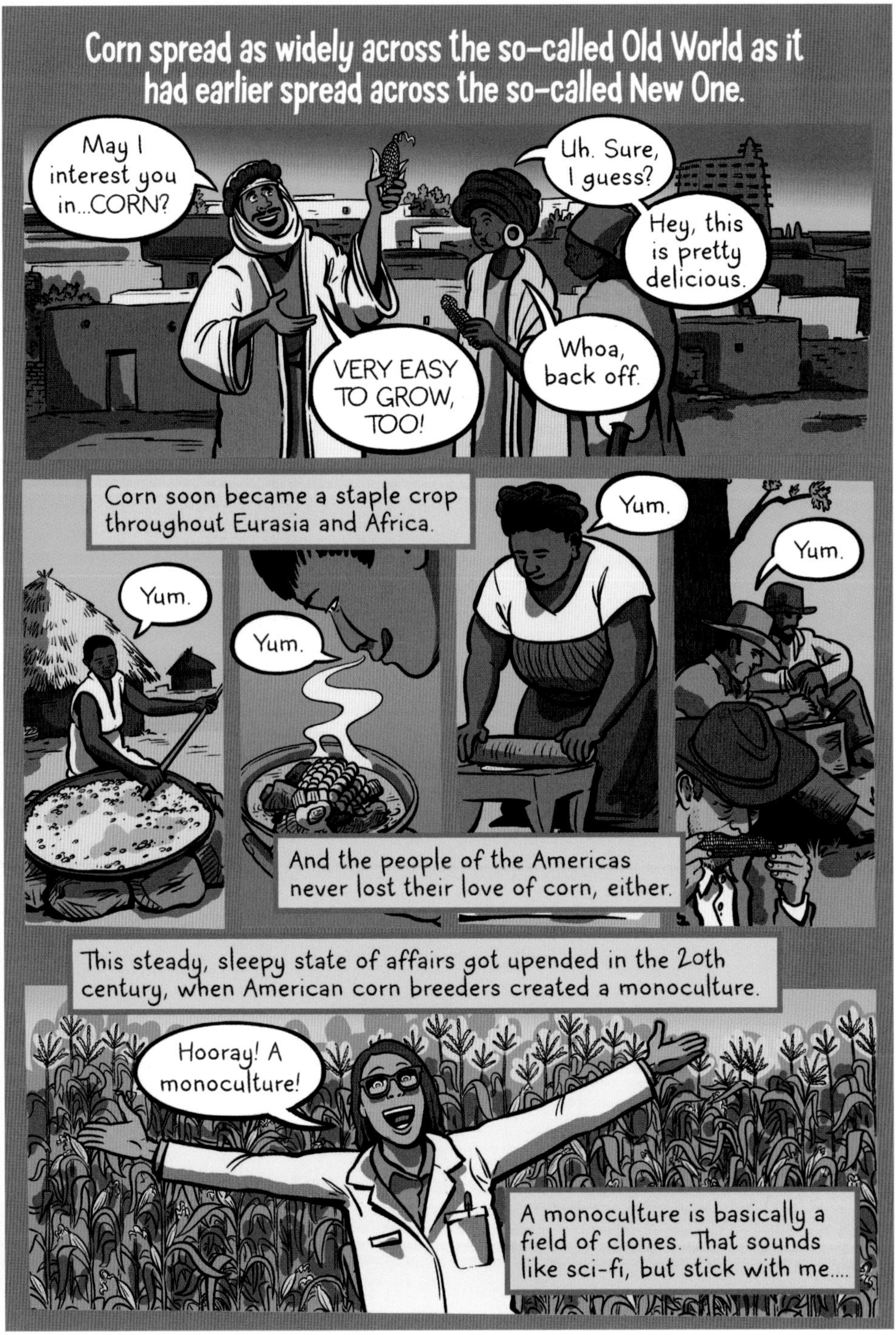
Corn spread as widely across the so-called Old World as it had earlier spread across the so-called New One.
May I interest you in...CORN?
Uh. Sure, I guess?
Hey, this is pretty delicious.
VERY EASY TO GROW, TOO!
Whoa, back off.
Corn soon became a staple crop throughout Eurasia and Africa.
Yum.
Yum.
Yum.
Yum.
And the people of the Americas never lost their love of corn, either.
This steady, sleepy state of affairs got upended in the 20th century, when American corn breeders created a monoculture.
Hooray! A monoculture!
A monoculture is basically a field of clones. That sounds like sci-fi, but stick with me....

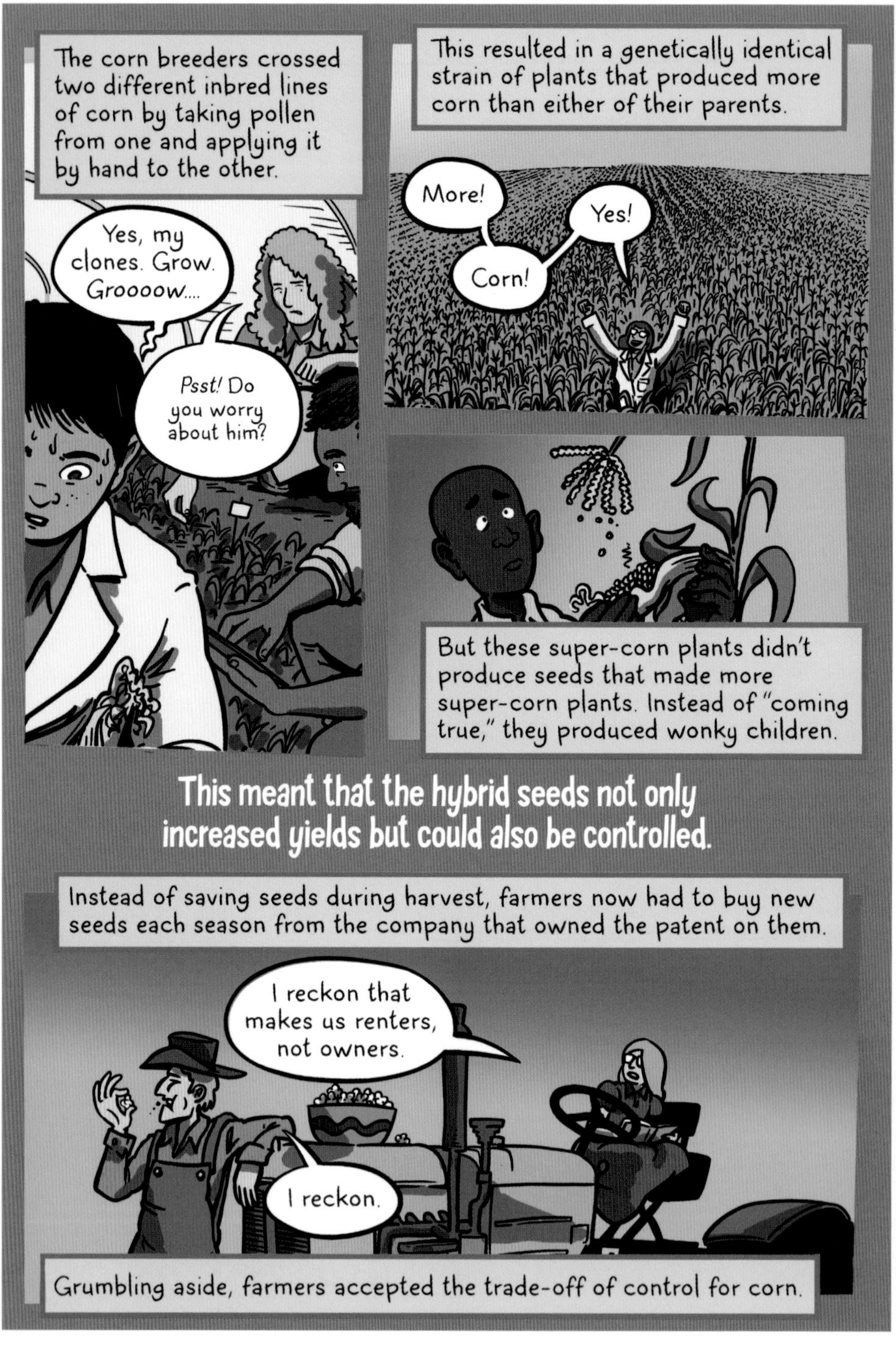
The corn breeders crossed two different inbred lines of corn by taking pollen from one and applying it by hand to the other.
Yes, my clones. Grow. Groooow....
Psst! Do you worry about him?
This resulted in a genetically identical strain of plants that produced more corn than either of their parents.
More!
Corn!
Yes!
But these super-corn plants didn't produce seeds that made more super-corn plants. Instead of "coming true," they produced wonky children.
This meant that the hybrid seeds not only increased yields but could also be controlled.
Instead of saving seeds during harvest, farmers now had to buy new seeds each season from the company that owned the patent on them.
I reckon that makes us renters, not owners.
I reckon.
Grumbling aside, farmers accepted the trade-off of control for corn.

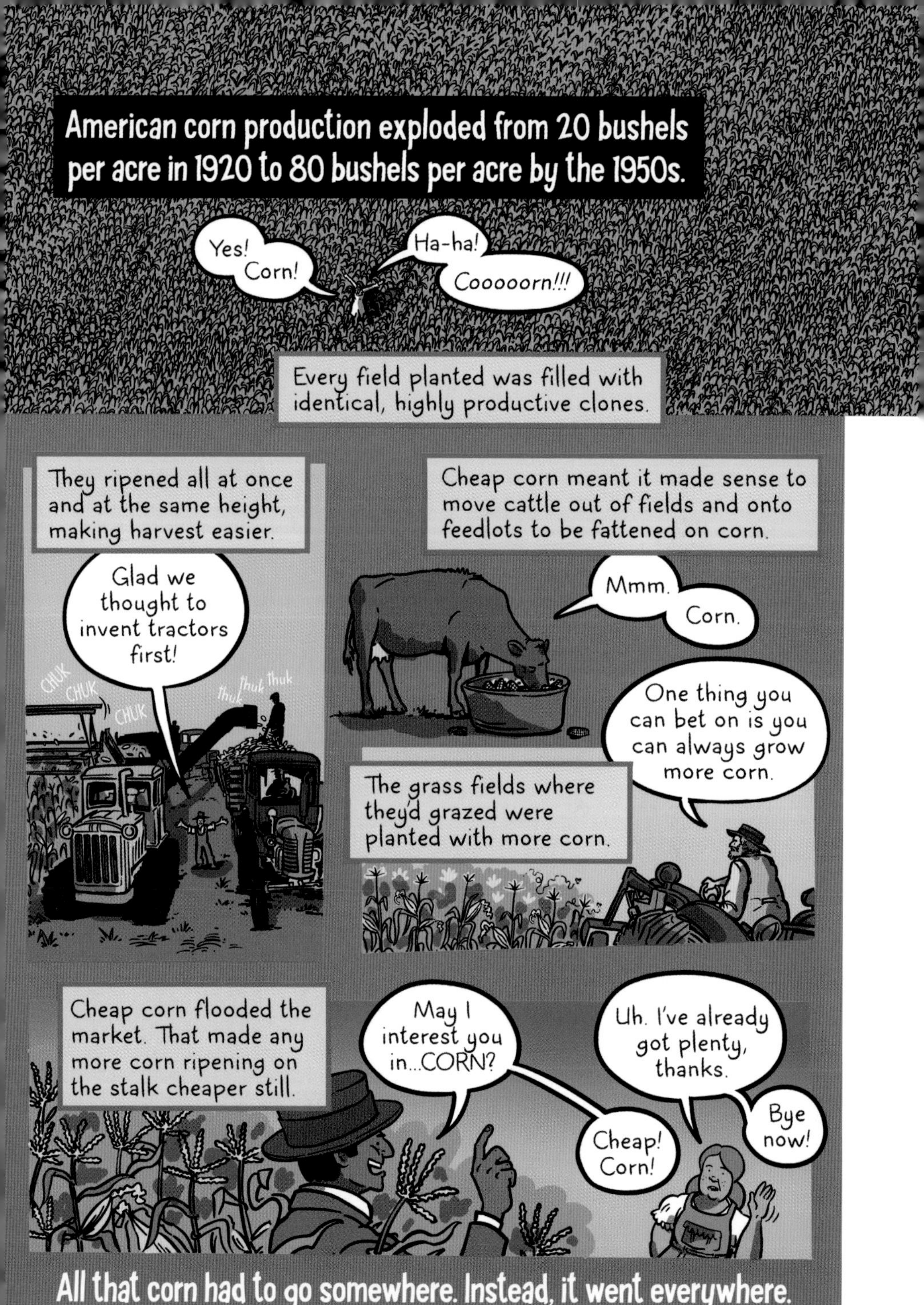
American corn production exploded from 20 bushels per acre in 1920 to 80 bushels per acre by the 1950s.
Yes! Corn!
Ha-ha! Cooooorn!!!
Every field planted was filled with identical, highly productive clones.
They ripened all at once and at the same height, making harvest easier.
Glad we thought to invent tractors first!
CHUK CHUK CHUK
thuk thuk thuk
Cheap corn meant it made sense to move cattle out of fields and onto feedlots to be fattened on corn.
Mmm. Corn.
One thing you can bet on is you can always grow more corn.
The grass fields where they'd grazed were planted with more corn.
Cheap corn flooded the market. That made any more corn ripening on the stalk cheaper still.
May I interest you in...CORN?
Cheap! Corn!
Uh. I've already got plenty, thanks.
Bye now!
All that corn had to go somewhere. Instead, it went everywhere.

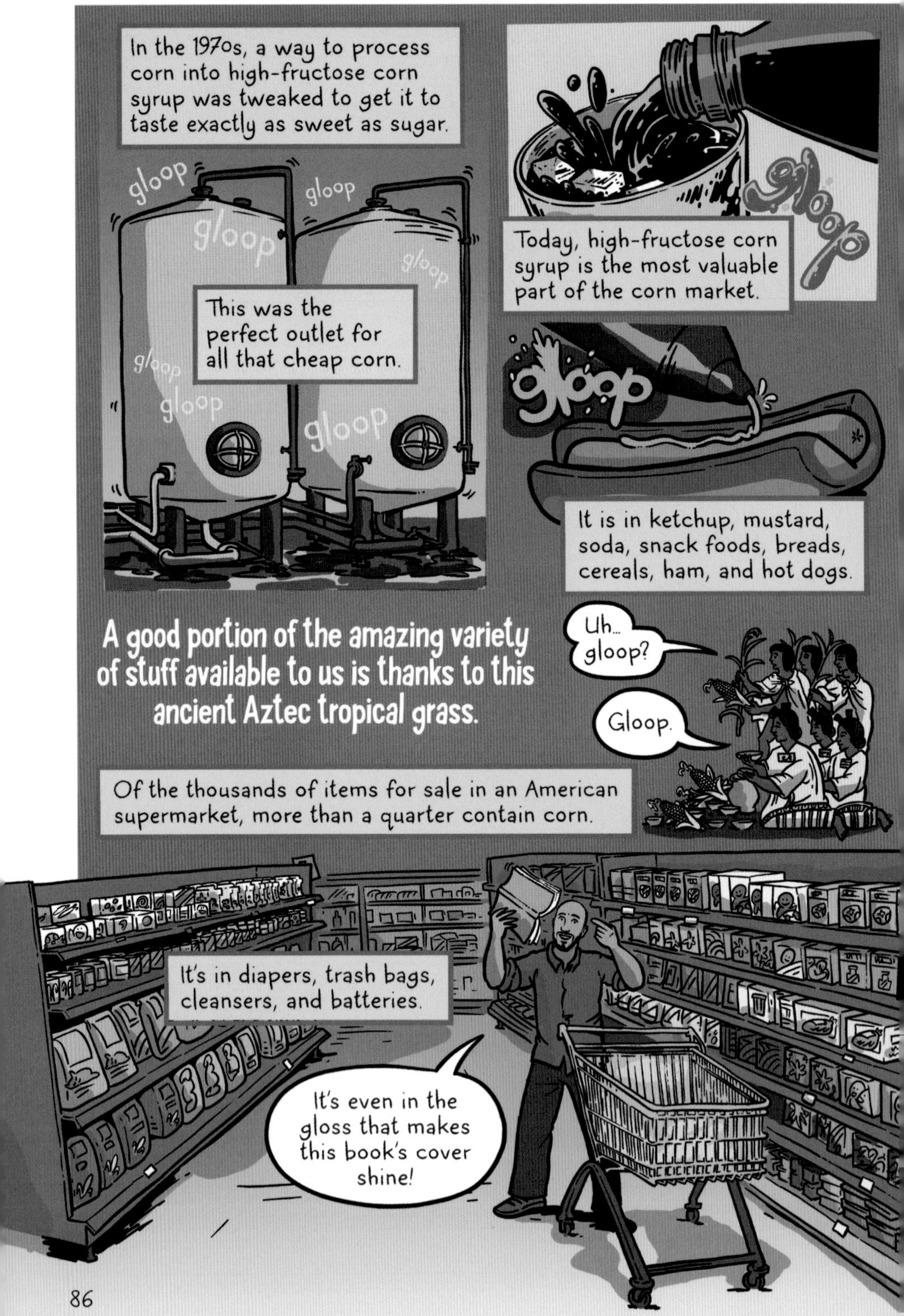
In the 1970s, a way to process corn into high-fructose corn syrup was tweaked to get it to taste exactly as sweet as sugar.
gloop
gloop
gloop
gloop
This was the perfect outlet for all that cheap corn.
gloop
gloop
gloop
gloop
Today, high-fructose corn syrup is the most valuable part of the corn market.
gloop
It is in ketchup, mustard, soda, snack foods, breads, cereals, ham, and hot dogs.
A good portion of the amazing variety of stuff available to us is thanks to this ancient Aztec tropical grass.
Uh... gloop?
Gloop.
Of the thousands of items for sale in an American supermarket, more than a quarter contain corn.
It's in diapers, trash bags, cleansers, and batteries.
It's even in the gloss that makes this book's cover shine!

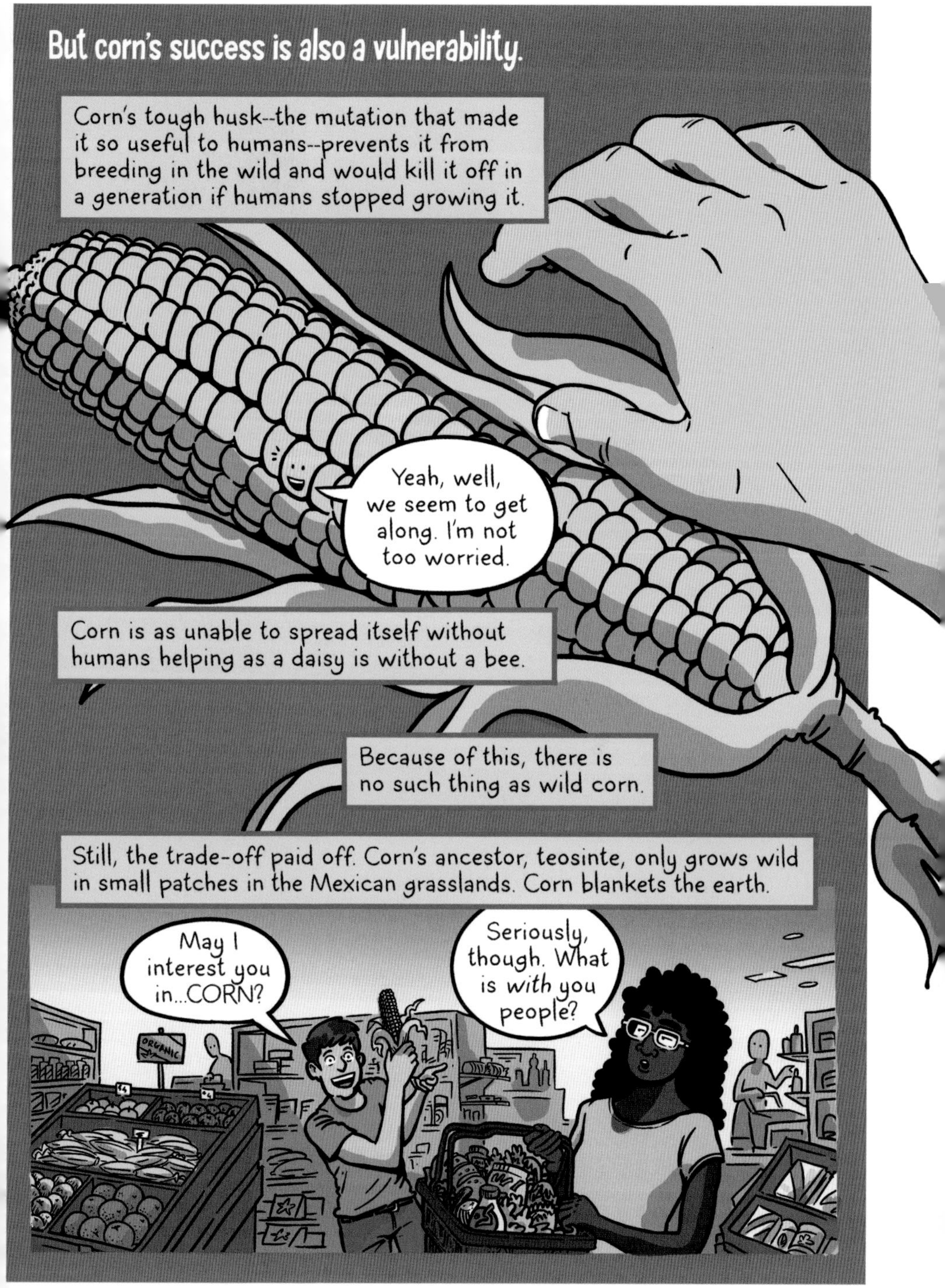
But corn's success is also a vulnerability.
Corn's tough husk--the mutation that made it so useful to humans--prevents it from breeding in the wild and would kill it off in a generation if humans stopped growing it.
Yeah, well, we seem to get along. I'm not too worried.
Corn is as unable to spread itself without humans helping as a daisy is without a bee.
Because of this, there is no such thing as wild corn.
Still, the trade-off paid off. Corn's ancestor, teosinte, only grows wild in small patches in the Mexican grasslands. Corn blankets the earth.
May I interest you in...CORN?
Seriously, though. What is *with* you people?
ORGANIC

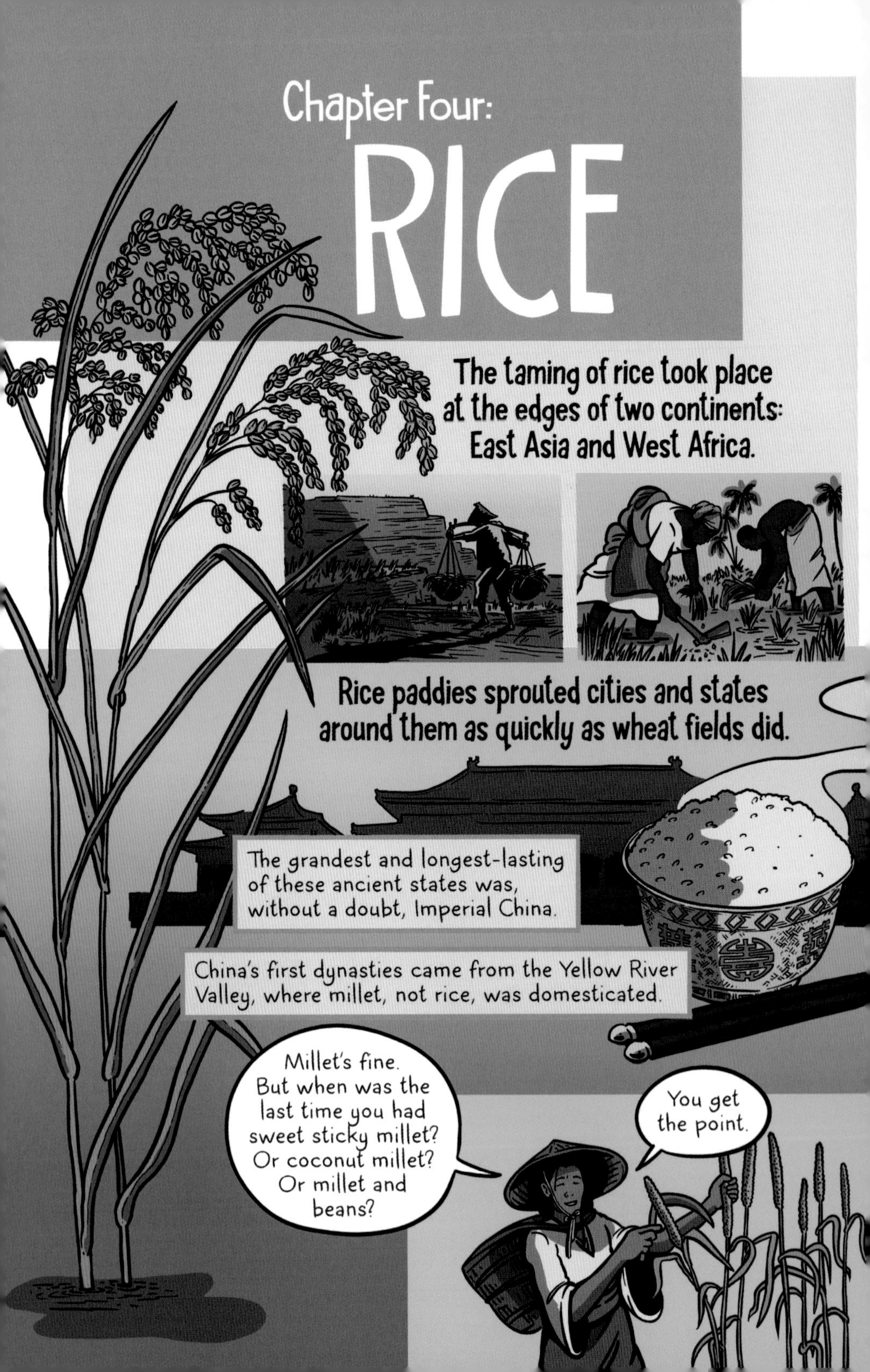

Chapter Four:
RICE
The taming of rice took place at the edges of two continents: East Asia and West Africa.
Rice paddies sprouted cities and states around them as quickly as wheat fields did.
The grandest and longest-lasting of these ancient states was, without a doubt, Imperial China.
China's first dynasties came from the Yellow River Valley, where millet, not rice, was domesticated.
Millet's fine. But when was the last time you had sweet sticky millet? Or coconut millet? Or millet and beans?
You get the point.

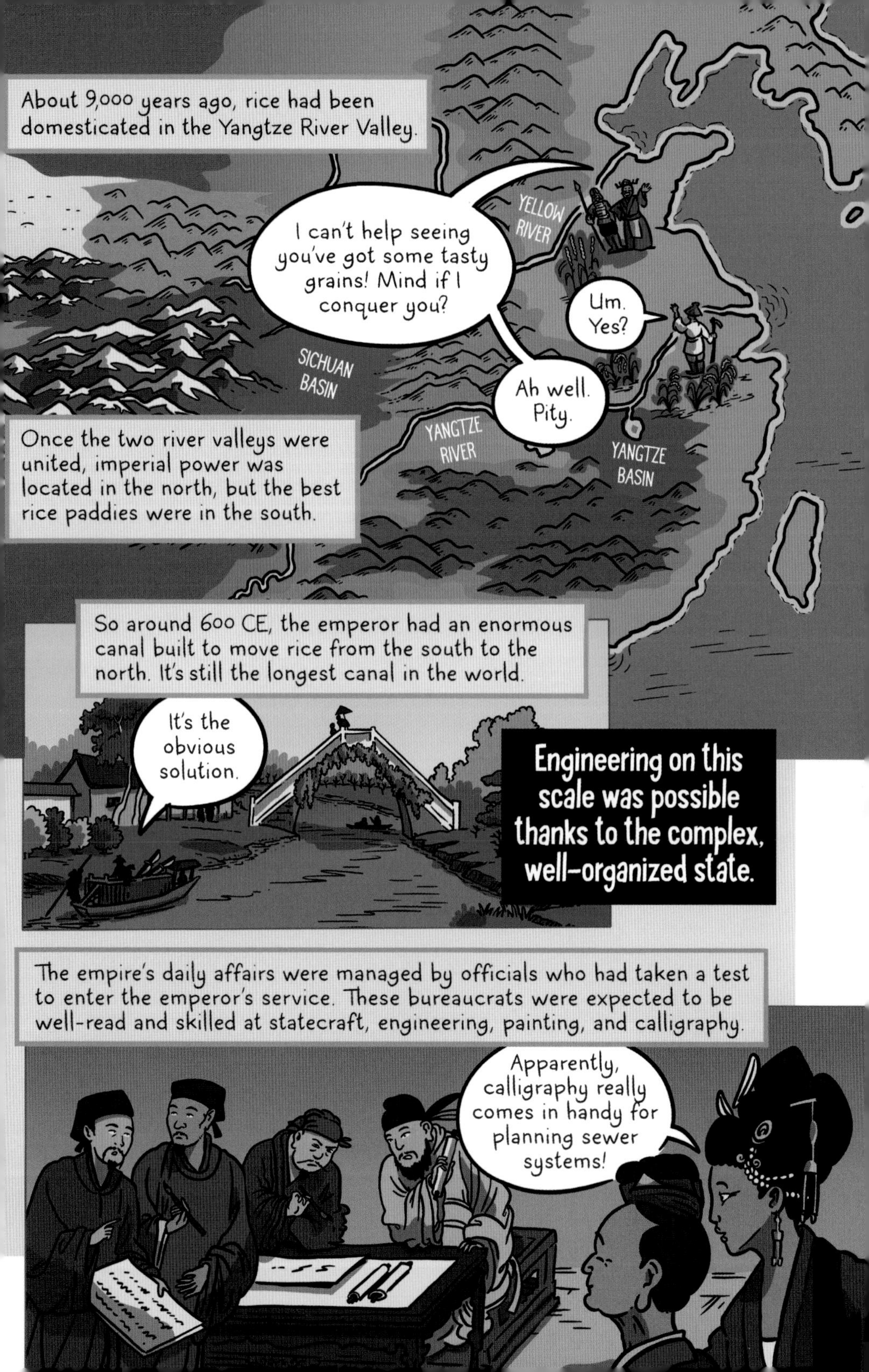
About 9,000 years ago, rice had been domesticated in the Yangtze River Valley.
I can't help seeing you've got some tasty grains! Mind if I conquer you?
YELLOW RIVER
Um. Yes?
SICHUAN BASIN
Ah well. Pity.
YANGTZE RIVER
YANGTZE BASIN
Once the two river valleys were united, imperial power was located in the north, but the best rice paddies were in the south.
So around 600 CE, the emperor had an enormous canal built to move rice from the south to the north. It's still the longest canal in the world.
It's the obvious solution.
Engineering on this scale was possible thanks to the complex, well-organized state.
The empire's daily affairs were managed by officials who had taken a test to enter the emperor's service. These bureaucrats were expected to be well-read and skilled at statecraft, engineering, painting, and calligraphy.
Apparently, calligraphy really comes in handy for planning sewer systems!

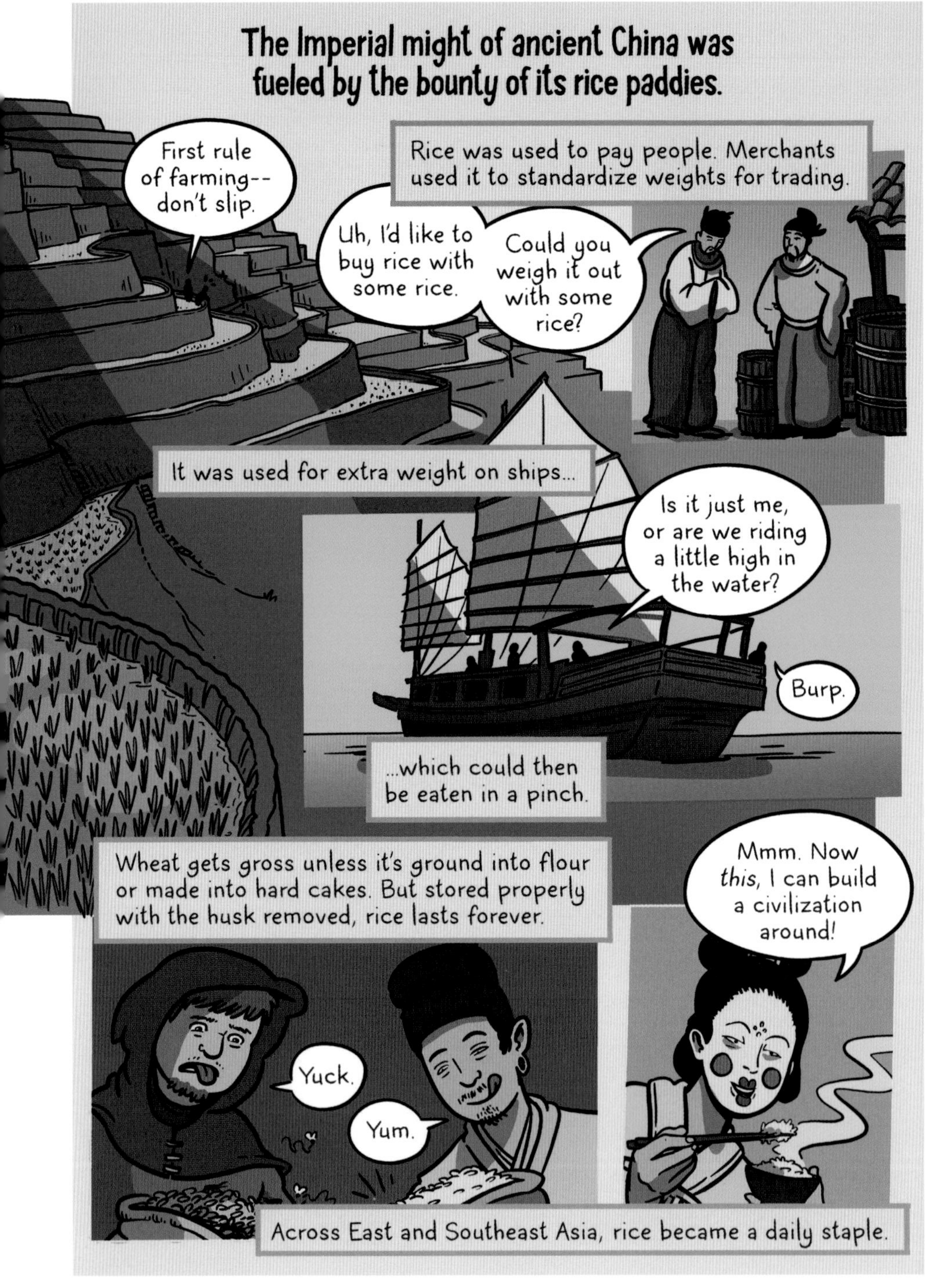
The Imperial might of ancient China was fueled by the bounty of its rice paddies.
First rule of farming-- don't slip.
Rice was used to pay people. Merchants used it to standardize weights for trading.
Uh, I'd like to buy rice with some rice.
Could you weigh it out with some rice?
It was used for extra weight on ships...
Is it just me, or are we riding a little high in the water?
Burp.
...which could then be eaten in a pinch.
Wheat gets gross unless it's ground into flour or made into hard cakes. But stored properly with the husk removed, rice lasts forever.
Mmm. Now *this*, I can build a civilization around!
Yuck.
Yum.
Across East and Southeast Asia, rice became a daily staple.

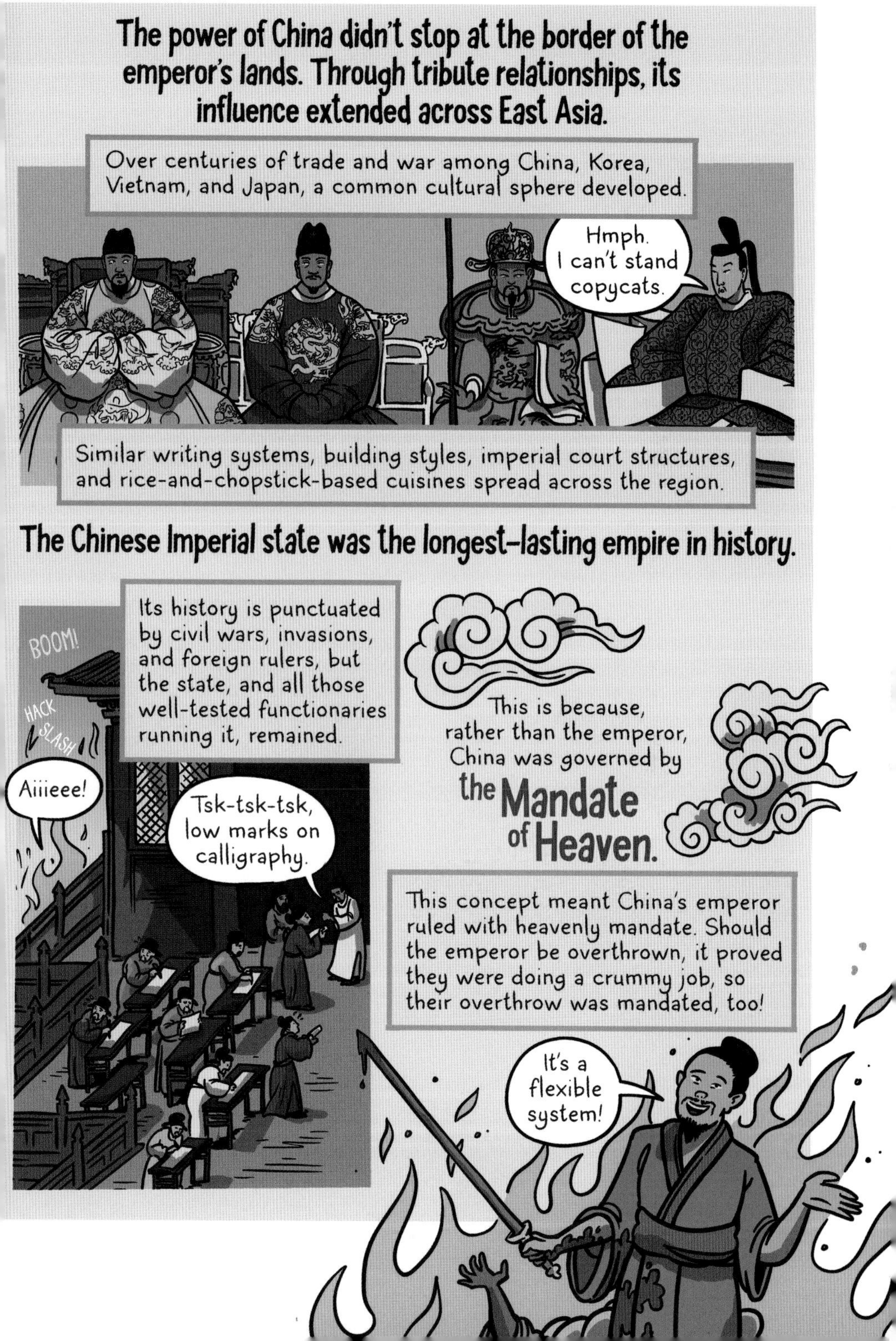
The power of China didn't stop at the border of the emperor's lands. Through tribute relationships, its influence extended across East Asia.
Over centuries of trade and war among China, Korea, Vietnam, and Japan, a common cultural sphere developed.
Hmph. I can't stand copycats.
Similar writing systems, building styles, imperial court structures, and rice-and-chopstick-based cuisines spread across the region.
The Chinese Imperial state was the longest-lasting empire in history.
BOOM!
HACK
SLASH
Its history is punctuated by civil wars, invasions, and foreign rulers, but the state, and all those well-tested functionaries running it, remained.
Aiiieee!
Tsk-tsk-tsk, low marks on calligraphy.
This is because, rather than the emperor, China was governed by
the Mandate of Heaven.
This concept meant China's emperor ruled with heavenly mandate. Should the emperor be overthrown, it proved they were doing a crummy job, so their overthrow was mandated, too!
It's a flexible system!

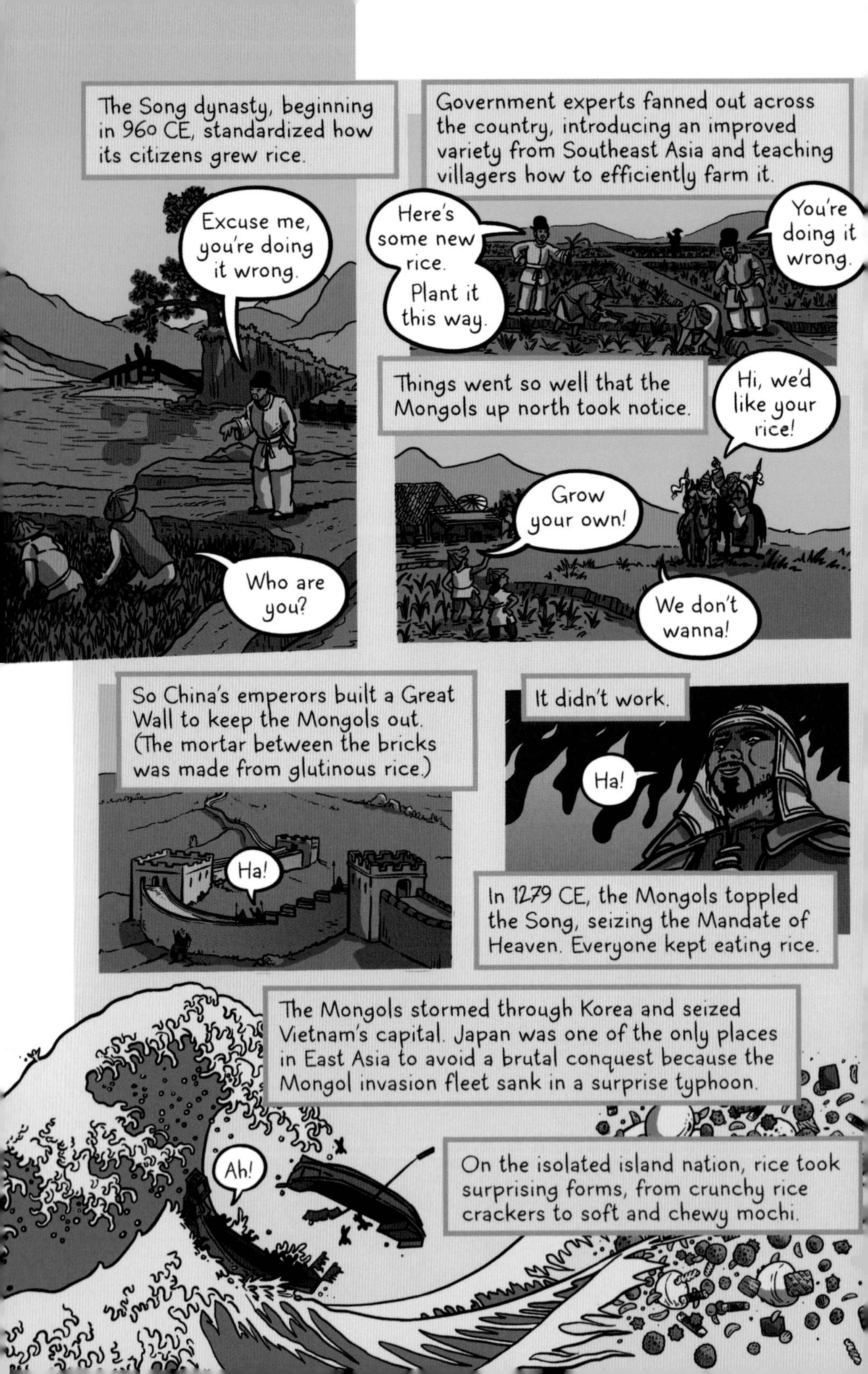
The Song dynasty, beginning in 960 CE, standardized how its citizens grew rice.
Excuse me, you're doing it wrong.
Who are you?
Government experts fanned out across the country, introducing an improved variety from Southeast Asia and teaching villagers how to efficiently farm it.
Here's some new rice.
Plant it this way.
You're doing it wrong.
Things went so well that the Mongols up north took notice.
Hi, we'd like your rice!
Grow your own!
We don't wanna!
So China's emperors built a Great Wall to keep the Mongols out. (The mortar between the bricks was made from glutinous rice.)
Ha!
It didn't work.
Ha!
In 1279 CE, the Mongols toppled the Song, seizing the Mandate of Heaven. Everyone kept eating rice.
The Mongols stormed through Korea and seized Vietnam's capital. Japan was one of the only places in East Asia to avoid a brutal conquest because the Mongol invasion fleet sank in a surprise typhoon.
Ah!
On the isolated island nation, rice took surprising forms, from crunchy rice crackers to soft and chewy mochi.

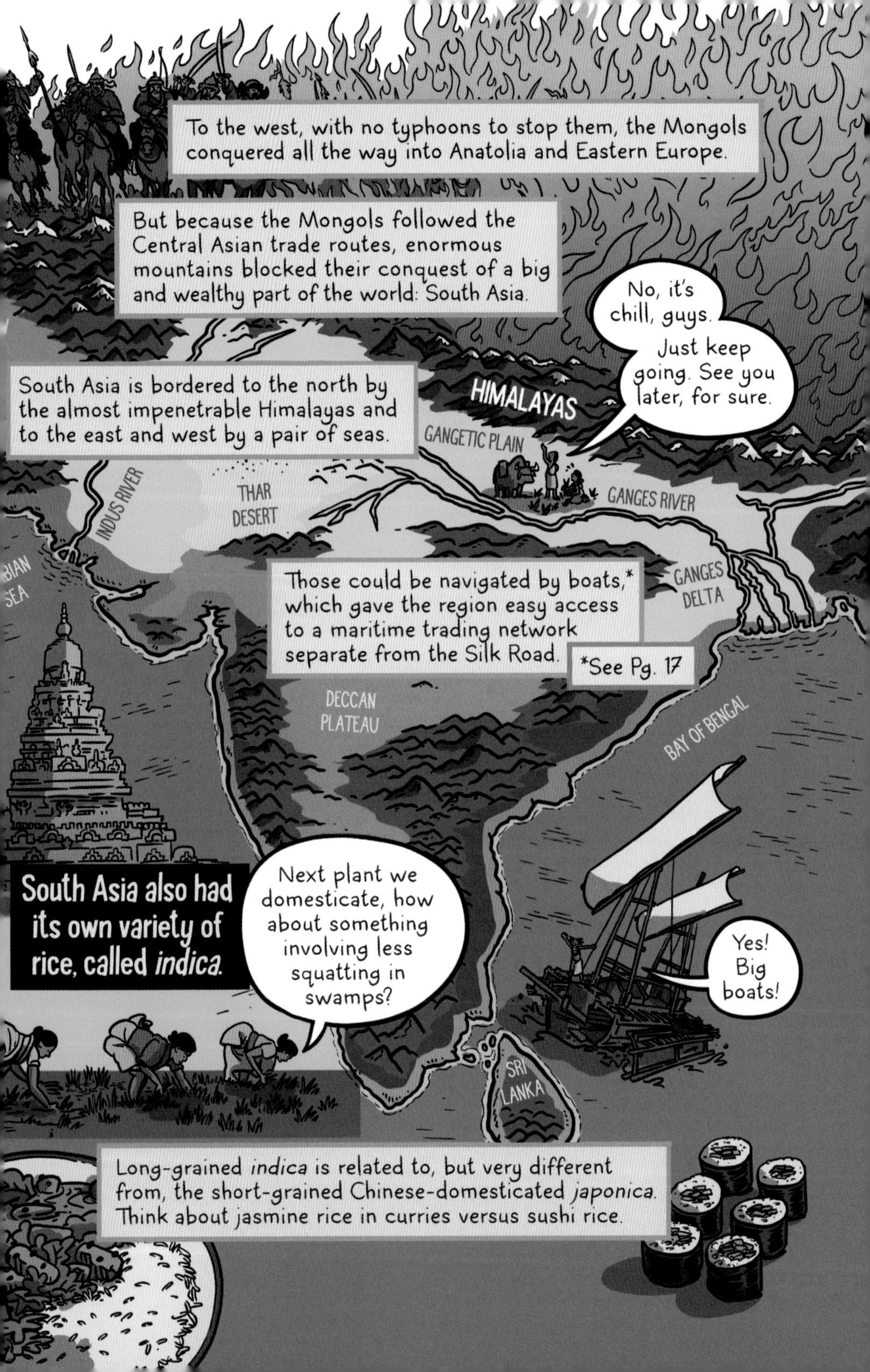
To the west, with no typhoons to stop them, the Mongols conquered all the way into Anatolia and Eastern Europe.
But because the Mongols followed the Central Asian trade routes, enormous mountains blocked their conquest of a big and wealthy part of the world: South Asia.
No, it's chill, guys.
Just keep going. See you later, for sure.
South Asia is bordered to the north by the almost impenetrable Himalayas and to the east and west by a pair of seas.
HIMALAYAS
GANGETIC PLAIN
INDUS RIVER
THAR DESERT
GANGES RIVER
GANGES DELTA
SEA
Those could be navigated by boats,* which gave the region easy access to a maritime trading network separate from the Silk Road.
*See Pg. 17
DECCAN PLATEAU
BAY OF BENGAL
South Asia also had its own variety of rice, called *indica*.
Next plant we domesticate, how about something involving less squatting in swamps?
Yes! Big boats!
SRI LANKA
Long-grained *indica* is related to, but very different from, the short-grained Chinese-domesticated *japonica*. Think about jasmine rice in curries versus sushi rice.

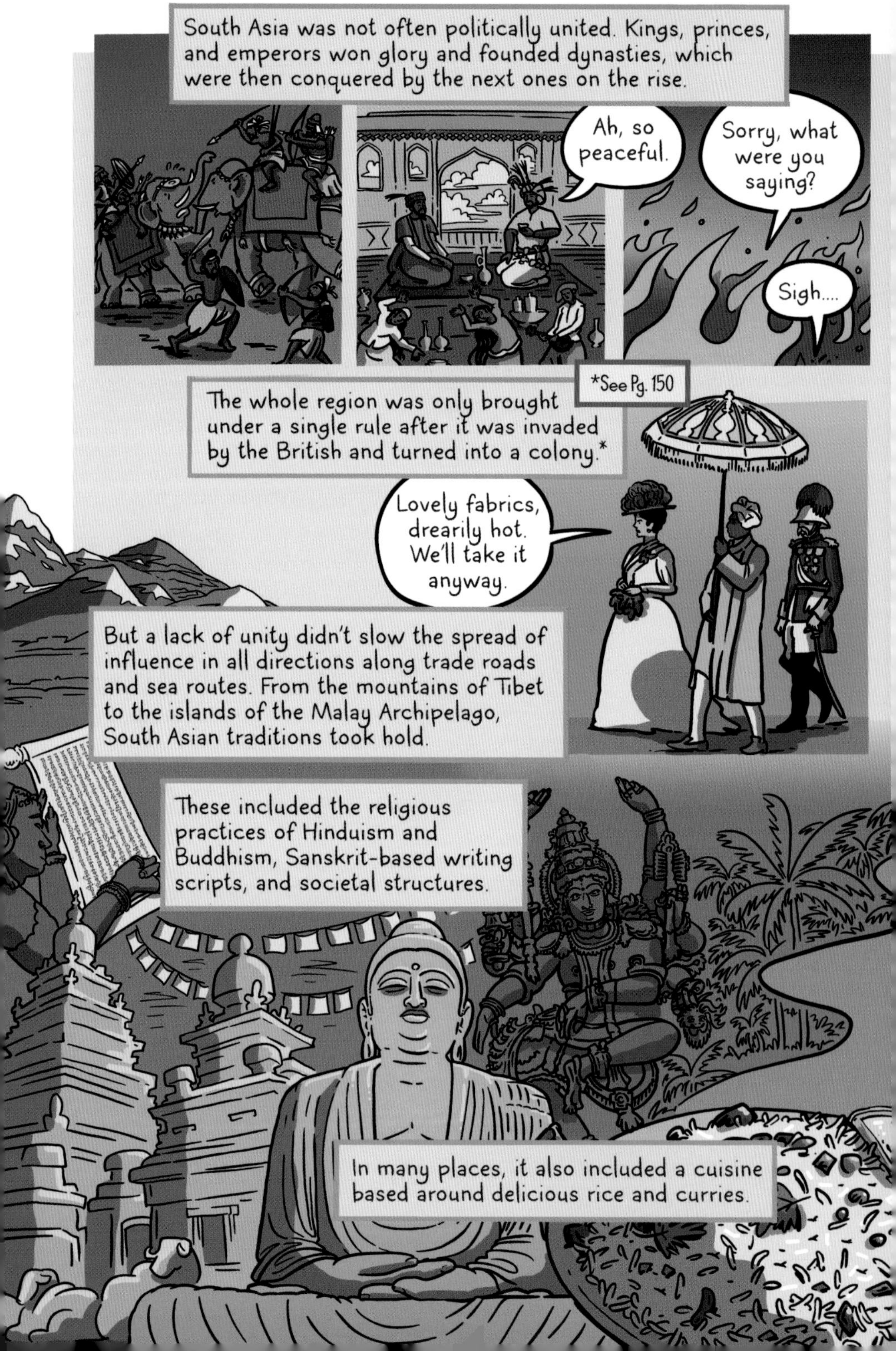
South Asia was not often politically united. Kings, princes, and emperors won glory and founded dynasties, which were then conquered by the next ones on the rise.
Ah, so peaceful.
Sorry, what were you saying?
Sigh....
The whole region was only brought under a single rule after it was invaded by the British and turned into a colony.*
*See Pg. 150
Lovely fabrics, drearily hot. We'll take it anyway.
But a lack of unity didn't slow the spread of influence in all directions along trade roads and sea routes. From the mountains of Tibet to the islands of the Malay Archipelago, South Asian traditions took hold.
These included the religious practices of Hinduism and Buddhism, Sanskrit-based writing scripts, and societal structures.
In many places, it also included a cuisine based around delicious rice and curries.

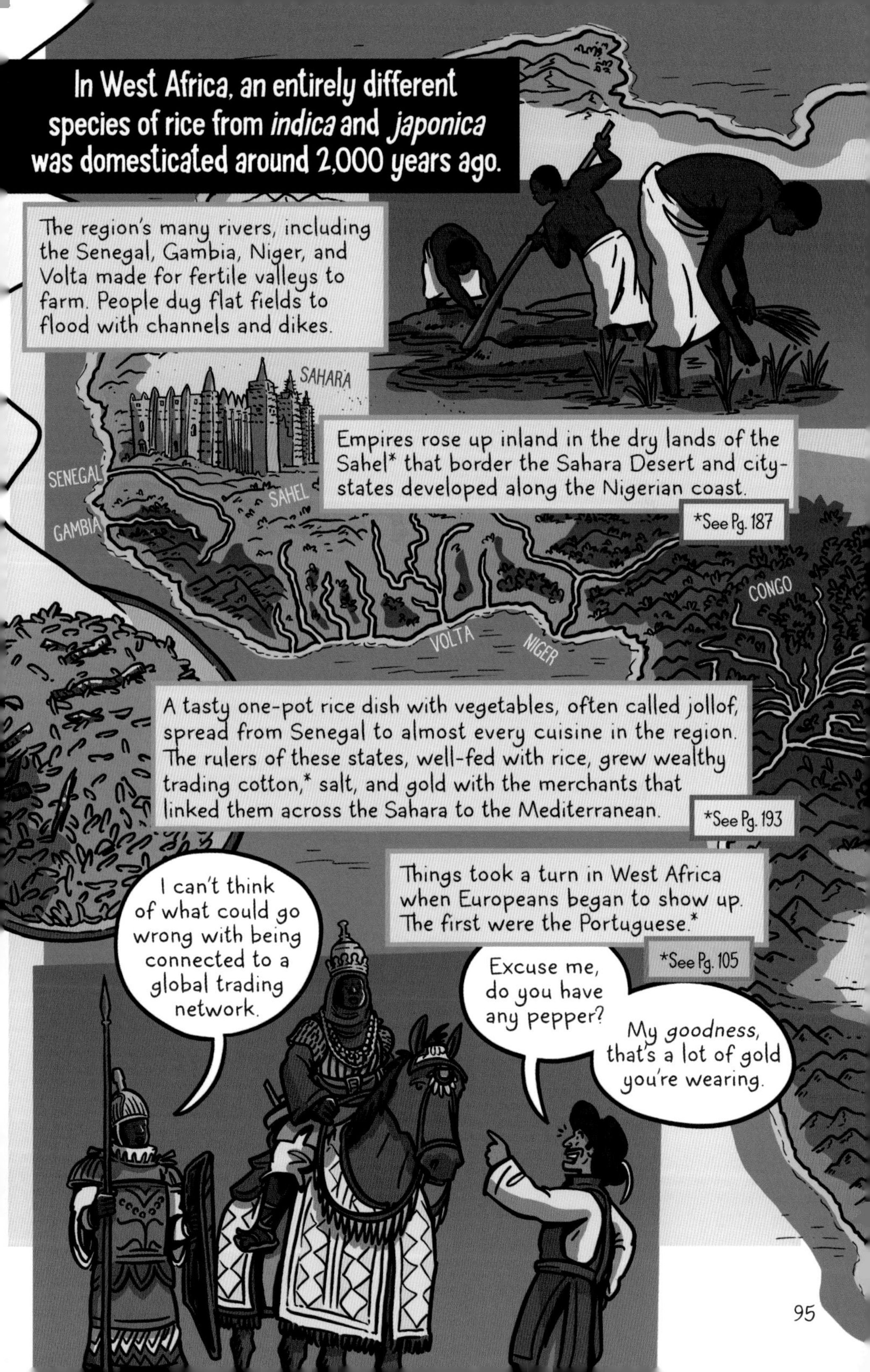

In West Africa, an entirely different species of rice from *indica* and *japonica* was domesticated around 2,000 years ago.
The region's many rivers, including the Senegal, Gambia, Niger, and Volta made for fertile valleys to farm. People dug flat fields to flood with channels and dikes.
SAHARA
SENEGAL
SAHEL
GAMBIA
Empires rose up inland in the dry lands of the Sahel* that border the Sahara Desert and city-states developed along the Nigerian coast.
*See Pg. 187
CONGO
VOLTA
NIGER
A tasty one-pot rice dish with vegetables, often called jollof, spread from Senegal to almost every cuisine in the region. The rulers of these states, well-fed with rice, grew wealthy trading cotton,* salt, and gold with the merchants that linked them across the Sahara to the Mediterranean.
*See Pg. 193
Things took a turn in West Africa when Europeans began to show up. The first were the Portuguese.*
*See Pg. 105
I can't think of what could go wrong with being connected to a global trading network.
Excuse me, do you have any pepper?
My *goodness*, that's a lot of gold you're wearing.

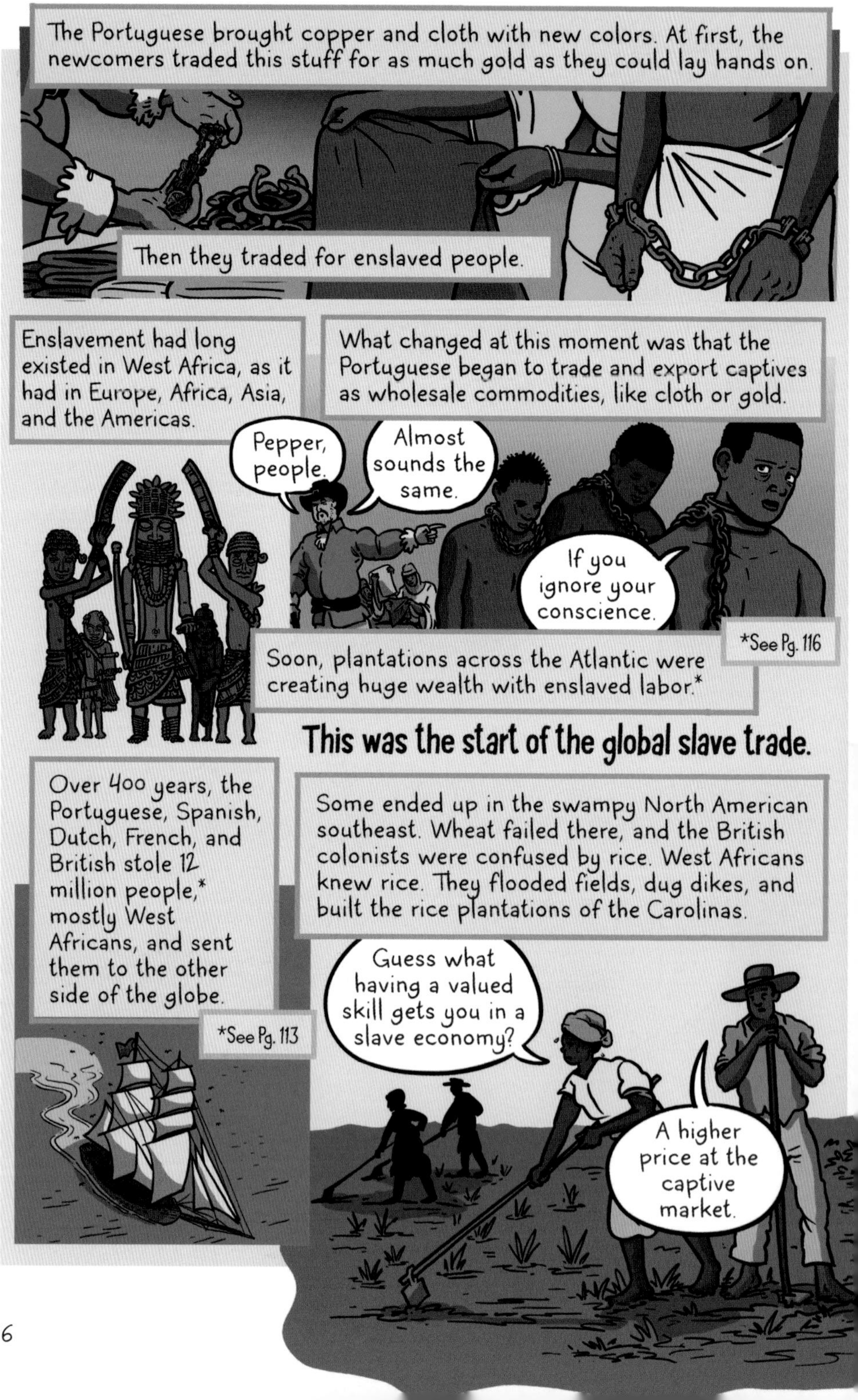
The Portuguese brought copper and cloth with new colors. At first, the newcomers traded this stuff for as much gold as they could lay hands on.
Then they traded for enslaved people.
Enslavement had long existed in West Africa, as it had in Europe, Africa, Asia, and the Americas.
What changed at this moment was that the Portuguese began to trade and export captives as wholesale commodities, like cloth or gold.
Pepper, people.
Almost sounds the same.
If you ignore your conscience.
Soon, plantations across the Atlantic were creating huge wealth with enslaved labor.*
*See Pg. 116
This was the start of the global slave trade.
Over 400 years, the Portuguese, Spanish, Dutch, French, and British stole 12 million people,* mostly West Africans, and sent them to the other side of the globe.
*See Pg. 113
Some ended up in the swampy North American southeast. Wheat failed there, and the British colonists were confused by rice. West Africans knew rice. They flooded fields, dug dikes, and built the rice plantations of the Carolinas.
Guess what having a valued skill gets you in a slave economy?
A higher price at the captive market.

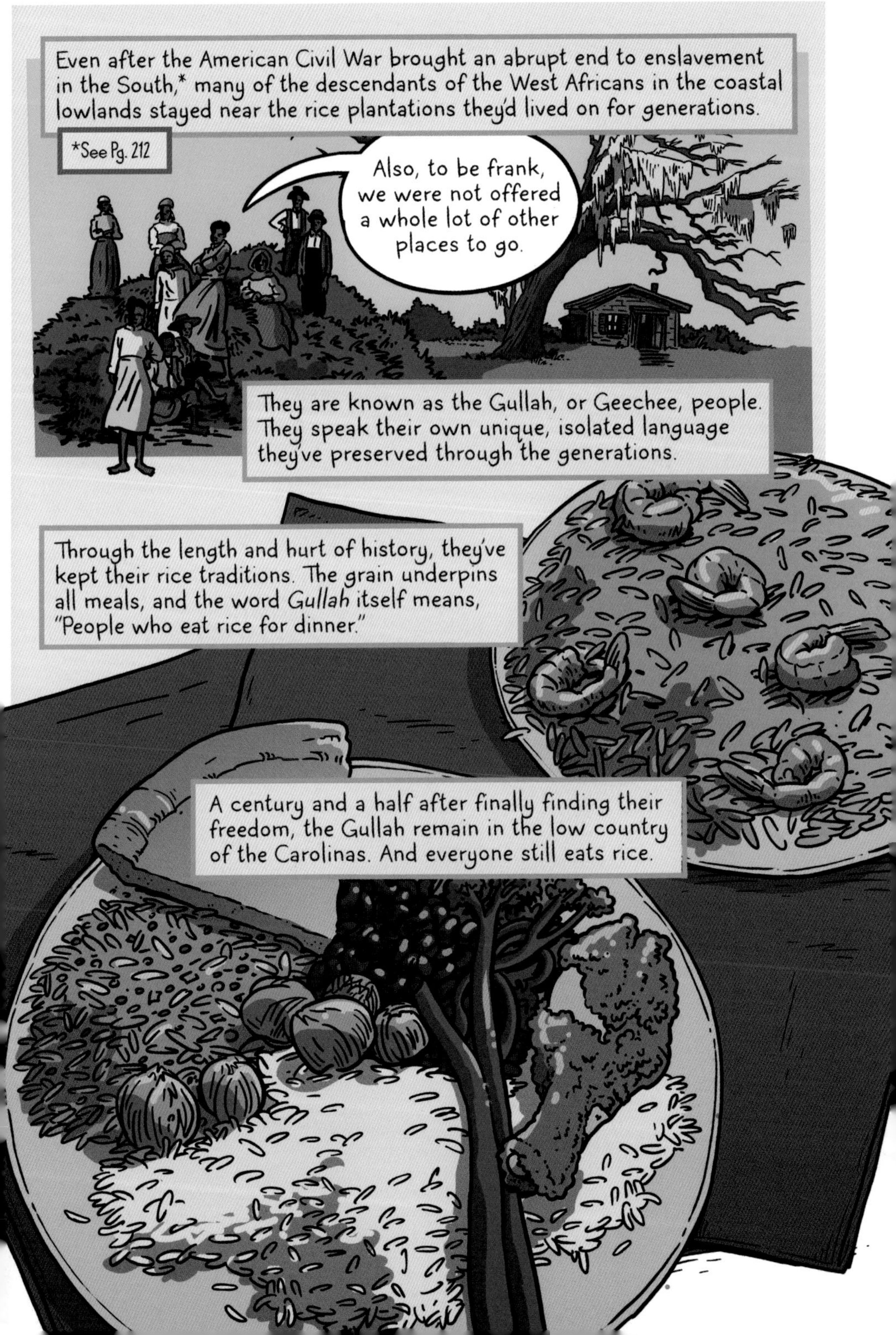
Even after the American Civil War brought an abrupt end to enslavement in the South,* many of the descendants of the West Africans in the coastal lowlands stayed near the rice plantations they'd lived on for generations.
*See Pg. 212
Also, to be frank, we were not offered a whole lot of other places to go.
They are known as the Gullah, or Geechee, people. They speak their own unique, isolated language they've preserved through the generations.
Through the length and hurt of history, they've kept their rice traditions. The grain underpins all meals, and the word *Gullah* itself means, "People who eat rice for dinner."
A century and a half after finally finding their freedom, the Gullah remain in the low country of the Carolinas. And everyone still eats rice.

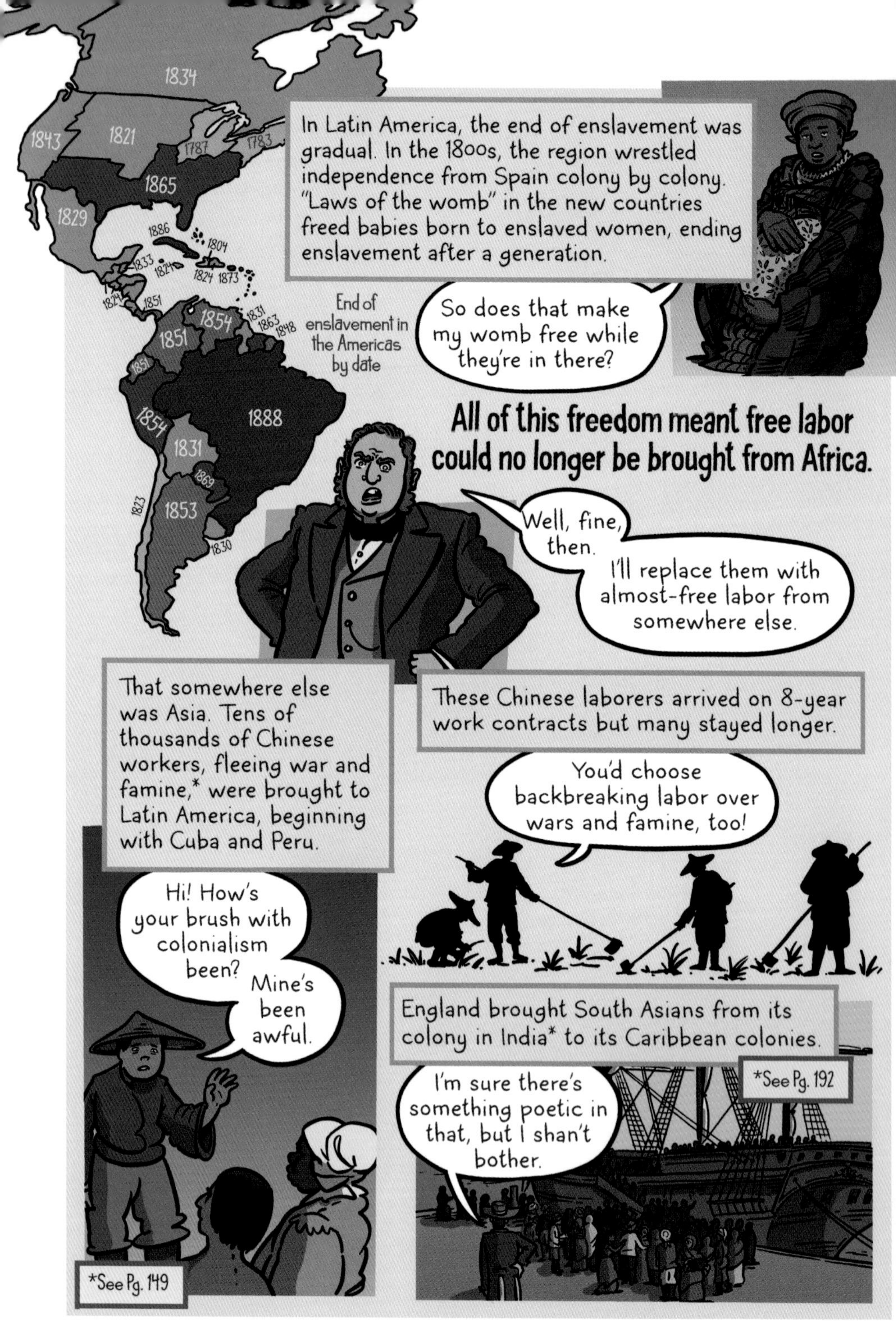
1834
1843
1821
1787
1783
1865
1829
1886
1804
1833
1824
1824
1873
1824
1851
1854
1831
1863
1848
1851
1851
1888
1854
1831
1869
1823
1853
1830
End of enslavement in the Americas by date
In Latin America, the end of enslavement was gradual. In the 1800s, the region wrestled independence from Spain colony by colony. "Laws of the womb" in the new countries freed babies born to enslaved women, ending enslavement after a generation.
So does that make my womb free while they're in there?
All of this freedom meant free labor could no longer be brought from Africa.
Well, fine, then.
I'll replace them with almost-free labor from somewhere else.
That somewhere else was Asia. Tens of thousands of Chinese workers, fleeing war and famine,* were brought to Latin America, beginning with Cuba and Peru.
These Chinese laborers arrived on 8-year work contracts but many stayed longer.
You'd choose backbreaking labor over wars and famine, too!
Hi! How's your brush with colonialism been?
Mine's been awful.
*See Pg. 149
England brought South Asians from its colony in India* to its Caribbean colonies.
*See Pg. 192
I'm sure there's something poetic in that, but I shan't bother.

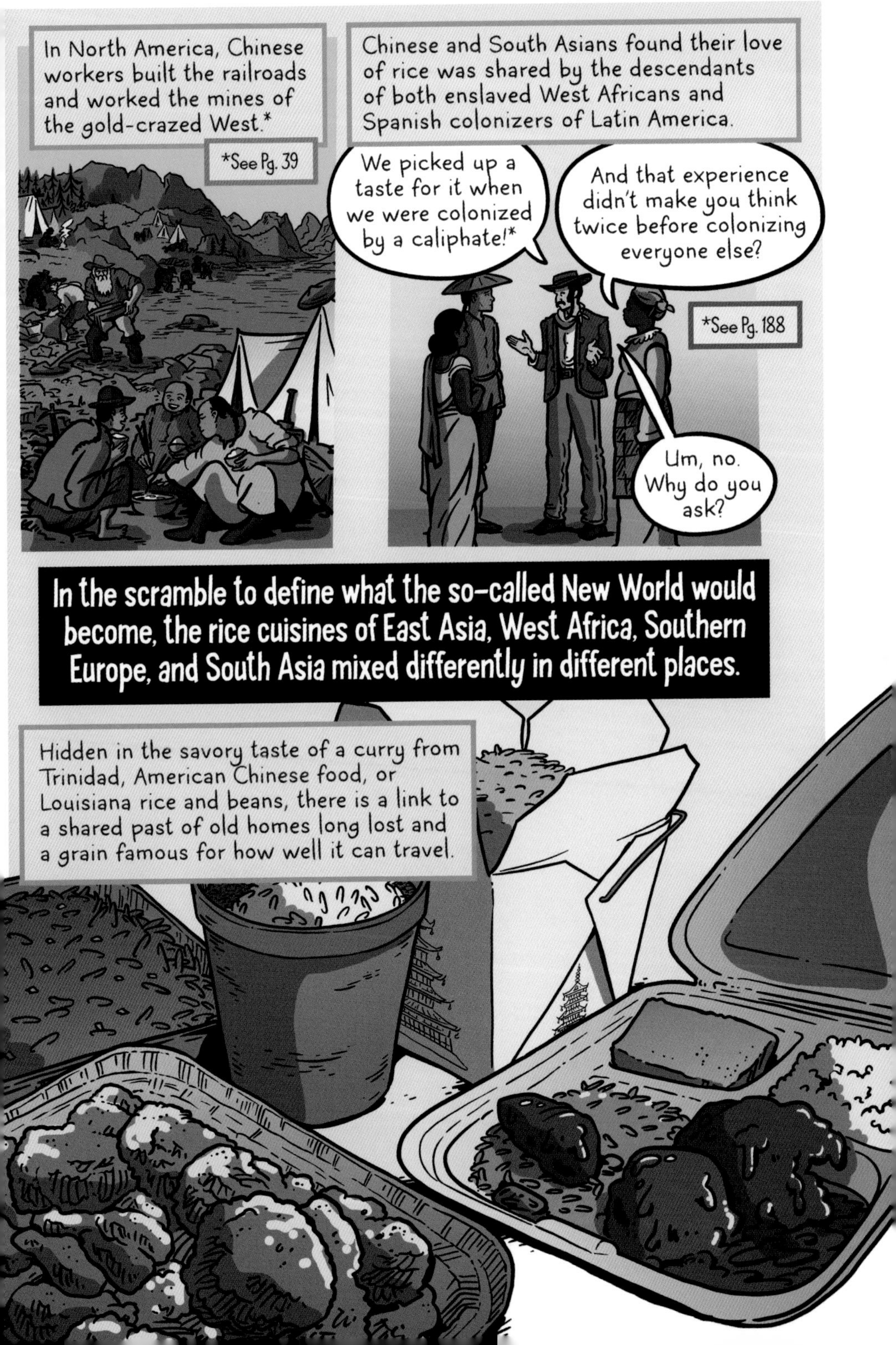
In North America, Chinese workers built the railroads and worked the mines of the gold-crazed West.*
*See Pg. 39
Chinese and South Asians found their love of rice was shared by the descendants of both enslaved West Africans and Spanish colonizers of Latin America.
We picked up a taste for it when we were colonized by a caliphate!*
And that experience didn't make you think twice before colonizing everyone else?
*See Pg. 188
Um, no. Why do you ask?
In the scramble to define what the so-called New World would become, the rice cuisines of East Asia, West Africa, Southern Europe, and South Asia mixed differently in different places.
Hidden in the savory taste of a curry from Trinidad, American Chinese food, or Louisiana rice and beans, there is a link to a shared past of old homes long lost and a grain famous for how well it can travel.

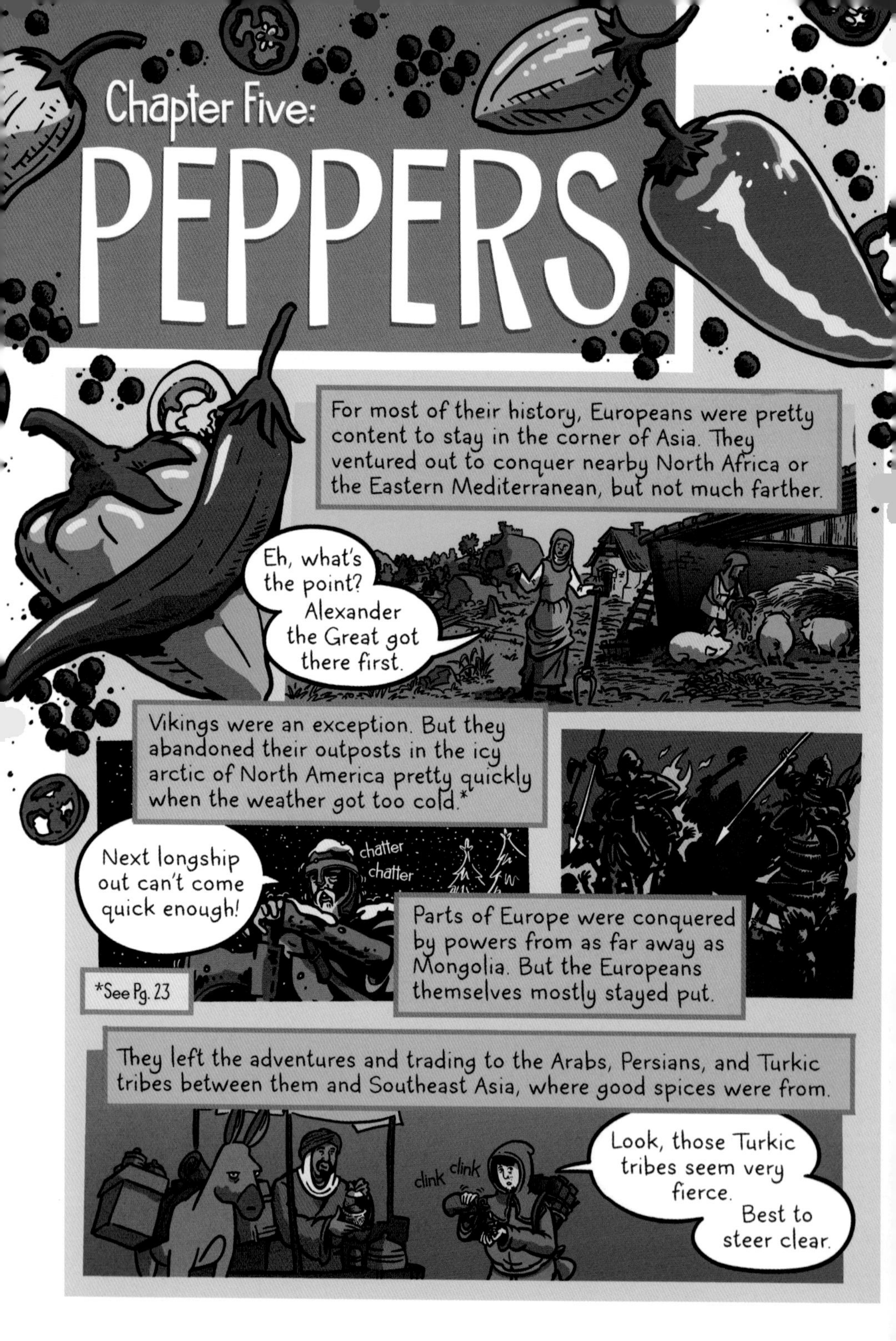
Chapter Five:
PEPPERS
For most of their history, Europeans were pretty content to stay in the corner of Asia. They ventured out to conquer nearby North Africa or the Eastern Mediterranean, but not much farther.
Eh, what's the point? Alexander the Great got there first.
Vikings were an exception. But they abandoned their outposts in the icy arctic of North America pretty quickly when the weather got too cold.*
Next longship out can't come quick enough!
chatter chatter
*See Pg. 23
Parts of Europe were conquered by powers from as far away as Mongolia. But the Europeans themselves mostly stayed put.
They left the adventures and trading to the Arabs, Persians, and Turkic tribes between them and Southeast Asia, where good spices were from.
clink clink
Look, those Turkic tribes seem very fierce. Best to steer clear.

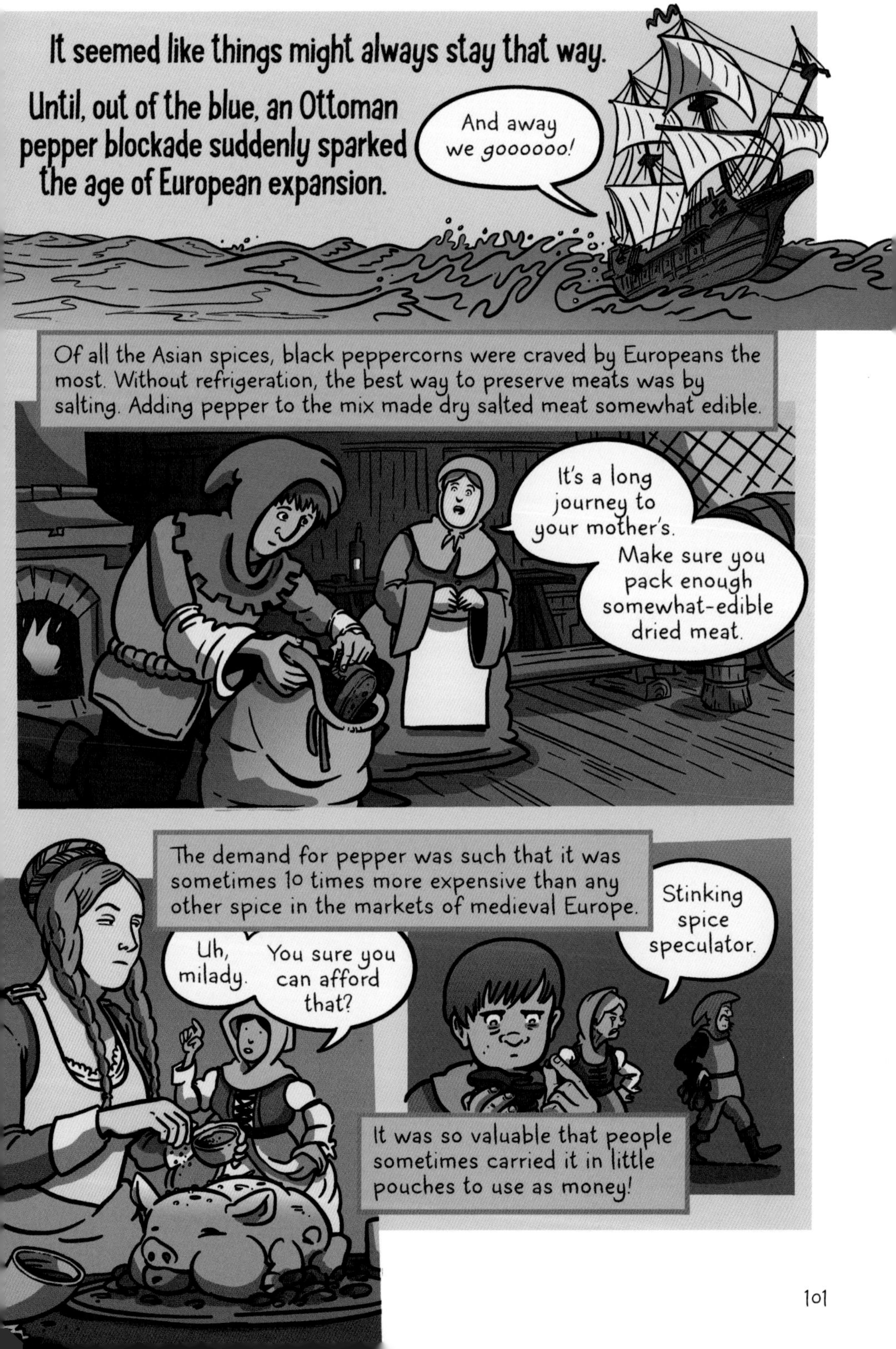
It seemed like things might always stay that way.
Until, out of the blue, an Ottoman pepper blockade suddenly sparked the age of European expansion.
And away we *goooooo!*
Of all the Asian spices, black peppercorns were craved by Europeans the most. Without refrigeration, the best way to preserve meats was by salting. Adding pepper to the mix made dry salted meat somewhat edible.
It's a long journey to your mother's.
Make sure you pack enough somewhat-edible dried meat.
The demand for pepper was such that it was sometimes 10 times more expensive than any other spice in the markets of medieval Europe.
Uh, milady.
You sure you can afford that?
Stinking spice speculator.
It was so valuable that people sometimes carried it in little pouches to use as money!

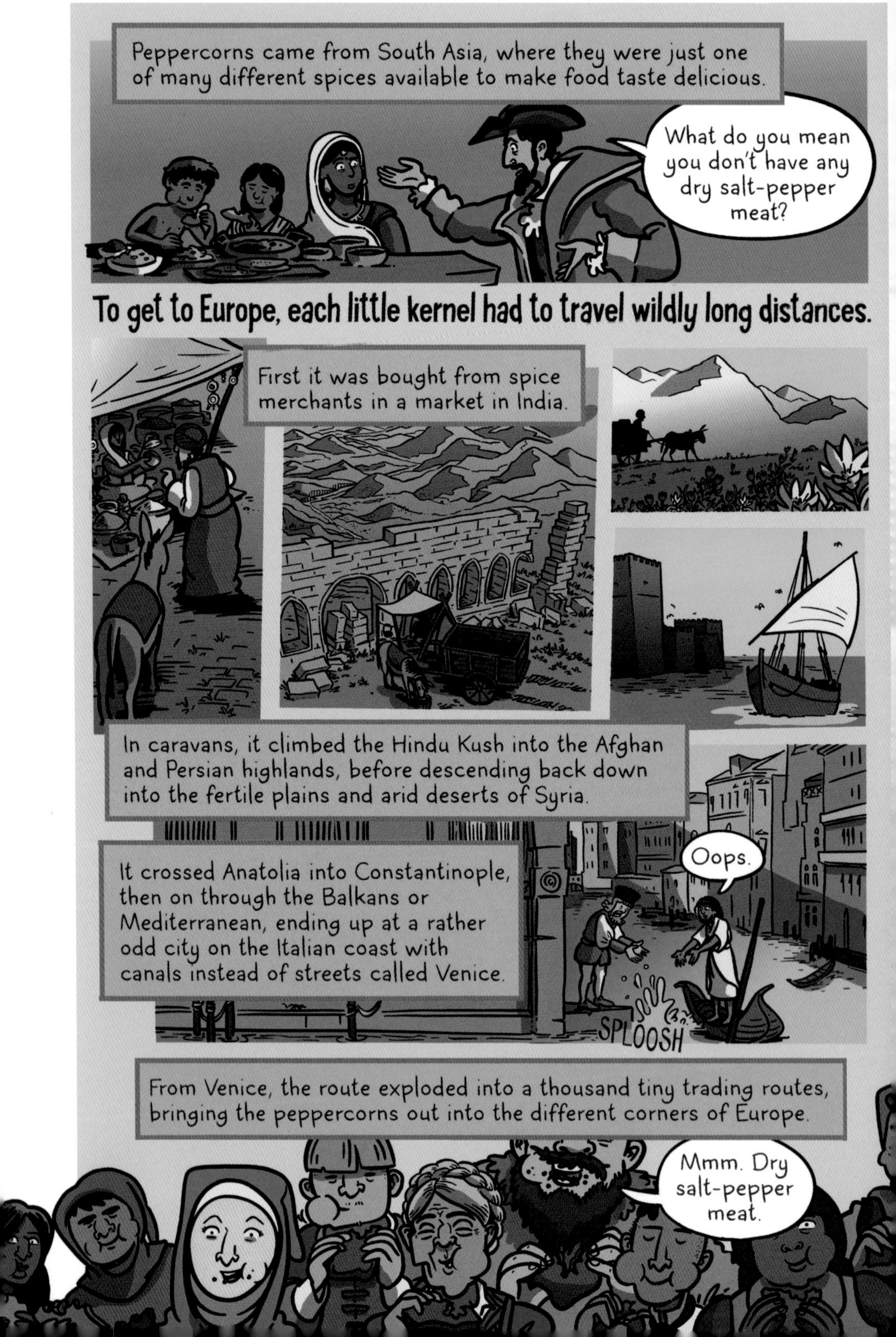
Peppercorns came from South Asia, where they were just one of many different spices available to make food taste delicious.
What do you mean you don't have any dry salt-pepper meat?
To get to Europe, each little kernel had to travel wildly long distances.
First it was bought from spice merchants in a market in India.
In caravans, it climbed the Hindu Kush into the Afghan and Persian highlands, before descending back down into the fertile plains and arid deserts of Syria.
It crossed Anatolia into Constantinople, then on through the Balkans or Mediterranean, ending up at a rather odd city on the Italian coast with canals instead of streets called Venice.
Oops.
SPLOOSH
From Venice, the route exploded into a thousand tiny trading routes, bringing the peppercorns out into the different corners of Europe.
Mmm. Dry salt-pepper meat.

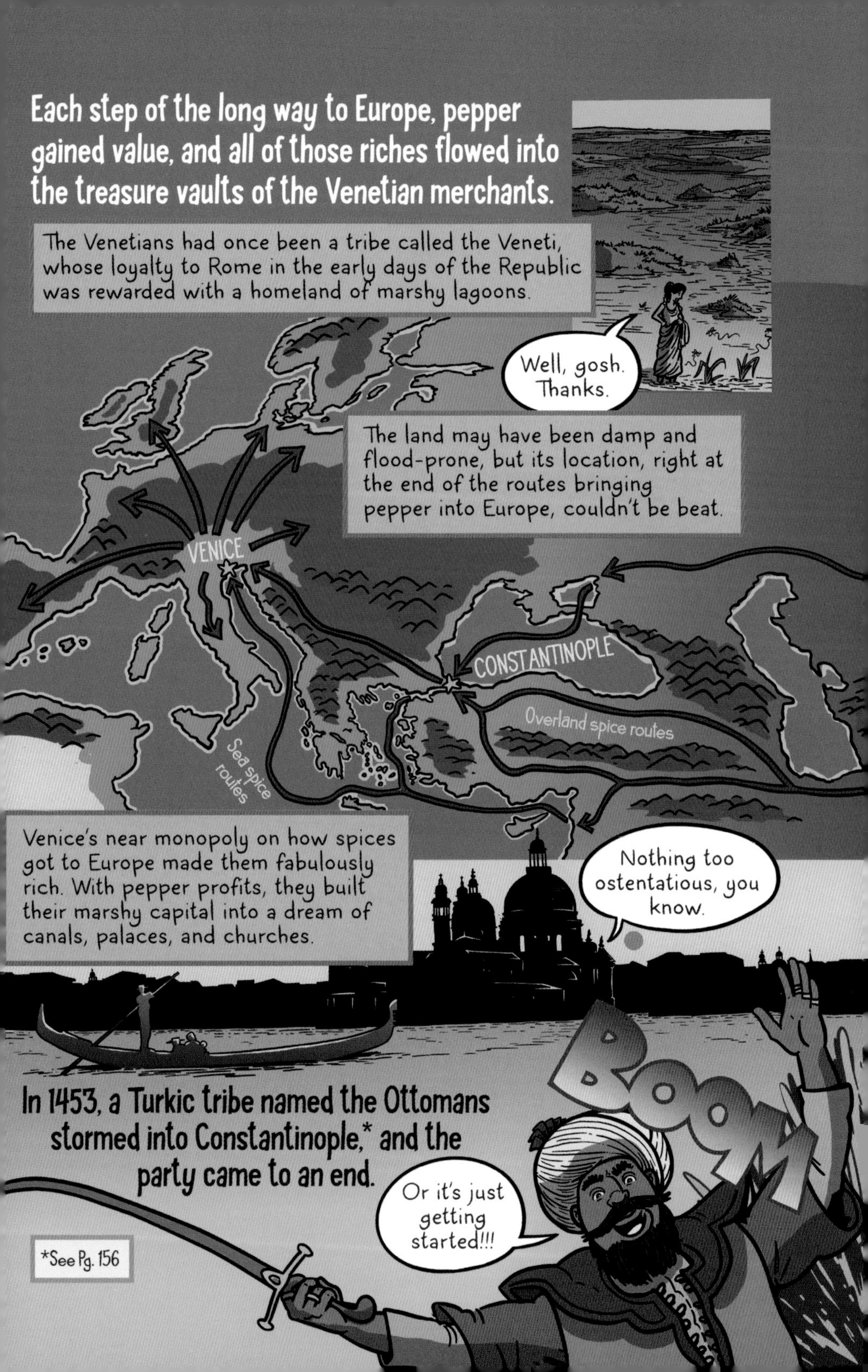

Each step of the long way to Europe, pepper gained value, and all of those riches flowed into the treasure vaults of the Venetian merchants.
The Venetians had once been a tribe called the Veneti, whose loyalty to Rome in the early days of the Republic was rewarded with a homeland of marshy lagoons.
Well, gosh. Thanks.
The land may have been damp and flood-prone, but its location, right at the end of the routes bringing pepper into Europe, couldn't be beat.
VENICE
CONSTANTINOPLE
Overland spice routes
Sea spice routes
Venice's near monopoly on how spices got to Europe made them fabulously rich. With pepper profits, they built their marshy capital into a dream of canals, palaces, and churches.
Nothing too ostentatious, you know.
In 1453, a Turkic tribe named the Ottomans stormed into Constantinople,* and the party came to an end.
BOOM
Or it's just getting started!!!
*See Pg. 156

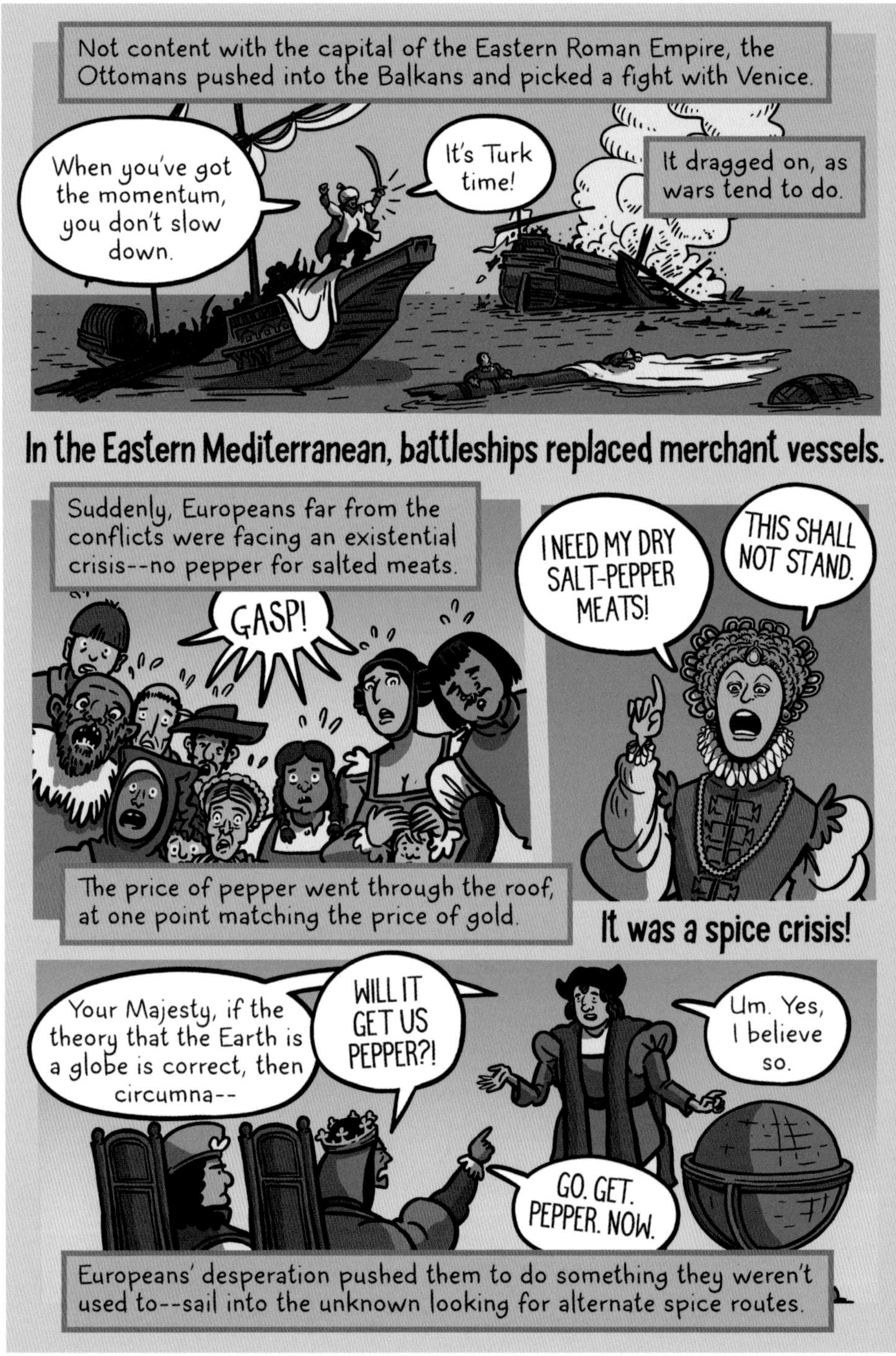
Not content with the capital of the Eastern Roman Empire, the Ottomans pushed into the Balkans and picked a fight with Venice.
When you've got the momentum, you don't slow down.
It's Turk time!
It dragged on, as wars tend to do.
In the Eastern Mediterranean, battleships replaced merchant vessels.
Suddenly, Europeans far from the conflicts were facing an existential crisis--no pepper for salted meats.
GASP!
The price of pepper went through the roof, at one point matching the price of gold.
I NEED MY DRY SALT-PEPPER MEATS!
THIS SHALL NOT STAND.
It was a spice crisis!
Your Majesty, if the theory that the Earth is a globe is correct, then circumna--
WILL IT GET US PEPPER?!
Um. Yes, I believe so.
GO. GET. PEPPER. NOW.
Europeans' desperation pushed them to do something they weren't used to--sail into the unknown looking for alternate spice routes.

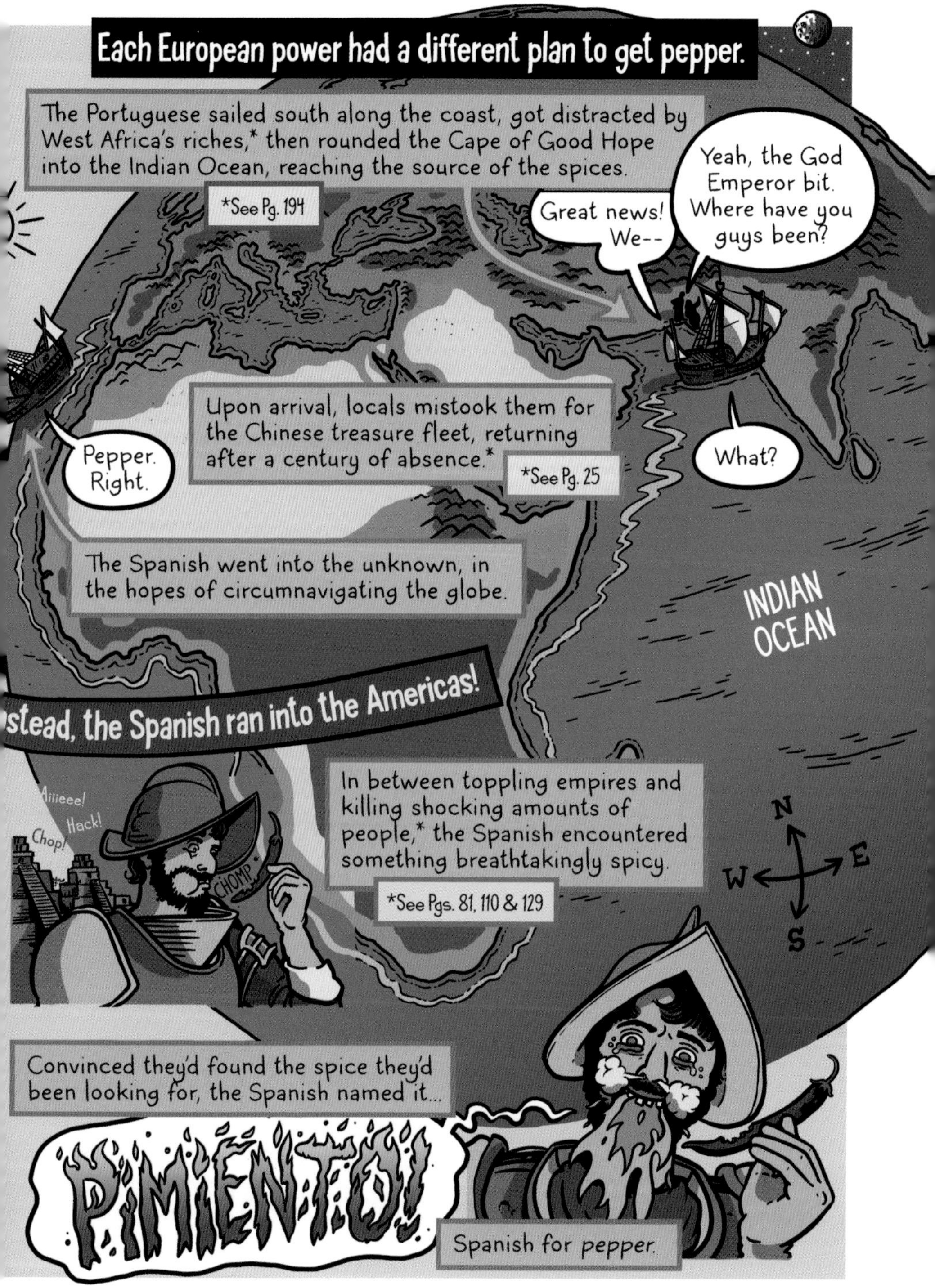
Each European power had a different plan to get pepper.
The Portuguese sailed south along the coast, got distracted by West Africa's riches,* then rounded the Cape of Good Hope into the Indian Ocean, reaching the source of the spices.
*See Pg. 194
Great news! We--
Yeah, the God Emperor bit. Where have you guys been?
What?
Upon arrival, locals mistook them for the Chinese treasure fleet, returning after a century of absence.*
*See Pg. 25
Pepper. Right.
The Spanish went into the unknown, in the hopes of circumnavigating the globe.
INDIAN OCEAN
stead, the Spanish ran into the Americas!
Aiiieee!
Hack!
Chop!
CHOMP
In between toppling empires and killing shocking amounts of people,* the Spanish encountered something breathtakingly spicy.
*See Pgs. 81, 110 & 129
N
W
E
S
Convinced they'd found the spice they'd been looking for, the Spanish named it...
PIMIENTO!
Spanish for pepper.

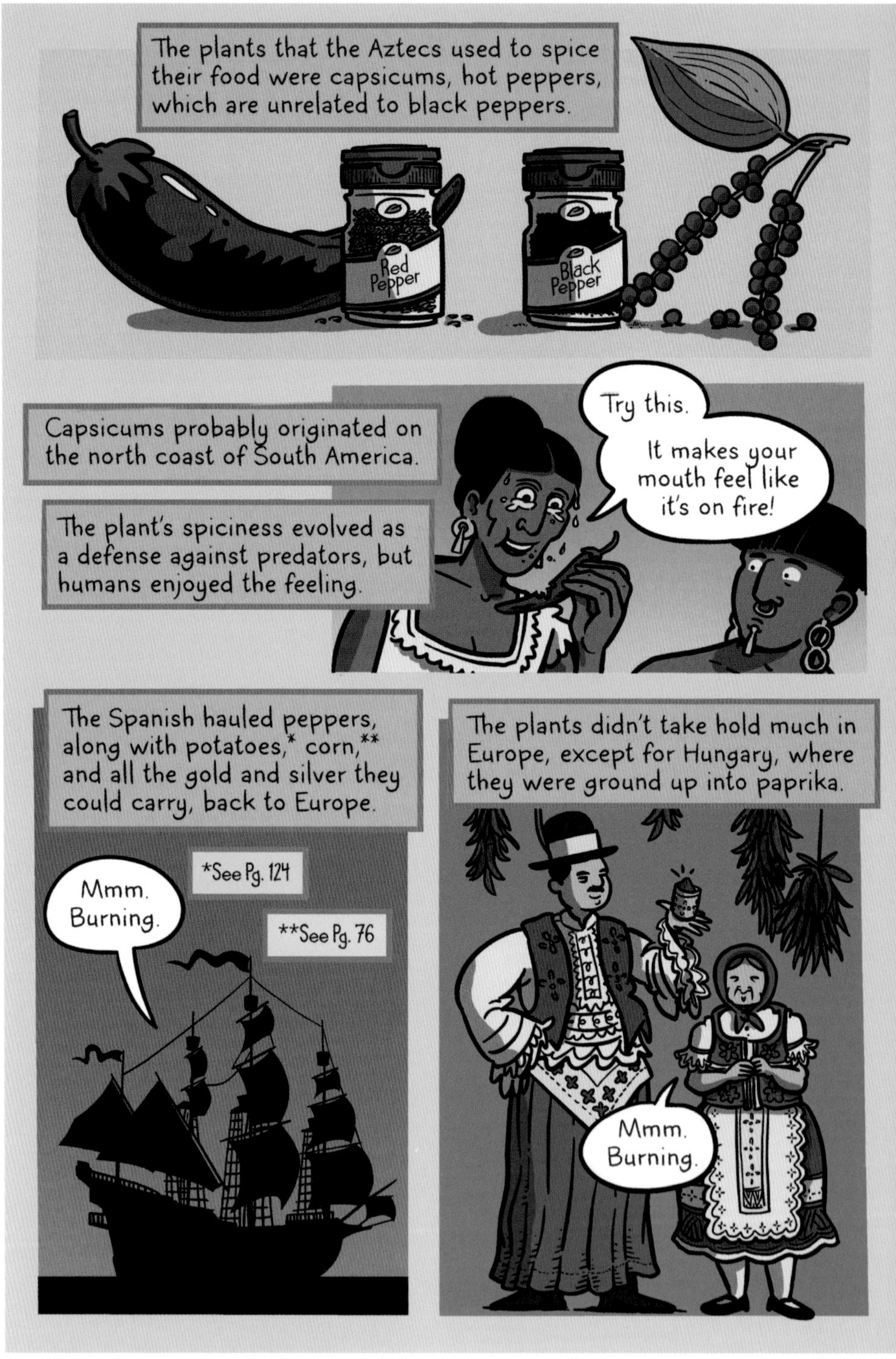
The plants that the Aztecs used to spice their food were capsicums, hot peppers, which are unrelated to black peppers.
Red Pepper
Black Pepper
Capsicums probably originated on the north coast of South America.
The plant's spiciness evolved as a defense against predators, but humans enjoyed the feeling.
Try this.
It makes your mouth feel like it's on fire!
The Spanish hauled peppers, along with potatoes,* corn,** and all the gold and silver they could carry, back to Europe.
*See Pg. 124
**See Pg. 76
Mmm. Burning.
The plants didn't take hold much in Europe, except for Hungary, where they were ground up into paprika.
Mmm. Burning.

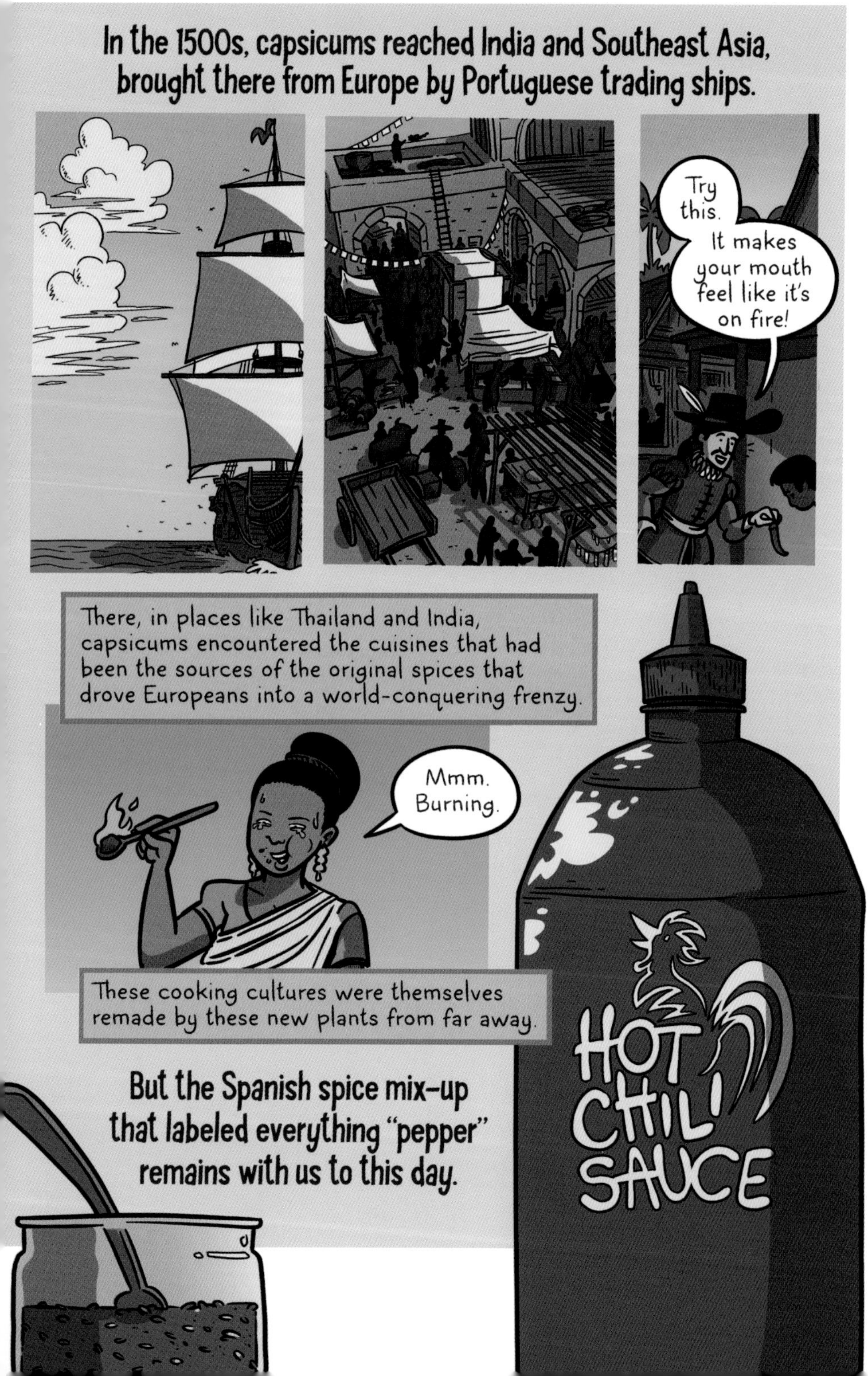
In the 1500s, capsicums reached India and Southeast Asia, brought there from Europe by Portuguese trading ships.
Try this.
It makes your mouth feel like it's on fire!
There, in places like Thailand and India, capsicums encountered the cuisines that had been the sources of the original spices that drove Europeans into a world-conquering frenzy.
Mmm. Burning.
These cooking cultures were themselves remade by these new plants from far away.
But the Spanish spice mix-up that labeled everything "pepper" remains with us to this day.
HOT CHILI SAUCE

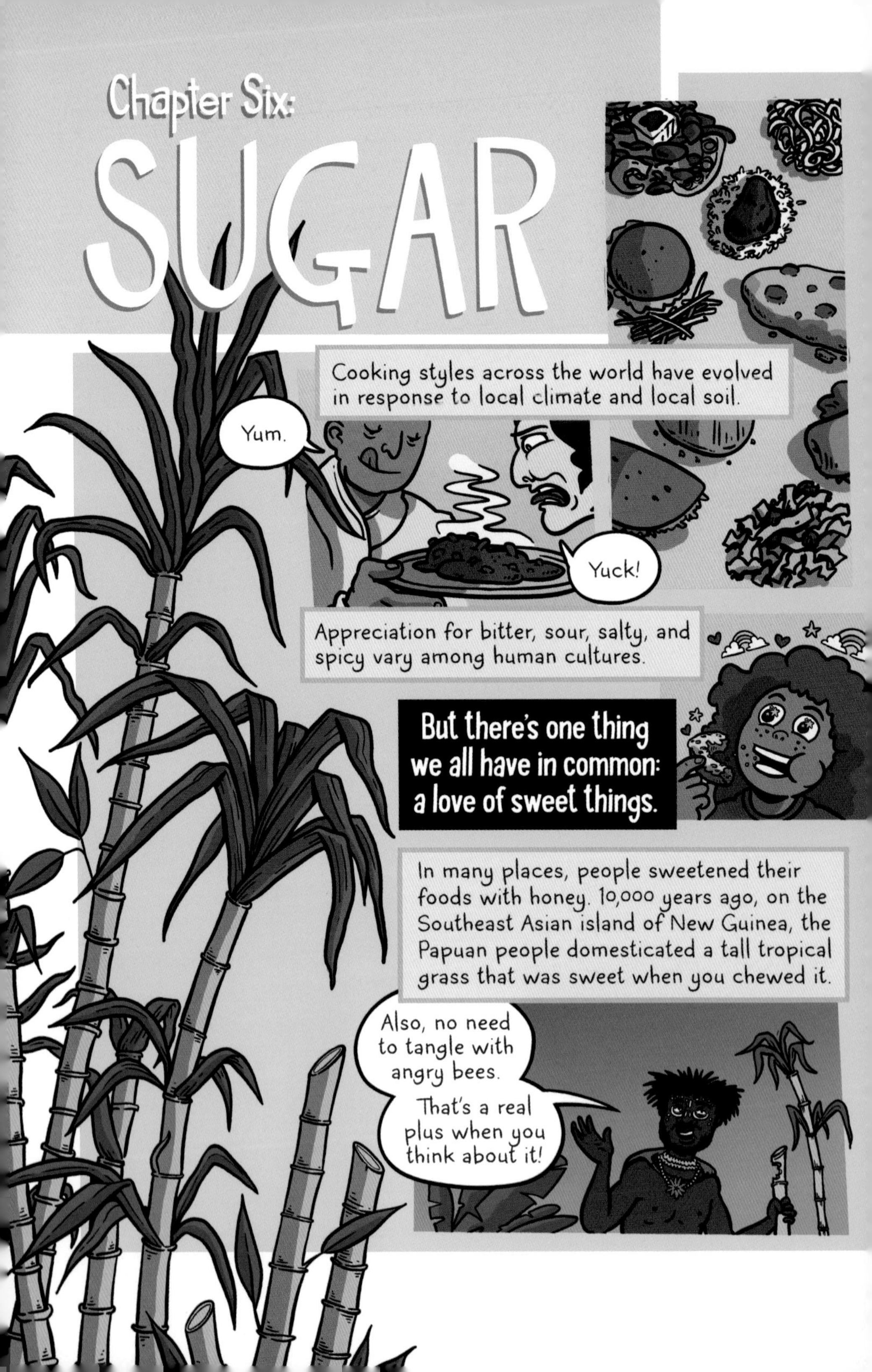
Chapter Six:
SUGAR
Cooking styles across the world have evolved in response to local climate and local soil.
Yum.
Yuck!
Appreciation for bitter, sour, salty, and spicy vary among human cultures.
But there's one thing we all have in common: a love of sweet things.
In many places, people sweetened their foods with honey. 10,000 years ago, on the Southeast Asian island of New Guinea, the Papuan people domesticated a tall tropical grass that was sweet when you chewed it.
Also, no need to tangle with angry bees.
That's a real plus when you think about it!

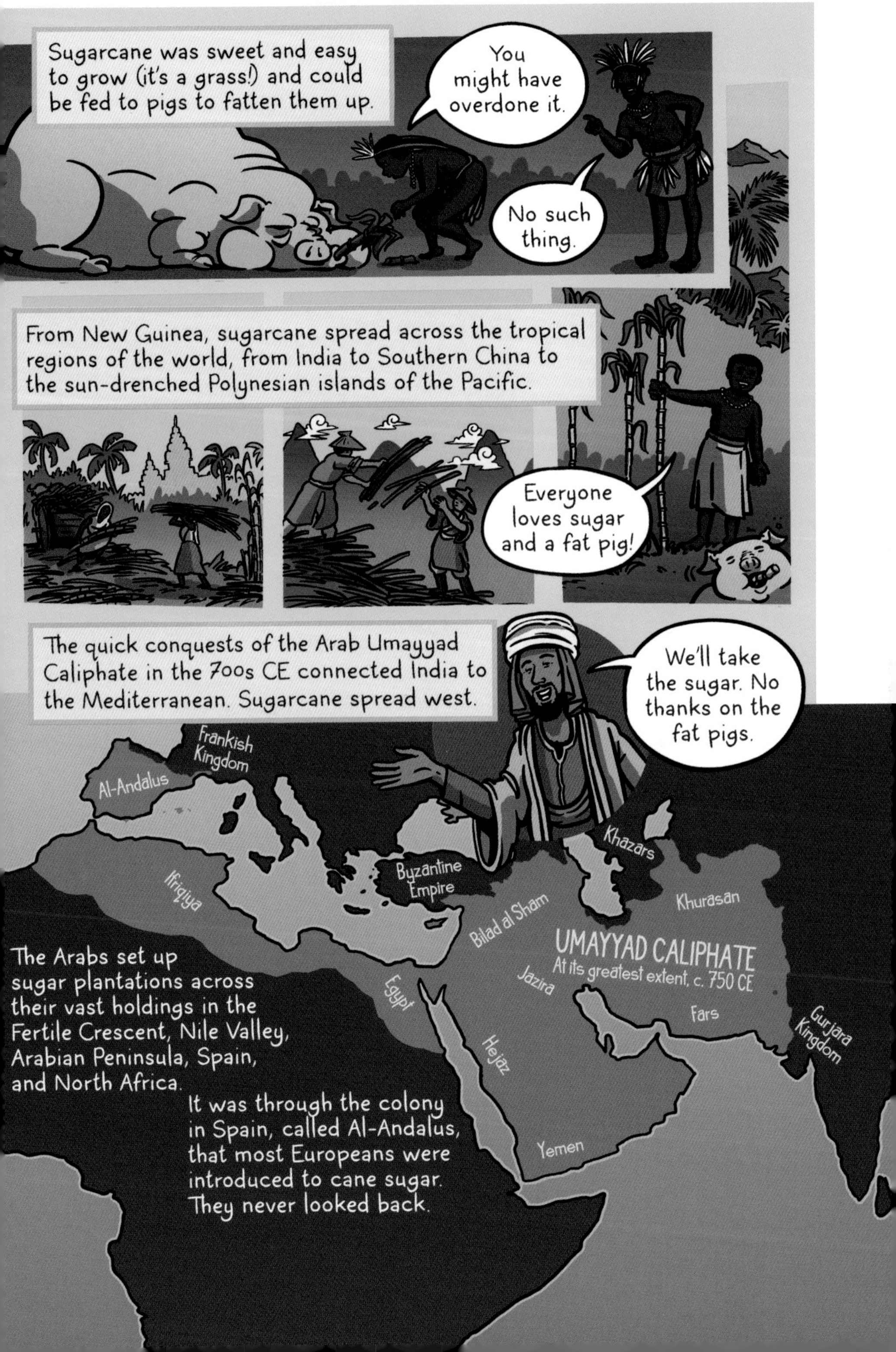
Sugarcane was sweet and easy to grow (it's a grass!) and could be fed to pigs to fatten them up.
You might have overdone it.
No such thing.
From New Guinea, sugarcane spread across the tropical regions of the world, from India to Southern China to the sun-drenched Polynesian islands of the Pacific.
Everyone loves sugar and a fat pig!
The quick conquests of the Arab Umayyad Caliphate in the 700s CE connected India to the Mediterranean. Sugarcane spread west.
We'll take the sugar. No thanks on the fat pigs.
Frankish Kingdom
Al-Andalus
Ifriqiya
Byzantine Empire
Khazars
Khurasan
Bilad al Sham
UMAYYAD CALIPHATE
At its greatest extent, c. 750 CE
Egypt
Jazira
Fars
Gurjara Kingdom
Hejaz
Yemen
The Arabs set up sugar plantations across their vast holdings in the Fertile Crescent, Nile Valley, Arabian Peninsula, Spain, and North Africa.
It was through the colony in Spain, called Al-Andalus, that most Europeans were introduced to cane sugar. They never looked back.

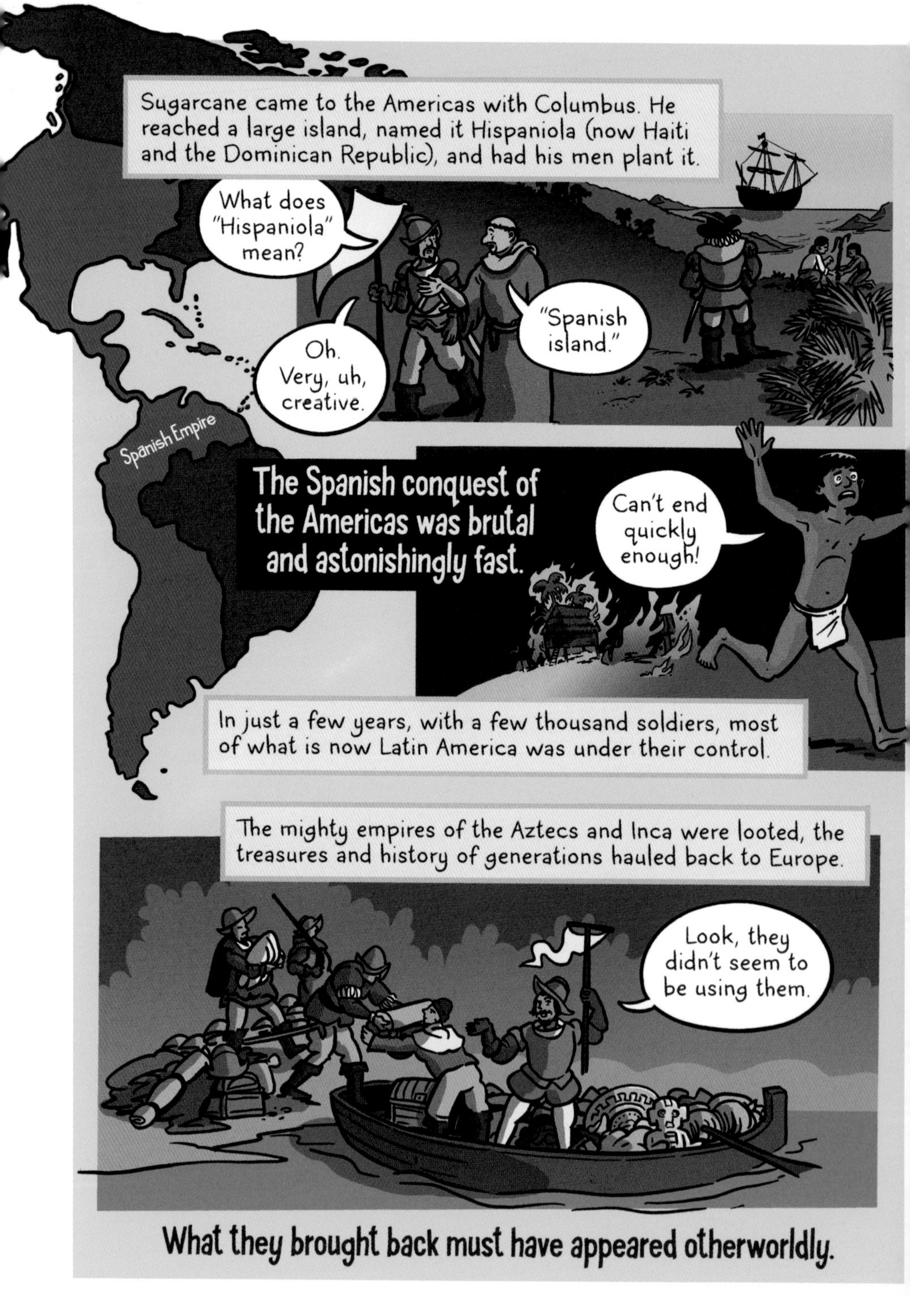

Sugarcane came to the Americas with Columbus. He reached a large island, named it Hispaniola (now Haiti and the Dominican Republic), and had his men plant it.
What does "Hispaniola" mean?
"Spanish island."
Oh. Very, uh, creative.
Spanish Empire
The Spanish conquest of the Americas was brutal and astonishingly fast.
Can't end quickly enough!
In just a few years, with a few thousand soldiers, most of what is now Latin America was under their control.
The mighty empires of the Aztecs and Inca were looted, the treasures and history of generations hauled back to Europe.
Look, they didn't seem to be using them.
What they brought back must have appeared otherworldly.

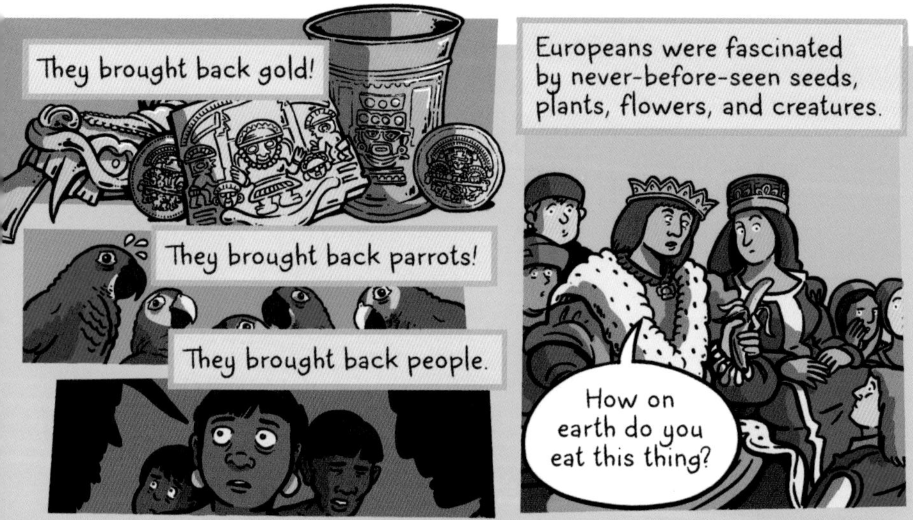
They brought back gold!
Europeans were fascinated by never-before-seen seeds, plants, flowers, and creatures.
They brought back parrots!
They brought back people.
How on earth do you eat this thing?

The Spanish found profit practically everywhere in the New World.

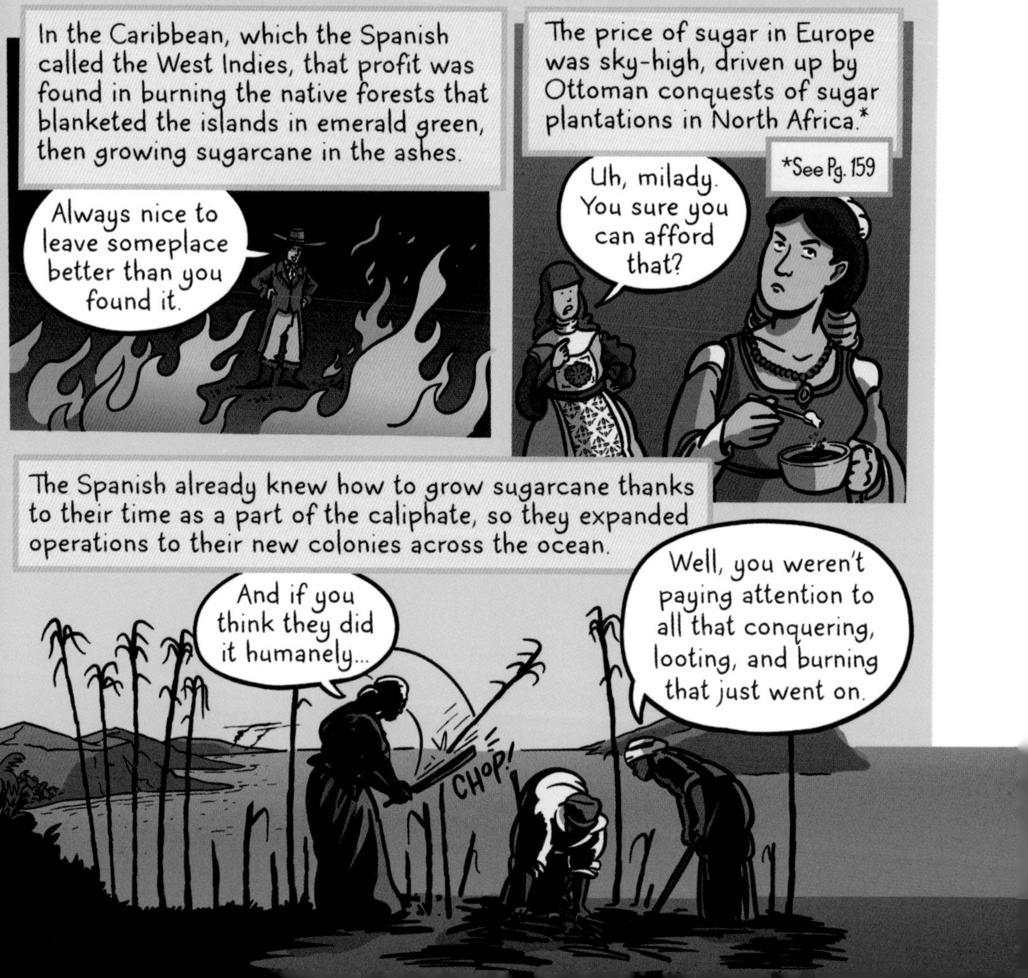
In the Caribbean, which the Spanish called the West Indies, that profit was found in burning the native forests that blanketed the islands in emerald green, then growing sugarcane in the ashes.
Always nice to leave someplace better than you found it.
The price of sugar in Europe was sky-high, driven up by Ottoman conquests of sugar plantations in North Africa.*
*See Pg. 159
Uh, milady. You sure you can afford that?
The Spanish already knew how to grow sugarcane thanks to their time as a part of the caliphate, so they expanded operations to their new colonies across the ocean.
And if you think they did it humanely...
Well, you weren't paying attention to all that conquering, looting, and burning that just went on.
CHOP!

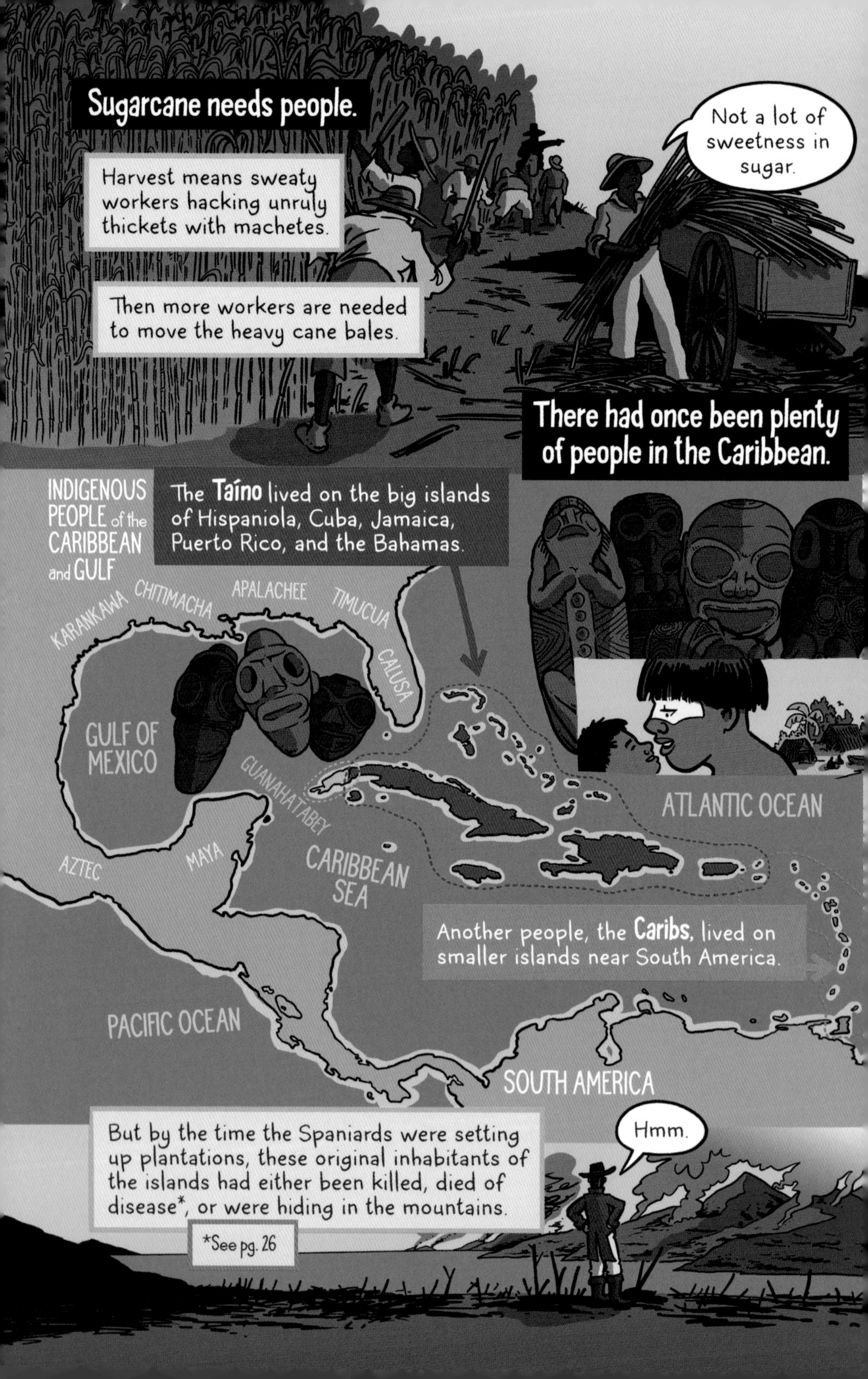
Sugarcane needs people.
Harvest means sweaty workers hacking unruly thickets with machetes.
Then more workers are needed to move the heavy cane bales.
Not a lot of sweetness in sugar.
There had once been plenty of people in the Caribbean.
INDIGENOUS PEOPLE of the CARIBBEAN and GULF
The Taíno lived on the big islands of Hispaniola, Cuba, Jamaica, Puerto Rico, and the Bahamas.
KARANKAWA
CHITIMACHA
APALACHEE
TIMUCUA
CALUSA
GULF OF MEXICO
GUANAHATABEY
ATLANTIC OCEAN
AZTEC
MAYA
CARIBBEAN SEA
Another people, the Caribs, lived on smaller islands near South America.
PACIFIC OCEAN
SOUTH AMERICA
But by the time the Spaniards were setting up plantations, these original inhabitants of the islands had either been killed, died of disease*, or were hiding in the mountains.
*See pg. 26
Hmm.

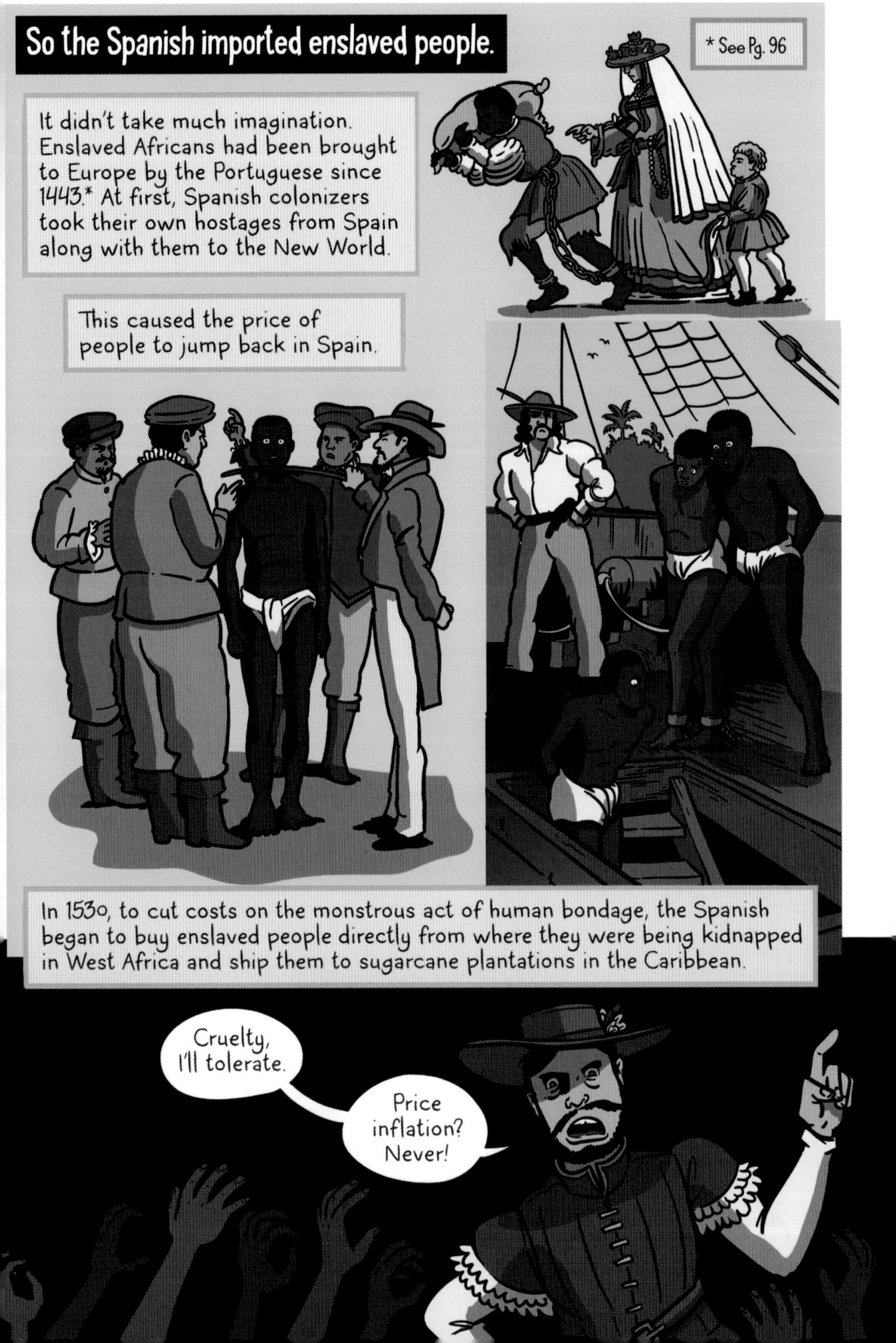
So the Spanish imported enslaved people.
* See Pg. 96
It didn't take much imagination. Enslaved Africans had been brought to Europe by the Portuguese since 1443.* At first, Spanish colonizers took their own hostages from Spain along with them to the New World.
This caused the price of people to jump back in Spain.
In 1530, to cut costs on the monstrous act of human bondage, the Spanish began to buy enslaved people directly from where they were being kidnapped in West Africa and ship them to sugarcane plantations in the Caribbean.
Cruelty, I'll tolerate.
Price inflation? Never!

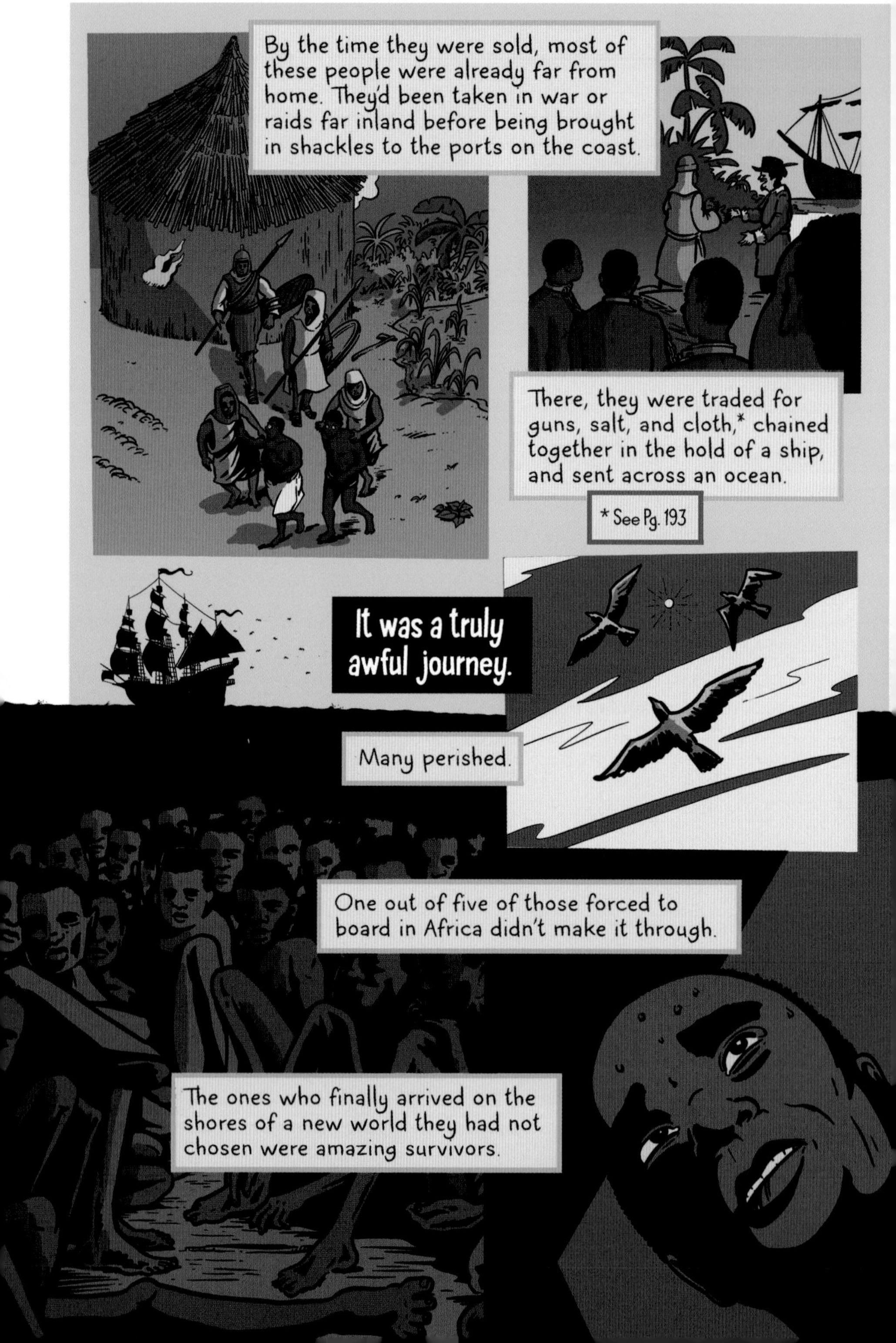
By the time they were sold, most of these people were already far from home. They'd been taken in war or raids far inland before being brought in shackles to the ports on the coast.
There, they were traded for guns, salt, and cloth,* chained together in the hold of a ship, and sent across an ocean.
* See Pg. 193
It was a truly awful journey.
Many perished.
One out of five of those forced to board in Africa didn't make it through.
The ones who finally arrived on the shores of a new world they had not chosen were amazing survivors.

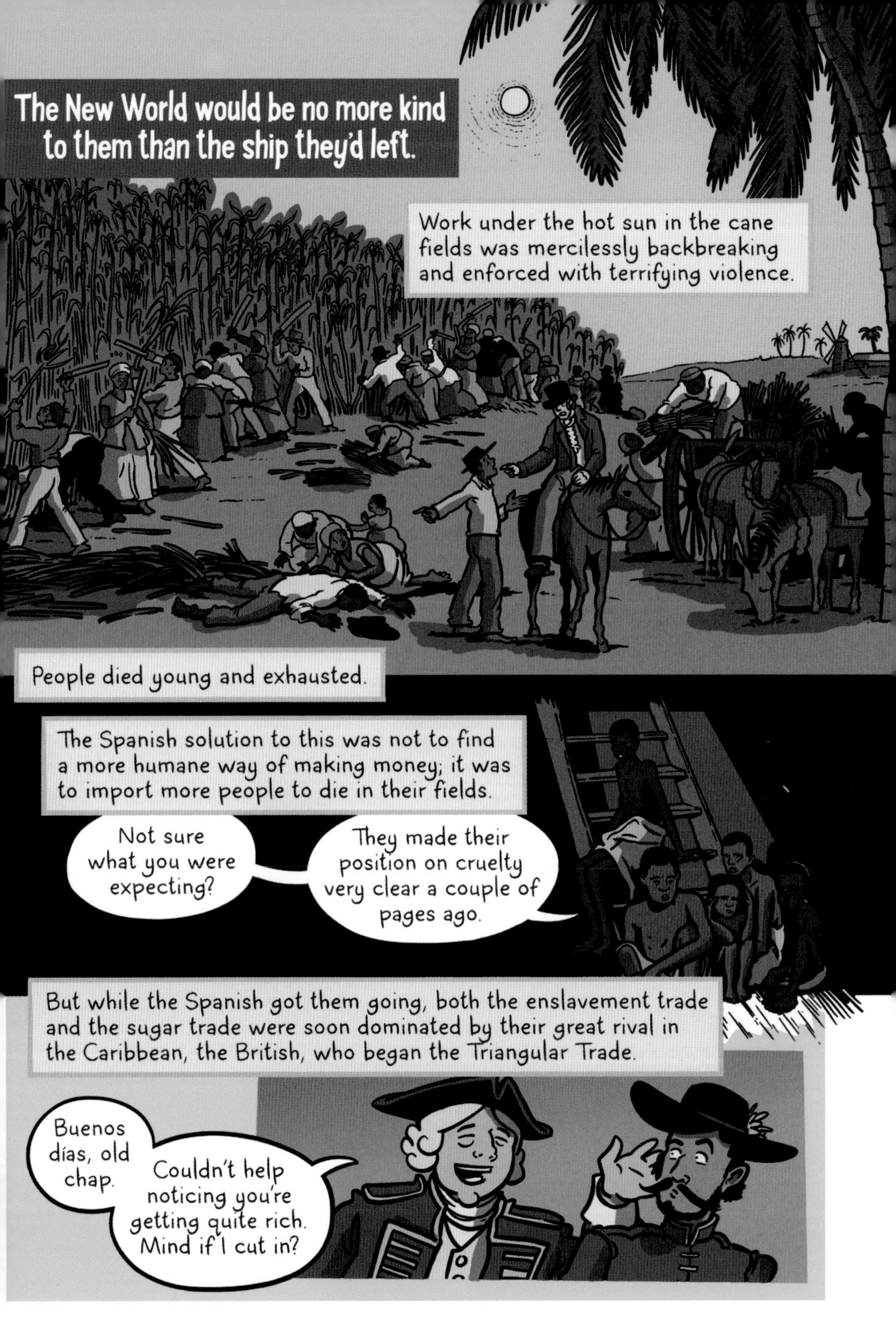

The New World would be no more kind to them than the ship they'd left.
Work under the hot sun in the cane fields was mercilessly backbreaking and enforced with terrifying violence.
People died young and exhausted.
The Spanish solution to this was not to find a more humane way of making money; it was to import more people to die in their fields.
Not sure what you were expecting?
They made their position on cruelty very clear a couple of pages ago.
But while the Spanish got them going, both the enslavement trade and the sugar trade were soon dominated by their great rival in the Caribbean, the British, who began the Triangular Trade.
Buenos días, old chap.
Couldn't help noticing you're getting quite rich. Mind if I cut in?

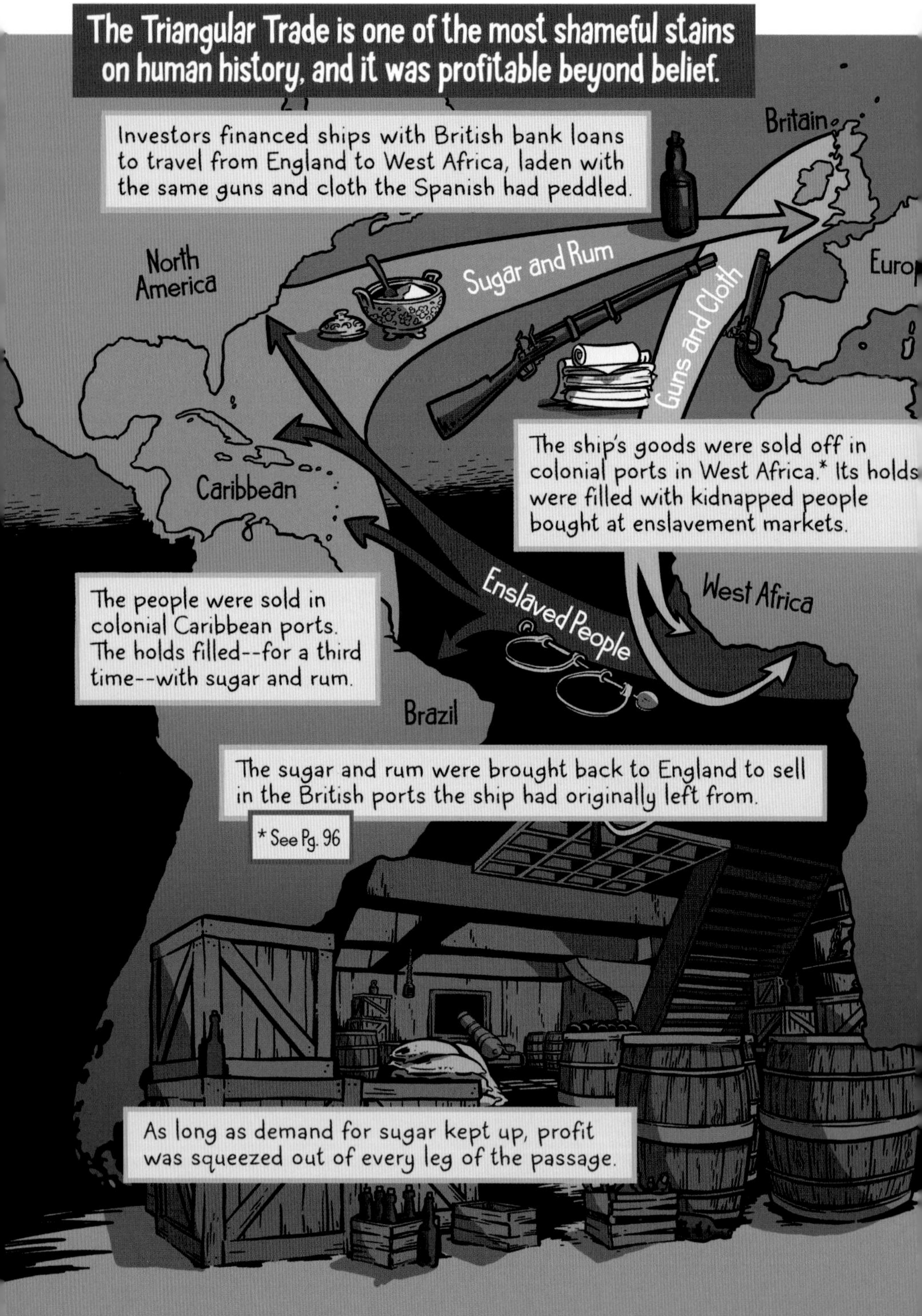
The Triangular Trade is one of the most shameful stains on human history, and it was profitable beyond belief.
Investors financed ships with British bank loans to travel from England to West Africa, laden with the same guns and cloth the Spanish had peddled.
Britain
North America
Europ
Sugar and Rum
Guns and Cloth
Caribbean
The ship's goods were sold off in colonial ports in West Africa.* Its holds were filled with kidnapped people bought at enslavement markets.
West Africa
Enslaved People
The people were sold in colonial Caribbean ports. The holds filled--for a third time--with sugar and rum.
Brazil
The sugar and rum were brought back to England to sell in the British ports the ship had originally left from.
* See Pg. 96
As long as demand for sugar kept up, profit was squeezed out of every leg of the passage.

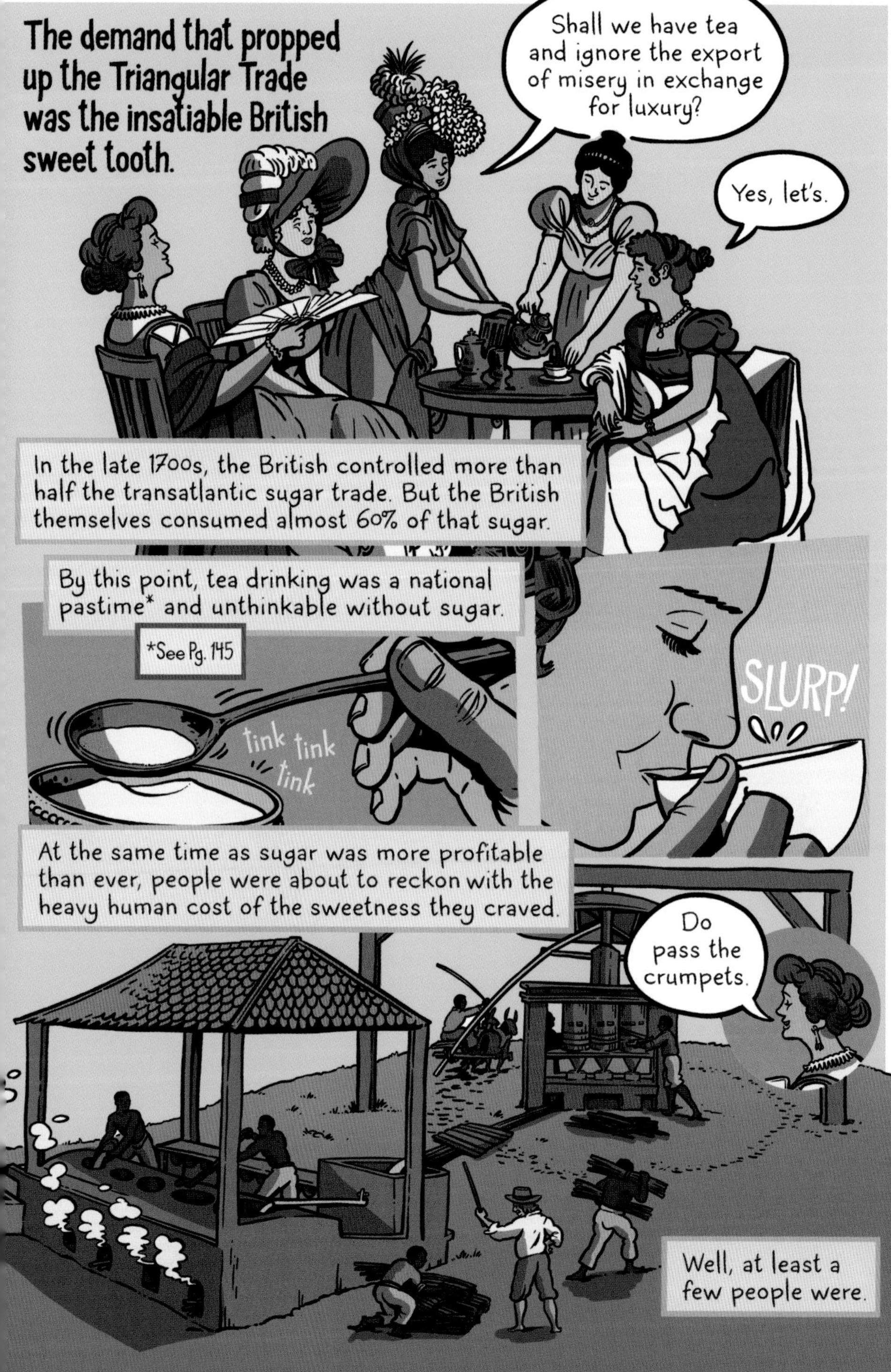

The demand that propped up the Triangular Trade was the insatiable British sweet tooth.
Shall we have tea and ignore the export of misery in exchange for luxury?
Yes, let's.
In the late 1700s, the British controlled more than half the transatlantic sugar trade. But the British themselves consumed almost 60% of that sugar.
By this point, tea drinking was a national pastime* and unthinkable without sugar.
*See Pg. 145
tink tink tink
SLURP!
At the same time as sugar was more profitable than ever, people were about to reckon with the heavy human cost of the sweetness they craved.
Do pass the crumpets.
Well, at least a few people were.

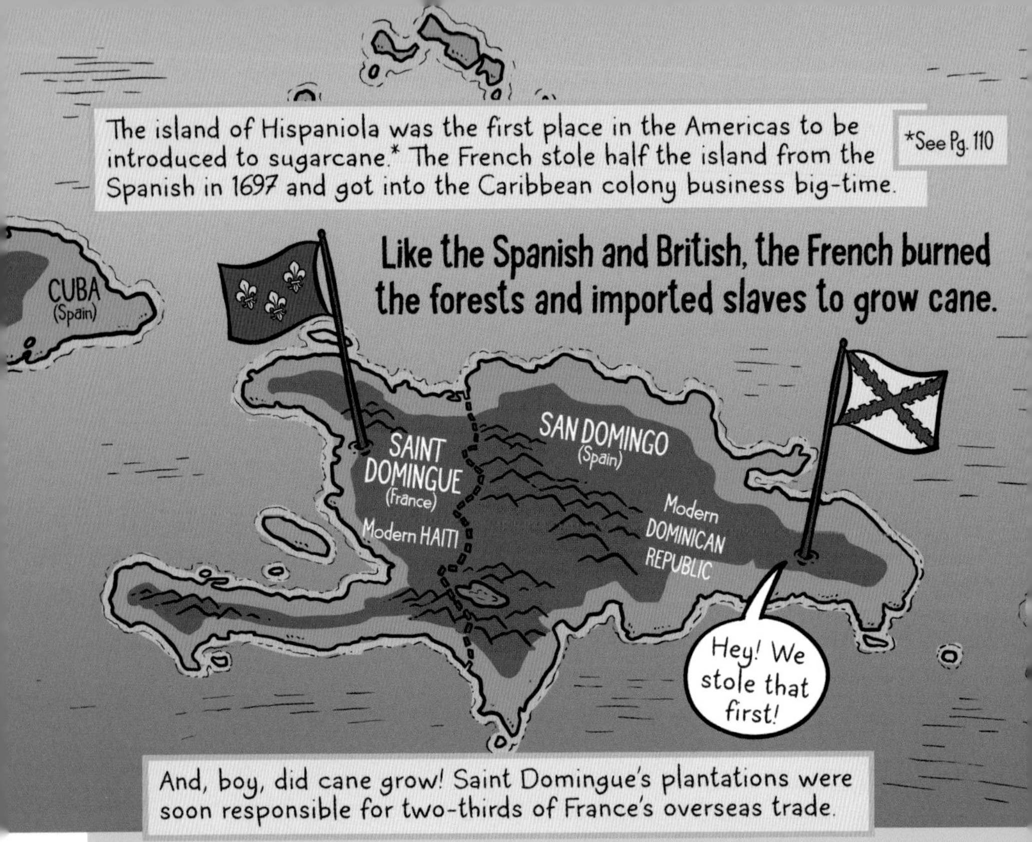
The island of Hispaniola was the first place in the Americas to be introduced to sugarcane.* The French stole half the island from the Spanish in 1697 and got into the Caribbean colony business big-time.
*See Pg. 110
Like the Spanish and British, the French burned the forests and imported slaves to grow cane.
CUBA (Spain)
SAINT DOMINGUE (France)
Modern HAITI
SAN DOMINGO (Spain)
Modern DOMINICAN REPUBLIC
Hey! We stole that first!
And, boy, did cane grow! Saint Domingue's plantations were soon responsible for two-thirds of France's overseas trade.

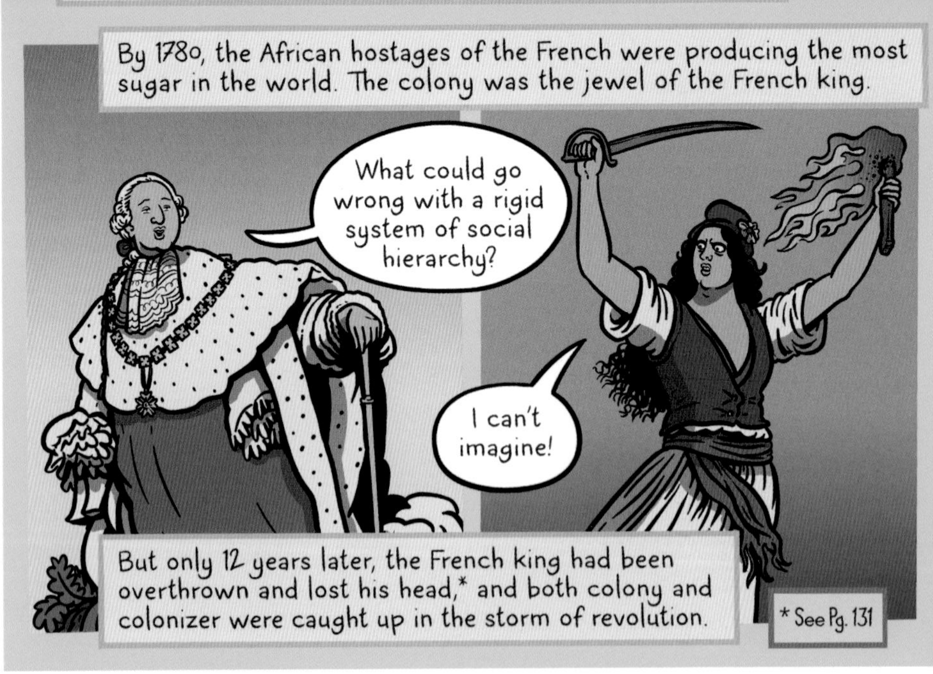
By 1780, the African hostages of the French were producing the most sugar in the world. The colony was the jewel of the French king.
What could go wrong with a rigid system of social hierarchy?
I can't imagine!
But only 12 years later, the French king had been overthrown and lost his head,* and both colony and colonizer were caught up in the storm of revolution.
* See Pg. 131

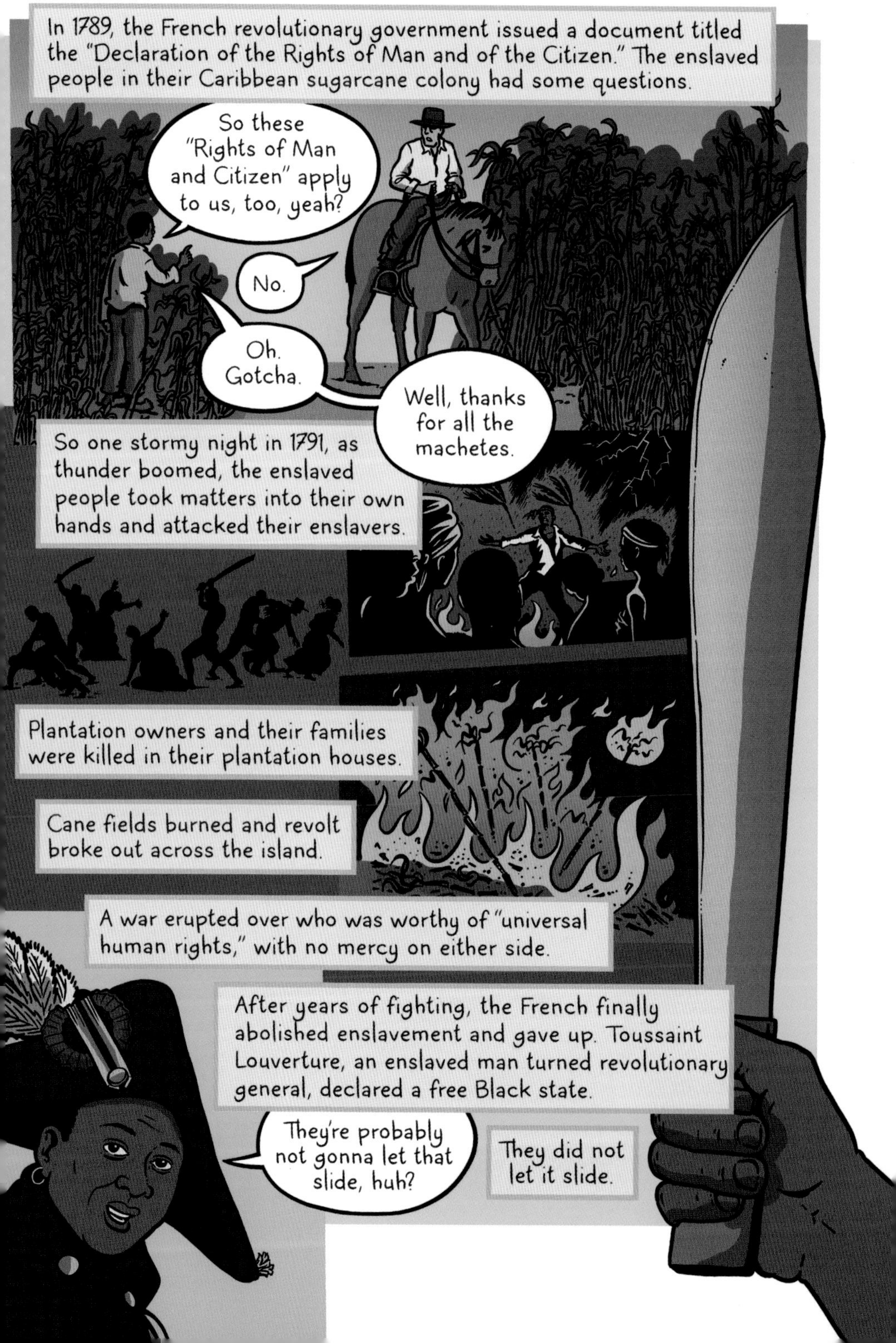
In 1789, the French revolutionary government issued a document titled the "Declaration of the Rights of Man and of the Citizen." The enslaved people in their Caribbean sugarcane colony had some questions.
So these "Rights of Man and Citizen" apply to us, too, yeah?
No.
Oh. Gotcha.
Well, thanks for all the machetes.
So one stormy night in 1791, as thunder boomed, the enslaved people took matters into their own hands and attacked their enslavers.
Plantation owners and their families were killed in their plantation houses.
Cane fields burned and revolt broke out across the island.
A war erupted over who was worthy of "universal human rights," with no mercy on either side.
After years of fighting, the French finally abolished enslavement and gave up. Toussaint Louverture, an enslaved man turned revolutionary general, declared a free Black state.
They're probably not gonna let that slide, huh?
They did not let it slide.

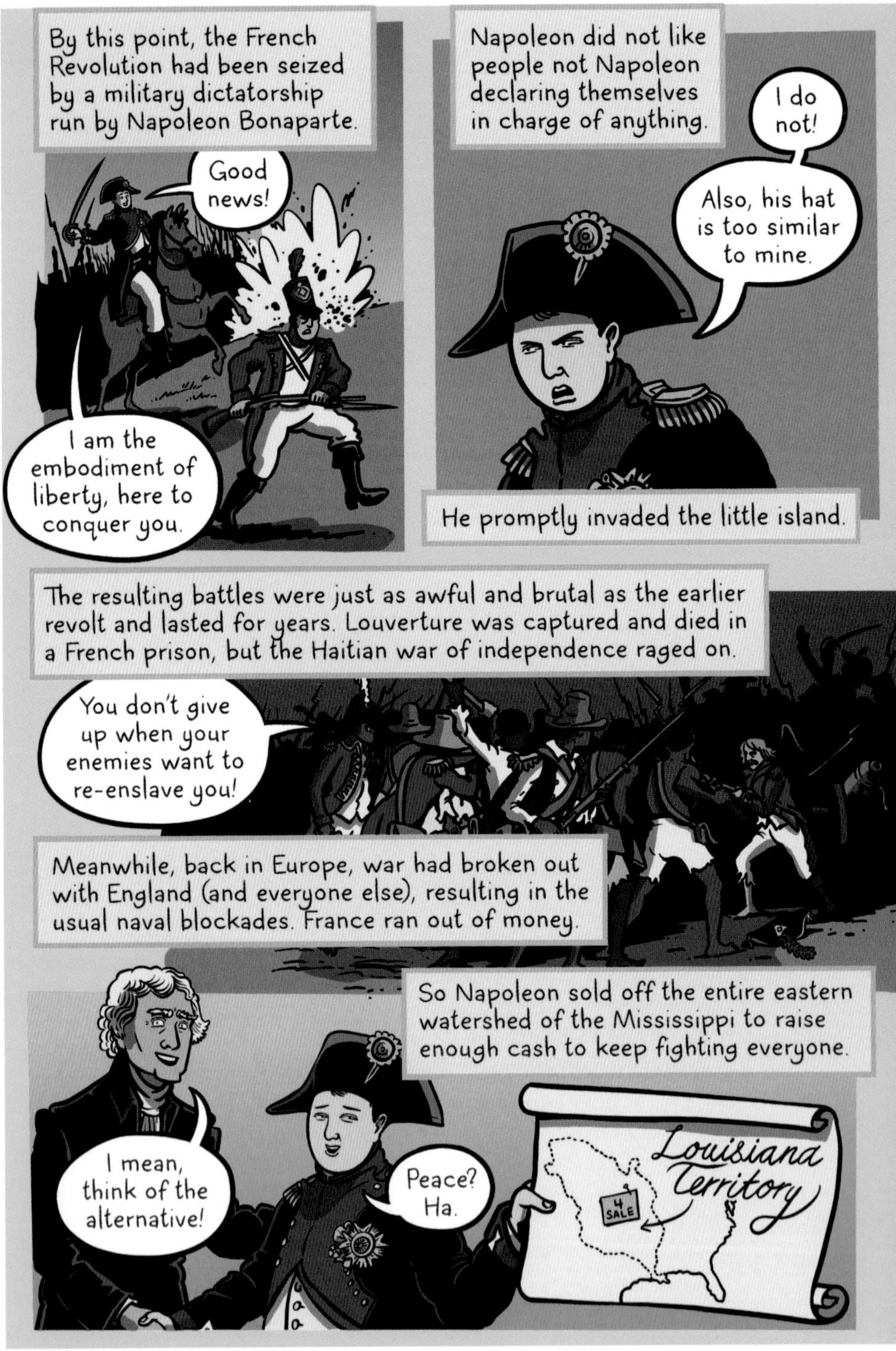
By this point, the French Revolution had been seized by a military dictatorship run by Napoleon Bonaparte.
Good news!
I am the embodiment of liberty, here to conquer you.
Napoleon did not like people not Napoleon declaring themselves in charge of anything.
I do not!
Also, his hat is too similar to mine.
He promptly invaded the little island.
The resulting battles were just as awful and brutal as the earlier revolt and lasted for years. Louverture was captured and died in a French prison, but the Haitian war of independence raged on.
You don't give up when your enemies want to re-enslave you!
Meanwhile, back in Europe, war had broken out with England (and everyone else), resulting in the usual naval blockades. France ran out of money.
So Napoleon sold off the entire eastern watershed of the Mississippi to raise enough cash to keep fighting everyone.
I mean, think of the alternative!
Peace? Ha.
Louisiana Territory
4 SALE

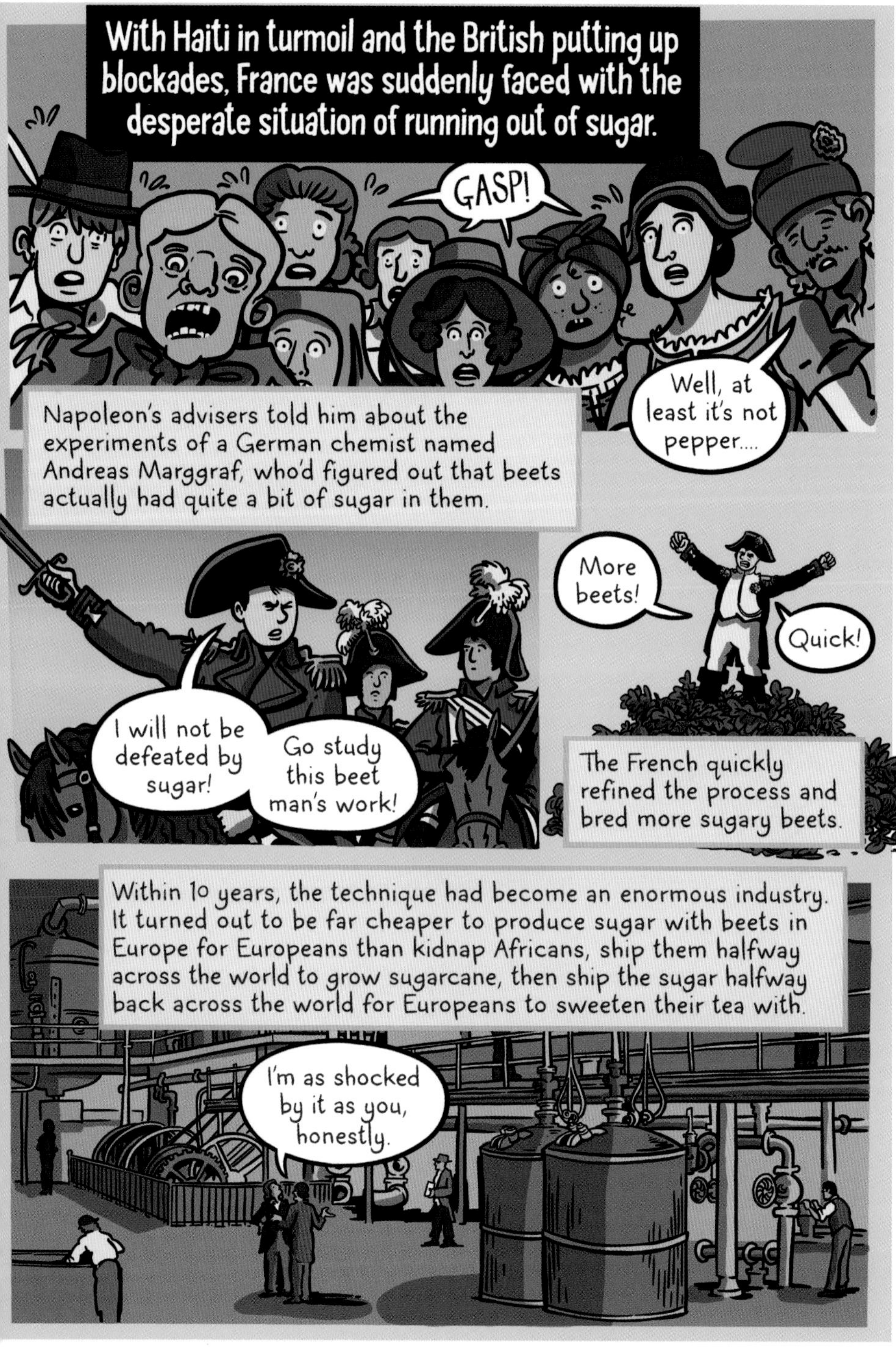

With Haiti in turmoil and the British putting up blockades, France was suddenly faced with the desperate situation of running out of sugar.
GASP!
Well, at least it's not pepper....
Napoleon's advisers told him about the experiments of a German chemist named Andreas Marggraf, who'd figured out that beets actually had quite a bit of sugar in them.
I will not be defeated by sugar!
Go study this beet man's work!
More beets!
Quick!
The French quickly refined the process and bred more sugary beets.
Within 10 years, the technique had become an enormous industry. It turned out to be far cheaper to produce sugar with beets in Europe for Europeans than kidnap Africans, ship them halfway across the world to grow sugarcane, then ship the sugar halfway back across the world for Europeans to sweeten their tea with.
I'm as shocked by it as you, honestly.

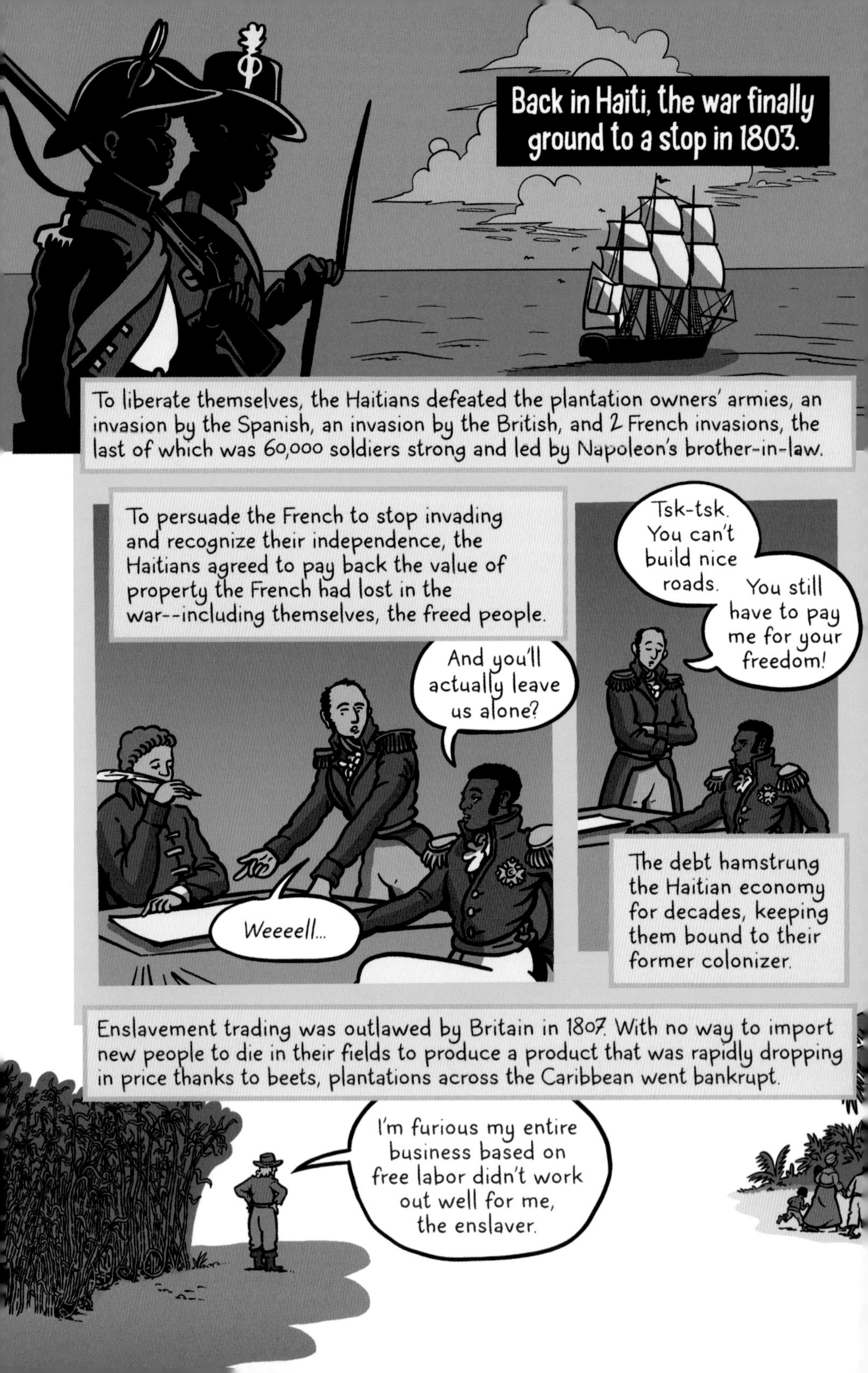
Back in Haiti, the war finally ground to a stop in 1803.
To liberate themselves, the Haitians defeated the plantation owners' armies, an invasion by the Spanish, an invasion by the British, and 2 French invasions, the last of which was 60,000 soldiers strong and led by Napoleon's brother-in-law.
To persuade the French to stop invading and recognize their independence, the Haitians agreed to pay back the value of property the French had lost in the war--including themselves, the freed people.
And you'll actually leave us alone?
Weeeell...
Tsk-tsk. You can't build nice roads.
You still have to pay me for your freedom!
The debt hamstrung the Haitian economy for decades, keeping them bound to their former colonizer.
Enslavement trading was outlawed by Britain in 1807. With no way to import new people to die in their fields to produce a product that was rapidly dropping in price thanks to beets, plantations across the Caribbean went bankrupt.
I'm furious my entire business based on free labor didn't work out well for me, the enslaver.

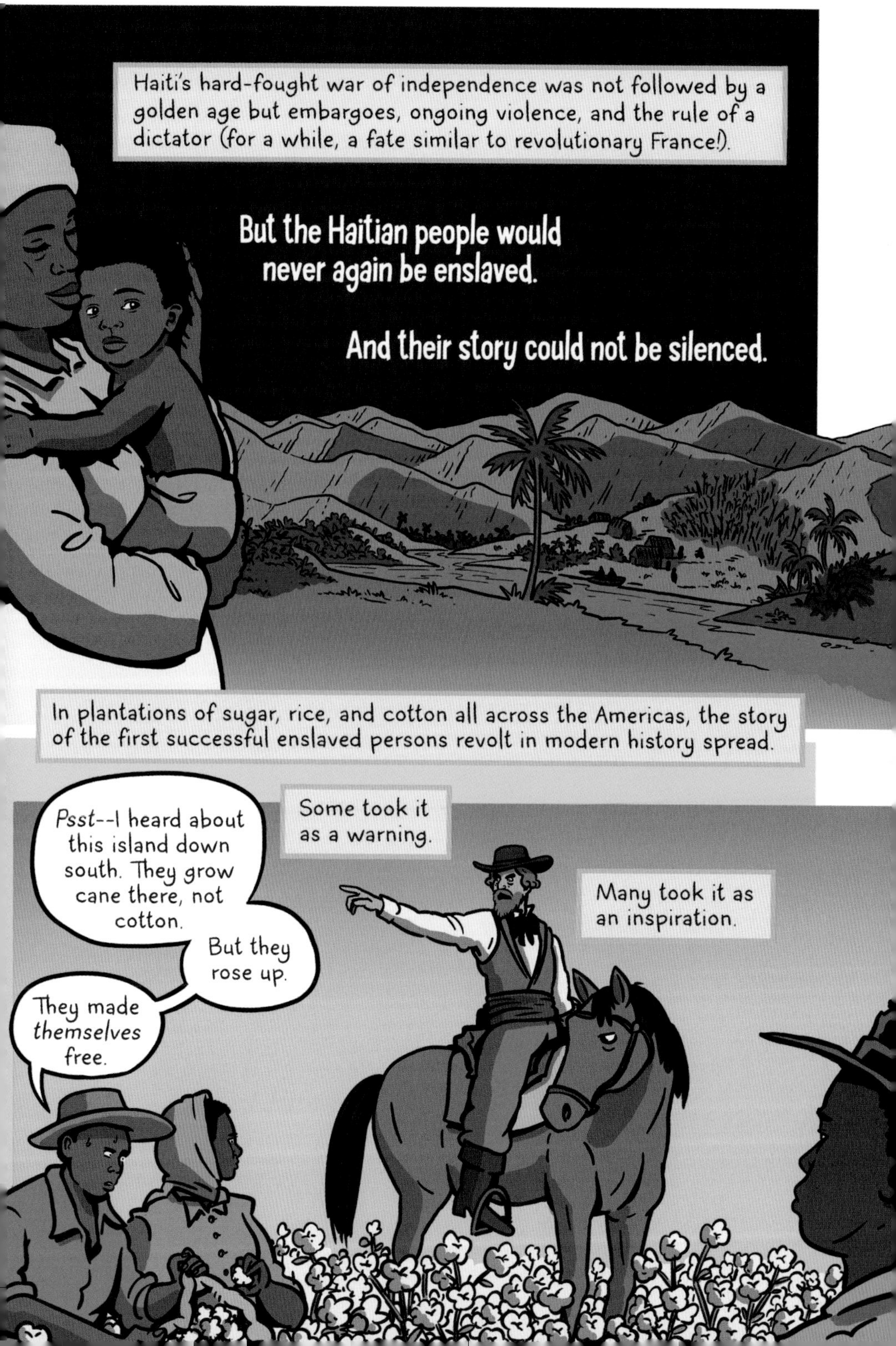
Haiti's hard-fought war of independence was not followed by a golden age but embargoes, ongoing violence, and the rule of a dictator (for a while, a fate similar to revolutionary France!).
But the Haitian people would never again be enslaved.
And their story could not be silenced.
In plantations of sugar, rice, and cotton all across the Americas, the story of the first successful enslaved persons revolt in modern history spread.
Psst--I heard about this island down south. They grow cane there, not cotton.
But they rose up.
They made *themselves* free.
Some took it as a warning.
Many took it as an inspiration.

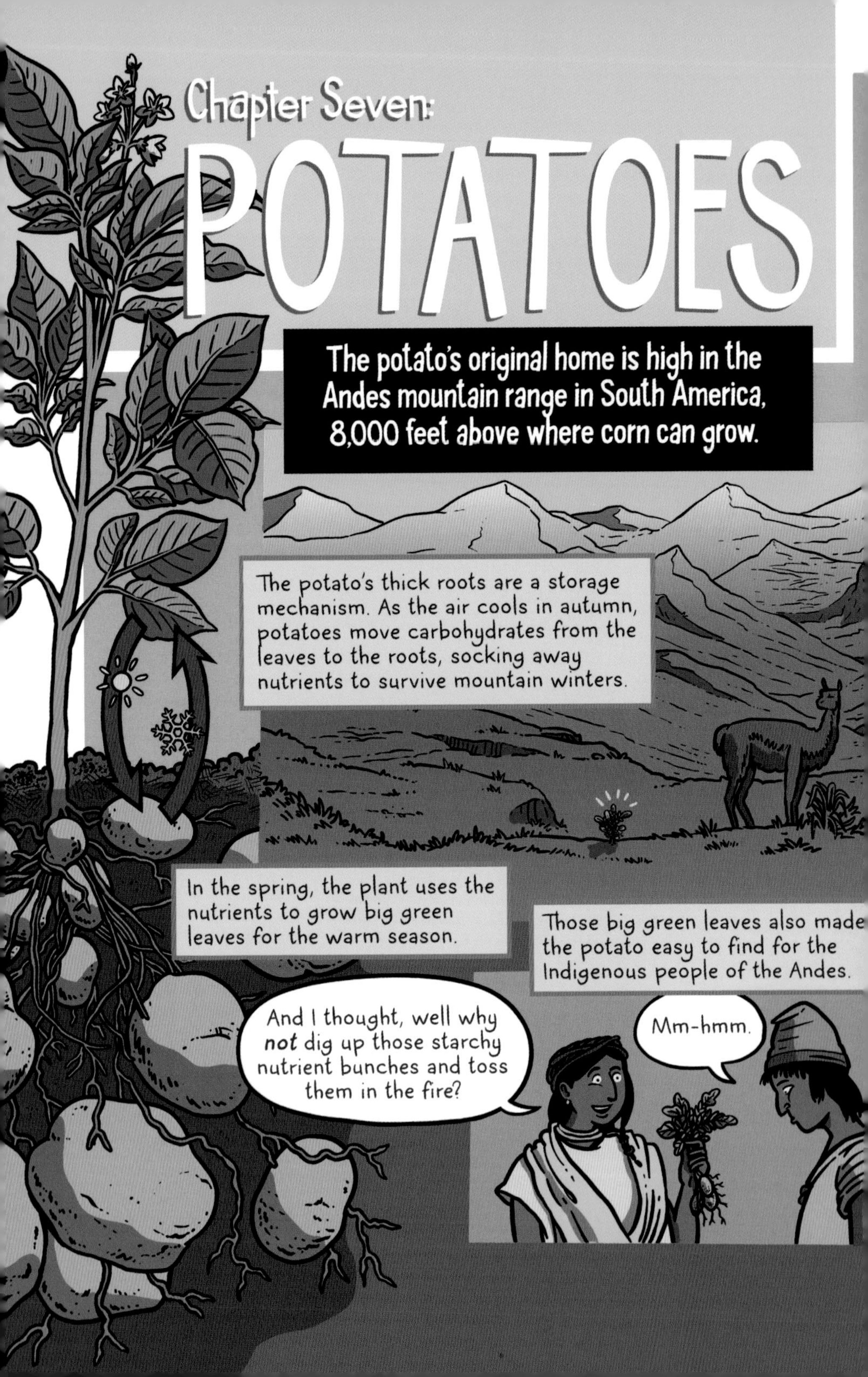

Chapter Seven:
POTATOES
The potato's original home is high in the Andes mountain range in South America, 8,000 feet above where corn can grow.
The potato's thick roots are a storage mechanism. As the air cools in autumn, potatoes move carbohydrates from the leaves to the roots, socking away nutrients to survive mountain winters.
In the spring, the plant uses the nutrients to grow big green leaves for the warm season.
Those big green leaves also made the potato easy to find for the Indigenous people of the Andes.
And I thought, well why *not* dig up those starchy nutrient bunches and toss them in the fire?
Mm-hmm.

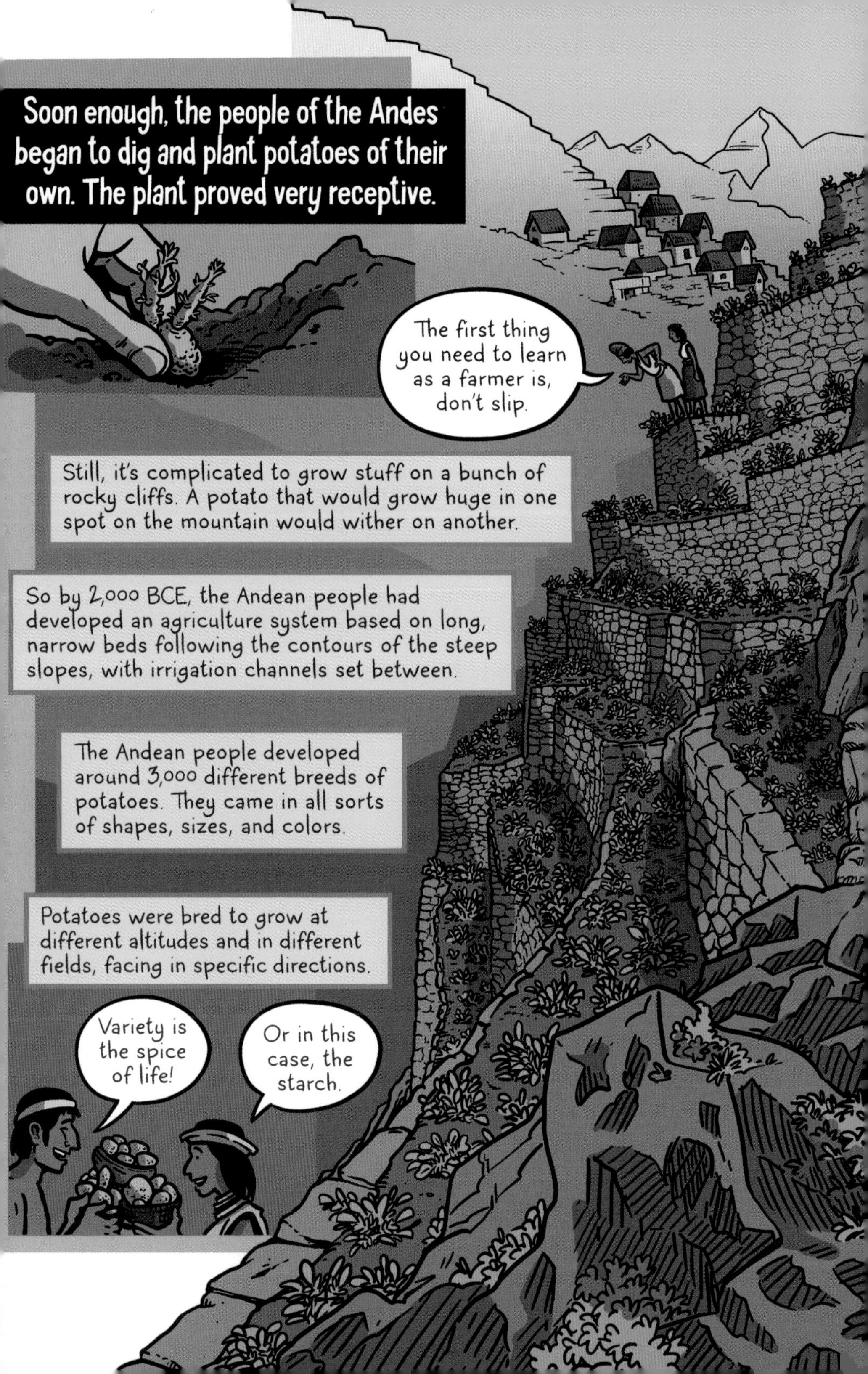
Soon enough, the people of the Andes began to dig and plant potatoes of their own. The plant proved very receptive.
The first thing you need to learn as a farmer is, don't slip.
Still, it's complicated to grow stuff on a bunch of rocky cliffs. A potato that would grow huge in one spot on the mountain would wither on another.
So by 2,000 BCE, the Andean people had developed an agriculture system based on long, narrow beds following the contours of the steep slopes, with irrigation channels set between.
The Andean people developed around 3,000 different breeds of potatoes. They came in all sorts of shapes, sizes, and colors.
Potatoes were bred to grow at different altitudes and in different fields, facing in specific directions.
Variety is the spice of life!
Or in this case, the starch.

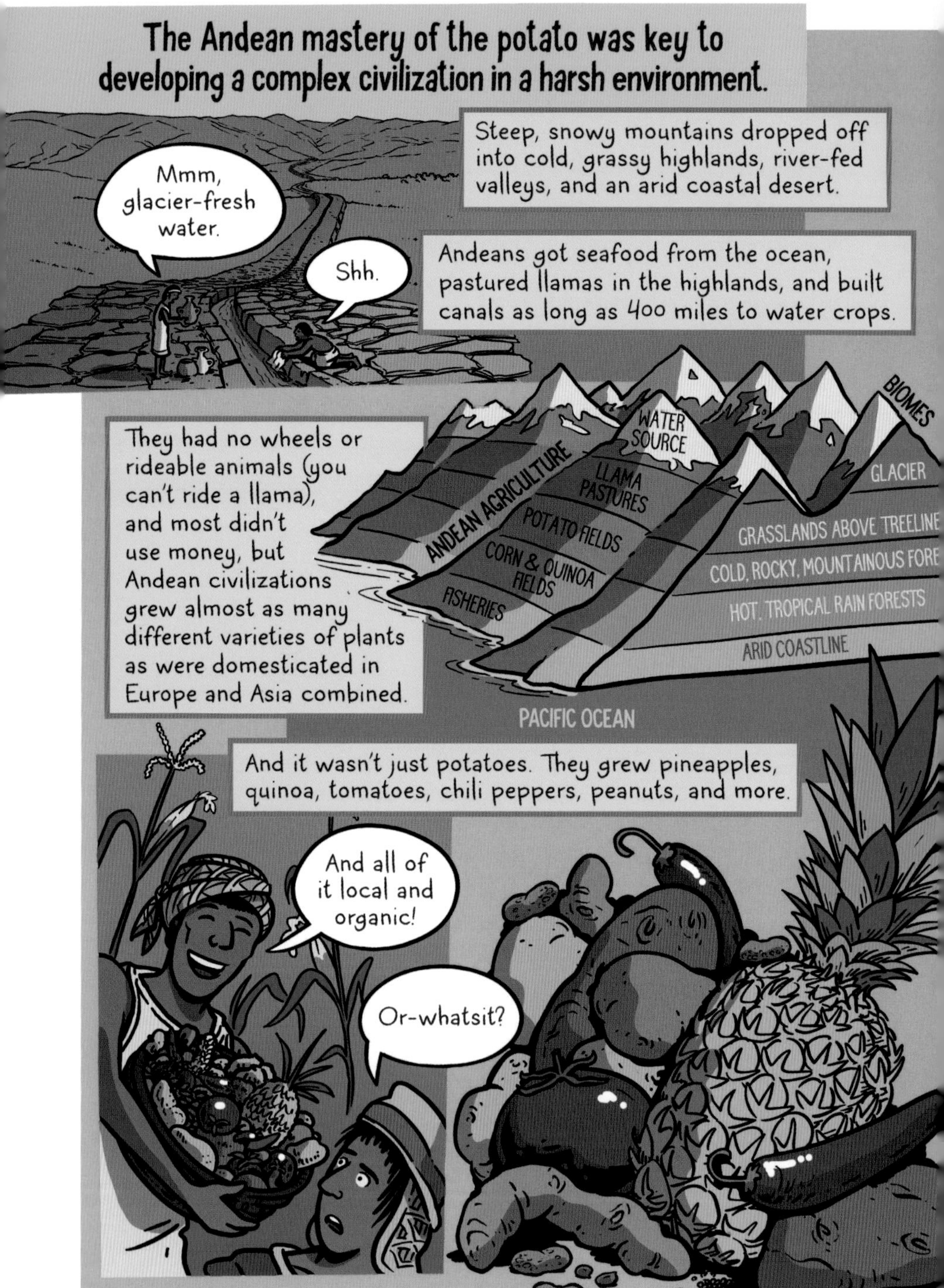

The Andean mastery of the potato was key to developing a complex civilization in a harsh environment.
Steep, snowy mountains dropped off into cold, grassy highlands, river-fed valleys, and an arid coastal desert.
Mmm, glacier-fresh water.
Shh.
Andeans got seafood from the ocean, pastured llamas in the highlands, and built canals as long as 400 miles to water crops.
They had no wheels or rideable animals (you can't ride a llama), and most didn't use money, but Andean civilizations grew almost as many different varieties of plants as were domesticated in Europe and Asia combined.
ANDEAN AGRICULTURE
WATER SOURCE
LLAMA PASTURES
POTATO FIELDS
CORN & QUINOA FIELDS
FISHERIES
BIOMES
GLACIER
GRASSLANDS ABOVE TREELINE
COLD, ROCKY, MOUNTAINOUS FORE
HOT, TROPICAL RAIN FORESTS
ARID COASTLINE
PACIFIC OCEAN
And it wasn't just potatoes. They grew pineapples, quinoa, tomatoes, chili peppers, peanuts, and more.
And all of it local and organic!
Or-whatsit?

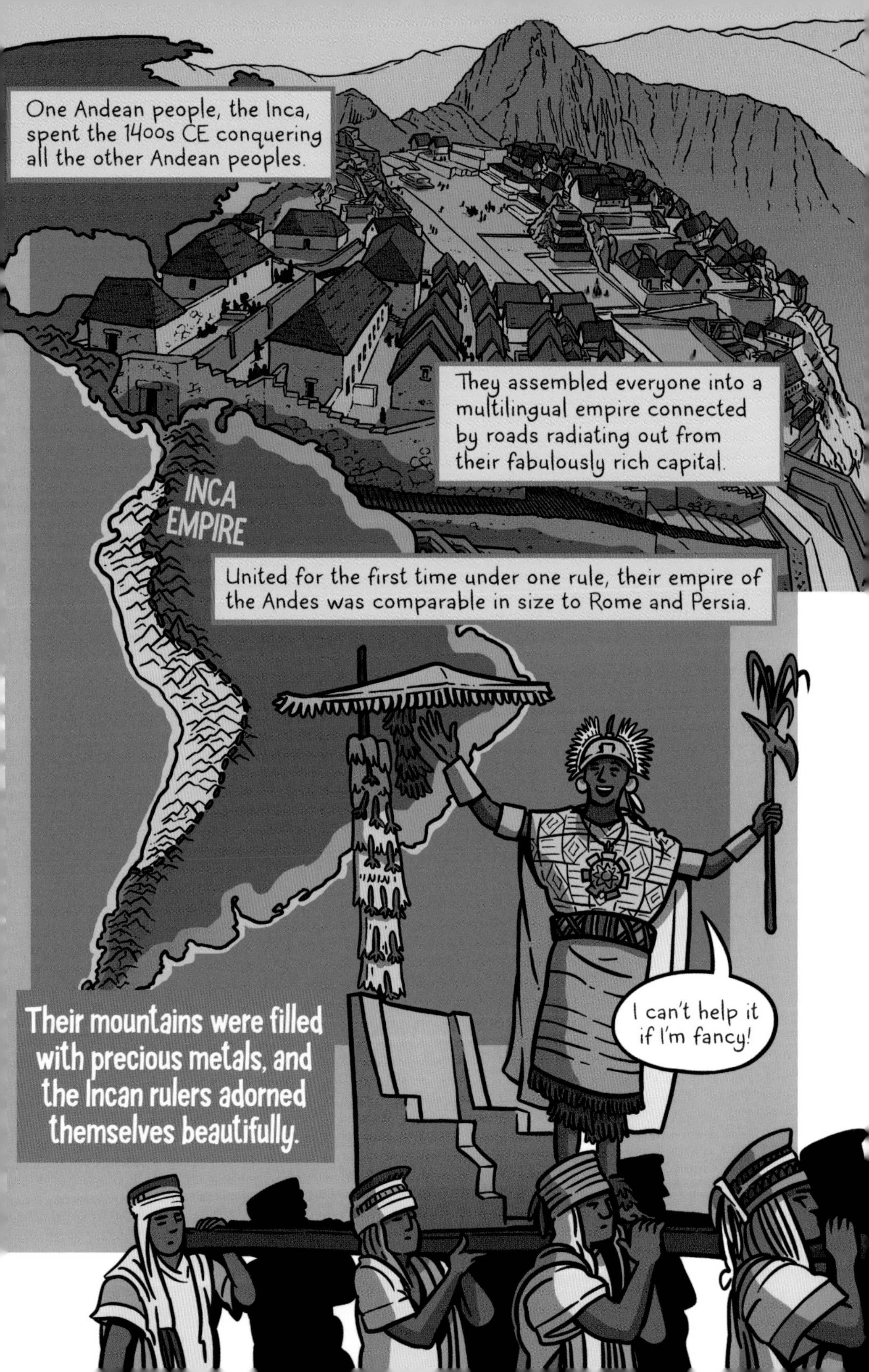
One Andean people, the Inca, spent the 1400s CE conquering all the other Andean peoples.
They assembled everyone into a multilingual empire connected by roads radiating out from their fabulously rich capital.
INCA EMPIRE
United for the first time under one rule, their empire of the Andes was comparable in size to Rome and Persia.
Their mountains were filled with precious metals, and the Incan rulers adorned themselves beautifully.
I can't help it if I'm fancy!

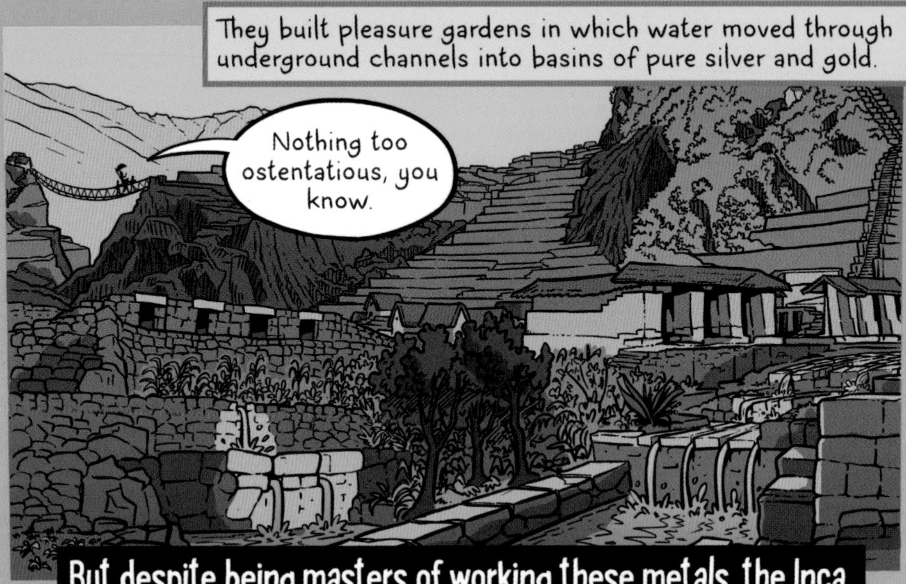
They built pleasure gardens in which water moved through underground channels into basins of pure silver and gold.
Nothing too ostentatious, you know.

But despite being masters of working these metals, the Inca did not use gold or silver as a way to buy and sell things.

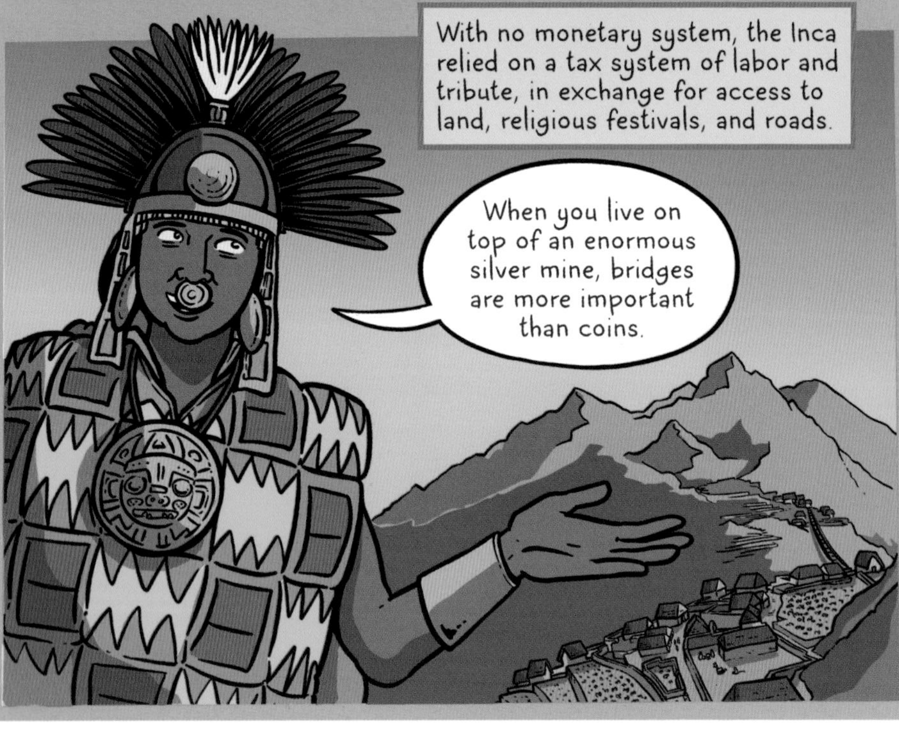
With no monetary system, the Inca relied on a tax system of labor and tribute, in exchange for access to land, religious festivals, and roads.
When you live on top of an enormous silver mine, bridges are more important than coins.

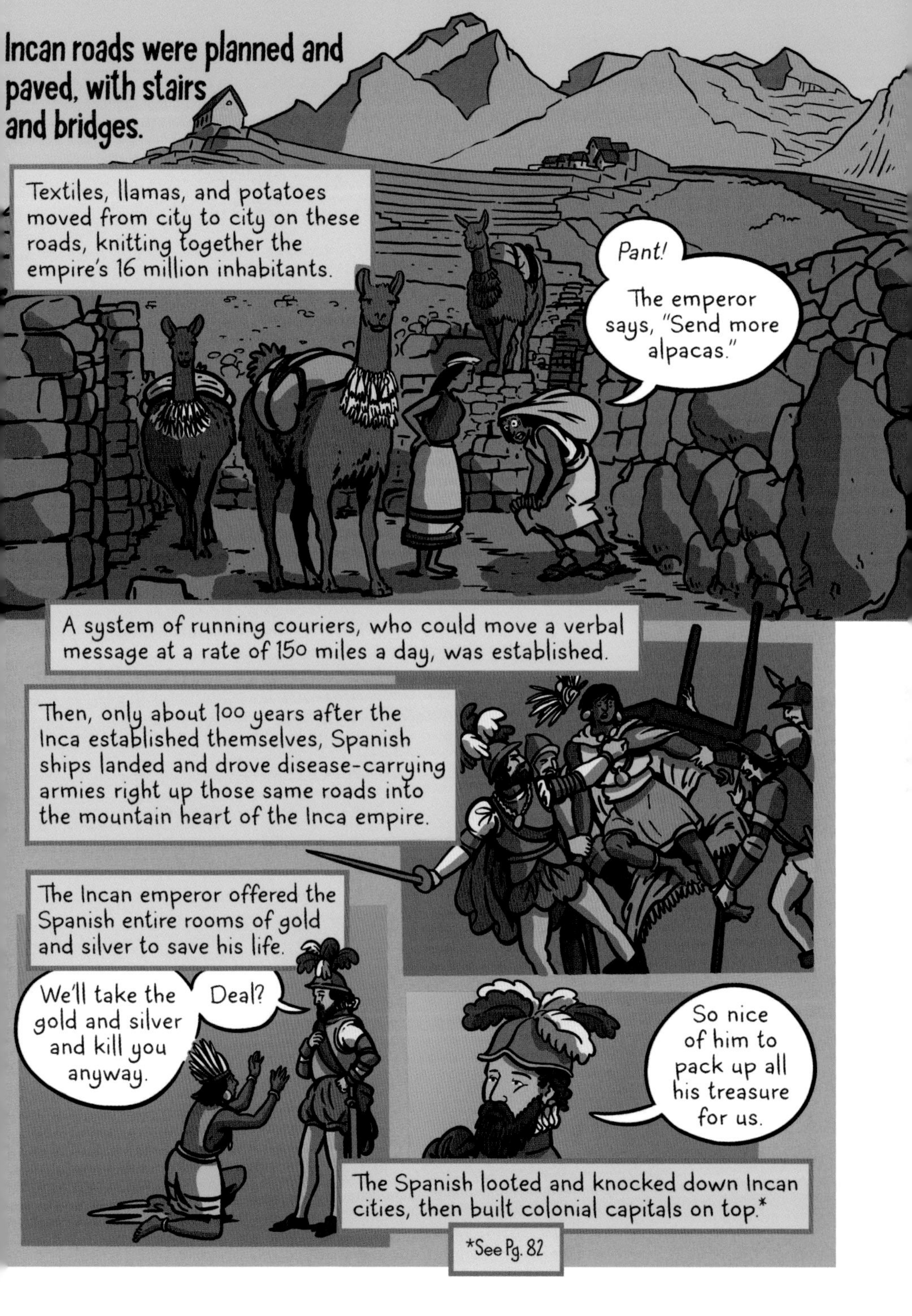

Incan roads were planned and paved, with stairs and bridges.
Textiles, llamas, and potatoes moved from city to city on these roads, knitting together the empire's 16 million inhabitants.
Pant!
The emperor says, "Send more alpacas."
A system of running couriers, who could move a verbal message at a rate of 150 miles a day, was established.
Then, only about 100 years after the Inca established themselves, Spanish ships landed and drove disease-carrying armies right up those same roads into the mountain heart of the Inca empire.
The Incan emperor offered the Spanish entire rooms of gold and silver to save his life.
Deal?
We'll take the gold and silver and kill you anyway.
So nice of him to pack up all his treasure for us.
The Spanish looted and knocked down Incan cities, then built colonial capitals on top.*
*See Pg. 82

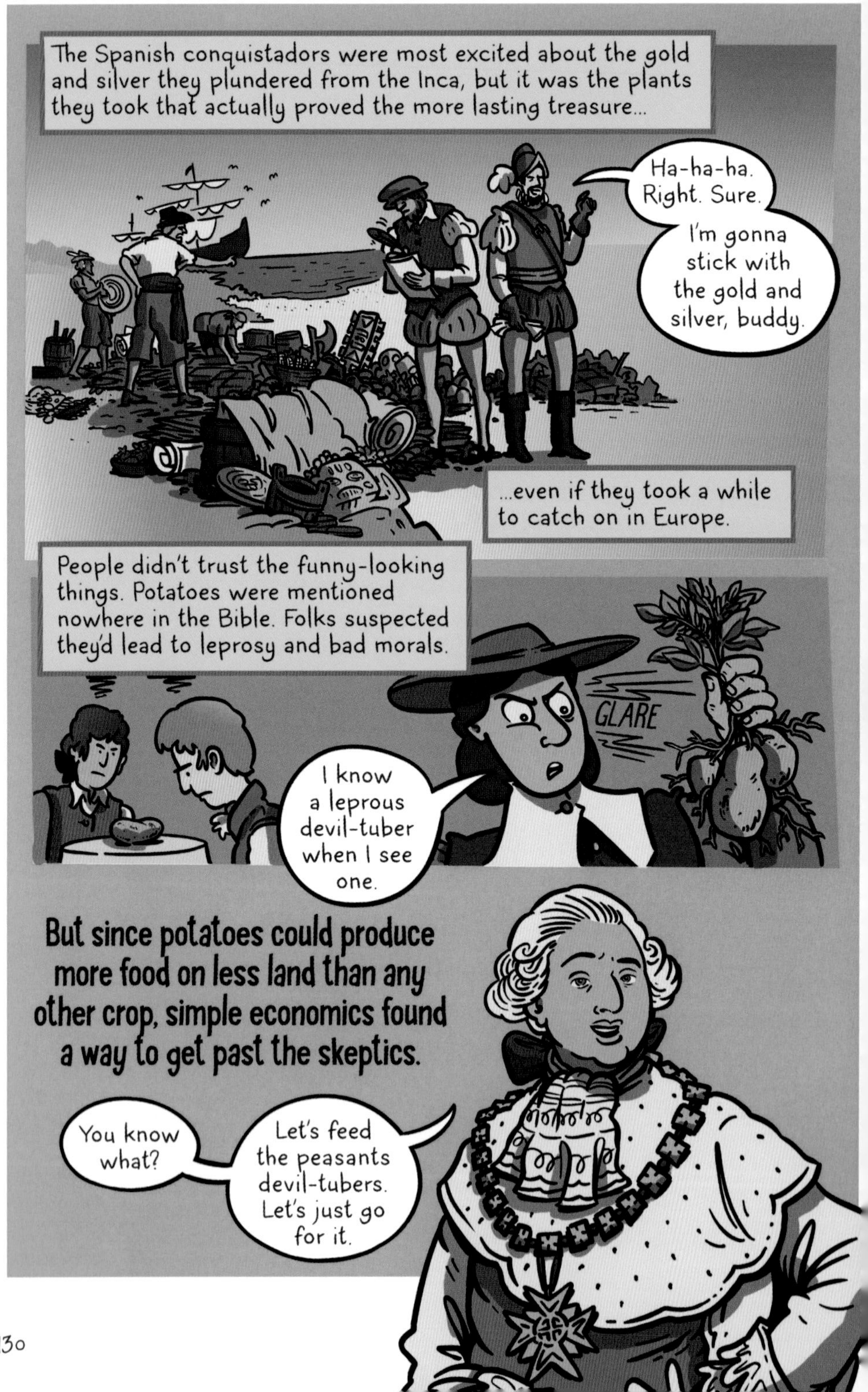

The Spanish conquistadors were most excited about the gold and silver they plundered from the Inca, but it was the plants they took that actually proved the more lasting treasure...
Ha-ha-ha. Right. Sure.
I'm gonna stick with the gold and silver, buddy.
...even if they took a while to catch on in Europe.
People didn't trust the funny-looking things. Potatoes were mentioned nowhere in the Bible. Folks suspected they'd lead to leprosy and bad morals.
GLARE
I know a leprous devil-tuber when I see one.
But since potatoes could produce more food on less land than any other crop, simple economics found a way to get past the skeptics.
You know what?
Let's feed the peasants devil-tubers. Let's just go for it.

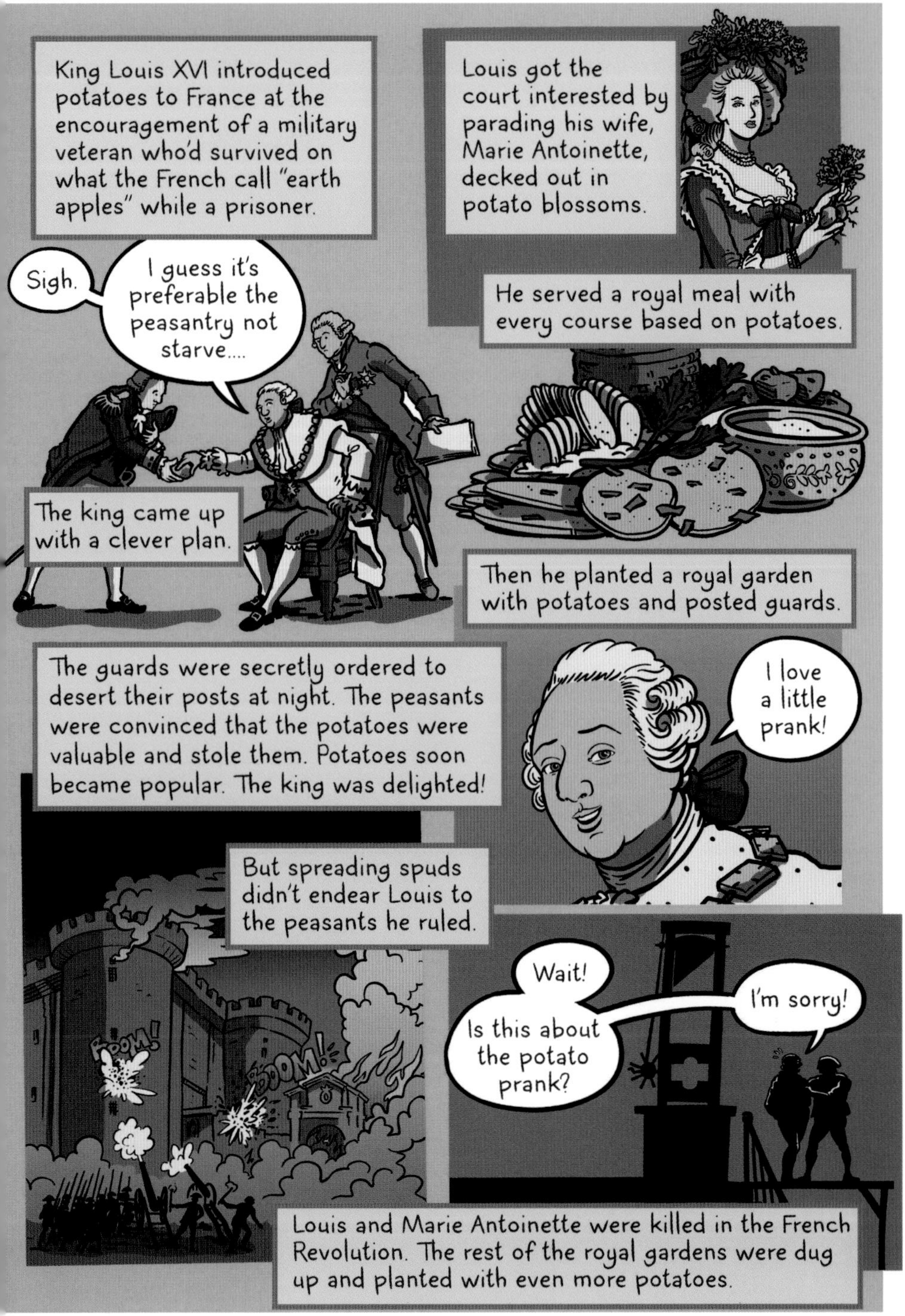
King Louis XVI introduced potatoes to France at the encouragement of a military veteran who'd survived on what the French call "earth apples" while a prisoner.
Louis got the court interested by parading his wife, Marie Antoinette, decked out in potato blossoms.
Sigh.
I guess it's preferable the peasantry not starve....
He served a royal meal with every course based on potatoes.
The king came up with a clever plan.
Then he planted a royal garden with potatoes and posted guards.
The guards were secretly ordered to desert their posts at night. The peasants were convinced that the potatoes were valuable and stole them. Potatoes soon became popular. The king was delighted!
I love a little prank!
But spreading spuds didn't endear Louis to the peasants he ruled.
BOOM!
BOOM!
Wait!
Is this about the potato prank?
I'm sorry!
Louis and Marie Antoinette were killed in the French Revolution. The rest of the royal gardens were dug up and planted with even more potatoes.

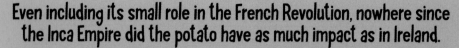

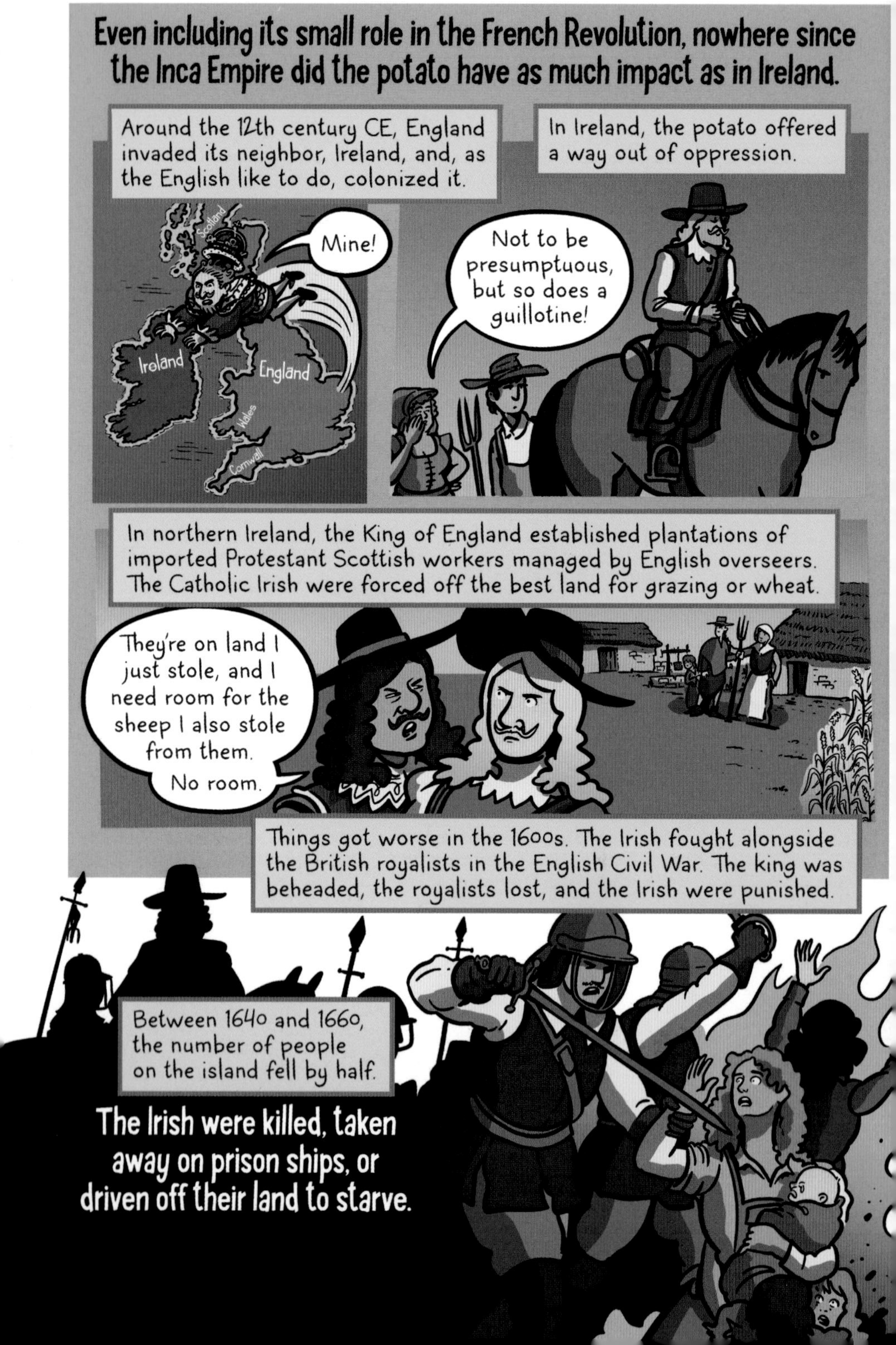

Even including its small role in the French Revolution, nowhere since the Inca Empire did the potato have as much impact as in Ireland.
Around the 12th century CE, England invaded its neighbor, Ireland, and, as the English like to do, colonized it.
Scotland
Mine!
Ireland
England
Wales
Cornwall
In Ireland, the potato offered a way out of oppression.
Not to be presumptuous, but so does a guillotine!
In northern Ireland, the King of England established plantations of imported Protestant Scottish workers managed by English overseers. The Catholic Irish were forced off the best land for grazing or wheat.
They're on land I just stole, and I need room for the sheep I also stole from them.
No room.
Things got worse in the 1600s. The Irish fought alongside the British royalists in the English Civil War. The king was beheaded, the royalists lost, and the Irish were punished.
Between 1640 and 1660, the number of people on the island fell by half.
The Irish were killed, taken away on prison ships, or driven off their land to starve.

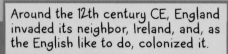

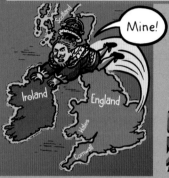

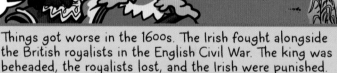

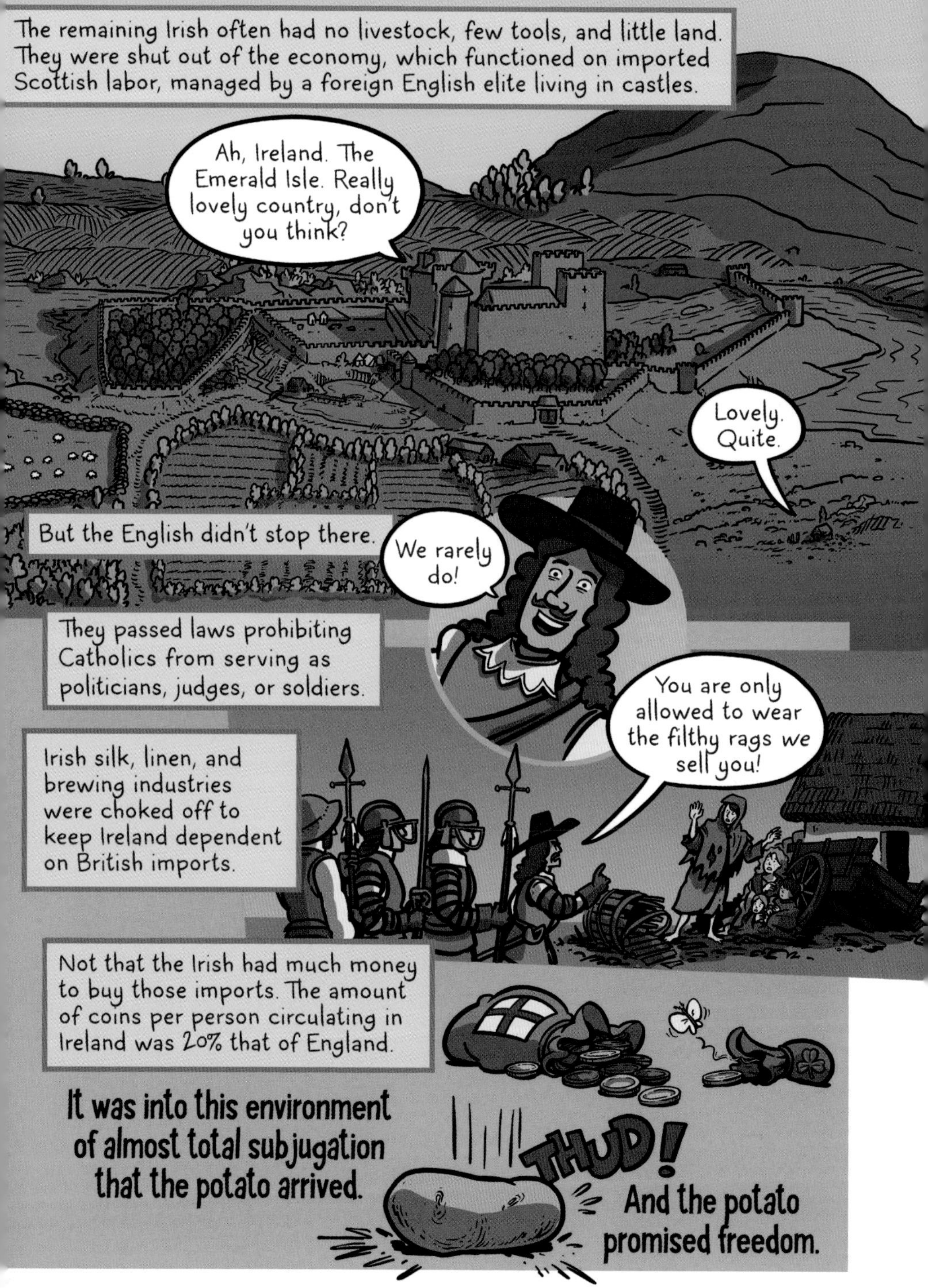

The remaining Irish often had no livestock, few tools, and little land. They were shut out of the economy, which functioned on imported Scottish labor, managed by a foreign English elite living in castles.
Ah, Ireland. The Emerald Isle. Really lovely country, don't you think?
Lovely. Quite.
But the English didn't stop there.
We rarely do!
They passed laws prohibiting Catholics from serving as politicians, judges, or soldiers.
You are only allowed to wear the filthy rags we sell you!
Irish silk, linen, and brewing industries were choked off to keep Ireland dependent on British imports.
Not that the Irish had much money to buy those imports. The amount of coins per person circulating in Ireland was 20% that of England.
It was into this environment of almost total subjugation that the potato arrived.
THUD!
And the potato promised freedom.

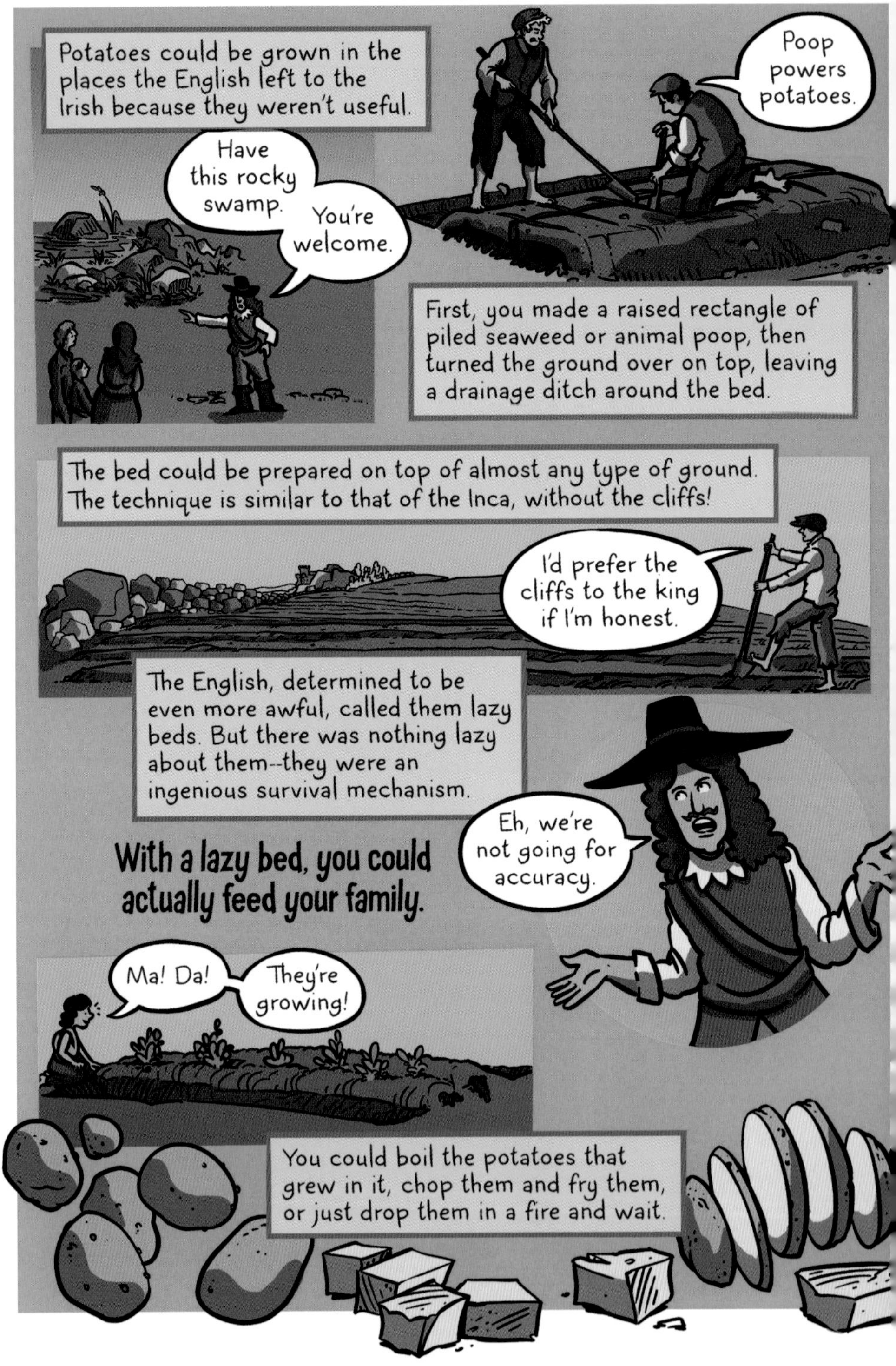
Potatoes could be grown in the places the English left to the Irish because they weren't useful.
Have this rocky swamp.
You're welcome.
Poop powers potatoes.
First, you made a raised rectangle of piled seaweed or animal poop, then turned the ground over on top, leaving a drainage ditch around the bed.
The bed could be prepared on top of almost any type of ground. The technique is similar to that of the Inca, without the cliffs!
I'd prefer the cliffs to the king if I'm honest.
The English, determined to be even more awful, called them lazy beds. But there was nothing lazy about them--they were an ingenious survival mechanism.
With a lazy bed, you could actually feed your family.
Eh, we're not going for accuracy.
Ma! Da!
They're growing!
You could boil the potatoes that grew in it, chop them and fry them, or just drop them in a fire and wait.

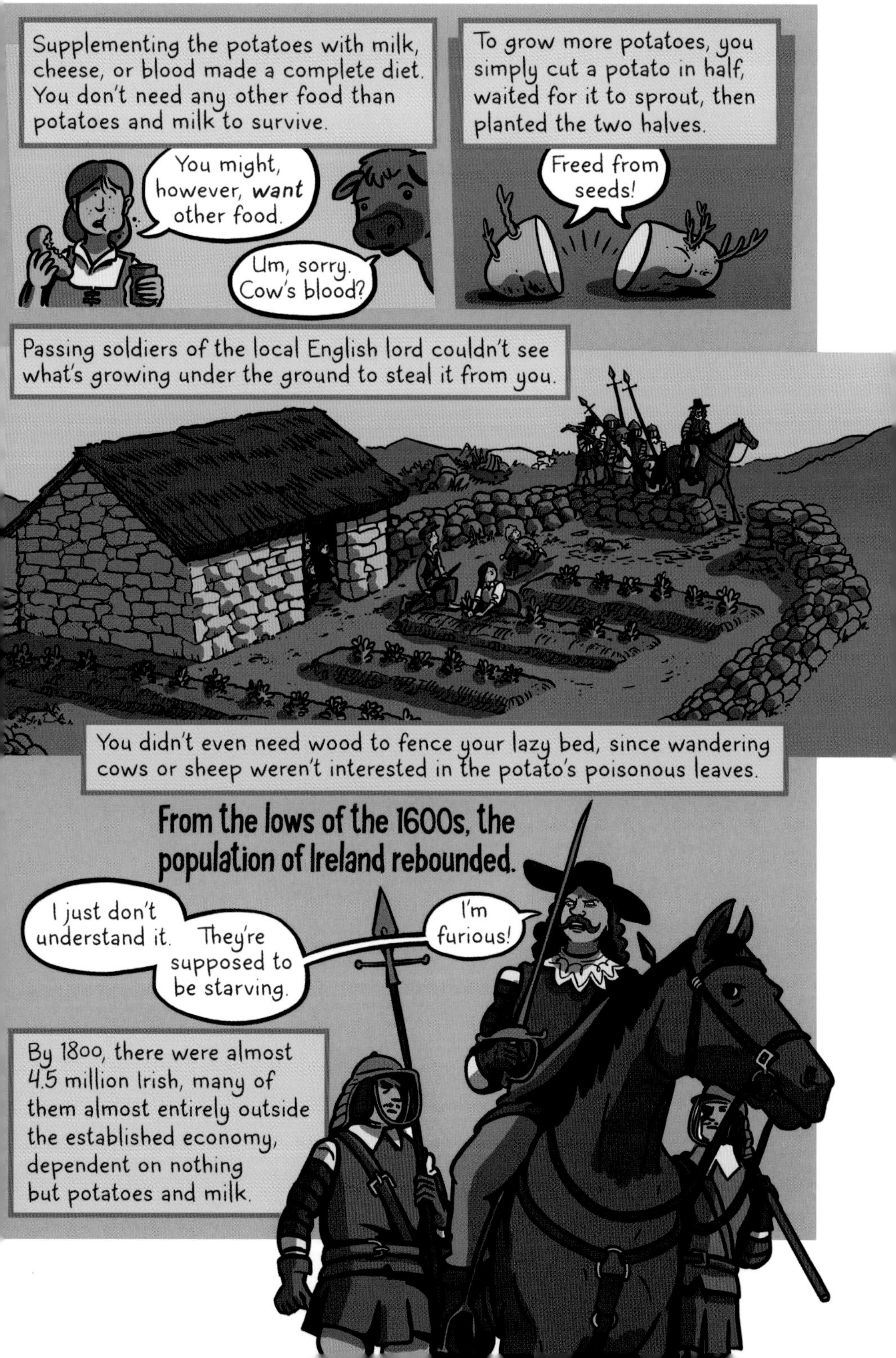

Supplementing the potatoes with milk, cheese, or blood made a complete diet. You don't need any other food than potatoes and milk to survive.
You might, however, **want** other food.
Um, sorry. Cow's blood?
To grow more potatoes, you simply cut a potato in half, waited for it to sprout, then planted the two halves.
Freed from seeds!
Passing soldiers of the local English lord couldn't see what's growing under the ground to steal it from you.
You didn't even need wood to fence your lazy bed, since wandering cows or sheep weren't interested in the potato's poisonous leaves.
From the lows of the 1600s, the population of Ireland rebounded.
I just don't understand it. They're supposed to be starving.
I'm furious!
By 1800, there were almost 4.5 million Irish, many of them almost entirely outside the established economy, dependent on nothing but potatoes and milk.

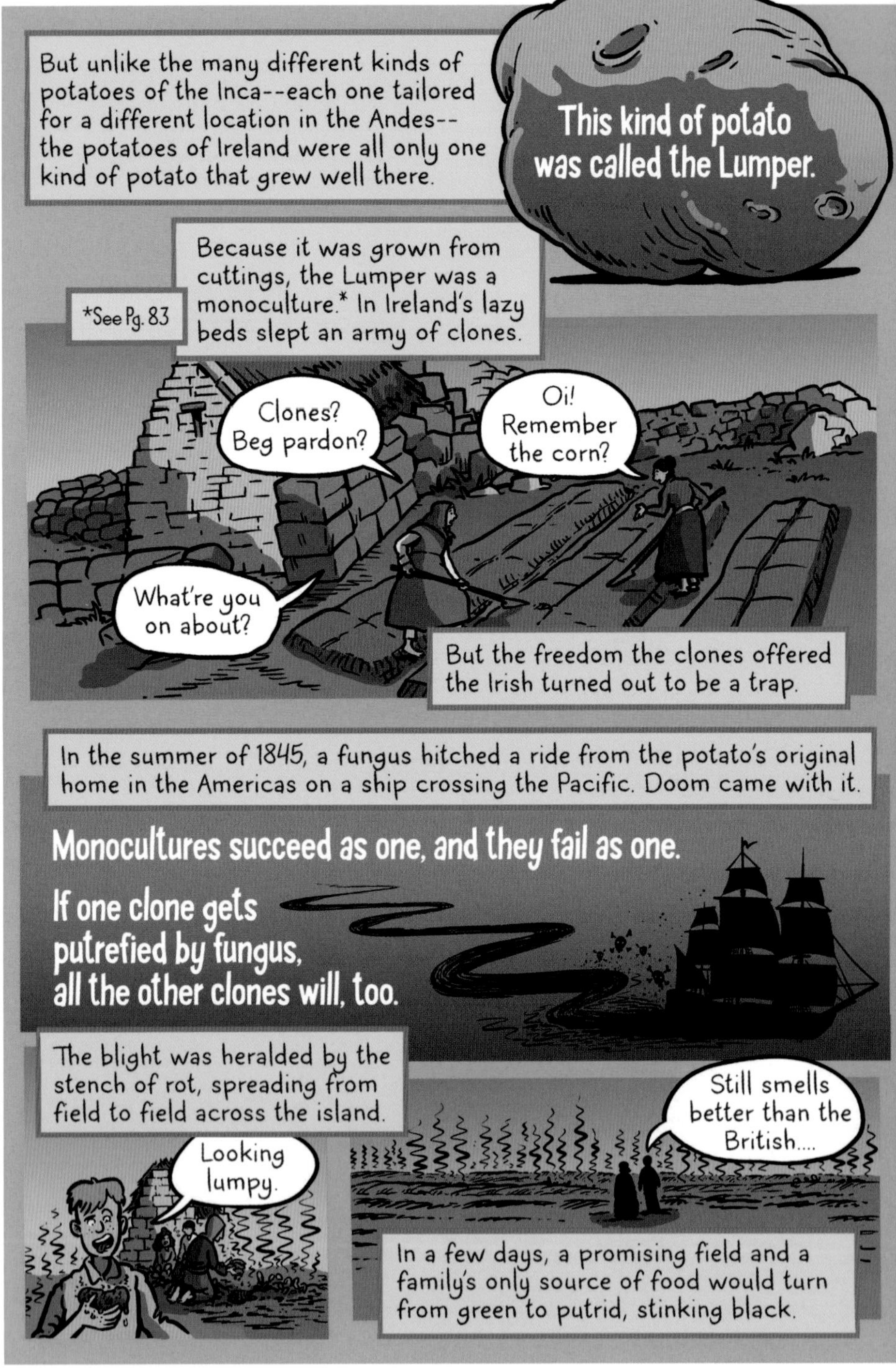

But unlike the many different kinds of potatoes of the Inca--each one tailored for a different location in the Andes--the potatoes of Ireland were all only one kind of potato that grew well there.
This kind of potato was called the Lumper.
Because it was grown from cuttings, the Lumper was a monoculture.* In Ireland's lazy beds slept an army of clones.
*See Pg. 83
Clones? Beg pardon?
Oi! Remember the corn?
What're you on about?
But the freedom the clones offered the Irish turned out to be a trap.
In the summer of 1845, a fungus hitched a ride from the potato's original home in the Americas on a ship crossing the Pacific. Doom came with it.
Monocultures succeed as one, and they fail as one.
If one clone gets putrefied by fungus, all the other clones will, too.
The blight was heralded by the stench of rot, spreading from field to field across the island.
Looking lumpy.
Still smells better than the British....
In a few days, a promising field and a family's only source of food would turn from green to putrid, stinking black.

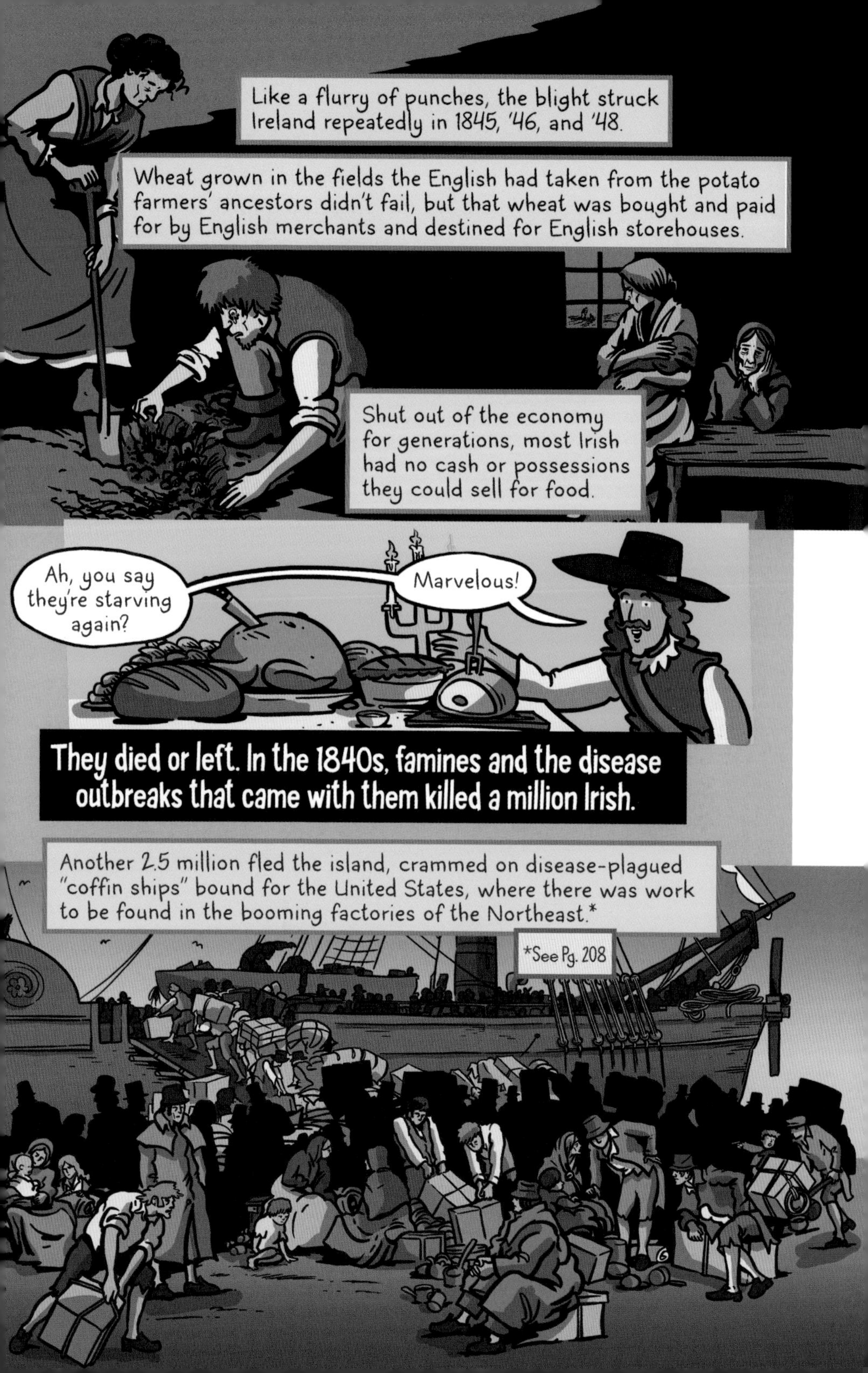
Like a flurry of punches, the blight struck Ireland repeatedly in 1845, '46, and '48.
Wheat grown in the fields the English had taken from the potato farmers' ancestors didn't fail, but that wheat was bought and paid for by English merchants and destined for English storehouses.
Shut out of the economy for generations, most Irish had no cash or possessions they could sell for food.
Ah, you say they're starving again?
Marvelous!
They died or left. In the 1840s, famines and the disease outbreaks that came with them killed a million Irish.
Another 2.5 million fled the island, crammed on disease-plagued "coffin ships" bound for the United States, where there was work to be found in the booming factories of the Northeast.*
*See Pg. 208

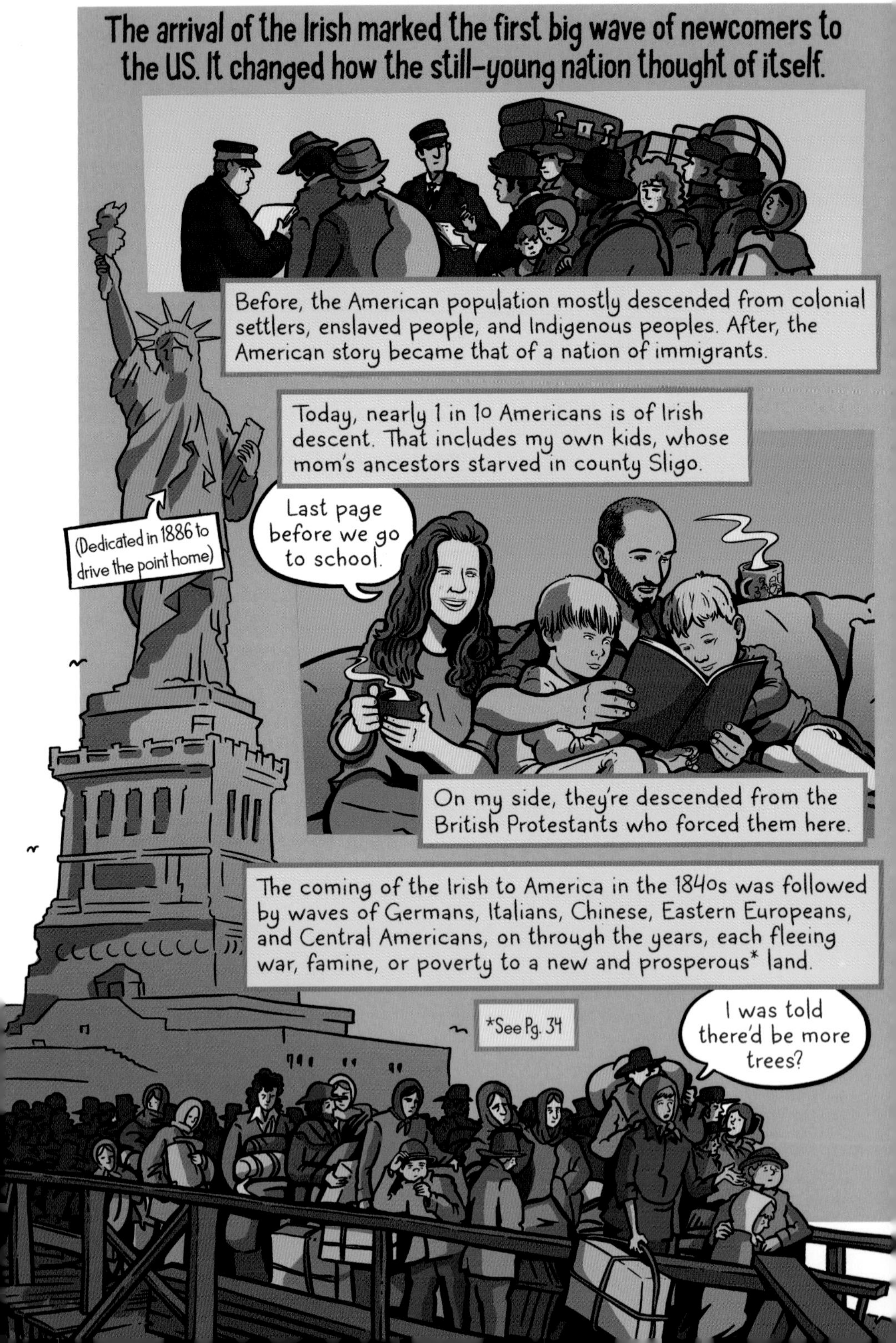
The arrival of the Irish marked the first big wave of newcomers to the US. It changed how the still-young nation thought of itself.
Before, the American population mostly descended from colonial settlers, enslaved people, and Indigenous peoples. After, the American story became that of a nation of immigrants.
Today, nearly 1 in 10 Americans is of Irish descent. That includes my own kids, whose mom's ancestors starved in county Sligo.
(Dedicated in 1886 to drive the point home)
Last page before we go to school.
On my side, they're descended from the British Protestants who forced them here.
The coming of the Irish to America in the 1840s was followed by waves of Germans, Italians, Chinese, Eastern Europeans, and Central Americans, on through the years, each fleeing war, famine, or poverty to a new and prosperous* land.
*See Pg. 34
I was told there'd be more trees?

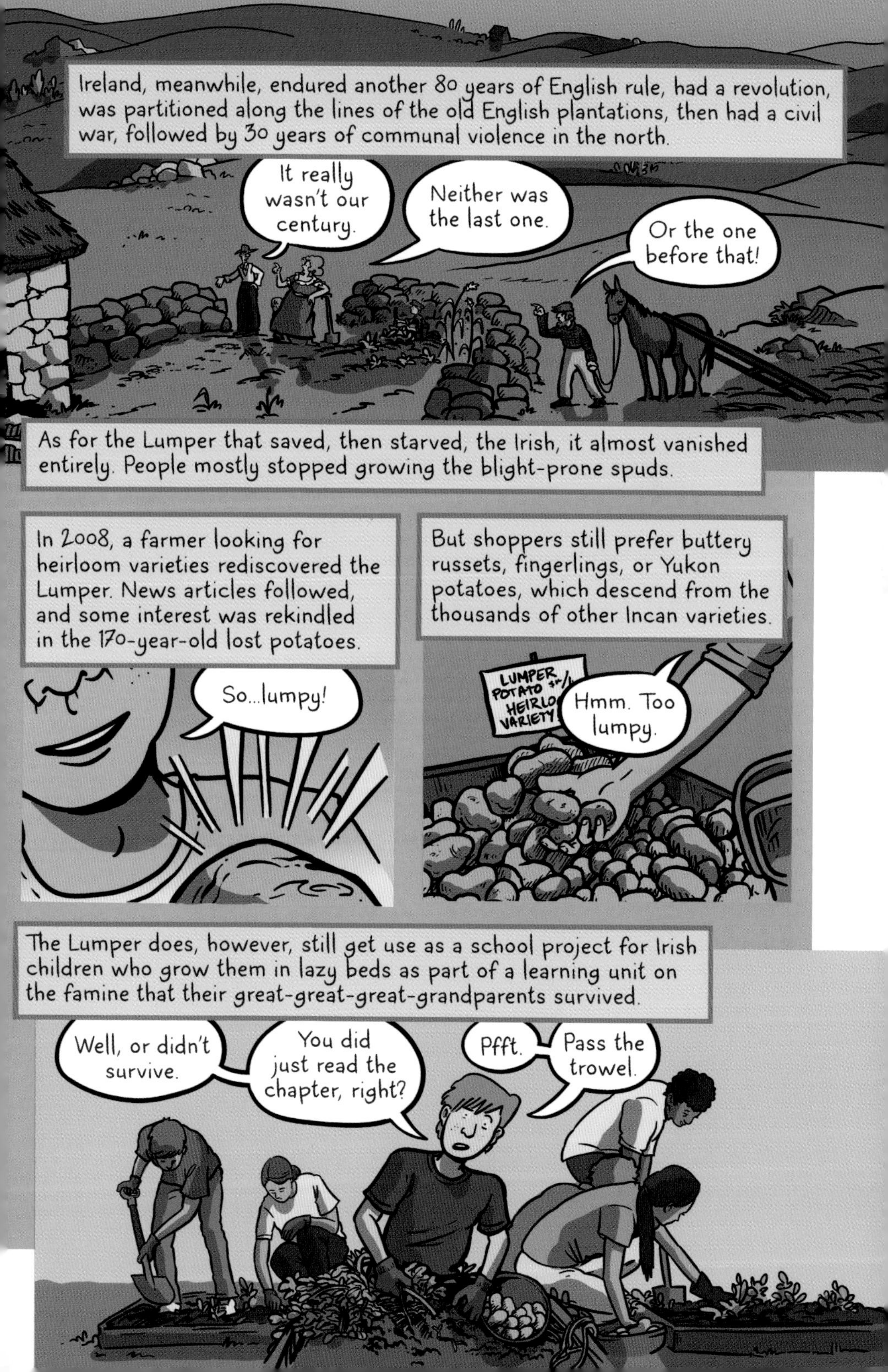
Ireland, meanwhile, endured another 80 years of English rule, had a revolution, was partitioned along the lines of the old English plantations, then had a civil war, followed by 30 years of communal violence in the north.
It really wasn't our century.
Neither was the last one.
Or the one before that!
As for the Lumper that saved, then starved, the Irish, it almost vanished entirely. People mostly stopped growing the blight-prone spuds.
In 2008, a farmer looking for heirloom varieties rediscovered the Lumper. News articles followed, and some interest was rekindled in the 170-year-old lost potatoes.
So...lumpy!
But shoppers still prefer buttery russets, fingerlings, or Yukon potatoes, which descend from the thousands of other Incan varieties.
LUMPER POTATO
Hmm. Too lumpy.
The Lumper does, however, still get use as a school project for Irish children who grow them in lazy beds as part of a learning unit on the famine that their great-great-great-grandparents survived.
Well, or didn't survive.
You did just read the chapter, right?
Pfft.
Pass the trowel.

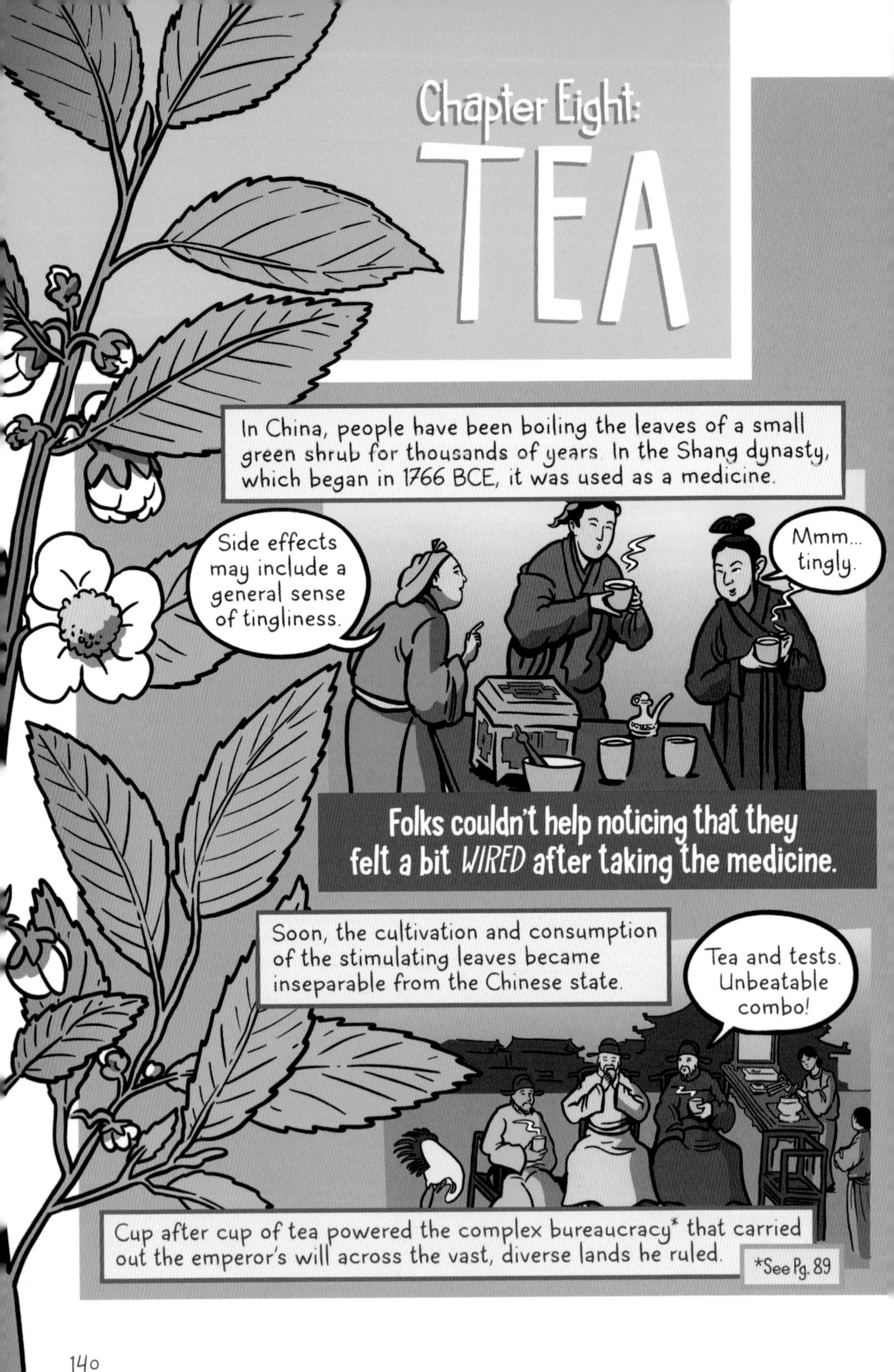

Chapter Eight:
TEA
In China, people have been boiling the leaves of a small green shrub for thousands of years. In the Shang dynasty, which began in 1766 BCE, it was used as a medicine.
Side effects may include a general sense of tingliness.
Mmm... tingly.
Folks couldn't help noticing that they felt a bit WIRED after taking the medicine.
Soon, the cultivation and consumption of the stimulating leaves became inseparable from the Chinese state.
Tea and tests. Unbeatable combo!
Cup after cup of tea powered the complex bureaucracy* that carried out the emperor's will across the vast, diverse lands he ruled.
*See Pg. 89

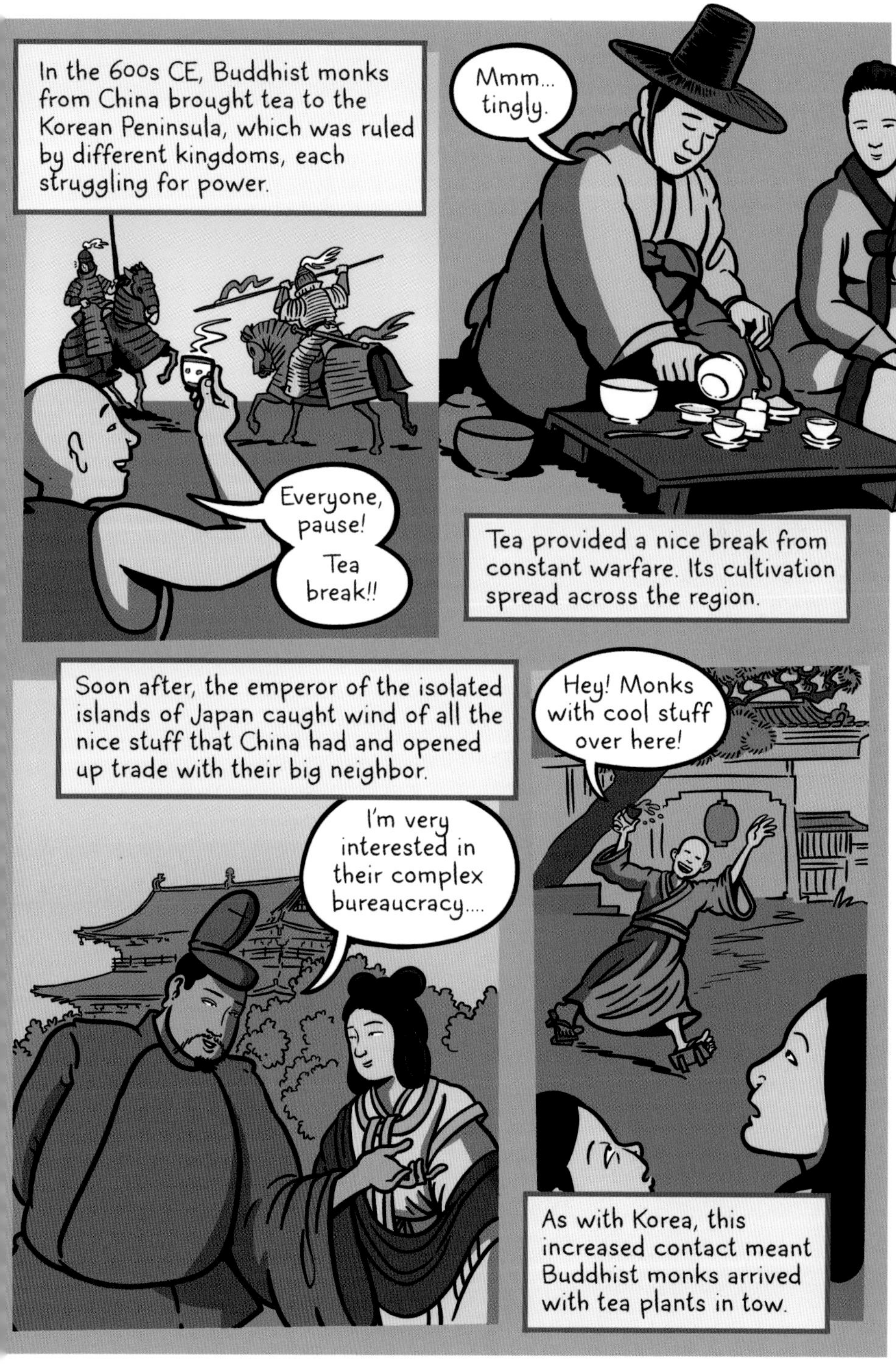
In the 600s CE, Buddhist monks from China brought tea to the Korean Peninsula, which was ruled by different kingdoms, each struggling for power.
Everyone, pause!
Tea break!!
Mmm... tingly.
Tea provided a nice break from constant warfare. Its cultivation spread across the region.
Soon after, the emperor of the isolated islands of Japan caught wind of all the nice stuff that China had and opened up trade with their big neighbor.
I'm very interested in their complex bureaucracy....
Hey! Monks with cool stuff over here!
As with Korea, this increased contact meant Buddhist monks arrived with tea plants in tow.

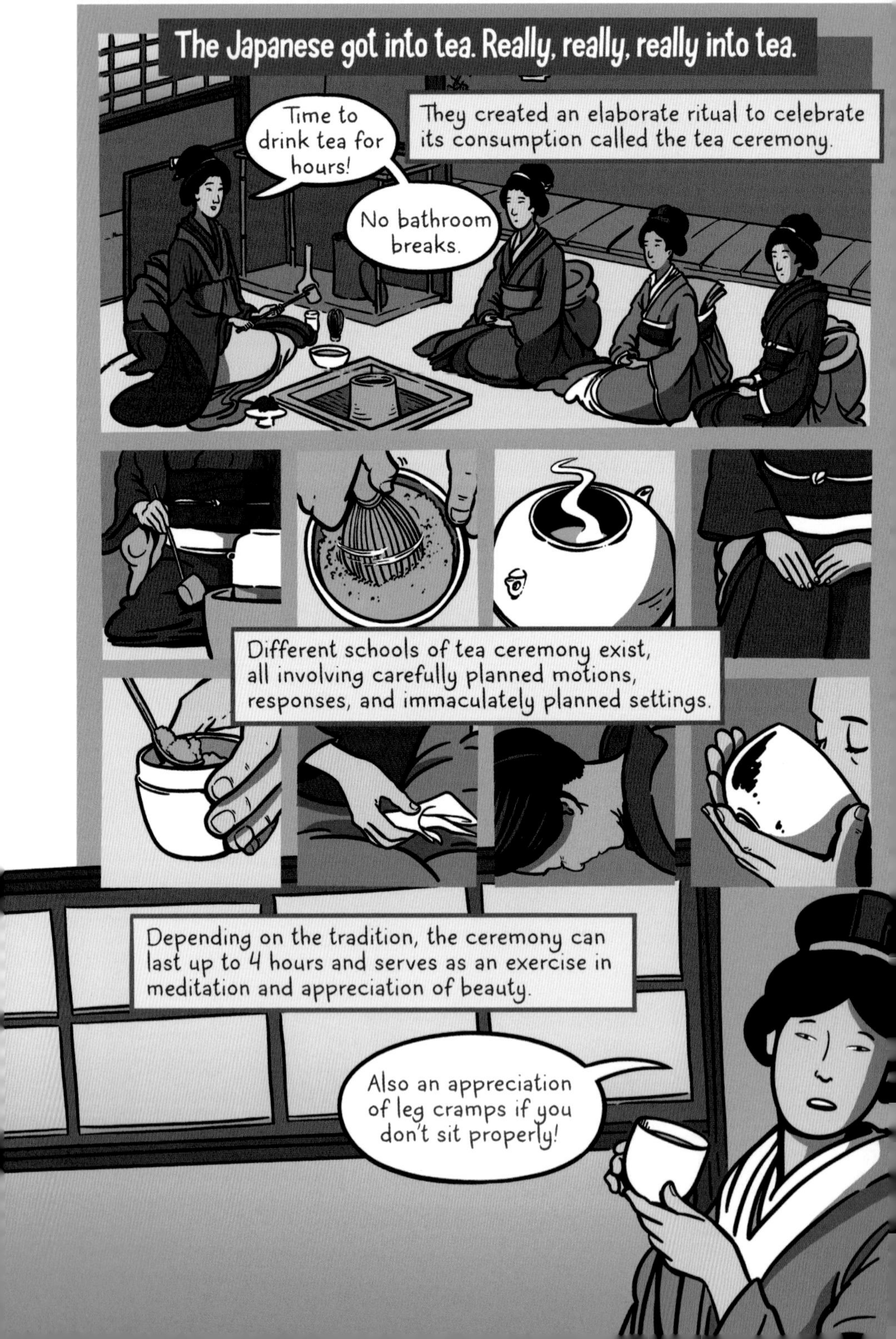
The Japanese got into tea. Really, really, really into tea.
Time to drink tea for hours!
They created an elaborate ritual to celebrate its consumption called the tea ceremony.
No bathroom breaks.
Different schools of tea ceremony exist, all involving carefully planned motions, responses, and immaculately planned settings.
Depending on the tradition, the ceremony can last up to 4 hours and serves as an exercise in meditation and appreciation of beauty.
Also an appreciation of leg cramps if you don't sit properly!

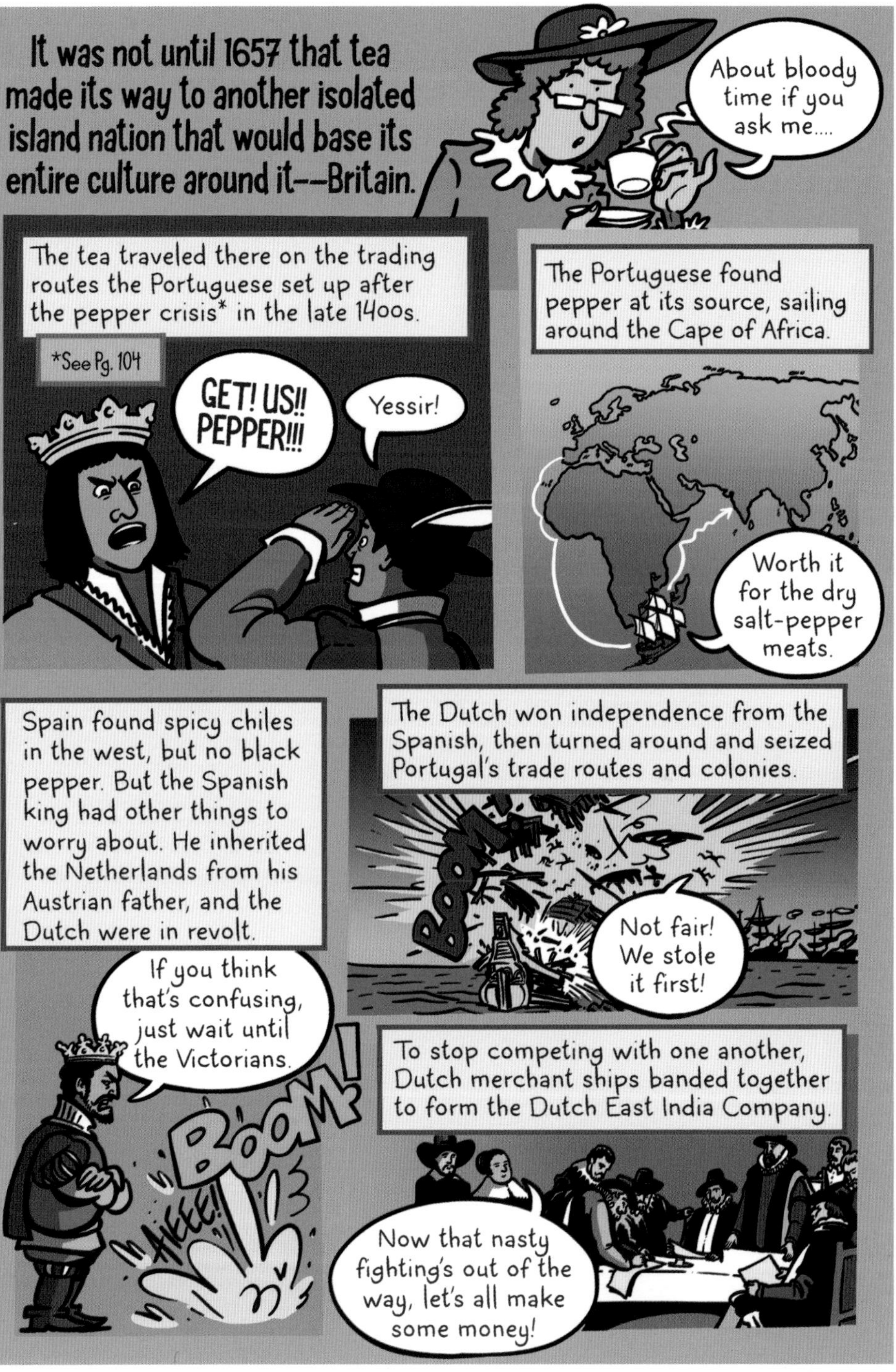
It was not until 1657 that tea made its way to another isolated island nation that would base its entire culture around it--Britain.
About bloody time if you ask me....
The tea traveled there on the trading routes the Portuguese set up after the pepper crisis* in the late 1400s.
*See Pg. 104
GET! US!! PEPPER!!!
Yessir!
The Portuguese found pepper at its source, sailing around the Cape of Africa.
Worth it for the dry salt-pepper meats.
Spain found spicy chiles in the west, but no black pepper. But the Spanish king had other things to worry about. He inherited the Netherlands from his Austrian father, and the Dutch were in revolt.
If you think that's confusing, just wait until the Victorians.
BOOM!
AIEEE!
The Dutch won independence from the Spanish, then turned around and seized Portugal's trade routes and colonies.
BOOM
Not fair! We stole it first!
To stop competing with one another, Dutch merchant ships banded together to form the Dutch East India Company.
Now that nasty fighting's out of the way, let's all make some money!

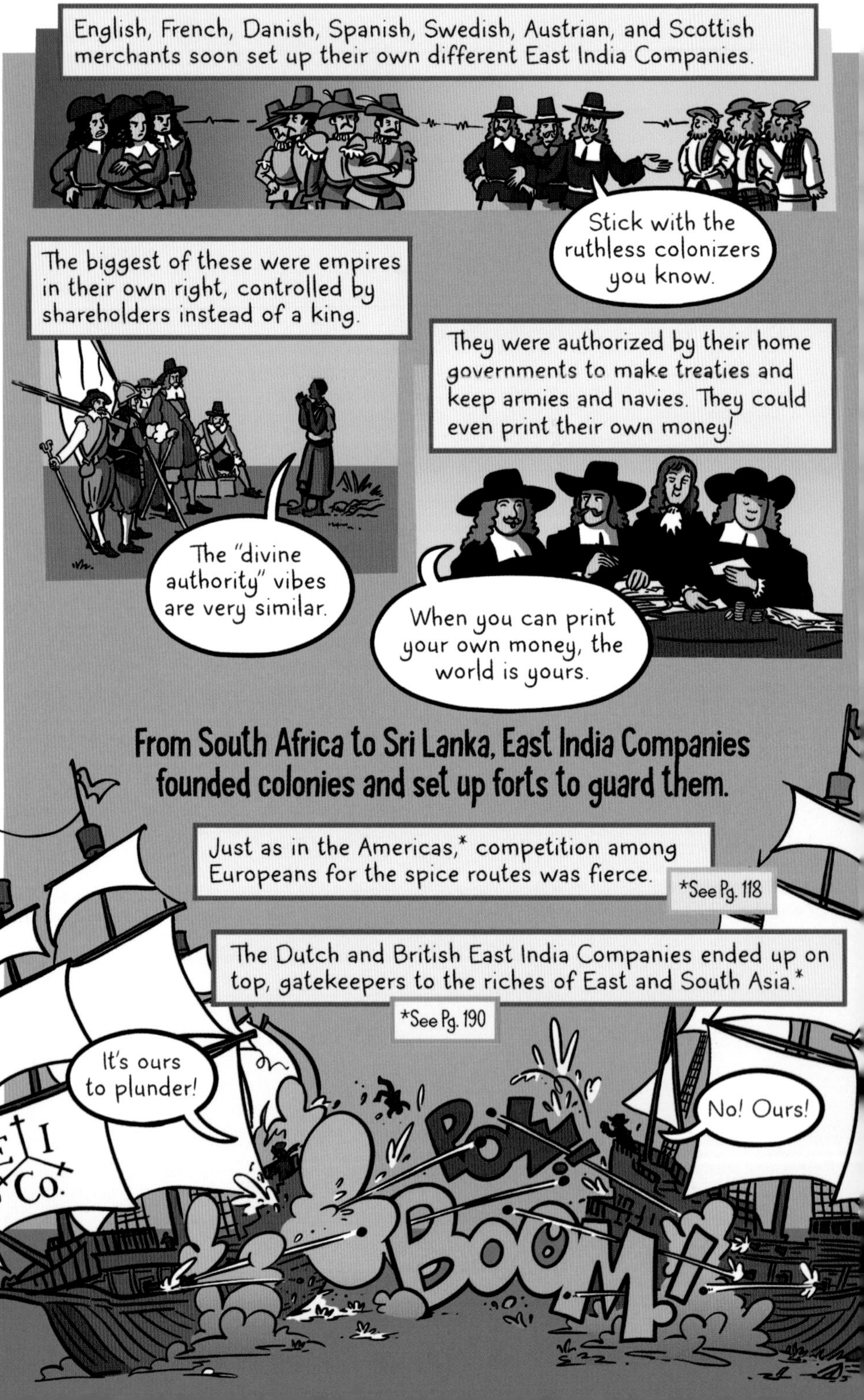
English, French, Danish, Spanish, Swedish, Austrian, and Scottish merchants soon set up their own different East India Companies.
Stick with the ruthless colonizers you know.
The biggest of these were empires in their own right, controlled by shareholders instead of a king.
The "divine authority" vibes are very similar.
They were authorized by their home governments to make treaties and keep armies and navies. They could even print their own money!
When you can print your own money, the world is yours.
From South Africa to Sri Lanka, East India Companies founded colonies and set up forts to guard them.
Just as in the Americas,* competition among Europeans for the spice routes was fierce.
*See Pg. 118
The Dutch and British East India Companies ended up on top, gatekeepers to the riches of East and South Asia.*
*See Pg. 190
It's ours to plunder!
E I Co.
POW
BOOM!
No! Ours!

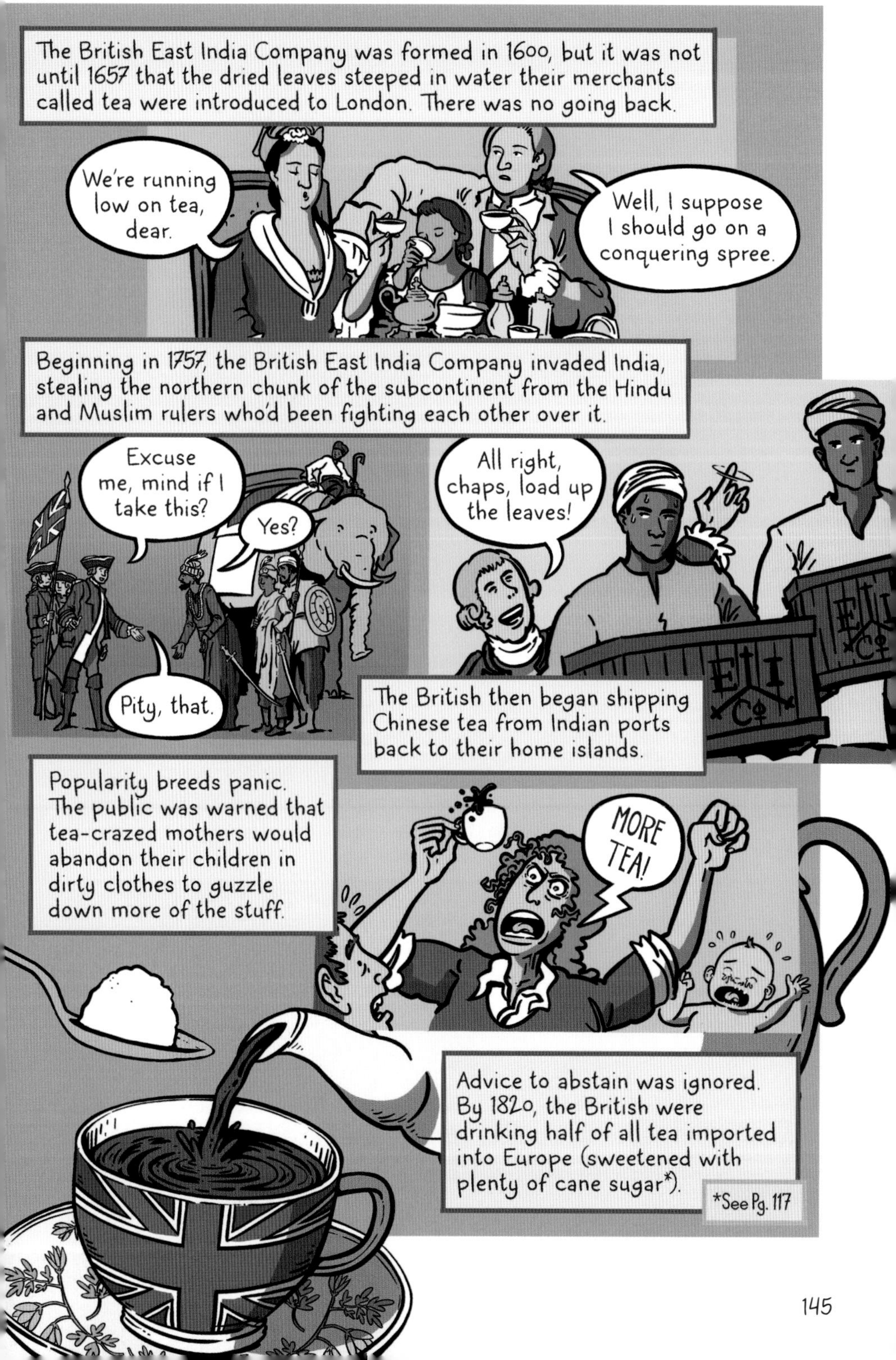
The British East India Company was formed in 1600, but it was not until 1657 that the dried leaves steeped in water their merchants called tea were introduced to London. There was no going back.
We're running low on tea, dear.
Well, I suppose I should go on a conquering spree.
Beginning in 1757, the British East India Company invaded India, stealing the northern chunk of the subcontinent from the Hindu and Muslim rulers who'd been fighting each other over it.
Excuse me, mind if I take this?
Yes?
Pity, that.
All right, chaps, load up the leaves!
E I I C°
The British then began shipping Chinese tea from Indian ports back to their home islands.
Popularity breeds panic. The public was warned that tea-crazed mothers would abandon their children in dirty clothes to guzzle down more of the stuff.
MORE TEA!
Advice to abstain was ignored. By 1820, the British were drinking half of all tea imported into Europe (sweetened with plenty of cane sugar*).
*See Pg. 117

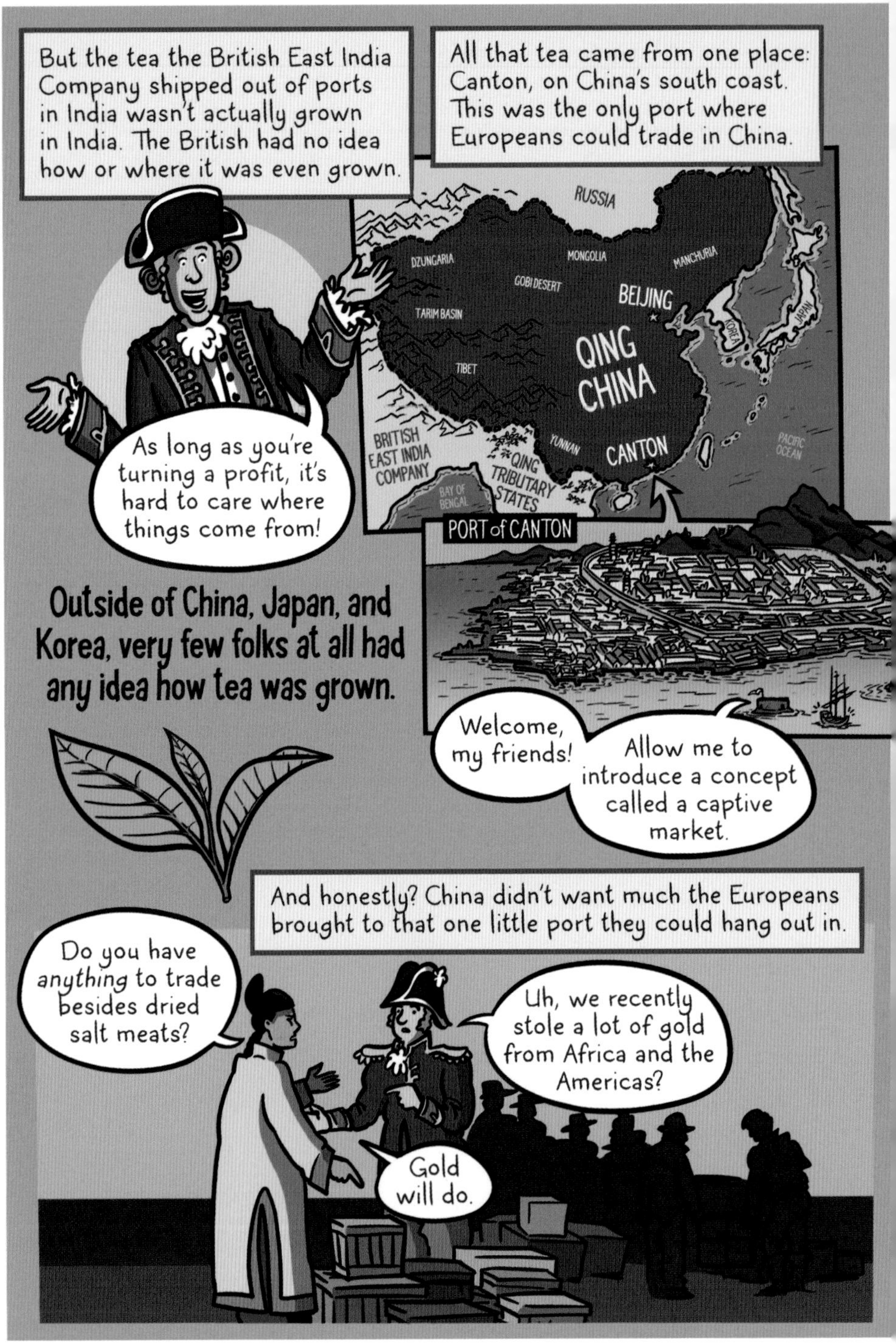

But the tea the British East India Company shipped out of ports in India wasn't actually grown in India. The British had no idea how or where it was even grown.
All that tea came from one place: Canton, on China's south coast. This was the only port where Europeans could trade in China.
RUSSIA
DZUNGARIA
MONGOLIA
MANCHURIA
GOBI DESERT
BEIJING
TARIM BASIN
KOREA
JAPAN
QING CHINA
TIBET
YUNNAN
CANTON
PACIFIC OCEAN
BRITISH EAST INDIA COMPANY
QING TRIBUTARY STATES
BAY OF BENGAL
As long as you're turning a profit, it's hard to care where things come from!
PORT of CANTON
Outside of China, Japan, and Korea, very few folks at all had any idea how tea was grown.
Welcome, my friends!
Allow me to introduce a concept called a captive market.
And honestly? China didn't want much the Europeans brought to that one little port they could hang out in.
Do you have anything to trade besides dried salt meats?
Uh, we recently stole a lot of gold from Africa and the Americas?
Gold will do.

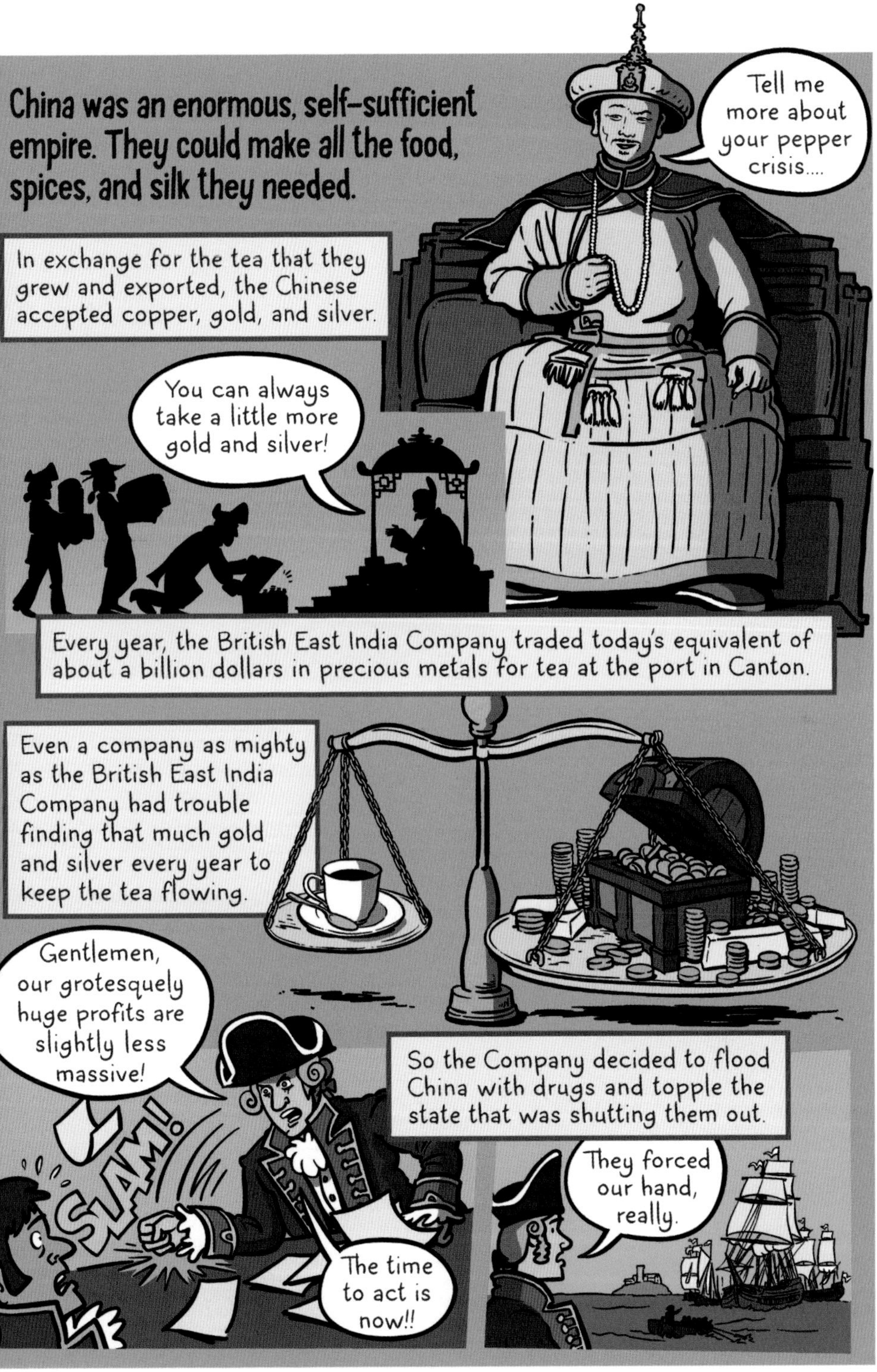
China was an enormous, self-sufficient empire. They could make all the food, spices, and silk they needed.
Tell me more about your pepper crisis....
In exchange for the tea that they grew and exported, the Chinese accepted copper, gold, and silver.
You can always take a little more gold and silver!
Every year, the British East India Company traded today's equivalent of about a billion dollars in precious metals for tea at the port in Canton.
Even a company as mighty as the British East India Company had trouble finding that much gold and silver every year to keep the tea flowing.
Gentlemen, our grotesquely huge profits are slightly less massive!
SLAM!
The time to act is now!!
So the Company decided to flood China with drugs and topple the state that was shutting them out.
They forced our hand, really.

The drug the British used to tip the tea balance was opium, which is made from flowers. Poppies to be precise, first grown in ancient times in the valleys of the Hindu Kush and widely used across Asia.

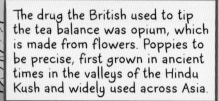

Opium dulls pain, makes you feel blissful, and is very, very addictive.

Opium had been used in China as a medicine for a long time. It became trendy to smoke it at court, and in 1729, the emperor banned the stuff.

As it happened, the chunk of India the British East India Company conquered a few pages ago was where most of the world's opium was grown and processed.

Very stinky.

Did you know that banning something almost always increases its value?

CHINA

DO NOT ENTER!

BANG

With a near monopoly on drug production, the British East India Company scaled up operations.

The Company's smugglers ran the opium into China and hooked the empire. Nearly a million people in India made opium for China, directed from company headquarters in London.

The first rule of setting up a drug-running operation in order to topple a state that won't trade with you is, don't slip.

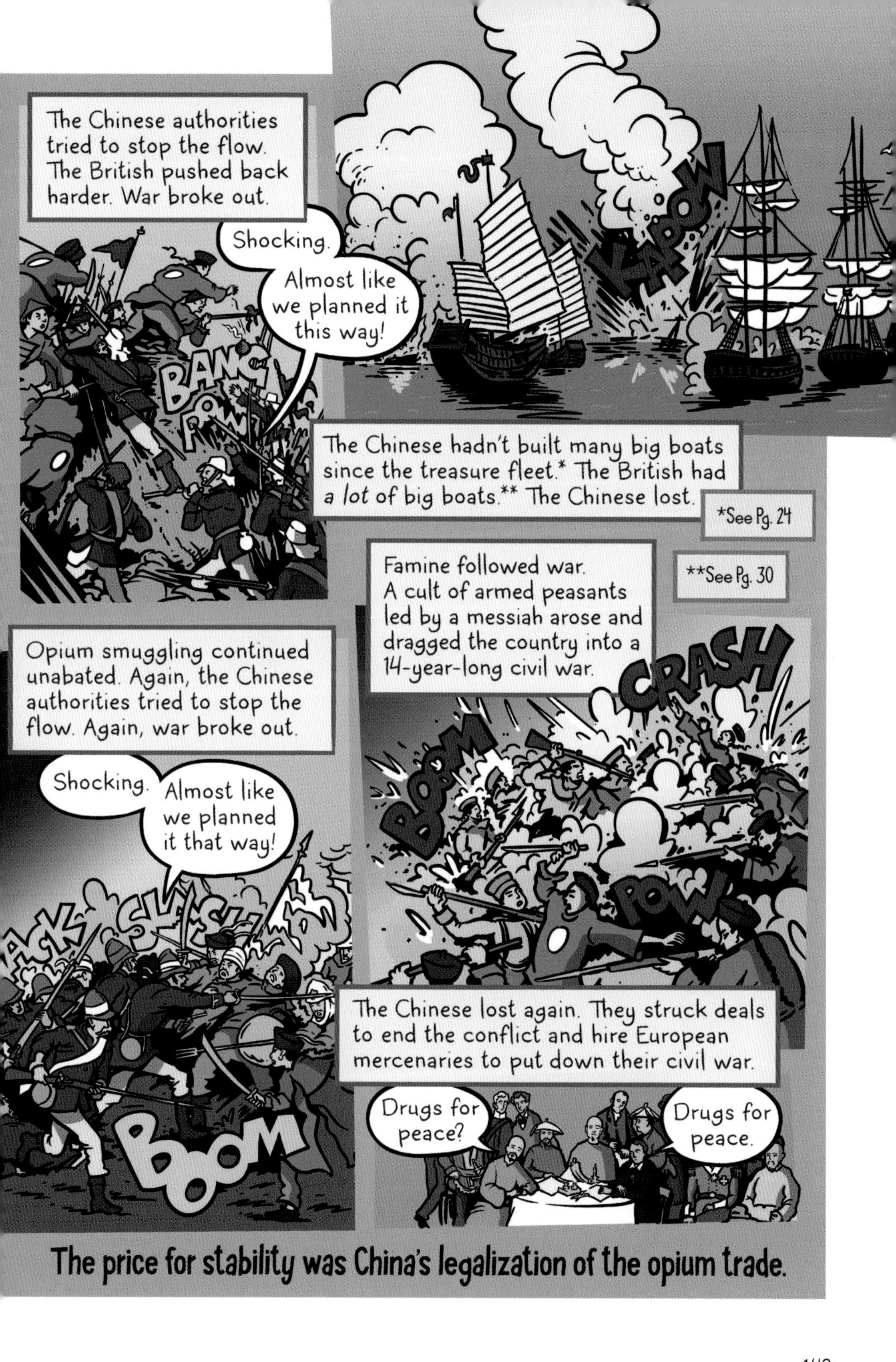

The Chinese authorities tried to stop the flow. The British pushed back harder. War broke out.
Shocking.
Almost like we planned it this way!
KAPOW
BANG
POW
The Chinese hadn't built many big boats since the treasure fleet.* The British had a *lot* of big boats.** The Chinese lost.
*See Pg. 24
**See Pg. 30
Famine followed war. A cult of armed peasants led by a messiah arose and dragged the country into a 14-year-long civil war.
CRASH
BOOM
POW
Opium smuggling continued unabated. Again, the Chinese authorities tried to stop the flow. Again, war broke out.
Shocking.
Almost like we planned it that way!
BOOM
The Chinese lost again. They struck deals to end the conflict and hire European mercenaries to put down their civil war.
Drugs for peace?
Drugs for peace.
The price for stability was China's legalization of the opium trade.

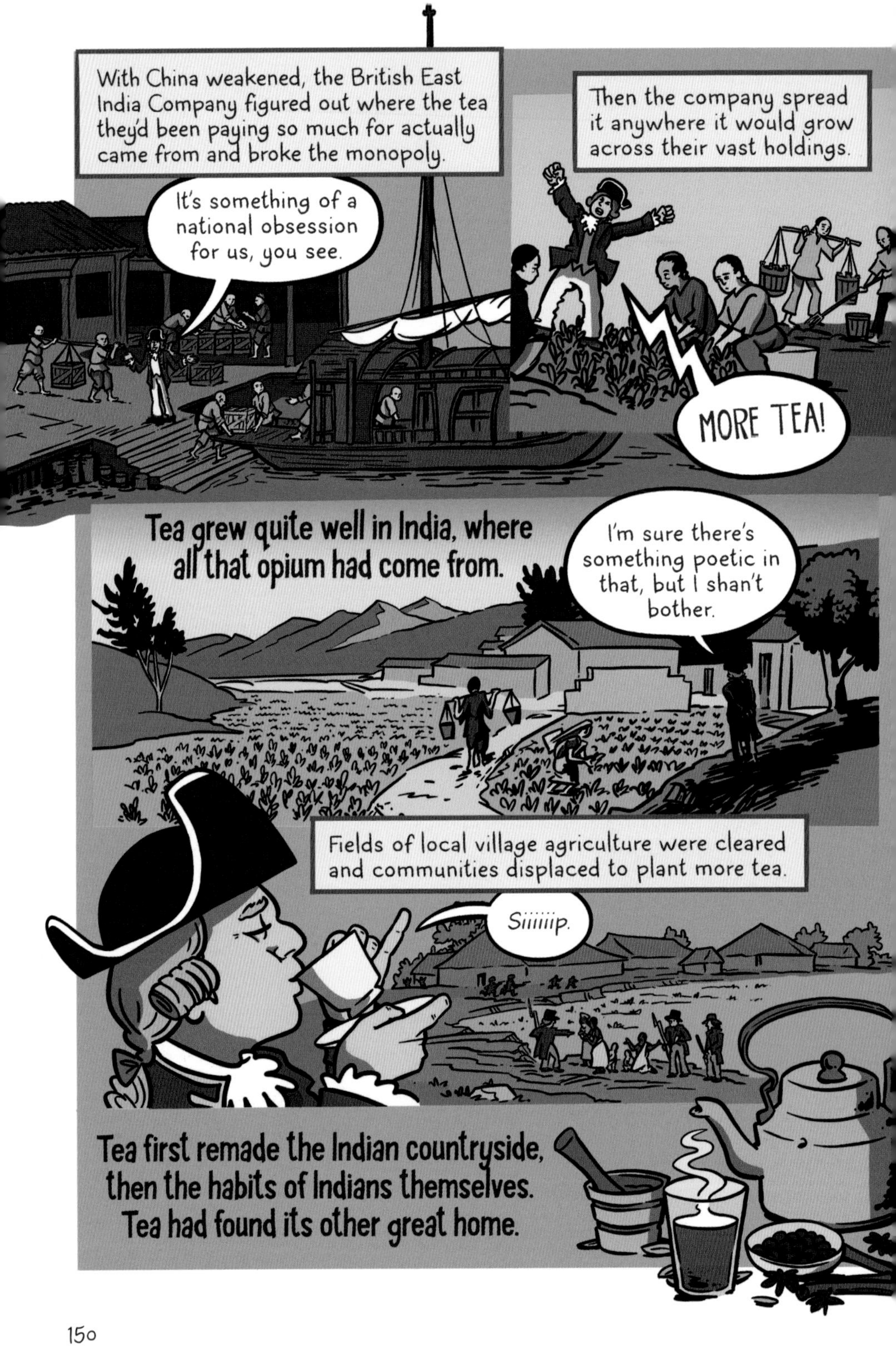
With China weakened, the British East India Company figured out where the tea they'd been paying so much for actually came from and broke the monopoly.
It's something of a national obsession for us, you see.
Then the company spread it anywhere it would grow across their vast holdings.
MORE TEA!
Tea grew quite well in India, where all that opium had come from.
I'm sure there's something poetic in that, but I shan't bother.
Fields of local village agriculture were cleared and communities displaced to plant more tea.
Siiiiiip.
Tea first remade the Indian countryside, then the habits of Indians themselves. Tea had found its other great home.

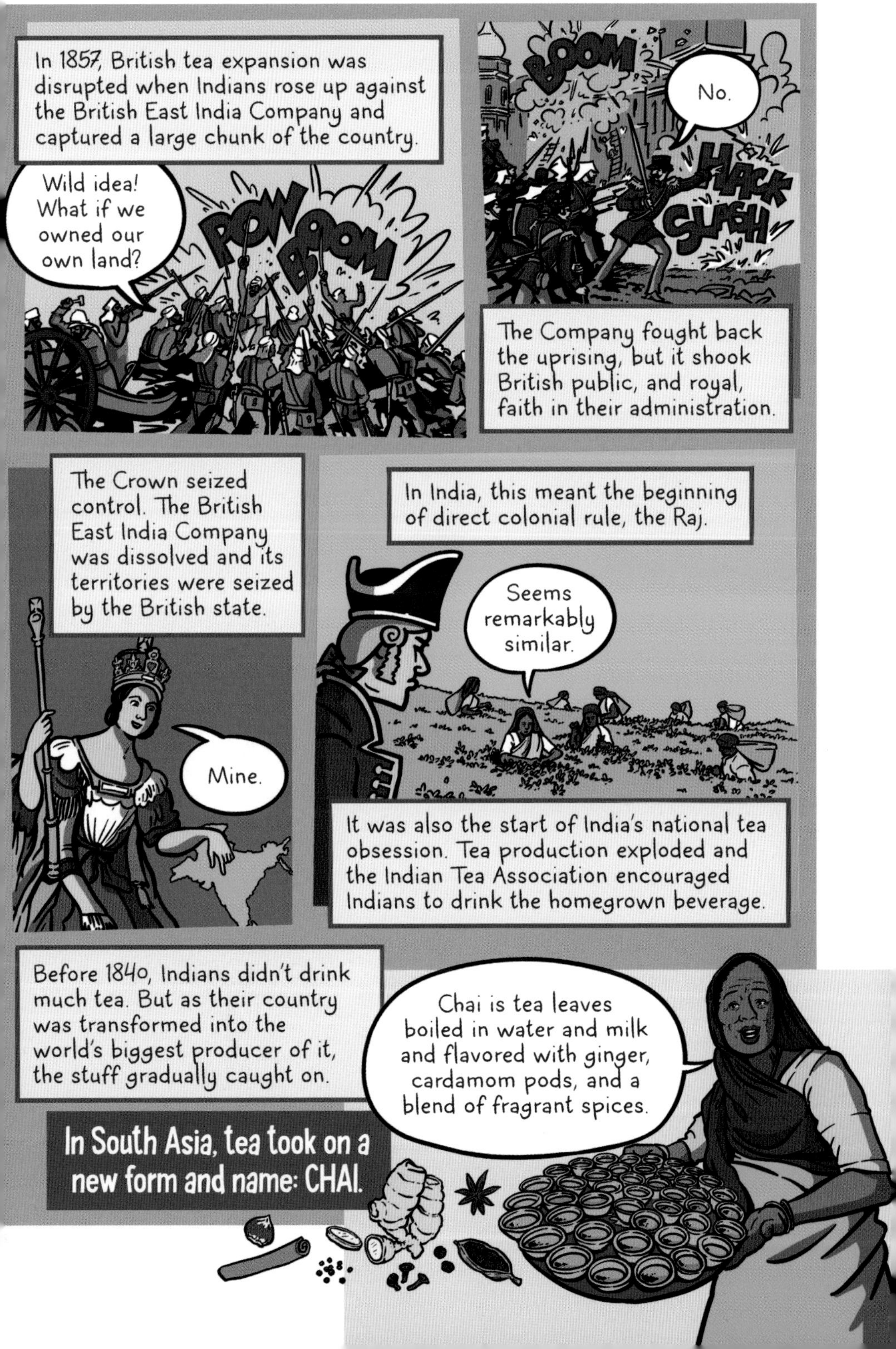
In 1857, British tea expansion was disrupted when Indians rose up against the British East India Company and captured a large chunk of the country.
Wild idea! What if we owned our own land?
POW
BOOM
BOOM
No.
HACK
SLASH
The Company fought back the uprising, but it shook British public, and royal, faith in their administration.
The Crown seized control. The British East India Company was dissolved and its territories were seized by the British state.
Mine.
In India, this meant the beginning of direct colonial rule, the Raj.
Seems remarkably similar.
It was also the start of India's national tea obsession. Tea production exploded and the Indian Tea Association encouraged Indians to drink the homegrown beverage.
Before 1840, Indians didn't drink much tea. But as their country was transformed into the world's biggest producer of it, the stuff gradually caught on.
Chai is tea leaves boiled in water and milk and flavored with ginger, cardamom pods, and a blend of fragrant spices.
In South Asia, tea took on a new form and name: CHAI.

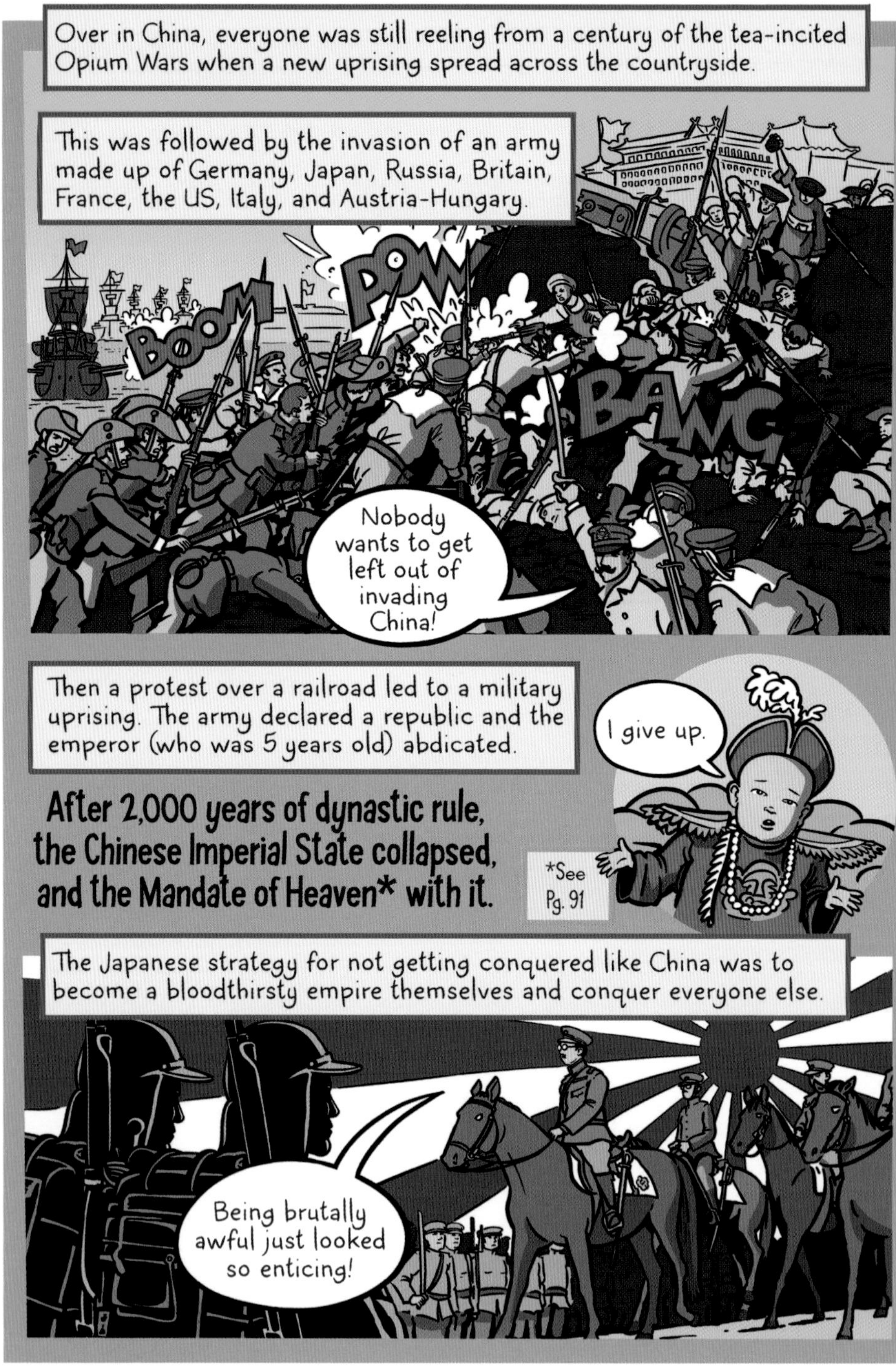
Over in China, everyone was still reeling from a century of the tea-incited Opium Wars when a new uprising spread across the countryside.
This was followed by the invasion of an army made up of Germany, Japan, Russia, Britain, France, the US, Italy, and Austria-Hungary.
BOOM
POW
BANG
Nobody wants to get left out of invading China!
Then a protest over a railroad led to a military uprising. The army declared a republic and the emperor (who was 5 years old) abdicated.
I give up.
After 2,000 years of dynastic rule, the Chinese Imperial State collapsed, and the Mandate of Heaven* with it.
*See Pg. 91
The Japanese strategy for not getting conquered like China was to become a bloodthirsty empire themselves and conquer everyone else.
Being brutally awful just looked so enticing!

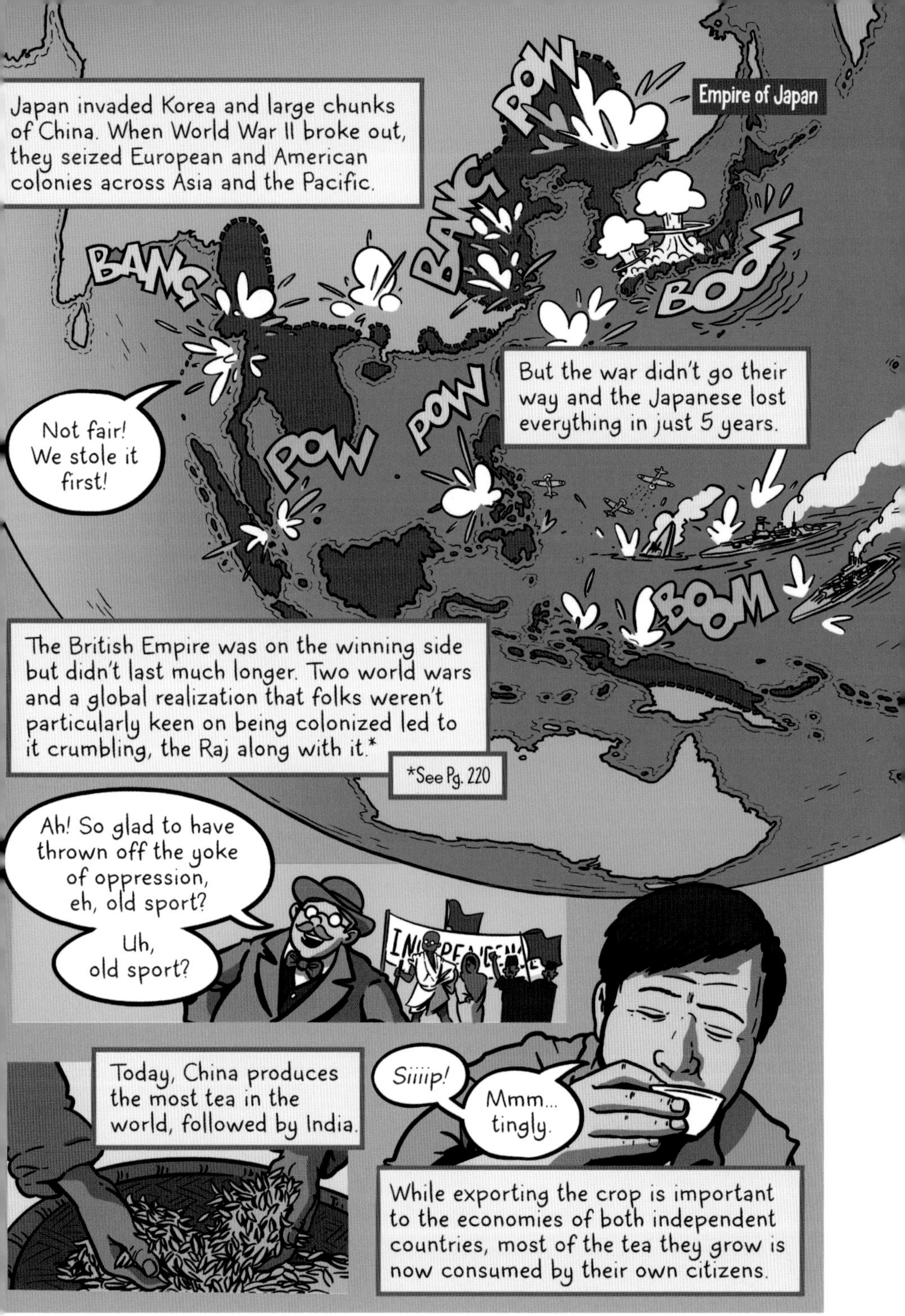
Japan invaded Korea and large chunks of China. When World War II broke out, they seized European and American colonies across Asia and the Pacific.
Empire of Japan
POW
BANG
BANG
BOOM
POW
POW
Not fair! We stole it first!
But the war didn't go their way and the Japanese lost everything in just 5 years.
BOOM
The British Empire was on the winning side but didn't last much longer. Two world wars and a global realization that folks weren't particularly keen on being colonized led to it crumbling, the Raj along with it.*
*See Pg. 220
Ah! So glad to have thrown off the yoke of oppression, eh, old sport?
Uh, old sport?
Today, China produces the most tea in the world, followed by India.
Siiiip!
Mmm... tingly.
While exporting the crop is important to the economies of both independent countries, most of the tea they grow is now consumed by their own citizens.

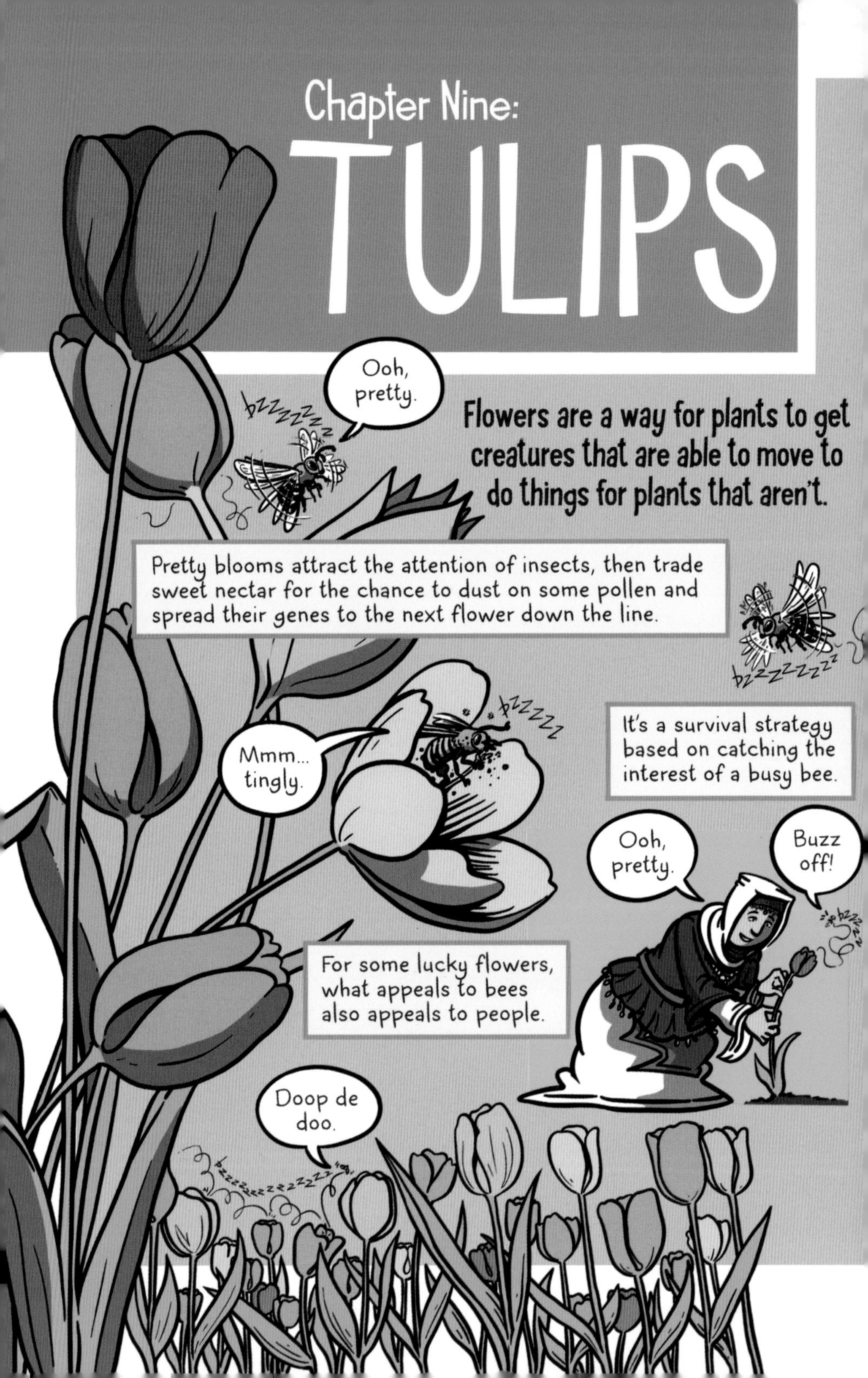

Chapter Nine:
TULIPS
Ooh, pretty.
bzzzzzzz
Flowers are a way for plants to get creatures that are able to move to do things for plants that aren't.
Pretty blooms attract the attention of insects, then trade sweet nectar for the chance to dust on some pollen and spread their genes to the next flower down the line.
bzzzzzzzz
bzzzzz
Mmm... tingly.
It's a survival strategy based on catching the interest of a busy bee.
Ooh, pretty.
Buzz off!
For some lucky flowers, what appeals to bees also appeals to people.
Doop de doo.

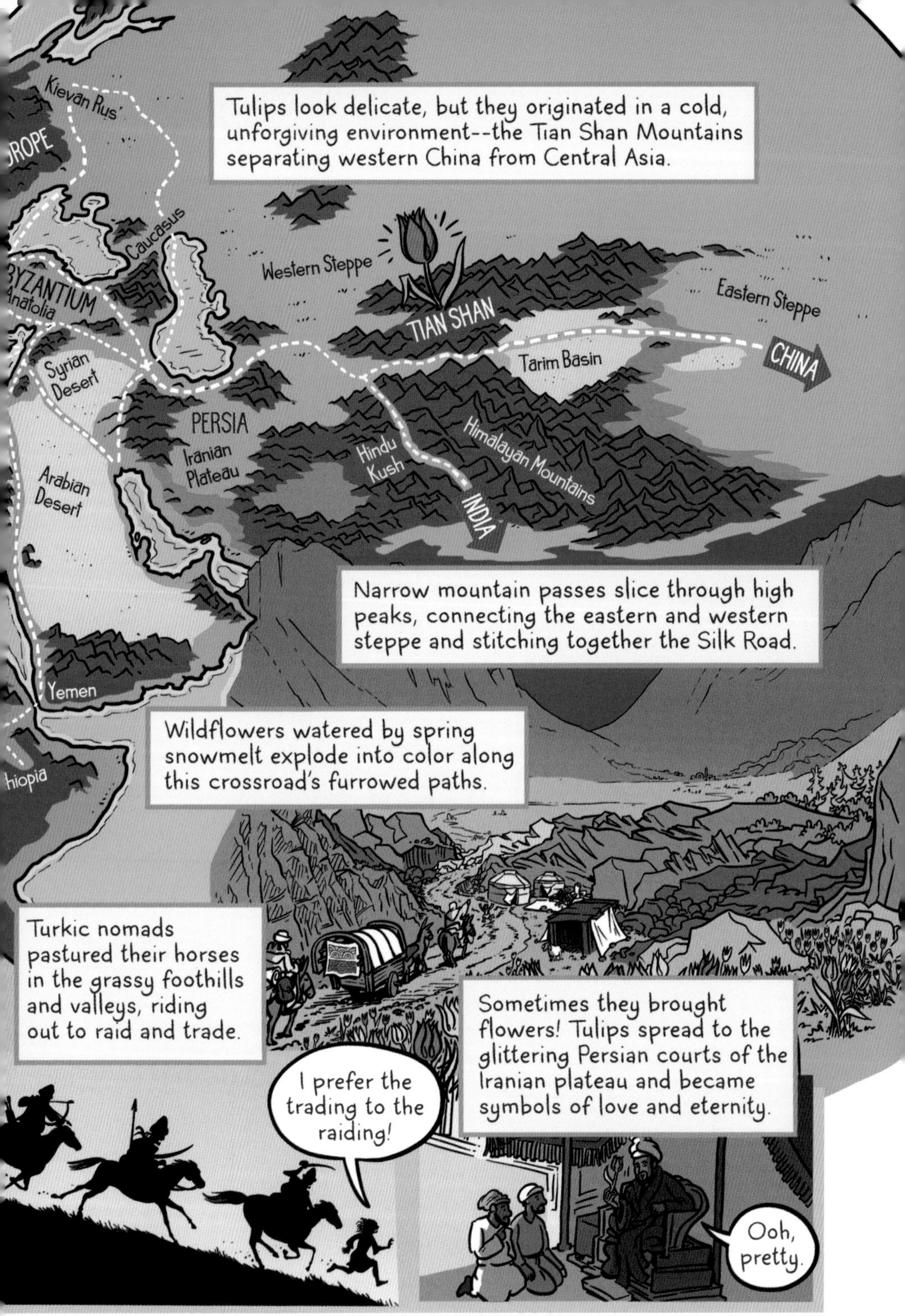
Tulips look delicate, but they originated in a cold, unforgiving environment--the Tian Shan Mountains separating western China from Central Asia.
Kievan Rus'
UROPE
Caucasus
Western Steppe
Eastern Steppe
BYZANTIUM
Anatolia
TIAN SHAN
Tarim Basin
CHINA
Syrian Desert
PERSIA
Iranian Plateau
Hindu Kush
Himalayan Mountains
INDIA
Arabian Desert
Yemen
hiopia
Narrow mountain passes slice through high peaks, connecting the eastern and western steppe and stitching together the Silk Road.
Wildflowers watered by spring snowmelt explode into color along this crossroad's furrowed paths.
Turkic nomads pastured their horses in the grassy foothills and valleys, riding out to raid and trade.
I prefer the trading to the raiding!
Sometimes they brought flowers! Tulips spread to the glittering Persian courts of the Iranian plateau and became symbols of love and eternity.
Ooh, pretty.

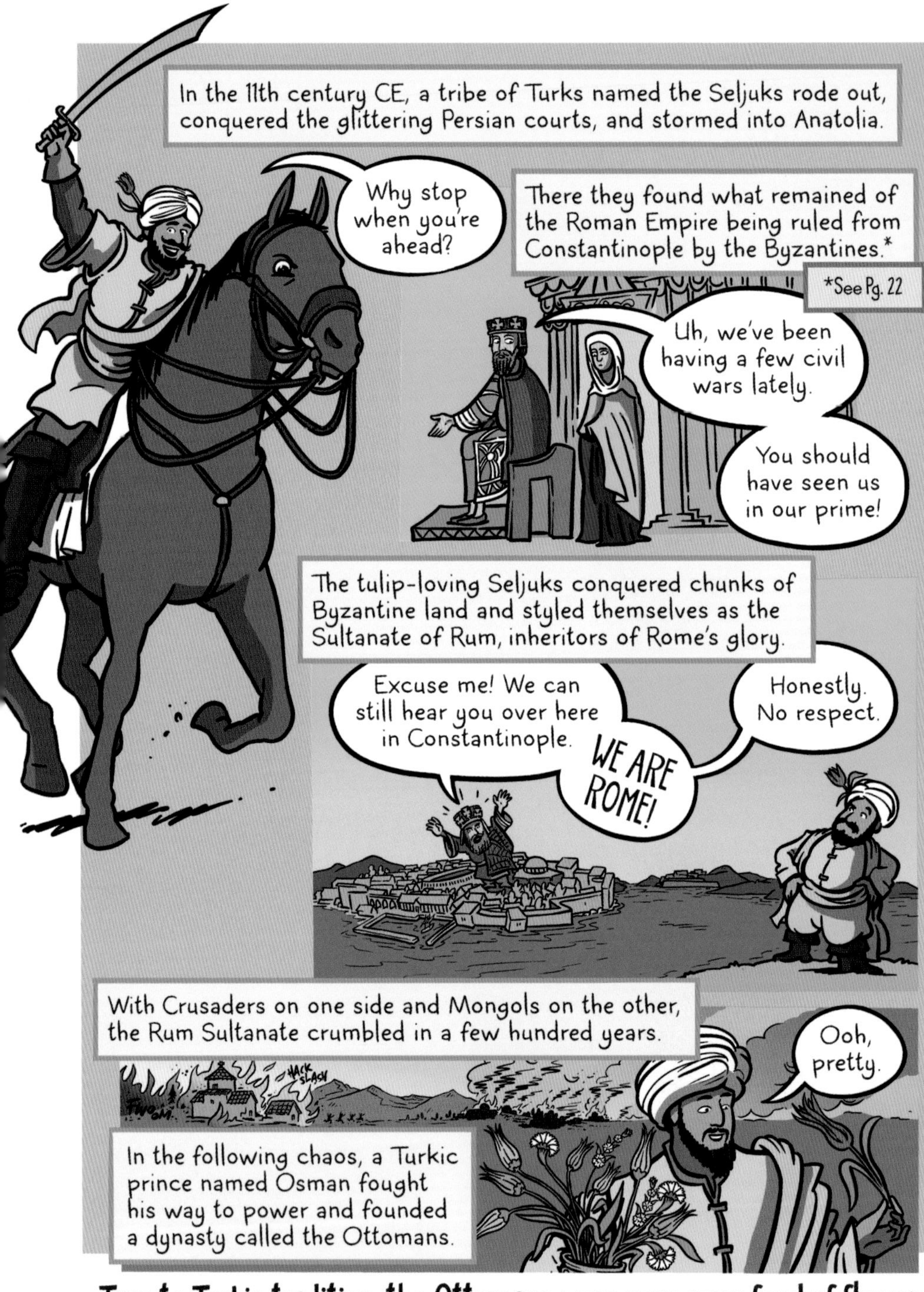
In the 11th century CE, a tribe of Turks named the Seljuks rode out, conquered the glittering Persian courts, and stormed into Anatolia.
Why stop when you're ahead?
There they found what remained of the Roman Empire being ruled from Constantinople by the Byzantines.*
*See Pg. 22
Uh, we've been having a few civil wars lately.
You should have seen us in our prime!
The tulip-loving Seljuks conquered chunks of Byzantine land and styled themselves as the Sultanate of Rum, inheritors of Rome's glory.
Excuse me! We can still hear you over here in Constantinople.
WE ARE ROME!
Honestly. No respect.
With Crusaders on one side and Mongols on the other, the Rum Sultanate crumbled in a few hundred years.
HACK
SLASH
Ooh, pretty.
In the following chaos, a Turkic prince named Osman fought his way to power and founded a dynasty called the Ottomans.

True to Turkic tradition, the Ottomans were very, very fond of flowers.

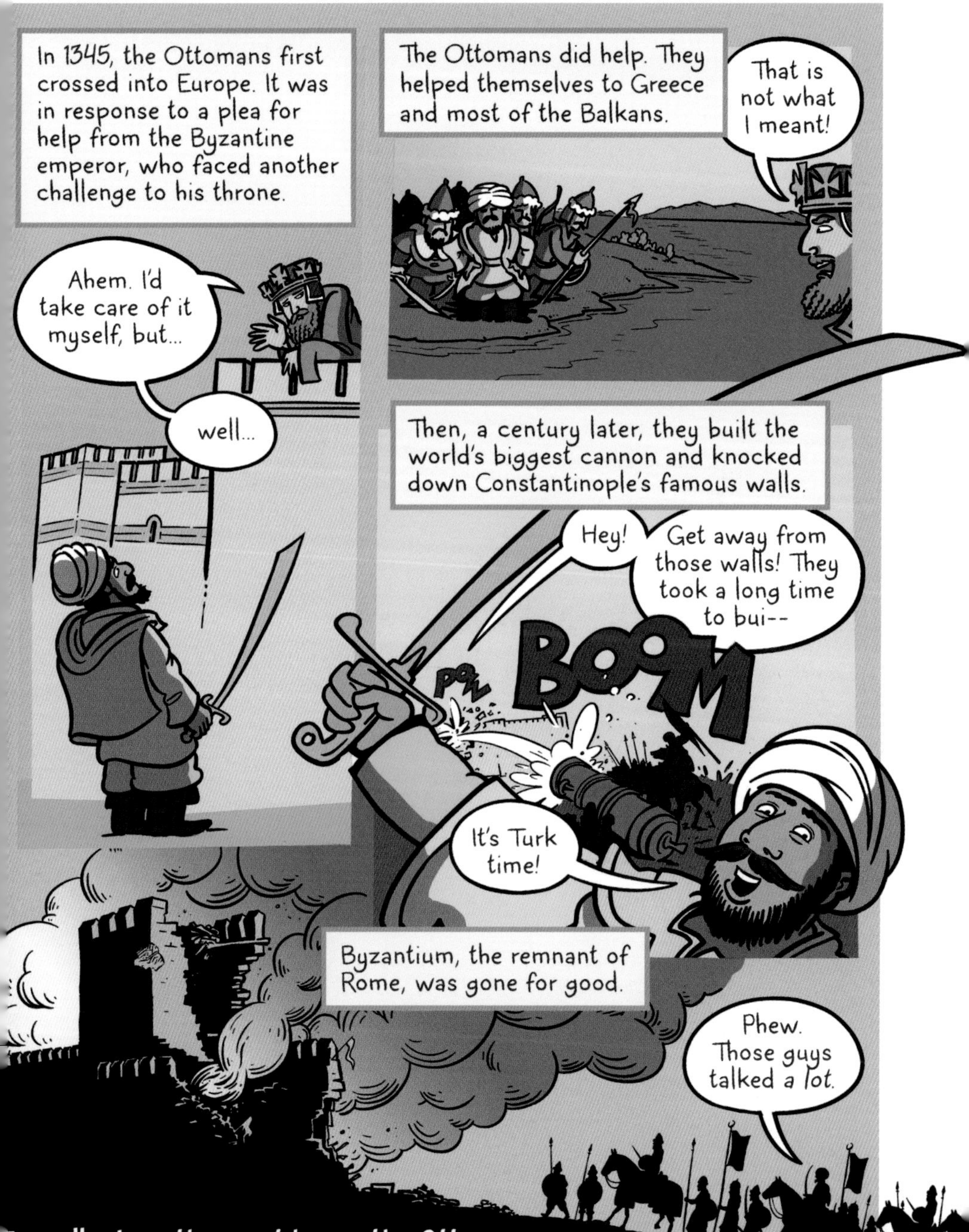
In 1345, the Ottomans first crossed into Europe. It was in response to a plea for help from the Byzantine emperor, who faced another challenge to his throne.
Ahem. I'd take care of it myself, but...
well...
The Ottomans did help. They helped themselves to Greece and most of the Balkans.
That is not what I meant!
Then, a century later, they built the world's biggest cannon and knocked down Constantinople's famous walls.
Hey!
Get away from those walls! They took a long time to bui--
POW
BOOM
It's Turk time!
Byzantium, the remnant of Rome, was gone for good.
Phew. Those guys talked a lot.

To really drive the point home, the Ottomans even
hanged the city's name from Constantinople to Istanbul

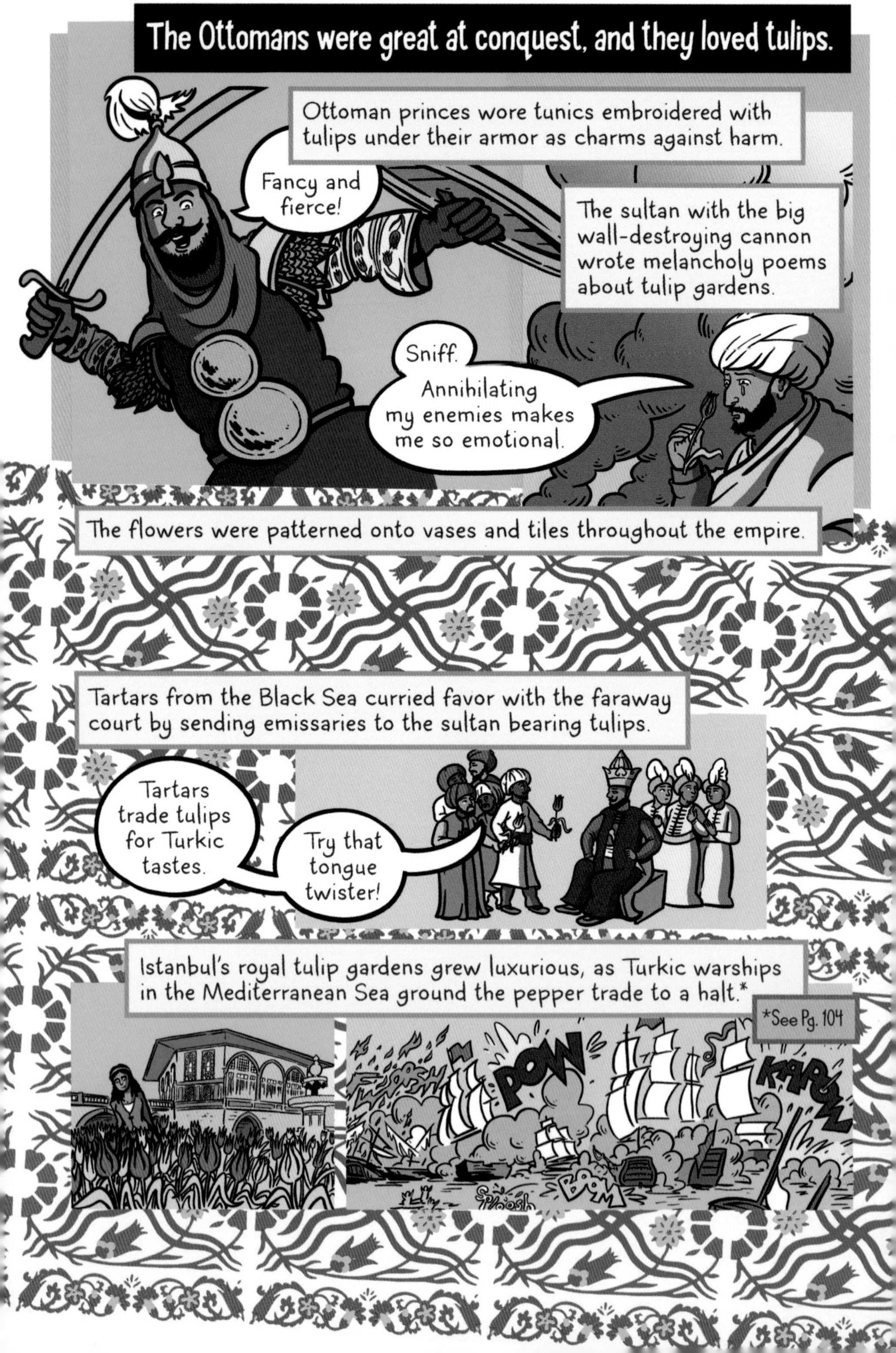
The Ottomans were great at conquest, and they loved tulips.
Ottoman princes wore tunics embroidered with tulips under their armor as charms against harm.
Fancy and fierce!
The sultan with the big wall-destroying cannon wrote melancholy poems about tulip gardens.
Sniff.
Annihilating my enemies makes me so emotional.
The flowers were patterned onto vases and tiles throughout the empire.
Tartars from the Black Sea curried favor with the faraway court by sending emissaries to the sultan bearing tulips.
Tartars trade tulips for Turkic tastes.
Try that tongue twister!
Istanbul's royal tulip gardens grew luxurious, as Turkic warships in the Mediterranean Sea ground the pepper trade to a halt.*
*See Pg. 104
POW
KAPOW
BOOM

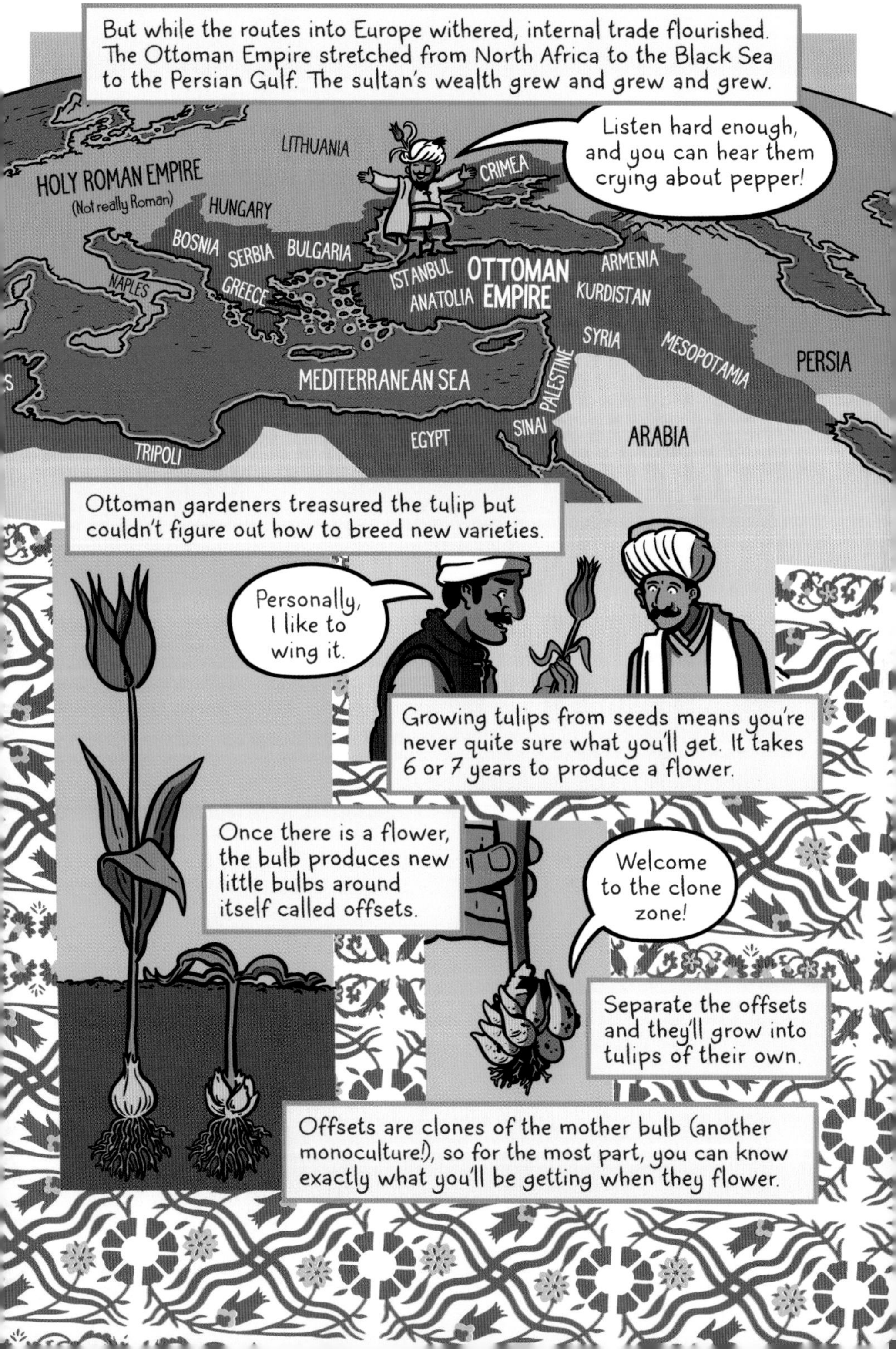

But while the routes into Europe withered, internal trade flourished. The Ottoman Empire stretched from North Africa to the Black Sea to the Persian Gulf. The sultan's wealth grew and grew and grew.
Listen hard enough, and you can hear them crying about pepper!
LITHUANIA
HOLY ROMAN EMPIRE
(Not really Roman)
HUNGARY
CRIMEA
BOSNIA
SERBIA
BULGARIA
NAPLES
GREECE
ISTANBUL
OTTOMAN EMPIRE
ANATOLIA
ARMENIA
KURDISTAN
SYRIA
MESOPOTAMIA
PERSIA
PALESTINE
MEDITERRANEAN SEA
SINAI
EGYPT
ARABIA
TRIPOLI
Ottoman gardeners treasured the tulip but couldn't figure out how to breed new varieties.
Personally, I like to wing it.
Growing tulips from seeds means you're never quite sure what you'll get. It takes 6 or 7 years to produce a flower.
Once there is a flower, the bulb produces new little bulbs around itself called offsets.
Welcome to the clone zone!
Separate the offsets and they'll grow into tulips of their own.
Offsets are clones of the mother bulb (another monoculture!), so for the most part, you can know exactly what you'll be getting when they flower.

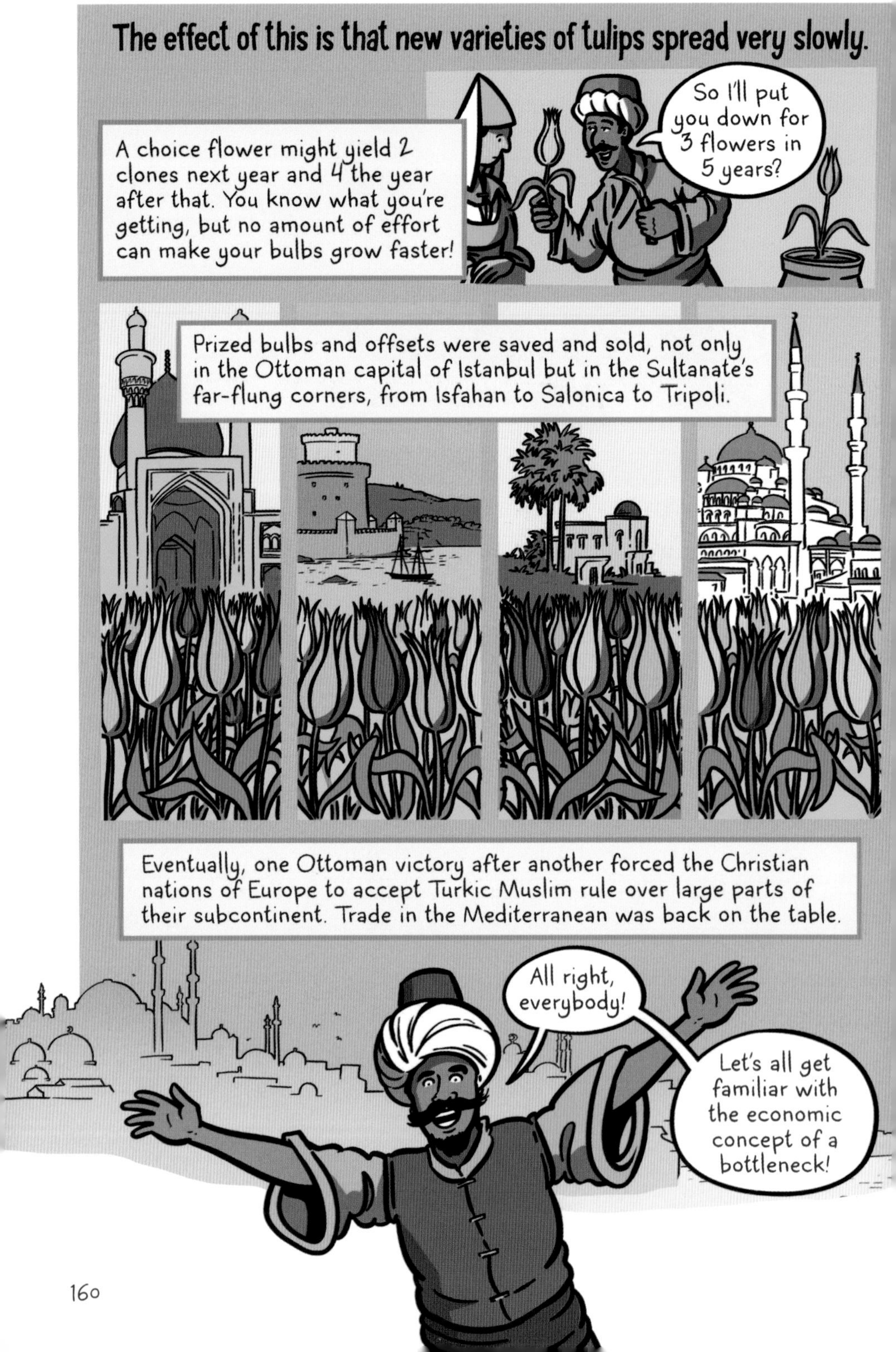
The effect of this is that new varieties of tulips spread very slowly.
A choice flower might yield 2 clones next year and 4 the year after that. You know what you're getting, but no amount of effort can make your bulbs grow faster!
So I'll put you down for 3 flowers in 5 years?
Prized bulbs and offsets were saved and sold, not only in the Ottoman capital of Istanbul but in the Sultanate's far-flung corners, from Isfahan to Salonica to Tripoli.
Eventually, one Ottoman victory after another forced the Christian nations of Europe to accept Turkic Muslim rule over large parts of their subcontinent. Trade in the Mediterranean was back on the table.
All right, everybody!
Let's all get familiar with the economic concept of a bottleneck!

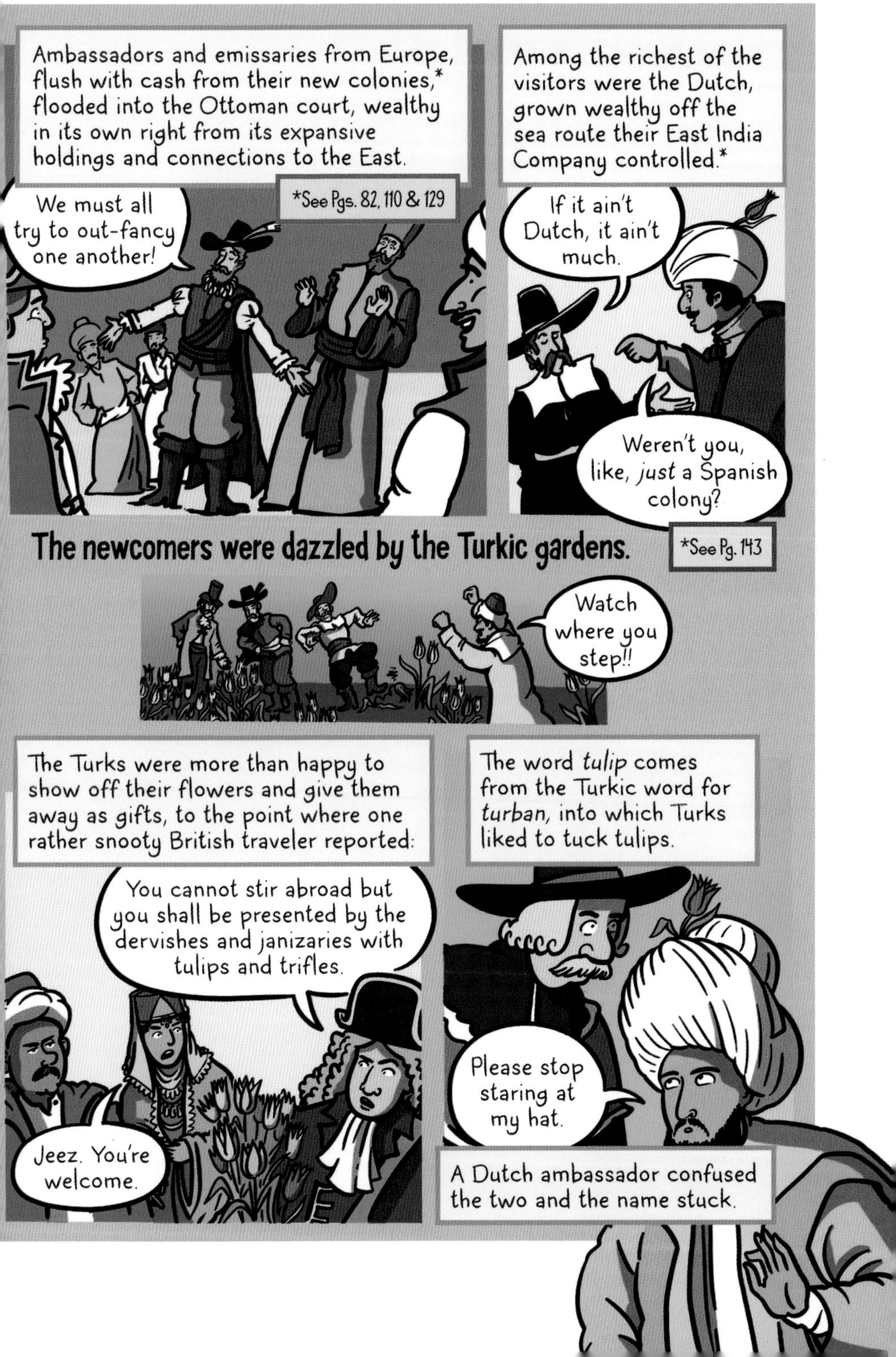
Ambassadors and emissaries from Europe, flush with cash from their new colonies,* flooded into the Ottoman court, wealthy in its own right from its expansive holdings and connections to the East.
*See Pgs. 82, 110 & 129
We must all try to out-fancy one another!
Among the richest of the visitors were the Dutch, grown wealthy off the sea route their East India Company controlled.*
If it ain't Dutch, it ain't much.
Weren't you, like, *just* a Spanish colony?
*See Pg. 143
The newcomers were dazzled by the Turkic gardens.
Watch where you step!!
The Turks were more than happy to show off their flowers and give them away as gifts, to the point where one rather snooty British traveler reported:
You cannot stir abroad but you shall be presented by the dervishes and janizaries with tulips and trifles.
Jeez. You're welcome.
The word *tulip* comes from the Turkic word for *turban*, into which Turks liked to tuck tulips.
Please stop staring at my hat.
A Dutch ambassador confused the two and the name stuck.

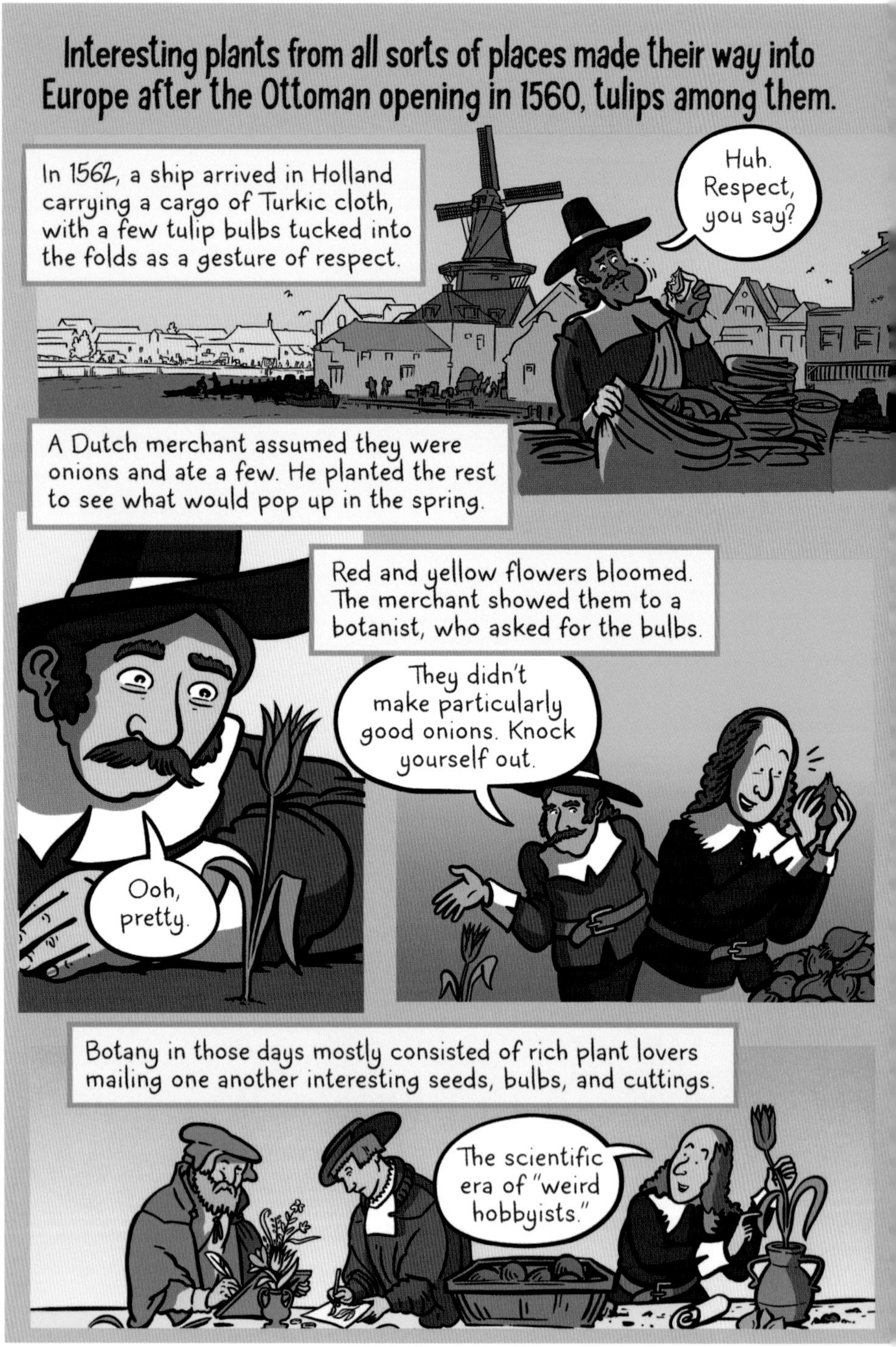
Interesting plants from all sorts of places made their way into Europe after the Ottoman opening in 1560, tulips among them.
In 1562, a ship arrived in Holland carrying a cargo of Turkic cloth, with a few tulip bulbs tucked into the folds as a gesture of respect.
Huh. Respect, you say?
A Dutch merchant assumed they were onions and ate a few. He planted the rest to see what would pop up in the spring.
Ooh, pretty.
Red and yellow flowers bloomed. The merchant showed them to a botanist, who asked for the bulbs.
They didn't make particularly good onions. Knock yourself out.
Botany in those days mostly consisted of rich plant lovers mailing one another interesting seeds, bulbs, and cuttings.
The scientific era of "weird hobbyists."

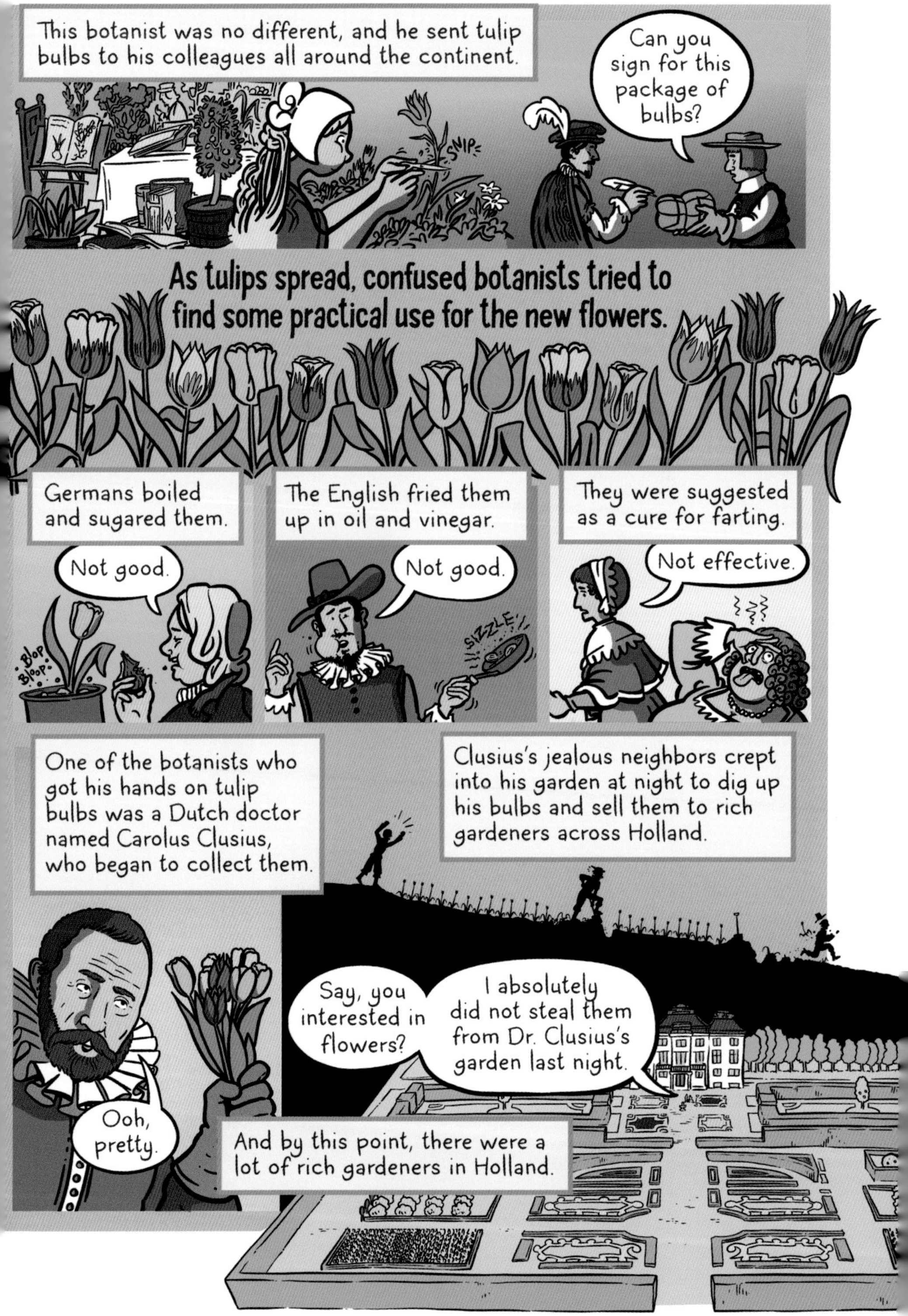
This botanist was no different, and he sent tulip bulbs to his colleagues all around the continent.
Can you sign for this package of bulbs?
As tulips spread, confused botanists tried to find some practical use for the new flowers.
Germans boiled and sugared them.
Not good.
The English fried them up in oil and vinegar.
Not good.
They were suggested as a cure for farting.
Not effective.
One of the botanists who got his hands on tulip bulbs was a Dutch doctor named Carolus Clusius, who began to collect them.
Ooh, pretty.
Clusius's jealous neighbors crept into his garden at night to dig up his bulbs and sell them to rich gardeners across Holland.
Say, you interested in flowers?
I absolutely did not steal them from Dr. Clusius's garden last night.
And by this point, there were a lot of rich gardeners in Holland.

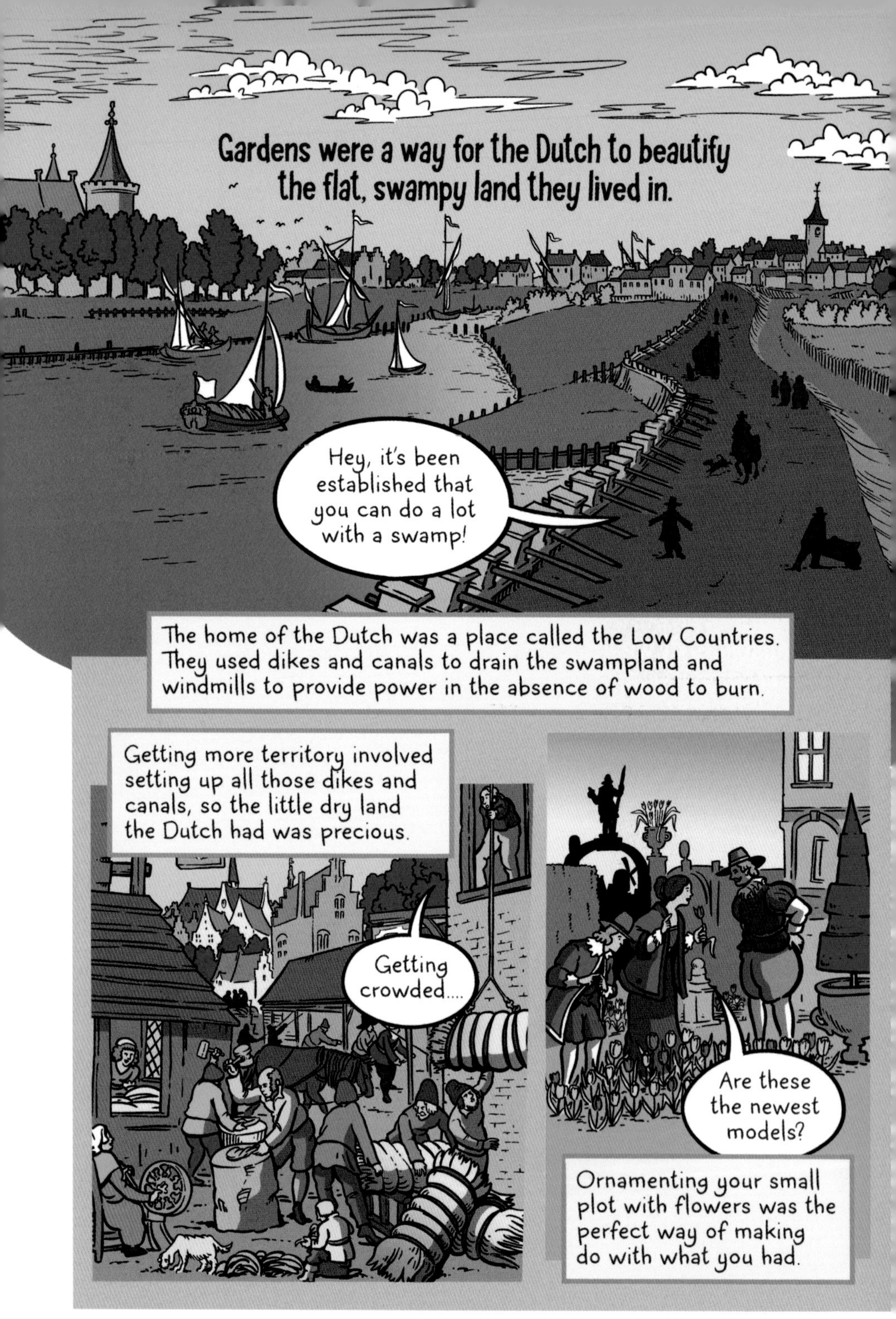
Gardens were a way for the Dutch to beautify the flat, swampy land they lived in.
Hey, it's been established that you can do a lot with a swamp!
The home of the Dutch was a place called the Low Countries. They used dikes and canals to drain the swampland and windmills to provide power in the absence of wood to burn.
Getting more territory involved setting up all those dikes and canals, so the little dry land the Dutch had was precious.
Getting crowded....
Are these the newest models?
Ornamenting your small plot with flowers was the perfect way of making do with what you had.

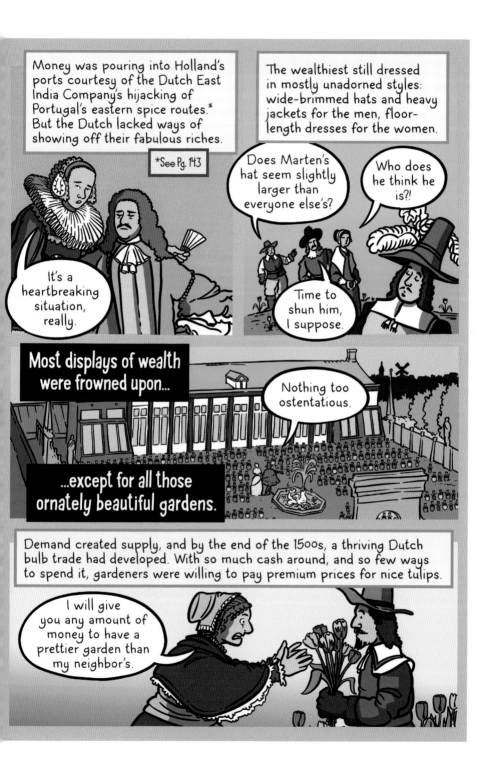

Money was pouring into Holland's ports courtesy of the Dutch East India Company's hijacking of Portugal's eastern spice routes.* But the Dutch lacked ways of showing off their fabulous riches.

*See Pg. 143

The wealthiest still dressed in mostly unadorned styles: wide-brimmed hats and heavy jackets for the men, floor-length dresses for the women.

Does Marten's hat seem slightly larger than everyone else's?

Who does he think he is?!

It's a heartbreaking situation, really.

Time to shun him, I suppose.

Most displays of wealth were frowned upon...

Nothing too ostentatious.

...except for all those ornately beautiful gardens.

Demand created supply, and by the end of the 1500s, a thriving Dutch bulb trade had developed. With so much cash around, and so few ways to spend it, gardeners were willing to pay premium prices for nice tulips.

I will give you any amount of money to have a prettier garden than my neighbor's.

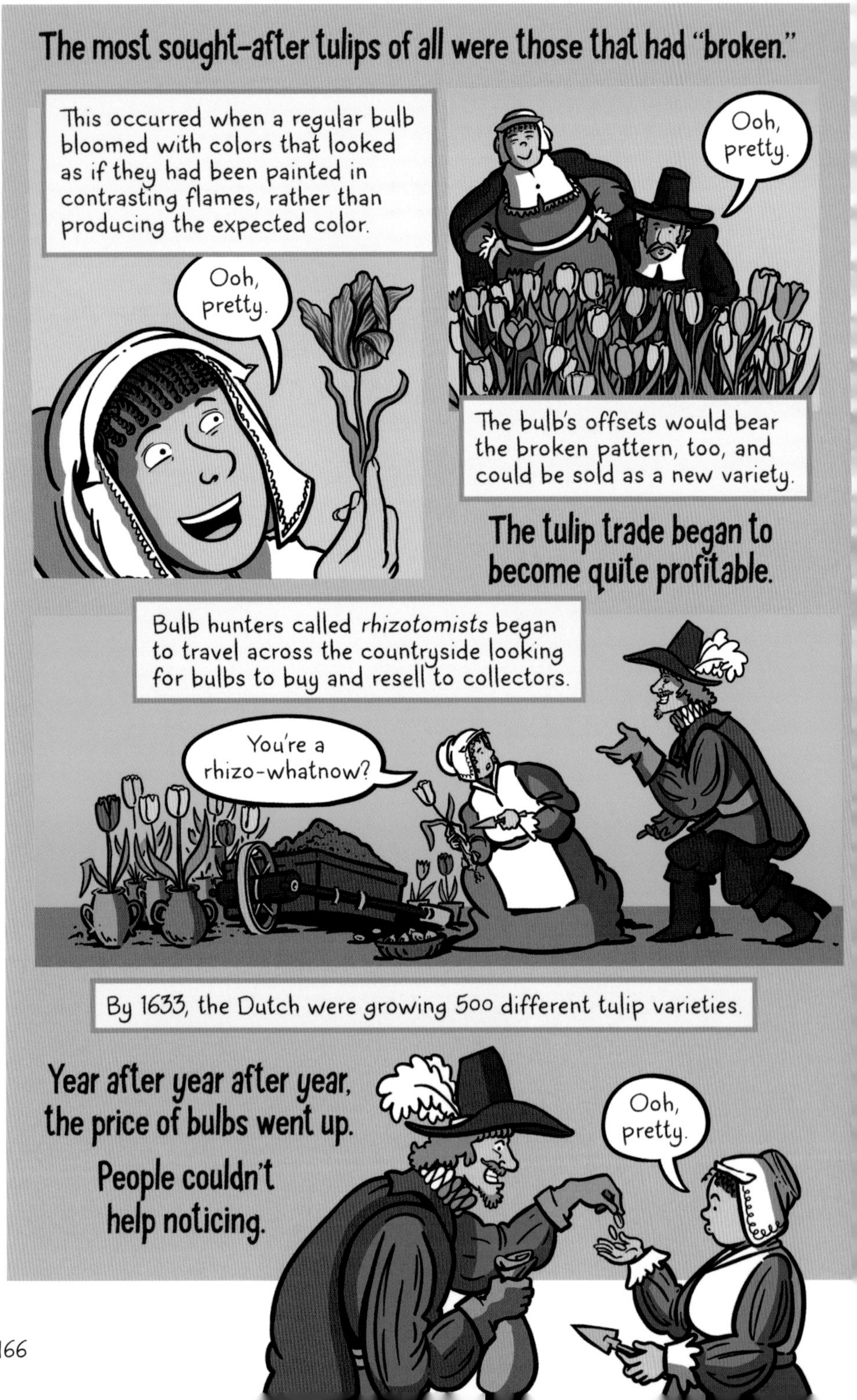

The most sought-after tulips of all were those that had "broken."
This occurred when a regular bulb bloomed with colors that looked as if they had been painted in contrasting flames, rather than producing the expected color.
Ooh, pretty.
Ooh, pretty.
The bulb's offsets would bear the broken pattern, too, and could be sold as a new variety.
The tulip trade began to become quite profitable.
Bulb hunters called *rhizotomists* began to travel across the countryside looking for bulbs to buy and resell to collectors.
You're a rhizo-whatnow?
By 1633, the Dutch were growing 500 different tulip varieties.
Year after year after year, the price of bulbs went up.
People couldn't help noticing.
Ooh, pretty.

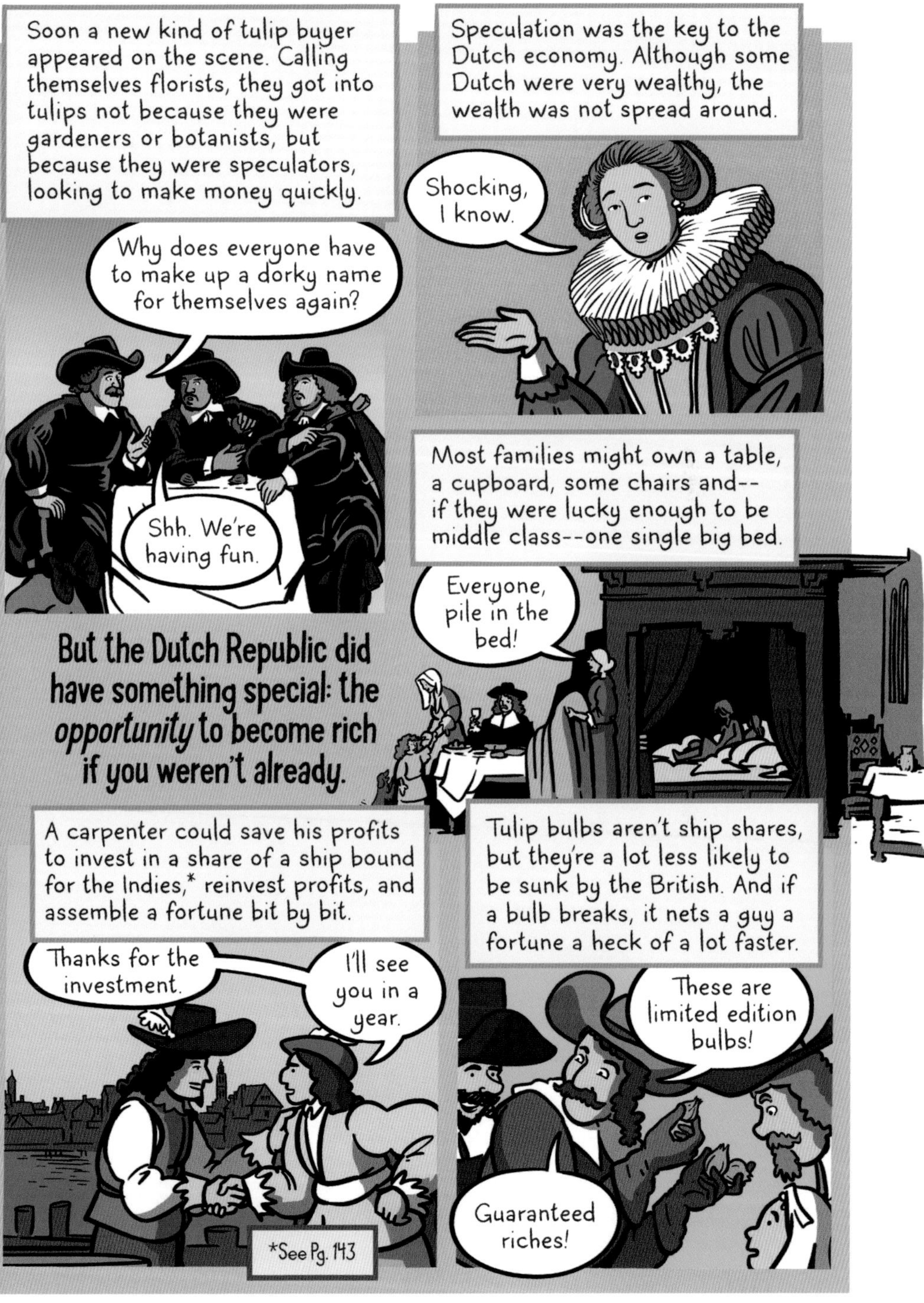
Soon a new kind of tulip buyer appeared on the scene. Calling themselves florists, they got into tulips not because they were gardeners or botanists, but because they were speculators, looking to make money quickly.
Why does everyone have to make up a dorky name for themselves again?
Shh. We're having fun.
Speculation was the key to the Dutch economy. Although some Dutch were very wealthy, the wealth was not spread around.
Shocking, I know.
Most families might own a table, a cupboard, some chairs and--if they were lucky enough to be middle class--one single big bed.
Everyone, pile in the bed!
But the Dutch Republic did have something special: the opportunity to become rich if you weren't already.
A carpenter could save his profits to invest in a share of a ship bound for the Indies,* reinvest profits, and assemble a fortune bit by bit.
Thanks for the investment.
I'll see you in a year.
*See Pg. 143
Tulip bulbs aren't ship shares, but they're a lot less likely to be sunk by the British. And if a bulb breaks, it nets a guy a fortune a heck of a lot faster.
These are limited edition bulbs!
Guaranteed riches!

The tulip trade was unregulated and easy to get into.

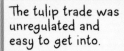

You just gotta have money and know some guy who sells tulip bulbs!

Getting money wasn't hard. If you were a blacksmith, weaver, or carpenter, you could sell your tools.

What could go wrong with selling the tools I use to make a living?

Your finest... whatever!

Then you bought bulbs.

Because so many other people were also getting into the tulip trade, you could bet that there would be buyers for your bulbs.

That'll be one guilder.

Your finest... whatever!

A lot of buyers meant bidding wars, which meant prices rose.

Your finest... whatever!

Your finest... whatever!

Your finest... whatever!

When prices rose, people couldn't help noticing. And so on and so forth.

You say they're making all this money from flowers?

Tulip bulb varieties, because they are cloned so slowly from offsets, are most scarce when they are new and most valued.

This cap meant that the people with the most money would end up paying higher and higher prices for the limited number of the hot new thing.

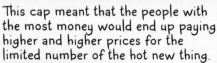

I must have those fancy bulbs!

In 1633, an entire house was exchanged for 3 rare bulbs.

I will definitely not have regrets about this!

For 2 years, prices climbed and climbed. More people couldn't help noticing.

This seems like something we can just sustain forever, right?

Absolutely.

In 1635, florists began to sell bulbs still in the ground by exchanging signed notes, rather than physically trading the actual bulbs.

Now traders could bet on the future value of a bulb before it even flowered.

Why trade bulbs when you can trade paper?

This is known as the time of the Wind Trade, or *windhandel* in Dutch. What would come to be called tulipmania was in full swing.

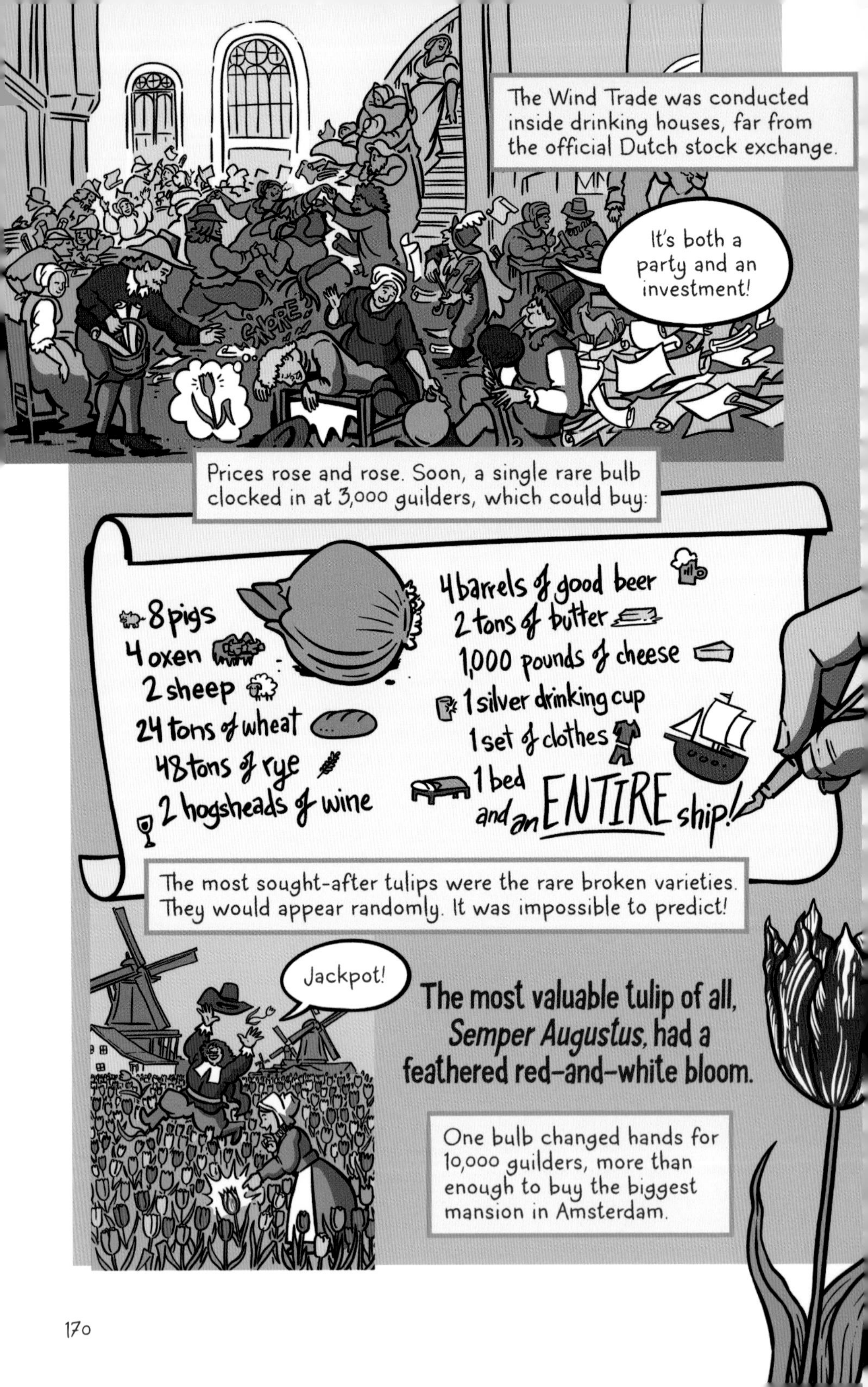

The Wind Trade was conducted inside drinking houses, far from the official Dutch stock exchange.
It's both a party and an investment!
SNORE
Prices rose and rose. Soon, a single rare bulb clocked in at 3,000 guilders, which could buy:
8 pigs
4 oxen
2 sheep
24 tons of wheat
48 tons of rye
2 hogsheads of wine
4 barrels of good beer
2 tons of butter
1,000 pounds of cheese
1 silver drinking cup
1 set of clothes
1 bed
and an ENTIRE ship!
The most sought-after tulips were the rare broken varieties. They would appear randomly. It was impossible to predict!
Jackpot!
The most valuable tulip of all, *Semper Augustus*, had a feathered red-and-white bloom.
One bulb changed hands for 10,000 guilders, more than enough to buy the biggest mansion in Amsterdam.

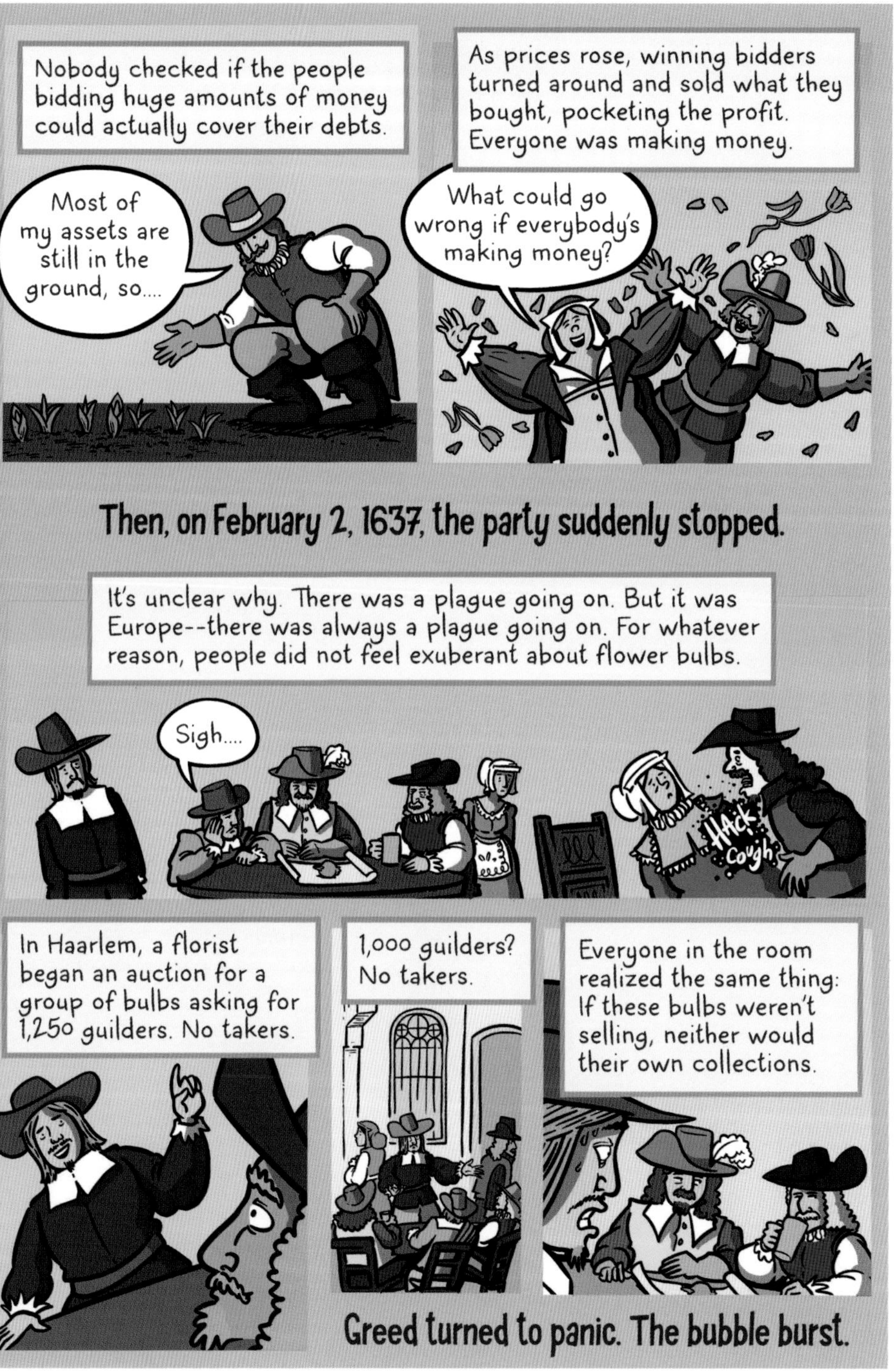
Nobody checked if the people bidding huge amounts of money could actually cover their debts.
Most of my assets are still in the ground, so....
As prices rose, winning bidders turned around and sold what they bought, pocketing the profit. Everyone was making money.
What could go wrong if everybody's making money?
Then, on February 2, 1637, the party suddenly stopped.
It's unclear why. There was a plague going on. But it was Europe--there was always a plague going on. For whatever reason, people did not feel exuberant about flower bulbs.
Sigh....
HACK
Cough
In Haarlem, a florist began an auction for a group of bulbs asking for 1,250 guilders. No takers.
1,000 guilders? No takers.
Everyone in the room realized the same thing: If these bulbs weren't selling, neither would their own collections.
Greed turned to panic. The bubble burst.

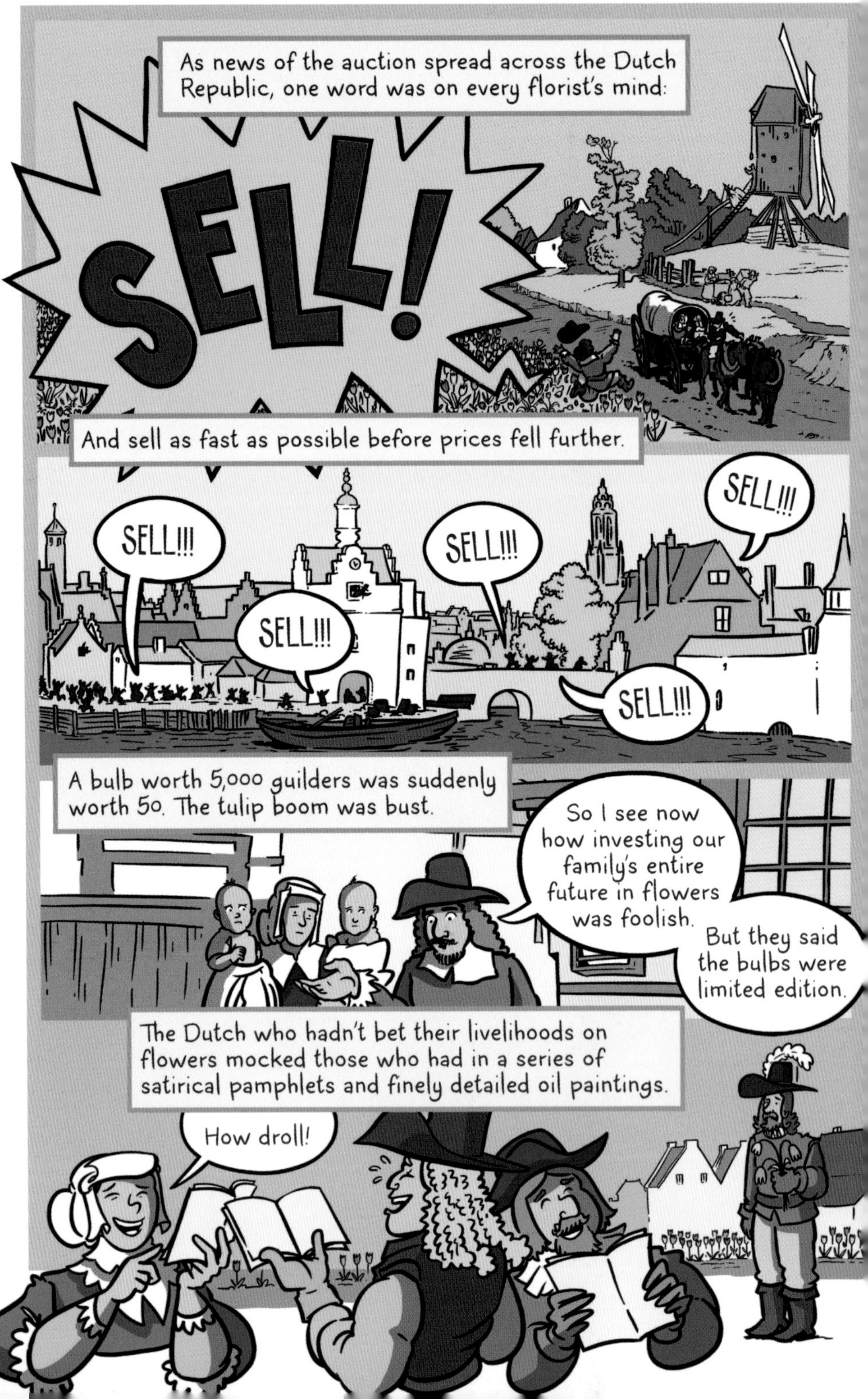
As news of the auction spread across the Dutch Republic, one word was on every florist's mind:
SELL!
And sell as fast as possible before prices fell further.
SELL!!!
SELL!!!
SELL!!!
SELL!!!
SELL!!!
A bulb worth 5,000 guilders was suddenly worth 50. The tulip boom was bust.
So I see now how investing our family's entire future in flowers was foolish.
But they said the bulbs were limited edition.
The Dutch who hadn't bet their livelihoods on flowers mocked those who had in a series of satirical pamphlets and finely detailed oil paintings.
How droll!

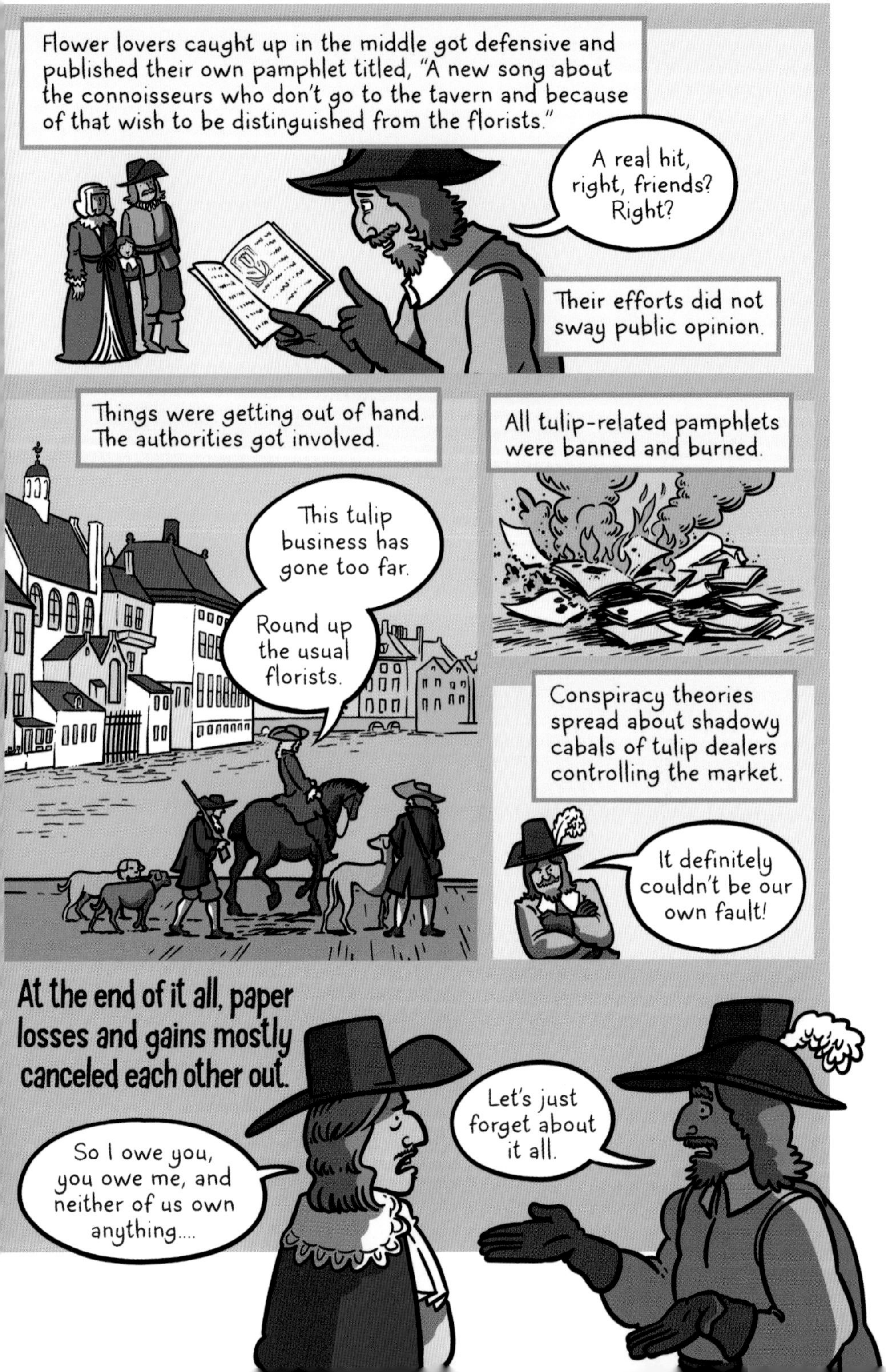

Flower lovers caught up in the middle got defensive and published their own pamphlet titled, "A new song about the connoisseurs who don't go to the tavern and because of that wish to be distinguished from the florists."
A real hit, right, friends? Right?
Their efforts did not sway public opinion.
Things were getting out of hand. The authorities got involved.
This tulip business has gone too far.
Round up the usual florists.
All tulip-related pamphlets were banned and burned.
Conspiracy theories spread about shadowy cabals of tulip dealers controlling the market.
It definitely couldn't be our own fault!
At the end of it all, paper losses and gains mostly canceled each other out.
So I owe you, you owe me, and neither of us own anything....
Let's just forget about it all.

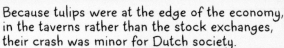
Because tulips were at the edge of the economy, in the taverns rather than the stock exchanges, their crash was minor for Dutch society.

You heard something happened in the drinking houses with the flower weirdos?

But tulipmania was funny! News of the absurd episode spread quickly across Europe.

Curiosity led to desire.

Have you heard about this Dutch tulip nonsense?

I must have those silly flowers!

Soon, the Dutch were selling bulbs abroad for a reasonable profit. Tulips no longer commanded outlandish prices, but the flower's infamy had created a healthy export market.

Just, uh, like we planned.

A major destination for Dutch bulbs was the Ottoman court in Istanbul, from where the Dutch had obtained tulips in the first place.

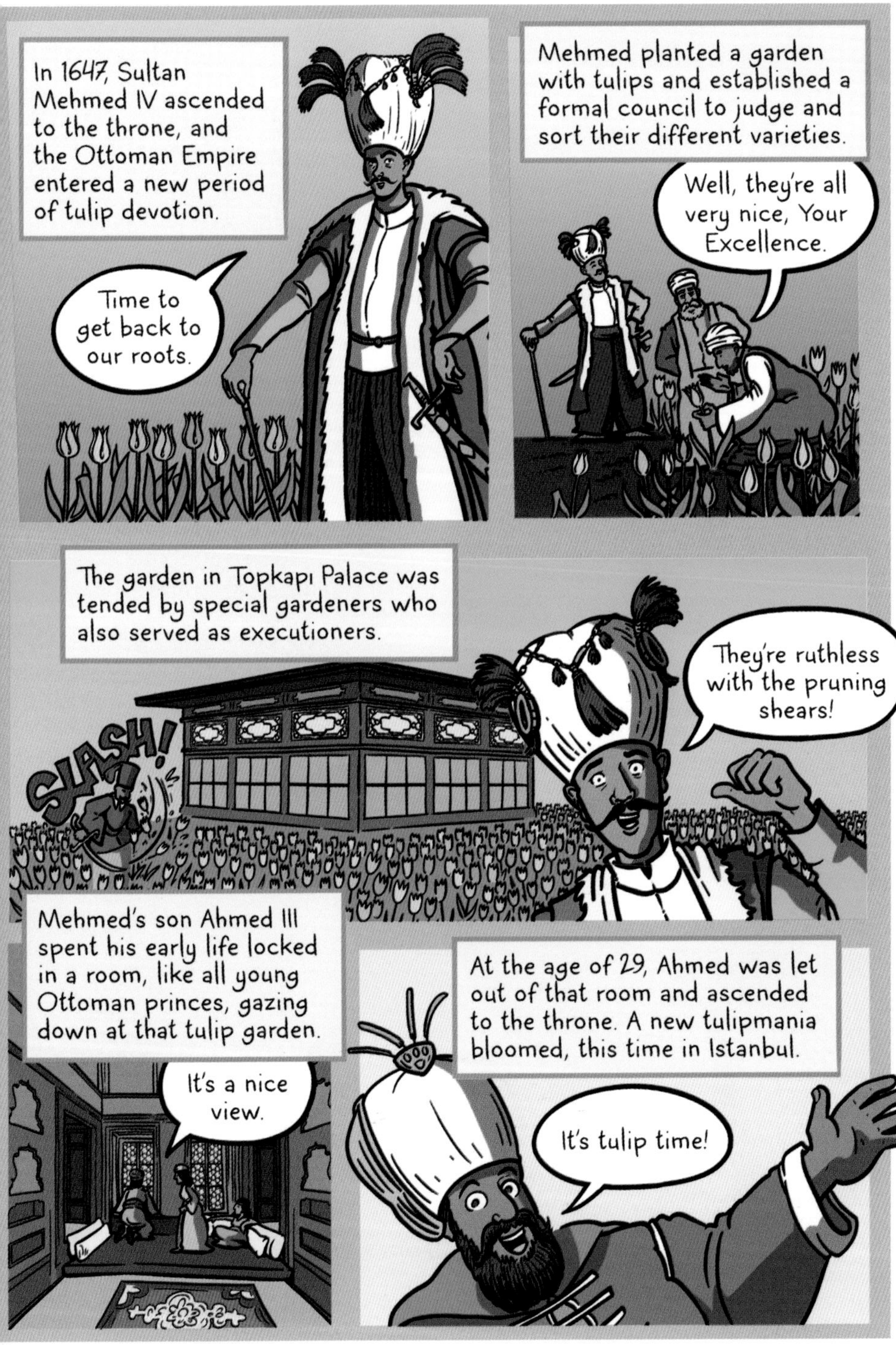

In 1647, Sultan Mehmed IV ascended to the throne, and the Ottoman Empire entered a new period of tulip devotion.
Time to get back to our roots.
Mehmed planted a garden with tulips and established a formal council to judge and sort their different varieties.
Well, they're all very nice, Your Excellence.
The garden in Topkapı Palace was tended by special gardeners who also served as executioners.
SLASH!
They're ruthless with the pruning shears!
Mehmed's son Ahmed III spent his early life locked in a room, like all young Ottoman princes, gazing down at that tulip garden.
It's a nice view.
At the age of 29, Ahmed was let out of that room and ascended to the throne. A new tulipmania bloomed, this time in Istanbul.
It's tulip time!

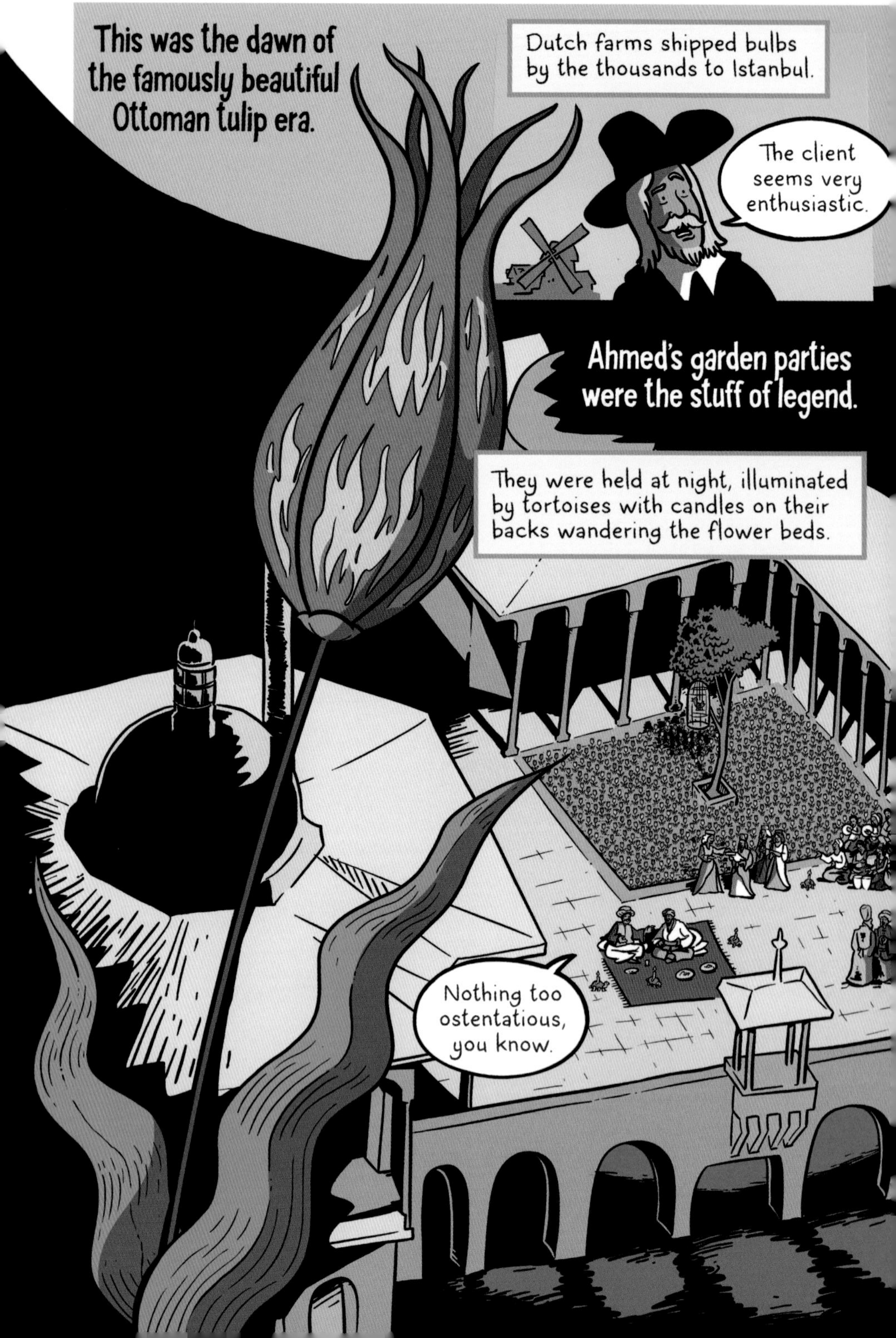
This was the dawn of the famously beautiful Ottoman tulip era.
Dutch farms shipped bulbs by the thousands to Istanbul.
The client seems very enthusiastic.
Ahmed's garden parties were the stuff of legend.
They were held at night, illuminated by tortoises with candles on their backs wandering the flower beds.
Nothing too ostentatious, you know.

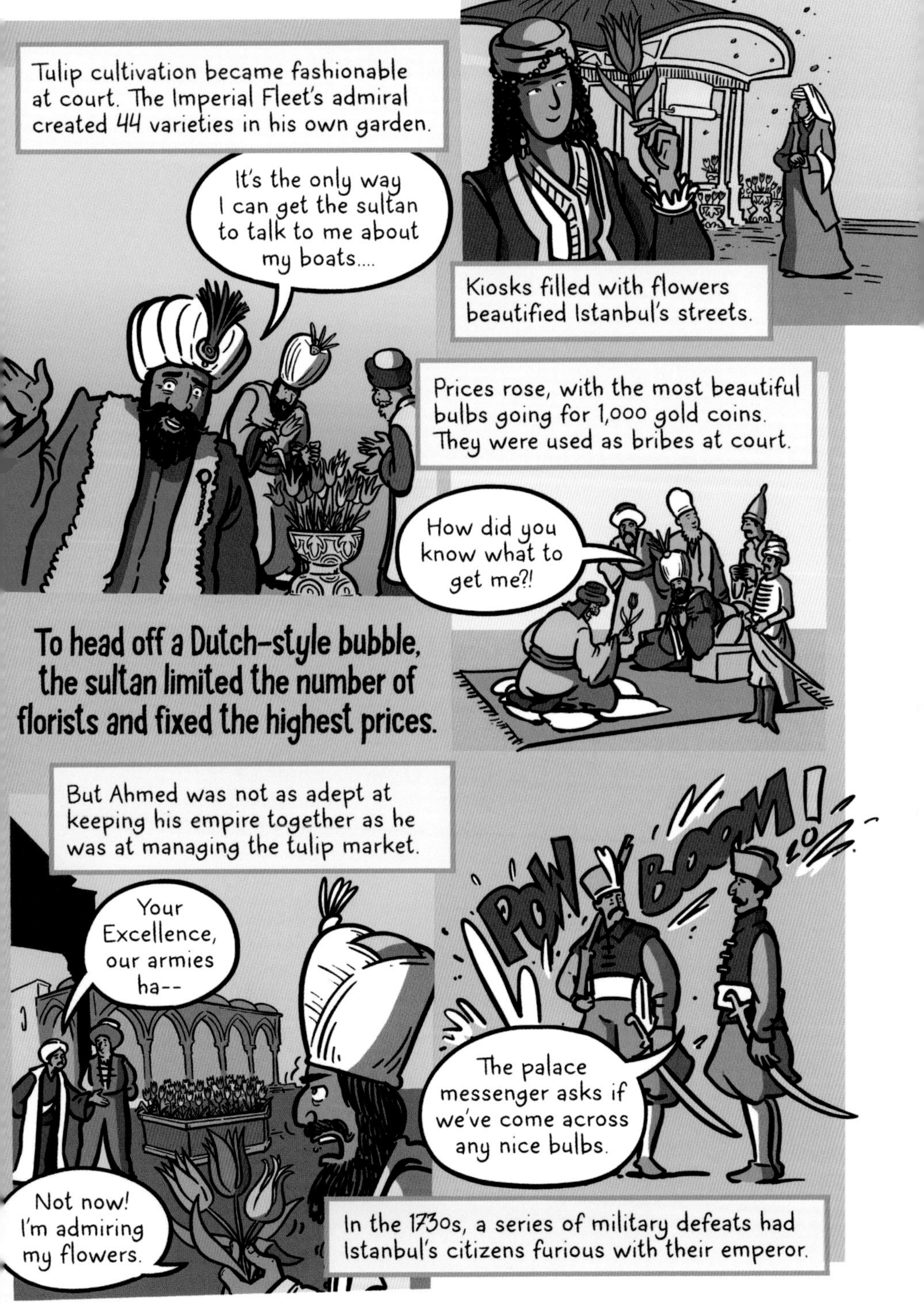
Tulip cultivation became fashionable at court. The Imperial Fleet's admiral created 44 varieties in his own garden.
It's the only way I can get the sultan to talk to me about my boats....
Kiosks filled with flowers beautified Istanbul's streets.
Prices rose, with the most beautiful bulbs going for 1,000 gold coins. They were used as bribes at court.
How did you know what to get me?!
To head off a Dutch-style bubble, the sultan limited the number of florists and fixed the highest prices.
But Ahmed was not as adept at keeping his empire together as he was at managing the tulip market.
Your Excellence, our armies ha--
Not now! I'm admiring my flowers.
POW
BOOM!
The palace messenger asks if we've come across any nice bulbs.
In the 1730s, a series of military defeats had Istanbul's citizens furious with their emperor.

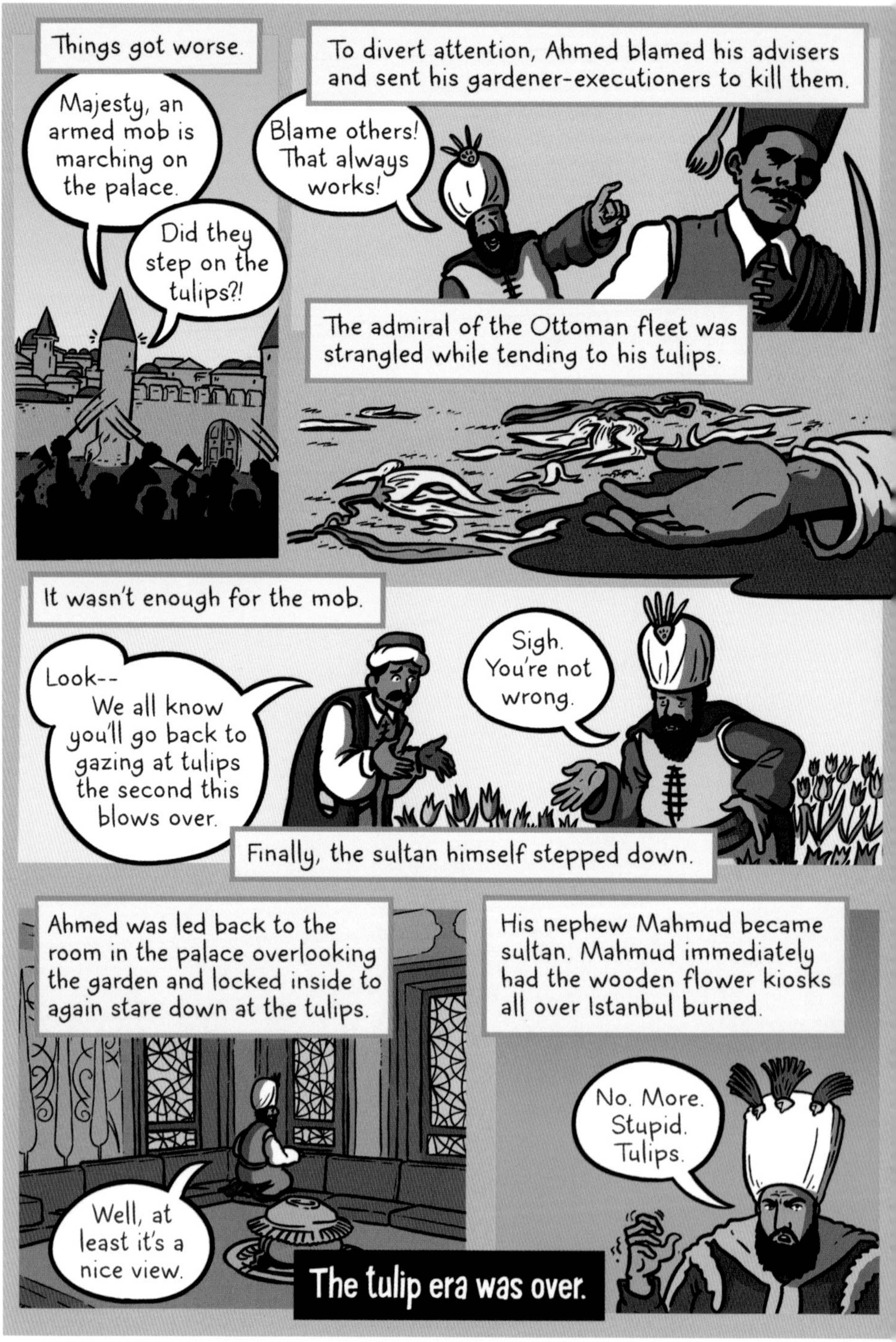
Things got worse.
Majesty, an armed mob is marching on the palace.
Did they step on the tulips?!
To divert attention, Ahmed blamed his advisers and sent his gardener-executioners to kill them.
Blame others! That always works!
The admiral of the Ottoman fleet was strangled while tending to his tulips.
It wasn't enough for the mob.
Look-- We all know you'll go back to gazing at tulips the second this blows over.
Sigh. You're not wrong.
Finally, the sultan himself stepped down.
Ahmed was led back to the room in the palace overlooking the garden and locked inside to again stare down at the tulips.
Well, at least it's a nice view.
His nephew Mahmud became sultan. Mahmud immediately had the wooden flower kiosks all over Istanbul burned.
No. More. Stupid. Tulips.
The tulip era was over.

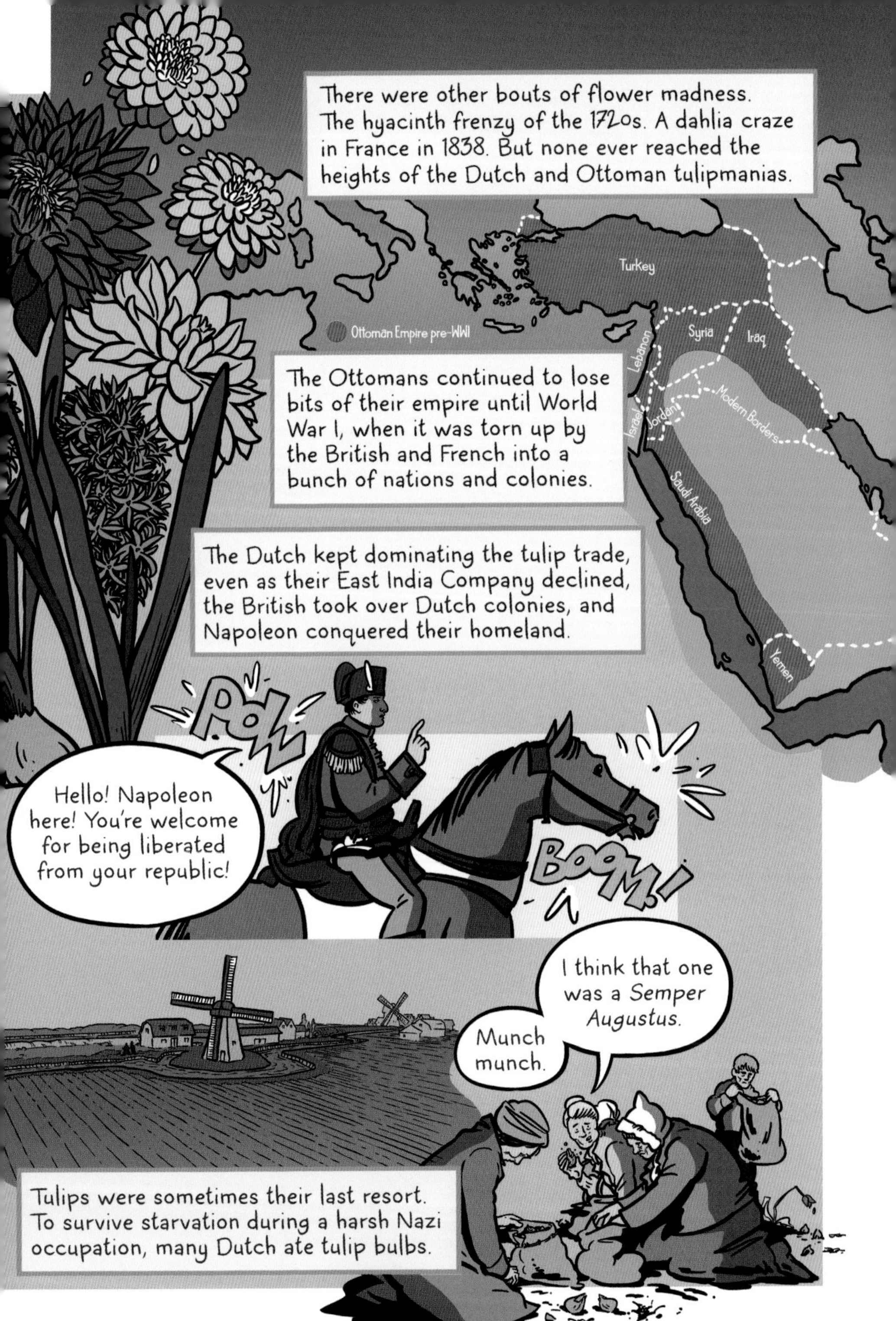
There were other bouts of flower madness. The hyacinth frenzy of the 1720s. A dahlia craze in France in 1838. But none ever reached the heights of the Dutch and Ottoman tulipmanias.
Turkey
Ottoman Empire pre-WWI
Lebanon
Syria
Iraq
Israel
Jordan
Modern Borders
Saudi Arabia
Yemen
The Ottomans continued to lose bits of their empire until World War I, when it was torn up by the British and French into a bunch of nations and colonies.
The Dutch kept dominating the tulip trade, even as their East India Company declined, the British took over Dutch colonies, and Napoleon conquered their homeland.
POW
Hello! Napoleon here! You're welcome for being liberated from your republic!
BOOM!
I think that one was a *Semper Augustus*.
Munch munch.
Tulips were sometimes their last resort. To survive starvation during a harsh Nazi occupation, many Dutch ate tulip bulbs.

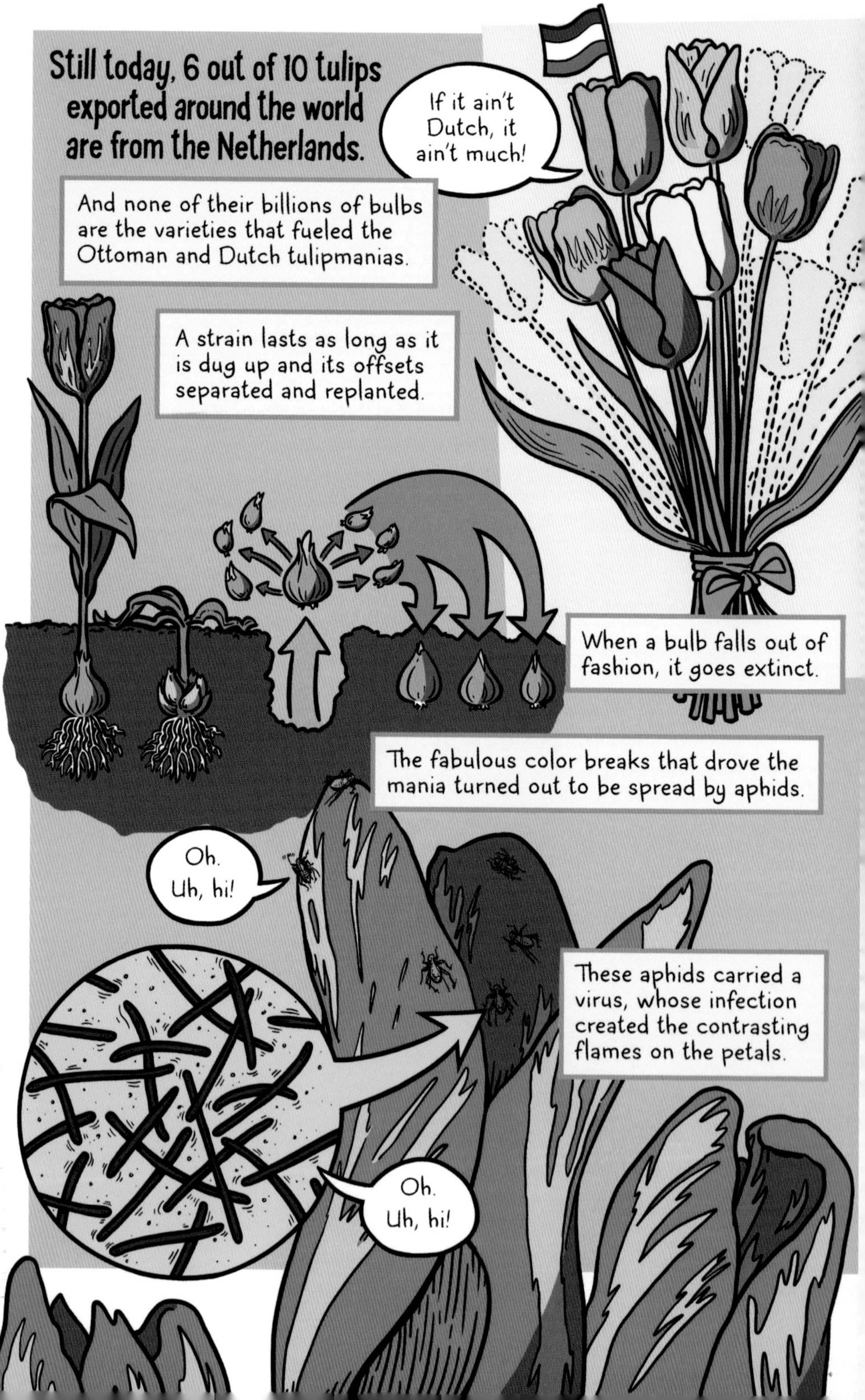
Still today, 6 out of 10 tulips exported around the world are from the Netherlands.
If it ain't Dutch, it ain't much!
And none of their billions of bulbs are the varieties that fueled the Ottoman and Dutch tulipmanias.
A strain lasts as long as it is dug up and its offsets separated and replanted.
When a bulb falls out of fashion, it goes extinct.
The fabulous color breaks that drove the mania turned out to be spread by aphids.
Oh. Uh, hi!
These aphids carried a virus, whose infection created the contrasting flames on the petals.
Oh. Uh, hi!

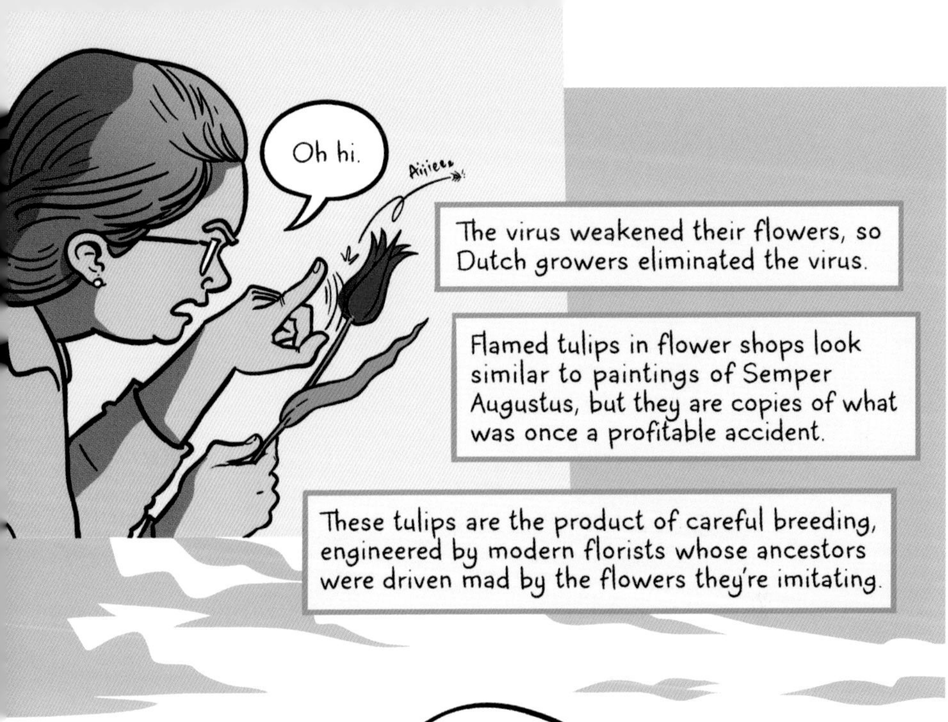
Oh hi.
Aiiieee
The virus weakened their flowers, so Dutch growers eliminated the virus.
Flamed tulips in flower shops look similar to paintings of Semper Augustus, but they are copies of what was once a profitable accident.
These tulips are the product of careful breeding, engineered by modern florists whose ancestors were driven mad by the flowers they're imitating.

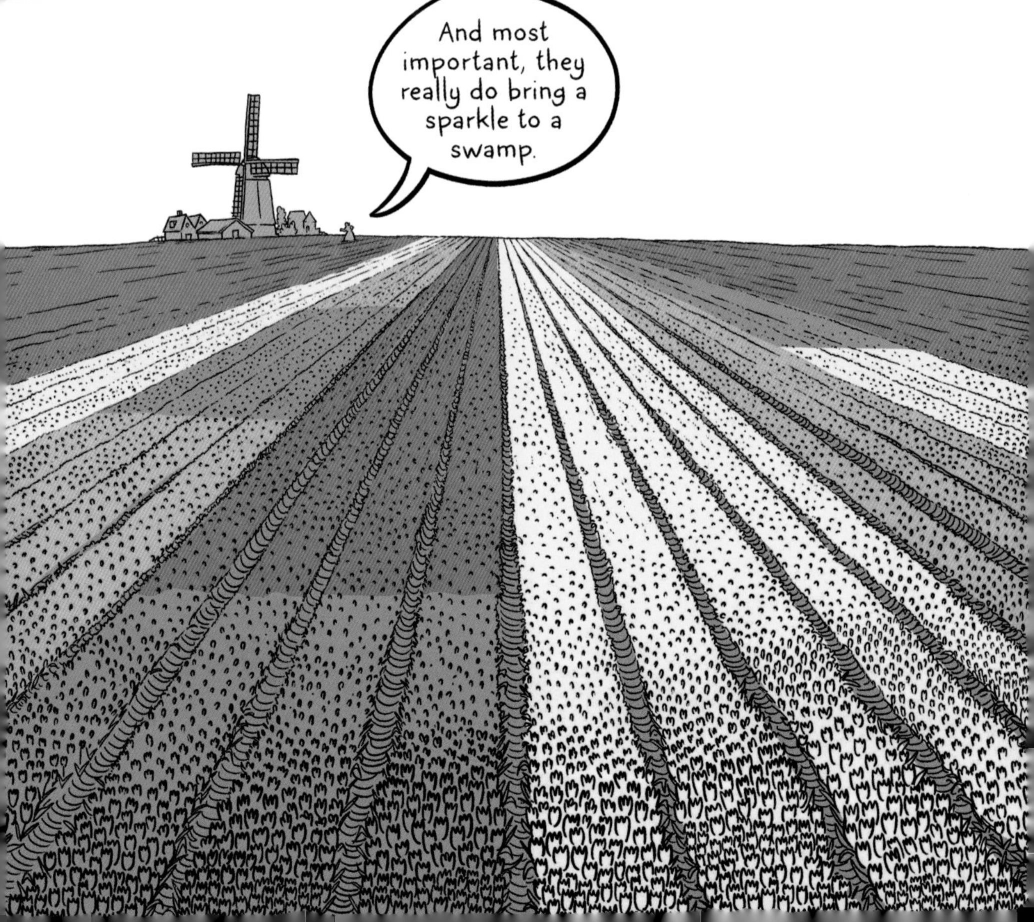
And most important, they really do bring a sparkle to a swamp.

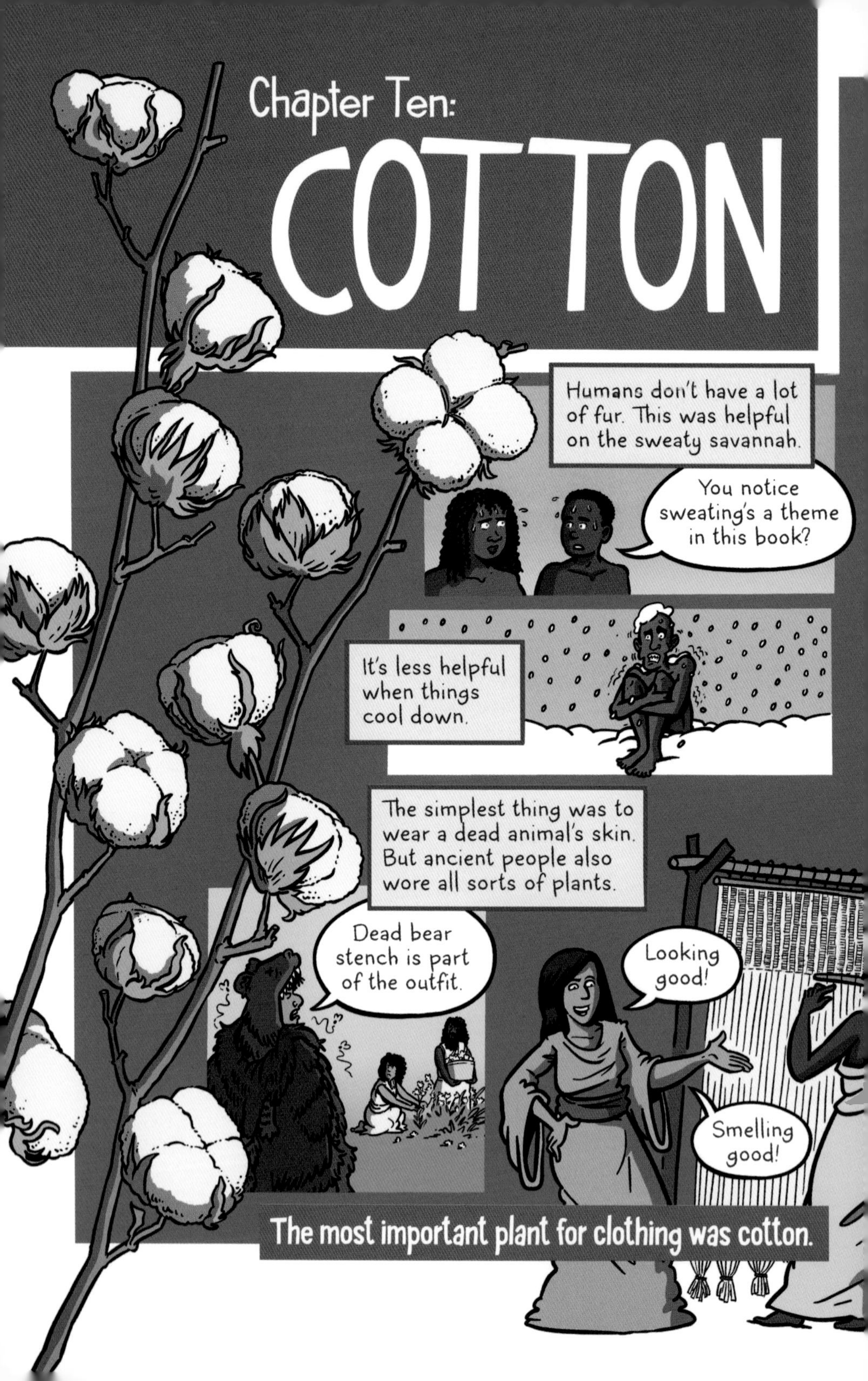
Chapter Ten:
COTTON
Humans don't have a lot of fur. This was helpful on the sweaty savannah.
You notice sweating's a theme in this book?
It's less helpful when things cool down.
The simplest thing was to wear a dead animal's skin. But ancient people also wore all sorts of plants.
Dead bear stench is part of the outfit.
Looking good!
Smelling good!
The most important plant for clothing was cotton.

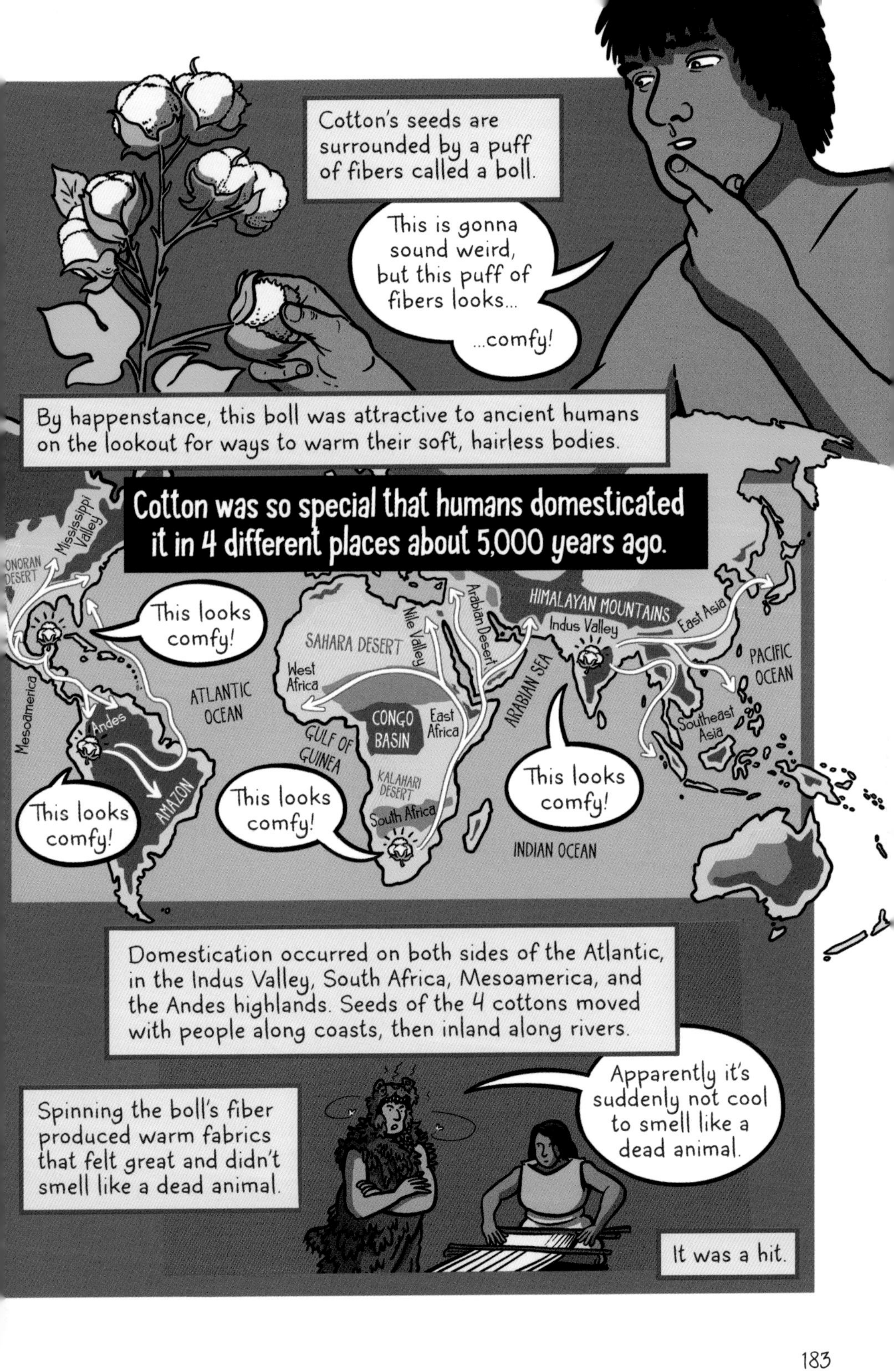

Cotton's seeds are surrounded by a puff of fibers called a boll.
This is gonna sound weird, but this puff of fibers looks...
...comfy!
By happenstance, this boll was attractive to ancient humans on the lookout for ways to warm their soft, hairless bodies.
Cotton was so special that humans domesticated it in 4 different places about 5,000 years ago.
Mississippi Valley
SONORAN DESERT
This looks comfy!
Mesoamerica
ATLANTIC OCEAN
Andes
This looks comfy!
AMAZON
SAHARA DESERT
West Africa
Nile Valley
Arabian Desert
CONGO BASIN
East Africa
GULF OF GUINEA
KALAHARI DESERT
South Africa
This looks comfy!
HIMALAYAN MOUNTAINS
Indus Valley
East Asia
PACIFIC OCEAN
ARABIAN SEA
Southeast Asia
This looks comfy!
INDIAN OCEAN
Domestication occurred on both sides of the Atlantic, in the Indus Valley, South Africa, Mesoamerica, and the Andes highlands. Seeds of the 4 cottons moved with people along coasts, then inland along rivers.
Spinning the boll's fiber produced warm fabrics that felt great and didn't smell like a dead animal.
Apparently it's suddenly not cool to smell like a dead animal.
It was a hit.

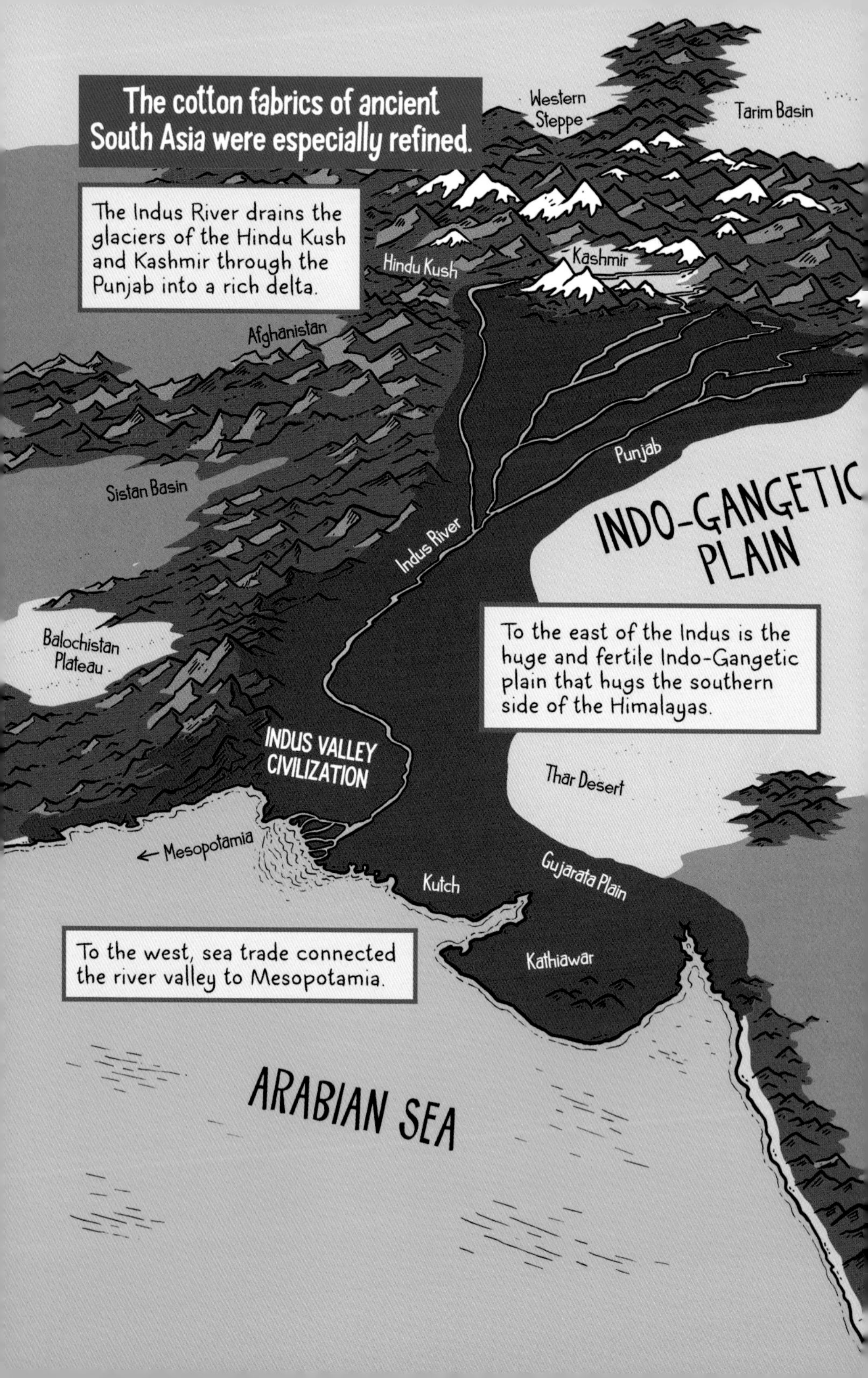
The cotton fabrics of ancient South Asia were especially refined.
The Indus River drains the glaciers of the Hindu Kush and Kashmir through the Punjab into a rich delta.
Western Steppe
Tarim Basin
Hindu Kush
Kashmir
Afghanistan
Punjab
Sistan Basin
INDO-GANGETIC PLAIN
Indus River
Balochistan Plateau
To the east of the Indus is the huge and fertile Indo-Gangetic plain that hugs the southern side of the Himalayas.
INDUS VALLEY CIVILIZATION
Thar Desert
← Mesopotamia
Kutch
Gujarata Plain
Kathiawar
To the west, sea trade connected the river valley to Mesopotamia.
ARABIAN SEA

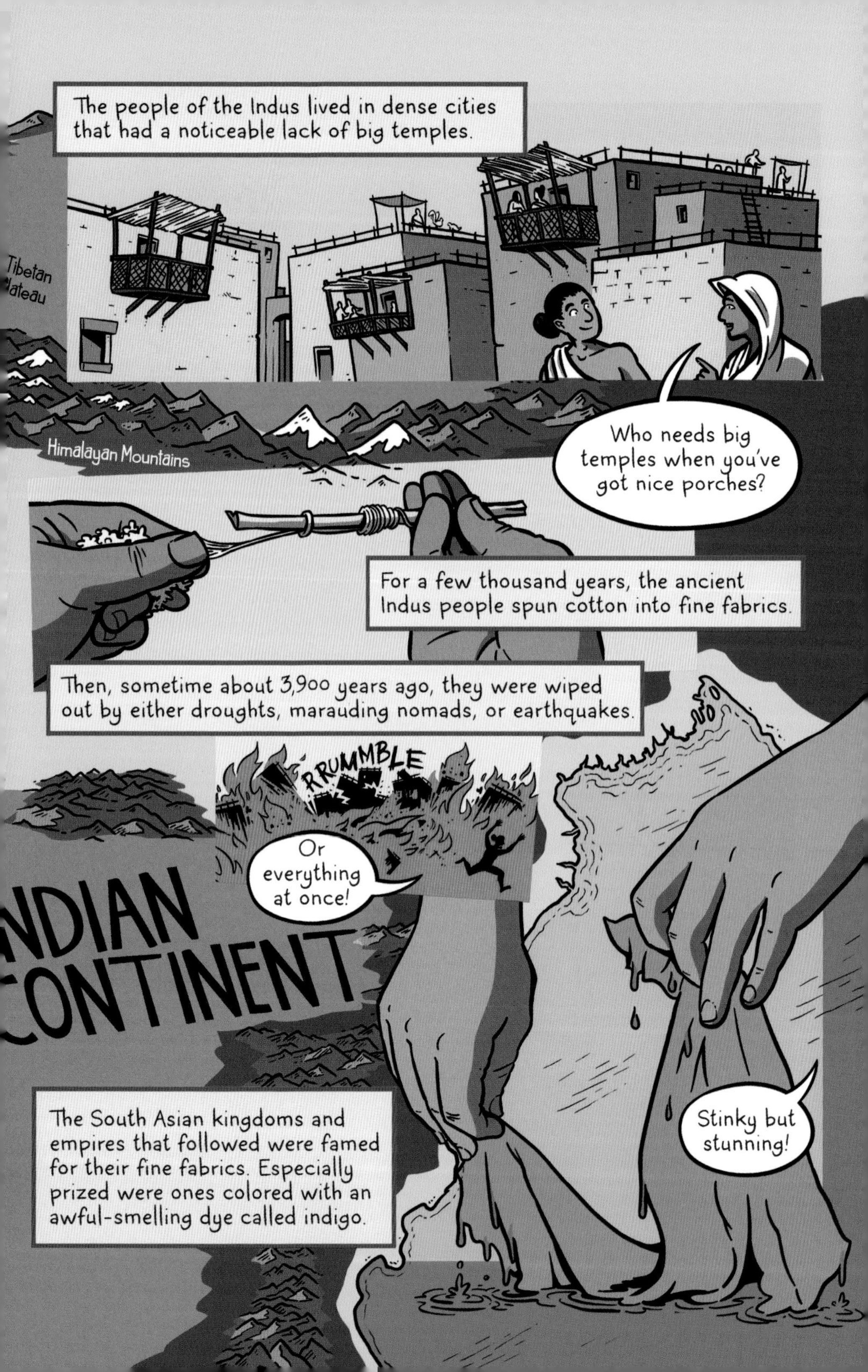
The people of the Indus lived in dense cities that had a noticeable lack of big temples.
Tibetan Plateau
Himalayan Mountains
Who needs big temples when you've got nice porches?
For a few thousand years, the ancient Indus people spun cotton into fine fabrics.
Then, sometime about 3,900 years ago, they were wiped out by either droughts, marauding nomads, or earthquakes.
RRUMMBLE
Or everything at once!
NDIAN
CONTINENT
The South Asian kingdoms and empires that followed were famed for their fine fabrics. Especially prized were ones colored with an awful-smelling dye called indigo.
Stinky but stunning!

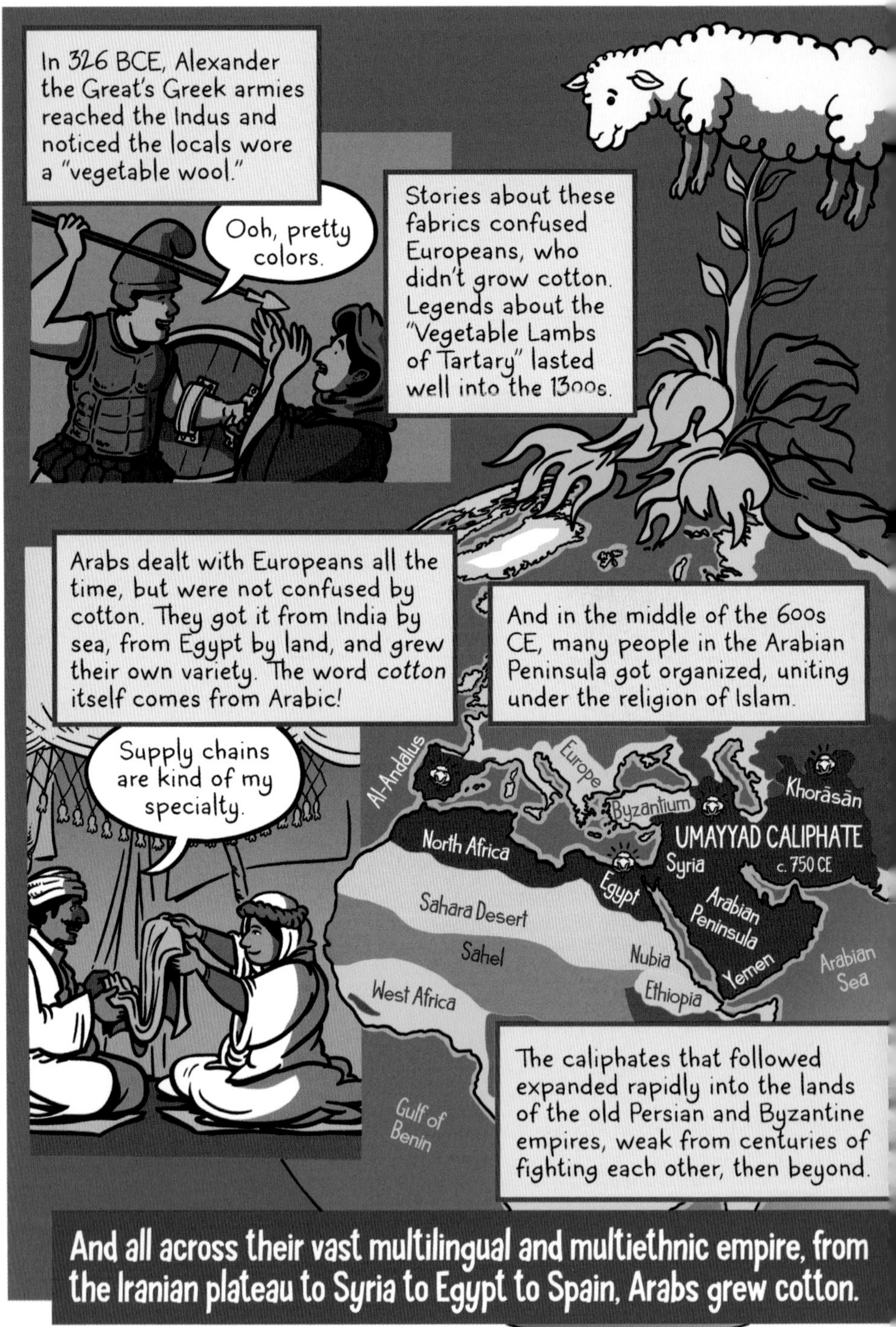

In 326 BCE, Alexander the Great's Greek armies reached the Indus and noticed the locals wore a "vegetable wool."
Ooh, pretty colors.
Stories about these fabrics confused Europeans, who didn't grow cotton. Legends about the "Vegetable Lambs of Tartary" lasted well into the 1300s.
Arabs dealt with Europeans all the time, but were not confused by cotton. They got it from India by sea, from Egypt by land, and grew their own variety. The word *cotton* itself comes from Arabic!
And in the middle of the 600s CE, many people in the Arabian Peninsula got organized, uniting under the religion of Islam.
Supply chains are kind of my specialty.
Al-Andalus
Europe
Byzantium
Khorāsān
UMAYYAD CALIPHATE
c. 750 CE
North Africa
Syria
Egypt
Arabian Peninsula
Sahara Desert
Sahel
Nubia
Yemen
Arabian Sea
West Africa
Ethiopia
Gulf of Benin
The caliphates that followed expanded rapidly into the lands of the old Persian and Byzantine empires, weak from centuries of fighting each other, then beyond.
And all across their vast multilingual and multiethnic empire, from the Iranian plateau to Syria to Egypt to Spain, Arabs grew cotton.

Connecting the caliphate's heartlands with its far-flung colonies in Spain was a narrow coastal strip of North Africa between the Mediterranean Sea and Sahara Desert called the Maghreb.

The Berber tribes of the Maghreb had lived through Roman, Egyptian, and Phoenician occupations.

Thanks for the cloth! We're off to the desert. We'll be back in, like, 5 or 6 months.

They happily traded with the empires that passed through their lands but resisted assimilation into them.

Maybe never.

The trade routes of the Berbers weren't on the seas where their conquerors came from but south through the sands of the Sahara.

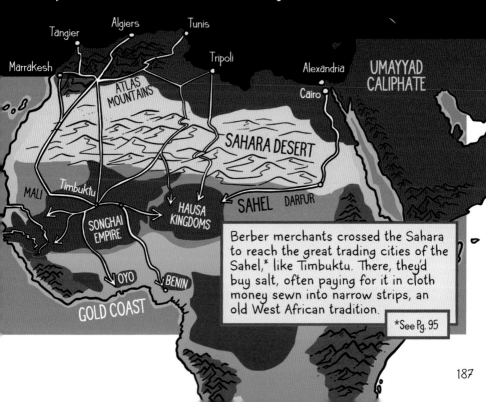

Tangier
Algiers
Tunis
Marrakesh
Tripoli
Alexandria
Cairo
UMAYYAD CALIPHATE
ATLAS MOUNTAINS
SAHARA DESERT
MALI
Timbuktu
SAHEL
DARFUR
HAUSA KINGDOMS
SONGHAI EMPIRE
OYO
BENIN
GOLD COAST

Berber merchants crossed the Sahara to reach the great trading cities of the Sahel,* like Timbuktu. There, they'd buy salt, often paying for it in cloth money sewn into narrow strips, an old West African tradition.

*See Pg. 95

187

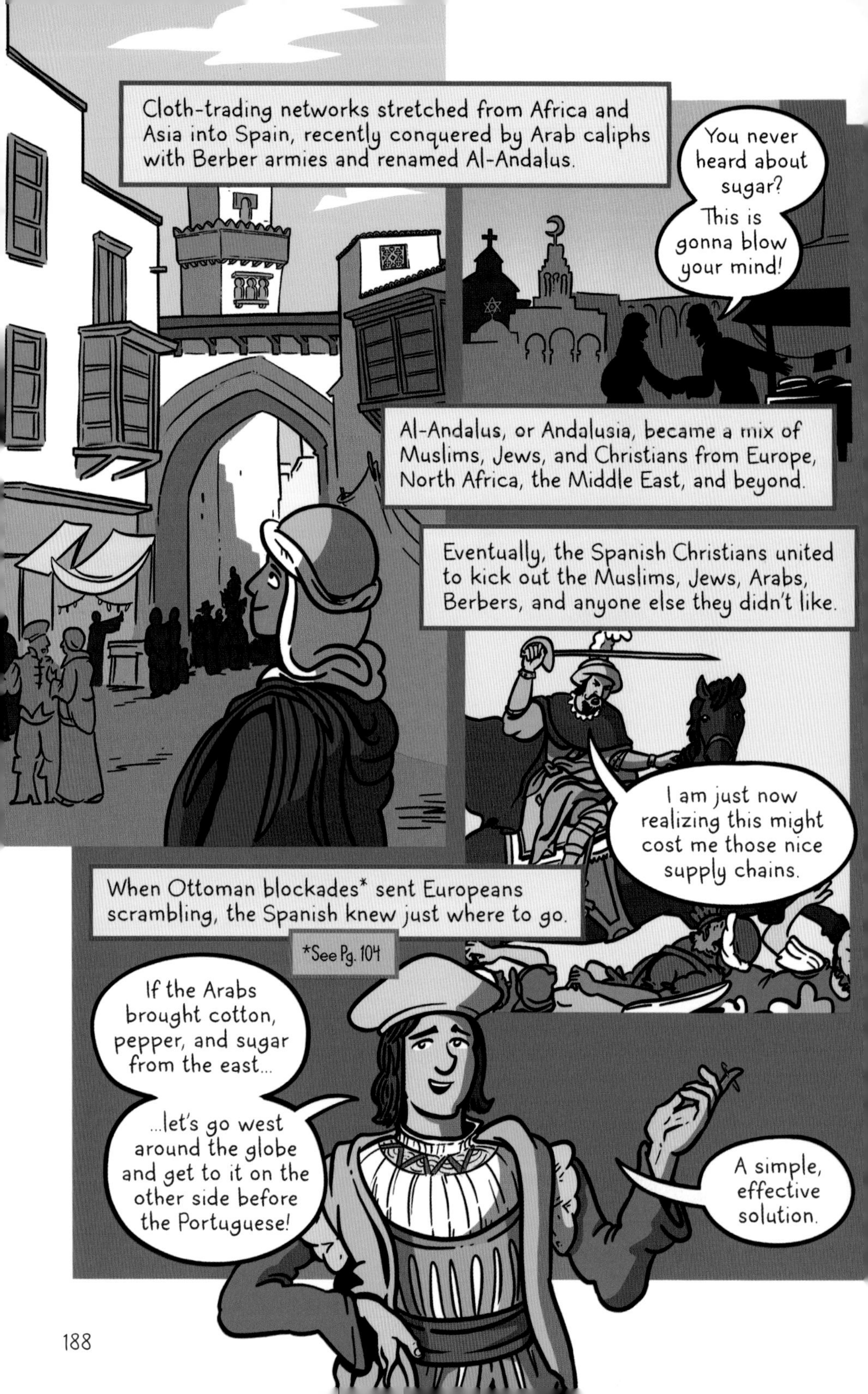
Cloth-trading networks stretched from Africa and Asia into Spain, recently conquered by Arab caliphs with Berber armies and renamed Al-Andalus.
You never heard about sugar? This is gonna blow your mind!
Al-Andalus, or Andalusia, became a mix of Muslims, Jews, and Christians from Europe, North Africa, the Middle East, and beyond.
Eventually, the Spanish Christians united to kick out the Muslims, Jews, Arabs, Berbers, and anyone else they didn't like.
I am just now realizing this might cost me those nice supply chains.
When Ottoman blockades* sent Europeans scrambling, the Spanish knew just where to go.
*See Pg. 104
If the Arabs brought cotton, pepper, and sugar from the east...
...let's go west around the globe and get to it on the other side before the Portuguese!
A simple, effective solution.

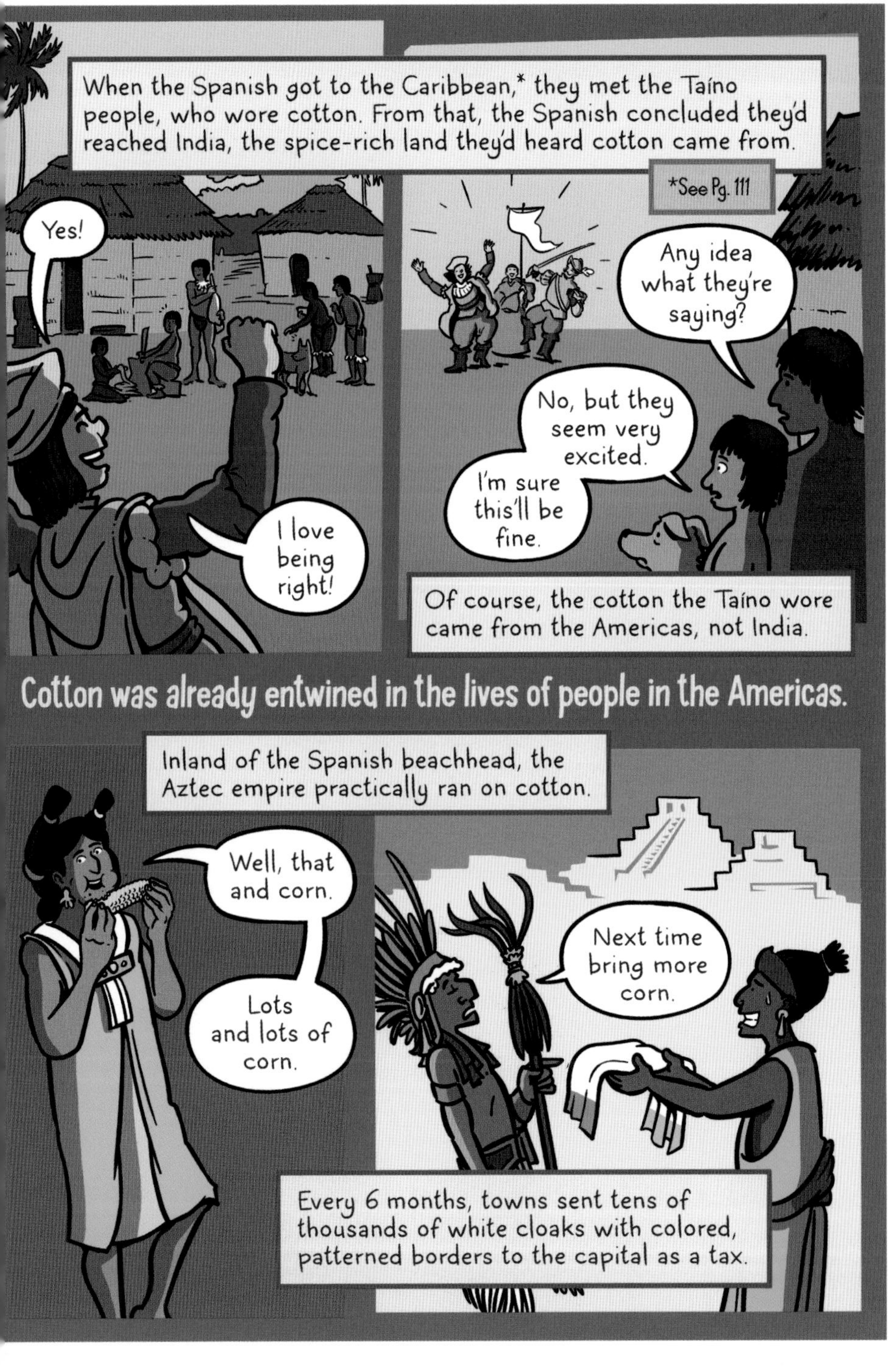
When the Spanish got to the Caribbean,* they met the Taíno people, who wore cotton. From that, the Spanish concluded they'd reached India, the spice-rich land they'd heard cotton came from.
*See Pg. 111
Yes!
I love being right!
Any idea what they're saying?
No, but they seem very excited.
I'm sure this'll be fine.
Of course, the cotton the Taíno wore came from the Americas, not India.
Cotton was already entwined in the lives of people in the Americas.
Inland of the Spanish beachhead, the Aztec empire practically ran on cotton.
Well, that and corn.
Lots and lots of corn.
Next time bring more corn.
Every 6 months, towns sent tens of thousands of white cloaks with colored, patterned borders to the capital as a tax.

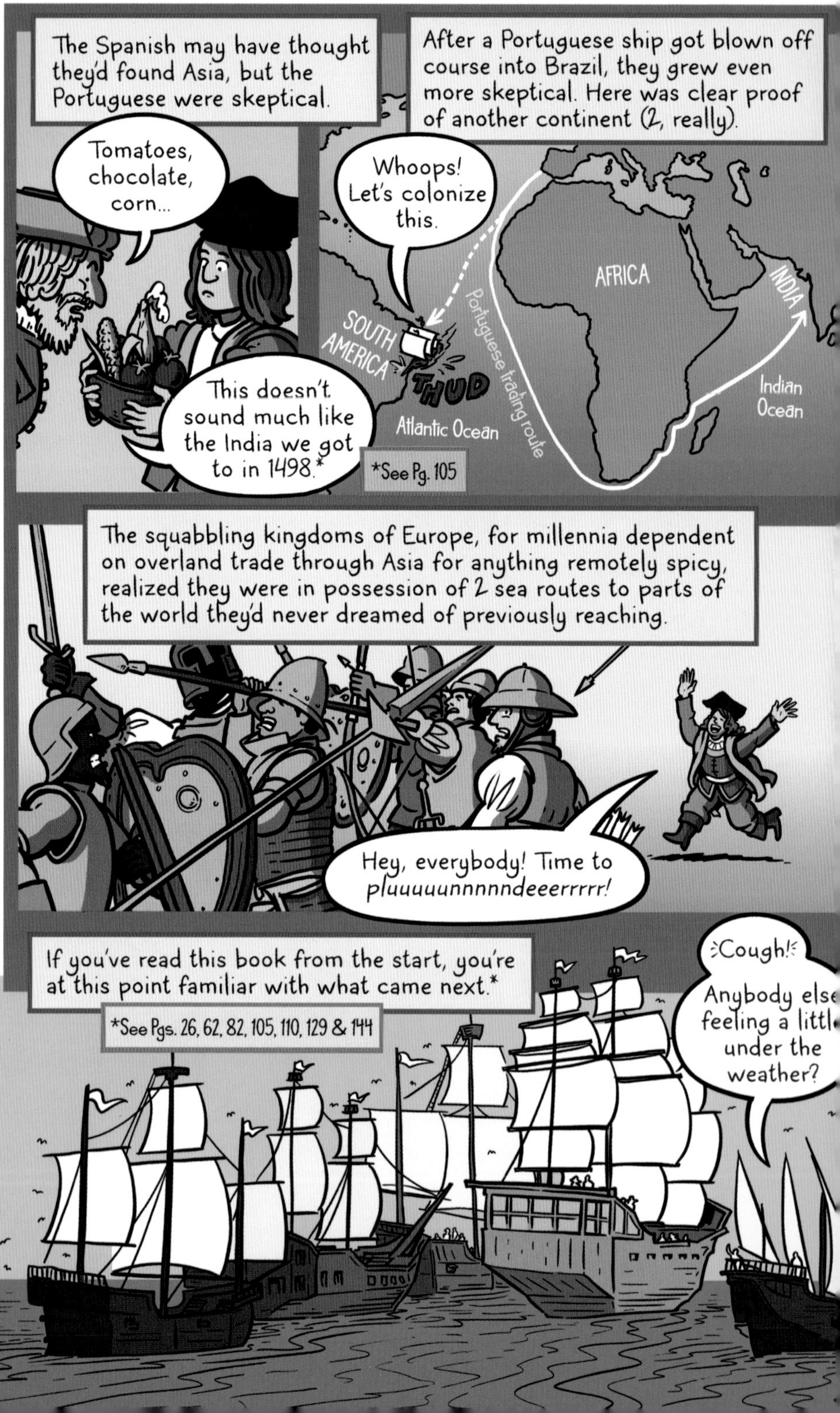

The Spanish may have thought they'd found Asia, but the Portuguese were skeptical.
Tomatoes, chocolate, corn...
This doesn't sound much like the India we got to in 1498.*
After a Portuguese ship got blown off course into Brazil, they grew even more skeptical. Here was clear proof of another continent (2, really).
Whoops! Let's colonize this.
SOUTH AMERICA
THUD
Atlantic Ocean
Portuguese trading route
AFRICA
INDIA
Indian Ocean
*See Pg. 105
The squabbling kingdoms of Europe, for millennia dependent on overland trade through Asia for anything remotely spicy, realized they were in possession of 2 sea routes to parts of the world they'd never dreamed of previously reaching.
Hey, everybody! Time to pluuuuunnnndeeerrrrr!
If you've read this book from the start, you're at this point familiar with what came next.*
*See Pgs. 26, 62, 82, 105, 110, 129 & 144
Cough!
Anybody else feeling a little under the weather?

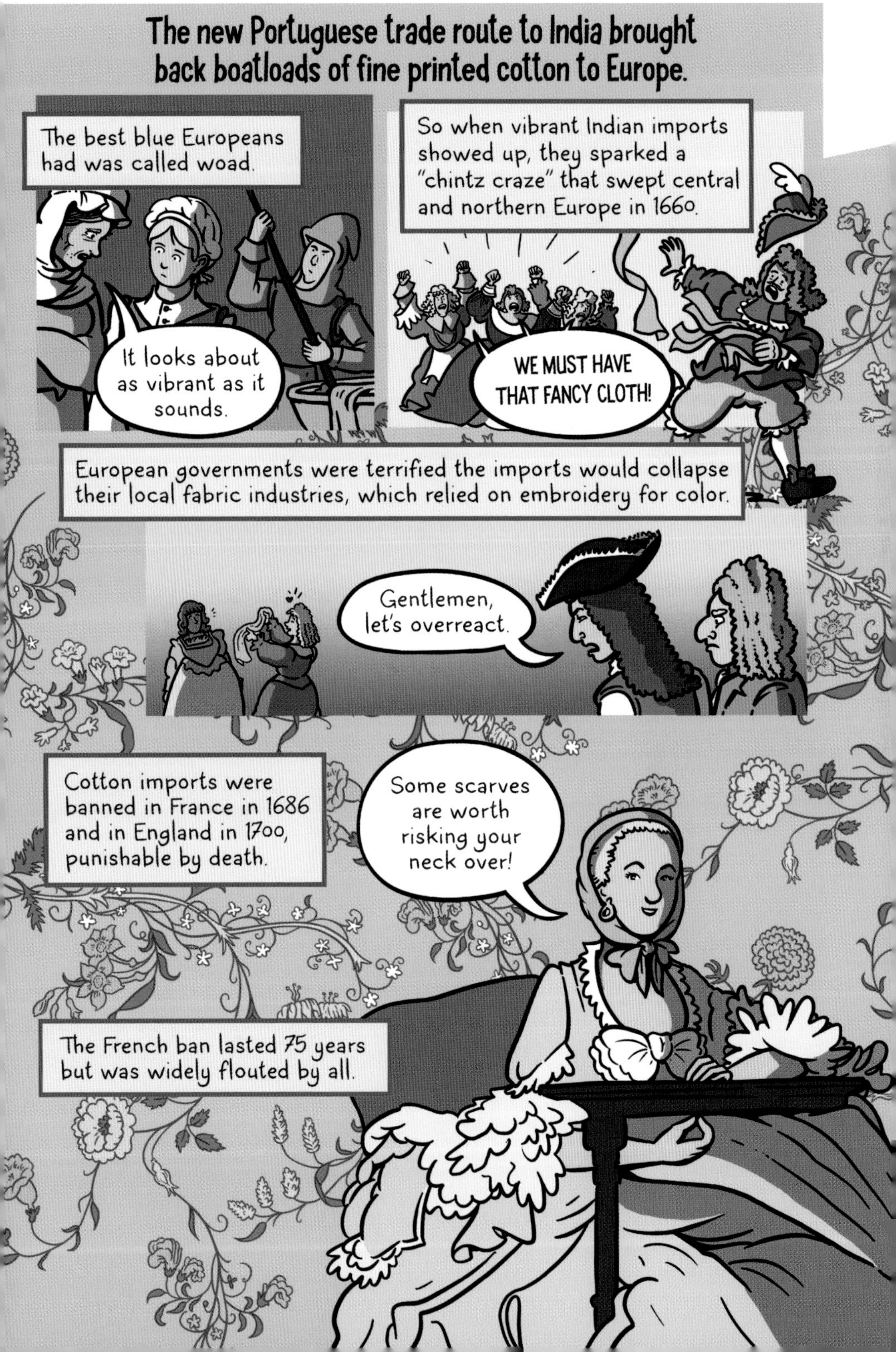
The new Portuguese trade route to India brought back boatloads of fine printed cotton to Europe.
The best blue Europeans had was called woad.
It looks about as vibrant as it sounds.
So when vibrant Indian imports showed up, they sparked a "chintz craze" that swept central and northern Europe in 1660.
WE MUST HAVE THAT FANCY CLOTH!
European governments were terrified the imports would collapse their local fabric industries, which relied on embroidery for color.
Gentlemen, let's overreact.
Cotton imports were banned in France in 1686 and in England in 1700, punishable by death.
Some scarves are worth risking your neck over!
The French ban lasted 75 years but was widely flouted by all.

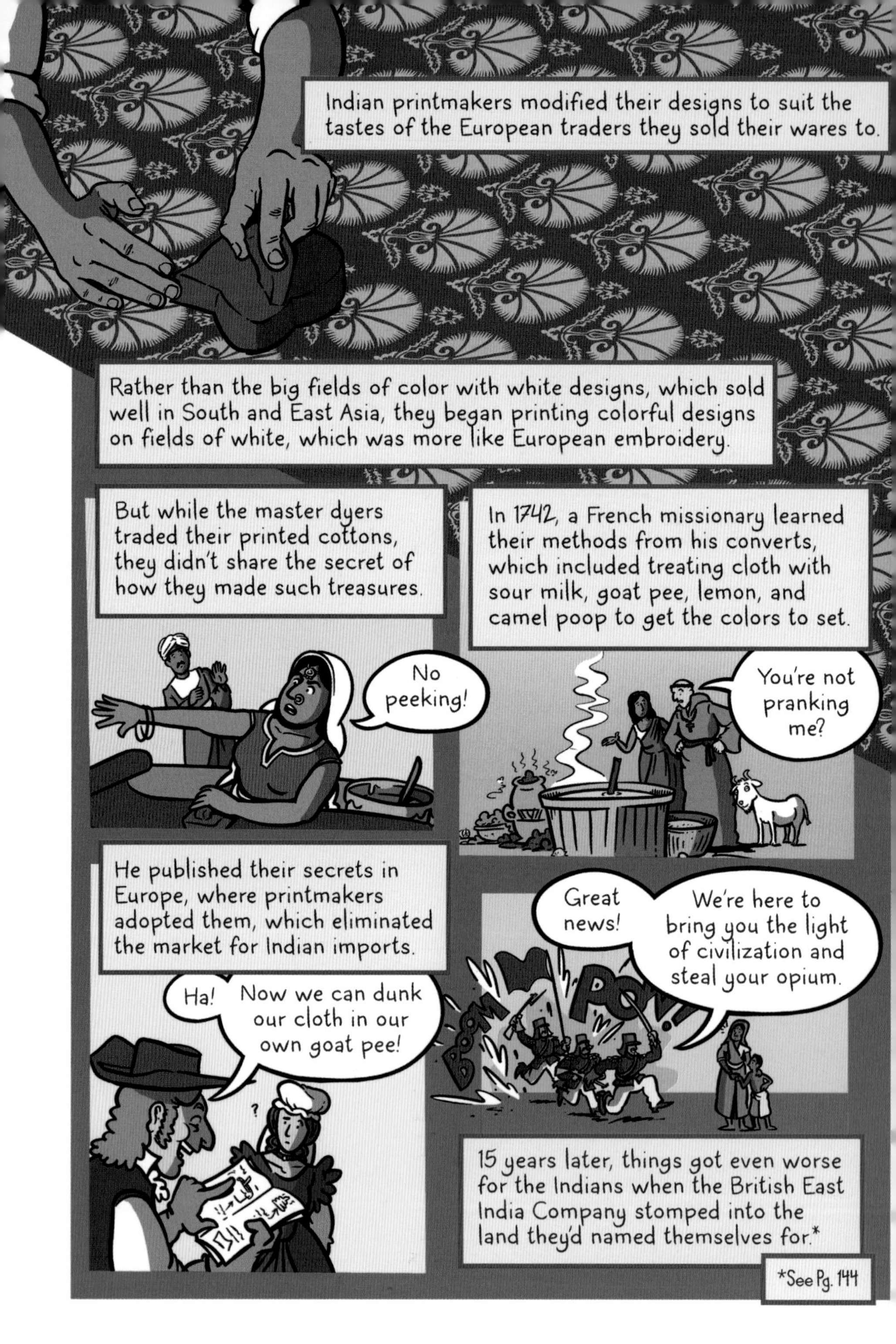

Indian printmakers modified their designs to suit the tastes of the European traders they sold their wares to.
Rather than the big fields of color with white designs, which sold well in South and East Asia, they began printing colorful designs on fields of white, which was more like European embroidery.
But while the master dyers traded their printed cottons, they didn't share the secret of how they made such treasures.
No peeking!
In 1742, a French missionary learned their methods from his converts, which included treating cloth with sour milk, goat pee, lemon, and camel poop to get the colors to set.
You're not pranking me?
He published their secrets in Europe, where printmakers adopted them, which eliminated the market for Indian imports.
Ha!
Now we can dunk our cloth in our own goat pee!
?
Great news!
We're here to bring you the light of civilization and steal your opium.
BOOM
POW
15 years later, things got even worse for the Indians when the British East India Company stomped into the land they'd named themselves for.*
*See Pg. 144

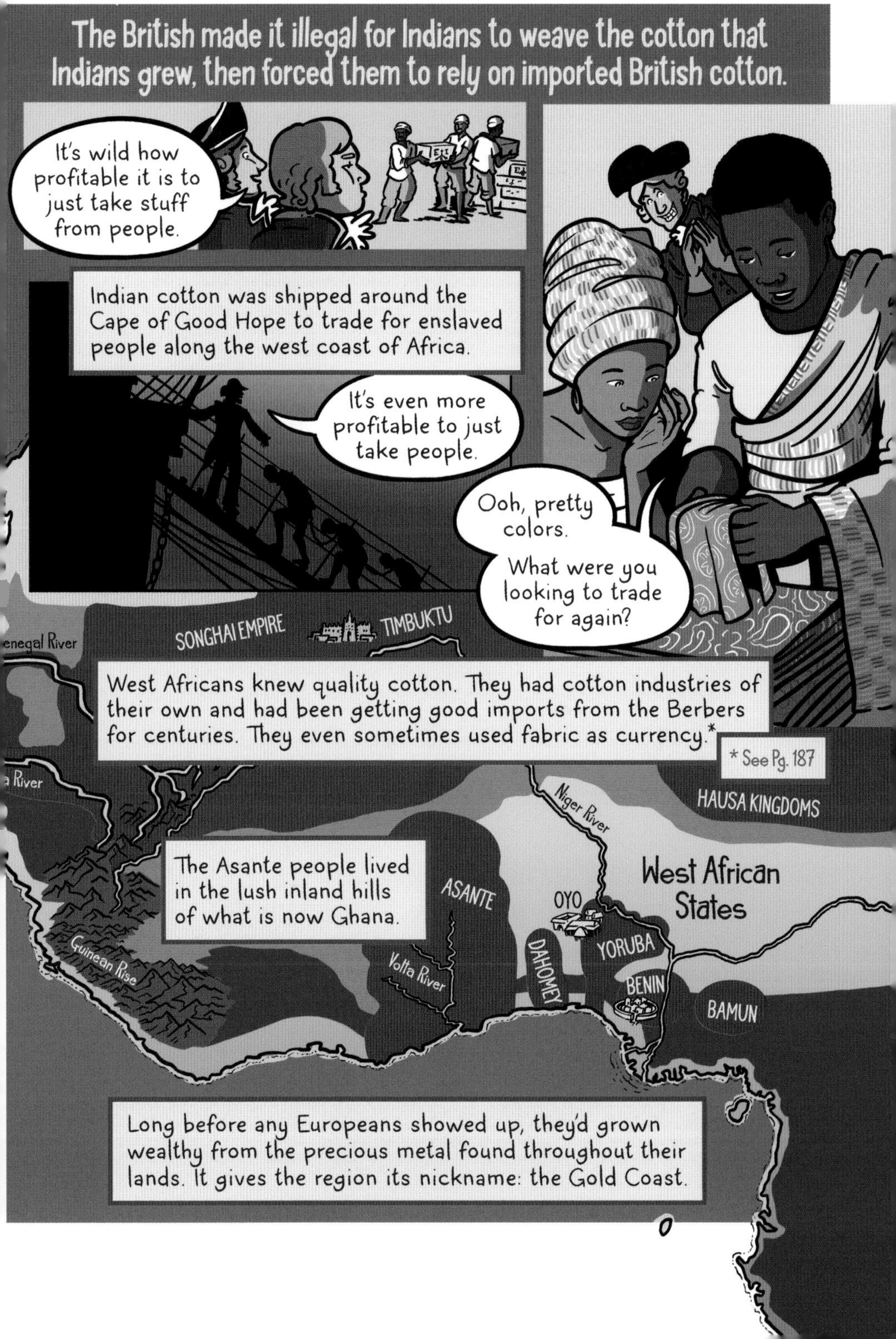

The British made it illegal for Indians to weave the cotton that Indians grew, then forced them to rely on imported British cotton.
It's wild how profitable it is to just take stuff from people.
Indian cotton was shipped around the Cape of Good Hope to trade for enslaved people along the west coast of Africa.
It's even more profitable to just take people.
Ooh, pretty colors.
What were you looking to trade for again?
SONGHAI EMPIRE
TIMBUKTU
enegal River
West Africans knew quality cotton. They had cotton industries of their own and had been getting good imports from the Berbers for centuries. They even sometimes used fabric as currency.*
* See Pg. 187
a River
Niger River
HAUSA KINGDOMS
The Asante people lived in the lush inland hills of what is now Ghana.
ASANTE
West African States
OYO
YORUBA
DAHOMEY
BENIN
BAMUN
Guinean Rise
Volta River
Long before any Europeans showed up, they'd grown wealthy from the precious metal found throughout their lands. It gives the region its nickname: the Gold Coast.

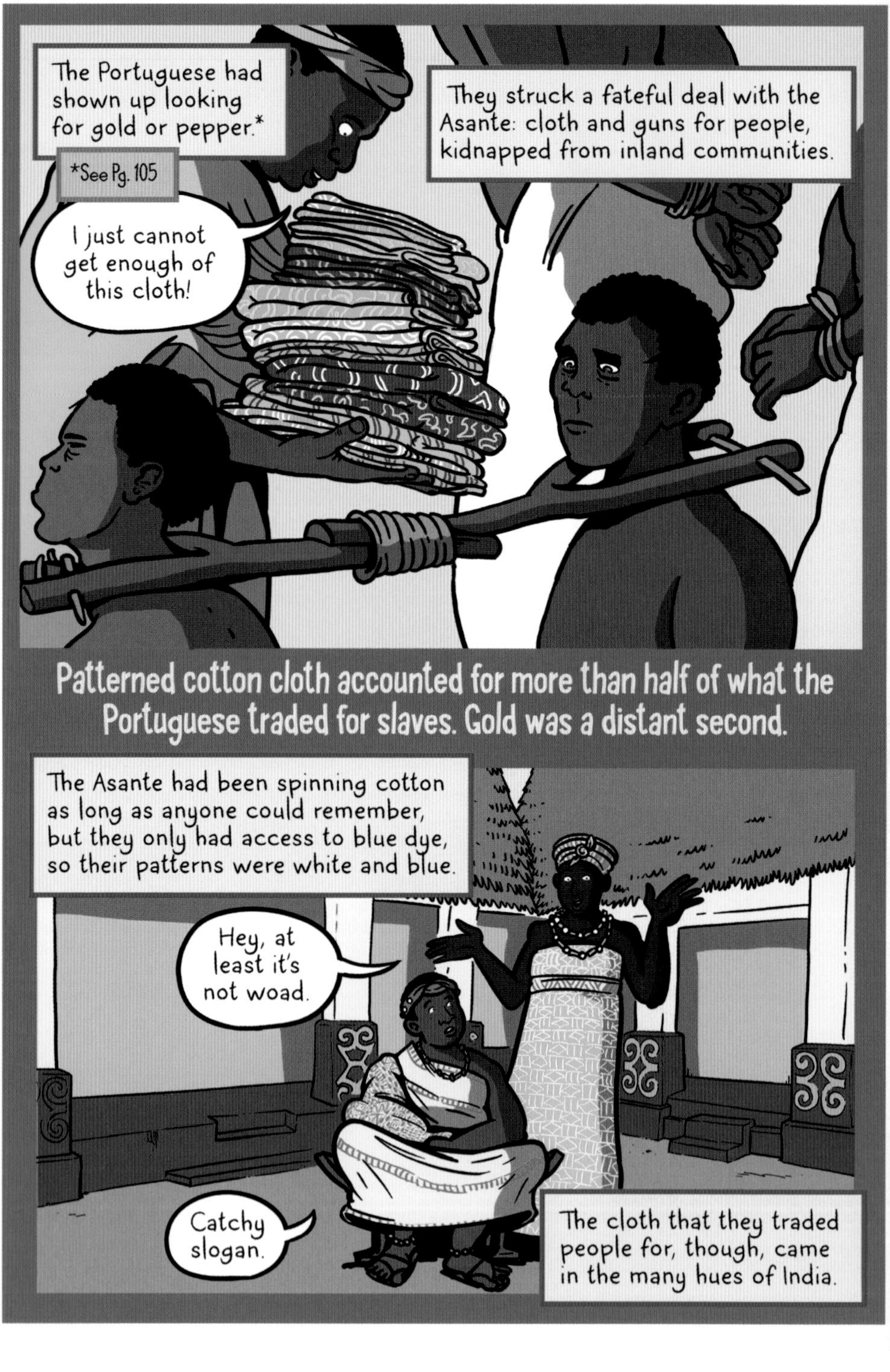
The Portuguese had shown up looking for gold or pepper.*
*See Pg. 105
They struck a fateful deal with the Asante: cloth and guns for people, kidnapped from inland communities.
I just cannot get enough of this cloth!
Patterned cotton cloth accounted for more than half of what the Portuguese traded for slaves. Gold was a distant second.
The Asante had been spinning cotton as long as anyone could remember, but they only had access to blue dye, so their patterns were white and blue.
Hey, at least it's not woad.
Catchy slogan.
The cloth that they traded people for, though, came in the many hues of India.

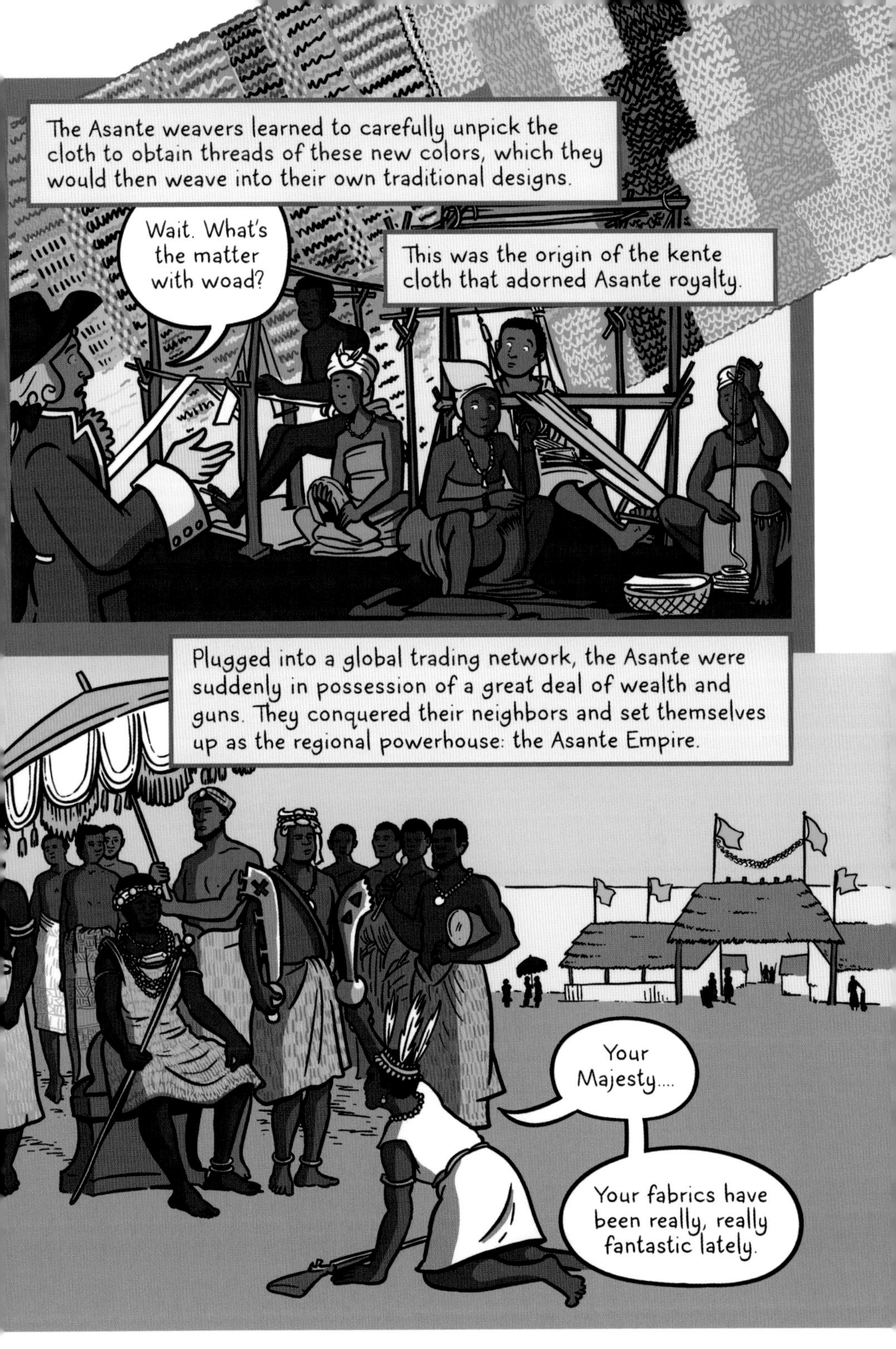
The Asante weavers learned to carefully unpick the cloth to obtain threads of these new colors, which they would then weave into their own traditional designs.
Wait. What's the matter with woad?
This was the origin of the kente cloth that adorned Asante royalty.
Plugged into a global trading network, the Asante were suddenly in possession of a great deal of wealth and guns. They conquered their neighbors and set themselves up as the regional powerhouse: the Asante Empire.
Your Majesty....
Your fabrics have been really, really fantastic lately.

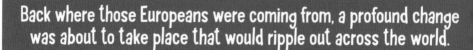

Back where those Europeans were coming from, a profound change was about to take place that would ripple out across the world.

This change would be ushered in by an ill-tempered wigmaker named Richard Arkwright, who traveled the hills of Lancashire, England, buying women's hair.

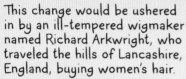

It sounds weird when you put it that way.

When wigs went out of style, Arkwright got into the cotton business, designing an efficient mill that ran off water power.

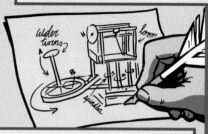

Arkwright became known for betraying business partners, but he could build a fine cotton mill.

It's the results that matter.

Arkwright's efficient new mills also put a bunch of inefficient handweavers out of work, who proceeded to efficiently burn down Arkwright's mill.

It's the results that matter.

Did you know you could just buy your own army? It's fantastic!

Arkwright hired 1,500 troops, bought some cannons, and built even more cotton mills.

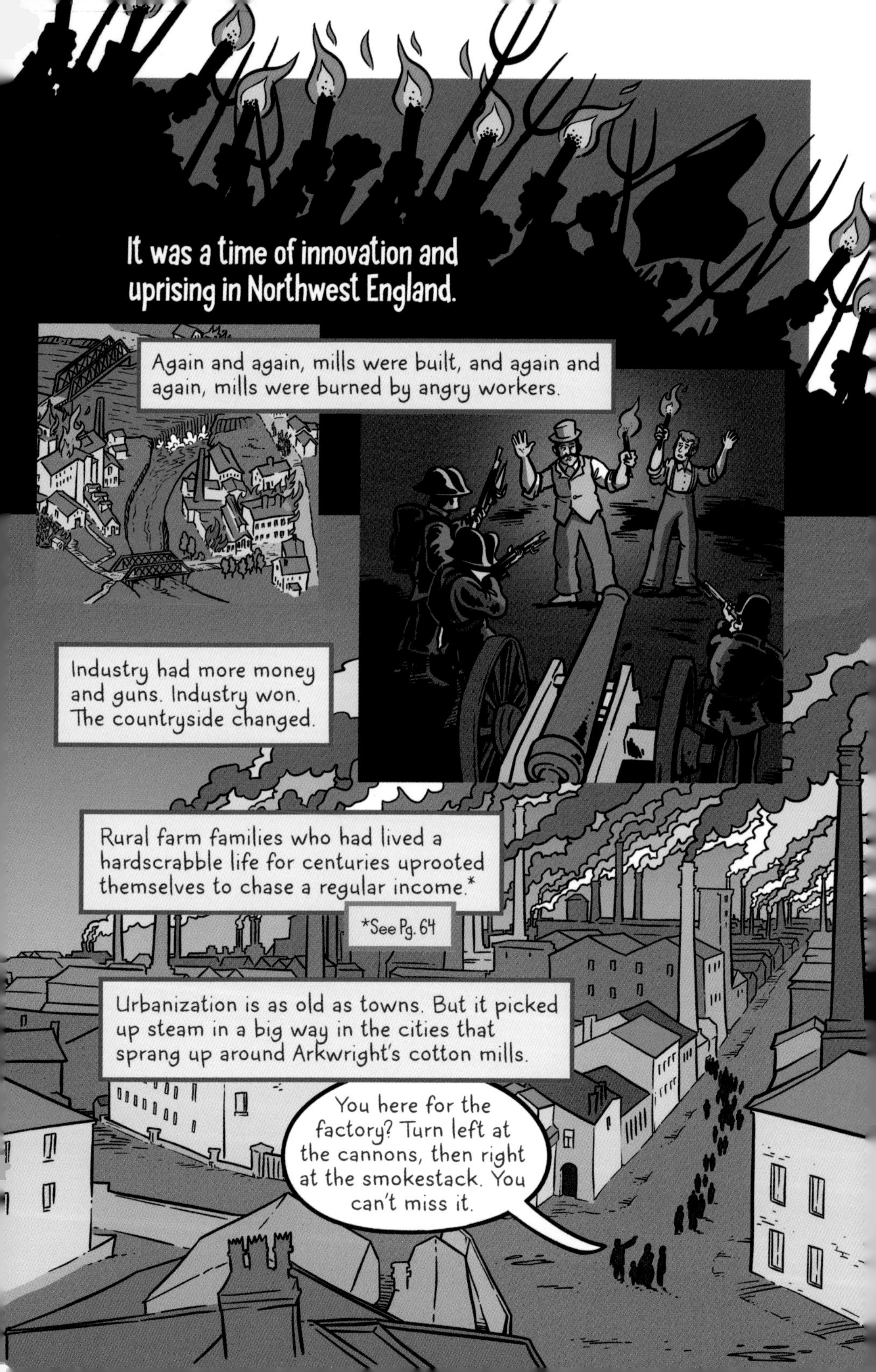
It was a time of innovation and uprising in Northwest England.
Again and again, mills were built, and again and again, mills were burned by angry workers.
Industry had more money and guns. Industry won. The countryside changed.
Rural farm families who had lived a hardscrabble life for centuries uprooted themselves to chase a regular income.*
*See Pg. 64
Urbanization is as old as towns. But it picked up steam in a big way in the cities that sprang up around Arkwright's cotton mills.
You here for the factory? Turn left at the cannons, then right at the smokestack. You can't miss it.

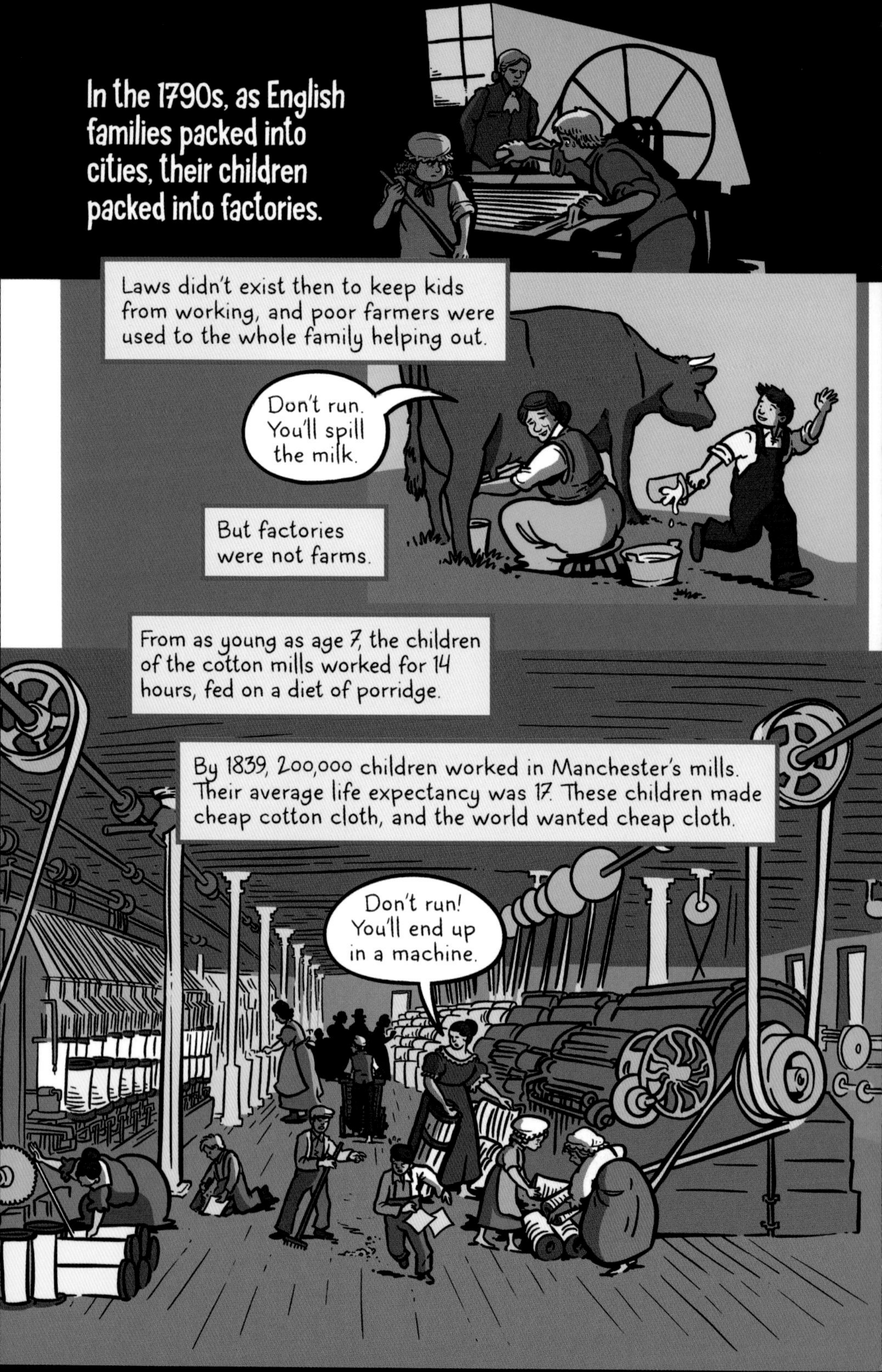
In the 1790s, as English families packed into cities, their children packed into factories.
Laws didn't exist then to keep kids from working, and poor farmers were used to the whole family helping out.
Don't run. You'll spill the milk.
But factories were not farms.
From as young as age 7, the children of the cotton mills worked for 14 hours, fed on a diet of porridge.
By 1839, 200,000 children worked in Manchester's mills. Their average life expectancy was 17. These children made cheap cotton cloth, and the world wanted cheap cloth.
Don't run! You'll end up in a machine.

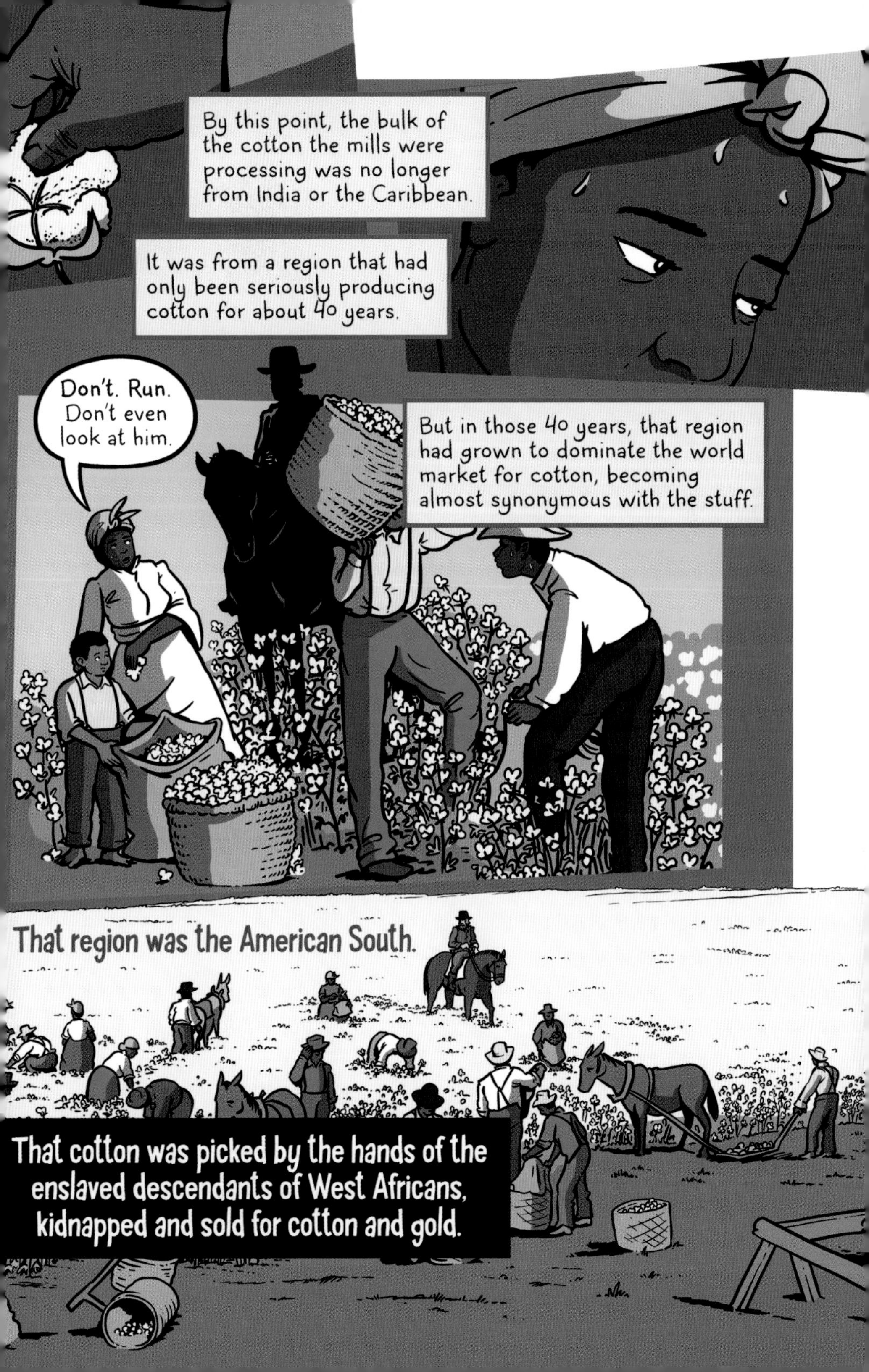

By this point, the bulk of the cotton the mills were processing was no longer from India or the Caribbean.
It was from a region that had only been seriously producing cotton for about 40 years.
Don't. Run. Don't even look at him.
But in those 40 years, that region had grown to dominate the world market for cotton, becoming almost synonymous with the stuff.
That region was the American South.
That cotton was picked by the hands of the enslaved descendants of West Africans, kidnapped and sold for cotton and gold.

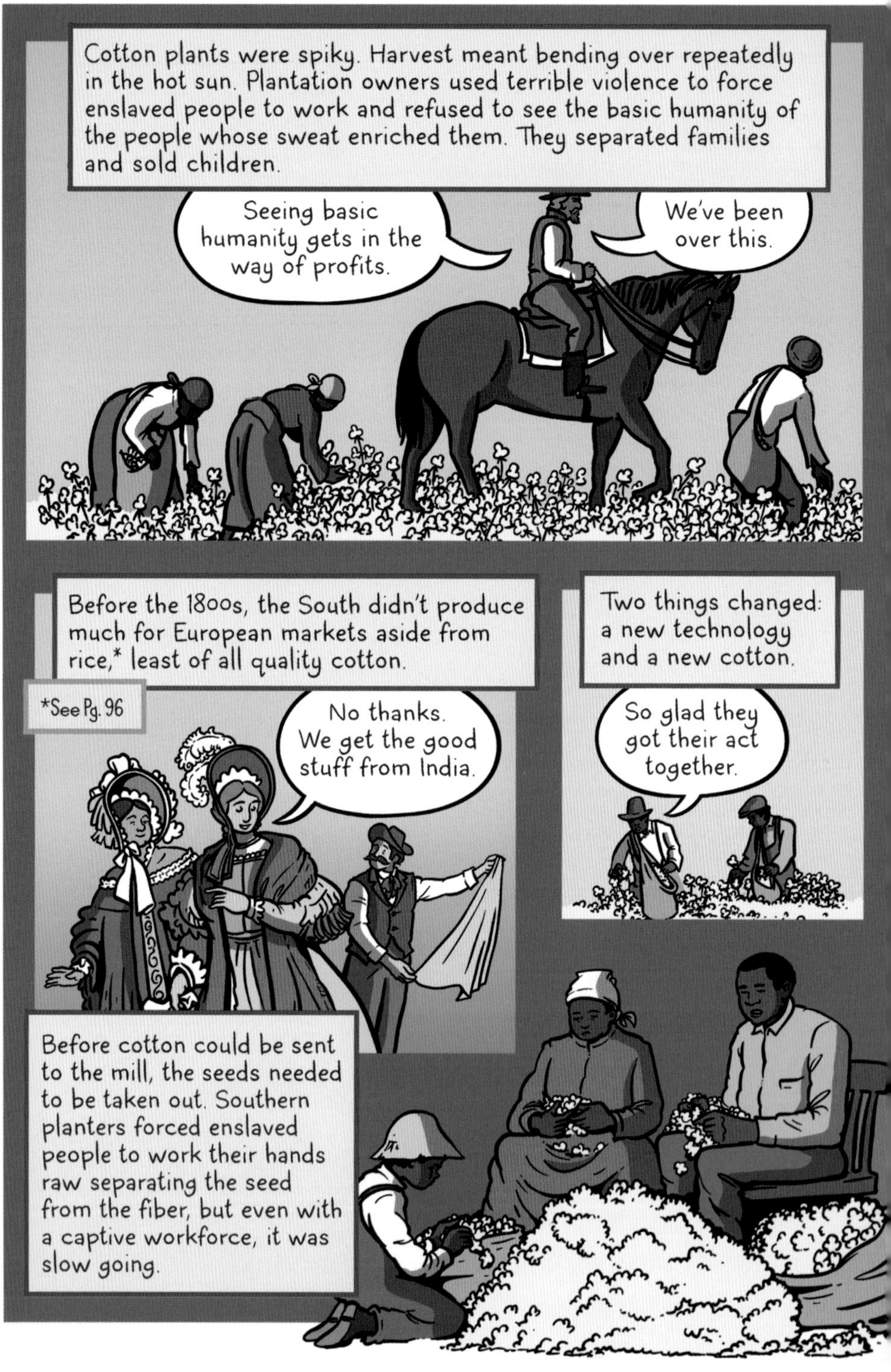

Cotton plants were spiky. Harvest meant bending over repeatedly in the hot sun. Plantation owners used terrible violence to force enslaved people to work and refused to see the basic humanity of the people whose sweat enriched them. They separated families and sold children.
Seeing basic humanity gets in the way of profits.
We've been over this.
Before the 1800s, the South didn't produce much for European markets aside from rice,* least of all quality cotton.
*See Pg. 96
No thanks. We get the good stuff from India.
Two things changed: a new technology and a new cotton.
So glad they got their act together.
Before cotton could be sent to the mill, the seeds needed to be taken out. Southern planters forced enslaved people to work their hands raw separating the seed from the fiber, but even with a captive workforce, it was slow going.

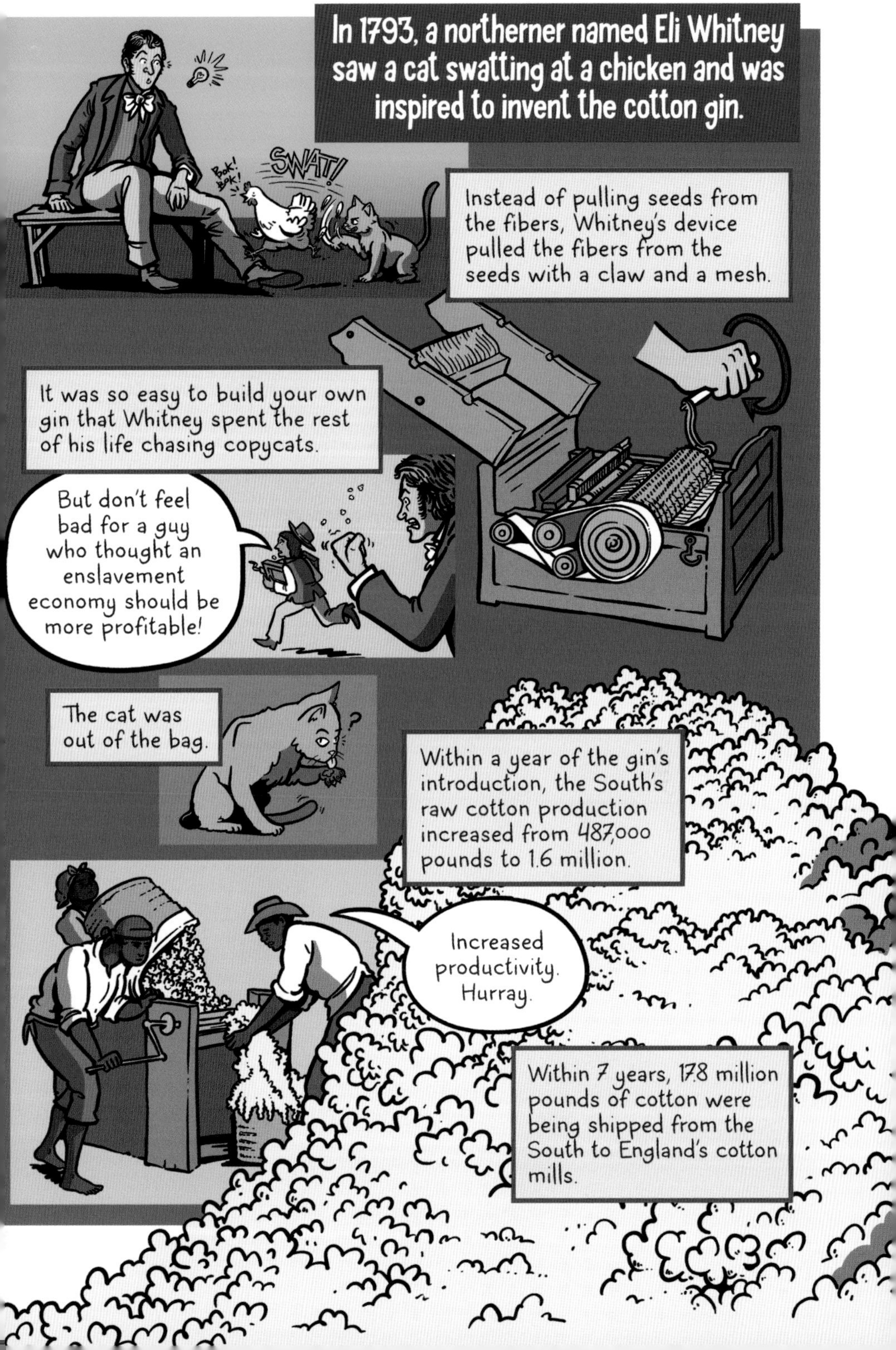
In 1793, a northerner named Eli Whitney saw a cat swatting at a chicken and was inspired to invent the cotton gin.
BOK! BOK!
SWAT!
Instead of pulling seeds from the fibers, Whitney's device pulled the fibers from the seeds with a claw and a mesh.
It was so easy to build your own gin that Whitney spent the rest of his life chasing copycats.
But don't feel bad for a guy who thought an enslavement economy should be more profitable!
The cat was out of the bag.
?
Within a year of the gin's introduction, the South's raw cotton production increased from 487,000 pounds to 1.6 million.
Increased productivity. Hurray.
Within 7 years, 17.8 million pounds of cotton were being shipped from the South to England's cotton mills.

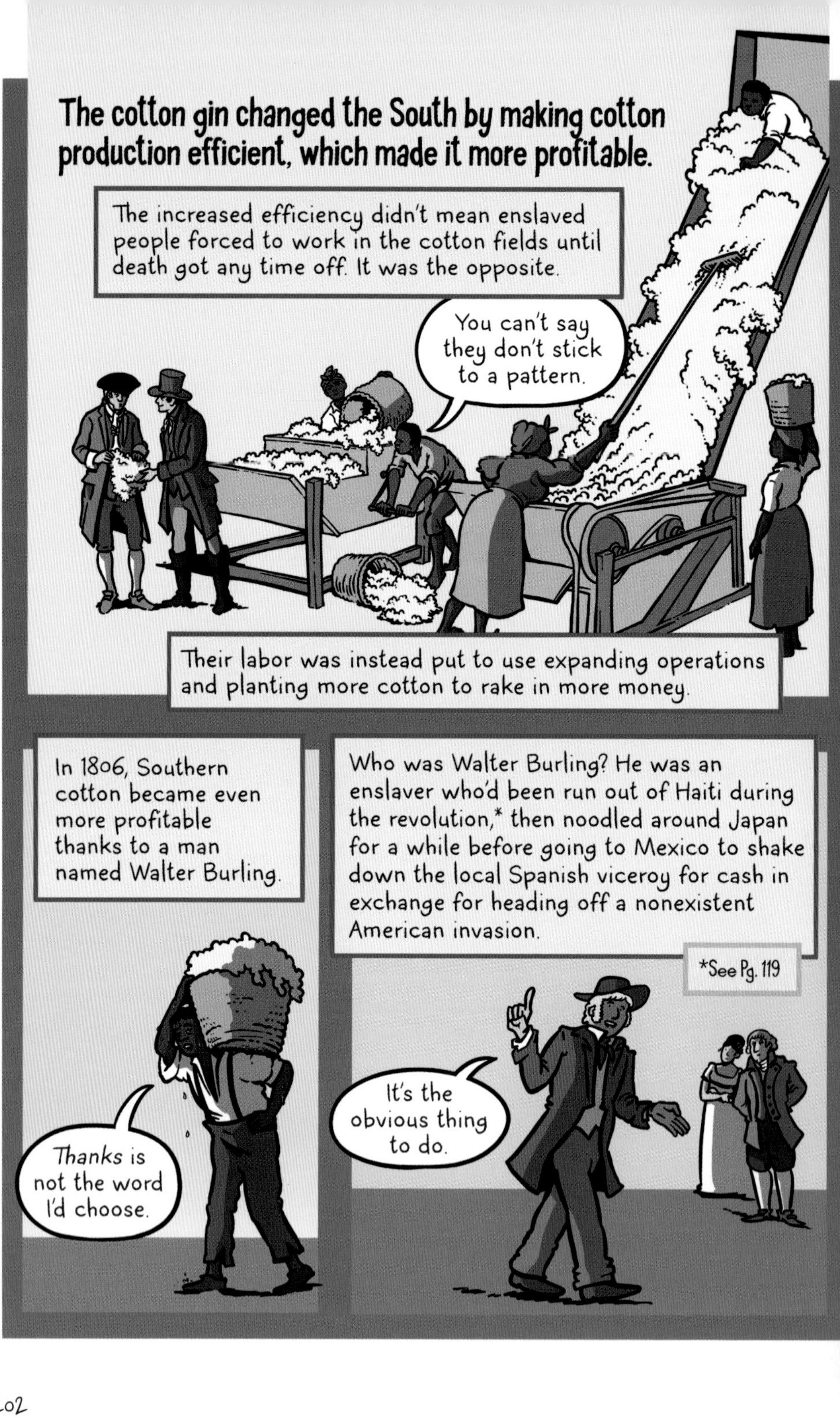
The cotton gin changed the South by making cotton production efficient, which made it more profitable.
The increased efficiency didn't mean enslaved people forced to work in the cotton fields until death got any time off. It was the opposite.
You can't say they don't stick to a pattern.
Their labor was instead put to use expanding operations and planting more cotton to rake in more money.
In 1806, Southern cotton became even more profitable thanks to a man named Walter Burling.
Thanks is not the word I'd choose.
Who was Walter Burling? He was an enslaver who'd been run out of Haiti during the revolution,* then noodled around Japan for a while before going to Mexico to shake down the local Spanish viceroy for cash in exchange for heading off a nonexistent American invasion.
*See Pg. 119
It's the obvious thing to do.

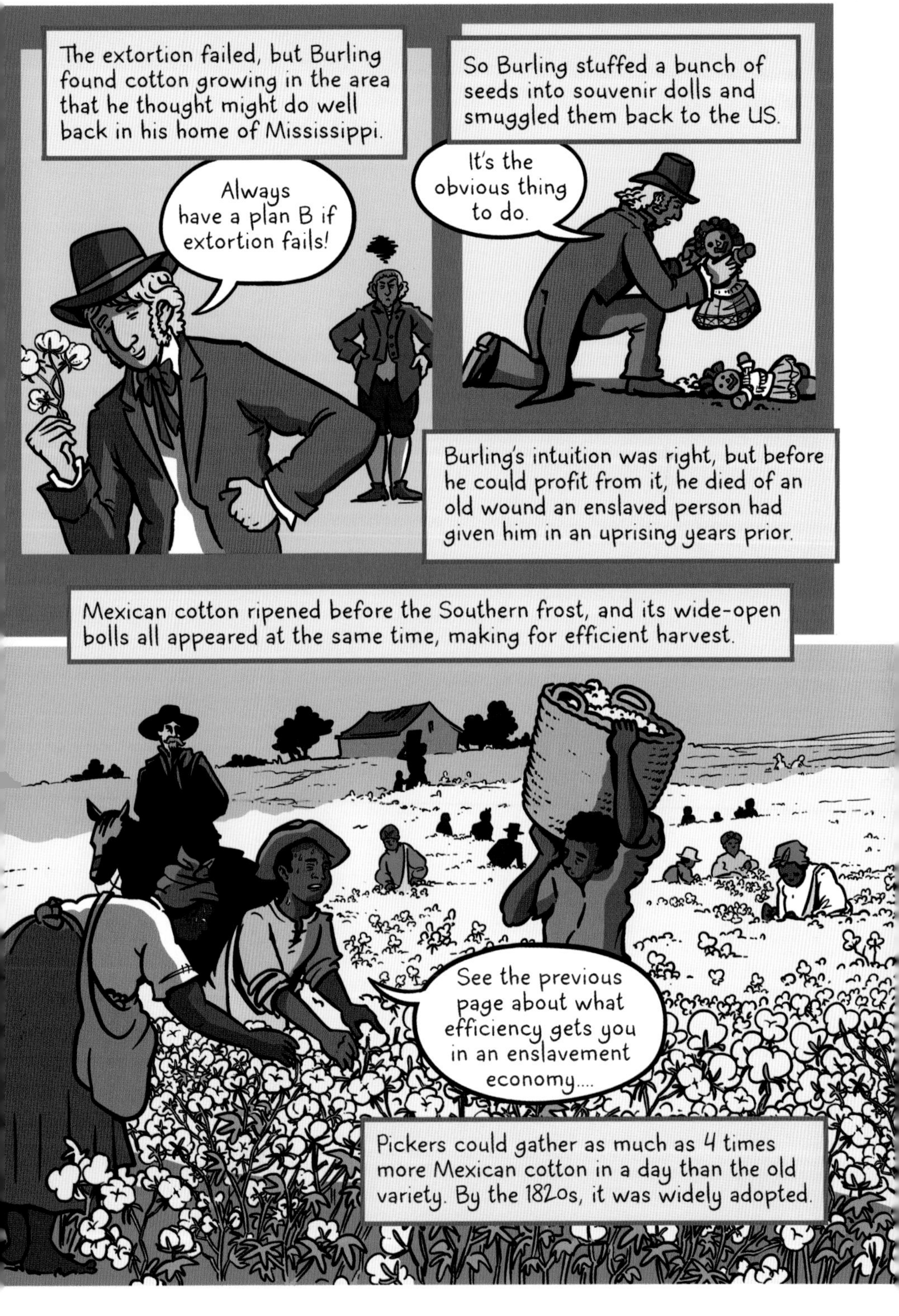
The extortion failed, but Burling found cotton growing in the area that he thought might do well back in his home of Mississippi.
Always have a plan B if extortion fails!
So Burling stuffed a bunch of seeds into souvenir dolls and smuggled them back to the US.
It's the obvious thing to do.
Burling's intuition was right, but before he could profit from it, he died of an old wound an enslaved person had given him in an uprising years prior.
Mexican cotton ripened before the Southern frost, and its wide-open bolls all appeared at the same time, making for efficient harvest.
See the previous page about what efficiency gets you in an enslavement economy....
Pickers could gather as much as 4 times more Mexican cotton in a day than the old variety. By the 1820s, it was widely adopted.

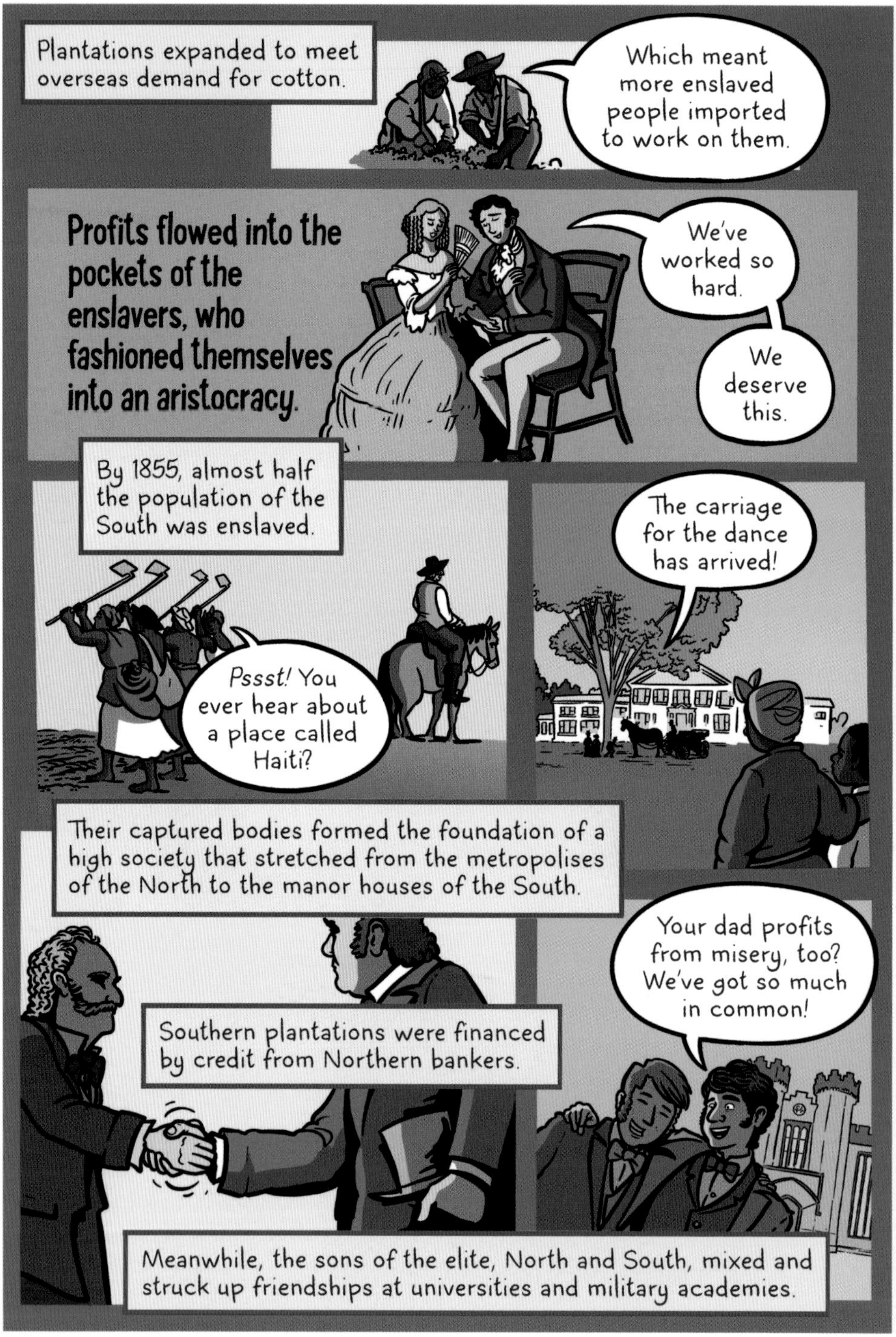
Plantations expanded to meet overseas demand for cotton.
Which meant more enslaved people imported to work on them.
Profits flowed into the pockets of the enslavers, who fashioned themselves into an aristocracy.
We've worked so hard.
We deserve this.
By 1855, almost half the population of the South was enslaved.
Pssst! You ever hear about a place called Haiti?
The carriage for the dance has arrived!
Their captured bodies formed the foundation of a high society that stretched from the metropolises of the North to the manor houses of the South.
Southern plantations were financed by credit from Northern bankers.
Your dad profits from misery, too? We've got so much in common!
Meanwhile, the sons of the elite, North and South, mixed and struck up friendships at universities and military academies.

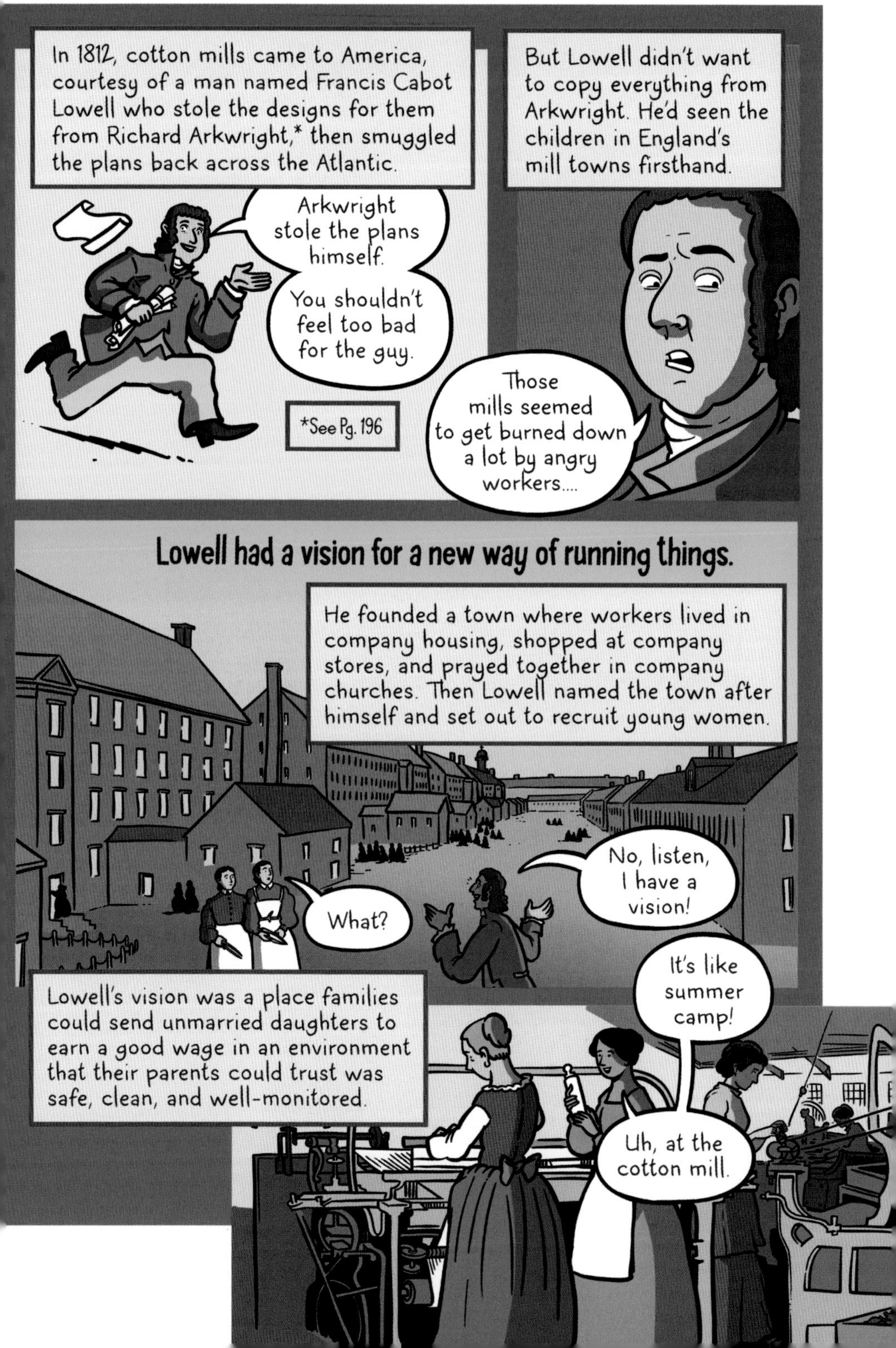
In 1812, cotton mills came to America, courtesy of a man named Francis Cabot Lowell who stole the designs for them from Richard Arkwright,* then smuggled the plans back across the Atlantic.
Arkwright stole the plans himself.
You shouldn't feel too bad for the guy.
*See Pg. 196
But Lowell didn't want to copy everything from Arkwright. He'd seen the children in England's mill towns firsthand.
Those mills seemed to get burned down a lot by angry workers....
Lowell had a vision for a new way of running things.
He founded a town where workers lived in company housing, shopped at company stores, and prayed together in company churches. Then Lowell named the town after himself and set out to recruit young women.
What?
No, listen, I have a vision!
Lowell's vision was a place families could send unmarried daughters to earn a good wage in an environment that their parents could trust was safe, clean, and well-monitored.
It's like summer camp!
Uh, at the cotton mill.

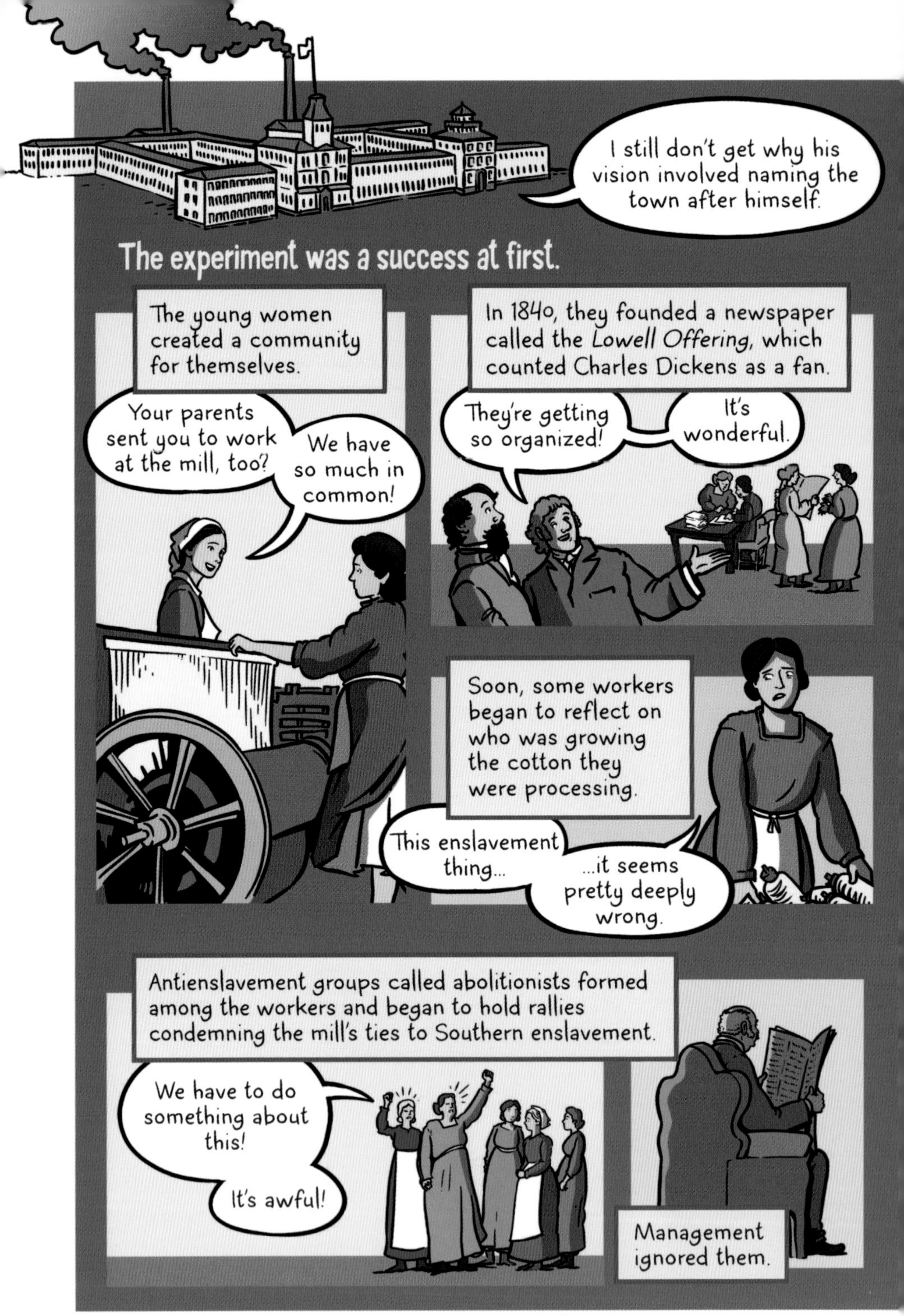
I still don't get why his vision involved naming the town after himself.
The experiment was a success at first.
The young women created a community for themselves.
Your parents sent you to work at the mill, too?
We have so much in common!
In 1840, they founded a newspaper called the *Lowell Offering*, which counted Charles Dickens as a fan.
They're getting so organized!
It's wonderful.
Soon, some workers began to reflect on who was growing the cotton they were processing.
This enslavement thing...
...it seems pretty deeply wrong.
Antienslavement groups called abolitionists formed among the workers and began to hold rallies condemning the mill's ties to Southern enslavement.
We have to do something about this!
It's awful!
Management ignored them.

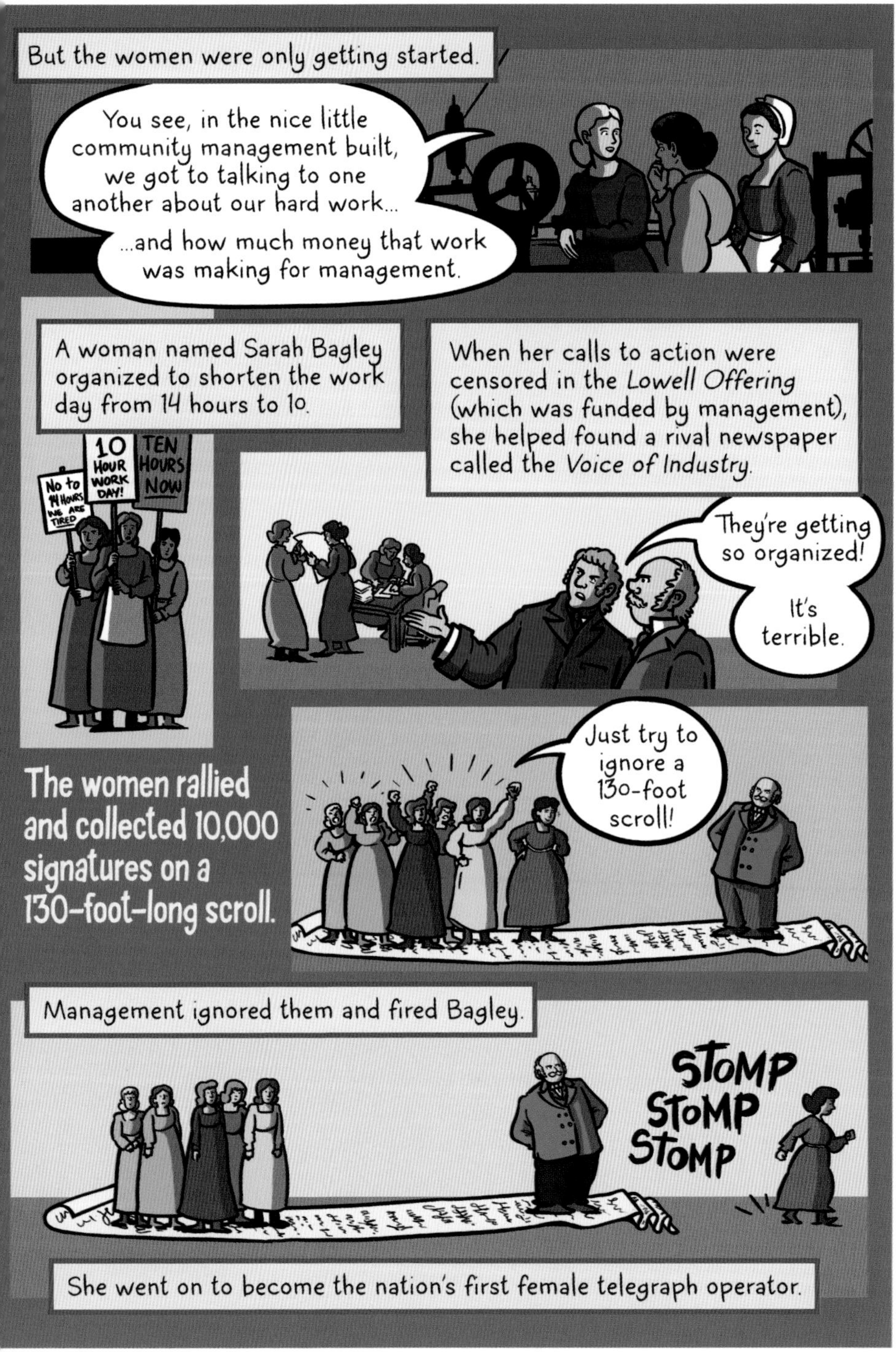

But the women were only getting started.
You see, in the nice little community management built, we got to talking to one another about our hard work...
...and how much money that work was making for management.
A woman named Sarah Bagley organized to shorten the work day from 14 hours to 10.
10 HOUR WORK DAY!
TEN HOURS NOW
No to 14 HOURS WE ARE TIRED
When her calls to action were censored in the Lowell Offering (which was funded by management), she helped found a rival newspaper called the Voice of Industry.
They're getting so organized!
It's terrible.
The women rallied and collected 10,000 signatures on a 130-foot-long scroll.
Just try to ignore a 130-foot scroll!
Management ignored them and fired Bagley.
STOMP
STOMP
STOMP
She went on to become the nation's first female telegraph operator.

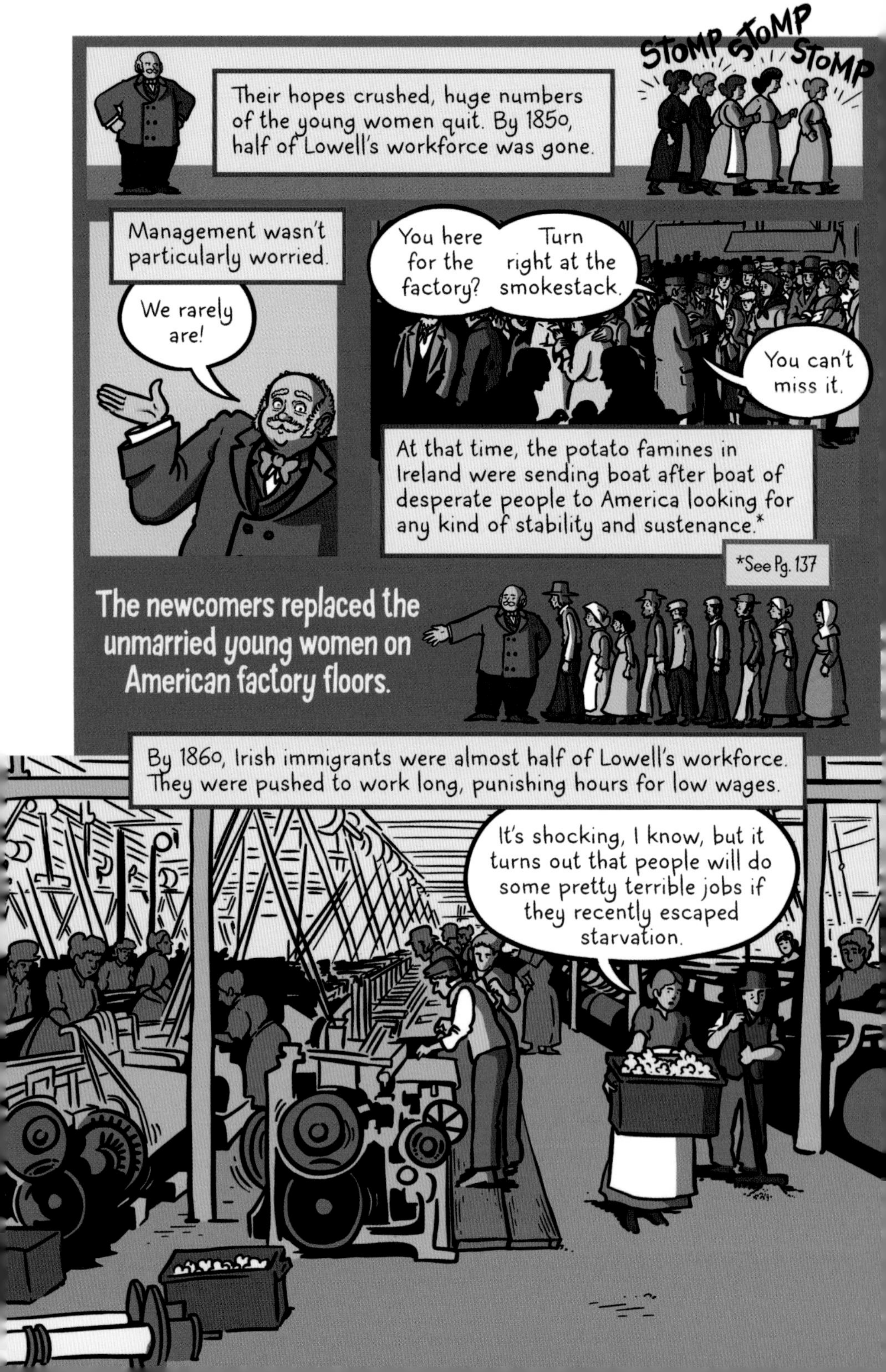
STOMP STOMP STOMP
Their hopes crushed, huge numbers of the young women quit. By 1850, half of Lowell's workforce was gone.
Management wasn't particularly worried.
We rarely are!
You here for the factory?
Turn right at the smokestack.
You can't miss it.
At that time, the potato famines in Ireland were sending boat after boat of desperate people to America looking for any kind of stability and sustenance.*
*See Pg. 137
The newcomers replaced the unmarried young women on American factory floors.
By 1860, Irish immigrants were almost half of Lowell's workforce. They were pushed to work long, punishing hours for low wages.
It's shocking, I know, but it turns out that people will do some pretty terrible jobs if they recently escaped starvation.

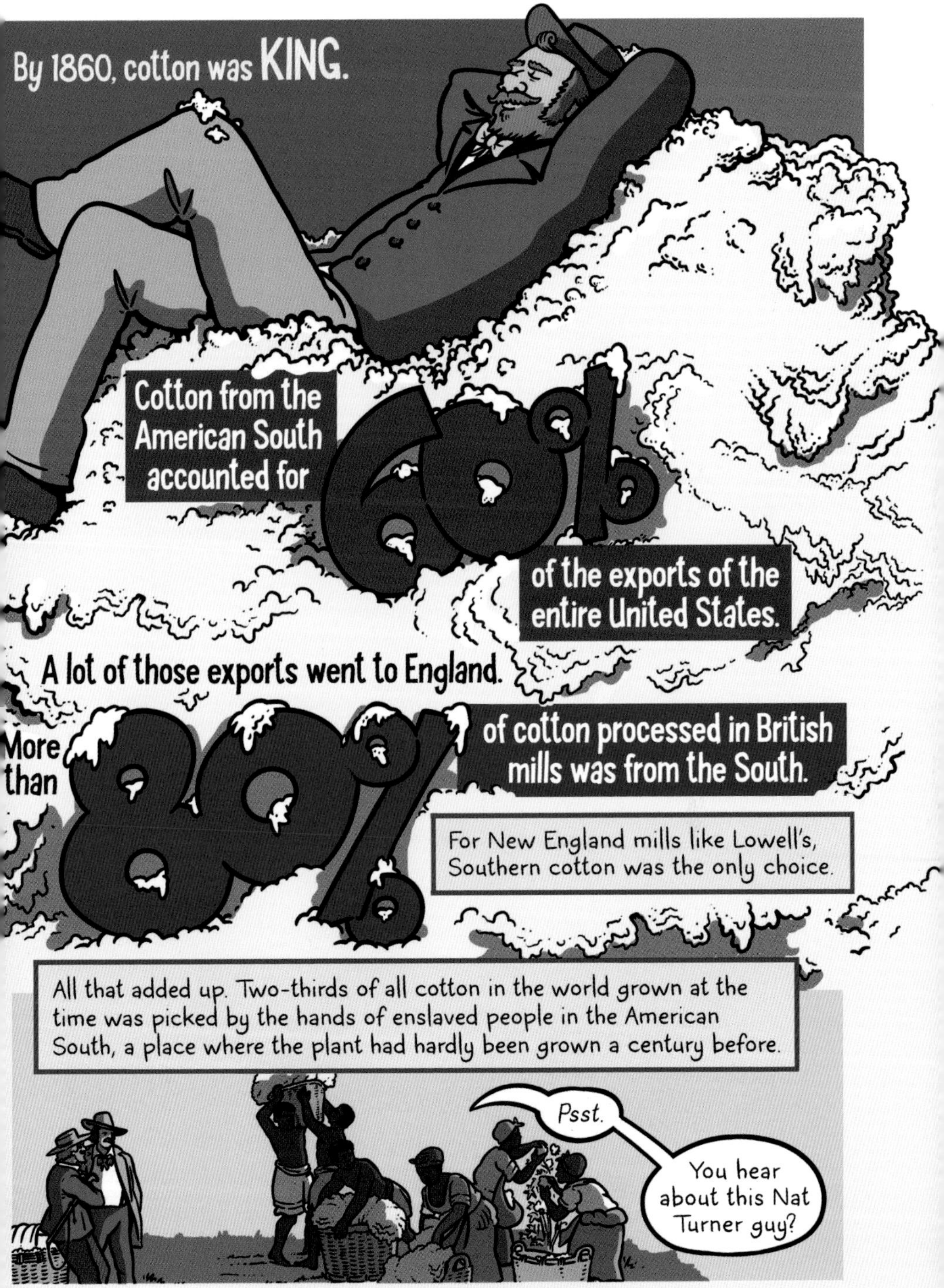

By 1860, cotton was KING.
Cotton from the American South accounted for
60%
of the exports of the entire United States.
A lot of those exports went to England.
More than
80%
of cotton processed in British mills was from the South.
For New England mills like Lowell's, Southern cotton was the only choice.
All that added up. Two-thirds of all cotton in the world grown at the time was picked by the hands of enslaved people in the American South, a place where the plant had hardly been grown a century before.
Psst.
You hear about this Nat Turner guy?

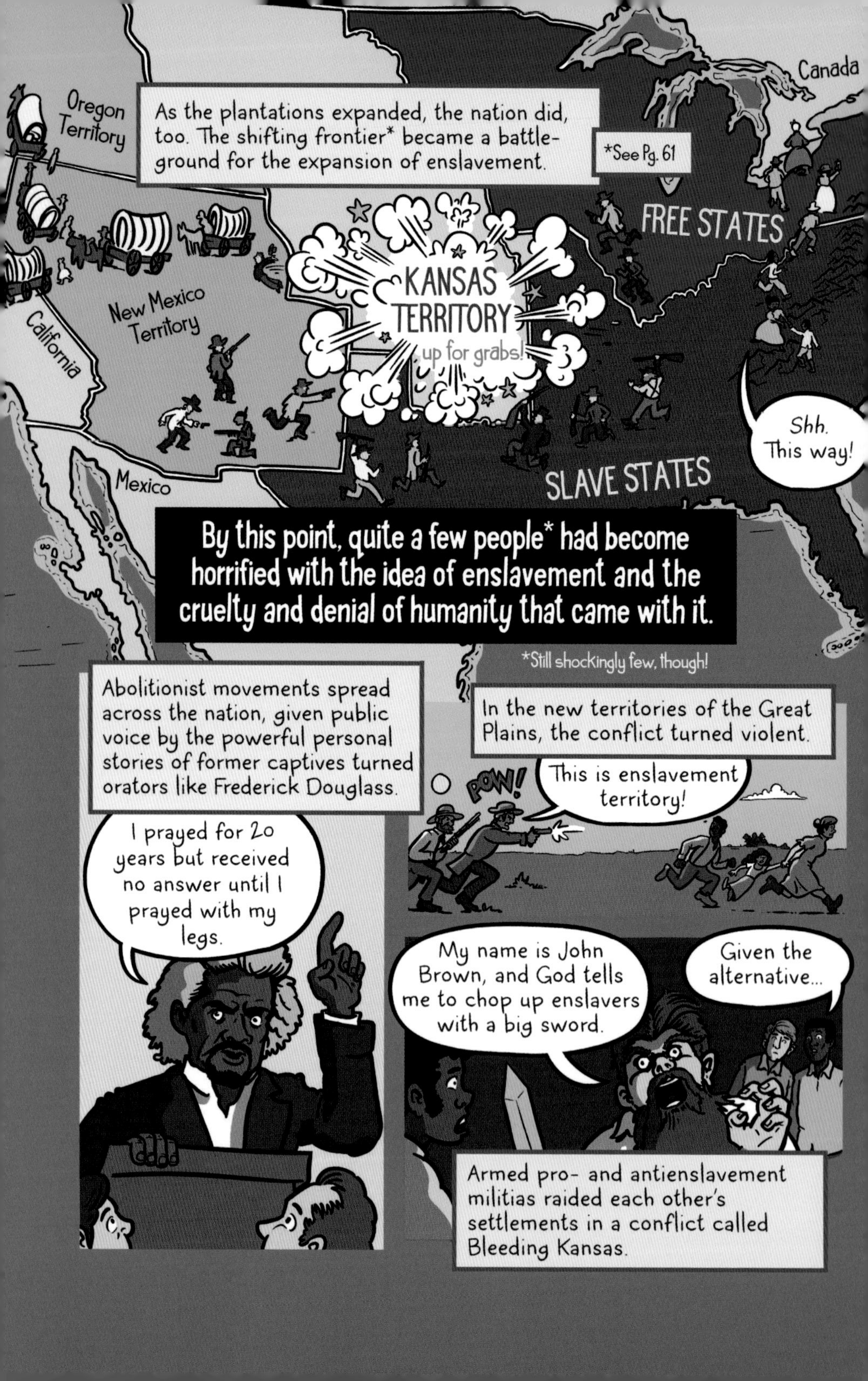

Oregon Territory
As the plantations expanded, the nation did, too. The shifting frontier* became a battleground for the expansion of enslavement.
*See Pg. 61
Canada
FREE STATES
New Mexico Territory
California
KANSAS TERRITORY
up for grabs!
Mexico
SLAVE STATES
Shh. This way!
By this point, quite a few people* had become horrified with the idea of enslavement and the cruelty and denial of humanity that came with it.
*Still shockingly few, though!
Abolitionist movements spread across the nation, given public voice by the powerful personal stories of former captives turned orators like Frederick Douglass.
I prayed for 20 years but received no answer until I prayed with my legs.
In the new territories of the Great Plains, the conflict turned violent.
POW!
This is enslavement territory!
My name is John Brown, and God tells me to chop up enslavers with a big sword.
Given the alternative...
Armed pro- and antienslavement militias raided each other's settlements in a conflict called Bleeding Kansas.

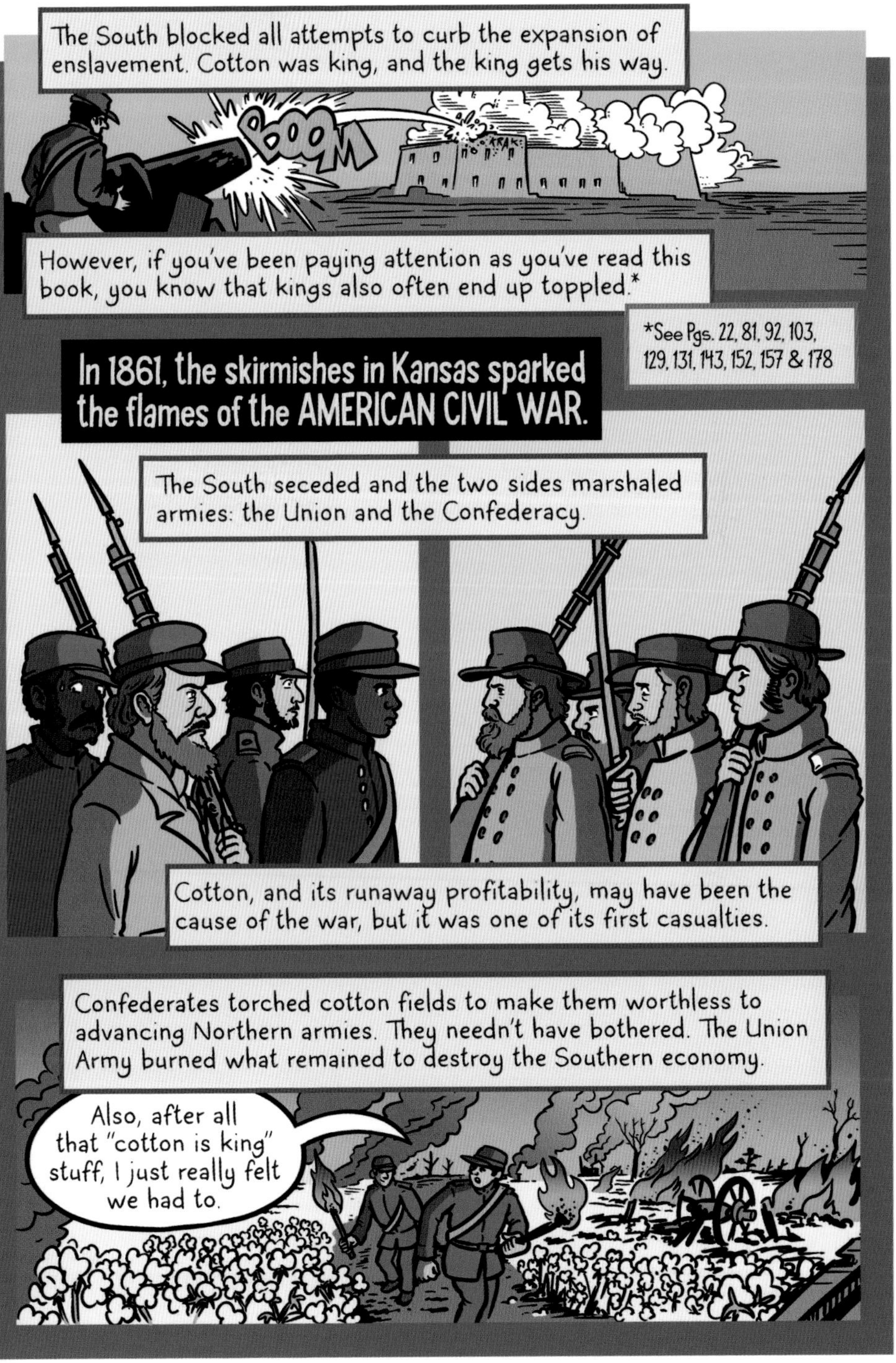
The South blocked all attempts to curb the expansion of enslavement. Cotton was king, and the king gets his way.
BOOM
KRAK
However, if you've been paying attention as you've read this book, you know that kings also often end up toppled.*
*See Pgs. 22, 81, 92, 103, 129, 131, 143, 152, 157 & 178
In 1861, the skirmishes in Kansas sparked the flames of the AMERICAN CIVIL WAR.
The South seceded and the two sides marshaled armies: the Union and the Confederacy.
Cotton, and its runaway profitability, may have been the cause of the war, but it was one of its first casualties.
Confederates torched cotton fields to make them worthless to advancing Northern armies. They needn't have bothered. The Union Army burned what remained to destroy the Southern economy.
Also, after all that "cotton is king" stuff, I just really felt we had to.

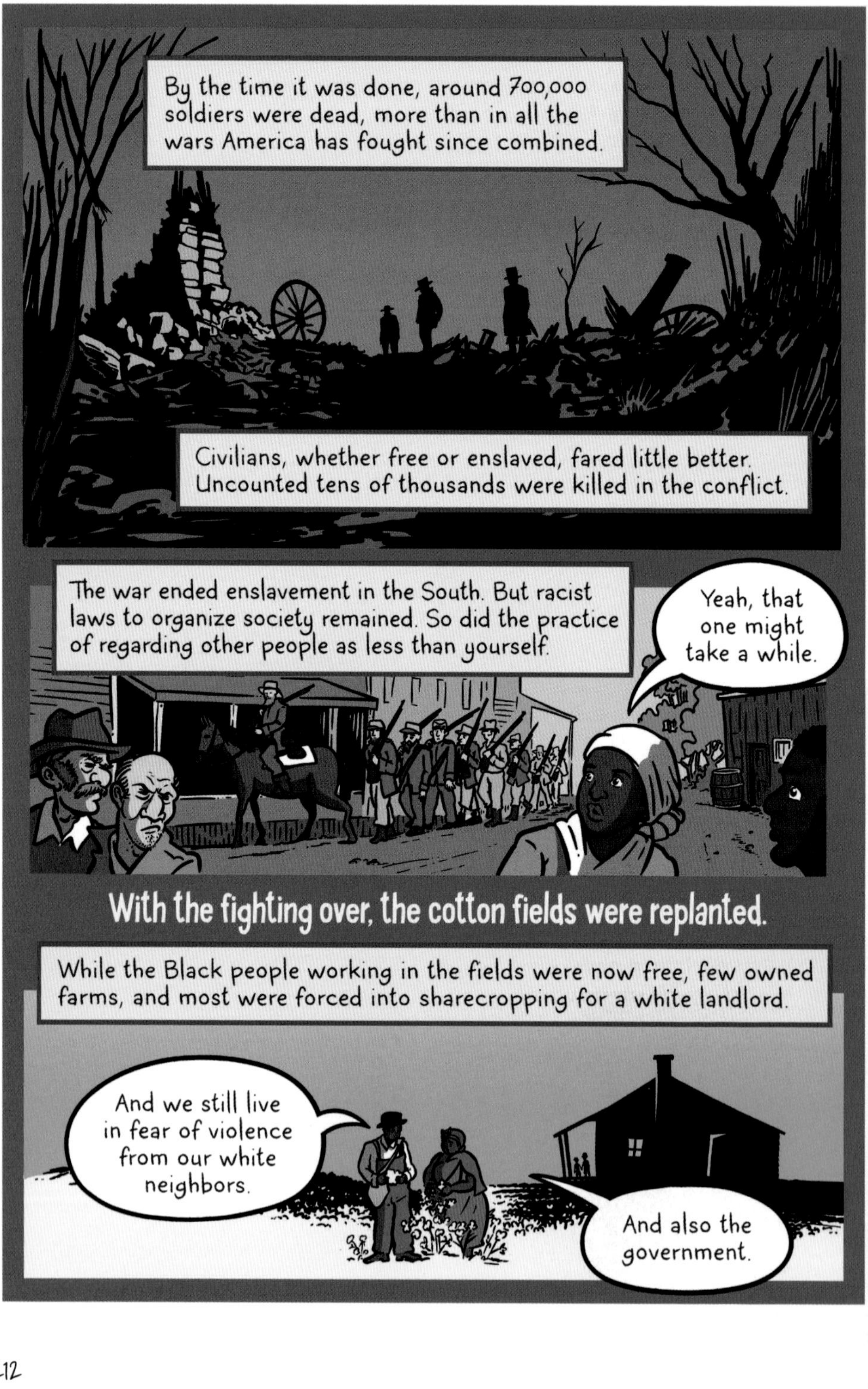
By the time it was done, around 700,000 soldiers were dead, more than in all the wars America has fought since combined.
Civilians, whether free or enslaved, fared little better. Uncounted tens of thousands were killed in the conflict.
The war ended enslavement in the South. But racist laws to organize society remained. So did the practice of regarding other people as less than yourself.
Yeah, that one might take a while.
With the fighting over, the cotton fields were replanted.
While the Black people working in the fields were now free, few owned farms, and most were forced into sharecropping for a white landlord.
And we still live in fear of violence from our white neighbors.
And also the government.

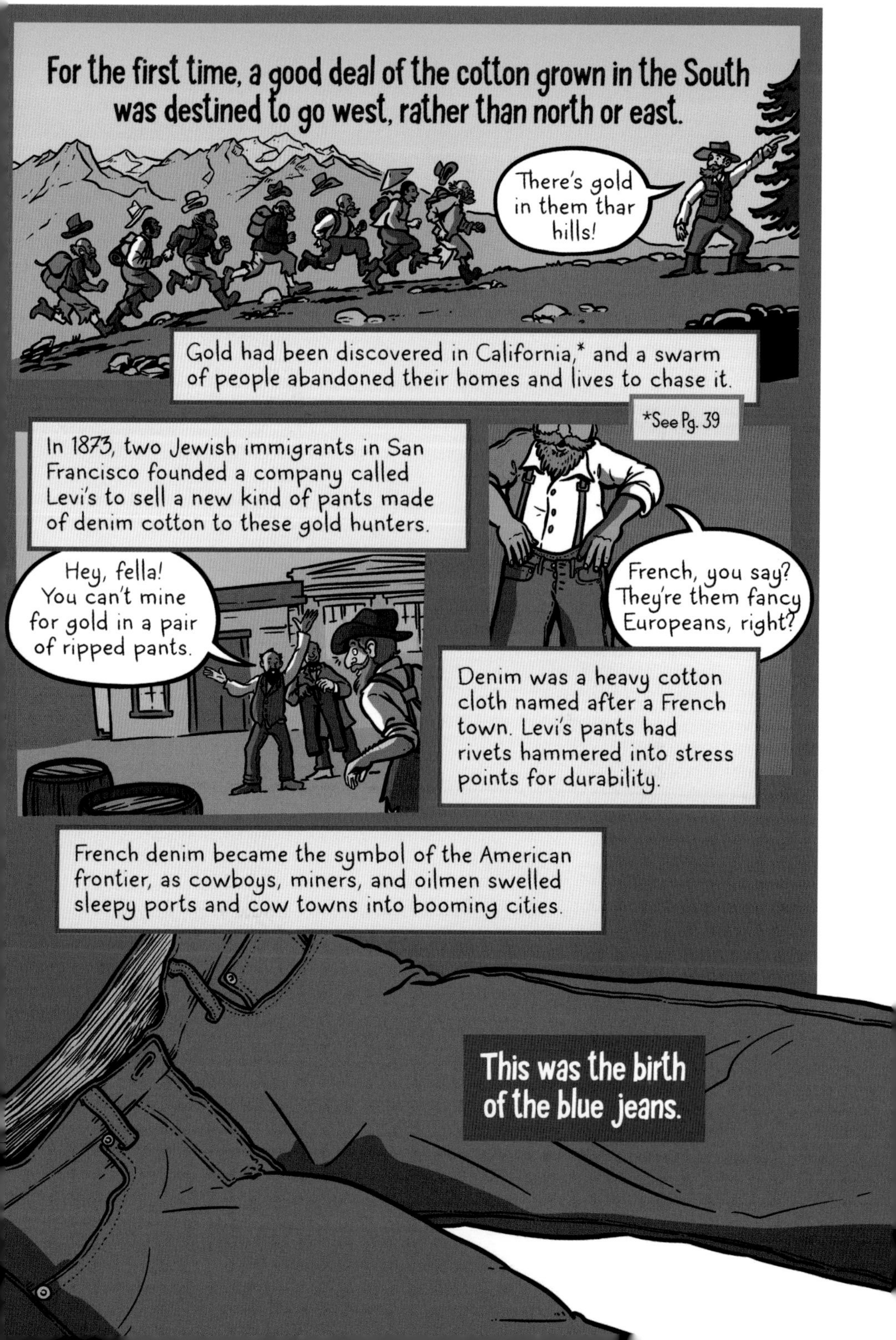
For the first time, a good deal of the cotton grown in the South was destined to go west, rather than north or east.
There's gold in them thar hills!
Gold had been discovered in California,* and a swarm of people abandoned their homes and lives to chase it.
*See Pg. 39
In 1873, two Jewish immigrants in San Francisco founded a company called Levi's to sell a new kind of pants made of denim cotton to these gold hunters.
Hey, fella! You can't mine for gold in a pair of ripped pants.
French, you say? They're them fancy Europeans, right?
Denim was a heavy cotton cloth named after a French town. Levi's pants had rivets hammered into stress points for durability.
French denim became the symbol of the American frontier, as cowboys, miners, and oilmen swelled sleepy ports and cow towns into booming cities.
This was the birth of the blue jeans.

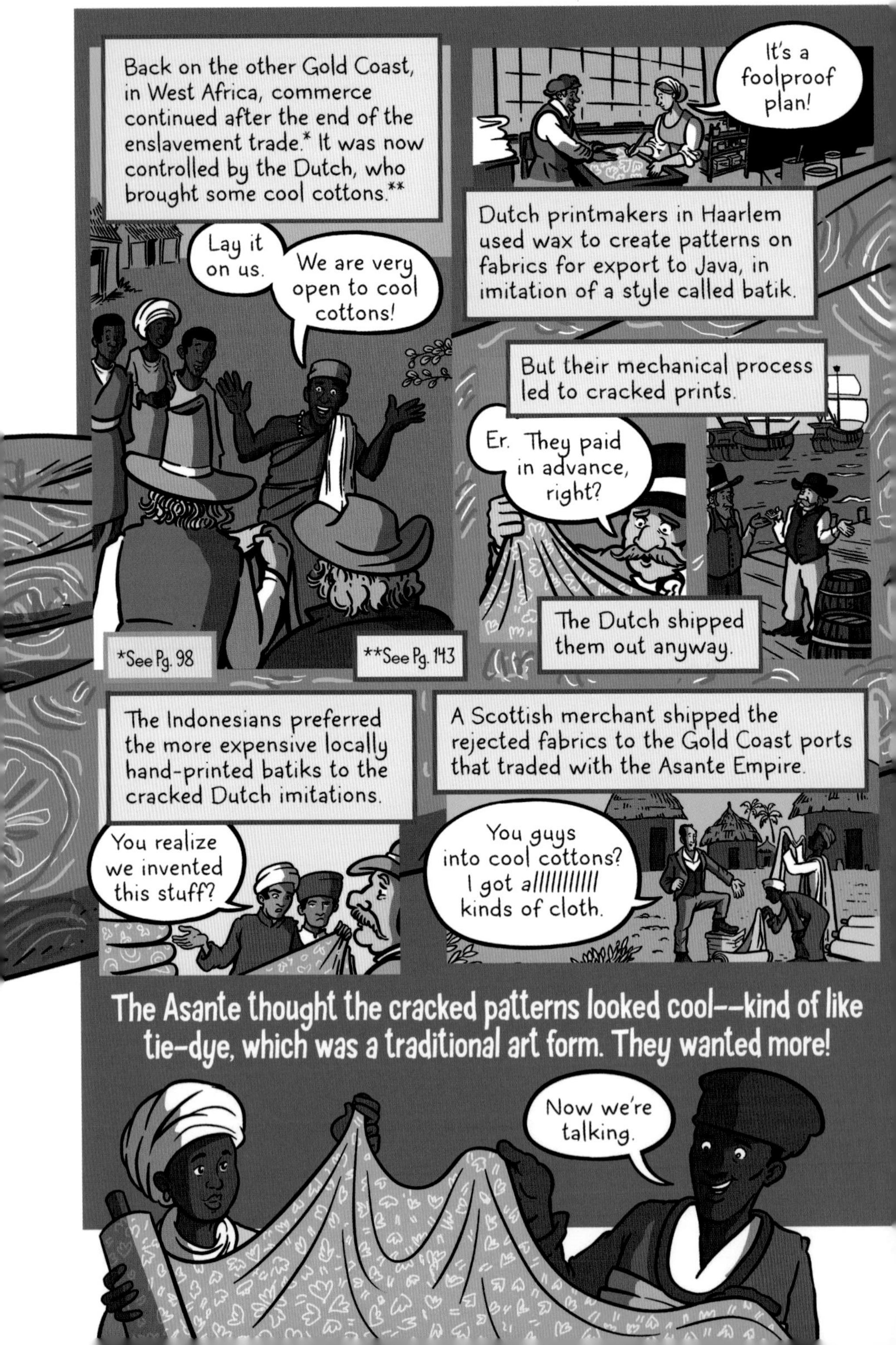

Back on the other Gold Coast, in West Africa, commerce continued after the end of the enslavement trade.* It was now controlled by the Dutch, who brought some cool cottons.**
Lay it on us.
We are very open to cool cottons!
*See Pg. 98
**See Pg. 143
It's a foolproof plan!
Dutch printmakers in Haarlem used wax to create patterns on fabrics for export to Java, in imitation of a style called batik.
But their mechanical process led to cracked prints.
Er. They paid in advance, right?
The Dutch shipped them out anyway.
The Indonesians preferred the more expensive locally hand-printed batiks to the cracked Dutch imitations.
You realize we invented this stuff?
A Scottish merchant shipped the rejected fabrics to the Gold Coast ports that traded with the Asante Empire.
You guys into cool cottons? I got alllllllllll kinds of cloth.
The Asante thought the cracked patterns looked cool--kind of like tie-dye, which was a traditional art form. They wanted more!
Now we're talking.

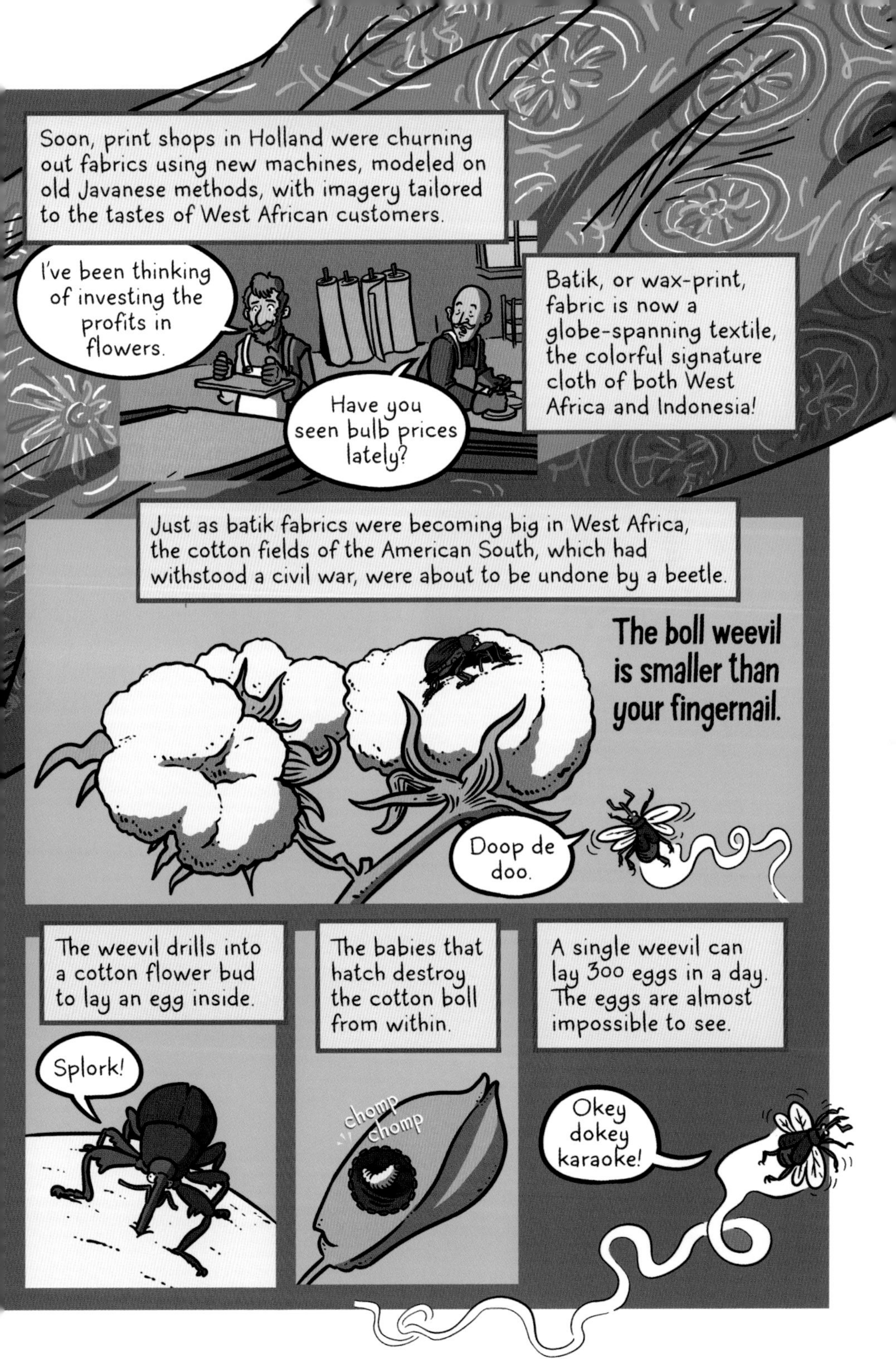

Soon, print shops in Holland were churning out fabrics using new machines, modeled on old Javanese methods, with imagery tailored to the tastes of West African customers.
I've been thinking of investing the profits in flowers.
Have you seen bulb prices lately?
Batik, or wax-print, fabric is now a globe-spanning textile, the colorful signature cloth of both West Africa and Indonesia!
Just as batik fabrics were becoming big in West Africa, the cotton fields of the American South, which had withstood a civil war, were about to be undone by a beetle.
The boll weevil is smaller than your fingernail.
Doop de doo.
The weevil drills into a cotton flower bud to lay an egg inside.
Splork!
The babies that hatch destroy the cotton boll from within.
chomp chomp
A single weevil can lay 300 eggs in a day. The eggs are almost impossible to see.
Okey dokey karaoke!

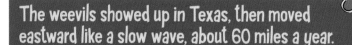

The weevils showed up in Texas, then moved eastward like a slow wave, about 60 miles a year.

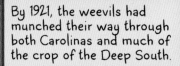

By 1921, the weevils had munched their way through both Carolinas and much of the crop of the Deep South.

As tends to happen, the losses flowed down to the people with the least power or money--the Black sharecroppers and tenant farmers.

"As tends to happen."

Why stop when you're ahead?

Their economic ruin was compounded by the racist violence of the Jim Crow era.

We'll stay with your cousin just until we find our footing.

Many left.

Between 1916 and 1928, more than 1.2 million Black people left the South and its cotton for the urban areas of the North and Midwest.

Chicago alone gained 70,000 Black residents in the space of 12 years.

Are we there yet?

Shh.

After WWII, this Great Migration continued. People packed into cars, trains, and wagons and left the only homes they'd known since their ancestors were dragged there. From Oakland to Detroit, New York to LA, Youngstown to Milwaukee, Black families grew America's cities.

A world away, in 1 of the 4 ancient cradles of cotton domestication, another movement was stirring.

What a jolly little system where we get to take everyone else's stuff.

India had remained under British dominion since the British East India Company used its stolen opium fields to break China.*

*See Pg. 147

Indians were forced to buy imported British cotton to prop up British mills.

Sigh. We know what the good stuff looks like.

The cotton Indians actually grew was exported to make the British rich.

One musn't leave cash on the table.

But every colony is a liberation story waiting to be told. India's time came with the birth of Mohandas Gandhi in 1869.

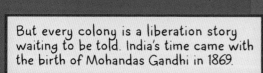

Gandhi grew up in India, trained as a lawyer in London, then traveled to work in South Africa, which had been a Dutch colony until 1806 when the British stole it while the Dutch were distracted by being conquered by Napoleon.*

*See Pg. 179

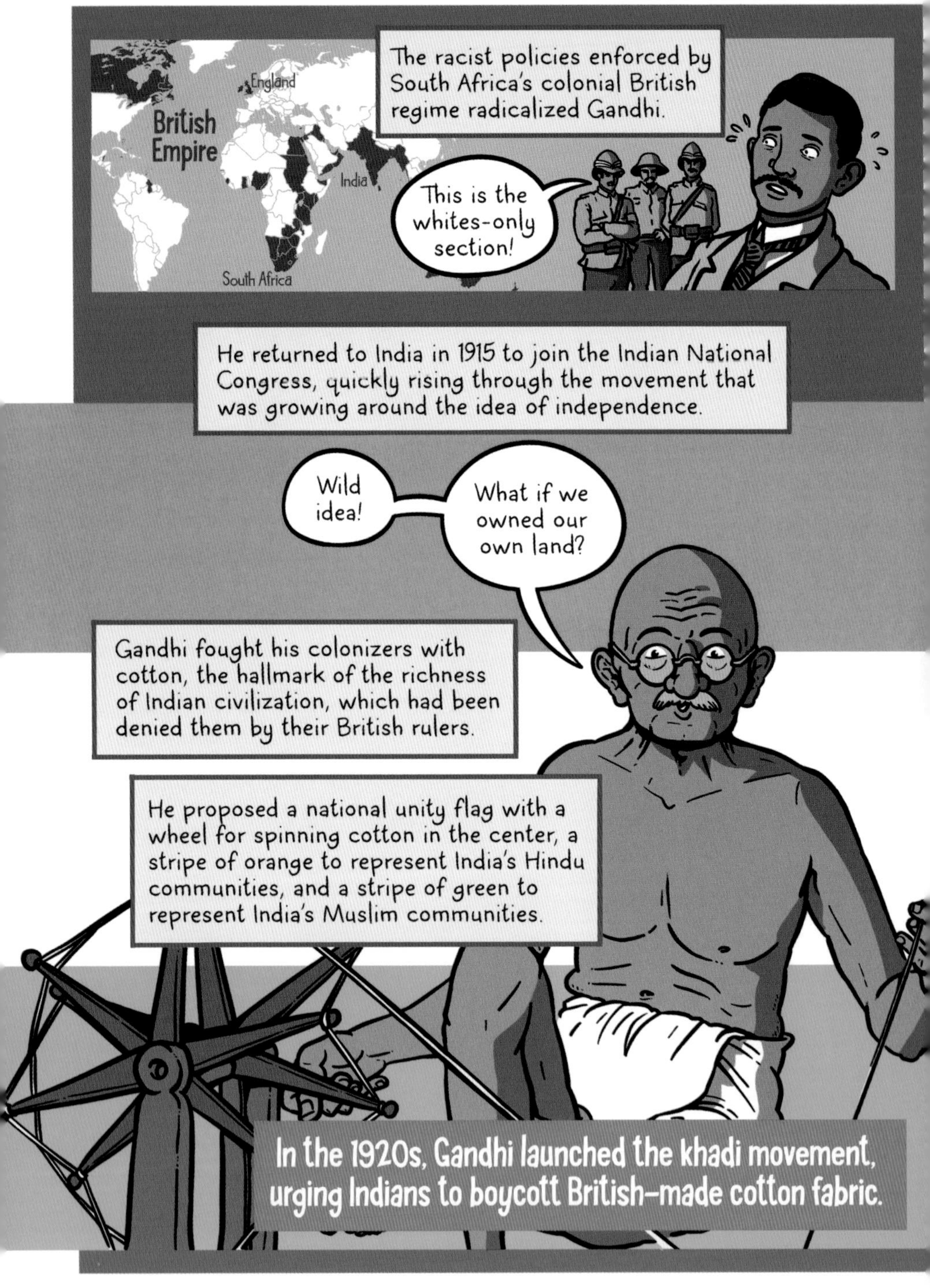
England
British Empire
India
South Africa
The racist policies enforced by South Africa's colonial British regime radicalized Gandhi.
This is the whites-only section!
He returned to India in 1915 to join the Indian National Congress, quickly rising through the movement that was growing around the idea of independence.
Wild idea!
What if we owned our own land?
Gandhi fought his colonizers with cotton, the hallmark of the richness of Indian civilization, which had been denied them by their British rulers.
He proposed a national unity flag with a wheel for spinning cotton in the center, a stripe of orange to represent India's Hindu communities, and a stripe of green to represent India's Muslim communities.
In the 1920s, Gandhi launched the khadi movement, urging Indians to boycott British-made cotton fabric.

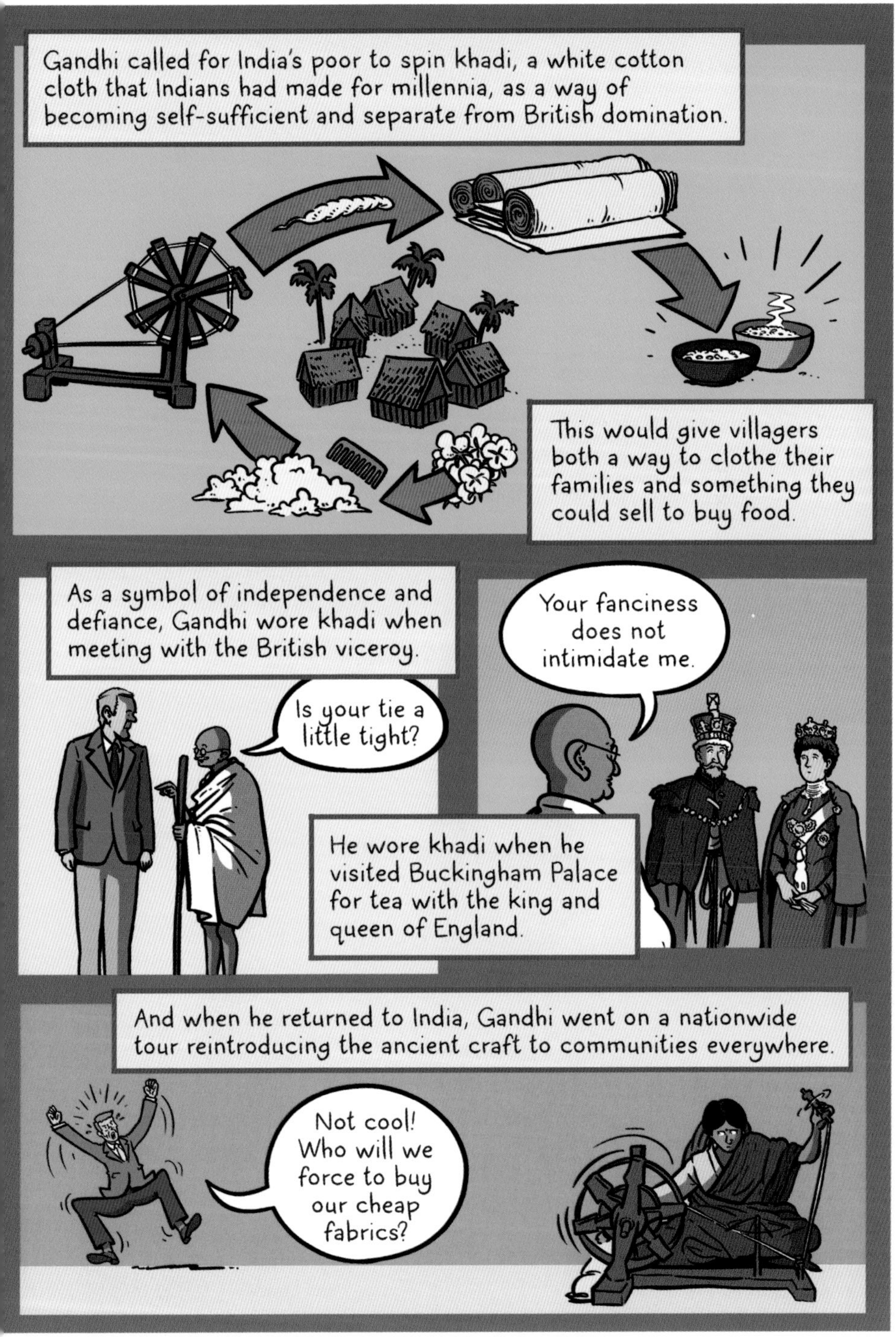
Gandhi called for India's poor to spin khadi, a white cotton cloth that Indians had made for millennia, as a way of becoming self-sufficient and separate from British domination.
This would give villagers both a way to clothe their families and something they could sell to buy food.
As a symbol of independence and defiance, Gandhi wore khadi when meeting with the British viceroy.
Is your tie a little tight?
Your fanciness does not intimidate me.
He wore khadi when he visited Buckingham Palace for tea with the king and queen of England.
And when he returned to India, Gandhi went on a nationwide tour reintroducing the ancient craft to communities everywhere.
Not cool! Who will we force to buy our cheap fabrics?

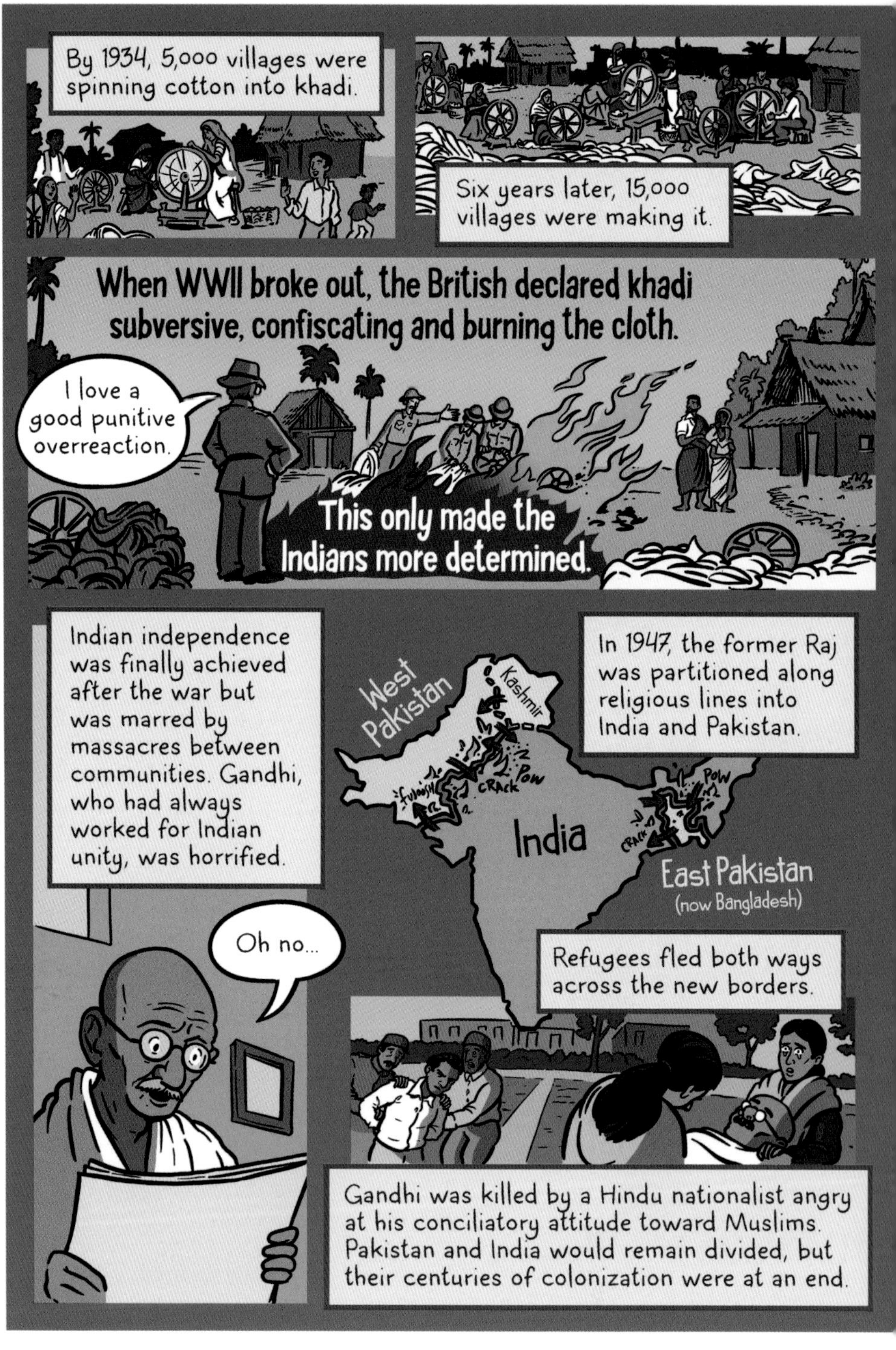
By 1934, 5,000 villages were spinning cotton into khadi.
Six years later, 15,000 villages were making it.
When WWII broke out, the British declared khadi subversive, confiscating and burning the cloth.
I love a good punitive overreaction.
This only made the Indians more determined.
Indian independence was finally achieved after the war but was marred by massacres between communities. Gandhi, who had always worked for Indian unity, was horrified.
West Pakistan
Kashmir
In 1947, the former Raj was partitioned along religious lines into India and Pakistan.
FWOOSH
CRACK
POW
POW
CRACK
India
East Pakistan
(now Bangladesh)
Oh no...
Refugees fled both ways across the new borders.
Gandhi was killed by a Hindu nationalist angry at his conciliatory attitude toward Muslims. Pakistan and India would remain divided, but their centuries of colonization were at an end.

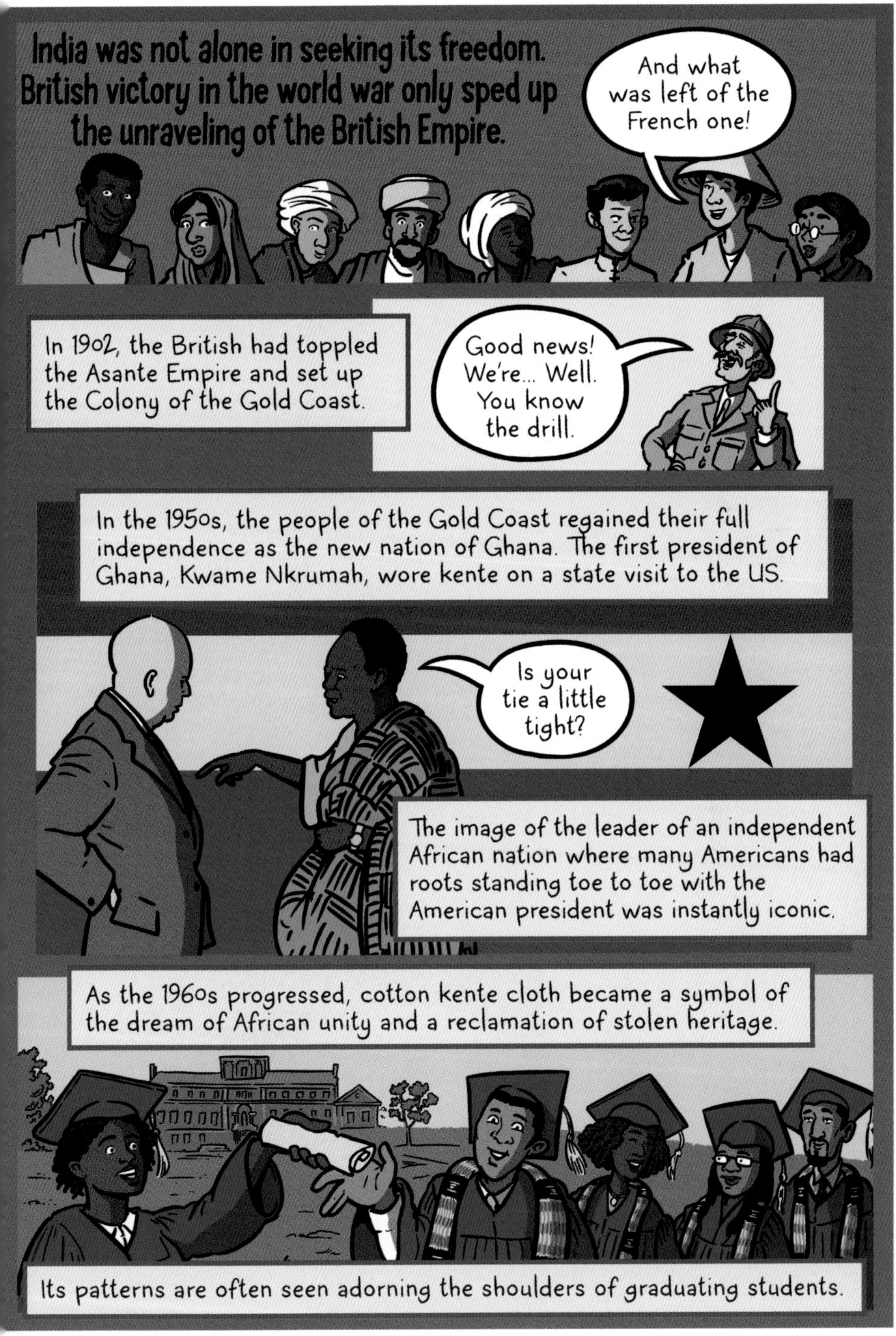

India was not alone in seeking its freedom. British victory in the world war only sped up the unraveling of the British Empire.
And what was left of the French one!
In 1902, the British had toppled the Asante Empire and set up the Colony of the Gold Coast.
Good news! We're... Well. You know the drill.
In the 1950s, the people of the Gold Coast regained their full independence as the new nation of Ghana. The first president of Ghana, Kwame Nkrumah, wore kente on a state visit to the US.
Is your tie a little tight?
The image of the leader of an independent African nation where many Americans had roots standing toe to toe with the American president was instantly iconic.
As the 1960s progressed, cotton kente cloth became a symbol of the dream of African unity and a reclamation of stolen heritage.
Its patterns are often seen adorning the shoulders of graduating students.

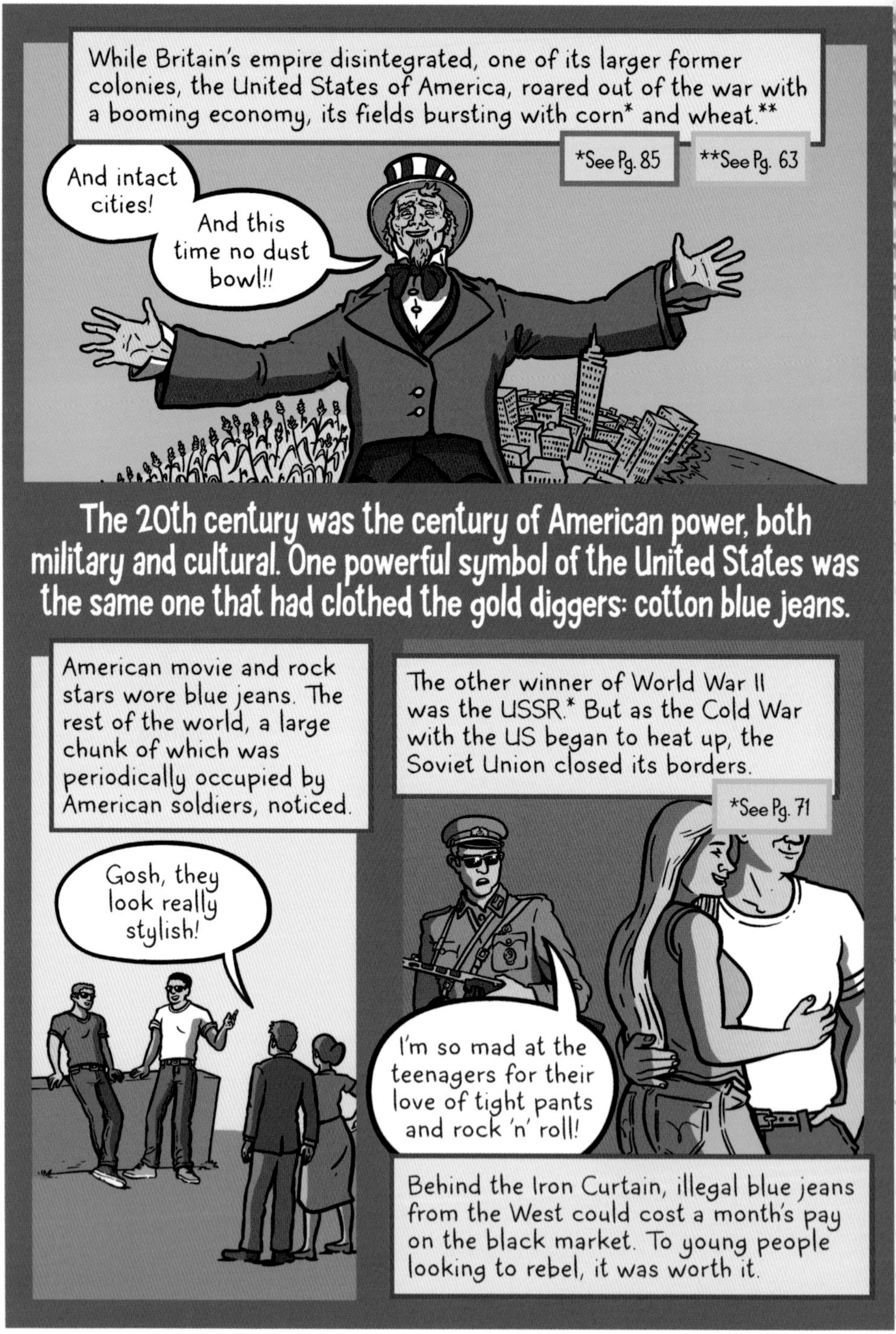
While Britain's empire disintegrated, one of its larger former colonies, the United States of America, roared out of the war with a booming economy, its fields bursting with corn* and wheat.**
*See Pg. 85
**See Pg. 63
And intact cities!
And this time no dust bowl!!
The 20th century was the century of American power, both military and cultural. One powerful symbol of the United States was the same one that had clothed the gold diggers: cotton blue jeans.
American movie and rock stars wore blue jeans. The rest of the world, a large chunk of which was periodically occupied by American soldiers, noticed.
Gosh, they look really stylish!
The other winner of World War II was the USSR.* But as the Cold War with the US began to heat up, the Soviet Union closed its borders.
*See Pg. 71
I'm so mad at the teenagers for their love of tight pants and rock 'n' roll!
Behind the Iron Curtain, illegal blue jeans from the West could cost a month's pay on the black market. To young people looking to rebel, it was worth it.

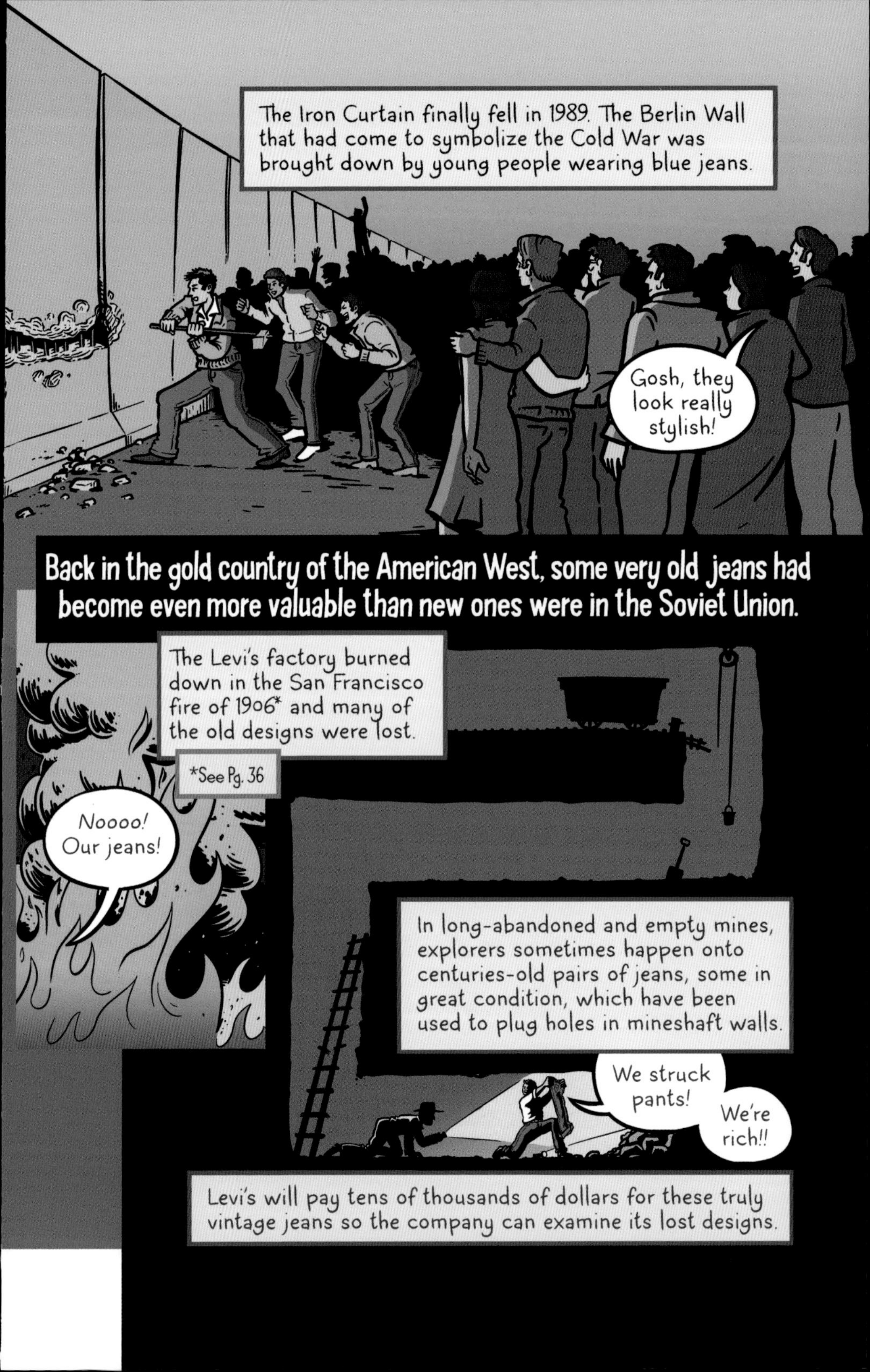

The Iron Curtain finally fell in 1989. The Berlin Wall that had come to symbolize the Cold War was brought down by young people wearing blue jeans.
Gosh, they look really stylish!
Back in the gold country of the American West, some very old jeans had become even more valuable than new ones were in the Soviet Union.
The Levi's factory burned down in the San Francisco fire of 1906* and many of the old designs were lost.
*See Pg. 36
Noooo! Our jeans!
In long-abandoned and empty mines, explorers sometimes happen onto centuries-old pairs of jeans, some in great condition, which have been used to plug holes in mineshaft walls.
We struck pants!
We're rich!!
Levi's will pay tens of thousands of dollars for these truly vintage jeans so the company can examine its lost designs.

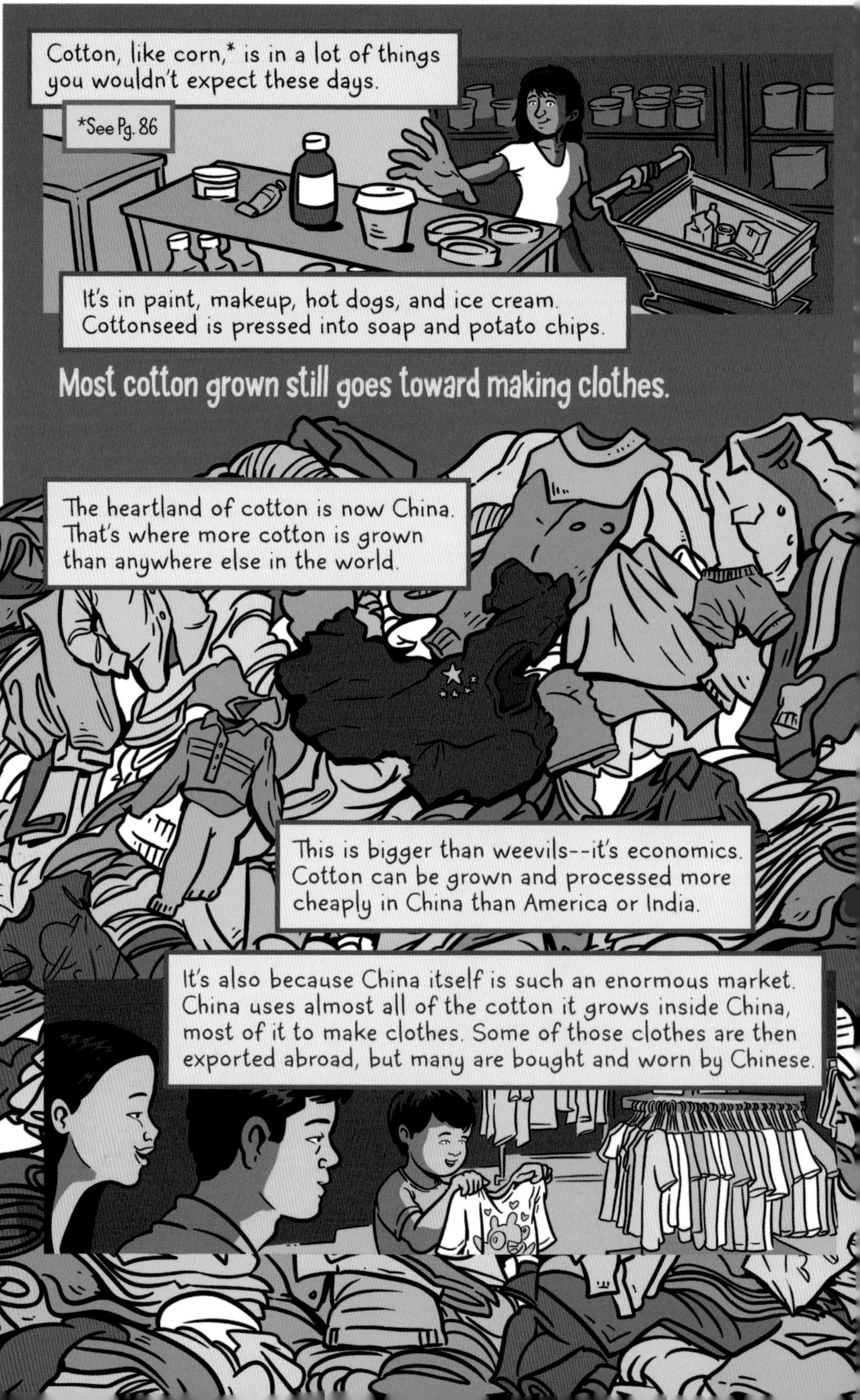
Cotton, like corn,* is in a lot of things you wouldn't expect these days.
*See Pg. 86
It's in paint, makeup, hot dogs, and ice cream. Cottonseed is pressed into soap and potato chips.
Most cotton grown still goes toward making clothes.
The heartland of cotton is now China. That's where more cotton is grown than anywhere else in the world.
This is bigger than weevils--it's economics. Cotton can be grown and processed more cheaply in China than America or India.
It's also because China itself is such an enormous market. China uses almost all of the cotton it grows inside China, most of it to make clothes. Some of those clothes are then exported abroad, but many are bought and worn by Chinese.

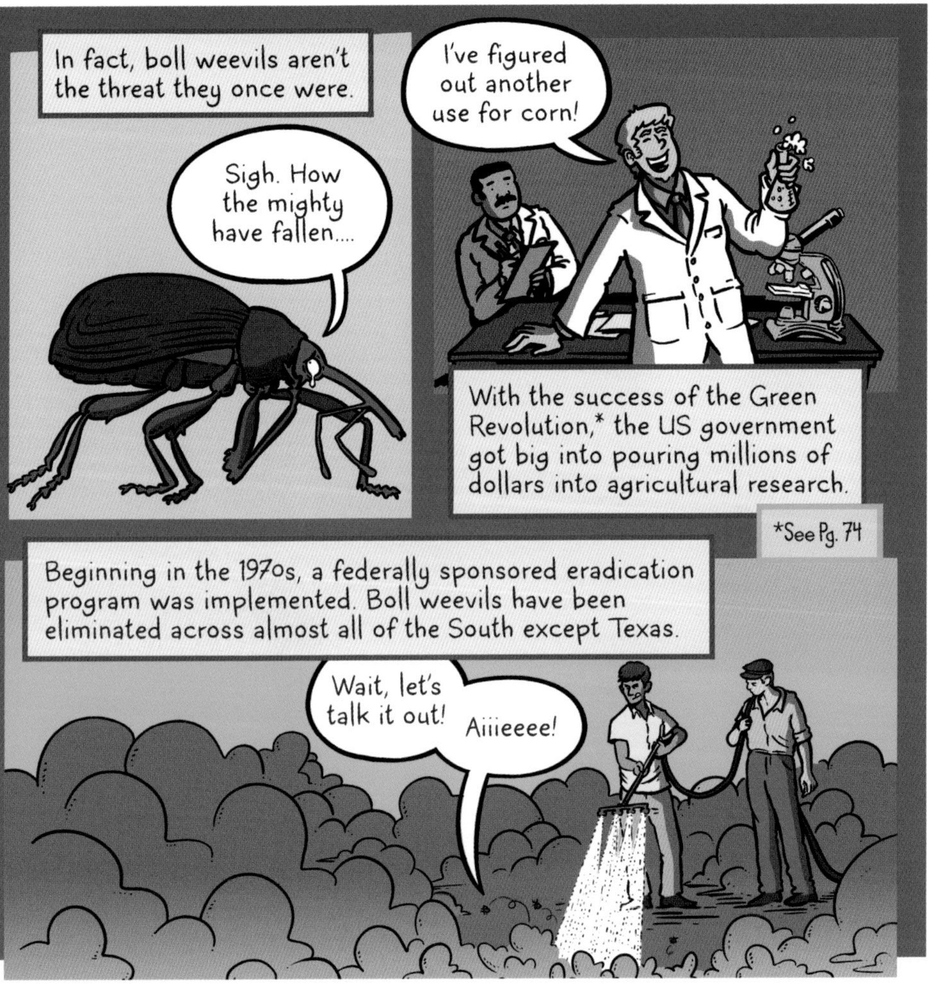
In fact, boll weevils aren't the threat they once were.
Sigh. How the mighty have fallen....
I've figured out another use for corn!
With the success of the Green Revolution,* the US government got big into pouring millions of dollars into agricultural research.
*See Pg. 74
Beginning in the 1970s, a federally sponsored eradication program was implemented. Boll weevils have been eliminated across almost all of the South except Texas.
Wait, let's talk it out!
Aiiieeee!

But like any conqueror, the weevils left their mark, even as their hold on the land receded.

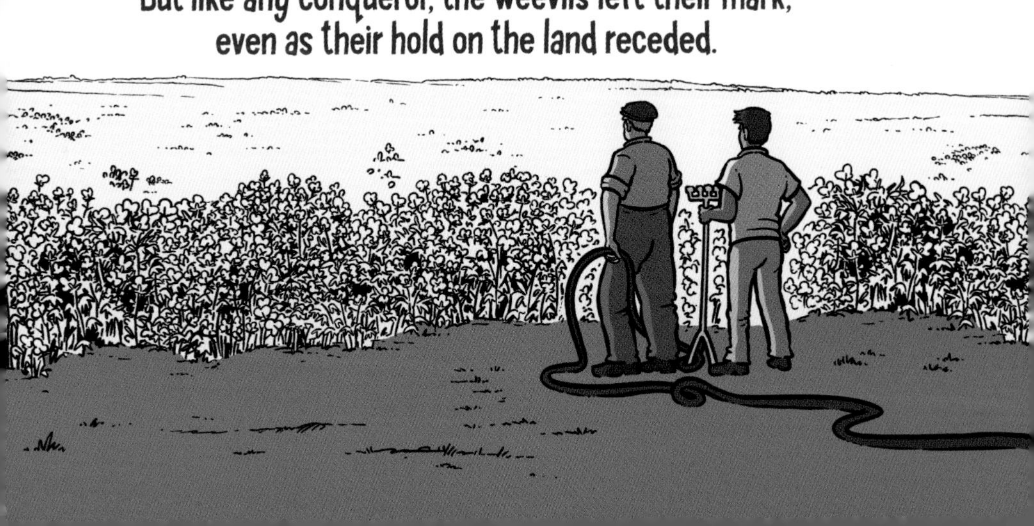

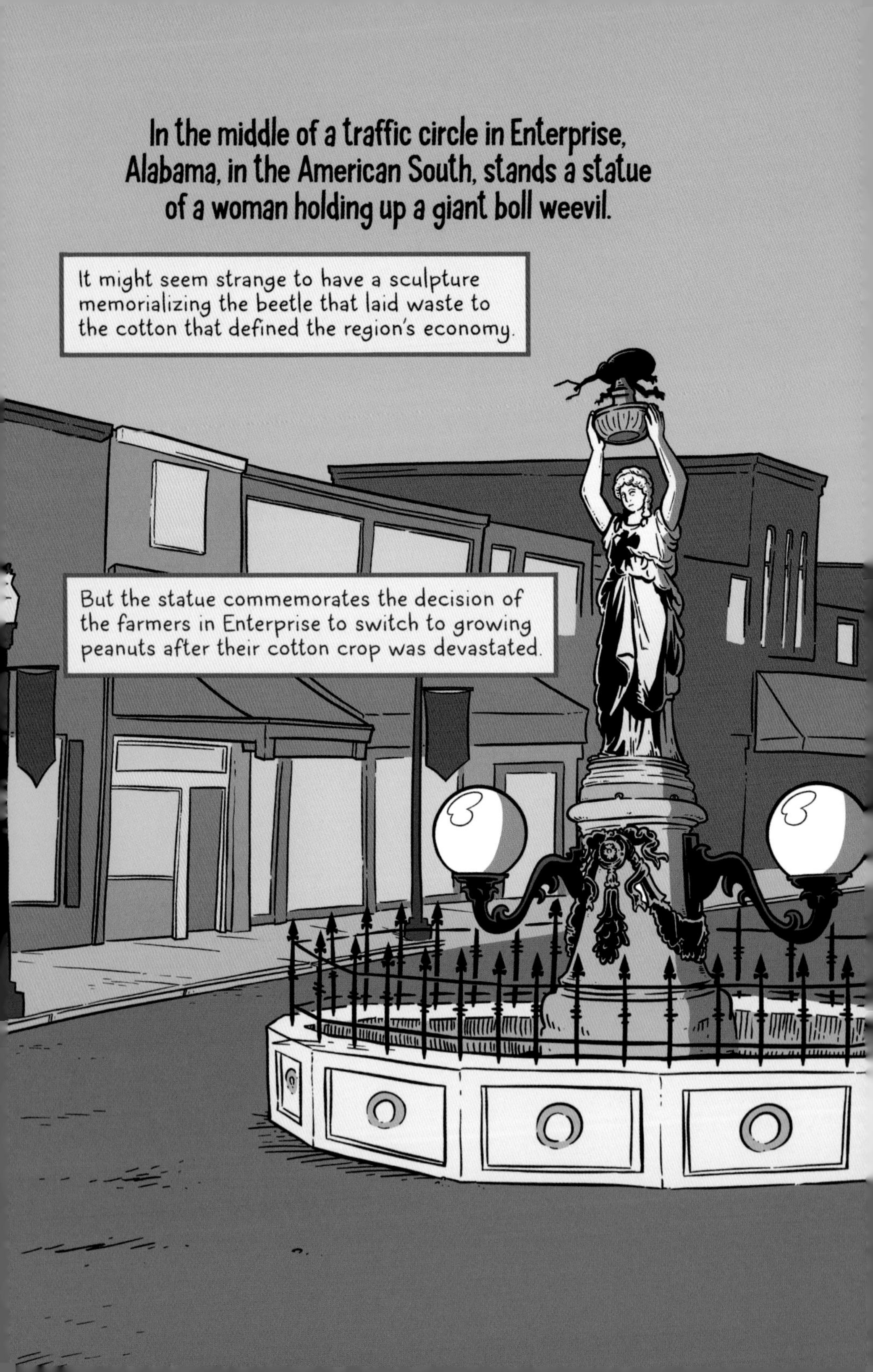
In the middle of a traffic circle in Enterprise, Alabama, in the American South, stands a statue of a woman holding up a giant boll weevil.
It might seem strange to have a sculpture memorializing the beetle that laid waste to the cotton that defined the region's economy.
But the statue commemorates the decision of the farmers in Enterprise to switch to growing peanuts after their cotton crop was devastated.

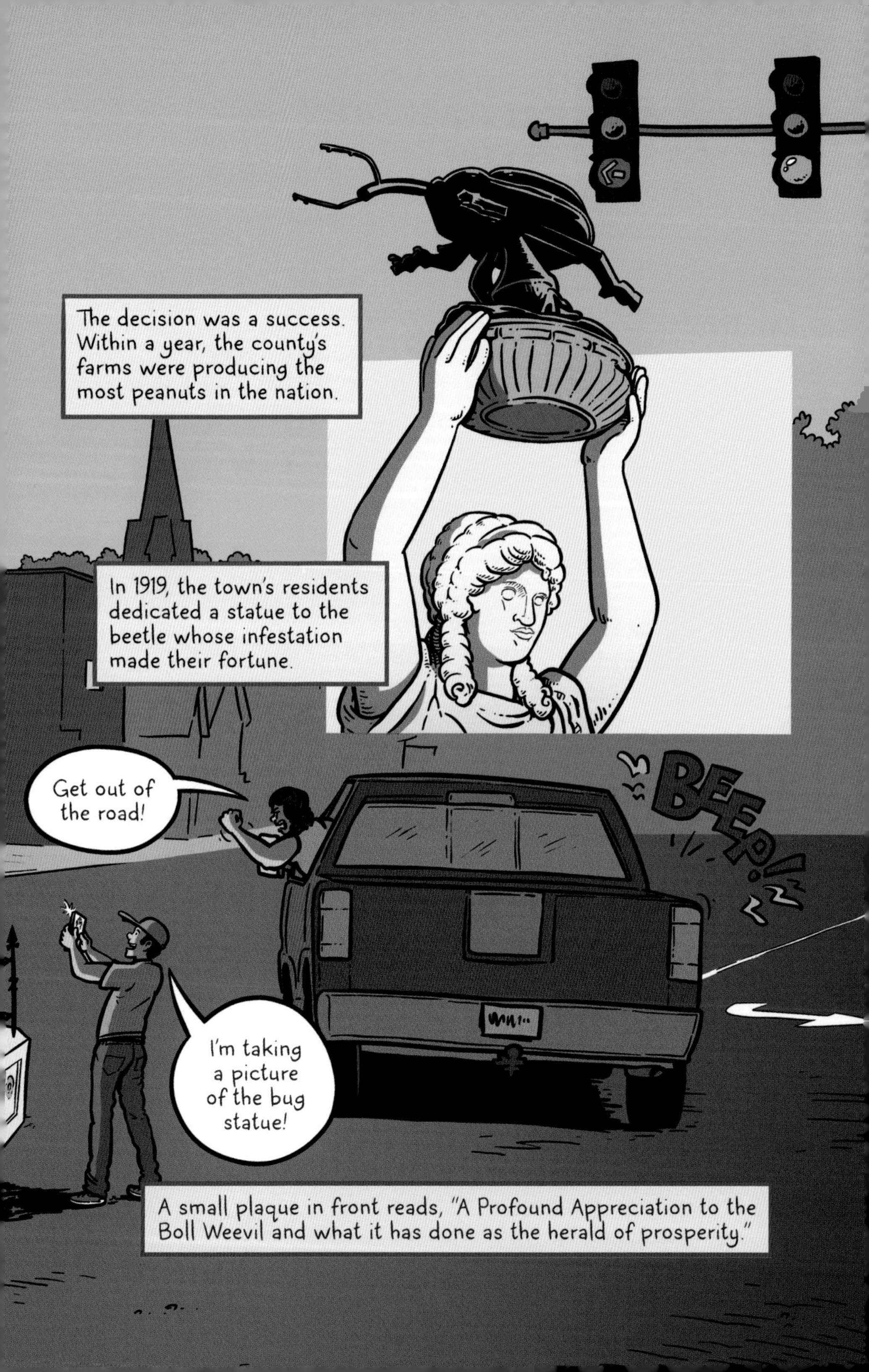
The decision was a success. Within a year, the county's farms were producing the most peanuts in the nation.
In 1919, the town's residents dedicated a statue to the beetle whose infestation made their fortune.
Get out of the road!
BEEP!
I'm taking a picture of the bug statue!
A small plaque in front reads, "A Profound Appreciation to the Boll Weevil and what it has done as the herald of prosperity."

AFTERWORD

Telling history is tough if you try to get somewhere honest. That's as true for big stuff as it is for things like potatoes and peppers.

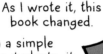

As I wrote it, this book changed.

From a simple story about plants, it became a history of empires, colonies, and how we depend on one another.

I think that's because plants are useful tools for us humans to build complexity and connection.

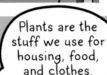

We trade them with one another for their beauty or usefulness.

Plants are the stuff we use for housing, food, and clothes.

More plants mean more people and bigger cities.

But the honest truth is that people do amazing things when they are connected to one another.

But they also often act in ways that are unforgivable.

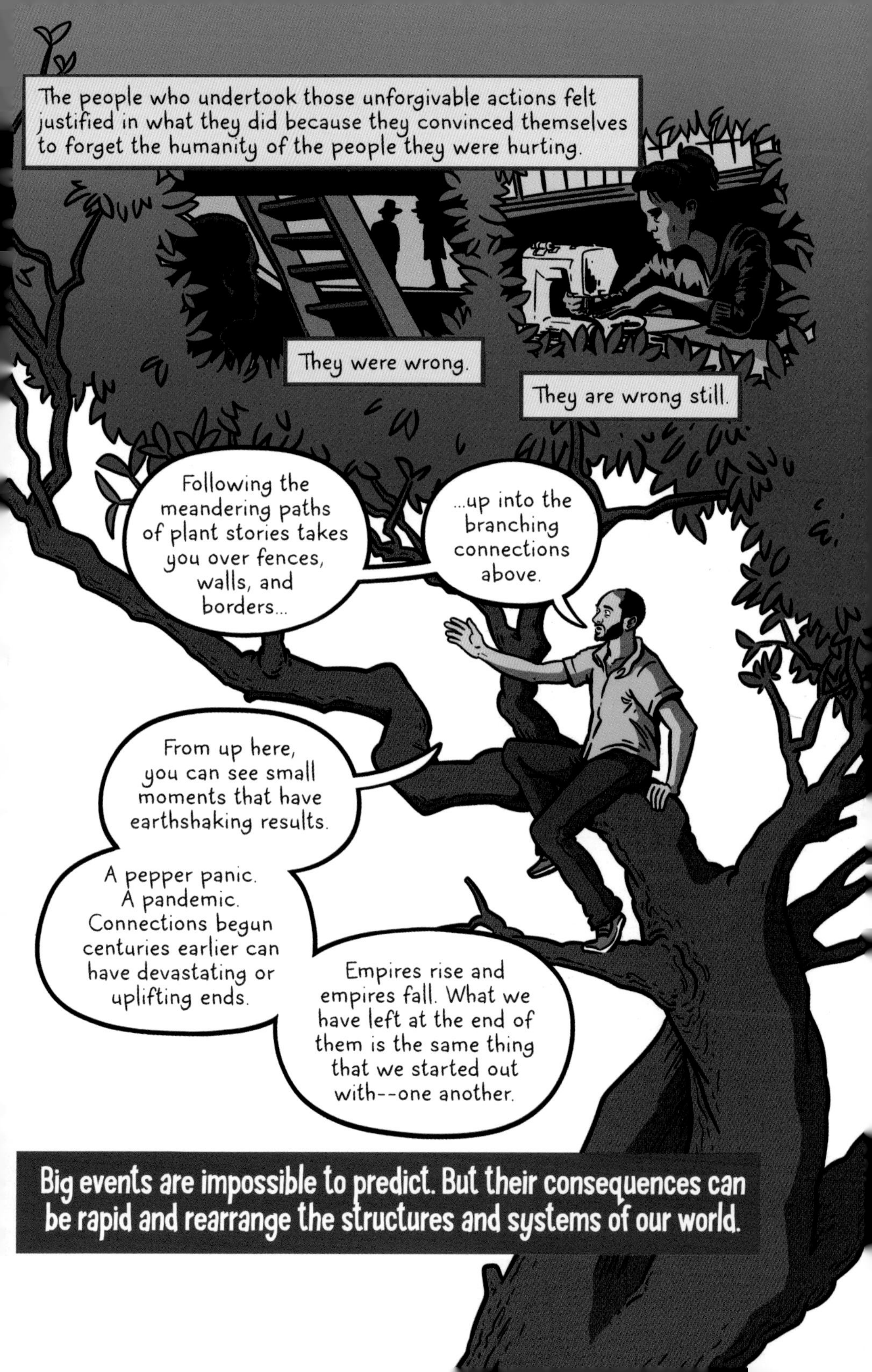
The people who undertook those unforgivable actions felt justified in what they did because they convinced themselves to forget the humanity of the people they were hurting.
They were wrong.
They are wrong still.
Following the meandering paths of plant stories takes you over fences, walls, and borders...
...up into the branching connections above.
From up here, you can see small moments that have earthshaking results.
A pepper panic. A pandemic. Connections begun centuries earlier can have devastating or uplifting ends.
Empires rise and empires fall. What we have left at the end of them is the same thing that we started out with--one another.
Big events are impossible to predict. But their consequences can be rapid and rearrange the structures and systems of our world.

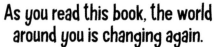

As you read this book, the world around you is changing again.

This very moment is a turning point in the relationship between people, plants, and everything.

For generations, people have worked to figure out how to grow more and better plants.

The past century has seen agricultural advances at such a pace that large-scale famines have been all but eliminated, even as small-scale hunger still haunts us.

But having achieved that dream, we dug deeper.

The quest to increase crop yields has led to humanity cracking open the building blocks of life itself with gene editing.*

*See Pg. 75

230

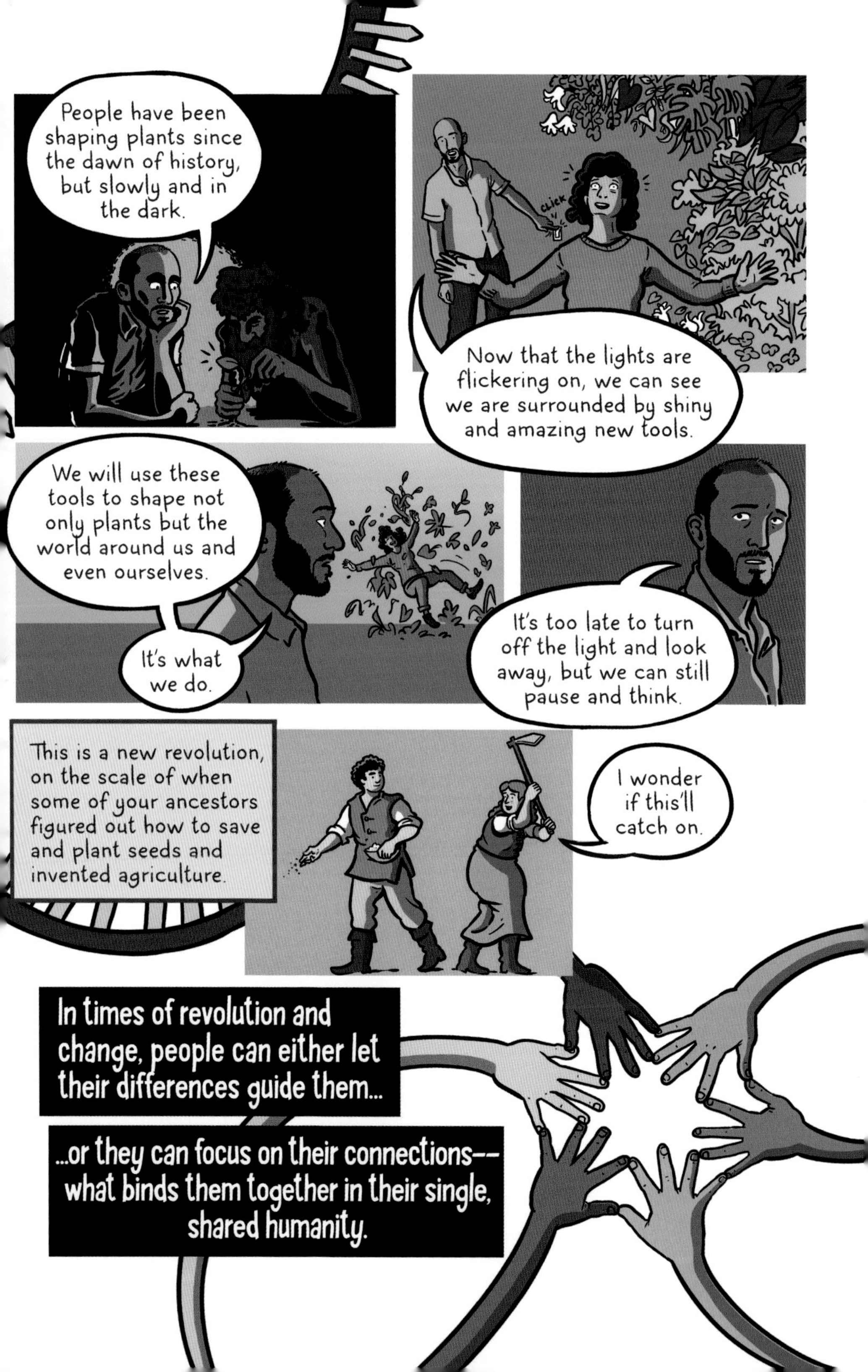
People have been shaping plants since the dawn of history, but slowly and in the dark.
CLICK
Now that the lights are flickering on, we can see we are surrounded by shiny and amazing new tools.
We will use these tools to shape not only plants but the world around us and even ourselves.
It's what we do.
It's too late to turn off the light and look away, but we can still pause and think.
This is a new revolution, on the scale of when some of your ancestors figured out how to save and plant seeds and invented agriculture.
I wonder if this'll catch on.
In times of revolution and change, people can either let their differences guide them...
...or they can focus on their connections-- what binds them together in their single, shared humanity.

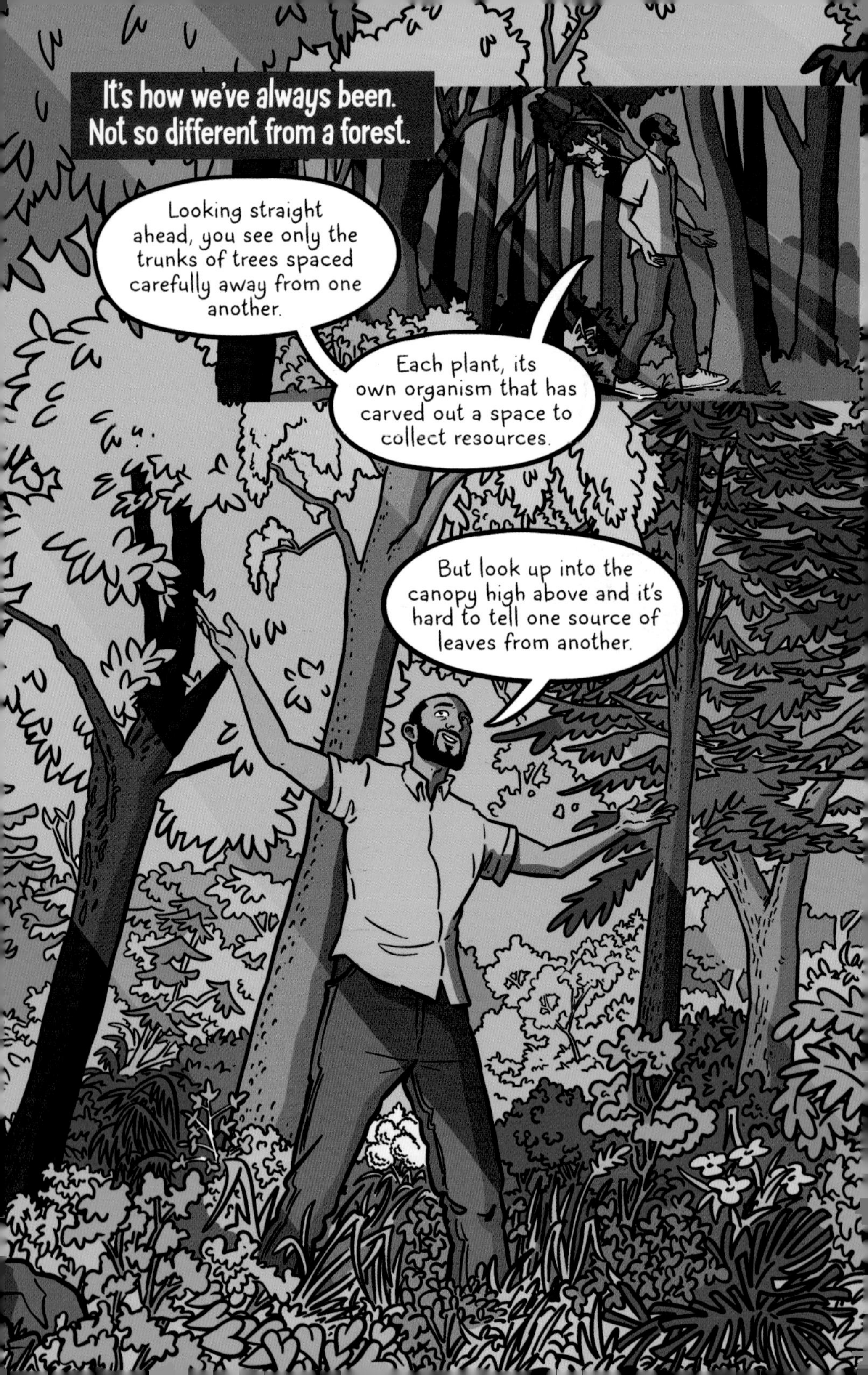
It's how we've always been. Not so different from a forest.
Looking straight ahead, you see only the trunks of trees spaced carefully away from one another.
Each plant, its own organism that has carved out a space to collect resources.
But look up into the canopy high above and it's hard to tell one source of leaves from another.

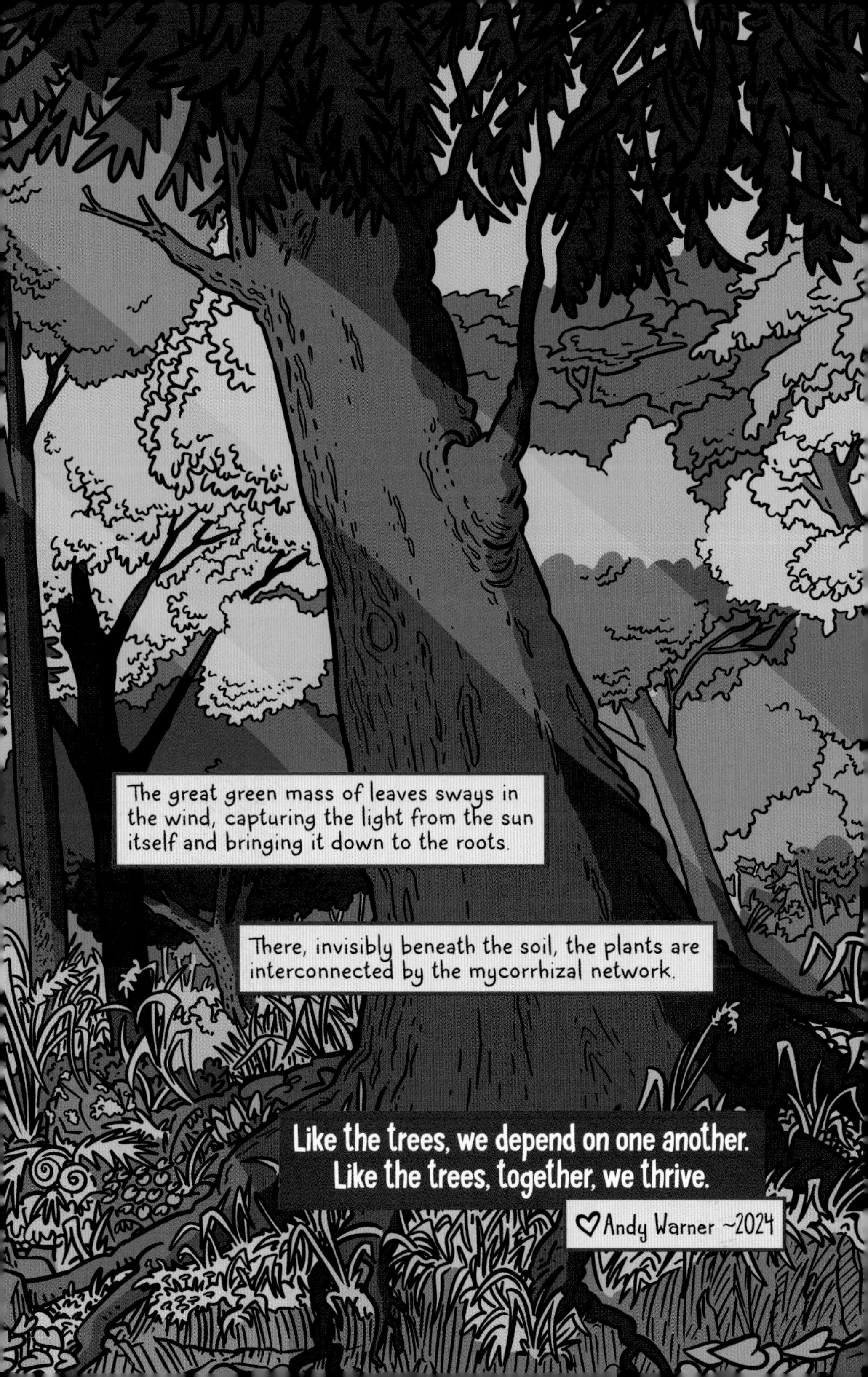
The great green mass of leaves sways in the wind, capturing the light from the sun itself and bringing it down to the roots.
There, invisibly beneath the soil, the plants are interconnected by the mycorrhizal network.
Like the trees, we depend on one another.
Like the trees, together, we thrive.
♡Andy Warner ~2024

INDEX

A

abolitionism, 206, 210-11
agriculture and farming, 14, 50, 53,
  125-26
  Green Revolution, 74-75, 225, 230
Ahmed III, 175, 177-78
Al-Andalus, 109, 188
Alexander the Great, 100, 186
American Chinese food, 99
American Civil War, 97, 211-12
American colonies
  wheat and, 60-61
  wood and, 31-33
American South and cotton, 199-204, 209
  boll weevils, 226-27
  enslavement and, 199-201, 203-4
ammonium nitrate, 74
ancient Egypt (Egyptians)
  wheat, 56-58
  wood and, 19
ancient Greeks and cotton, 186
ancient Rome. See Roman Empire
Andean peoples and potatoes, 125-28
Anglo-French Wars, 32, 120
aqueducts, 58
Arabian Peninsula
  cotton and, 186-88
  sugar and, 109
Archimedes, 20
Arkwright, Richard, 196, 205
Asante Empire, 194-95, 214-15, 221-22
Austronesians, 16
Aztec Empire, 78-82, 110
  corn and, 78-82
  cotton and, 188, 189
  peppers and, 106

B

Bagley, Sarah, 207
batik, 214-15
bees and flowers, 154
beets, 121

Berbers, 187, 193
Berlin Wall, 223
big boats. See boats
bird poop (guano), 73
bison (buffalo), 62-63, 68
Black Death, 22
black peppercorns, 101-6
Bleeding Kansas, 210
bloodthirsty conquering sprees, 23, 29
  82, 92, 100, 103-5, 110, 129, 132, 144,
  152-53, 156-58, 190
blue jeans, 213, 222-23
boats, 93, 104, 149
  wheat and, 64
  wood and, 15-17, 20, 23-24, 26, 29
boll, 183
boll weevils, 215-16, 225-27
book burning, 173
books and paper, 42
bottlenecks, 160
brain size, 13
Britain (British Empire)
  cotton and, 191, 193, 196-99, 217-18,
    221-22
  rice and, 94
  sugar and, 115-17
  tea and, 143-51, 153
  wheat and, 65
  wood and, 29-33
British East India Company, 144-46, 147,
  148, 150, 151, 192, 217
British Raj, 151, 220
bronze technology, 17
Brown, John, 210
Buddhism, 94, 141
Burling, Walter, 202-3
Byzantine Empire, 156, 186
Byzantium, 157

C

California Gold Rush, 39, 99, 213
California redwoods, 38-39, 43, 45

Caligula, 21
calligraphy, 89
canals, 57, 79-81, 89
Cape of Good Hope, 105
capsicums, 106-7
captive markets, 146
carbon dioxide, 27, 44
carbon reserve, 44
Caribs and sugar, 112
Carthage, 20
cattle and corn, 85
cedars of Lebanon, 18, 20
Central Asia, tulips, 155
chai, 151
charcoal, 17
Chicago, 36
China (Chinese Empire)
    cotton and, 224
    Mandate of Heaven, 91, 92, 152
    Opium Wars, 147-49, 150, 152
    rice and, 88-93
    tea and, 140-41, 146-50, 152
    tulips and, 155
    wheat and, 53
    wood and, 24-25
chinampas, 80-81
Chinese Civil War, 149
Chinese laborers and rice, 98-99
"chintz craze," 191
chloroplasts, 4
cities
    Great Migration, 216
    wheat and, 57, 64
    wood and, 36
climate change, 44
Clusius, Carolus, 163
"coffin ships," 137
Cold War, 72, 75, 222-23
Columbus, Christopher, 110
Confederacy, 211-12
Constantinople, 102, 103, 157
controlled burns, 49
corn, 76-87
corn husks, 77, 87
corn syrup, 86
cotton, 182-227

cotton gin, 201-2
cotton mills, 196, 198-99, 205
crop failures, 27
    Great Famine of Ireland, 136-37, 208
Crusaders, 156
Cuba, 98

D

dahlias, 179
"Declaration of the Rights of Man and of
    the Citizen," 119
deforestation, 44-45
denim, 213
detective stories, 42
Dickens, Charles, 206
dikes, 164
diseases. See also plant diseases that
    changed history
    indigenous peoples and, 26, 112
dispersal methods of plants, 48, 63, 76,
    157
domestication, 7, 48
    corn, 78
    cotton, 183
    rice, 89, 93
Douglass, Frederick, 210
dragons, 2
droughts, 51
Dust Bowl, 68-69
Dutch East India Company,
    143-44, 161, 165
Dutch Republic
    cotton and, 214-15
    tea and, 143-44
    tulipmania, 165-74
    tulips and, 161-74, 179-80

E

Easter Island, 16
Egyptians, ancient. See ancient Egypt
Eight-Nation Alliance, 152
English Civil War, 132
enslavement and captive trade, 8
    cotton and, 193, 194, 199-204, 206,
        209-12
    rice and, 96-97, 98
    sugar and, 111, 113-17, 122
environmentalism, 45

"Epic of Gilgamesh," 19
evolution, 4
    grasses and wheat, 48, 49
    trees and wood, 10-11, 13

F

famines, 27, 51, 65, 74
    Great Famine of Ireland, 136-37, 208
farming. See agriculture and farming
fascism, 70
Fertile Crescent, 49-50, 53, 109
fertilizer, 72-74, 75, 81
fire, 11, 13, 51
flammability, 11
floodplains, 55
floods, 55
florists, 167
French Empire
    cotton and, 191-92
    potatoes and, 131
    sugar and, 118-22
    wheat and, 61
    wood and, 30, 32
French Revolution, 118, 120, 131

G

Gandhi, Mohandas, 217-20
gene editing, 230
genetic modifications, 52, 74-75, 159,
    169, 181
Germany
    World War I, 65, 67
    World War II, 70-71
get-rich-quick-schemes, Dutch
    merchants and tulipmania, 166-74
goat pee, 192
Gold Rush, 39, 99, 213
grains, 48
granaries, 58
grasses, 48-52
Great Dying, 27
Great Famine of Ireland, 136-37, 208
Great Fire of Chicago, 36
Great Fire of London, 29
Great Migration, 216
Great Plains, 61-63
    Dust Bowl, 68-69
    enslavement and abolitionist

movement, 210
    wheat and, 61-62, 68
    wood and, 35
Great Wall of China, 92
Green Revolution, 74-75, 225, 230
Gullah, 97

H

Haitian Revolution, 119, 120, 122-23, 202
Hawai'i, 16
Hearst, William Randolph, 41
high-fructose corn syrup, 86
high-yield crops, 74-75
Hill, Julia "Butterfly," 45
Hinduism, 94
Hindu Kush, 102, 184
Hispaniola, 110, 118
Hitler, Adolf, 70-71
honey, 108
human migration, 13-14
Hungarian paprika, 106
Hunger Plan, 71
hunter-gatherers, 49
hyacinths, 179

I

Inca Empire, 110, 127-29
    bird poop as fertilizer, 73
    corn and, 78
    potatoes and, 127-29
India
    cotton and, 191-93, 217-20
    peppers and, 107
    tea and, 145, 150-51
Indian independence movement, 218-20
Indian National Congress, 218
Indian Tea Association, 151
indica rice, 93
indigenous peoples
    corn and, 78
    sugar and, 112
    wheat and, 62-63
    wood and, 26-27, 30, 32, 39, 44
indigo, 185
Indus River, 55, 184-86
industrialization, 197-98
insects and flowers, 154
Ireland and potatoes, 132-37, 139

Great Famine, 136-37, 208
  lazy beds, 134-35, 139
Irish immigration, 137-38, 208
Irish War of Independence, 139
Iron Curtain, 222-23
irrigation, 57
Islam, 186

J
Japan
  rice and, 92
  tea and, 141-42, 152-53
Japanese invasions of Korea, 153
Japanese tea ceremony, 142
japonica rice, 93
jasmine rice, 93
jollof, 95

K
kente cloth, 221
khadi movement, 218-20
"King's Broad Arrow," 31
Korea
  rice and, 92
  tea and, 141

L
labor rights, 207
"Laws of the womb," 98
lazy beds, 134-35, 139
leprous devil-tubers, 130
Levant, 53
levees, 57
Levi's, 213, 223
Little Ice Age, 27
logging, 43-45
Louisiana Purchase, 61, 120
Louisiana rice and beans, 99
Louis XVI of France, 131
Lowell (town), 205-8
Lowell, Francis Cabot, 205-6
Lowell Offering, 206, 207
Lumper potato, 136, 139

M
Maghreb, 187
Mahmud II, 178
Mandate of Heaven, 91, 92, 152
marauding lions, 11
Marggraf, Andreas, 121
Marie Antoinette, 131
Maya and corn, 78
Mediterranean and trade, 18, 59
Mehmed IV, 175
Mesopotamia, 58
millet, 88
Ming dynasty, 24-25
mochi, 92
Mongol Empire, 92-93, 156
monocultures, 83-85, 136
mycorrhizal networks, 46-47

N
Napoleon Bonaparte, 61, 120-21, 179, 217
National Association of Master Bakers, 66
National Housewives League, 66
Nazi Germany, 70-71, 179
nectar, 154
Netherlands. *See* Dutch Republic
New Guinea and sugar, 108-9
newspapers, 40-41, 206
Nile River Valley, 53, 55-56, 109
Nineveh, 58
nitrogen, 73
Nkrumah, Kwame, 221

O
offsets, 159, 166, 169, 180
Opium Wars, 147-49, 150, 152
Osman I, 156
Ottoman Empire
  cotton and, 188
  peppers and, 103-4
  sugar and, 111
  tulips and, 156-61, 174-78, 179
Ottoman-Venetian wars, 104

P
palace intrigue, 177-78
Panama Canal, 43

paper, 40-42
paprika, 106
Papuans, 108
peanuts, 126, 227
peppercorns, 101-6
peppers, 100-107, 126
Persia, 155, 186
Peru, 98
Phoenicians, 18-20
photosynthesis, 4-5
pimiento, 105
pineapples, 126
plantations, 96, 112-13, 118, 119, 132, 204, 210
plant diseases that changed history.
  See also diseases
  cotton and boll weevils, 215-16, 225-27
  potato blight, 136-37
  tulips and aphids, 180-81
Polynesians, 16, 26
Portuguese
  cotton and, 190-91, 193, 194
  peppers and, 105, 107
  rice and, 95-96
  sugar and, 113
  tea and, 143
potato blight, 136-37
potatoes, 124-39
Pulitzer, Joseph, 41
Puritans
  wheat and, 60
  wood and, 28

Q

quinoa, 126

R

railroads, 35, 63, 99, 152
Redwood Summer of 1990, 45
redwood trees, 38-39, 43, 45
rhizotomists, 166
rice, 88-99
rice paddies, 88, 89
roads, 21, 128-29
Roman Empire
  wheat and, 59
  wood and, 21-22

Royal Navy, 29-30
rum, 116
Rum Sultanate, 156
Rwanda, 56

S

Sahara Desert, 95, 187
Sahel, 95, 187
Saint Domingue, 118
salt, 187
San Francisco, 36
science fiction, 42
seeds, 48-53
Seljuks, 156
Semper Augustus, 170, 179
Shang dynasty, 140
ship masts, 30, 33
Sierra Nevada redwoods, 38-39, 45
Silk Road, 53, 93, 155
Simard, Suzanne, 46
Song dynasty, 92
South Africa, 217-18
South Asia
  chai and, 151
  cotton and, 184-85
  peppercorns and, 102
  rice and, 92-94
Southeast Asia
  peppers and, 107
  sweeteners and, 108
Soviet Union, 74
  Cold War, 72, 75, 222-23
  World War II, 70-71
Spanish conquest of the Americas, 81-82, 105-6, 110-15, 129-30, 189-90
Spanish Empire
  corn and, 81-82
  cotton and, 188-90
  peppers and, 105-6
  potatoes and, 129-30
  rice and, 98

sugar and, 110-15
tea and, 143
wheat and, 60
speculation, 167
Stalin, Joseph, 70
Stone Age, 11
sugar, 108-23
sugar beets, 121
Sultanate of Rum, 156
Sumerians, 19, 54-55
sunlight and plants, 3-4
supply and demand, 18, 165
supply chains, 186, 188
sushi rice, 93
swamps, utility of, 79, 93, 95-96, 164, 181
sweatiness, 13, 60, 63, 112, 182
sweet potatoes, 26
sycamore tree, 6
Syria, 102

T

Taíno peoples, 112
Tartars, 158
tea, 140-53
tea ceremony, 142
Tenochtitlan, 79-81
teosinte, 76, 87
Thailand and peppers, 107
Tian Shan Mountains, 155
Timbuktu, 187
tomatoes, 126
Topkapı Palace, 175
trade, 8, 18, 64, 228
    cotton, 184, 187, 190-91, 209
    opium, 148-49, 150
    peppers, 100, 102-3, 105, 106
    potatoes, 129
    rice, 90, 91, 95-96
    Silk Road, 53, 93, 155
    sugar, 115-17
    tea, 143-49
    tulips, 165, 167-70

wheat, 53, 57, 59, 64
Treaty of Versailles, 67
trees. See wood
Triangular Trade, 115-17
tulips, 154-81
    aphids and, 180-81
    history of cultivation, 158-64
    offsets, 159, 166, 169, 180
    origins of, 155-56
tulipmania
    Dutch Republic, 165-74
    Ottoman Empire, 174-78
Turkey. See also Ottoman Empire
    tulips, 155-56
Turk time, 104, 157
Turner, Nat, 209

U

Ukraine wheat, 70
Umayyad Caliphate, 109
uprisings, 98, 197
    French Revolution, 118, 120, 131
    Haitian Revolution, 119, 120, 122-23, 202
    urbanization, 197-98

V

Vegetable Lambs of Tartary, 186
Venetians, 102-4
Verne, Jules, 42
Vietnam and rice, 92
Vikings
    peppers and, 100
    wood and, 23
Virguna Mountains, 56
Voice of Industry, 207

W

wealth extraction, 43-45, 202-4
Wells, H.G., 42
West Africa
    cotton and, 187, 193, 194-95, 214
    rice and, 95-97
western novels, 42
West Indies and sugar, 111
wheat, 50-75, 90
wheels, 21
Whitney, Eli, 201

wigs, 196
Wind Trade, 169-70
wood, 10-47
    boats, 15-17, 20, 23-24, 26, 29
    history of use of, 17-46
    human evolution and migration, 10-17
    logging, 43-45
    paper, 40-42
    trees and mycorrhizal networks, 46-
        47
Wood Age, 11
wooden tools, 12, 15
work hours, 207
World War I, 65-67, 73, 179
World War II, 70-71, 153, 179, 220, 222

Y
Yangtze River Valley, 89
Yellow River Valley, 88, 89

BIBLIOGRAPHY

Dash, Mike. *Tulipomania: The Story of the World's Most Coveted Flower & the Extraordinary Passions It Aroused*. New York: The Crown Publishing Group, 2001.

Ennos, Roland. *The Age of Wood: Our Most Useful Material and the Construction of Civilization*. New York: Scribner, 2021.

Hobhouse, Henry. *Seeds of Change: Six Plants That Transformed Mankind*. Washington, DC: Shoemaker & Hoard, 2005.

Hobhouse, Henry. *Seeds of Wealth: Four Plants That Made Men Rich*. Washington, DC: Shoemaker & Hoard, 2005.

Hobhouse, Penelope. *The Story of Gardening*. New York: Princeton Architectural Press, 2020.

Laws, Bill. *A History of the Garden in Fifty Tools*. Chicago: The University of Chicago Press, 2014.

Laws, Bill. *Fifty Plants That Changed the Course of History*. Richmond Hill, Ontario: Firefly Books, 2015.

Marton, Renee. *Rice: A Global History*. London: Reaktion Books Ltd., 2014.

Pollan, Michael. *Second Nature: A Gardener's Education*. New York, Grove Press, 2003.

Pollan, Michael. *The Botany of Desire: A Plant's-Eye View of the World*. New York: Random House, 2022.

Postrel, Virginia. *The Fabric of Civilization: How Textiles Made the World*. New York: Basic Books, 2021.

Yafa, Stephen. *Cotton: The Biography of a Revolutionary Fiber*. New York: Penguin Books, 2006.

Zabinski, Catherine. *Amber Waves: The Extraordinary Bibliography of Wheat, from Wild Grass to World Megacrop*. Chicago: The University of Chicago Press, 2022.

ACKNOWLEDGMENTS

First, thank you to all the researchers and writers whose work I referenced to put this book together. Thanks to Kathy for reading my drafts, and to my kids for inspiring me with their overwhelming curiosity. Thank you to Eleri and Luke for their beautiful coloring work, and to Aron for helping out in a pinch. Thanks to Lisa for distracting the beasts, and thanks to Ginger for giving me a reason to take a break and go for a walk outside every once in a while. Thanks to my editor, Andrea Colvin, and to my agent, Farley Chase, for making it possible for me to create an entire book about how human history is shaped by our relationship with domesticated plants.

Andy Warner

is the *New York Times* bestselling author of *Brief Histories of Everyday Objects* and *This Land Is My Land.* He is a contributing editor at the Nib and teaches cartooning at Stanford University and the Animation Workshop in Denmark. His comics have been published by *Slate, Fusion,* American Public Media, popsci.com, KQED, IDEO, The Center for Constitutional Rights, UNHCR, UNRWA, UNICEF, and Buzzfeed. He was a recipient of the 2018 Berkeley Civic Arts Grant and was the 2019, 2021, and 2023 Hawai'i Volcanoes National Park Artist-in-Residence. He works in a garret room in South Berkeley and comes from the sea.